COUNTRY LIVING
MAGAZINE

Guide to Rural England

THE WEST COUNTRY

Cornwall, Devon, Dorset and Somerset

By David Gerrard

Published by:
Travel Publishing Ltd
Airport Business Centre, 10 Thornbury Road,
Estover, Plymouth PL6 7PP

ISBN13   9781904434948

© Travel Publishing Ltd

Country Living is a registered trademark of The National
Magazine Company Limited.

First Published: 2001   Second Edition: 2004
Third Edition: 2006   Fourth Edition: 2008
Fifth Edition 2010

COUNTRY LIVING GUIDES:

East Anglia	Scotland
Heart of England	The South of England
Ireland	The South East of England
The North East of England	The West Country
The North West of England	Wales

PLEASE NOTE:

All advertisements in this publication have been accepted in good faith by Travel Publishing and they have not necessarily been endorsed by *Country Living* Magazine.

All information is included by the publishers in good faith and is believed to be correct at the time of going to press. No responsibility can be accepted for errors.

Editor:	David Gerrard
Printing by:	Latimer Trend, Plymouth
Location Maps:	© Maps in Minutes ™ (2010) © Collins Bartholomews 2010 All rights reserved.
Cover Photo:	Fishing Boats at Penberth © Britain on View Photo Library
Text Photos:	see page 402

Foreword

From a bracing walk across the hills and tarns of The Lake District to a relaxing weekend spent discovering the unspoilt hamlets of East Anglia, nothing quite matches getting off the beaten track and exploring Britain's areas of outstanding beauty.

Each month, *Country Living Magazine* celebrates the richness and diversity of our countryside with features on rural Britain and the traditions that have their roots there. So it is with great pleasure that I introduce you to the *Country Living Magazine Guide to Rural England* series. Packed with information about unusual and unique aspects of our countryside, the guides will point both fair-weather and intrepid travellers in the right direction.

Each chapter provides a fascinating tour of the West Country area, with insights into local heritage and history and easy-to-read facts on a wealth of places to visit, stay, eat, drink and shop.

I hope that this guide will help make your visit a rewarding and stimulating experience and that you will return inspired, refreshed and ready to head off on your next countryside adventure.

Susy Smith

Susy Smith
Editor, Country Living magazine

PS To subscribe to *Country Living Magazine* each month, call 01858 438844

Introduction

This is the fifth edition of *The Country Living Guide to Rural England - The West Country* and we are sure that it will be as popular as its predecessors. David Gerrard, a very experienced travel writer has, of course, completely updated the contents of the guide and ensured that it is packed with vivid descriptions, historical stories, amusing anecdotes and interesting facts on hundreds of places in Cornwall, Devon, Dorset and Somerset. In this respect we would like to thank all the Tourist Information Centres who helped us to provide you with up-to-date information. The advertising panels within each chapter provide further information on places to see, stay, eat, drink, shop and even exercise!

The guide however is not simply an "armchair tour". Its prime aim is to encourage the reader to visit the places described and discover much more about the wonderful towns and villages as well as the beauty and charm of the varied rural landscapes and coastlines of the West Country. Whether you decide to explore this region by wheeled transport or on foot we are sure you will find it a very uplifting experience.

We are always interested in receiving comments on places covered (or not covered) in our guides so please do not hesitate to use the reader reaction forms provided at the rear of this guide to give us your considered comments. This will help us refine the content of the next edition. We also welcome any general comments which will help improve the overall presentation of the guides themselves.

For more information on other titles in the Country Living Rural Guide series and the full range of travel guides published by Travel Publishing please refer to the order form at the rear of this guide or log on to our website (see below).

Travel Publishing

Did you know that you can also search our website for details of thousands of places to see, stay, eat or drink throughout Britain and Ireland? Our site has become increasingly popular and now receives hundreds of thousands of visits. Try it!

website: www.findsomewhere.co.uk

Contents

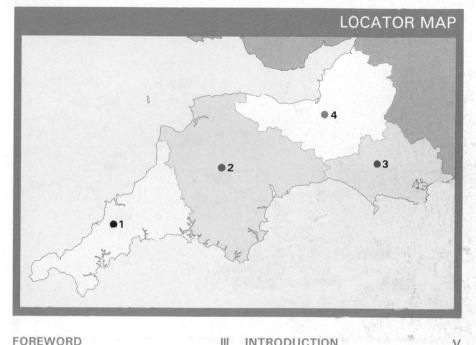

LOCATOR MAP

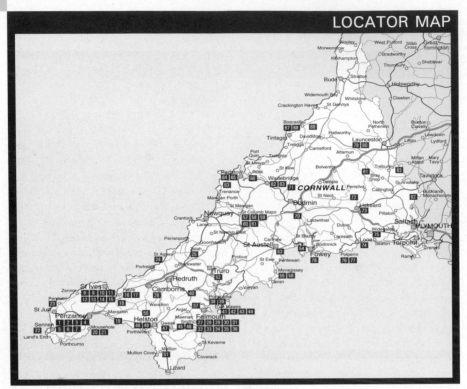

LOCATOR MAP

ADVERTISERS AND PLACES OF INTEREST

Continued on Page 4

🏛 historic building   🏛 museum and heritage   🏛 historic site   🐾 scenic attraction   🐾 flora and fauna

1| Cornwall

"I like Cornwall very much. It is not England," wrote DH Lawrence. That was more than 80 years ago, but the ancient Duchy of Cornwall remains stubbornly distinct from the rest of England, not just in its dramatic and spectacular scenery, but in its strong Celtic heritage. The landscape is dotted with ancient monuments, crosses and holy wells, and ancient legends – especially those relating to King Arthur and the Knights of the Round Table – appear to have been hot-wired into the Cornish psyche.

Cornish people have been recognised as a separate identity by the Commission for Racial Equality and they have their own distinctive and attractive dialect. According to the Cornish Language Board, around 2600 people still speak Kernuack, the original language of the peninsula. A firm in Helston occasionally publishes books in the ancient language and Kernuack has been recognised as a living language by the European Commission. Elements of Kernuack still survive in the names of Cornish places and people – as Sir Walter Scott put it: "By Tre-, Pol and Pen-, You shall know all true Cornishmen."

One simple fact about the county helps to explain its distinct character. Wherever you are in Cornwall, you are never more than 20 miles from the sea. Maritime trade started early here – in the days of King Solomon, the Cornish people were already trading tin with the Phoenicians. Cornish eyes, it seems, were always turned seawards rather than inland, and the people's cultural affinity was with the Celtic diaspora of Ireland and Brittany rather than their mainland neighbours.

Added to this cultural separation was the county's physical distance from major centres of population. Even today, Cornwall's population of around 500,000 is less than that of the city of Bristol. There's not a single mile of motorway within its boundaries and long stretches of the main through route, the A30 from Penzance to London, are still single carriageway.

It was this isolation – and the luminous light of the area – that attracted major artists to the little seaside resort of St Ives, which now boasts a world-class art gallery in the Tate St Ives. More recently, an abandoned china clay pit has been transformed into what has been described as the Eighth Wonder of the World, the inspired – and phenomenally successful – Eden Project, whose enormous bio-spheres celebrate the complex relationship between plants, people and resources.

Elsewhere, the county boasts the third largest natural harbour in the world, Falmouth; acres of glorious gardens such as the Lost Gardens of Heligan; King Arthur's legendary fortress at Tintagel, and other medieval castles at St Mawes, Falmouth and St Michael's Mount; the wonderful Elizabethan mansion of Prideaux Place at Padstow; and, of course, Land's End where the granite bulwark overlooks the Atlantic waters beneath which lies the legendary Land of Lyonesse.

Tintagel Castle Remains

ADVERTISERS AND PLACES OF INTEREST (CONT.)

🏛 historic building 🏛 museum and heritage 🏛 historic site 🌾 scenic attraction 🌷 flora and fauna

Penzance

🏛 Market House	🏛 Egyptian House		
🏛 Union Hotel	🏛 Maritime Museum		
🏛 National Lighthouse Centre			
🎨 Penlee House Art Gallery	🎨 Mazey Day		
🌿 Trengwainton Gardens			
🏛 Cornwall Geological Museum			

Penzance's famous promenade, the longest in Cornwall, runs from the open air art deco-style Jubilee Swimming Pool around the broad curve of Mount's Bay. Just along from the Jubilee Pool are the harbour and docks, still busy with fishing and pleasure boats. The town's main street is Market Jew Street whose curious name is believed to be a corruption of the old Cornish Marghas Yow, meaning Thursday Market. This busy shopping area leads gently uphill to the handsome classical building of the silver-domed **Market House** (1836), which now serves as a bank. In front of this granite structure stands a statue to Penzance's most famous son, Sir Humphry Davy, the scientist best remembered for inventing the miners' safety lamp. Born in a nearby street, the son of a local woodcarver, Davy was one of the foremost chemists of the 19th century and, along with his contribution to miners' safety, he also founded both the Athenaeum Club and London Zoo.

Leading downhill from the Market House is the town's most interesting area, Chapel Street. Along this thoroughfare stands the exotic **Egyptian House**, created from two cottages in the 1830s by John Lavin, to entice customers into his shop. Although the designer of the magnificent façade is unknown, it is believed to have been inspired by the Egyptian Hall in Piccadilly, London.

IRISS

66 Chapel Street, Penzance,
Cornwall TR18 4AD
Tel: 01736 366568
e-mail: sales@iriss.co.uk
website: www.iriss.co.uk

The historic street in which **Iriss** stands is one of the most interesting in Penzance and has not been significantly changed since the mid 19th century. It is now a fascinating area to explore with a wealth of independent and specialist shops and a good selection of restaurants, coffee shops and public houses.

Iriss is just one of the many independent shops worth a look along the main thoroughfare from the harbour to the town centre. Owned by Mariarosa Martin, this delightful shop is a fantastic find for creative people fond of knitting and other crafts. Iriss specialises in rug making equipment, knitting wool, silk painting, tapestry and kneedle work. It is popular with locals and visitors to the area and for those who don't have the pleasure of having this shop on their doorstep Mariarosa has a comprehensive website, where she sells products online.

Iriss can be found in a four-storey building, which dates back to the 1800s and was originally run by a tailor. The present shop was established in 1985 and is definitely worth a look for keen crafters.

🎬 stories and anecdotes　🐦 famous people　🎨 art and craft　🎭 entertainment and sport　👣 walks

THE ALVERTON GALLERY

5 Alverton Street, Penzance,
Cornwall TR18 2QW
Tel: 01736 351668
e-mail: info@thealvertongallery.co.uk
website: www.thealvertongallery.co.uk

Located in the heart of Penzance with plenty of parking nearby, **The Alverton Gallery** is a gallery with a difference for the discerning art lover. The large picture window frontage invites the passer-by to pause, and then step inside the spacious gallery where they will be welcome to watch the resident artists at work, ask questions and sample the coffee and biscuits while you browse! The owners, Diana and Tim Wayne, are both makers themselves. Diana works at her etching press or with screen prints; Tim exhibits his own woodcut prints and ceramic sculpture in the gallery.

Their working studio gallery offers an unusual blend of contemporary fine art, featuring artists and makers predominantly from West Cornwall. There's an ever-changing wall display of west country and other artists with a variety of landscape, seascape and figurative paintings in oil, acrylic, watercolour and mixed media. Also on display are original wood engravings, etchings, screen prints and lithographs. Then there's the glassware, featuring designer and hand-formed pieces using fused techniques and decals.

The jewellery exhibits include designer and hand-made necklaces, bracelets, rings and brooches in silver with gold, copper and semi precious stones, along with Venetian murano glass and beaded jewellery. The gold items include new and second-hand necklaces, bracelets, brooches and rings. Another section of the gallery is devoted to contemporary decorative, sculptural and everyday pottery, ranging from traditional tableware to unusual, unique and experimental ceramics, using stoneware, porcelain, terracotta and crank clays.

The gallery also features sculptures - unique pieces carved and hand moulded from bronze, wood, clay and marble and other stone. Items in wood include turned wooden bowls and plates, keepsake and jewellery boxes in exotic, native and recycled wood.

Then there are the objets d'art, the French term for the eclectic mix of bygones, collectables and pieces of past times that intrigue us. These might include treen, pewter, sculpture, crockery, figurines and boxes.

With so much on display and of such quality, this outstanding gallery should not be missed. It is open from 9.30am to 5pm, Monday to Saturday.

🏛 historic building 🏛 museum and heritage 🏛 historic site 🜨 scenic attraction 🌱 flora and fauna

Egyptian House

mainland England of the victory of Trafalgar and the death of Lord Nelson. Chapel Street was also the childhood home of Marie Branwell, the mother of the Brontë sisters.

For centuries, a remote market town that made its living from fishing, mining and smuggling, Penzance today is popular with holidaymakers as well as being the ferry port for the Isles of Scilly. Along with its near neighbours, Newlyn and Mousehole, Penzance was sacked by the Spanish in 1595. Having supported the Royalist cause during the Civil War, it suffered the same fate again less than 60 years later. A major port in the 19th century for the export of tin, the fortunes of Penzance were transformed by the railway's arrival in 1859. Not only could the direct despatch of early flowers, vegetables and locally caught fish to the rest of Britain be undertaken, but the influx of holidaymakers boosted the town's fledgling tourist industry.

The house is now owned by the Landmark Trust and its upper floors can be rented for holiday stays.

Opposite this splendid building stands the **Union Hotel** whose Georgian façade hides an impressive Elizabethan interior. From the Minstrel's Gallery in the sumptuous dining room was made the first announcement in

Penzance celebrates its long-standing links with the sea at the **Maritime Museum**, which houses a fascinating collection of artefacts that illustrate the ferocity of the waters along this stretch of coast. The museum's interior re-creates an 18th-century four-deck man-of-war, complete with creaking floorboards, and contains displays of pieces of eight and other

📖 stories and anecdotes   🐿 famous people   ✍ art and craft   🎭 entertainment and sport   🚶 walks

BOHEMIA GUILD

54 Market Jew Street, Penzance, Cornwall TR18 2HZ
Tel: 01736 363919
e-mail: bohemiaguild@aol.com
website: www.bohemiaguild.com

'A Gallery with a Conscience'

Bohemia Art, Craft and Re-Makers Guild is as much about the
people as their art. It opened its doors in November 2009 on
Market Jew Street, opposite the railway station. Bohemia Guild
exhibits for sale the functional and decorative work of a wide
cross-section of Cornish and West Country makers of all ages.
Works on display come from people who are just starting out or
simply enjoy the act of creating beautiful things, and from others
who have successfully made their life's work in art or come to art
late in life. Together, Bohemia Guild and these makers are united
in their quest for and commitment to the highest standards of
work in all its diverse forms, both decorative and practical.

The range is truly amazing, from painting, prints and
photography to ceramics, pottery, wood turning and carving,
children's crafts, toys and clothing, gloves, scarves, booties,
glass-making and stained glass, découpage, bags and baskets,
textiles, jewellery and much more. The gallery places particular
emphasis on re-making, whether it is in the people who have left
previous careers and re-invented themselves as artists, or in the
objects they have taken from the past to re-create something new
and out of the ordinary.

Art is sometimes born out of a case of 'needs must'. Art in
Adversity is another aspect which the Bohemia Guild is
enthusiastic about. Some of the local fishermen are a case in
point. Many have found themselves unable to work due to ill
health, accidents or changed and reduced circumstances. Turning
their heads from fish to art has given many a new meaning and
purpose in life; it is hoped that Bohemia Guild can help those in
adversity to achieve an alternative income stream as well.

A gallery with a conscience, Bohemia Guild not only tells the
story behind the art but also ensures that those exhibiting gain
the maximum financial benefits from the sale of their work.
Business hours are 10am to 5pm Monday to Saturday.

🏠 historic building 🏛 museum and heritage 🏚 historic site 🐾 scenic attraction 🐾 flora and fauna

HOTEL PENZANCE

Britons Hill, Penzance, Cornwall TR18 3AE
Tel: 01736 363117   Fax: 01736 350970
e-mail: enquiries@hotelpenzance.com
website: www.hotelpenzance.com

Sometimes in life you are lucky enough to find a special place that forces you to leave behind the hectic pace and endless schedules of modern life, enabling you to slow down and relax. **Hotel Penzance** provides just such a place, converted from two Edwardian merchant's houses in the 1920s. All rooms retain their original proportions and atmosphere. Its location is set in a Mediterranean style garden around an outdoor heated pool perched high above the rooftops of Penzance overlooking the waterfront activity of the harbour and Mounts Bay.

The warmth of the hotel is enhanced by the very special team of people who welcome you, never pompous always genuinely caring nothing is ever too much trouble.

A superb base for exploring; Enjoy the rugged cliffs of Land's End and the surrounding coastal paths. Learn to surf at Sennen Cove or relax on Britain's best blue flag beaches. Watch open-air performances at the Minnack Theatre. Swim in the Art-deco Jubilee Pool. Take boat trips from Penzance Marina. Explore artisan Chapel Street and the town's many galleries – so much to do!

THE BAY RESTAURANT (Two Rosettes) combines the very finest cuisine with an excellent wine cellar, welcoming residents and non-residents alike.

Under the guidance of Head Chef Ben Reeves, the restaurant offers a seasonally changing menu, taking advantage of immediate local availability. By doing this it offers you the best of regional produce in its peak condition... Fish from Newlyn and St Ives...meats, poultry and dairy produce from local farms... vegetables and herbs grown especially and wild produce foraged from the shores and woodlands.

Ben is always quick to instil his values in his brigade; 'we have to become far more aware of our responsibilities to the environment, especially sustainability and provenance. Great ingredients are necessary to the creation of great food, so we need to ensure that what we are using today will be sustainable and therefore available for the chefs of tomorrow and the future. As a guiding principal, searching for quality, always begins closest to home'

Number 36

No. 4 Causeway Head, Penzance, Cornwall   TR18 2SN
Tel: 01736 367590   e-mail: andrea@no36.fsworldco.uk

Number 36 is located in the old pedestrianised street of Causeway Head with its Victorian cinema, speciality shops, galleries and eateries that spill out onto the street in summer. This fashion, accessories and gift shop was established in 2007 by Andrea Simmons who has many years experience in the trade. The shop occupies a traditional building of Penzance stone with a huge picture window displaying samples of the colourful and vibrant stock available inside. Here, there is clothing appealing to all ages and purses, with a large range of sizes. There are some wonderful accessories on offer, especially the huge selection of scarves which are personally sourced by Andrea directly from which she visits twice yearly. The extensive range of jewellery includes some items designed and made by Andrea herself. Also on sale is an intriguing selection of quality gifts, including some novelty items such as bath bombs in the shape of cup cakes. Finally, there's a range of crockery and a tasteful selection of cards, including humorous ones.

🏚 historic building 📷 museum and heritage 🏛 historic site 🌳 scenic attraction 🦋 flora and fauna

Harbour Lighthouse

Museum. The county's long association with the mining industry is highlighted at the **Cornwall Geological Museum**, which has some intriguing fossil displays and surveys 400 million years of Cornwall's past.

At the end of June, the town celebrates **Mazey Day**, a revival of the St John's Eve celebrations abolished in Queen Victoria's reign. Mazey Day is now the climax of Golowan Week and the Golowan Festival when large numbers of visitors join local revellers to take part in the music, dance, drama and pageantry.

artefacts recovered from wrecks off the Isles of Scilly.

Down at the harbour, at the **National Lighthouse Centre**, the story of lighthouse keeping is told. Opened by Prince Andrew in 1991, the centre has assembled what is the probably the largest and finest collection of lighthouse equipment in the world. Visitors can operate the 100-year-old apparatus, blast off a foghorn, or just sit back and watch a video about the history of the lighthouse.

Elsewhere in Penzance, local history and the work of the Newlyn School of artists can be seen at the **Penlee House Art Gallery and**

Just to the northwest of the town, and close to the village of Madron, lie **Trengwainton Gardens**, the National Trust-owned woodland gardens that are known for their spring-flowering shrubs, their exotic trees and the walled garden that contains plants that cannot be grown in the open anywhere else in the country. The walled garden was built in the early 19th century by the then owner Sir Rose Price, the son of a wealthy Jamaican sugar planter.

Two miles west of Penzance, Trewidden

UNION HOTEL

Chapel Street, Penzance, Cornwall TR18 4AE
Tel: 01736 362319
e-mail: enquiries@unionhotel.co.uk
website: www.unionhotel.co.uk

During its long history, the **Union Hotel** has provided accommodation for Royalty, Prime Ministers and some great artistes. The hotel occupies a prime position in the centre of Penzance, in what is considered to be one of the finest streets in Cornwall. It has a bar offering a tempting bar menu and a Theatre Bar Restaurant serving superb food cooked to your liking by a qualified chef. In the en suite bedrooms you'll find crisp white sheets, fluffy white towels, direct dial telephone, colour TV, hospitality tray and hair dryer. Breakfast is served in an impressive room that was once the town's Assembly Rooms and in which the death of Nelson at Trafalgar was first proclaimed in England.

There are two sister hotels - The White Hart Hotel in Hayle and the Angel Hotel in Helston (see pages 22 and 53)

Gardens is one of the finest informal gardens in Cornwall and contains one of the best collections of camellias in the country.

Around Penzance

ZENNOR

5½ miles N of Penzance on the B3306

🏠 Wayside Folk Museum   🏛 Zennor Quoit

🏛 Chysauster Ancient Village

This delightful ancient village, situated between moorland and coastal cliffs, shows evidence of Bronze Age settlers. It also has a 12th-century church, famous for its carved bench end depicting a mermaid holding a comb and mirror. A local legend tells of a mysterious young maiden who was drawn to the church by the beautiful singing of a chorister, the churchwarden's son Matthew Trewhella. An enchanting singer herself, the maiden lured Matthew down to nearby Pendour Cove where he disappeared. On warm summer evenings, it is said that their voices can be heard rising from the waves.

By the porch in the church is a memorial to John Davey, who died in 1891, stating that he was the last person to have any great knowledge of the native Cornish language Kernuack. It is said that he remained familiar with the language by speaking it to his cat. There has recently been a revival of interest in Kernuack, and visitors to Cornwall who chance upon a Kernuack speaker might impress him by asking, "Plema'n diwotti?" and with any luck directed to the nearest pub. Another useful entry in the Cornish phrasebook is, "Fatell yu an pastyon yn gwerthji ma? A wrons I ri dhymn drog goans?" which means, "What are the pasties like in this shop? Will they give me indigestion?"

For an insight into the history of Zennor and the surrounding area, the **Wayside Folk Museum** is a unique private museum, founded in 1935, that covers every aspect of life in Zennor and district from 3000BC to the 1930s. On display are waterwheels, a millhouse, a wheelwright's and blacksmith's premises, a miller's cottage with kitchen and parlour, and exhibits on tin mining. The collection has more than 5000 items in 16 display areas and includes an extensive collection of photographs and information on people who have lived in the area.

Tin mining is also referred to in the name of the local inn, The Tinners Arms, whose name DH Lawrence borrowed as the title of a short story. Lawrence spent many hours at this pub while living in the village with his wife Frieda during World War One. It was during his stay here, under police surveillance, that Lawrence wrote *Women in Love*. However, his pacifist tendencies and Frieda's German heritage (her cousin was the flying ace the Red Baron von Richthofen) caused them to be 'moved on' in October 1917. Lawrence refers to the episode in his semi-autobiographical novel *Kangaroo* (1923).

To the southeast of the village are the

Wayside Folk Museum

🏠 historic building   🏛 museum and heritage   🏛 historic site   🌣 scenic attraction   🌿 flora and fauna

dilapidated remains of the Neolithic chamber tomb, **Zennor Quoit**, believed to be some 4500 years old. One of many ancient monuments in the area, the tomb has a huge capstone that was once supported on five broad uprights.

A couple of miles to the south of Zennor, on a windy hillside, stands **Chysauster Ancient Village** (English Heritage), the best-preserved prehistoric settlement in the southwest. This Romano-Cornish village, built around 2000 years ago, has one of the oldest identifiable streets in the country. The site was only discovered during archaeological excavations in the 1860s. Villagers here were farmers, as cattle sheds have been unearthed. They also worked tin beside the nearby stream. Their housing consisted of stone-walled homesteads, each with an open central courtyard surrounded by several circular living rooms topped with thatch or turf. Eight of these have survived.

St Ives

7 miles NE of Penzance on the A3074

- Tate St Ives Gallery
- Barbara Hepworth Sculpture Garden
- Leach Gallery   St Ives Museum
- Knill Steeple   St Ives Festival
- Trewyn Subtropical Gardens   Carbis Bay

This lovely old fishing town with its maze of narrow streets and picturesque harbour, has been showered with various awards in the past few years. It won the Gold Award in the international Entente Florale, has made off with more Britain in Bloom top prizes than any other UK town, and a recent University of

I SHOULD COCO

39 Fore Street, St Ives, Cornwall TR26 1HF.
Tel: 01736 798756 / 07811 647738
website: www.ishouldcoco.co.uk

Founded in 2009, I Should Coco is a unique little chocolate boutique overlooking the harbour in St Ives. This beautifully light and airy shop has a fascinating glass wall to the workshop, where you can watch the chocolatiers at work. The smell in the shop is wonderful, and there are always tasters of the work in progress. All the products are hand made on site by a team of artisan chocolatiers, headed up by founders Andrea and Kevin Parsons. Fresh cream truffles – a treat very difficult to find these days – are a speciality and the team make full use of the wonderful ingredients available on their doorstep to make these sublime creations, including Cornish Cream; Honey; Strawberries; Raspberries; Elderflowers and even Cornish Seasalt ! For the more adventurous, Chilli and Tequila truffles are a revelation not to be missed.

Other exciting original products include a range of single origin chocolates from Peru; Mexico; Madagascar and many other exotic locations and award winning infused chocolates such as Nutmeg and Vanilla and Habanero chilli pepper. Bespoke chocolate creations can be undertaken on commission for Birthdays , Weddings and other special occasions and these can range from a personal message to a picture hand painted in chocolate.

Its a very creative atmosphere but just to help things along, original works by local artists have been used on the wrappers and boxes and adorn the walls of the shop. Not surprisingly this unique enterprise has garnered many awards including most recently 4 Gold Awards from the Taste of the West. With undoubtedly many more to follow!

stories and anecdotes   famous people   art and craft   entertainment and sport   walks

THE SPRUCE TREE

11 Fore Street, St Ives, Cornwall TR26 1AB
Tel: 01736 794713
e-mail: thesprucetree@chessbroadband.co.uk

Located in St Ives main cobbled street with a wide variety of interesting shops, **The Spruce Tree** specialises in quality items made of wood, glass and ceramic. Many of these items are individually sourced from around the world. In the shop's unusually shaped semi-circular display window is a range of Moorcroft Pottery from Burslem in Staffordshire and a selection of items to be found inside. The ground and first floor galleries have beautifully displayed wooden pieces from around the world. There are hand-carved, hand-painted wooden figures for Nativity scenes from Italy, Noah's Arks and other wooden gifts are sourced in the USA, while the range of coloured boxes come from a co-operative in Columbia. The wooden vases made of lignum vitae - the 'tree of life' are from Bolivia while the wooden puzzle trees are sourced in Worcester, England. Lladro porcelain from Spain is another well known product available in this shop.

This shop prides itself on having highly unusual items, Swedish glass sculptures and glass flowers from Wales being good examples. It also supports local artists and craftsmen, the hallmarked solid silver jewellery coming from a nearby village.

The Spruce Tree is also a Steiff Club Store with a good selection of Steiff and other collectable teddy bears.

Surrey survey, using a complex formula to decide which were the best beach destinations globally, placed St Ives at the top of its UK list, and fourth in the world. An organisation called The Most Beautiful Bays in the World has declared St Ives Bay one of its select few, on a par with Caribbean, Asian and American beauty spots. Another two of St Ives' five sandy beaches have also qualified for a Blue Flag award. And in 2010 the town received the Coast Award as Best Family Holiday Destination.

Culturally, the town is famous worldwide as an artists' colony. They were drawn here by the special quality of the light – ultra-violet radiation is greater here than anywhere else in the country. JMW Turner was the first major artist to arrive, in 1811, to be followed in later decades by Whistler, Sickert, McNeill, Munnings, Ben Nicholson, the sculptor Barbara Hepworth and the potter Bernard

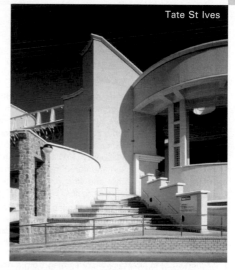

Tate St Ives

Leach. Art still dominates and, along with the numerous private galleries, there is the **Tate St Ives Gallery** where the work of 20th-century

KUIAMA CRAFTS

42 Fore Street, St Ives,
Cornwall TR26 1HE
Tel: 01736 798009
website: www.kuiamacrafts.com

Kuiama Crafts owned and run by Heidi Kuiama Moore, is a vibrant, friendly and informative gift and lifestyle shop on the main shopping street in St Ives. Opening in 2005 selling a selection of unique gifts, they have since expanded the range year by year with handcrafted gifts from home and world sources. The range includes interiors with a nautical theme; hand woven and dyed silk accessories from a Fairtrade source in an exciting spectrum of colours; and Dunoon Ceramics Fine Bone China mugs. Kuiama Crafts also stock an expanding range of hand knitting yarns and accessories, in particular a Fairtrade range by Manos del Uruguay in pure wool, silk, cashmere and merino blends, all hand dyed. There are also available yarns in alpaca, cotton and speciality yarns for sock and lace knitting. Heidi is a trained artist and has a passion for all textiles, in particular felt making. The shop always carries a selection of her unique hand felted and embroidered pictures of local landscape scenes. Heidi's mother Norma is a very talented quilter producing lovely soft furnishings and interior decorations that will enhance any home, for any time of the year. Styles include vintage, nautical, traditional and contemporary Christmas.

stories and anecdotes 🖾 famous people 𝒫 art and craft 🖉 entertainment and sport 🏃 walks

FORE STREET DELI

30a Fore Street, St Ives, Cornwall TR26 1HE
Tel: 01736 794578
e-mail: info@forestdeli.co.uk
website: www.forestdeli.co.uk

There has been a delicatessen here on the main shopping street for many years, but since being acquired by Peter Williams in 2008 the **Fore St Deli** has gone from strength to strength. An eyecatching array of fresh fruit and vegetables outside the shop tempts shoppers into a world of fine food, from meat, poultry, fish and shellfish to cheese and dairy, cooked and cured meats, chutneys, pickles and preserves, oils and vinegars, chocolates, beers, wines, spirits and fruit juices.

    The owner is dedicated to sourcing and promoting the best of local produce, so naturally Cornwall's specialities are all to be found – honey, fairings, Yarg, cheddar, camembert, cider, sea salt and many more. The Deli also has touches that really set it apart from the norm: they marinade and flavour olives and keep an oil drum from which customers can draw the finest olive oil into their own bottles. Fore St Deli is also a haven for those with an intolerance for gluten, and Peter has spent many years perfecting his range of gluten-free delights. He has found the ideal base in Doves Farm self-raising flour, and the selection of cakes includes banana, chocolate, lemon polenta and coconut St Clements. He also prepares a range of frozen ready meals, including pies and lasagne.

    The Deli offers a range of Welcome Packs (including ready assembled or pick and mix) and Hampers that make wonderful gifts – the Luxury Hamper contains Camel Valley 'Champagne', Worthy Farm Cheddar, Cornish Camembert, Bath Oliver biscuits, Crellow chutney and chocolates.

THE ORGANIC PANDA

1 Pendolver Terrace, St Ives, Cornwall TR26 2EL
Tel: 01736 793890

In the same ownership as Fore St Deli, the **Organic Panda** is a unique and totally delightful B&B and Art Gallery in an elegant Victorian house a short walk from the Blue Flag Porthminster Beach. The three bedrooms are stylish and contemporary, designed on environmental principles, with eco-friendly materials, wool carpets and organic cotton bedding. Also on the premises is a vibrant art exhibition with original artwork for sale by Peter Williams and others.

🏛 historic building   🏛 museum and heritage   🏛 historic site   🦢 scenic attraction   🌱 flora and fauna

TREMAYNE APPLIED ARTS

Street an Pol, St Ives, Cornwall TR26 2DS
Tel: 01736 797779
e-mail: tonkinson@btinternet.com

Tremayne Applied Arts was founded in 1997 and is still run with great knowledge and enthusiasm by owners Roger and Eileen Tonkinson. Set on a narrow street right in the heart of the artistic community of St Ives, their gallery is housed in a Victorian/Edwardian building that was originally a bakery. Two of its three rooms still have the original slate floors, while the third room opens out onto a pleasant little slate-paved courtyard. It's a lovely setting for a gallery where you might be able to find original works for sale by some of the famous artists who made St Ives their home.

Visitors are often surprised by some of the artists whose work can be found at Tremayne Applied Arts. The renowned and influential potter Bernard Leach is one such name, alongside his wife Janet Leach and Bernard's son, David, who made up a St Ives pottery dynasty. Ben Nicholson and Patrick Heron are two more of the famous names associated with St Ives, and their work can be found in the Tremayne Gallery too. The work of Dame Lucie Rie, whose pottery is on display in places such as the Museum of Modern Art in New York, can also be found at Tremayne, as can the abstract pioneer Victor Pasmore.

The gallery doesn't only show local artists, though, as work by international names including Lalique, Braque, Tapio Wirkkala and Le Corbusier can also be seen here in what is almost a Design Museum as much as an art gallery. The owners like to cover all the major design periods of the 20th and 21st centuries, from the Arts and Crafts Movement at the turn of the 20th century through to the present day. You're therefore likely to find work here from the 1920s and 1930s, and the 1950s-1970s, in all areas of the Applied Arts.

Tremayne displays and sells not just paintings, prints and ceramics, but also furniture, sculptures, glassware and fabrics too. If you don't find what you're looking for then Roger and Eileen will be happy to help you try to find it through their search service. As well as their regular displays there are also occasional exhibitions, often coinciding with the St Ives September Festival, though any time is a good time to visit this exceptional gallery.

GAUGE GALLERY
26 Fore Street, St Ives, Cornwall TR26 1HE
Tel: 01736 795107
e-mail: info@gaugegallery.co.uk website: www.gaugegallery.co.uk

In light, spacious premises the **Gauge Gallery** exhibits the work of world-renowned jewellers, showcasing original works rarely seen outside prestigious galleries in the world's capitals and major cities. Many of the artists whose work cab be seen here have exhibited at the Victoria & Albert Museum and the British Museum in London and in Museums in Tokyo and New York – so quality is very much to the fore in this amazing place. Clients of the gallery have a unique opportunity to become totally involved in designing and creating their own pieces of jewellery with the owner and in-house silversmith/jeweller Ed Wilson. He is always on hand and ready with his extensive knowledge and experience to assist with commissions or to help clients choose just the right piece from the wonderful items on display. Ed's interest in design began while studying as an architectural student, during which time he started making his own jewellery. In 2002 he began an apprenticeship with Timothy (Tim) Lukes, a silversmith based in St Ives. Ed's work is greatly influenced by the environment – the seasons, the energy of the sea, the ebb and flow of the tide, all symbolising contrast and movement. His pieces display an elegant simplicity; each piece is unique, handcrafted and finished to the highest quality.

Tim Lukes learned his trade at Garrard's in London, then gained experience in many workshops in the UK and overseas before returning to St Ives in 1994 to his original interest, design. His beautifully crafted silverware and designer jewellery is widely admired and he is always ready to discuss commissions, visualising ideas with clients and recreating them in precious metals.

Paul Spurgeon is an inventive, award-winning designer/goldsmith known for his imaginative use of platinum and white and natural coloured diamonds, with minute attention to detail evident in his elegant, stylish work, which is inspired by the visual arts, literature and nature.

Shaun Leane is a Member of the Institute of Professional Goldsmiths and a multiple winner of UK Designer of the Year. After spending many years in a traditional workshop with a focus on diamond mounting and antique restoration he started his own business in 1999. he works at his bench as often as possible, creating bespoke pieces and iconic catwalk pieces in collaboration with leading fashion designers.

The craftsmen described above are just four of the major personalities linked with the Gauge Gallery. The Gallery's excellent website provides profiles and examples of the work of many other designer/artists.

🏠 historic building 🏛 museum and heritage 🏚 historic site 🍃 scenic attraction 🐦 flora and fauna

painters and sculptors is permanently on display in a rather austere three-storey building backing directly into the cliff face. Opened in 1993, the gallery offers a unique introduction to contemporary and modern art, and many works can be viewed in the surroundings that inspired them.

The Tate also manages the **Barbara Hepworth Sculpture Garden and Museum** at Trewyn Studio where she both lived and worked until her tragic death in a fire in 1975. Sculptures in bronze, stone and wood are on display in the museum and garden, along with paintings, drawings and archive material. Many of her other works are exhibited in the Tate St Ives Gallery; still more are dotted around the town.

The famous potter, Bernard Leach, is celebrated at the **Leach Gallery** housed in his former studio at Higher Stennack, about three-quarters of a mile west of the town centre. The original workshops Leach used are still in place, and there's also an exhibition room, a gallery of contemporary work, and a shop. A new purpose-built studio houses a number of resident 'start-up' potters and student potters who make the new range of high-fired Leach tableware designed by Lead Potter Jack Doherty.

The original settlement at St Ives takes its name from the 6th-century missionary St Ia, who is said to have landed here from Ireland on an ivy leaf. The 15th-century parish church bears her name along with those of the two fishermen Apostles, St Peter and St Andrew.

One of the most important pilchard fishing centres in Cornwall until the early 20th century, St Ives holds a record dating back to 1868 for the greatest number of fish caught in a single seine net. Known locally as The Island, St Ives Head is home to a Huer's Hut, from where a lookout would scan the sea looking for shoals of pilchards. A local speciality, heavy or *hevva* cake, was traditionally made for the seiners on their return from fishing. As well as providing shelter for the fishing fleet, the harbour was also developed for exporting locally mined ores and minerals. The town's two industries led the labyrinthine narrow streets to become divided into two communities: 'Downalong' where the fishing families lived and 'Upalong', the home of the mining families.

Housed in a building that once belonged to a mine, **St Ives Museum** displays a range of artefacts chronicling the natural, industrial and maritime history of the area. There is also a display dedicated to John Knill, mayor of the town in the 18th century. A customs officer by profession, he was also rumoured to be an energetic smuggler. Certainly one of the

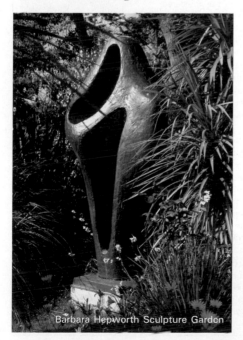
Barbara Hepworth Sculpture Garden

THE LEACH POTTERY

Higher Stennack, St Ives, Cornwall TR26 2HE
Tel: 01736 799703
e-mail: office@leachpottery.com
website: www.leachpottery.com

The year 2010 marks the 90th anniversary of the founding of **The Leach Pottery** which was established in 1820 by Bernard Leach and Shoji Hamada. One of the great figures of 20th century art, Leach played a crucial pioneering role in creating an identity for artist potters in Britain and around the world. In March 2008, a £1.7 million capital project was completed, giving new life to the Leach Pottery and enabling it to set up in production and open its doors to the public once again.

The Leach Pottery is managed by the Bernard Leach (St Ives) Trust whose primary purposes of the trust are to advance the education of the public in the life and work of Bernard Leach and his circle, and the development of studio pottery, and to provide training in the art, craft and making of pottery.

At the Trust's premises in Higher Stennack, visitors can see the Old Workshop where pots were thrown, decorated and glazed. The fireplace where Bernard used to hold impromptu debates on the nature of craft pottery is still in place. Up to 8 people would work in here. The Clay Room is where the clay was prepared and recycled. Here you can see the clay mixers, the pug machine for creating 'slugs' of clay for using on the wheel, and the bins for the powdered clay and glaze materials. Also on display are the Leach Wheels, were designed by David Leach and Dicon Nance. The flywheel is driven by

the potter's foot via a cranked pedal and provides steady momentum to the wheel head.

The Kiln Room, once open-sided to the south, was the first building on the site. The climbing kiln, built in 1923, was the first of its kind in the western world and was in use until the 1970s.

A new building hosts annually changing exhibitions, examining the Leach legacy and the history of studio pottery. Also new is the production studio where recently established potters and ceramics students work under the guidance of lead potter Jack Doherty. Housed in the old cottage is the Gallery where the selling exhibition changes regularly and features the best of British and international craft pottery.

Finally, the shop provides the opportunity to buy 'Standard Ware' created on site, and to see work from featured Cornish potters.

🏠 historic building   🖼 museum and heritage   🏛 historic site   🐾 scenic attraction   🌿 flora and fauna

Porthmeor Beach, St Ives

A more conventional celebration is the **St Ives Festival** in September each year which brings together musicians, artists and writers of the highest calibre from all over the country, and beyond.

If you feel the need to escape the busy streets, seek out **Trewyn Subtropical Gardens**, just off the High Street. Wooden sculptures of musicians stand on lawns surrounded by banana trees and other exotic flora.

town's most memorable citizens, he built the **Knill Steeple** monument to the south of the town to be his mausoleum, but it also served to guide ships carrying contraband safely to the shore. Knill left a bequest to the town so that every five years, a ceremony would be held at the Steeple when 10 girls and two widows would first sing the 100th Psalm and then dance around the monument for 15 minutes to the tune of a fiddler. For performing this strange ceremony the participants received 10 shillings (50p). The custom is still maintained - the next will take place on 25 July 2011.

It is not only artists who have been inspired by the beautiful surroundings of St Ives: Virginia Woolf recaptures the happy mood of her childhood holidays here in her novel *To the Lighthouse*; and Rosamunde Pilcher, famous for her books set in Cornwall, was born near the town in 1924.

Just to the southeast of the town, easy to reach on foot and a great favourite with families, lies the sheltered beach of **Carbis Bay** where various water sports are also available. To the west of St Ives is a wonderful and remote coastline of coves, cliffs and

stories and anecdotes   famous people   art and craft   entertainment and sport   walks

headland that provides a wealth of wildlife and archaeological interest. Following the network of footpaths from St Ives to Pendeen, walkers can discover small wooded valleys, rich bogs, old industrial remains and prehistoric features such as the cliff castles at Gurnard's Head and Bosigran.

HAYLE

7½ miles NE of Penzance on the B3301

🐦 Paradise Park

Established in the 18th century as an industrial village, Hayle was also a seaport with a harbour in the natural shelter of the Hayle estuary. It was here, in the early 1800s, that the Cornish inventor Richard Trevithick built an early version of the steam locomotive. A short time later, one of the first railways in the world was constructed here to carry tin and copper from Redruth down to the port. With its industrial past, Hayle is not a place naturally associated with cosmetics, but it was Hayle-born Florence

Nightingale Graham who set up her own beauty parlour on New York's Fifth Avenue under the name Elizabeth Arden.

The Hayle estuary and sands around the town are an ornithologist's delight. Some of the world's rarest and most beautiful birds can be seen at **Paradise Park** (see panel on page 21), a leading conservation zoo located on the southern outskirts of the town. As well as providing a sanctuary for tropical birds and exotic animals, the park also has a huge indoor play centre and a special toddlers area.

Across the estuary is Lelant, a thriving seaport in the Middle Ages that suffered a decline as the estuary silted up. Now a popular holiday village with a golf course, Lelant is particularly loved by bird-watchers, who come to see the wide variety of wildfowl and waders on the mud and salt flats. Lelant was the birthplace of Rosamunde Pilcher who celebrated her native county in enormously popular novels, including *The Shell Seekers*.

WHITE HART HOTEL

10 Foundry Square, Hayle, Cornwall TR27 4HQ
Tel: 01736 752322
e-mail: bookings@whitehearthayle.demon.uk
website: www.whitehearthotel-hayle.co.uk

Occupying an elegant Grade II listed building dating back to 1838, the **White Hart Hotel** is the oldest hotel in the town and offers period charm together with modern amenities. It has an attractive bar and a restaurant serving an appetising menu based on fresh local produce. The accommodation comprises 25 attractively furnished and decorated rooms, all with en suite facilities and provided with hospitality tray, mini-fridge and TV with Freeview. The owner of the hotel is an avid art collector so all the rooms feature original works of art from various artists. and a range of paintings and statuettes from his collection can be found decorating the rooms of the hotel. Naturally, the hotel has its own ghosts - if you feel inclined to find out for yourself, ask for Room 9!

There are two sister hotels - The Union Hotel in Penzance and the Angel Hotel in Helston (see pages 11 and 53).

🏛 historic building 🏛 museum and heritage 🏛 historic site 🦆 scenic attraction 🐦 flora and fauna

WILDLIFE WOOD CARVER

Steppy Downs Studio, 13 St Erth Hill, Hayle, Cornwall TR27 6EX
Tel: 01736 753342 / 07855 602183
website: www.wildlifewoodcarver.co.uk

Established more than twenty years ago, **Wildlife Wood Carver** was the brainchild of Roy Hewson who, at his workplace Steppy Downs Studio, just outside the small village of St Erth, worked in the creative art form of decorative wildlife woodcarving. The business has now been taken over by his son Andrew who continues to produce top quality wood carvings. They are predominantly of birds, - terns, seagulls, mallards, puffins, owls - with flying birds as a speciality. The pieces are finely balanced to produce a wing cadence close to the characteristics of the species chosen. But Andrew is happy to accept commissions for any kind of wood carving. One commission he received was for a birthday present, a carving of one man's prize possession, his racing car. He can work from photographs and has done many family portraits of children and pets.

Andrew also continues his father's use of "pyrography', a very ancient and precise art form whose name comes from the Greek for 'burning onto wood'. Combining skills learnt as an instrument maker in the aviation industry, Roy created his wildlife pieces in fine detail, using a technique that he termed 'painting with heat' . This uses the 'Firefly' control unit that Roy manufactured which provides a calibrated control of the hand piece temperature over the range from 0 to 2000 degrees Fahrenheit, a range of temperature which Roy considered as his temperature/palette producing a range of texturing colour which is very pleasing to the eye.

Steppy Downs Studio enjoys extensive views of the Hayle Estuary to the north and St. Michael's Mount and Penzance to the south west. To find it, leave the A30 at St Erth Station, just south of Hayle, and continue to the T junction. Turn left, continue through the village and up St Erth Hill. Steppy Downs House and Studio are situated on the left hand side at the brow of the hill.

St Michael's Mount

MARAZION
5 miles E of Penzance off the A394

🌿 Marazion Marsh   🔾 St Michael's Mount

🏛 St Michael's Mount Castle

Cornwall's oldest charter town (dating from 1257), Marazion was for many centuries the most important settlement around Mount's Bay. The legacy of this harbour town is its fine old inns and residential houses overlooking the sandy beach. The town is now a windsurfing and sailing centre, but to the northwest is **Marazion Marsh & RSPB Reserve**, an extensive area of wetland and reed beds behind Marazion Beach on the Penzance road. More than 450 plant species have been recorded here, and the reserve is home to many nesting and roosting birds, including herons, reed and sedge warblers and Cetti's warbler.

Situated a third of a mile offshore, **St Michael's Mount** rises dramatically out of the waters of Mount's Bay. It is connected to Marazion by a cobbled causeway that is exposed at low tide; at other times you can travel there on one of the three small ferries. Inhabited since prehistoric times, this granite rock is named after the Archangel St Michael who, according to legend, appeared to a party of fishermen in a vision in the 5th century. In the 11th century, Edward the Confessor founded a priory on the mount in tribute to the famous Benedictine Mont St Michel in Normandy. The remains of that building are incorporated into the marvellous **St Michael's Mount Castle** owned by the St Aubyn family from 1660 until 1954 when it was donated to the National Trust. The St Aubyn family remain in residence however, with a 999-year lease. Along with the impressive medieval remains, the castle incorporates architectural styles from the 17th to the 19th century. A fine plaster frieze of 1641 depicting scenes of bear and deer hunting, and some elegant Chippendale furniture are amongst the heritage treasures; a model of the castle made out of discarded champagne corks by the St Aubyns' butler, Henry Lee, is amongst the quirkier attractions.

When an earlier St Aubyn resident, the 4th Lord St Levan, was asked what had been his most significant contribution to the family home, he replied, "The 10 tons of manure I had brought to the island." They were used to fertilise the extraordinary maritime garden created in terraces just above the sea. Sub-tropical plants flourish here in abundance and even in winter fuchsias and hydrangeas are still in bloom.

GODOLPHIN CROSS
9 miles E of Penzance off the B3302

🏛 Godolphin House   🏚 Wheal Prosper Mine

🔾 Praa Sands

To the northwest of the village stands **Godolphin House**, an exceptional part-Tudor, part-Stuart house that still retains its original Elizabethan stables. The former home of the Earls of Godolphin, the house has many splendid features. However the family members, who made their fortune in mining, are more interesting; Sidney, the poet, was killed during the Civil War fighting for the king; Sidney, the 1st earl, was a Lord High Treasurer to both William III and Queen Anne; the 2nd earl imported the famous Godolphin Arabian, one of three stallions from which all British thoroughbreds are descended. While the house remains in private ownership, the Godolphin estate is owned by the National Trust and this historic landscape includes more than 400 recorded archaeological features.

To the south of Godolphin lies the hamlet of Rinsey where evidence of tin mining can be seen in the restored 19th century engine house of **Wheal Prosper** and the ruins of a copper mine, Wheal Trewavas. Just to the west of Rinsey, two headlands enclose the mile long crescent of **Praa Sands**, one of the finest family beaches in Cornwall. Further west again is Prussia Cove, a clifftop settlement named after a notorious 18th-century smuggler, John Carter, who modelled himself on Frederick the Great of Prussia.

NEWLYN
1 mile S of Penzance on the B3315

🎨 Newlyn Art Gallery

The largest fish-landing port in England and Wales, Newlyn has a long association with fishing. Its massive jetties, built in the 1880s, embrace not only the existing 15th-century harbour, but also 40 acres of Mount's Bay. The arrival of the railway in 1859 allowed the swift transportation of fresh fish and seafood to London and beyond. Newlyn is still a base for around 200 vessels. Cornish sardines are landed in the early hours each morning, ready

🎭 stories and anecdotes 🦜 famous people 🎨 art and craft 🖌 entertainment and sport 🚶 walks

for processing and canning the same day.

In late August, the Newlyn Fish Festival celebrates the value and importance of the fishing industry to the local community. Fishing boats in the harbour are decked with flags and there are spectacular displays of fish, while the quayside is thrown open to craft markets and entertainment.

It was not fish, but the exceptionally clear natural light that drew Stanhope Forbes to Newlyn in the 1880s. He was soon joined by other artists, keen to experience the joys of painting outside. The Newlyn School of art was founded with the help of other artists such as Lamorna Birsh, Alfred Munnings and Norman Garstin, but to see their work you have to visit the Penlee House Gallery in Penzance. The **Newlyn Art Gallery** exhibits a wide variety of work with special emphasis on the work of local artists, past and present.

MOUSEHOLE
2 miles S of Penzance off the B3315

Mousehole (pronounced Mowzel) was described by Dylan Thomas, who honeymooned here in 1937, as "the loveliest village in England". Still largely unspoilt, it fulfils the popular image of what a Cornish fishing village should look like, complete with a picturesque harbour where a small number of fishing boats off-load their daily catch. At the southern end of the quay, rising from the water, is Merlin's Rock. Here the great wizard is supposed to have prophesied:

*There shall land on the Rock of Merlin
Those who shall burn Paul, Penzance and Newlyn.*

In July 1595, four Spanish galleys fulfilled his prophecy. Every house in the village except one was destroyed - the sole survivor, Keigwin House (private), can still be seen.

🏛 historic building 🏛 museum and heritage 🏛 historic site 🏞 scenic attraction 🌿 flora and fauna

Stargazey

Mill Lane, Mousehole, Cornwall TR19 6RP
Tel: 01736 731115
e-mail: gifts@stargazey.plus.com
website: www.stargazey.co.uk

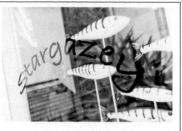

Stockists of coast & country inspired home accessories, soft furnishings & stylish designer gifts from Gisela Graham, Archipelago, Bill Brown and many more...

Take home a little piece of Cornwall from our locally sourced candles, soaps, and slate. Discover stunning sculptured driftwood fresh from a Cornish beach, tastefully combined with new ideas & inspiration from around the world. Cool, calm & co-ordinated New England colours...breathe in the sea air, relax & enjoy the experience in our pretty courtyard setting.

Fabulous interiors at affordable prices, don't miss us on your next visit to Mousehole. **Find us nextdoor to Pam's Pantry & The Little Picture Gallery.**

Dolly Pentreath, reputedly the last person to speak only the Cornish language, lived in Mousehole. She died in the early 1800s and there is a memorial to her in the churchyard at Paul, a small village just above Mousehole.

In winter, the entrance to Mousehole harbour is closed by sturdy wooden beams to keep the force of the sea at bay. In past times, the village has suffered ferocious winter storms and one of these events is

Mousehole Harbour

remembered annually shortly before Christmas on 23 December, Tom Bawcock's Eve, when a huge fish pie - Starry Gazey Pie - is baked and consumed by the patrons of the inn on the quayside. This event commemorates the catch landed by Tom Bawcock ,which saved villagers who were close to starvation as storms had prevented other fishermen from leaving harbour.

ST BURYAN

5 miles SW of Penzance on the B3283

🏯	Church of St Buriana
🏛	Boscawen-Un Stone Circle
🏛 Tretyn Dinas	🐚 Logan Rock

The landscape around this village is dominated by the 14th-century tower of one of the finest churches in Cornwall, the **Church of St Buriana**. It also provides a day mark for shipping around Land's End and can be seen from the Scilly Isles. Its major treasure is a beautiful medieval screen, painted in dazzling gold, red and green.

To the north of St Buryan is the isolated **Boscawen-Un Stone Circle** whose central standing stone is an attractive leaning pillar of sparkling quartz.

To the southwest, and sheltered in a shallow valley, is the unspoilt hamlet of Treen. A short walk away is the spectacularly sited Iron Age coastal fort, **Tretyn Dinas**. Also on this headland stands the famous **Logan Rock**, a massive 60-ton granite boulder that was once so finely balanced it could be rocked by hand.

PORTHCURNO
7½ miles SW of Penzance off the B3315

🏛	Porthcurno Telegraph Museum

🎭	Minack Theatre

A recent survey by the *Sunday Times* listed the beach at Porthcurno as one of the Top Ten Best Beaches in the World. It praised its "secret coves, craggy cliffs, soft sand and proper rock pools".

It was from this dramatic cove, protected by Gwennap Head and Cribba Head, that the first telegraph cable was laid in 1870 linking Britain with the rest of the world. The **Porthcurno Telegraph Museum**, housed in a secret underground wartime communications centre, explains the technology that has been developed from Victorian times to the present.

This interesting village is also home to the **Minack Theatre**. This open-air amphitheatre cut into the cliffside looks as if it might have been created by the Romans, but in fact it was founded by a very determined lady, Rowena Cade, in the 1930s. Appropriately, with Porthcurno Bay providing a not always serene

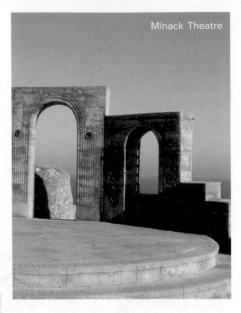

Minack Theatre

backdrop, the first play produced here, in 1931, was Shakespeare's *The Tempest*. Since then the Bard's plays have provided the central focus for each season's performances, along with other classics, avant-garde plays and the perennially popular *Pirates of Penzance*. Daytime visitors can explore the Rowena Cade Exhibition Centre, which tells the story of how Rowena spent decades developing the 750-seat theatre.

LAND'S END
9 miles SW of Penzance on the A30

🌿	Land's End Experience

Mainland England's most westerly point, Land's End was once a mystical place. Somewhere beyond its craggy cliffs lay the Lost Land of Lyonesse and the stark, treeless surroundings often draped in sea mist spoke eloquently of elemental, hostile forces. Then in 1982, a London businessman, Peter de Savary, outbid the National Trust to buy the

FIRST AND LAST COTTAGES

Treeve Moor House, Sennen, Penzance,
Cornwall TR19 7AE
Tel: 01736 871284
Mobile: 07771 914660
e-mail: info@firstandlastcottages.co.uk
website: www.firstandlastcottages.co.uk

A very personal service is offered at **First and Last Cottages** owned by Liz Trenary. The selection of self-catering holiday cottages, apartments and barn conversions are all set within an Area of Outstanding Natural Beauty in West Cornwall. Stunning scenery surrounds the properties, which are close to the breathtaking coastline and nearby fishing villages.

Liz has a wide range of self-catering accommodation available in a variety of locations including Porthcurno, Porthgwarra, St Buryan, Sennen Cove and St Just. It is Liz who takes the bookings here, meets and greets all guests and answers any enquiries. She also owns Treeve Moor House, which is the closest bed and breakfast to Land's End. It is in an ideal location for visiting the outdoor Minack Theatre, walking the coastal path and it's just four miles from Land's End airport.

There is plenty in West Cornwall to keep visitors occupied. Tourists can indulge in water sports, bird watching, the lively arts scene, visiting sub-tropical gardens and eating fabulous food. There are currently 19 self-catering properties available in the area. Ring for details.

120-acre site. At the same time he bought John o'Groats, 874 miles away near the northern tip of Scotland. "Cornwall is a goldmine," he declared and proceeded to make Land's End into a kind of theme park with a huge hotel, amusements complex and car parks. The evocative name still draws many thousands here each year and the coastline itself, swarming with herring gulls and fulmars, remains as awe-inspiring as ever. From this headland can be seen Longships Lighthouse, just off shore, and Wolf Rock Lighthouse, nine miles to the southwest.

There's almost always a queue jostling to be photographed in front of the signpost showing the distances to various cities around the world, while the **Land's End Experience** is a flashy video presentation that is certainly an experience of a kind. More acceptable are an exhibition telling the story of the men of the RNLI and state-of-the-art displays of local tales and legends and the lives of the Cornish farmers and craftsmen.

SANCREED

3½ miles W of Penzance off the A30

| 🏛 St Credan's Church | ⛲ Sancreed Holy Well |
| 🗿 Carn Euny | 🌿 Bartinney Downs |

The best example of an ancient Celtic Cross in Cornwall stands nine feet high in the churchyard of 15th-century **St Credan's Church**. In the surrounding area are two Bronze Age monuments, the Blind Fiddler and the Two Sisters. Like many Cornish menhirs, they are said to represent humans turned to stone for committing irreligious acts on the Sabbath.

Just outside the village, steps lined with glowing moss-green phosphoresce lead down

---

🎭 stories and anecdotes 🦜 famous people 🎨 art and craft 🎟 entertainment and sport 🚶 walks to **Sancreed Holy Well**, which was re-discovered by the local vicar in1879. it is in a sheltered pine and holly grove. In his book, *Holy Wells of Cornwall,* the Rev A Lane-Davies wrote, "This spot always seems to me to possess a greater air of mystery and sanctity than any other in Cornwall." Above the well is the remains of an old chapel.

To the southwest of the village is **Carn Euny**, a fascinating Iron Age courtyard farming settlement that was founded around 200BC. By far the most impressive building here is the Fogou, which was first discovered by miners in the 19th century and takes its name from the Cornish for cave. This underground chamber was constructed in three separate stages, and the 65-foot-room was entered by a low 'creep' passage at one end.

Immediately west of Carn Euny is **Bartinney Downs**, a large area of heathland where programmes are in place to preserve wildlife habitats, archaeological sites and historic features, including old china clay works, abandoned quarries and the ruins of Bartinney Castle.

ST JUST-IN-PENWITH

7 miles W of Penzance on the A3071

🚶 The Tinners' Way   🏛 The Count House

The westernmost town in mainland Britain, St Just was a copper and tin mining centre and the surrounding area is littered with industrial remains. A narrow road leads from this rather sombre town westwards to Cape Cornwall, the only cape in England, passing the last remnant of Cape Cornwall mine – its tall chimney. On the southern side of this headland lies Priest's Cove, a quiet boulder-strewn beach, while, further along, the South West Coast Path follows the cliff tops. The coastal road from St Just to St Ives, the

B3306, is regarded by many as the most spectacular coastal route in England.

For a town its size, St Just is well-supplied with art galleries displaying the work of local artists. There are four in the town itself and another, the Tregeseal Gallery, just outside.

St Just marks the start (or the end) of **The Tinners' Way**, an ancient track way between the town and St Ives. The track follows ancient moorland paths that were certainly used more than 2000 years ago and may originally have been part of a network of paths dating back to Neolithic times.

To the northeast of the town lies Botallack, where the remains of Three Crowns Mine rise dramatically on the clifftop. Here, tunnels were cut over half a mile out to sea, under the seabed, to extract rich copper lode. **The Count House** (National Trust) was formerly the acounts office for the mine and now contains exhibits detailing the area's mining history, geology and wild life.

PENDEEN

8 miles NW of Penzance on the B3306

🏛 Geevor Tin Mine 🏛 Levant Steam Engine

Tin has been mined at Pendeen since prehistoric times. At the Geevor Mine tin was still being extracted until 1985 when the international crash in tin prices sounded its death knell. The mine closed in 1990 but has been preserved as the **Geevor Tin Mine and Heritage Centre**. It not only preserves the mine but offers visitors the chance to experience the claustrophobic conditions of miners underground, while former miners relate their own stories of working here.

Close by, housed in a tiny building perched high on the cliff, is the National Trust-owned **Levant Steam Engine**, Cornwall's oldest beam engine. It has been restored and is once

PENDEEN POTTERY & ART GALLERY

Pendeen, nr Penzance, Cornwall TR19 7DN
Tel: 01736 788070
e-mail: pendeenpottery@tiscali.co.uk
website: www.pendeenpottery.co.uk

Situated in the former mining village of Pendeen, on the exceptionally scenic B3306 St Ives to Lands End road, **Pendeen Pottery and Art Gallery** is a working pottery run the husband and wife team of John and Gemma Swan.

They produce an interesting and varied range of domestic and gardenware, all hand-thrown by John and hand-decorated on the premises. As well as decorating John's white earthenware in a variety of styles, Gemma paints landscapes and still life and botanical subjects and teaches botanical and flower painting at Penzance Art School. They supply various galleries and outlets, including the Lost Gardens of Heligan, the Eden Project and National Trust properties, and John also supplies jars for the cider industry.

Paintings and crafts by other invited Cornish artists are exhibited at the pottery, which is close to Geevor Mine and Heritage Centre as well as Levant Mine and Botallack, owned by the National Trust.

again producing power. Further to the north, on the slate promontory of Pendeen Watch, stands Pendeen Lighthouse, which has been guiding ships for nearly a century.

Redruth

🪝 The Tin Miner 🐿 William Murdoch 🏔 Carn Brea
🏔 Hell's Mouth   🏛 Gwennap Pit

Redruth was once the capital of the largest and richest metal mining area in Britain. The deep mining of copper after the 1730s brought prosperity to the town – at the peak of production in the 1850s, two-thirds of the world's copper came from Cornwall. Some pockets of Victorian, Georgian and earlier buildings bear witness to those days of comparative affluence for some. The miners themselves endured dreadful conditions. Children started work as young as eight and fatal accidents were frequent. The average life span of a miner was less than 40 years. Until recently, the only memorials they had were the ruined mine buildings and chimney stacks dotted across the countryside around Redruth. But in 2008, a 6-foot-high bronze

sculpture by David Stannard of **The Tin Miner** was erected in Fore Street.

In the late 1790s, Redruth was the home of the Scottish inventor **William Murdoch** who is famous for such innovations as coal-gas lighting and vacuum powered tubes. His home, Murdoch House, was the first private house to have gas lighting installed, in 1792. It now houses the Global Migration Project where visitors with Cornish roots can trace their forebears.

Immediately south of the town rises dramatic **Carn Brea**, a granite hill that reaches some 738 feet above sea level and is crowned by a 90-foot monument to Francis Basset, a local benevolent mine and land owner. Once the site of an early Neolithic settlement, Carn Brea is also home to a small, part-medieval castle and it is still the site of the pagan ritual of the Midsummer Bonfire ceremony.

To the north, along the coast, are the two thriving holiday centres of Porthtowan and Portreath. Although they developed as a copper mining village and ore-exporting port respectively, they are now favoured by surfers and families during the summer season. Near Portreath is the startling natural feature known as **Hell's Mouth**. The geology of the cliffs here causes the inrushing seawater to make a loud booming noise as the caves fill with surging waves.

Just to the southeast of Redruth is the mysterious **Gwennap Pit**, a round, grass-covered amphitheatre, thought to have been created by the collapse of a subterranean mine shaft. Once used as a pit for the staging of cock fights,

Gwennap Pit, nr Redruth

this curious theatre is sometimes known as the Methodist Cathedral, as John Wesley preached here on many occasions. Methodists from all around the world still gather here on Spring Bank Holiday.

A few miles further southeast of Redruth, the village of Ponsonooth is home to a rather special Cornish delicacy, Cornish Yarg Cheese. This famous cheese, with its distinctive flavour somewhere between Cheddar and Caerphilly, comes wrapped in a nettle leaf covering. This local delicacy reaches many of the best restaurants and delicatessen counters around the country.

Tin Mine, nr St Agnes

Around Redruth

ST AGNES
5 miles N of Redruth on the B3285

🏚 Stippy-Stappy 🏚 Wheal Coates

🏛 St Agnes Parish Museum

🏚 Blue Hills Tin Streams ⛰ St Agnes Beacon

This picturesque coastal resort, with some of the finest surfing beaches in the UK, was once known as the source of the finest tin in Cornwall. It still retains many of its original miners' cottages and grander mine owners' houses. Of particular interest is the steeply terraced row of 18th-century cottages known as **Stippy-Stappy**, the Cornish dialect term for walking uphill. Surrounding the village are many haunting ruins of old mine workings, including the clifftop buildings of one of Cornwall's best known mines – **Wheal Coates**

(National Trust). The mine operated between 1860 and 1890 and its derelict Engine House is one of the more exceptional landmarks along this stretch of coast. The walk to the remains of Wheal Kitty provides panoramic views over this once industrial area.

Visitors coming to this now popular seaside resort can learn more about the village's heritage through the displays on mining, seafaring and local natural history at the **St Agnes Parish Museum**. Those with an interest in learning about the tin production processes should join one of the guided tours around **Blue Hills Tin Streams** at nearby Trevellas where production still continues on a small scale. Items made with the tin mined here are on sale in the shop.

Noted as the birthplace of the Georgian society painter, John Opie, St Agnes was also introduced to thousands of readers through the *Poldark* novels of Winston Graham in which the village appeared as St Ann.

From the village, a footpath takes walkers out to St Agnes Head and **St Agnes Beacon** from whose summit may be seen 30 parish

PAPER MOUNTAIN AND SCRAP ANGELS CRAFT SUPPLIES

Unit 9, Great Western Railway Yard, St Agnes, Cornwall TR5 0PD
Tel: 01872 554405
e-mail: scrapangels@btinternet.com
website: www.scrapangels.co.uk

Paper Mountain and Scrap Angels Craft Supplies is the first dedicated scrap book specialist in Cornwall. Standing in the quaint village of St Agnes, on the north coast of the Duchy, it stocks a wide range of products for those interested in scrapbooking, card making and paper crafts.

This delightful independent shop is owned by Kerry Grant who also offers a variety of classes in the shop's very own workshop (ring for details). The cost of the class includes a generous class kit, two hours tuition and another hour to complete the project.

A fun evening of scrapbooking can be enjoyed every third Wednesday and Thursday of the month at the Scrapangels shop from 7pm-10pm. The Scrapangels Scrapbook Club gives keen scrapbookers the opportunity to meet people with a similar passion for paper crafts. Those attending can work on their own projects or try one of the Page Kits on offer.

If a trip to the pretty seaside village is not on the cards you can always reap the benefits of secure shopping on the scrapangels website, which has new products added every week.

churches, both Cornish coasts, part of Devon and, at night, the lights of 12 lighthouses. There are also spectacular views over the old mine workings and remains from both the Bronze and Iron Ages. Now the home of some rare and localised plants and a wide variety of bird life, this area is criss-crossed by footpaths and is owned by the National Trust.

PENHALLOW
8 miles NE of Redruth on the A3075

🗝 Cornish Cyder Farm

Acclaimed by the English Tourist Board as The Nation's Favourite Farm Visit, the family run **Cornish Cyder Farm** just south of Penhallow offers a fully guided tour of the site and orchards. Visitors can sample some of the 40 different fruit products made here, including jams, country wines, cider, cider brandy and traditional Cornish Scrumpy. The Cyder Museum tells the history of cider-making through displays of old equipment and artefacts, and the Mowhay Restaurant serves Cornish cream teas and home-made food.

PERRANPORTH
10 miles NE of Redruth on the B3285

🗝 Lowender Peran Festival   🗝 Millennium Sundial

🏛 St Piran's Oratory

This pleasant holiday resort, with its three-mile stretch of golden sand, much favoured by surfers, was at one time a pilchard fishing and mining village that also harboured smuggling gangs. Though little has survived from those days, the small town's Celtic heritage is still remembered during the annual **Lowender Peran Festival** in mid October, which brings all the Celtic nations together through music and dance.

🏛 historic building 📷 museum and heritage 🏛 historic site 🌱 scenic attraction 🌿 flora and fauna

High on the cliff above the village rises the **Millennium Sundial**, a giant construct, which is adjusted to indicate Cornish time - 20 minutes earlier than GMT.

High up in the dunes overlooking Penhale Sands is **St Piran's Oratory**, a ruined 6th or 7th-century building constructed on the site of St Piran's grave. The ruins lay beneath the sand until it was uncovered in 1835. It's the oldest known church in the southwest, but the shifting sands have once again claimed the remains. A simple plaque now marks the burial place of the saint who is said to have travelled from Ireland to the Cornish coast on a millstone.

Perranporth rather surprisingly has its own airfield. It served as a Spitfire base during World War Two and is regarded by English Heritage as one of the most important remaining airfields of that period. The field is now used as a base for parachuting and gliding clubs. Scenic flights are also available.

ST ALLEN
9½ miles NE of Redruth off the A30

Chyverton Garden

As in many parts of the country with a Celtic tradition, Cornwall has its own 'little people' – the piskies. One legend tells of a boy from St Allen who failed to return home after going out to pick flowers in a nearby wood. His frantic mother began a search and eventually he was found, three days later, dazed but unharmed. All the boy could remember was being led deep into the forest, to a fantastic cave filled with jewels, and being fed the

Chyverton Garden

Zelah, nr Truro, Cornwall TR4 9HD
Tel: 01872 540324   Fax: 01872 540648

The core of the house at Chyverton was built in 1730 and in 1770 two wings were added by John Thomas, a wealthy mine owner. Over the next 55 years he created a Georgian landscape garden on the property: he dammed a small stream to form a lake, built a bridge and a walled garden and planted 94 acres of woodland.

The first rhododendrons, for which **Chyverton Garden** is renowned, were planted in 1890; most of them are the old hybrid Cornish Red and many are of an immense size, perhaps the largest in cultivation in Europe. The garden also has notable magnolias and camellias and a fine collection of conifers. In 1924 the estate changed hands for the first time and became the home of Treve and Muriel Holman, keen gardeners who added many exotic plants brought back from plant hunting trips to the Far East and who created a woodland garden.

The whole garden is looked after by their son Nigel, who has encouraged the wild and natural appearance that is such a feature. Some of the plants are named after Treve Holman and Nigel's late wife Elisabeth, and in the memorial garden is a wooden bridge designed by Nigel that commemorates the death of Treve in 1959.

stories and anecdotes   famous people   art and craft   entertainment and sport   walks

purest honey by the piskies.

Just to the north of St Allen, at the village of Zelah, is **Chyverton Garden** (see panel on page 35) which is centred around a grand Georgian house (private) built by a wealthy local mine owner. The landscaped garden is renowned for its rhododendrons, the first of which were planted in 1890, and for its magnolias, camellias and conifers. Admission to the garden is by appointment only and the best time to visit is during April and May.

POOL
2 miles SW of Redruth on the A3047

📷	Cornish Mines & Engines
📷	Cornwall Industrial Discovery Centre
🌱	Shire Horse Farm

Now subsumed into the Camborne and Redruth conurbation, this village was very much at the heart of Cornwall's mining industry. **Cornish Mines and Engines** (National Trust) displays two huge engines that were used to pump water from the mines. At the nearby Cornwall **Industrial Discovery Centre** the secrets of the county's dramatic heritage are revealed.

Before the days of steam, heavy work was carried out by horses, and the **Shire Horse Farm and Carriage Museum**, at nearby Treskillard, pays a living tribute to these gentle giants. The farm is also one of the very few remaining breeders of the Suffolk Punch horse. The museum has an interesting collection of private carriages and horse-drawn commercial vehicles (including the largest collection of horse-drawn omnibuses in the country), farming implements and hand tools used by previous generations. There are wheelwright and blacksmith shops, and wagon rides are available.

CAMBORNE
3 miles SW of Redruth on the A3047

📷	Geological Museum	🌱	Richard Trevithick
🏛	Trevithick Cottage	🌱	Godrevy Point

Once the capital of Cornwall's tin and copper mining area - in the 19th century the land around Camborne was the most intensely mined in the world. In the 1850s, more than 300 mines were producing some two thirds of the world's copper. However, the discovery of extensive mineral deposits in the Americas, South Africa and Australia led to the industry's decline in Cornwall in the early 1900s. Before the industry took off in the 18th century, Camborne was a small place and the traces of rapid expansion can still be seen in the numerous terraces of 18th and 19th-century miners' houses.

As the town's livelihood has depended on mining for several hundred years, it is not surprising that Camborne is home to the world-famous School of Mines. Its **Geological Museum** displays rocks and minerals from all over the world. Outside the town's library is a statue to **Richard Trevithick**, a talented amateur wrestler known as the Cornish Giant who was responsible for developing the high pressure steam engine, the screw propeller and an early locomotive that predated Stephenson's Rocket by 12 years. His achievements are celebrated in Camborne on Trevithick Day, towards the end of April, and his childhood home, **Trevithick Cottage** (National Trust), is open on Wednesday afternoons during the season.

To the northwest of Camborne is **Godrevy Point** whose low cliffs mark the northern edge of St Ives Bay. It's a popular beauty spot from where seals can be sighted offshore. Just off the point lies Godrevy Island with the

POOLEYS MEAT PANTRY

103 Trelowarren Street, Camborne,
Cornwall TR14 8AW
Tel: 01209 712350

The town of Camborne is lucky enough to boast a truly traditional butcher's shop, **Pooleys Meat Pantry**. There has been a butcher's shop on this site since 1930. It was established by the late William Pooley, continued by Douglas Pooley and then over in 2007 by Roy Clemens of the Meat Pantry and Leonard Tresidder who has worked in the town for 20 years. They make their own sausages and championship Hoggs Pudding on site and also supply hotels and other catering outlets.

Customers here have come to expect knowledgeable service from the well-trained and pleasant staff as they select their steaks, pork and poultry. Popular products here are the shop's own Cornish Porker Sausages, Pork & Apple Burgers and Black Cracked Pepper Sausages, all of which are made from locally sourced ingredients. The shop also sells Cornish Heavy Cake, Pickled Eggs and Picked Onions. If you are not able to get to the shop Pooleys operates a daily home delivery service.

lighthouse that featured in Virginia Woolf's novel *To the Lighthouse*. Much of the coastline from Godrevy eastwards to Navax Point is owned by the National Trust and the clifftops support some of the botanically richest maritime heath in Europe.

Falmouth

🏰 Pendennis Castle	🌿 Fox Rosehill Gardens
🏛 National Maritime Museum Cornwall	
🦆 Jacob's Ladder	

Falmouth has grown up around a spectacular deep-water anchorage that is the world's third largest natural harbour – only Sydney and Rio de Janeiro are more extensive. The town lies in Britain's Western Approaches and guards the entrance into Carrick Roads. First settled centuries ago, it was not until the 17th century that the port was properly developed, although Henry VIII, 100 years earlier, sought to

defend the harbour from invasion. Impressively sited on a 200-foot promontory overlooking the entrance to Carrick Roads, Henry's **Pendennis Castle** (English Heritage) is one of Cornwall's great fortresses. Along with St Mawes Castle on the opposite bank, it served as a powerful deterrent against enemy attack. Strengthened further during the threat of a second Spanish Armada, Pendennis was one of the last Royalist strongholds to fall during the Civil War. It remained in use until

Blockhouse at Pendennis Castle

🎬 stories and anecdotes   🎭 famous people   🎨 art and craft   ✏ entertainment and sport   🚶 walks

JUST LIKE THIS

37 High Street, Falmouth, Cornwall TR11 2AF
Tel/Fax: 01326 212895

In a handsome period building on Falmouth's bustling High Street, **Just Like This** is stocked with an eclectic mix of ladies' designer clothes and footwear, gifts, jewellery and accessories large and small. Fun is the name of the game here, with words like quirky, zany and fabulously funky describing the bright, colourful items on show. It's worth a visit just to meet the bubbly owner Jane Thomas, who had been in the retail business in Truro for 25 years before opening here in 2006. Since then she has been adding fun and colour to the clothes and the lives of the good ladies of Falmouth and the many visitors who spend time in this lovely place every year. Almost everything in stock is just that little bit different, great to wear and guaranteed to turn heads. Clothes and shoes are naturally the main items, but the accessories are a big part of the business, from zany bright bathing hats in vintage style to Funky umbrellas, crazy hair dyes, hair brushes and feather boas. The following are among the British and Continental brand names to be found at Just Like This, very different from each other in many respects but sharing a sense that choosing a wardrobe is something to enjoy:

Desigual, established in 1984, makes colourful Spanish clothing and accessories for ladies and girls in distinctive style. The range includes shirts, tank tops, T-shirts, blouses, skirts, dresses and coats.

Irregular Choice was founded by design entrepreneur in 1994 to maintain and encourage creativity and individuality in what he saw as a world of increasing conformity. His shoes – flats, heels, boots and trainers – have been dubbed 'the lifestyle choice of fashion footwear'.

Iron Fist, founded in 2001 by two friends from South Africa, makes shoes that are unique and stylish, with individual artwork on every item. Ideas come from skateboarding, surfing, art, music and street culture, and the artwork sets iron Fist shoes apart from streetwear counterparts.

The founders of Vendula, which was established in London in 2003, saw a gap in interesting and unusual accessories and started designing and making a range of colourful, witty bags – cute 'apple' bags, clutch bags, pearl bags, evening bags and purses. Open from 10 to 5.30pm Monday to Saturday.

the end of World War Two. Now, through a variety of displays and exhibitions, the 450-year history of the fortress is explained.

During its heyday in the early 1800s, Falmouth was the home of almost 40 packet ships, which carried passengers, cargo and mail to every corner of the globe. The introduction of steam-powered vessels put paid to Falmouth's days as a major port and, by the 1850s, the packet service had moved to Southampton. A charming legacy of the packet ships' prosperous days is **Fox Rosehill Gardens**, which are stocked with many exotic plants from around the world brought back by various ships' captains, including one named Fox. Blessed by the mild Cornish climate, banana, eucalyptus, bamboos, agaves and a wide variety of palms flourish here – and in many private gardens.

Although the docks continue to be used by

SPARKLES

15 Theydon Road, Falmouth, Cornwall TR11 2RG
Tel: 01326 314138/0783 7770013
e-mail: moirasparkles2000@yahoo.co.uk

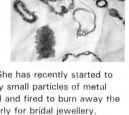

Moira McCullough produces beautiful, unique pieces of jewellery at her home in Falmouth. Her speciality is beaded jewellery, with beads in glass, crystal, pearl or wood threaded on virtually unbreakable thread. She has recently started to produce pieces from Precious metal Clay – a clay-like medium with very small particles of metal mixed with an organic binder and water. This can be shaped, then dried and fired to burn away the binder, leaving the pure metal. She also accepts commissions, particularly for bridal jewellery.

SISLEY

28 Church Street, Falmouth, Cornwall TR11 3EQ
Tel: 01326 315090
e-mail: shop@sisleycornwall.co.uk
website: www.sisleycornwall.co.uk

Located on Falmouth's main shopping street, with easy parking nearby, **Sisley** is the only retail outlet in the South West for the internationally renowned Sisley brand of ladies fashionwear. Proprietor Veronique Eastham buys this range of modern classics to cater for all ages and sizes, and the displays, beautifully laid out in colour tones, and the friendly, helpful staff make it a pleasure to shop here. The Sisley brand, a division of Benetton, covers a wide range of dresses and tops, skirts and trousers, knitwear, shoes, bags and accessories, all of the highest quality, with the finest attention to detail.

Ladies who wear Sisley will look and feel a million dollars, but considering the quality and the undoubted touch of class the prices are really competitive. Services offered by the shop include a wardrobe makeover and image consultancy. Shop hours are 10am to 5pm (to 5.30 Saturday, 12 to 4 Sunday). The website shows the Sisley range and shoppers who can't get to Falmouth can shop by mail order. An e-mail to the shop will get the latest news, offers, sales dates and new stock details.

THE COURTYARD DELI

2 Bells Court, Falmouth, Cornwall TR11 3AZ
Tel: 01326 319526
e-mail: courtyarddeli@btconnect.com

The **Courtyard Deli** is housed in traditional slate-hung stone building dating from 1764, set back behind the main street up the slipway opposite Marks & Spencer. Just thirty seconds from the hustle and bustle of Market Street, it provides an air of peace and seclusion that's prefect for a relaxing coffee and a snack or taking time to choose something to take away from the mouth-watering array of top-quality fare. The premises are light and inviting, with some easy chairs and sofas and the work of local artists on the walls. Outside is a sunny, sheltered courtyard set with tables and chairs and also offering full waiter/waitress service. It's equally popular with locals meeting friends for a chat or taking a break from work or shopping and with the many visitors who come to Falmouth throughout the year. The deli is owned and run by Lyn Pollard, who opened here in 2006. She sources as much as possible locally, using her extensive knowledge of the top producers/suppliers in the area, and has established contacts with all the suppliers of goods that come from further afield. The bread and many of the cakes, pastries and pies are made on the premises, and customers return time and again for the home-cooked ham, the zingy fresh salads, the pork pies, the homity pies, the apple pies, the meringues, the bread-and-butter pudding, the Origin organic coffee, the ice cream and the Cornish cream teas. The Deli also caters for dietary requirements, including a gluten free menu. There's also a good selection of Continental goods, including olives and olive oil, chorizo, salami and other cooked and cured meats, houmus and taramasalata.

Sandwiches with home-baked white or seedy bread tempt with generous fillings like Cornish Brie with onion marmalade, home-cooked ham with piccalilli, and sweet chilli crayfish tails. Served with chips and a salad garnish, they make tasty, satisfying snacks or lunches. Equally popular are the platters – Greek, tapas, fish, cheese and a Cornish selection.

The Deli offers a bespoke catering service that includes picnic and gift hampers, with orders taken for parties, weddings and other special occasions and cakes themed for the event.

Lyn is happy to share her passion for good food with her customers and outside the usual shop hours (daytimes Monday to Saturday) she organises occasional informal deli talks, discussions and workshops, which take place from 7 to 9 in the evening – see the website for details of upcoming evenings.

🏛 historic building 🖼 museum and heritage 🏛 historic site 🦋 scenic attraction 🌿 flora and fauna

merchant shipping, the town's traditional activities are being overtaken by yachting and tourism. Falmouth's nautical and notorious past is revealed at the **National Maritime Museum Cornwall** where the wealth of displays explain the rise in popularity of the town due to the packet ships. The museum's collection includes 120 historic British and international boats, as well as contemporary vessels, prototypes and future designs. In the vast Flotilla Gallery, an array of vessels is displayed suspended in mid-air and can be viewed from three different levels. A great way to arrive at the museum is to use the Park & Float service, located on the A39 at the northern end of the town, and sail to the museum on a classic ferry. Opposite the museum stands the town's oldest residence,

National Maritime Museum

Arwenack House (private), parts of which date back to the 14th century - most of the house, however, was remodelled in the 16th and 17th centuries.

From Killigrew Street a flight of 111 stone steps, known as **Jacob's Ladder**, climbs up the hillside to reveal sweeping views across the town and harbour. The Ladder is not named

---

THE WATERMEN'S GALLERY

Custom House Quay, Falmouth, Cornwall TR11 3JT
Tel: 01326 312165 Mob: 07971 283975
e-mail: sophi@beharrell.net
website: www.sophiart.co.uk

SOPHI BEHARRELL is a long-standing artist based in Falmouth.

She has sold in some of the leading galleries in the South west for over 13yrs, selling her canvases to all kinds of people from here and abroad.

Sophi has always managed to capture the essence of Cornwall whether it be in her **Cliffscapes** enhancing the beauty of the wildflowers or the majestic **Beachscapes** that go on forever, right through to the tranquil **Creeks and Coves.**

Come and Visit Sophi working on her latest canvas in her beautiful waterside studio overlooking Falmouth Docks.

The Watermen's Gallery also shows a wide range of local artists work and a wonderful array of crafts and giftware to suit everybody's pockets.

So, next time you are in Falmouth pop into see Sophi and her incredible studio.

"Pure Escapism, Pure Inspiration"

🎬 stories and anecdotes 🐦 famous people 🎨 art and craft ✏ entertainment and sport 🚶 walks

THE CORNISH STORE

11 Arwenack Street, Falmouth, Cornwall TR11 3JA
Tel: 01326 315514
e-mail: sales@thecornishstore.com
*   or store@cornishtreats.com*
website: www.thecornishstore.com or www.cornishtreats.com

The Cornish Store is a family run business based in the historic maritime town of Falmouth.

Keven and Anne Ayres aim to provide their customers with the very best merchandise that Cornwall has to offer – an impressive variety of gifts, crafts and souvenirs both traditional and contemporary. With a combined experience in the trade of over forty years they are true professionals with a passion for both their business and Cornwall. Ninety-nine percent of everything they sell comes from Cornwall and the UK and they are currently supporting over ninety Cornish producers. Many items are designed and produced exclusively for the Cornish Store and with prices starting at 50p there is something to suit all budgets.

The range is truly amazing, from clothing, household textiles and pottery to jewellery, clocks and watches, or from books maps and CD's to greetings cards, soft toys and delicious food and drink items. Stock changes constantly but among the perennial favourites are Cornish retro rugby shirts, T-shirts featuring Kernowman, Kernowgirl and the Cornish Mafia, Pasty Peeps soft toys, Cornish Tartan accessories, Dreckly Clocks, St.Piran Flag beach towels and Cornish sayings mugs. Cornish food and drink products are incredibly popular, who could resist delicious homemade chutneys, preserves and breakfast marmalades or luxurious fudge and handmade chocolates? You will also find the famous Furniss Fairings, Cornish Sea Salt and Tregothnan Tea. Selections of all these delectable items can be purchased in the pretty Cornish Treat Gift Baskets available in a range of prices. There are unique Camel Valley Wines, Cornish Mead and Cider and locally produced beers and liqueurs, with occasional tastings on high days and holidays. Cornish tin and pewter is seen in a wide variety of handsome jewellery that makes a fine souvenir of a visit to Cornwall. CD's cover the spectrum of Cornish music, male voice choirs, brass bands, sea shanty groups, folk, humour, dialect and the traditional Cornish carols.

A trip to the Cornish Store – a light, airy space in a Gradell listed 17th century building, is a must on any visit to Falmouth – shop hours are 9.30am – 5.30pm Monday to Saturday all year round and 11am – 4pm on Sundays between Easter and Christmas. Shoppers who can't get to the Cornish Store can browse the excellent and comprehensive websites and order on line, where, you can be assured, delivery is never Dreckly!

CHELSEA HOUSE HOTEL

Emslie Road, Falmouth, Cornwall TR11 4BG
Tel: 01326 212230 Fax: 05600 764160
e-mail: info@chelseahousehotel.com
website: www.chelseahousehotel.com

Chelsea House is a high-quality Bed & breakfast establishment in a quiet, peaceful setting off the main road but just 100 metres from the seafront. The guest accommodation has recently been refurbished to a very high standard, and most of the ten rooms have smart new bathrooms. Each of the rooms has its own theme, most enjoy fine views and three have south-facing private balconies. Guests have the use of beautiful gardens and a terrace set with tables and comfortable chairs.

The house was built in 1908 for a Dutch packet boat captain, and many attractive original features have been retained while providing modern comfort and facilities. The day starts with an excellent breakfast that includes full English and vegetarian options, several ways with eggs, kippers, Danish pastries and home-made marmalade.

Owner Donna Barbett knows everything there is to know about the area and is always happy to help guests plan their stay here. Gyllyngvase Beach and the National Maritime Museum Cornwall are close by, and Henry VIII's Pendennis Castle is a gentle stroll away.

stories and anecdotes 🕯 famous people 🎨 art and craft 🎭 entertainment and sport 🚶 walks

THE MARCH HARE

20 Church Street, Falmouth,
Cornwall TR11 3EG
Tel: 01326 312106

Specialising in high quality
ladies fashion, **The March Hare**
was one of the first
"boutiques" to open in the
picturesque Cornish town of
Falmouth. It first started
trading in 1967 and owner
Angela Cortis has been here
since the beginning, which explains her good hospitality and expertise.

It is a real delight to shop in Falmouth, with its cobbled streets, independent shops and seaside
location. It is an all year round working port and the town bustles with people in the summer
months. From the main shopping street there are side streets which lead down to the sea and so a
coastal view is never far away.

Angela offers a large range of occasion wear for weddings, cruises and dances and caters for
sizes 10 – 24. There is a beautiful selection of accessories such as hats, bags, scarves and
jewellery as well as shoes, and German and Danish casual wear. Tivoli, Zele, Peruzzi, Chianti,
Michaela Louisa and Steilmann are just some of the ranges stocked here.

The staff members are extremely friendly and accommodating and take pleasure in ensuring
each visitor has an enjoyable experience.

TYTO

3 Tidemill House, Discovery Quay, Falmouth TR11 3XP
Tel: 01326 313260
e-mail: gem@tytoboutique.co.uk
website: www.tytoboutique.co.uk

Tyto can be found just footsteps from the National Maritime
Museum Cornwall, Falmouth, and stocks a tempting range of hand-
picked products.

Founded in July 2009 and with a team of creative staff they
pride themselves on offering a space for local artists and
craftspeople to display their wares alongside great designer brands
like Marimekko.

Always on the hunt for new and exciting treats they stock a
wide selection of clothing for ladies and gentlemen as well as
desirable accessories, fabulous footwear and lovely gift and
homewares. Currently in store there are delights from brands such
as Terra Plana, Emily and Fin, COMUNE, Gentle Fawn, Loreak
Mendian and Stolen Thunder to name a few! There are also a few
carefully selected vintage treasures to look out for.

Tyto is a fantastic find at Discovery Quay in this bustling
fishing town, famous for its cobbled streets, the 16th century
Pendennis Castle and thriving independent stores.

Open Tuesday to Saturday 10-6 and Sunday to Monday 12-4.

after the biblical character but after the local businessman, Jacob Hamblen, who commissioned the steps.

In recent years the town has become a thriving centre for the arts. The Poly in Church Street is a general arts centre; the Falmouth Art Gallery has a small but interesting collection of contemporary art; the Falmouth Arts Centre offers a varied programme of film, drama, dance, recitals and live music events; and the Princess Pavilion hosts various shows during the season.

Pirates and smugglers were of course drawn to Falmouth. On Custom House Quay, stands an early 19th-century brick-built incinerator known as the Queen's Pipe. It was here that contraband tobacco seized by Falmouth's customs men was burnt. Another unusual memorial can be found on Fish Strand Quay; the tall granite obelisk here was erected in 1852 as a memorial to the men of the Post Office Packet Service, which delivered mail all over the world in 'packet boats'.

From Falmouth's busy harbour, ferries and cruise boats ply the local waters to St Mawes, Flushing, Truro and other enticing destinations, and also offer whale and dolphin spotting trips.

Around Falmouth

MYLOR
2 miles N of Falmouth off the A39

🏛 Celtic Cross

The two attractive waterside villages of Mylor Churchtown and Mylor Bridge have now blended into one another as a yachting and water sports centre. They are also home to the last remaining fleet of oyster fishermen. It was at Mylor Churchtown that the packet ships

called, and in the village's ancient churchyard lie the graves of many sea captains. Also in the churchyard, by the south porch, stands a 10-foot-high **Celtic Cross**, one of the tallest in Cornwall. A further seven feet of the cross extends underground.

Just to the southwest of Mylor is another popular yachting centre, Flushing, which was given its distinctive look by Dutch settlers from Vlissingen who arrived here in the 17th century.

PENRYN
2 miles NE of Falmouth off the A39

🏛 Glasney College of Priory

🏛 Camborne School of Mines

🦜 The Penryn Tragedy

Penryn is perhaps one of the oldest towns in the Cornwall districts. It first was founded in 1216; later being incorporated in 1621 by King James I. Before Falmouth's rise to prominence in Tudor times, Penryn was the controlling port at the mouth of Carrick Roads. At one time, granite quarried close by was shipped from here all over the world, in fact, some of the most prominent dwellings and world renowned monuments were built from the granite stone from Penryn; to name a few- the London Bridge and Singapore harbour.

Centuries ago, the small port town served as home and educational quarters for many priests in training. The **Glasney College of Priory** was founded in the mid 12th century; but later demolished in the 15th century. Today, visitors are permitted to view the relics of what is left of the famous college. Since Penryn's beginnings were built on education it seemed only right when Penryn was asked to be the new home of the Institute of Cornish Studies and the University of Exeter's world-renowned **Camborne School of Mines**. One of the specialists in mining education, Robert

JUST DELIGHTS

Commercial Road, Penryn, nr Falmouth,
Cornwall TR10 8AQ
Tel: 01326 379075
e-mail: justdelights@hotmail.co.uk
website: www.justdelights.co.uk

The owner of **Just Delights**, Gemma Guilmard, did what many people do – came to Cornwall and fell in love with the place. In Gemma's case, though, she loved it so much she moved here and opened her truly delightful and unique shop four years ago.

What makes Just Delights different is the range of pottery from Poland that it stocks. More specifically the pottery and ceramics come from the historic town of Boleslawiec in south-west Poland, the town where the first Polish pottery was made some 500 years ago. Today the industry still thrives, and the traditional local clay is what makes these items truly unique. The beautiful ivory and blue baking dishes could be used purely for display, although they are also fully safe for use in microwaves, ovens and dishwashers. For smaller gifts there are jugs, coffee-pots, salt and pepper pots, or mugs and cups, all in the same lovely Polish style.

The range of items in Just Delights has now expanded and includes vintage furniture, cards and soft toys for children, as well as herb drawers that are truly irresistible.

Hunt, is remembered here in the school's impressive Geological Museum and Art Gallery, which displays minerals and rocks from all over the world.

Penryn was the home of Thomas Pellow (born circa 1704) who spent two decades as a white slave in Morroco. Pirates captured him in 1715 when he was just 11-years-old. He stayed 23 years as a captive before escaping back to England. Pellow's story is told in his autobiography, "The History of the Long Captivity and Adventures of Thomas Pellow" (1740) and in "White Gold: The Extraordinary Story of Thomas Pellow and Islam's One Million White Slaves" (2007) by Giles Milton. A fascinating insight into the local history can be found at the town museum, located under the town hall.

Another reminder of the town's maritime past is the illusive tale of a family wiped out through greed and forms the basis of the play,

The Penryn Tragedy. After years at sea, a young sailor from Penryn returned home to his parents' Bohelland Barn and, as a joke, he disguised himself as a rich man but not before telling his sister of his plan. His parents, overcome with temptation on meeting this rich stranger, murdered the young man for his money. Next morning, the sister came in search of her brother and the full horror of their crime caused her parents to commit suicide. The particulars connected with this horrid deed, were preserved in a small pamphlet, which was published in 1618, the same year the event is said to have taken place, however this curious pamphlet does not appear to be in existence.

PORTSCATHO
4½ miles NE of Falmouth off the A3078

This pleasant, unspoilt fishing village with its sandy beach on Gerrans Bay, may appear

---

🏛 historic building   📷 museum and heritage   🏛 historic site   ⌖ scenic attraction   🌱 flora and fauna

HIGHER ROSEVINE FARM

Rosevine, Portscatho, Truro, Cornwall TR2 5EW
Tel: 01872 580247
e-mail: info@higherrosevinefarm.co.uk
website: www.higherrosevinefarm.co.uk

These 4-star, thoughtfully converted and equipped barns at **Higher Rosevine Farm** both sleep up to 4 people in a twin and double room. The perfect location for those seeking the peace and convenience of a coastal and rural position. With sandy Porthcunick beach and the S.W.Coast Path on your doorstep, you'll enjoy your stay even more knowing that both barns have been designed on sustainable principals to help preserve the unspoilt beauty of the Roseland Peninsular. Surrounded by natural beauty and wildlife you can wake up spoilt for choice as to which breathtaking walk to take, quiet beach, harbour village, restaurant or famous garden to visit.

Choose single storey Smugglers Barn, suitable for those not wanting stairs, or Wreckers Barn with the bedrooms upstairs. The combination of rustic charm and modern technology provides each with open-plan living, dining, well equipped kitchen, wet room, under floor heating and shared courtyard for al fresco dining. TV, DVD, dishwasher, fridge, microwave, hob, and oven as standard, so you can be as creative or lazy with food as desired on your self-catering holiday. The ideal escape for families, walkers, mariners, beach and garden lovers. You won't be bored, do as much or as little as you like. Sorry no pets.

TREWITHIAN FARM

Portscatho, Truro, Cornwall TR2 5EJ
Tel: 01872 580293
e-mail: enquiries@trewithian-farm.co.uk
website: www.trewithian-farm.co.uk

Trewithian Farm is a grand 400-year-old ivy-clad stone house which manages to be both a working farm and to have earned a prestigious 4 star from Visit England for its luxurious accommodation. It couldn't have a better location, on Cornwall's beautiful Roseland peninsula, a peaceful area of Outstanding Natural Beauty, yet only 10 minutes from St Mawes where a passenger ferry takes you right to Falmouth's bustling harbour. This is famous as one of the three deepest harbours in the world, and the deepest in Western Europe.

Trewithian has six bedrooms – two family rooms, two twin rooms and two double rooms, with one of the doubles having an adjoining single room too. They are all either ensuite or have their own private adjoining bathrooms, while guests can also enjoy their own private lounge, the dining room, and the farmhouse grounds. Trewithian is also open all-year, and in the winter months a hearty home-cooked evening meal is available on request, or you can dine in one of the pubs in the nearby villages, or in St Mawes. In summer there are the nearby sandy beaches of Carne and Pendower, making Trewithian ideal for family holidays too.

🎞 stories and anecdotes 🦜 famous people 🎨 art and craft 🎭 entertainment and sport 🚶 walks

THE OLIVE GROVE

Cornish Garden Nurseries,
Barras Moor Farm,
Perranarworthal, Truro,
Cornwall TR3 7PE
Tel: 01872 870867

e-mail: theolivegrove@live.co.uk
website: www.the-olive-grove.co.uk

FULLY LICENSED TRADITIONAL BISTRO

THE OLIVE GROVE Bistro/Café has a real old fashioned feel to it, incorporating a Delicatessen, Farm Shop, offering **home cooked food and local produce** (Organic where possible).
Set within the wonderful surroundings of Cornish Garden Nurseries, Barras Moor Estate, Perranarworthal, Stocking fabulous items for the home, including flowers, cushions, paintings, etc! Hand crafted jewellery, garden paraphernalia & much more! With outside seating in a peaceful oasis surrounded by Mediterranean trees.
Open 7 days a week from 10am -5.30 Monday to Sunday, offering Breakfast Lunch & High Tea with **Gluten wheat & dairy free** options available, choice of two organic meats with seasonal veg with all the trimmings, vegetarian & vegan options available for **Sunday Lunch.**
Now Open for evening bookings on Thursday, Friday and Saturday from 6pm - Midnight

"**OLIVE GROVE EVENTS!** A purpose built marquee is available for hire for functions of all descriptions. Whether you're looking for a creative corporate, fundraising event, a weeding or bar mitzvah planner, we'll put together a worry free spectacular affair that will please all!...

Mawes Castle

...familiar to anyone who watched the TV drama, *The Camomile Lawn*, for which it provided a scenic location. To the west, at St Just in Roseland, stands an exquisite 13th-century church, surrounded by gardens containing many subtropical trees and shrubs first planted by the botanist John Treseder at the end of the 19th century.

ST MAWES

2 miles E of Falmouth by ferry, on the A3078

🏰 St Mawes Castle   🏰 St Anthony's Lighthouse

🔆 St Anthony's Head

This charming town, a popular and exclusive sailing centre in the shelter of Carrick Roads, is dominated by its pristine Tudor fort, **St Mawes Castle** (English Heritage). Built in the 1540s as part of Henry VIII's coastal defences, it is a fine example of Tudor military architecture. The castle's cloverleaf, or trefoil, design ensured that, whatever the direction of an attack, the castle could defend itself. However, a shot was never fired from here in anger. Today visitors can look around the Tudor interiors, which are in remarkably good condition, and shudder at the oubliette - a deep shaft where prisoners...

...were detained. Its opening is now covered by glass.

From the town, ferries take passengers across the river to Falmouth and, during the summer, a boat also takes passengers down the river to the remote and unspoilt area of Roseland around St Anthony. From St Anthony Head, the southernmost tip of the Roseland peninsula, there are wonderful views across Carrick Roads. At the foot of the headland stands **St Anthony's Lighthouse**, built in 1834 to warn sailors off the notorious Manacles rocks. It is open to the public during the season.

An excellent starting point for a number of coastal walks, **St Anthony's Head**, owned by the National Trust, also provides a scenic

St Anthony's Lighthouse

DELI-CIOUS OF ST MAWES

1/2 The Arcade, St Mawes, Truro, Cornwall, TR2 5DT
Tel: 01326 270045

Claire and James Brown bought **Deli-cious** 4 years ago with the aim of buying only the best of West Country foods. They have learned to appreciate local foods and their cheeses, crabs, scallops and fish truly are a joy to cook and serve. Local early vegetables are made into soups, preserves, chutneys and pickles which are enhanced by Italian Olive Oils and flavoured stuffed olives. To complete your fantastic culinary experience, a range of fine wines and chocolate are also available. Deli-cious offer a hamper service for Christmas, birthdays and other occasions all made from their exciting selection of local and home-made produce.

THE SQUARE GALLERY

5 The Arcade, St Mawes, Nr Truro, Cornwall TR2 5DT
Tel: 01326 270720
e-mail: squaregallery@mac.com website: www.thesquaregallery.co.uk

The Square Gallery with its beautiful harbour front location is much more than a place to hang paintings. Every inch of the cosy interior is occupied with an eclectic mix of individually selected arts and crafts, the majority of which are from Cornish artists. Painted silk scarves drape alongside collages and abstracts, hand-crafted jewellery twinkles next to boldly painted local scenes, ceramics and figurines line the walls beneath oil paintings and watercolours. There truly is a treasure for everyone and all can feel comfortable to browse for that unique piece of art. The Square Gallery is open from 10.30am to 5pm daily.

PHILIP MARTIN ESTATE AGENTS

3 The Arcade, St Mawes, Truro, Cornwall, TR2 5DT
Tel: 01326 270008   Fax: 01872 264007
e-mail: sales@philip-martin.co.uk website: www.philip-martin.co.uk

Opening the doors to their St Mawes office in 2007 Philip Martin is the only independent qualified Estate Agent in St Mawes. Coupled with the successful office in Truro which was established in 1986 the partners Philip Martin, Steven Jenkin and James Harvey along with their professional dedicated team offer advice and proactive marketing on all matters relating to property sales and purchases as well as advice on letting, auctions, valuations, planning, development and legal matters. With all partners having a strong Cornish background and over 70 years combined experience in the local property market the firm offers a high quality professional and personal service that is backed by the Royal Institution of Chartered Surveyors.

LOOK AGAIN ANTIQUES & COUNTRY FURNITURE

4 The Arcade, St Mawes, Truro, Cornwall TR2 5DT
Tel: 01326 270988 Fax: 01326 270792

For over 4 years Ken Walkers' harbour front shop has been brimming over with a wide range of beautiful furniture from many a different era. Inside the shop is treasure trove of collectable curiosities and small antique items nestled atop and alongside larger pieces such as chairs, tables and dressers. All tastes and periods are catered for amongst the vast range which frequently spills out of the front of shop creating a pavement display of furniture history. So whether you are looking for that vital piece to finish a special room or a unique gift for a loved one, a trip to **Look Again Antiques & Country Furniture** is not to be missed! Ken also runs a cycle hire business from his store, with all the bicycles outside.

setting for the remains of a military battery in use right up until the 1950s.

St Mawes itself provides a good base from which to explore the Roseland Peninsula, an enchanting area of narrow lanes and waterside villages.

ST KEVERNE
12 miles SE of Falmouth off the B3293

Something of a focal point on this part of the Lizard Peninsula, the pleasant village of St Keverne is rare in Cornwall in that it has a handsome village square. Its elevated position has led to its octagonal church spire being used as a landmark for ships attempting to negotiate the treacherous rocks, The Manacles, which lie offshore. In the churchyard, there are some 400 graves of those who have fallen victim to this dangerous reef.

Just outside the village a statue commemorates the 500th anniversary of the Cornish Rebellion of 1497, one of whose leaders was a blacksmith from St Keverne, while the church has a plaque in memory of the executed rebel leaders. Although St Keverne has been dominated by the sea for centuries, its agricultural heritage is continued in the ancient custom of Crying the Neck. It was believed that the corn spirit resided in the last wheat sheaf cut, so this was plaited and hung over the fireplace until spring.

MAWNAN SMITH
3 miles S of Falmouth off the A39

🌿 Glendurgan Garden 🌿 Trebah Garden

Just to the west of this pretty village is **Glendurgan Garden** (National Trust), created in the 1820s in a wonderful wooded valley that drops down to the shores of the Helford estuary. The garden contains many fine trees and exotic plants, and children will enjoy the famous Heade Maze, created in 1833 from laurels, as well as the Giant's Stride – a maypole.

To the southeast, the tower of the 15th-century church at Mawnan has been a local landmark for sailors for centuries. An excellent place from which to take in the sweeping coastline, the tower was also used as a lookout post during times of war.

Further up Helford Passage is the tiny fishing hamlet of Durgan, along with the sub-tropical **Trebah Garden** that has often been dubbed the 'garden of dreams'. On a 25-acre site that falls down to a private beach on the Helford Estuary, the owner at the time, Charles Fox, set out to create a garden of rare and exotic plants and trees collected from around the world. Reaching maturity in the early 1930s, and regarded at the time as one of the most beautiful in England, the garden was sold in 1939. There followed some 40 years of neglect before a massive restoration programme in the 1980s returned it to its original impressive state.

HELFORD
6 miles S of Falmouth off the B3293

🚶 Helford River Walk

A picture-postcard village standing on the secluded tree-lined southern banks of the Helford estuary, Helford must have one of the most attractive settings in the whole of the county. It was once the haunt of smugglers who took advantage of the estuary's many isolated creeks, one of which inspired Daphne du Maurier's novel *Frenchman's Creek*. She had spent her honeymoon in the area and the book is her only romantic novel.

Helford town is now a popular sailing centre. During the summer, it is linked to Helford Passage, on the northern bank, by a

BURDOCK VEAN HOTEL

*Budock Vean Hotel, nr Helford
Passage, Mawnan Smith, Falmouth,
Cornwall TR11 5LG
Tel: 01326 252100
website: www.budockvean.co.uk*

The Budock Vean Hotel is a four-star
country house hotel, set in 65
beautiful acres on the beautiful
Helford river. Awarded Considerate
Hotel of the Year 2010 it boasts its own golf course, tennis courts, large indoor pool, health spa
and award winning restaurant.

The hotel's superb restaurant offers an excellent and varied cuisine using local produce. Fresh
seafood and Cornish cream teas are naturally among the specialities. You'll find an atmosphere of
calm here, which allows you the space to recharge your batteries, spend some time with good
friends or simply indulge yourself.

Out in the fresh air, the James Braid golf course beckons. From the front door, walkers can
explore the river to Rosemullion Head or Porth Navas, across the river via ferry to Helford Village
and Frenchman's Creek or wander along to nearby Trebah and Glendurgan gardens.

The spectacular indoor heated pool with its open log fire and sauna is warm and welcoming
during the winter and in summer. The health spa offers a full range of massage and aromatherapy
treatments including Spiezia 100% organic spa range. Awards: Four-star AA and ETB.

SOUTH WEST INTERIORS – TREVARN BED AND BREAKFAST

*Trevarn, Carwinion Road, Mawnan Smith, Falmouth,
Cornwall TR11 5JD Tel: 01326 251245
e-mail: enquiries@trevarn.co.uk
website: www.trevarn.co.uk*

The picturesque village of Mawnan Smith is home to the
beautifully decorated **Trevarn Bed and Breakfast.** Friendly
owners Melanie and Geoffrey have their own interior design
company, **South West Interiors,** and so the whole place is
tastefully decorated and furnished.

The bed and breakfast is set in an idyllic location with
spectacular rural views. Being in the heart of Rosamund
Pilcher and Daphne du Maurier country, nowhere in the Duchy
is more than an hour away.

There are three well equipped guest rooms available here,
with one double, one twin and a single room. Each of the
rooms has its own private bathroom and two are located on
the ground floor, with easy access for disabled visitors. Ring for details.

Trevarn is perfectly situated for walking the coastal path, with the Helford River just down the
road at Carwinion, and the coastal path ten minutes' walk away at Nansidwell beach. Carwinion
Gardens can be found opposite the guest house, which is in a quiet location, with wonderful views
down to Mawnan Smith village and Maenporth.

ferry that has been in existence since the Middle Ages. The deep tidal creeks in the area have given rise to rumours that this is the home of Morgawr, the legendary Helford monster. The first recorded sighting of Morgawr was in 1926 and ever since then there have been numerous people who claim to have seen this "hideous, hump-backed creature with stumpy horns".

From the village, the five-mile **Helford River Walk** takes in several isolated hamlets and a 200-year-old fig tree in the churchyard at Manaccan before returning to the tearooms and pubs of Helford.

The rich mud of the Helford River, revealed at low tide, is a wonderful feeding ground for many birds including heron, cormorant and curlew, while the ancient natural woodlands along the shores support a wealth of plants and wildlife.

GWEEK
8 miles SW of Falmouth off the A394

🐾 National Seal Sanctuary

Set at the head of the Helford River, the picturesque village of Gweek developed as an important commercial port in the 13th century after Helston harbour became silted up. The same fate befell Gweek years later although it retains its links with its maritime past and the old harbour area is very much alive with craft shops and small boatyards.

Just a short distance from the centre of the village along the north side of the creek, is the **National Seal Sanctuary** (see panel below), the country's leading marine rescue centre established over 40 years ago. The sanctuary cares for sick, injured and orphaned seals. Visitors can witness the joyful antics of the seals at feeding time and explore the Woodland Nature Quest around an ancient coppiced wood.

HELSTON
10 miles SW of Falmouth on the A394

🏨 Blue Anchor Inn		🏨 Angel Hotel	
🏨 The Monument		🏛 Helston Folk Museum	
🦋 Festival of the Furry		🐾 Trevarno Estate	
🏛 National Museum of Gardening			
🦋 Flambards	🐾 Loe Pool	🎬 Lady of the Lake	

Dating back to Roman times when it was

National Seal Sanctuary

Gweek, near Helston, Cornwall TR12 6UG
Tel: 01326 221361
website: www.sealsanctuary.co.uk

The National Seal Sanctuary, set on the picturesque reaches of the Helford Estuary, is a haven for some of the world's most enchanting creatures. Every year the sanctuary rescues, rehabilitates and releases over 30 injured or abandoned seal pups. Following all the care and attention in the seal hospital, the pups are transferred to the convalescence pools once they are well enough and able to feed. In these pools they build up their strength before returning to the wild. By getting involved with the adoption scheme, your valuable contribution would directly benefit the seals in their recovery and, in most cases, eventual release.

🎬 stories and anecdotes 🐾 famous people 🎨 art and craft 🦋 entertainment and sport 🐾 walks

developed as a port, Helston is the westernmost of Cornwall's five medieval stannary towns. During the Middle Ages, tin was brought here for assaying and taxing before being shipped. However, in the 13th century a shingle bar formed across the mouth of the River Cober, cutting off the port's access to the sea. Helston's long history has left it with a legacy of interesting buildings. **The Blue Anchor Inn** was a hostel for monks before becoming an inn during the 15th century. It has its own private brewery, believed to be the oldest in the country. It's at the rear of the inn, next to the old skittle alley, and its beer, Spingo, comes in three strengths.

Another hostelry, the 16th-century **Angel Hotel** (see panel opposite), was originally the town house of the Godolphin family, but was converted into a hotel in the mid 1700s. Around that time, the Earl of Godolphin

provided funds for the parish church to be rebuilt after the previous structure had been struck by lightning and had to be demolished. In the churchyard stands a memorial to Henry Trengrouse, the Helston man who invented the rocket-propelled safety line that has saved so many lives around the British coast. Elsewhere, there are a surprising number of Georgian, Regency and Victorian buildings, which all help to give Helston a quaint and genteel air. One of the most striking architectural features in the town is **The Monument** in Coinagehall Street. A large arch bristling with pinnacles, it was erected in 1834 in memory of Humphrey Millet Grylls, a local banker and solicitor who was instrumental in saving the local tin mine from closing and thus preserving 1200 jobs.

Housed in one of the town's old market halls, close to the classical 19th-century

---

INSPIRATIONS

11 Wendron Street, Helston,
Cornwall TR13 8PT
Tel: 01326 572335
e-mail: paula.inspirations@google mail.com

Established by Paula Hendra in 2006, **Inspirations** provides exactly that - unusual and quirky gifts for all ages and pockets. They range from silver and costume jewellery, to handbags, scarves and accessories. There's an excellent selection of cards, along with some fascinating toys, soaps and bath bombs. Suppliers include Gisela Graham (interior décor), Jelly cat (soft toys and furnishings), East of India (hand-made cards and gifts), Vendula and Stone Bags (handbags and shoes),, Koziol (bathroom accessories) and Terramundi (money pots).

Helston itself is an ancient town which is best known for its Floral Dance which takes place on May 8th and attracts visitors from around the world. Many of the buildings in the town are built in the typical granite. The Inspirations shop is in this traditional style and stands on the same street where the famous world champion heavyweight boxer Bob Fitzsimmons was born in 1863. A plaque on his family's cottage in Wendron Street commemorates his achievements.

THE ANGEL HOTEL

16 Coinage Hall Street, Helston, Cornwall TR13 8EB
Tel: 01326 569393
website: www.theangelhotel-helston.co.uk

Dating back to the 16th century, **The Angel Hotel** was once the town house of Lord Sidney Godolphin who was First Minister to three monarchs. Later, it became a noted coaching inn and has been offering hospitality for more than 250 years. Under new management, it has recently been refurbished and has an elegant restaurant offering traditional meals and daily specials; a public bar and a superb lounge with weekly live entertainment; and a splendid Function Room/Ballroom with a minstrel's gallery catering for up to 150 guests. The hotel also offers comfortable accommodation in 13 double bedrooms, all with en suite facilities and beautifully appointed. The hotel ideally located in the heart of the high street of Helston, famous for its Floral Day and Furry Dance held in early May.

There are two sister hotels - The White Hart Hotel in Hayle and the Union Hotel in Penzance (see pages 11 and 22).

Grylls Monumnet

Guildhall, is the **Helston Folk Museum**, which covers many aspects of the town's and the local area's history. The displays range from archaeological finds and mineral specimens to the reconstruction of a blacksmith's shop, an 18th-century cider mill and a farm wagon from 1901.

Still very much a market town serving much of the Lizard Peninsula, Helston has managed to escape from the mass tourism that has affected many other Cornish towns. However, the famous Helston **Festival of the Furry**, or

Floral Dance, a colourful festival of music and dance, does bring people here in droves. The origins of the name are unknown, but it is clear that the festival has connections with ancient pagan spring celebrations as it is held on 8 May. The climax of the celebration is the midday dance when invited participants wearing top hat, tails and dress gowns, weave in and out of shops, houses and gardens.

Just to the northwest of the town lies **Trevarno Estate and Gardens** (see panel on page 56) – "the best excuse anyone could possibly want to go to Cornwall" according to *The Times*. This beautiful estate stocked with many rare shrubs and trees has a long history stretching back to 1296 when Randolphus de Trevarno first gave the land its name. Over the intervening centuries the gardens and grounds have been developed and extended so that, today, Trevarno is known as one of the finest gardens in a county with a great gardening

Trevarno Estate and Gardens

Trevarno, Crowntown, nr Helston, Cornwall TR13 0RU
Tel: 01326 574274 Fax: 01326 574282
e-mail: info@trevarno.co.uk
website: www.trevarno.co.uk

The jewel in the crown, at the heart of the estate, is 70 acres of enchanting gardens and grounds featuring one of Cornwall's largest and most diverse plant collections set within magnificent formal, informal and woodland areas. The gardens include numerous specimen shrubs and trees, a stunning bluebell valley, ornamental lake with picturesque Victorian Boathouse and formal cascade, Sunken Italian Garden, Serpentine Yew Tunnel, extensive Pinetum, Bamboo collection, atmospheric Rockery and Grotto, the Great Lawn and Summer Terrace and many other interesting features.

A remarkable celebration of Britain's gardening heritage can be found in the National Museum of Gardening, which features the country's largest and most comprehensive collection of gardening antiques, memorabilia and ephemera. A wide range of handmade soaps and skincare products are produced using the purest plant oils and materials available and visitors can sample the products, which are available for sale, in the Organic Herbal Workshop. Refreshments are available in the Fountain Garden Conservatory and there is a childrens adventure play are. A 2km walk takes you through the estate and offers excellent views.

tradition. The estate's **National Museum of Gardening** complements the grounds and highlights the ingenuity of gardeners down the ages by the range of gardening implements exhibited. Other attractions here include Soap and Skincare Workshops; a Vintage Soap Museum; the Colin Gregory Toy Museum; an adventure play area; a conservatory serving refreshments and a shop.

To the east of the town lies another interesting and award-winning family attraction, **Flambards**. Based around a faithful re-creation of a lamp-lit Victorian street, complete with more than 50 shops, it has numerous attractions for all the family. Exhibits include an undercover life-size re-creation of a World War Two blitzed street, an Anderson Shelter and a wartime pub. Wedding Fashions Down the Years features a romantic assembly of changing styles with a collection of wedding dresses and wedding cakes from 1870 to 1970. Rides and slides keep the youngsters happy, and for older children and adults the figure-of-eight karting circuit provides the opportunity to put driving skills to the test.

Close by is the Royal Navy's land and sea rescue headquarters at Culdrose, the largest and busiest helicopter base in Europe. Since the base was established here in 1947 as *HMS Seahawk*, it has carried out a great many successful search and rescue operations. There are guided tours and a special viewing area from which the comings and goings of the helicopters can be observed. In early August each year the base hosts Cornwall's largest one-day annual event, the Culdrose Air Day, which includes a five-hour flying display and attracts aircraft from around 20 countries.

When in the 13th century the shingle bar formed to the west of Helston and dammed the River Cober, it created the largest freshwater lake in Cornwall, **Loe Pool**. This is now owned by the National Trust and is a haven for sea birds as well as waterfowl such as mallard, mute swan, coot, teal and red-necked grebe. A Cornish folk tale links Loe Pool with the Arthurian legend of the **Lady of the Lake** – Tennyson himself favoured this site. As at Bodmin Moor's Dozmary Pool, a hand is said to have risen from the depths of the water to catch the dying King Arthur's sword. Another local story connects Loe Bar with the legendary rogue, Jan Tregeagle, who was set the task of weaving a rope from its sand as a punishment.

MULLION
12 miles SW of Falmouth on the B3296

| 🦀 Mullion Cove | 🐿 Guglielmo Marconi |
| 🏛 Future World @ Goonhilly | |

The largest settlement on the peninsula, Mullion has a 15th-century church and a 16th-century inn and is an ideal base from which to explore this remarkable part of Cornwall. A mile to the east lies the pretty, weather-worn harbour of **Mullion Cove** (National Trust), and just up the coast is the popular sandy beach of Poldhu Cove. It was from the clifftops above the beach in 1901 that the radio pioneer, **Guglielmo Marconi**, transmitted the first wireless message across the Atlantic. His Morse signal, the letter s repeated three times, was received in St John's,

---

SAVOY HOUSE GALLERY & HOLIDAY ACCOMMODATION

Churchtown, Mullion,
Cornwall TR12 7HQ
Tel: 01326 241271
e-mail: art.object@virgin.net

Located in a traditional double fronted Victorian house in the centre of the village of Mullion on the Lizard Peninsula, you will find Savoy House Gallery. Owned and run by Amanda Hopkins, the shop offers for sale well-chosen quality gifts, jewellery (costume and silver) and other ladies' accessories.

Amanda has been here for around three years and has established a lovely business, having previously worked in retail in London for many years.

Scarves, hand bags and purses are just some of the delightful products on sale in this spacious, airy and well stocked shop. Local ceramics and some local art work are available at Savoy House Gallery, which is open every day in the summer season, (winter opening times vary).

Above the gallery is a comfortable two bedroom holiday apartment (sleeping four), which has been decorated to a high standard. The apartment is available all year round. There are two free car parks in Mullion and on-street parking outside the shop.

🎭 stories and anecdotes 🐿 famous people 🎨 art and craft 🎟 entertainment and sport 🥾 walks

Newfoundland, quelling the doubts of the many who said that radio waves could not bend round the Earth's curvature. In 1905 a daily news service for ships was inaugurated, and in 1910 a message from Poldhu to the *SS Montrose* led to the arrest of the murderer Dr Crippen. A small granite obelisk, the Marconi Monument, was unveiled on the site of the wireless station by his daughter after the inventor's death.

Just a couple of miles inland, on the windswept heathland of Goonhilly Downs, is a monument to the very latest in telecommunications – **Future World @ Goonhilly**. It is the largest such station in the world and there have been few world events that have not been monitored through here since it opened in the 1960s. The guided tour around the station, which takes in all manner of telecommunications, including the internet and videophone links, is a fascinating and rewarding experience.

PORTHLEVEN
12 miles SW of Falmouth on the B3304

This pleasant fishing town developed from a small village in the 19th century. In 1811, London industrialists employed French prisoners-of-war to build a three-section harbour, which is arguably the most impressive in Cornwall. They planned to export tin and china clay and import mining machinery, and also to protect the growing fishing fleet. Sadly, this scheme to establish Porthleven as a major tin-exporting centre failed, but today the harbour is still busy with small fishing boats landing their daily catch. A number of the town's old industrial buildings have been converted into handsome craft galleries, restaurants and shops, and the charming old harbour is overlooked by an assortment of

attractive residential terraces and fishermen's cottages. A popular and attractive town, Porthleven is gaining a gastronomic reputation on account of the many excellent restaurants, cafés and inns to be found in such a small area. It also has a top quality fishmonger's shop located on the quayside.

LIZARD
14 miles SW of Falmouth on the A3083

🕏 South West Coast Path   🐟 Kynance Cove

Lizard is a place of craft shops, cafés and art galleries and lends its name to the Lizard Peninsula, the most southerly point of mainland Britain and also the country's warmest area. Just 14 miles by 14 miles, the peninsula's unique scenery has caused it to be designated an Area of Outstanding Natural Beauty. The **South West Coast Path** follows the coastline, much of which is cared for by the National Trust, and provides many opportunities for walkers of all abilities. In particular, there is a nine-mile, sometimes strenuous, walk to Mullion that takes in some of the most spectacular scenery as well as passing lowland Britain's largest National Nature Reserve.

The Lizard is also known for its unique Serpentine rock, a green mineral that became fashionable in the 19th century after Queen Victoria visited Cornwall and ordered many items made from the stone for her house, Osborne, on the Isle of Wight. The village is still the centre for polishing and fashioning the stone into souvenirs and objets d'art.

To the south of the village is Lizard Point, the tip of the peninsula, whose three sides are lashed by waves whatever the season. There has been a form of lighthouse here since the early 1600s. The present Lighthouse was built in 1751 despite protests from locals who feared that they would lose a regular source of income from looting wrecked ships. It now houses a light that is one of the most powerful in the world.

Just to the northeast of Lizard is the picturesque fishing village of Cadgwith, wedged in a rocky cove with fishing boats drawn up on the beach. With its cluster of pastel coloured thatched cottages and two shingle beaches, it is everyone's idea of a typical Cornish village. Life has not always been so peaceful here.

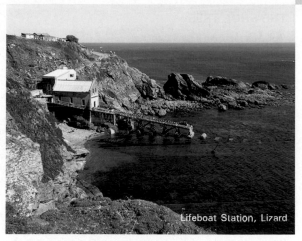
Lifeboat Station, Lizard

Throughout the 19th century, this was a busy pilchard fishing centre. In 1904, a record catch of nearly 1.8 million pilchards was landed in just four days. A small fleet of boats still sails from here, though their catch now is mainly lobster, crab, shark and mullet. Nearby is the curiously named Devil's Frying Pan, a collapsed sea cave with a spectacular blow-hole in the cliff.

To the northwest is the famous beauty spot, **Kynance Cove**, whose marvellous sandy beach and dramatic offshore rock formations have been a favoured destination ever since Prince Albert visited here with his children in 1846. The cove is the site of the largest outcrop of the Lizard Peninsula's curious Serpentine rock and there are caves to the west of the cove that can be explored, with care, at low tide.

WENDRON

8½ miles W of Falmouth on the B3297

🏛 Poldark Mine Heritage Complex

Close to this bleak village is one of the many mines that have been worked in this area since

the 15th century. It has now re-opened as the **Poldark Mine Heritage Complex**. Visitors to this interesting attraction can take an underground tour of the tunnels, see the famous 18th-century Poldark village and wander around the machinery exhibits, some of which are in working order. For a small charge, you can also try your hand at panning for gold.

Truro

🏛 Lemon Street   🏛 Truro Cathedral

🏛 Royal Cornwall Museum

This elegant small city at the confluence of three rivers – Tri-veru in Cornish – is the administrative and ecclesiastical centre of Cornwall. The city expanded from its ancient roots in medieval times following the prosperity originating from local mineral extractions. It was one of the first towns to be granted the rights of stannary (regulation of the tin trade), and several small medieval alleyways act as a reminder of those busy times before the silting up of the river saw

THE SHOE TREE

9 St Mary's Street, Truro, Cornwall TR1 2AF
Tel: 01872 320094
e-mail: downiedo@hotmail.com

Truro is an elegant little city where three rivers meet, with gracious Georgian streets and a Cathedral. It became a city when Cornwall was granted its own Bishop in 1877 and work began on the Cathedral in 1880. In the shadow of the Cathedral, on a corner site in St Mary's Street, Michelle Downie owns and runs the **Shoe Tree**, which sells a wide range of high-quality footwear for men and women, along with designer leather goods and luxury accessories. Some of the footwear brands have been household names for many years, while others are new on the scene, but all have quality and reliability in common, and all have the seal of approval from Michelle Downie, herself an accomplished footwear designer.

Sebago is best known for its Dockside range, introduced in 1970 and now available in a range of colours and limited edition designs. The name of Barkers, founded in 1880, is synonymous with classic British shoe design, and their shoes are still made by traditional methods, including uppers shaped on the last by hand. Van Dal is a Norwich-based firm making a wide range of ladies' shoes and boots that incorporate many comfort features. Mary G makes shoes for casual, everyday and special occasion wear, often distinguished by vibrant colours and luxurious fabrics. Other brands include Vic, Manila and Audley, and among the accessories sold by the Shoe Tree are sunglasses by Dior and Gucci, scarves and handbags. Trading hours are 10 to 5 Monday to Saturday.

Truro decline as a port and be overtaken by Falmouth. It was a fashionable place, rivalling Bath in the 18th century, and the short-lived recovery in mineral prices at that time saw the creation of the gracious Georgian streets and houses that are still so attractive today – **Lemon Street** in particular is regarded as one of the finest surviving Georgian streets in the country. Overlooking Lemon Street is a lofty memorial column to the African explorers Richard and John Lander who were born in Truro and who in the 1830s mapped the course of the River Niger.

Nearby is one of the city's most recent developments, Lemon Quay. It occupies the site of the original quay, which was covered over in 1923 and still remains beneath the surface. Above it, the pedestrianised piazza is busy with bars, restaurants and cafés, and

hosts various events such as the regular Arts, Crafts and Food Markets and the popular Made in Cornwall Fairs.

The arrival of the railway in 1859 confirmed Truro's status as the regional capital. In 1877, it became a city in its own right when the diocese of Exeter was divided and Cornwall was granted its own bishop. The foundation stone of **Truro Cathedral** was laid by the future Edward VII in 1880. This splendid Early English style building, with its celebrated Victorian stained glass window, was finally completed in 1910. Remnants of the earlier Perpendicular-style church that was demolished to make way for the cathedral include St Mary's Aisle and some striking Jacobean tombs. A curiosity in the south aisle is a matchstick model of the building that took 1600 hours and some 42,000 matches to

---

summer, concerts are held here. The park's peaceful atmosphere is occasionally disturbed by a train rumbling over the majestic granite viaduct nearby. Originally built by Isambard Kingdom Brunel, but replaced in 1904, the viaduct carries the main line from Paddington to Penzance.

During the summer months, river cruises to Falmouth and St Mawes are available.

FEOCK
4 miles S of Truro off the B3289

🏠 Smugglers Cottage 🏠 Trelissick

This is one of the prettiest small villages in Cornwall and there is a pleasant creek-side walk to the west. This follows the course of an old tramway, which dates from the time when this area was a bustling port. To the south of the village is Restronguet Point and the 17th-century Pandora Inn, named after the ship sent out to capture the mutineers from the *Bounty*.

From Tolverne, just north of Feock, Allied troops left for the Normandy coast during the D-day landings. On the shingle beach the remains of the concrete honeycombed mattresses can still be seen. While in the area, General Eisenhower stayed at **Smugglers Cottage**, a lovely Grade II listed thatched cottage, which is now a licensed tearoom serving lunches and cream teas in its riverside garden. Its owners have amassed a fascinating collection of memorabilia relating to that period.

Close by lies the estate of **Trelissick**, a grand 18th-century house with an imposing columned portico, surrounded by marvellous gardens and parkland with wonderful views over Carrick Roads. Although the house is not open to the public, the estate, which is owned by the National Trust, offers visitors tranquil

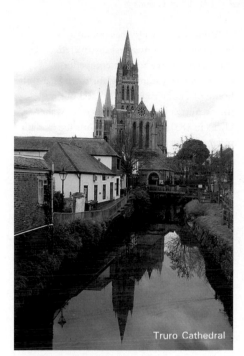
Truro Cathedral

complete. Outside, the cathedral's three spires soar high above a city in which high-rise buildings are still very much the exception.

Housed in one of Truro's fine Georgian buildings, the **Royal Cornwall Museum and Art Gallery** covers the history of the county from the Stone Age to the present day. Amongst its treasures are some early Bronze Age collars of beaten gold and the coffin of Ast Tayef Nakht dating from around 675BC, complete with unwrapped mummy. The Art Gallery, one of 10 scattered around the city, displays fine art from the Newlyn School to the present day.

The city has two major parks. The larger, Boscawen Park, sits beside the Truro River; Victoria Gardens, originally created to commemorate Queen Victoria's Diamond Jubilee, is filled with exotic trees, shrubs and flowers. On Sunday afternoons in the

gardens of exotic plants and the chance to walk along miles of paths through its extensive park and woodland beside the River Fal. Various outbuildings have been converted into restaurants, an art and craft gallery and a gift shop.

Feock can boast of sustaining one of only five remaining chain ferries operating in England. The King Harry Ferry has an all year round service and can take up to 28 cars per trip. It travels between Feock and Philleigh on the Roseland and cuts the journey time from Truro to the Roseland by up to 25-30 miles on a round trip.

St Austell

ᠪ Cornish Alps ᠉ St Austell Brewery Visitor Centre
ᠷ China Clay Country Park

"This strange white world of pyramid and pool," was Daphne du Maurier's response to the bizarre landscape around St Austell. The man ultimately responsible was William Cookworthy, a chemist from Plymouth, who discovered large deposits of kaolin, or china clay, here in 1748. Cookworthy realised the importance of the china clay, which is a constituent of many products including porcelain, glossy paper, textiles and pharmaceuticals. But for every ton of china clay extracted, another nine tons of spoil is created. Over the years, the waste material from the clay pits to the north and west of the town has been piled up into conical spoil heaps that led to these bare, bleached uplands being nicknamed the **Cornish Alps**. More recently the heaps and disused pits have been landscaped with acid-loving plants, such as rhododendrons, and they now have gently undulating footpaths and nature trails.

Although china clay has dominated St Austell since it was first discovered, and is still, despite fierce foreign competition, Cornwall's largest industry, the town is also the home of another important local business – the St Austell Brewery. Founded by Walter Hicks in 1851, the brewery flourished as the town expanded on the prosperity of the kaolin. Still thriving today, it remains a family business. The history of the company and an insight into the brewing process can be found at the informative **St Austell Brewery Visitor Centre**, from where visitors are also taken on a guided tour of the brewery.

A couple of miles north of the town, in the heart of the Cornish Alps, is Wheal Martyn, an old clay works, now transformed into the **China Clay Country Park**. Spread across 26 acres of woodland, this open air museum tells the 200-year-old story of the industry in Cornwall through a wide variety of displays. The land around this once busy mine has been replanted and now has a unique range of habitats. The nature trail through the surrounding countryside offers visitors the opportunity to discover many different birds, small mammals, plants and insects.

Around St Austell

ST BLAZEY
3½ miles NE of St Austell on the A390

ᠷ Eden Project

To the west of the village is the remarkable **Eden Project**, which, since its opening in May 2001, has been a huge international success. The project aims to "promote the understanding and responsible management of the vital relationship between plants, people and resources." The brain-child of former

Eden Project

CHARLESTOWN
1 mile SE of St Austell off the A390

🏛 Shipwreck & Heritage Centre

🌿 Tregrehan Gardens

This picturesque small fishing village, once named West Polmear, was transformed in the 1790s by Charles Rashleigh after whom the town was renamed. He was a local mine owner who built a harbour here to support the recently established china clay industry. Charlestown's harbour declined in the 19th century as other ports, such as Fowey and Plymouth, developed better facilities. However, what has been left is a harbour and village in a Georgian time capsule. As well as providing a permanent berth for square-rigged boats, it is a popular destination with holidaymakers and has been used as the location for TV series such as *Poldark* and *The Onedin Line*.

record producer Tim Smit, back in 1994, the Project took over an abandoned, 50-metre-deep china clay pit which, now contains the largest conservatories in the world. Three of the world's climate zones (Biomes) have been chosen for interpretation: the Humid Tropics (Rainforests and Tropical Islands) and the Warm Temperate regions (the Mediterranean, South Africa and California) are contained within the two giant conservatories that have already captured the public imagination. The third, or Outdoor Biome, is our own Temperate zone that thrives on the climatic advantages that Cornwall has to offer. More than three-quarters of Eden's plants are in this outdoor area the size of 30 football pitches with some 1900 different species and cultivars. Stunning at any time of year, these gardens are breathtaking in spring when daffodils, crocuses and spring-flowering shrubs present a spectacle that Tim Smit has described as "Picasso meets the Aztecs".

The Project can become quite congested at weekends, but you can avoid the queues by buying a combined bus and admission ticket in St Austell from First bus travel. Bikers and hikers can also claim a discount as well as going straight to the fast track ticket window.

Close to the docks is the **Shipwreck and Heritage Centre**. This offers an insight into the town's history, local shipwrecks and the various devices that have been developed over the years for rescuing and recovering those in peril at sea. There are hundreds of artefacts recovered from more than 150 shipwrecks and the many and varied exhibitions reflect village life in Charlestown, its history and the once thriving china clay industry. The exhibition displays a tremendous range of maritime history dating back to 1715 and has one of the largest underwater diving equipment collections in the country, including various suits used for treasure seeking and naval purposes.

Just to the northeast of Charlestown, close

CHARLESTOWN GALLERY

On The Quay, Charlestown, St Austell,
Cornwall PL25 3NJ
Tel: 01726 67886
e-mail: gemmaausten@hotmail.co.uk
website: www.flickr.com/photos/gemmaausten

Located close to the harbour in the picturesque coastal village of Charlestown, the **Charlestown Gallery** was established some 20 years ago by local artist Don Austen. His daughter Gemma has now taken over. An accomplished artist herself, Gemma shows her own work in the gallery along with that of many other local artists, among them Pete Fugler and Roy Steadman. The gallery is well laid out with an open plan display area and a workshop/working area at the back. The gallery also has a very reasonably priced framing service.

Charlestown itself is a delight to visit and its Shipwreck Heritage Museum is immensely popular. Noted as a home port for Tall Ships, the village has been extensively featured in many international films, most recently in *Alice in Wonderland* starring Johnny Depp.

THE DUCHY SMOKED FISH COMPANY

"The Smokehouse", The Causeway, Off Par Green, Par, Cornwall PL24 2AF
Tel: 01726 816063
e-mail: duchysmokedfish@live.co.uk
website: www.smokedfishcornwall.co.uk

The fact that many local restaurants, hotels, delis and fishmongers buy their smoked goods from **Duchy Smoked Fish** is a testament to their quality. Run by two local men, and only in business since 2009, their rapidly-growing reputation speaks for itself. They have their own 60-stone kiln in the smokehouse behind the shop, which enables them to smoke large quantities at the same time and whose heady aroma permeates the building making it impossible to resist buying.

Duchy Smoked Fish produces a cold-smoked mackerel, which is unique to them, so a rare chance to buy something you won't taste anywhere else. Smoked mussels are another of their special delicacies, as are the 2010 award winning smoked mackerel fillets and smoked haddock fillets.

to Tregrehan Mills, is **Tregrehan Gardens** where visitors can see many mature trees from as far afield as North America and Japan, along with rhododendrons and a range of Carlyon hybrid camellias. The garden has been created over the years since the early 1800s by the Carlyon family who have lived here since 1565.

MEVAGISSEY

5 miles S of St Austell on the B3273

🏛	Mevagissey Folk Museum
🚂	World of Model Railways Exhibition
🐟	Mevagissey Aquarium
🐟	Lost Gardens of Heligan
🐟	Caerhays Castle Gardens

Once aptly known as Porthilly, Mevagissey was renamed in the 14th century after the saints St Meva and St Issey. The largest fishing village on St Austell Bay, Mevagissey was an important centre of the pilchard industry and everyone who lived here was linked in some

way with either the fishing boats or processing the catch. This has led to a labyrinth of buildings all within easy reach of the harbour. The tiny Inner Harbour of today dates from the 1770s, while the Outer Harbour, built to increase the size of the port, was finally finished at the end of the 19th century.

On the East Quay is the **Mevagissey Folk Museum**, which shows how the village once looked when the pilchard industry was prospering. It also has a display on a local chemist, Mr Pears, who created the famous soap. During the season, a popular excursion from the harbour is to take the passenger ferry to Fowey, a crossing that takes about 35 minutes.

Elsewhere around the harbour, visitors can see the fascinating displays and models at the **World of Model Railways Exhibition**. It contains an impressive collection of 2000 models and a working display featuring more than 30 trains travelling through varied landscapes including town, country, seaside

THE BEAD STORE

11b Fore Street, St Austell, Cornwall, PL26 6UQ
Tel: 01726 844999
e-mail: info@thebeadstore.co.uk
website: www.thebeadstore.co.uk

The Bead Store is located in Mevagissey, a charming traditional Cornish fishing village. In the narrow streets, you will find gift shops, craft workshops, galleries, cafes and pubs. The Bead Store can be found on Fore Street, one street back from the harbour.

The Bead Store is an absolute treasure trove of fabulous beads and findings. Glass beads, pearls, gemstones and more fill every part of the shop. It really is a 'sweet shop' for grown-ups!

Don't fancy making it yourself? The staff at The Bead Store are accomplished jewellery makers and have hand-crafted jewellery for sale in the shop. If you would like to have a go at making your own jewellery, they will be pleased to answer any questions that you might have or to help pick out the best beads and findings for your project.

The Bead Store has specialized products, such as TierraCast pewter beads and findings, Toho seed beads, Fairtrade ceramic buttons and stunning Czech glass buttons. They also have bead kits and mixes, settings, cabochons, pendants, tools, books and more! In short, if you need something to make your own jewellery, The Bead Store has it all!

MEVAGISSEY FINE ART

4 St George's Square, Mevagissey, Cornwall PL26 6UB
Tel: 01726 844488
email: steve@ysellaart.co.uk
website: www.mevagisseyfineart.co.uk

Anyone who holidays or lives in the West Country, especially Cornwall, knows how spectacularly beautiful it is, and how it has not surprisingly always appealed to artists. At his shop in Mevagissey, Steve Elson (who took over the business from his parents in 2010) has one of the widest ranges of artworks in the region. He stocks the work of painters and craftsmen from all over the West Country, but predominantly Cornwall, as well as his own impressive framed photographs.

There are many limited edition prints as well as original paintings, alongside ceramics, jewellery, and colourful work in glass. Steve makes it his business to stock work in all price ranges, not just at the more expensive end of the market, so that anyone visiting his gallery on the heart of Mevagissey can find something to take away. Artists whose work you can find here include Tony Hogan, Kevin Platt and the cute cats, dogs, sheep and other animals of the ceramic artist Jane Adams.

and even an Alpine winter scene. The **Mevagissey Aquarium** features local sea life and is located in the old Lifeboat House just by the quay.

To the northwest of Mevagissey are the famous **Lost Gardens of Heligan,** one of the country's most interesting gardens. Originally laid out in 1780, the gardens lay undisturbed, or 'lost', for 70 years before being rediscovered in 1990. The 200-acre estate

Lost Gardens of Heligan

contains Victorian pleasure grounds with spring-flowering shrubs; a Japanese Garden; a lush 22-acre 'sub-tropical' jungle with exotic foliage; a pioneering wildlife conservation project and woodland and farm walks.

Gorran Haven, to the south of Mevagissey, was once a settlement to rival its neighbour. Those days were long ago and it is now an unspoilt village with a sandy beach, sheltered by Dodman

📰 stories and anecdotes 🐿 famous people 🎨 art and craft 🎭 entertainment and sport 🚶 walks

Point – a prominent headland where the remains of an Iron Age defensive earthwork can be seen.

To the west of Mevagissey, **Caerhays Castle Gardens** is an informal 60-acre woodland garden on the coast near Porthluney Cove. It was created in the late 1800s by JC Williams who sponsored plant-hunting expeditions to China to stock his grounds. The gardens are best known for their huge Asiatic magnolias, which are at their most magnificent in March and April. The castle itself was built in the Gothic style by John Nash between 1805 and 1807, and is open for conducted tours on certain days. Anyone familiar with Alfred Hitchcock's film *Rebecca* will recognise some of the interiors.

PROBUS
8 miles SW of St Austell off the A390

🌣 Trewithen House & Gardens

This large village is noted for having the tallest parish church tower in the county. Built of granite in the 16th century and richly decorated, it stands 124 feet high.

Just west of the village is **Trewithen House and Gardens**. The early Georgian house, whose name literally means 'house of the trees', stands in glorious woods and parkland and has gardens containing many rare species laid out in the early 20th century by George Johnstone. Of particular note are the magnificent collections of camellias, rhododendrons and magnolias. The interior of the house is filled with furniture and paintings collected by the Hawkins family over many years.

To the southeast of Probus lies **Tregony**, a small village that was an important river port long before Truro and Falmouth were developed; it is often called the 'Gateway to the Roseland Peninsula'. This indented tongue

of land, which forms the eastern margin of the Fal estuary, is always known by its Cornish name **Carrick Roads**. It has a network of footpaths that take in not only the craggy cliffs with their nesting seabirds but also the grasslands dotted with wildflowers and the ruined military fortresses that go back to the time of the Armada and beyond.

VERYAN
13 miles SW of St Austell off the A3078

🏠 Roundhouses

Set within a wooded hollow, this charming village is famous for the five **Roundhouses** that stand at its entrance. Built in the early 19th century for the daughters of the local vicar, the cottages' circular shape was believed to protect the residents from evil as there are no corners in which the Devil can hide.

Eastwards, on the coast, is the unspoilt fishing village of **Portloe** whose tiny harbour is completely overshadowed by steep cliffs. To the south lies **Carne Beacon**, one of the largest Bronze Age burial mounds in the country.

Newquay

🏵 Huer's Hut	🌣 Trenance Leisure Park
🌣 Newquay Zoo	🌣 Blue Reef Aquarium
🌣 Water World	🏛 Buccaneer Bay
🌣 Holywell Bay Fun Park	

Washed by the warm waters of the Gulf Stream, Newquay is now the UK's top surfing resort with a choice of no fewer than 14 beaches. Fistral Beach faces the Atlantic head on, so when the wind is coming from the southwest the billows arrive after an unbroken 3000-mile run – a worthy challenge for the top national and international surf riders. By contrast, the sheltered beaches at Towan,

Surfing at Fistral Beach

Great Western and Tolcarne provide a gentle start for beginners on belly-boards. On display in Alma Place is the world's longest surf board - a massive 36ft 6in long, it carried 11 people during a display marking the total solar eclipse of August 1999.

This busy resort has a long history. There is evidence of an Iron Age coastal fort among the cliffs and caves of Porth Island – the outcrop connected to the mainland by an elegant suspended footbridge. For centuries, the harbour lay at the heart of this once important pilchard fishing village The town takes its name from the New Kaye that was built in the mid 15th century by the villagers who wanted to protect the inlet here. On Towan Headland, the whitewashed **Huer's Hut** can still be seen; this was where the Huer would scan the sea looking for shoals of red pilchards. Once spotted, he would cry "hevva" to alert the fishing crews and then guide them to the shoals using a pair of bats known as bushes. As the fishing industry declined, (although you can still buy freshly caught shellfish on the quayside) Newquay became a major port for both china clay and mineral exports. However, today, its beautiful rocky coastline and acres of golden sands has seen it develop into a popular seaside resort,

famed throughout the world for its surfing.

Although there is some Regency architecture in Newquay, the rise of the town's fortunes in the 19th century saw a rapid expansion, and many of the large Victorian hotels and residential houses still remain. The Trenance Heritage Cottages, Newquay's oldest dwellings were built in the 1700s but have stood empty since 2002. A group was formed in 2007 and is currently developing plans for their restoration for use as a tearoom, small museum and artist's studio. The cottages stand within **Trenance Leisure Park**, which offers 26 acres of indoor and outdoor activities including bowling, boating, pitch & putt, crazy golf, horse-riding, tennis, ramp sports and a miniature railway. Also within the park is **Newquay Zoo** where conservation, education and entertainment go hand in hand, and hundreds of animals can be seen in sub-tropical lakeside gardens. Carpathian lynx are amongst the stars of the show, but the many other residents include African lions, red pandas, sloths, tapirs and capybara. Nearby, at the indoor **Water World** complex, the whole family can enjoy a range of pools and water activities in a tropical climate.

Adjacent to the harbour, the **Blue Reef Aquarium** is home to a huge variety of Cornish and tropical species including octopi, giant crabs, clownfish and lobsters. Some of them can be seen as you stroll among the colourful denizens of a coral reef through a spectacular underwater tunnel. There are more than 30 living displays including some graceful sharks and rays.

The characters and events that have shaped the history of this part of Cornwall can be

GINNY'S FLOWERS

7 Bank Street, St Columb Major, Cornwall TR9 6AT
Tel/Fax: 01637 881472
e-mail: ginnyscott@hotmail.co.uk website: www.ginnysflowers.co.uk

Ginny Scott trained as a florist at Falmouth Art College and gained knowledge and experience in many florist's shops before setting up here in 2007. **Ginny's Flowers** specialises in wedding floristry both traditional and contemporary, and Ginny is happy to discuss individual requirements and provide quotations. The shop handles all occasions. Ginny prides herself on providing personal service and sourcing the very best and freshest flowers from Holland.

THE COACHING INN

13 Bank Street, St Columb Major, Cornwall TR9 6AT
Tel: 01637 889767 e-mail: coachinginn@btconnect.com

The Coaching Inn is a handsome stone building with pretty hanging baskets adorning the frontage and low beamed ceilings. Cara Russell has built up a loyal clientele with her superb home cooking, which runs from curries and casseroles to omelettes, fajitas and pasta, with a good choice for vegetarians. Upstairs is a room used for pool or meetings. The Coaching Inn is also a popular place for a drink, with a good variety of local ales and ciders.

SIMPLY OCCASIONS

41 Fair Street, St Columb Major, Cornwall TR9 6RL
Tel: 01637 889212 e-mail: sales@simplyoccasions.info

In 2006 Mary Bird and Sonia Lucas set up **Simply Occasions**, which quickly became a popular source of cards, gifts and nice things for the home. They have filled the little shop with a wide variety of gifts, toys, jewellery, watches, photo frames, wedding presents, greetings cards, stationery and posters. They also sell a selection of jewellery, including the sought after Cornish silver Celtic jewellery.

THE CRIBBAGE

15 Fair Street, St Columb Major, Cornwall TR9 6RL
Tel: 01637 881729
e-mail: cmm.brown@virgin.net website: www.thecribbage.co.uk

Built in 1732 as two adjoining cottages, **The Cribbage** is now a comfortable, characterful guest house, owned and run by Caroline Brown. The accommodation comprises three beautifully appointed bedrooms that share a large bathroom with an unusual lion's foot bath. The day starts with a wonderful breakfast featuring Caroline's home-baked bread and the best local eggs, bacon and sausages. The house has a sitting room with a open fire and a pretty garden.

THE HEALTH & BEAUTY STUDIO

Union Square, St Columb Major, Cornwall TR9 6AU
Tel: 01637 889443/01637 881406

The **Health & Beauty Studio** in St Columb Major is owned and run by Pauline Bennett, who brings top qualifications, in-depth knowledge and many years' experience to the business. Among the services offered in the studio are various types of massage, manicures, pedicures, waxing, electrolysis, facials, dermatological skin care, bridal make-up, nail treatments and eye treatments.

discovered at **Buccaneer Bay**. More than 70 realistic life-size figures set in carefully constructed tableaux bring the days of smugglers and highwaymen, plague victims and miners, King Arthur and Merlin to life. The scariest part is the Dungeon of Despair where visitors can hear the screams of prisoners being tortured in the name of old-time 'justice'.

To the southwest of Newquay's famous beaches, Towan Beach and Fistral Beach, between the headlands of Pentire East and Pentire West, lies the quieter Gannel, home to notable populations of waders and wildfowl, which feed off the mudflats and saltings. Just a short distance further on is the pretty hamlet of Holywell with its attractive beach, towering sand dunes and **Holywell Bay Fun Park** offering a whole range of activities for young and old.

Around Newquay

ST COLUMB MAJOR
6 miles E of Newquay off the A39

🏛 Hurling the Silver Ball   🏰 Castle-an-Dinas

🐦 Cornish Birds of Prey Centre

Once in the running for consideration as the site of Cornwall's cathedral, this small town has an unusually large and flamboyant parish church with monumental brasses to the influential Arundell family. In the 14th century, Sir John Arundell was responsible for the town receiving its market charter. In 1850, the town's officials constructed a bishop's palace in anticipation of the county's cathedral being built here. Now called the Old Rectory (private) it retains much of its grandeur, though it does not play host to its originally intended guests.

Twice a year, the town is the venue for

Hurling the Silver Ball, a medieval game once common throughout Cornwall but now only played in St Columb and St Ives - played on Shrove Tuesday and then again on the Saturday 11 days later. The game involves two teams of several hundred people (the 'townsmen' and the 'countrymen') who endeavour to carry a silver ball made of apple wood to goals set two miles apart.

A couple of miles southeast of St Columb Major, on Castle Downs, are the remains of a massive Iron Age hill fort. **Castle-an-Dinas** was a major defence of the Dumnonia tribe who occupied this area around the 2nd century BC. The earthwork ramparts enclose an area of more than six acres. Anyone climbing to the gorse-covered remains will be rewarded with panoramic views over the leafy Vale of Mawgan to the northwest and the unearthly landscape created by china clay extraction to the south.

To the northeast of St Columb Major, at Winnards Perch, is the **Cornish Birds of Prey Centre** where visitors can see more than 50 hawks, falcons and buzzards fly freely during demonstrations. There are also waterfowl, ducks, pheasants, peacocks, emus, rheas, kookaburras, fallow deer, dwarf zebus and Shetland ponies. Also within the centre are three well-stocked fishing lakes, a tearoom and gift shop.

INDIAN QUEENS
8 miles E of Newquay off the A30

🐦 Screech Owl Sanctuary

Close to an area dominated by china clay quarries, this chiefly Victorian village is home to the **Screech Owl Sanctuary**, just to the northeast. A rehabilitation, conservation and education centre, the sanctuary has the largest collection of owls in the southwest of

England – more than 170 owls of 46 different species. As well as offering visitors the chance to see hand-tame owls at close quarters, the centre runs courses on owl welfare. Harry Potter would approve. A recent addition to the sanctuary's residents is a trio of young emus.

The village's unusual name appears to have come from a pub named The Indian Queen, which operated here in the 19th century. It has since been demolished, but its stone lintel recently reappeared on a house in the village, It bears the name and the words "Licensed Brewer and Retailer of Beer, Cyder, Wine and Tobacco. Licensed to the Post Horses".

KESTLE MILL
3m SE of Newquay on the A3058

🌱 DairyLand Farm World	🏛 Trerice
🏛 Lawnmower Museum	

Just to the south of Kestle Mill is a family attraction that has welcomed more than two million visitors since opening in 1975. **DairyLand Farm World** is a working dairy farm where visitors can see the 120 cows being milked to music; try their hand at milking a life-size model cow; explore the nature trail; and look around the Heritage Centre and Alternative Energy Centre.

Hidden away in the country lanes two miles west of Kestle Mill is the delightful small Elizabethan manor house **Trerice** (National Trust). A real architectural gem, it was built in 1571 for the influential Arundell family. As well as the hint of Dutch styling in the gables, and the beautiful window in the Great Hall with 576 small panes of 16th-century glass, Trerice is noted for its huge, ornate fireplaces, elaborate plasterwork and fine English oak and walnut furniture. Several rooms contain superb English and Oriental porcelain, and among the more esoteric collections are clocks

and drinking glasses. There are portraits by the renowned Cornish painter John Opie and an unusual set of early wooden skittles. Within the charming grounds, a former hayloft houses the **Lawnmower Museum** which traces the history of the lawnmower and contains more than 100 machines.

ST NEWLYN EAST
5 miles S of Newquay off the A3075

🌿 Lappa Valley Steam Railway
🏚 East Wheal Rose mine

A mile or so south of this sizeable village is the **Lappa Valley Steam Railway**. This narrow gauge railway (15 inch gauge) was opened in 1849 as a mineral line from Newquay to East Wheal Rose, and later became part of Great Western Railway's Newquay to Chacewater branch line. This line closed in 1963, but part of the track was re-opened in 1974 as a narrow gauge railway. Two steam locos, Muffin and Zebedee, work the line, running from Benny Halt on a two mile return journey to East Wheal Rose. The

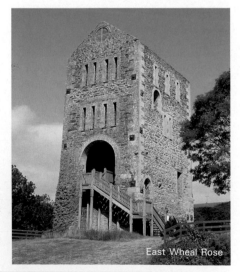
East Wheal Rose

railway is open from the beginning of April to the end of September and runs between seven and 11 trains a day, depending on the season.

At the northern terminus of the line are the imposing engine house and chimney stack of **East Wheal Rose** mine, Cornwall's richest lead mine that was the scene, in 1846, of the county's worst mining disaster. Following a flash flood caused by a sudden, unexpected cloudburst, 39 miners were drowned. The village cockpit, where cockfighting had taken place for centuries, was restored as a memorial to the dead; the mine was re-opened a year after the tragedy but closed for good in 1885.

Wadebridge

📗 Wadebridge Folk Festival	🎋 Camel Trail		
🏛 John Betjeman Centre	📗 Royal Cornwall Show		

Attractively sited on the banks of the River Camel at its lowest bridging point, this ancient port and busy market town is now a popular holiday centre, also renowned for its craftware. Linking the north and south coasts of Cornwall and the moorland with the sea, Wadebridge has always been a bustling place, and its establishment as a trading centre began in earnest in the 15th century. The Rev Lovibond, the vicar of St Petroc's, was looking for a means of conveying his flock of sheep safely across the river. So, in the 1460s, he built the 320-feet-long and now 14-arched bridge that can still be seen today. One of the longest bridges in Cornwall, it originally had 17 arches and it is said that this bridge, nicknamed the Bridge on Wool, was constructed on bridge piers that were sunk on a foundation of woolsacks. The bridge still carries the main road that links the town's two ancient parishes.

With a permanent river crossing there was a

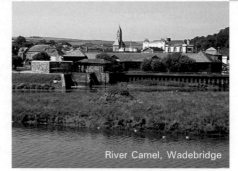
River Camel, Wadebridge

steady growth in trade through the town and its port, but the arrival of the railway in the 19th century saw Wadebridge really thrive. As a result, much of the town's architecture dates from the Victorian era.

Wadebridge maintains its links with farming and each June, to the west of the town centre, the **Royal Cornwall Show** is held. This extravaganza presents a wealth of attractions - a steam fair, military bands, parachute teams, acts of daring and hundreds of trade stalls selling thousands of products.

Another popular annual event is the **Wadebridge Folk Festival**, a feast of dance, music and fun that takes place over the August Bank Holiday weekend.

The town's former railway station is now home to the **John Betjeman Centre**, dedicated to the life and work of the much-loved Poet Laureate. Among the tributes and intimate artefacts on display are the poet's desk, his chair and drafts of his works. Many of his books are for sale, plus videos, post cards and other mementos.

Although the railway line, which opened in 1899, closed in the 1960s, a stretch of the track bed has been used to create the superb **Camel Trail**, a 17-mile traffic-free footpath and cycleway that leads up into the foothills of Bodmin Moor to the east, and westwards

COUNTRYWISE

5 Eddystone Road, Wadebridge, Cornwall PL27 7AL
Tel: 01208 812423

Countrywise is the perfect shop to stock up on your classic country clothing, and much more. This surprisingly spacious store also sells footwear and accessories for all outdoor occasions, as well as more rugged gear for walkers and hikers. At the other end of the scale is a new line in stylish handbags from Coccinelle which, like the rest of the Countrywise ranges, combines good looks with practicality.

Based not far from the River Camel in the historic town of Wadebridge, Countrywise is a family-run store whose team is both professional and friendly. They all know their country clothing, and are happy to offer practical help and advice whether you're looking to buy walking shoes or a rucksack. All the major, quality outdoor brands are stocked, including Dubarry, Musto and of course Barbour. The store spreads over two floors and upstairs can be found names including Berghaus, Royal Robbins and the ever-popular North Face range. You'll also find gear from Rohan, Crag Hopper and Lowe Alpine, Brasher and other walking boots, and a new range of Patagonia outdoor clothing. And if they don't have it in stock, they'll get it for you, usually within a few days. It's that kind of old-fashioned service that makes Countrywise special.

along the River Camel to Padstow.

Just to the west of Wadebridge, close to the hamlet of St Breock, stands the St Breock Downs Monolith, a striking Bronze Age longstone that is also known as the Men Gurta (the Stone of Waiting). Originally five metres (16 feet) high and weighing some 16.75 tonnes, this is Cornwall's largest and heaviest prehistoric monolith. Other prehistoric remains, such as the Nine Maidens stone row, can also be found on St Breock Downs.

Around Wadebridge

PENCARROW
4 miles SE of Wadebridge off the A389

🌱 Pencarrow

A fine Georgian country house completed in 1775, **Pencarrow** is the home of the

Molesworth-St Aubyn family and has a Grade II* listed garden containing more than 600 varieties of rhododendron, along with rock and woodland gardens. A notable feature is the avenue of araucaria whose English name is said to have originated at Pencarrow in 1834 when a guest examined the prickly leaves and declared, "It would puzzle a monkey!" During the season, the gardens are open daily, and guided tours of the house with its superb collections of paintings, furniture, porcelain and antique dolls are available Sunday to Thursday.

PORTHCOTHAN
8 miles W of Wadebridge on the B3276

🌱 Bedruthan Steps   🌱 Trevose Head

This tiny village overlooks a deep, square, sheltered cove with a sandy beach that was once the haunt of smugglers, but today is just

🏛 historic building 🏛 museum and heritage 🏛 historic site 🌱 scenic attraction 🌱 flora and fauna

one part of a stretch of coastline owned by the National Trust. A footpath over the southern headland leads to Porth Mear, another secluded cove beyond which, on a low plateau, is a prehistoric earthwork of banks and ditches. Further south again lie the **Bedruthan Steps**, a curious beach rock formation that is best viewed from the grassy clifftops. The giant slate rocks have been eroded over the centuries and their uniform shape has caused them, according to local legend, to be thought of as the stepping stone used by the Cornish giant Bedruthan.

To the north, the South West Coast Path leads walkers around Constantine Bay and past a succession of sandy beaches that are ideal for surfing. Unfortunately, the strong currents along this stretch make swimming hazardous. Beyond Constantine Bay stretches the remote headland of **Trevose Head** from where there are wonderful views down the coast, taking in bay after bay. At the tip of the headland stands Trevose Lighthouse, which has been warning mariners away from its sheer granite cliffs since 1847 with a beam that, today, can be seen up to 27 miles away.

PADSTOW

6 miles W of Wadebridge on the A389

🚶 Saints Way	🦞 National Lobster Hatchery
🏠 Raleigh Cottage	🐦 Charles Dickens
🖌 May Day	🏠 Prideaux Place

Padstow's sheltered position, on the western side of the Camel estuary, has made it a welcome haven for vessels for centuries and the area has been settled by many different people over the years, including the prehistoric Beaker folk, Romans, Celtic saints and marauding Vikings. Originally named Petroc-stow, it was here that the Welsh missionary St Petroc landed in the 6th

🎭 stories and anecdotes   🐦 famous people   🖌 art and craft   🖌 entertainment and sport   🚶 walks

century and, before moving on to Bodmin Moor to continue his missionary work, founded a Celtic Minster. Beginning at the door of the town's 13th-century parish Church of St Petroc, the **Saints' Way** is a 30-mile footpath that follows the route taken by travellers and pilgrims crossing Cornwall on their way from Brittany to Ireland.

The silting up of the River Camel in the 19th century, and the evocatively named Doom Bar, which restricts entry into the estuary mouth, put paid to Padstow's hopes of continuing as a major port.

Today, the picturesque harbour still teems with people and the influence of the sea is never far away. Since 1975, Padstow has been closely linked with the famous chef, restaurateur and ardent promoter of seafood, Rick Stein, whose empire now includes a seafood restaurant, a bistro café, a seafront delicatessen, a patisserie, fish & chip shop, a cooking school, accommodation and even a gift shop.

More seafood is on display at the **National Lobster Hatchery** (see panel opposite) on South Quay. In 2005, the Hatchery released more than 15,000 juvenile lobsters into the sea – for just £1 you can adopt one of them, name it and receive a certificate and information pack. There's also a gift shop area with sea-life related goods, and a range of books about marine life and Cornwall.

The Hatchery is close to the harbour, which remains the town's focal point. Here can be found many of Padstow's older buildings including the 16th-century **Raleigh Cottage**, where Sir Walter Raleigh lived while he was Warden of Cornwall.

As well as the annual Fish and Ships Festival, Padstow continues to celebrate **May Day** in a traditional manner that has it roots in pagan times. It begins at midnight on the eve of May Day and lasts throughout the

🏚 historic building 🏛 museum and heritage 🏛 historic site ♧ scenic attraction 🌱 flora and fauna

next day. The townsfolk sing in the new morning and then follow the prancing Obby Oss through the town in a procession of musicians, singers, drummers and dancers. The celebrations continue until midnight when the Obby Oss dies.

It was while visiting Padstow in 1842 that **Charles Dickens** was inspired to write *A Christmas Carol* in which he mentions the lighthouse at Trevose Head. His good friend, Dr Miles Marley, whose son Henry Marley, practised as a doctor at Padstow for 51 years, provided the surname for Scrooge's partner, Jacob.

On the northern outskirts of the town, and built on the site of St Petroc's monastery stands **Prideaux Place**, a magnificent Elizabethan mansion that has been the home of the ancient Cornish Prideaux-Brune family for more than 400 years. Along with family portraits and memorabilia, and remarkably ornate ceilings, the house contains many artefacts illustrating the history of this area and the country. The mansion is surrounded by glorious gardens and parkland overlooking the Camel estuary

that were laid out in the style of Capability Brown in the 18th century.

POLZEATH AND NEW POLZEATH
6 miles NW of Wadebridge off the B3314

🏛 Rumps Cliff Castle	🏠 Church of St Enadoc
🐾 Sir John Betjeman	

Surfers and holidaymakers flock to these two small resorts as the broad west-facing beach is not only ideal for surf, but the fine sands, caves and tidal rock pools make it a fascinating place for children. This was also a place much loved by Sir John Betjeman. To the north of the villages is a beautiful coastal path that takes in the cliffs and farmland of Pentire Point and Rumps Point – where stands **Rumps Cliff Castle**, an Iron Age fortification. The remains of four defensive ramparts can still be seen. The area is known for its wild tamarisk, an elegant flowering shrub that is more commonly found around the shores of the Mediterranean Sea. In the 1930s, Pentire Head was saved from commercial development by local fund-raisers who bought the land and donated it to the National Trust.

The National Lobster Hatchery

South Quay, Padstow, Cornwall PL28 8BL
Tel: 01841 533877
e-mail: hatchery@NationalLobsterHatchery.co.uk
website: www.hatchery.freeserve.co.uk

The National Lobster Hatchery promotes and contributes to the responsible management of coastal marine resources, as well as offering a resource for education, conservation and research. At the forefront, is a lobster restocking project, where fishermen bring egg laden female lobsters in to enable them to release their offspring where there are no predators. The young lobsters are then raised to a size where they can look after themselves and are released back into the sea. One of the main aims is education and groups from schools and colleges can be provided with activities and workshops. Open all year 7 days a week.

📖 stories and anecdotes   🐾 famous people   🎨 art and craft   🎭 entertainment and sport   🚶 walks

PORTHILLY GALLERY

Rock, Wadebridge, Cornwall PL27 6JX
Tel: 01208 863844
e-mail: info@porthillygallery.co.uk
website: www.porthillygallery.co.uk

Jethro Jackson has lived in Cornwall all his life, and he celebrates the county's beauty in his original and atmospheric work in both ceramics and paintings. He has an especial affinity with the North Cornish Coast, where his gallery in the little hamlet of Porthilly showcases his own work and that of many other talented artists Most of Jackson's paintings capture the North Coast's drama and beauty, while some of his pots swirl with the shape of the waves.

Other artists whose work can be seen and bought, or commissioned, at the gallery include Danka Napiorkowska, who specialises in decorative tiling but also paints colourful pastels showing the rich harvest of the Cornish seas. Roy reed is a photographic artist who produces panoramic landscapes, especially of the North Cornish Coast, by stitching together a series of prints. Hamish Mackie grew up on a Cornish farm and his sculptures have been displayed and acquired by public and private collectors all over the world.

A visit to the Porthilly Gallery is not only a chance to see a pretty part of Cornwall but also to admire and perhaps acquire some beautiful pieces of art.

This stretch of dramatic coastline, which runs round to Port Quin, includes sheltered bays and coves, ancient field patterns, old lead mines and Iron Age defensive earthworks. It is ideal walking country, and there are numerous footpaths taking walkers on circular routes that incorporate both coastal countryside and farmland.

The tiny hamlet of Port Quin suffered greatly when the railways took away the slate trade from its once busy quay, and the demise was so swift that, at one time, outsiders thought that the entire population had been washed away by a great storm. Overlooking the now repopulated hamlet is Doyden Castle, a squat 19th-century castellated folly that is now a holiday home.

To the southwest of Polzeath stands the delightful **Church of St Enodoc**, a Norman building that has on several occasions been virtually submerged by windblown sand. At those times the congregation would enter through an opening in the roof. The sand was finally cleared away in the 1860s when the church was restored, and the bell in the tower, which came from an Italian ship wrecked nearby, was installed in 1875. The beautiful churchyard contains many graves of shipwrecked mariners, but what draws many people to this quiet place is the grave of the poet **Sir John Betjeman**, who is buried here along with his parents. Betjeman spent many of his childhood holidays in the villages and coves around the Camel Estuary, and his affection for the local people and places was the inspiration for many of his works. The church is reached across a golf course that is regarded as one of the most scenic links courses in the country.

Tintagel

The romantic remains of **Tintagel Castle** (English Heritage), set on a wild and windswept headland that juts out into the Atlantic, are many people's abiding image of Cornwall. Throughout the year, many come to clamber up the wooden stairway to The Island to see the castle that legend claims was the birthplace of King Arthur. If the great king was born at this spot, it was certainly not in this castle, which was built in the 12th century. But in 1998 the discovery of a 6th-century slate bearing the Latin inscription Artognou – which translates as the ancient British name for Arthur – revitalised the belief that Tintagel was Arthur's home.

The legends were first written down by Geoffrey of Monmouth in the mid 1100s and over the years were reworked by many other writers, notably Sir Thomas Malory's *Morte d'Arthur* of around 1450, and Tennyson's epic poem *Idylls of the King* in 1859.

Tintagel village, of course, owes a lot to its Arthurian connections, so souvenir and themed shops have proliferated along its main street. You might prefer to pass on the 'genuine Excaliburgers' on offer in one pub, but an oddity worth visiting is **King Arthur's Great Hall**. It was built in 1933 of Cornish granite by a group calling themselves the Knights of King Arthur. They furnished the vast halls with a Round Table and 72 stained glass windows depicting their coats of arms and some of their adventures.

However, there is more to Tintagel than King Arthur. In the High Street, is the weather-beaten **Old Post Office** – a 14th-century small manor house that first became a post office in the 19th century. Purchased by the National Trust in 1903 for £100, the building is set within an enchanting cottage garden and still has its original stone-paved medieval hall and ancient fireplace, along with the ground-floor office of the former postmistress.

To the north of the village runs the mile-long **Rocky Valley**, a curious rock-strewn cleft in the landscape that has a character all of its own. In the wooded upper reaches can be found the impressive 40-foot waterfall known as **St Nectan's Kieve**. This was named after a Celtic hermit whose cell is believed to have stood beside the basin, or kieve, at the foot of the cascade. Here, too, can be seen the **Rocky Valley Carvings**, on a rock face behind a ruined building. Though it is suggested that

Old Post Office, Tintagel

the carvings date from early Christian times, around the same time that St Nectan was living here, it is impossible to be accurate, and other suggestions range from the 2nd century BC to the 17th century.

A little further north, and reached by a short footpath from the village of Bossiney, is the beautiful, sheltered beach of **Bossiney Haven**, surrounded by a semi-circle of cliffs. The views from the cliff tops are spectacular, but only the fit and agile should attempt to scramble down to the inviting beach below. Inland, at Bossiney Common, the outlines of ancient field patterns, or lynchets, can still be traced.

Around Tintagel

PORT ISAAC
6 miles SW of Tintagel on the B3267

🏛 Tregeare Rounds

🌿 Long Cross Victorian Gardens

A delightful fishing village that has retained much of its ancient charm, Port Isaac has become well-known to viewers of the ITV drama series, *Doc Martin*, for which it provides the major location as Port Wenn. The town is surrounded by open countryside, Heritage Coast and an Area of Outstanding Natural Beauty. Port Isaac has been a busy port since the Middle Ages. During its heyday in the 19th century, fish along with cargoes of stone, coal, timber and pottery were loaded and unloaded on its quayside. Following the arrival of the railways, pilchards were landed here in great numbers, gutted and processed in the village's many fish cellars before being packed

off to London and beyond by train. The centre of this conservation village is concentrated around the protected harbour where old fish cellars and fishermen's cottages line the narrow alleys and 'opes' that wend their way down to the coast. Crab and lobster fishing are still the major activity.

Two rather unusual attractions for summer visitors are the Thursday evening brass band concert and the Friday evening sing-song of shanties by the Port Isaac choir. Both take place on the beach from Whit Sunday until September.

Just to the east lies Port Gaverne, another busy 19th-century fishing port where, in one season, more than 1000 tons of pilchards were landed and processed in the village's fish cellars or 'pilchard palaces'. Today, most of the large stone buildings, including some of the old fish cellars, have been converted into holiday accommodation. Tourism has prospered here as the village has one of the safest beaches along the North Cornwall coast.

Just inland from the village can be found the double ramparts of **Tregeare Rounds**. This Celtic hill fort was excavated in 1904. Among the finds uncovered were pottery

Port Isaac Harbour

🏛 historic building 🏛 museum and heritage 🏛 historic site 🐾 scenic attraction 🌿 flora and fauna

fragments thought to be more than 2000 years old. It is believed to be the Castle Terrible in Thomas Malory's 15th-century epic, *Morte D'Arthur*. Here Uther Pendragon laid siege and killed the Earl of Cornwall because he had fallen in love with the earl's beautiful wife, Igerna.

Just over a mile inland, close to the village of Trelights, is the only public garden along this stretch of North Cornwall coast – **Long Cross Victorian Gardens**, a real garden lover's delight. Located next to the Long Cross Hotel, the gardens' imaginative planting and superb panoramic views make it a very special place. Other attractions here include a secret garden and a fascinating Victorian maze.

DELABOLE
3 miles S of Tintagel on the B3314

🗿 Delabole Slate Quarry

Home to the most famous slate quarry in Cornwall, Delabole is almost literally built of slate. It has been used here for houses, walls, steps and the church. The high quality dark blue slate has been quarried here uninterrupted since Tudor times, and it is known that, in around 2000BC, Beaker Folk on Bodmin Moor used slate as baking shelves. The huge crater of **Delabole Slate Quarry** is over half a mile wide and 500 feet deep – making it the largest man-made hole in the country. Although the demand for traditional building materials declined during the 20th century, the quarry is still worked and there are tours available and occasional slate splitting demonstrations.

To the southwest of the village stands the first wind farm to be built in Britain, Delabole Wind Farm, which became operational in 1991. It produces enough power each year to satisfy more than half the annual demands of both Delabole and Camelford.

CAMELFORD
4 miles SE of Tintagel on the A39

🏛 North Cornwall Museum

🏛 Arthurian Centre

This small and historic old market town, on the banks of the River Camel, prospered on the woollen trade. Around its central small square are some pleasant 18th and 19th-century houses. The **North Cornwall Museum and Gallery**, housed in a converted coach house, displays aspects of life in this area throughout the 20th century as well as the reconstruction of a 19th century moorland cottage.

North of the town, the **Arthurian Centre** houses the Land of Arthur exhibition and also contains an information room (including brass rubbing and a video presentation), a play area, a refreshment area and a shop stocked with Arthurian books and gifts. Close by, on the riverbank at Slaughter Bridge, lies an inscribed 6th-century slab that is said to mark the place where King Arthur fell at the Battle of Camlann in AD539, defeated by his nephew Mordred.

BOSCASTLE
3 miles NE of Tintagel on the B3263

🏛 Museum of Witchcraft   Thomas Hardy

On 16 August 2004, torrential rain fell on the hills above the picturesque fishing village of Boscastle and within hours its main street was filled with a turbulent torrent of water sweeping everything before it towards the sea. Vivid television pictures recorded the dramatic scenes as cars were jostled along like toys on the surging waves, and residents were winched by helicopters from their rooftops. Astonishingly, no one died and no one was seriously injured in the calamity, but most of the houses in the path of the flood were rendered uninhabitable. Insurance companies estimated that claims would exceed half a billion pounds. Six years on, the village has been painstakingly restored and bears no signs of the catastrophic flooding.

Before this disaster, Boscastle was best known for its picture-postcard qualities and its associations with the novelist Thomas Hardy. The village stands in a combe at the head of a remarkable S-shaped inlet that shelters it from the Atlantic Ocean. The only natural harbour between Hartland Point and Padstow, Boscastle's inner jetty was built by the renowned Elizabethan, Sir Richard Grenville, when the village was prospering as a fishing, grain and slate port. The outer jetty, or breakwater, dates from the 19th century when Boscastle had grown into a busy commercial

port handling coal, timber, slate and china clay. Because of the dangerous harbour entrance, ships were towed into it by rowing boats – a blowhole known as the Devil's Bellows in the outer harbour still sends up plumes of spray in bad weather.

Next to the slipway where the River Valency meets the sea is the **Museum of Witchcraft** (see panel below), which suffered badly in the flooding of August 2004. It reopened the following Easter and once again boasts the world's largest collection of witchcraft related artefacts and regalia. Visitors can also learn all about witches, their lives, their spells, their charms and their curses.

Even before the floods, Boscastle was becoming familiar to viewers of BBC2's documentary series, *A Seaside Parish,* which followed the arrival of a new vicar, the Rev

Museum of Witchcraft

The Harbour, Boscastle, Cornwall PL35 0HD
Tel: 01840 250111
e-mail: museumwitchcraft@aol.com
website: www.museumofwitchcraft.com

The **Museum of Witchcraft** in Boscastle houses the world's largest collection of witchcraft related artefacts and regalia. The museum has been located in Boscastle for over 40 years and despite severe damage in recent floods, it remains one of Cornwall's most popular museums.

The fascinating displays cover all aspects of witchcraft and include Divination, Sea Witchcraft, Spells and Charms, Modern Witchcraft, Herbs & Healing, Ritual Magic, Satanism and Hare & Shapeshifting.

One exhibit features the burial of Joan Wytte who was born in Bodmin, Cornwall, in 1775 and died of bronchial pneumonia in Bodmin Jail in 1813. She was a renowned clairvoyant and healer but became aggressive and impatient due to an untreated abscess in her tooth and people came to believe she was possessed by the devil. She became known as 'The Fighting Fairy Woman' and was imprisoned for grievous bodily harm.

Her skeleton came into the possession of the Museum of Witchcraft and was exhibited there for many years. Eight years ago the museum team believed she deserved a proper burial and Joan was finally laid to rest in 1998. Among the other artefacts to be seen here are an amazing collection of figures and dolls, carved plates and stones, jewellery, cauldrons, weapons and unpleasant devices used for extracting confessions! A stair lift is available for those with limited mobility.

Christine Musser, in the village and recorded her role in its various activities. The series later detailed the aftermath of the inundation that included visits by Prince Charles and the Rev Musser's fictional TV equivalent, Dawn French's *Vicar of Dibley*.

The spectacular slate headlands on either side of Boscastle's harbour mouth provide some excellent, if rather demanding, walking. This stretch of tortuous coastline is not only of ecological importance, but also historic. An Iron Age earthwork can be seen across the promontory at Willapark, and there is a 19th-century lookout tower on the summit.

From the village there is a footpath that follows the steep wooded Valency Valley to

HARBOUR LIGHT

The Harbour, Boscastle, Cornwall, PL35 0AG
Tel: 01840 250413 / 01840 250 374   Fax: 01840 250413
e-mail: harbourlightltd@hotmail.com
website: www.harbourlightltd@hotmail.com

Harbour Light is a wonderful independent shop selling a good selection of clothing and quality gifts. Owned by Trixie Webster, the shop was originally located on the other side of the stream, but was one of several independent shops completely destroyed during the devastating floods of August 2004, which attracted national media coverage. The shop, which also sells locally made gifts, now occupies another traditional building in the fishing village, which has made a remarkable recovery and returned to its picturesque routes. Popular with locals and visitors to the north Cornwall coast, Harbour Light is definitely worth a look.

THE OLD RECTORY ST JULIOT

St Juliot, Boscastle, Cornwall PL35 0BT
Tel: 01840 250225
e-mail: sally@stjuliot.com
website: www.stjuliot.com

The achievements of the luxury b&b **The Old Rectory** speak for themselves. *The Times* chose it as one of the 12 best b&b's in Britain, and for the last ten years it has earned itself five stars and a Gold Award from VisitEngland, the organisation's top accolade. The Rectory was built in 1847 and in 1870 was the place where the writer Thomas Hardy met his wife-to-be, Emma Lavinia Gifford, who was the Rector's sister-in-law.

Staying here is like stepping back in time, as guests can leave their cars behind and explore the lovely North Cornish scenery on foot from the door. England's highest cliffs are a short walk away, and here you can see seals basking on the rocks. In fact you don't even need to leave the Rectory to go exploring, as it has its own 3 acres of woodland garden. The four rooms are decorated in period style but with all the modern luxuries like whirlpool baths, power showers, and wireless internet. A full cooked breakfast is also included, much of the produce from their own walled kitchen garden.

🎭 stories and anecdotes 🦢 famous people 🎨 art and craft 🎭 entertainment and sport 🚶 walks

the hidden hamlet of St Juliot, which appears as Endelstow in **Thomas Hardy's** novel *A Pair of Blue Eyes*. As a young architect, Hardy worked on the restoration of the church and it was here, in 1870, that he met his future wife, Emma Gifford, the rector's sister-in-law. Emma later professed that the young architect had already appeared to her in a dream and wrote how, on first meeting him, she was "immediately arrested by his familiar appearance". Much of the couple's courtship took place along this wild stretch of coastline between Boscastle and Crackington Haven. When Emma died more than 40 years later, Hardy returned to St Juliot to erect a memorial to her in the church. Following his death in 1928, a similar memorial was erected to Hardy and, more than 70 years later, a Thomas Hardy Memorial window was installed to mark the millennium.

CRACKINGTON HAVEN
7½ miles NE of Tintagel off the B3263

One of the most dramatic places along this remarkable stretch of coastline, this tiny port is overlooked by towering 400-foot cliffs, which make it Cornwall's highest coastal point. The small and narrow sandy cove is approached down a steep-sided wooded combe. It is difficult to see how sizeable vessels once landed here to deliver their cargoes of limestone and Welsh coal. Just to the south of Crackington Haven the path leads to a remote beach, curiously named **The Strangles**, where at low tide large patches of sand are revealed amongst the vicious looking rocks. During one year alone in the 1820s, some 20 ships were said to have come to grief here. The

undercurrents are strong and swimming is always unsafe.

Bude

| å Bude Canal Trail | 🏛 Bude Castle |
| 🏛 Town Museum | ⚜ Bude Light 2000 |

A traditional seaside resort with sweeping expanses of sand, rock pools and Atlantic breakers, Bude has plenty to offer holidaymakers and coastal walkers. A popular surfing centre, said to be where British surfing began, the town is a much favoured holiday destination in summer.

The Bude Canal, built in the early 1820s, was an ambitious project that aimed to connect the Atlantic with the English Channel via the River Tamar. However, the only stretch to be finished was that between Bude and Launceston. It was a remarkable feat of engineering as the sea lock at the entrance to the canal was the only lock even though it ran for 35 miles and rose to a height of 350 feet in six miles. In order to achieve the changes in level, a series of inclined planes, or ramps, were used between the different levels, and a wheeled tub boat was pulled up the ramps on

Crooklets Beach, Bude

🏛 historic building 🏛 museum and heritage 🏛 historic site ⚜ scenic attraction 🌿 flora and fauna

metal rails. The canal finally closed to commercial craft in 1912 and now only two miles of the canal are passable. The **Bude Canal Trail** follows this tranquil backwater through some wonderfully peaceful and unspoilt countryside. Part of the redevelopment of the canal is the canal interpretation centre housed within the TIC building.

Close to the entrance to the canal stands battlemented **Bude Castle**, a small low building overlooking Summerleaze beach. It was designed by a local 19th-century physician, scientist and inventor, Sir Goldsworthy Gurney. Now called the Heritage Centre it is an attraction in its own right. The castle is interesting because it is thought to be the first building in Britain to be constructed on sand. The castle rests on a concrete raft - a technique developed by Gurney. Among his other inventions were a steam jet, a musical instrument consisting of glasses played as a piano, and the Bude Light, an intense light obtained by introducing oxygen into the interior flame and using mirrors. He used this to light his own house and also to light the House of Commons, where his invention replaced 280 candles and gave rise to the expression 'in the limelight'. The Bude Light served the House of Commons for 60 years and earned Gurney a knighthood. He is also remembered as being the first man to make a long journey in a mechanical vehicle when he drove a steam carriage from London to Bath and back.

To celebrate the new millennium, the town commissioned Carole Vincent and Anthony Fanshawe to design the **Bude Light 2000**, the first large-scale public sculpture to combine coloured concrete with fibre optic lighting. It stands close to the castle and was officially opened in June 2000 by the Duke of Gloucester.

The history of the town and its canal can be explored in the **Town Museum**, which stands on the canal side in a former blacksmith's forge. The story of Bude and the surrounding area, including shipwrecks, railways, farming and geology, is told in a series of vivid displays.

One of the high spots in the Bude calendar is the annual jazz festival, held in August and featuring numerous performances, street parades and jazz workshops - even jazz church services.

Around Bude

MORWENSTOW
5 miles N of Bude off the A39

🕊 Rev Stephen Hawker	🏛 Rectory
🏛 Hawker's Hut	🐚 Henna Cliff

Used to taking the full brunt of Atlantic storms, this tiny village lies on the harshest stretch of the north Cornwall coast. Although it can sometimes seem rather storm-lashed, it is a marvellous place from which to watch the changing moods of the ocean. Not surprisingly, shipwrecks have been common along this stretch of coast. Many came to grief in storms, but it was not unknown for local criminals to lure unsuspecting ships onto the rocks by lighting lanterns on the cliff tops or the shore.

The village's most renowned inhabitant was its eccentric vicar and poet, the **Rev Robert Stephen Hawker**, who came here in 1834 and remained among his flock of "smugglers, wreckers and dissenters" until his death in 1875. A colourful figure dressed in a purple

🎭 stories and anecdotes 🕊 famous people 🎨 art and craft 🎟 entertainment and sport 🥾 walks

frock coat, fisherman's jersey, and fishing boots beneath his cassock, Hawker spent much of his time walking through his beloved countryside. When not walking, he could often be found writing verses and smoking, opium by some accounts, in the driftwood hut that he built 17 steps from the top of the precipitous Vicarage Cliff. Now known as **Hawker's Hut**, it is the National Trust's smallest property.

Though a bizarre character, Hawker was also one of the first people to show concern at the number of ships coming to grief along this stretch of coastline. He spent hours monitoring the waves and would often climb down the cliffs to rescue shipwrecked crews or recover the bodies of those who had perished among the waves. After carrying the bodies back to the village, he would give them a proper Christian burial. Some 40 of these unfortunates lie buried in the churchyard. One of the many ships wrecked off Sharpnose headland was the *Caledonia*, whose figurehead stands above the grave of her captain in Morwenstow churchyard.

Hawker's other contribution to Morwenstow was the **Rectory**, which he built at his own expense and to his own design. As individual as the man himself, the house has chimneys that represent the towers of various churches and Oxford colleges; the broad kitchen chimney is in remembrance of his mother. His lasting contribution to the church was to introduce the annual Harvest Festival in 1843, and his most famous poem is the rousing Cornish anthem, *The Song of Western Men*. The National Trust-owned land, between the church and the cliffs, is dedicated to this remarkable man's memory.

To the north of the village is Welcombe Mouth, the graveyard of many ships that came to grief on its jagged rocks. Running back from the shore are the Welcombe and Marsland Valleys that are now a nature reserve and a haven for butterflies. To the south are the headlands of Higher and Lower Sharpnose Points. Rugged rocks, caused by erosion, lie above a boulder-strewn beach, while some of the outcrops of harder rock have begun to form tiny islands. Also north of the village is **Henna Cliff**, which has a sheer drop of 450 feet to the sea, making it the highest in Cornwall. From the cliff top there are spectacular views across to South Wales.

STRATTON
1 mile E of Bude on the A3072

🏚 Tree Inn

This ancient market town and one-time port is believed to have been founded by the Romans. During the Civil War, the town was a stronghold of the Royalists and their commander, Sir Bevil Greenville, made the **Tree Inn** his centre of operations. (The inn is of interest in its own right as it is constructed from the timbers of wrecked ships.) In May 1643, at the Battle of Stamford Hill, Greenville led his troops to victory over the Parliamentarians. The dead of both sides were buried in unmarked graves in Stratton churchyard. The battle is re-enacted in mid May each year by the Sealed Knot Society.

The Tree Inn was also the birthplace of the Cornish giant, Anthony Payne, Sir Bevil's bodyguard, who stood over seven feet tall. They fought together, both here and later at Lansdown Hill, near Bath, where Greenville was killed. After helping Greenville's son lead the Royalists to victory, Payne carried his master back to Stratton. After the war ended, Payne continued to live at the Greenville manor house until his death. When he died, the house had to be altered to allow his coffin to pass through the doorway.

LAUNCELLS

2½ miles E of Bude off the A3072

🏠 Church of St Swithin

Set in a delightful wooded combe, the 15th-century **Church of St Swithin** was acclaimed by Sir John Betjeman as "the least spoilt church in Cornwall". It is notable for its fine Tudor bench ends and for 15th-century floor tiles made in Barnstaple. In the churchyard is the grave of the remarkable Sir Goldsworthy Gurney (1793-1875) whose inventions included a prototype of incandescent lighting, the high-pressure steam jet, and steam-driven coaches that achieved a steady 15mph. There's lots more information about Gurney at the Bude Heritage Centre.

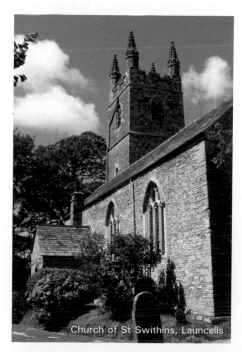
Church of St Swithins, Launcells

KILKHAMPTON

4 miles NE of Bude on the A39

The tall and elegant Church of St James contains monuments to the local Grenville family, many of them the work of Michael Chuke, a local man and a pupil of Grinling Gibbons. Equally notable are the magnificent carved bench ends, and the organ is one played by Henry Purcell when it was installed in Westminster Abbey.

Bodmin

🏰 Castle Canyke	⚔ Saints' Way		
🏠 St Petroc's Church	🕌 St Guran's Well		
🏠 Bodmin Jail	🎭 Courtroom Experience		
🎨 Shire Hall Gallery	🏛 Bodmin Town Museum		
🏠 Gilbert Memorial	🕌 Camel Valley Vineyard		
🏛 Duke of Cornwall's Regimental Museum			
🎭 Bodmin & Wenford Railway			
🏠 Lanhyrdrock House			

Situated midway between Cornwall's two coasts, and at the junction of two ancient trade routes, Bodmin has always been an important town used, particularly, by traders who preferred the overland journey to the sea voyage around Land's End. **Castle Canyke**, to the southeast, was built during the Iron Age to defend this important route. A few centuries later, the Romans erected a fort (one of a string they built to defend strategic river crossings) on a site here above the River Camel. The waymarked footpath, the **Saints' Way**, follows the ancient cross-country route. In the 6th century, St Petroc, one of the most influential of the early Welsh missionary saints, moved from Padstow to Bodmin and established a priory here. The present **St Petroc's Church** is the largest parish church in Cornwall at 151 feet long and 65 feet wide. Part of the tower contains masonry of the Norman period, but most of the present building was built between 1469 and 1472. It is one of the few churches of the period of which building records survive almost complete. The Mayor's accounts are preserved at the County Records Office in Truro. The total recorded cost was £196 7s 4d (about half a million pounds today). The 'furniture' - pulpit, screens and seats - cost £92 under a separate contract with one Mathy More in 1491. The timber was bought in Wales and some of this original woodwork is incorporated in the present screens and priests' seats. Amongst the church's treasures are the impressive Vyvian tomb commemorating one of the last priors, and a remarkable Norman font poised on a single column and carved with some alarming beasts. In the churchyard can be found one of the many holy wells in Bodmin – **St Guran's Well** – which dates from the 6th century.

The only market town in Cornwall to appear in the Domesday Book, Bodmin was chiefly an ecclesiastical town until the reign of Henry VIII. However, this did not mean that it was a quiet and peaceful place. During the Tudor reign, it was the scene of three uprisings: against the tin levy in 1496; in 1549, against the imposition of the English Prayer Book and in support of Perkin Warbeck against Henry VII in 1597. The town's failure to flourish when the railways arrived in Cornwall was due to its decision not to allow the Great Western Railway access to the town centre. Not only did it fail to expand as other towns did but, when Truro became the seat of the new bishopric, Bodmin missed out again.

During World War One, England's Crown Jewels and the Domesday Book were hidden

at **Bodmin Jail**, an austere 18th-century building, which continued as a prison up until 1909. Visitors can tour the cells, including the condemned cell, peopled now with rather dismal dummies. Part of the jail is now a licensed restaurant and lounge bar.

The imposing Shire Hall, built in 1837, served as the County Court until 1988. Now restored, it brings to life in **The Courtroom Experience** the notorious murder in 1844 of Charlotte Dymond on lonely Bodmin Moor and the trial of Matthew Weeks for the crime. Visitors can participate in the drama of the trial as jurors and enter the chilling holding cells where the accused awaited his trial.

In the jury rooms and public gallery on the first floor you will find the **Shire Hall Gallery**, which hosts a varied programme of Cornish and West County artists and craftspeople, as well as community exhibitions. **Bodmin Town Museum** provides an insight into the town's past and that of the surrounding area.

Just a short distance from the town centre is Bodmin Beacon Local Nature Reserve. At the beacon's summit stands the 144 foot high **Gilbert Memorial**, Commemorating Sir Walter Raleigh Gilbert, a descendant of Sir Walter Raleigh and a distinguished general in the Indian Army. From the beacon, there are exhilarating views over the town and moor.

Also easily reached from Bodmin is the Camel Trail, a walking and cycling path along the River Camel to Padstow, which follows the track bed of one of the country's first railways.

Housed in The Keep near the railway station in Bodmin, the **Duke of Cornwall's Light Infantry Regimental Museum** covers the military history of the County Regiment of Cornwall from its formation in 1702 to its eventual amalgamation with the Somerset Light Infantry in 1950. The Armoury contains a fine collection of small arms and machine guns. It also exhibits many of the colourful uniforms worn by the Regiment before 1914, as well as a permanent display of medals belonging to Harry Patch, one of the last survivors of World War One.

Nearby, Bodmin General Station is also the base for the **Bodmin and Wenford Railway**, a former branch line of the Great Western Railway. The line closed to passenger traffic in 1963 but has been splendidly restored. Today, steam locomotives take passengers on a 13-mile round trip along a steeply graded line through beautiful countryside. There are occasional luncheon and dinner specials, and driving instruction is also available.

To the south of the town, near the village of Cutmadoc, stands one of the most fascinating late 19th-century houses in England, the spectacular **Lanhydrock House** (National Trust - see panel below). Surrounded by wonderful formal gardens, woodland and parkland, it originally belonged to Bodmin's Augustinian priory. The extensive estate was bought in 1620 by Sir Richard Robarts (who made his fortune in tin and wool) and his family lived here until the estate was given to the Trust in 1953. Although partially destroyed by fire in 1881, the mansion has been fully restored and is now probably the grandest in Cornwall. Visitors can see that many of the rooms combine the building's original splendour with the latest in Victorian domestic comforts and amenities. One special bedroom belonged to Tommy Agar-Robarts, who was killed at the Battle of Loos in 1915; it contains many of his personal possessions. The grounds are equally magnificent and are known for the fabulous springtime displays of rhododendrons, magnolias and camellias, a superb avenue of ancient beech and sycamore trees, a cob-and-thatch summer house and a photogenic formal garden overlooked by the small estate church of St Hydroc. In the woods are many unusual flowers and ferns as well as owls, woodpeckers and many other birds.

Three miles northwest of Bodmin, the **Camel Valley Vineyard** offers tours, ending with a tasting, and there's a shop selling their still and sparkling wines.

Lanhydrock House

Lanhydrock, Bodmin, Cornwall PL30 5AD
Tel: 01208 265950
e-mail: lanhydrock@nationaltrust.org.uk
website: www.nationaltrust.org.uk

One of the most fascinating and complete late 19th-century houses in England, Lanhydrock is full of period atmosphere. Although the gatehouse and north wing (with magnificent 32yd-long gallery with plaster ceiling) survive from the 17th century, the rest of the house was rebuilt following a disastrous fire in 1881. The new house featured the latest in contemporary living, including central heating. The garden has a stunning collection of magnolias, rhododendrons and camellias, and offers fine colours right through into autumn. All this is set in a glorious estate of 364ha (900 acres) of woods and parkland running down to the River Fowey, with an extensive network of footpaths.

HELLAND BRIDGE POTTERY

Helland Bridge, Bodmin, Cornwall PL30 4QR
Tel: 01208 75240
e-mail: paul@paul-jackson.co.uk
website: www.paul-jackson.co.uk

The artist Paul Jackson settled in Cornwall in 1979 and has been selling his own exceptional work here at his **Helland Bridge Pottery** since 1989. From pots and vases to sensuous garden sculptures, Paul's work is always distinctive and he has been widely exhibited throughout England and Wales. At his own studio, however, there is chance not only to perhaps see the artist at work, but have him help you choose just the right piece for you from the largest and latest stock of his work.

His series of pots featuring sensitive nude studies has proved popular, as have his more recent saltglaze works. His Abstract series of pots and jugs will appeal to those like bright, striking colours, while his Wave series are clearly inspired by the sun, sea, rocks and surf of the Cornish coast. The artist's new series of sculptures can be placed inside or out, and with their flowing shapes in white, black, bronze or stone will stand out wherever they're placed.

Around Bodmin

BLISLAND
3 miles NE of Bodmin off the A30

🏛 Church of St Protus and St Hyacinth

Hidden in a maze of country lanes, this moorland village has a tree-lined village green that has stayed true to its original Saxon layout – an unusual sight on this side of the River Tamar. The part-Norman parish **Church of St Protus and St Hyacinth** is the only one in England dedicated to these brothers who were martyred in the 3rd century. This church was one of Sir John Betjeman's favourites, described by the poet as "dazzling and amazing". The church was restored with great sensitivity in the 1890s by the architect FC Eden, who also designed the sumptuously coloured Gothic screen that dominates the interior. A 17th-century carved pulpit was retained from the old church.

On the moorland to the north of the village are numerous ancient monuments, including the stone circle of Blisland Manor Common and Stipple Stone Henge Monument on Hawkstor Down.

BOLVENTOR
10 miles NE of Bodmin off the A30

🏛 Jamaica Inn	🕯 Daphne du Maurier		
🛢 Dozmary Pool	🏛 Museum of Smuggling		
🌿 Brown Willy	🌿 Roughtor		
🕯 King Arthur	🌿 Bodmin Moor		

Right at the heart of Bodmin Moor, this scenic village is the location of **Jamaica Inn**, the former coaching inn, immortalised by **Daphne du Maurier** in her famous 1936 novel of the same name. During the 18th and

19th-centuries this isolated hostelry, on the main route across the bleak moorland, provided an ideal meeting place for smugglers and other outlaws, as well as legitimate travellers journeying between Cornwall and the rest of England. Today, as well as providing hospitality, the inn has a **Museum of Smuggling** "devoted to the arts of concealment and evasion", which the arch villain, Demon Darvey, the vicar of Altarnum demonstrates with the aid of tableaux. There's also a room dedicated to the memory of Daphne du Maurier, which is full of memorabilia of the writer including her Sheraton writing desk on top of which is a packet of du Maurier cigarettes named after her father, the actor Gerald du Maurier. There's also a dish of Glacier Mints – Dame Daphne's favourite sweets.

Bodmin Moor, the bleak expanse of moorland surrounding Bolventor, is the smallest of the three great West Country moors and an Area of Outstanding Natural Beauty. Its granite upland is characterised by saturated moorland and weather-beaten tors. From here the rivers Inny, Lynher, Fowey, St Neot and De Lank flow to both the north and south coasts of Cornwall. In this wild countryside roams the Beast of Bodmin, an elusive catlike creature that could be an escaped puma or panther – or just another creation of the fertile Cornish imagination.

At 1377 feet, **Brown Willy** is the highest point of Bodmin Moor and Cornwall, while, just to the northwest, rises **Roughtor** (pronounced row tor to rhyme with now tor), the moor's second highest point. Standing on National Trust-owned land,

Roughtor is a magnificent viewing point and the site of a memorial to the men of the Wessex Regiment who were killed during World War Two.

Throughout this wild and beautiful moorland there are scattered Bronze Age hut circles and field enclosures and Iron Age hill forts. Many villages in and around the moor grew up around the monastic cells of Celtic missionaries and took the names of saints. Others were mining villages where ruined engine houses still stand out against the skyline.

To the south of Bolventor is the mysterious natural tarn, **Dozmary Pool**, a place firmly linked with the legend of **King Arthur**. Brought here following his final battle at Slaughter Bridge, the king lay dying at the water's edge, listening to *"the ripple washing in the reeds, and the wild water lapping on the crag"* as Tennyson described it in his poem *The Passing of Arthur*. Close to death, Arthur asked his friend, Sir Bedivere, to throw his sword Excalibur into the centre of the pool. As the knight did so a lady's arm *"clothed in white samite, mystic, wonderful"* rose from the waters to receive the sword. Dozmary is not the only lake to claim the Lady of the Lake – Loe Pool

Dozmary Pool

at Mount's Bay, and Bosherstone and Llyn Llydaw in Wales are also put forward as alternative resting places for Excalibur.

This desolate and isolated place is also linked with Jan Tregeagle, the wicked steward of the Earl of Radnor, whose many evil deeds included the murder of the parents of a young child whose estate he wanted. As a punishment, so the story goes, Tregeagle was condemned to spend the rest of time emptying the lake with a leaking limpet shell. His howls of despair are still said to be heard to this day.

By tradition, Dozmary Pool is bottomless, although it did dry up completely during a prolonged drought in 1869. Close by is the county's largest man-made reservoir, Colliford Lake. At 1000 feet above sea level, it is the perfect habitat for long tailed ducks, dippers and grey wagtails, and rare plants such as the heath-spotted and frog orchids.

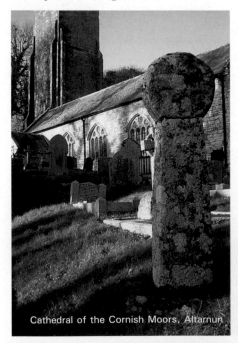

Cathedral of the Cornish Moors, Altarnun

TREWINT
13 miles NE of Bodmin off the A30

🦅 John Wesley   🏠 Wesley Cottage

This handsome village often played host to **John Wesley**, the founder of Methodism, on his preaching tours of Cornwall. One of the villagers, Digory Isbell, built an extension to his house for the use of Wesley and his preachers. Now known as **Wesley Cottage**, the rooms are open for visits during the summer months. The rooms, thought to be the smallest Methodist preaching place in the world, have been maintained as they were in the 18th century, and visitors can see the prophets' room and the pilgrims' garden. Digory Isbell and his wife are buried in Trewint churchyard.

ALTARNUN
14 miles NE of Bodmin off the A30

🏠 Cathedral of the Cornish Moors

This moorland village, charmingly situated in a steep-sided valley, is home to a splendid, 15th-century parish church that is often referred to as the **Cathedral of the Cornish Moors**. Dedicated to St Nonna, the mother of St David of Wales, the church has a 108-feet pinnacled tower that rises high above the river. Inside, it is surprisingly light and airy, with features ranging from Norman times through to some wonderful 16th-century bench end carvings. In the churchyard stands a Celtic cross, thought to date from the time of St Nonna's journey here from Wales in around AD527. The waters of nearby St Nonna's well were once thought to cure madness. After immersion in the waters, lunatics were carried into the church for mass. The process was repeated until the patient showed signs of recovery.

🏠 historic building   🖼 museum and heritage   🏚 historic site   🦆 scenic attraction   🌱 flora and fauna

Just to the northwest, near the peaceful village of St Clether, is another holy well, standing on a bracken-covered shelf above the River Inny beside its 15th-century chapel. To the north is **Laneast** where yet another of Bodmin Moor's holy wells is housed in a 16th-century building, close to a tall Celtic cross and the village's original Norman church. Laneast was also the birthplace of John Adams, the astronomer who discovered the planet Neptune.

The Cheesewring

MINIONS

16 miles NE of Bodmin off the B3254

Minions Heritage Centre   Golitha Falls
Hurlers Stone Circle   The Cheesewring

Boasting the highest pub in Cornwall, this moorland village was a thriving mining centre during the 19th and early 20th centuries with miners and quarrymen extracting granite, copper and lead from the surrounding area. It was also the setting for EV Thompson's historical novel, *Chase the Wind*. One of the now disused mine engine houses has become the **Minions Heritage Centre**. It covers more than 4000 years of life on the moorland, including the story of mining along with the life and times of much earlier settlers.

Close to the village stands the impressive **Hurlers Stone Circle**. This Bronze Age temple comprising three circles takes its name from the ancient game of hurling, the Celtic form of hockey. Legend has it that the circles were men who were caught playing the game on the Sabbath. As a punishment, they were turned to stone.

The Cheesewring, a natural pile of granite slabs whose appearance is reminiscent of a cheese press, also lies close to the village. Again, legends have grown up around these

stones. One, which is probably true, involves Daniel Gumb, a local stonecutter who was a great reader and taught himself both mathematics and astronomy. He married a local girl and they supposedly made their home in a cave under the Cheesewring. Before the cave collapsed, numerous intricate carvings could be seen on the walls, including the inscription D Gumb 1735. Another story tells that the Cheesewring was once the haunt of a Druid who would offer thirsty passersby a drink from a golden chalice that never ran dry. The discovery at nearby Rillaton Barrow, in 1890, of a ribbed cup of beaten gold lying beside a skeleton gave credence to the story. The chalice, known as the Rillaton Cup, is displayed in the British Museum.

South of Minions, and not far from the sizeable moorland village of St Cleer, is another holy well, St Cleer's Holy Well, covered by a beautiful 15th-century building. There used to be a total immersion (or bowssening) pool here that was used for the

stories and anecdotes   famous people   art and craft   entertainment and sport   walks

TASTE OF THE WEST COUNTRY

Fore Street, St Cleer, Liskeard, Cornwall PL14 5DA
Tel: 01579 345985
e-mail: tasteofthewestcountry@yahoo.co.uk
website: www.tasteofthewestcountry.co.uk

'Your Friendly Local Farm Shop'

Taste of the Westcountry was taken over in July 2010 by Rachel Cole, Sunshine and Chris Bolton. Rachel had previously been an employee of the Taste of the Westcountry and has extensive knowledge of the business and the products supplied. Sunshine and Chris had a delicatessen in Liskeard for three years before moving here in 2010 to expand their fantastic range of local and international deli products. At the **Taste of the West Country** they support local producers whenever they can, and are proud that many of the items come from field to shop in 2 hours, with no more than 10 food miles involved. They believe in fair prices for their suppliers, in the best possible quality and above all in tasty, healthy food and drink. The wide aisles allow plenty of space to fill up shoppers' trolleys with all the goodies on display, and the quality, the range and the friendly, helpful staff make this a great place to do the weekly shop. The locals love the place and visitors to the area regularly drop in, helping to enhance the success of a business that benefits the local community. Rachel, Chris and Sunshine intend to enhance the business by utilising their combined skills and experience to the full.

There's always a fine choice of fresh meat, seasonal game, and a good selection of smoked fish. Also to be found are free-range eggs; cheese, butter, milk, cream, ice cream and yoghurt; bread, cakes and super locally made pasties; jams and preserves and chutneys; speciality sauces, oils and condiments; Cornish chocolates and fudge; teas, coffees and herbal drinks; juices and smoothies; wines, ciders and real ales; organic, vegetarian,sugar free/ low sugar products suitable for diabetics and gluten-free ranges; dry goods and everyday shopping needs; plants and flowers; hand-made beauty products; and ecological household cleaning materials, washing powders and liquids and toilet rolls.

They constantly review and research the product range, and there are regular tasting days and special offers on selected lines. The Taste of the West Country, which is located 3 miles out of Liskeard close to the A38, is open until 6pm every day.

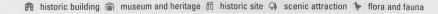

🏛 historic building   🏛 museum and heritage   🏛 historic site   🍃 scenic attraction   🌿 flora and fauna

attempted cure of the insane. There are several other reminders of the distant past. Dating back to Neolithic times, Trethevy Quoit is an impressive enclosed chamber tomb that originally formed the core of a vast earthwork mound. The largest such structure in Cornwall, this quoit is believed to be more than 5000 years old. Just to the west stands a tall stone cross, King Doniert's Stone, erected in memory of King Durngarth, a Cornish king, believed to have drowned in the River Fowey in AD875. Downstream from the Stone, the River Fowey descends through dense broadleaved woodland in a delightful series of cascades known as **Golitha Falls**. This outstanding and well-known beauty spot is a National Nature Reserve.

WARLEGGAN
11 miles E of Bodmin off the A38

🎞 Rev Frederick Densham   🌱 Cardinham Woods

Warleggan's most eccentric inhabitant was undoubtedly the **Rev Frederick Densham** who arrived at this tiny and remote hamlet in 1931. Immediately alienating his parishioners by closing the Sunday school, Densham continued by putting barbed wire around the rectory and patrolling the grounds with a pack of German Shepherd dogs. In response, his flock stayed away from his church and one record in the parish registry reads, "No fog. No wind. No rain. No congregation." Unperturbed, the rector fashioned his own congregation from cardboard, filled the pews and preached on as normal. It would, however, appear that Densham did have a gentler side to his nature, as he built a children's playground in the rectory garden.

To the north and west stretch the peaceful backwaters of **Cardinham Woods**, enjoyed by both walkers and cyclists. Acquired by the Forestry Commission in 1922, this attractive and varied woodland is a haven for a wide variety of wildlife, as well as producing high quality Douglas Fir for the timber industry. In medieval times, the woods were the location of an important Norman castle belonging to the Cardinham family, but all that remains today are an earthwork mound and a few traces of the original keep.

ST NEOT
11 miles E of Bodmin off the A38

🎞 St Neot   🎞 Carnglaze Slate Caverns

Once a thriving centre of the woollen industry, St Neot is famous for the splendid 15th-century Church of St Anietus and, in particular, its fabulous early 16th-century stained glass. Of the many beautiful scenes depicted here, perhaps the most interesting is that of **St Neot**, the diminutive saint after whom the village is named. Although only 15 inches tall, the saint became famous for his miracles involving animals. One story tells of an exhausted hunted doe that ran to St Neot's side. A stern look from the saint sent the pursuing hounds back into the forest while the huntsman dropped his bow and became a faithful disciple. Another tale depicted in the church window tells of an angel giving the saint three fish for his well and adding that as long as he only eats one fish a day there will always be fish to eat. Unfortunately, when St Neot fell ill, his servant took two fish and prepared them for his master. Horrified, Neot prayed over the meal, ordering the fish be returned to the well and, as they touched the water, they came alive again.

Tied to the tower outside the church is an oak branch that is replaced annually on Oak Apple Day. The ceremony was started by Royalists wishing to give thanks for the oak

BITTERSWEET

9 Fore Street, Liskeard, Cornwall PL14 3JA
Tel: 01579 349800
e-mail: info@bittersweetclothing.co.uk
website: www.bittersweetclothing.co.uk

Liskeard's **Bittersweet** clothing shop was started by Sandra Gilbride back in the 80s with a vintage/retro clothes and accessories shop in London. Sandra has always had an interest in vintage clothing which probably influences her selections. She offers her customers a wide range of carefully selected styles that won't go out of fashion and can be built on each season or when needed! Sandra really believes that clothes should not necessarily be kept for 'best occasions' and most of the clothes in her shop can be worn casually, like a special coat or jacket with jeans making you feel good on a daily basis, or dressed up for a special occasion with a piece of jewellery or wonderful shoes.

You'll find some 40 or so different designers featured on the racks here, ranging from Aganzi to Yumi, and including leading names such as Avoca, Komodo and Amazing Woman. Bittersweet also stocks a wide range of accessories: jewellery by Rosie Fox, Martine Wester, Jackie Brazil and Block; shoes by Fly London and Rascal; scarves from Lettuce; hats from Ignite and Braintree; bags by Owen Barry and Wrayfield; ; hand-made rag bags by Julia in Saltash; and much, much more.

Bittersweet has a very strong ethical stance. There are Fairtrade products from Kimodo, Braintree, Insight and Pants to Poverty, and store has its own sheep at St Brewerd whose wool they use to make throws and mittens. So if you are looking for something that's distinctive, durable and stylish all at the same time, Bittersweet is the store for you!

---

tree that hid Charles II during his flight from the country.

To the south of St Neot are the **Carnglaze Slate Caverns** where slate for use in the building trade was first quarried in the 14th century. Today, visitors can journey underground and see the large chambers that were once used by smugglers as rum stores. One of these chambers is occasionally used for concerts and can seat 300 people. There's also a subterranean lake, 18 feet deep, that is filled with the clearest blue-green water.

LISKEARD

13 miles E of Bodmin on the B3254

Looe Valley Line   Stuart House

Porfell Animal Land Wildlife Park

Situated on the undulating ground between the valleys of the East Looe and Seaton Rivers, this picturesque and lively market town was one of Cornwall's five medieval stannary towns – the others being Bodmin, Lostwithiel, Truro and Helston. The name comes from the Latin for tin, stannum, and these five towns were the only places licensed to weigh and stamp the metal. Liskeard had been a centre for the mining industry for centuries. By the early 19th century, after the construction of a canal linking the town with Looe, vast quantities of copper ore and granite joined the cargoes of tin. In the 1850s, the canal was replaced by the Looe Valley branch of the Great Western Railway. An eight-mile long scenic stretch of the **Looe Valley Line** is still open today, though the industrial wagons have long since been replaced with passenger carriages. The route hugs the steep-sided valley of the East Looe river and terminates in the coastal town of Looe.

Although it is a small town, Liskeard boasts some public buildings that act as a reminder of its past importance and prosperity. The Guildhall was constructed in 1859, while the Public Hall, opened in 1890, is still used as offices of the town council, as well as being home to a local Museum. Adjacent to the Passmore-Edwards public library stands **Stuart House**, a handsome Jacobean residence where Charles I stayed in 1644 while engaged in a campaign against Cromwell at nearby Lostwithiel. It is now an arts and heritage centre used for exhibitions, the sale of arts and crafts, and other events. Finally, in Well Street, is one of Liskeard's more curious features – an arched grotto that marks the site of Pipe Well, a medieval spring reputed to have had curative powers.

To the west of Liskeard is an attraction that will please all the family, **Porfell Animal Land Wildlife Park** at Trecongate. Within its 15 acres of fields bounded by streams and woodland, visitors can meet wallabies, marmosets, lemurs, zebra, meerkats and porcupines; feed the deer, goats, ducks and chickens; or just stroll through the woods or relax in the tearoom housed in an attractive old barn.

Looe

Old Guildhall Museum

Looe Island

The tidal harbour at Looe, created by two rivers, the East Looe and West Looe, made this an important fishing and seafaring port from the Middle Ages through to the 19th century. Originally two separate towns on either side of the estuary, East and West Looe were first connected by a bridge in the early 15th century. The present day seven-arched bridge, dating from the 19th century, carries the main road and links the two halves of the

GINGER

Fore Street, East Looe, Cornwall PL13 1AD
Tel: 01503 265065
e-mail: gingerinlooe@hotmail.com
website: www.gingerinlooe.co.uk

"**Ginger** is where East meets West Country!" So says owner Jayne Fox of her intriguing and exotic shop located in the main street of the charming riverside town of East Looe. She travels each year to India and other countries to buy stock from her regular suppliers thus cutting out the middle man and keeping costs down. Jayne buys as close to the source as possible, building up a strong relationship with her suppliers and their families, always looking to buy at fair trade prices, something that is reflected in Ginger's prices.

Amongst the unusual items on display here you'll find rare minerals from the Deccan Traps in Maharastra. Buyer Vilas Varade sources the minerals while travelling widely around the quarries of the magnificent Deccan Traps on his motorbike. Ginger buys all the best mineralogical samples which he collects and has funded Vilas to set up a shop in Ajanta. If you are seeking quality samples of Indian Zeolites, looking to increase your mineral/ fossil collection, or require tumble stones and crystals for alternative therapies, Ginger is the place to find them.

Other fascinating items on sale here include intricate carved stoneware from Uttar Pradesh; beautiful jewellery from Uttaranchal; hand painted papier-mache from Kashmir; stunning wall hangings and throws from Gujarat, and fashions from Goa.

Ginger are proud to offer a varied range of hand-made jewellery from places as diverse as New Zealand, Afghanistan, India, Peru and the UK.

Kesang and her mother in Utteranchal, India supply the shop with the most stunning silver mounted polished stones including lapis, labradorite, tiger eye and various quartz examples.

Ginger also sells wood ware originally from Indonesia, tumble-stones from Southern Africa, minerals from all around the world - in fact, everything from snake charmers flutes to shell boxes. There's also an exceptional range of clothing and accessories. So, whether you are looking for a special gift, or looking to add to your mineral collection, do visit or check out Ginger's website for ordering by mail.

TREDINNICK FARM SHOP

Widegates, Looe, Cornwall PL13 1QL
Tel: 01503 240992 Fax: 01503 240010
e-mail: sales@food4myholiday.com
website: **www.food4myholiday.com**

Tredinnick Farm Shop is a friendly, family-run enterprise situated on the B3152 between Looe and Hessenford. Visitors will discover an impressive range of locally sourced products, and the warm welcome and the ever-helpful staff make this a great place to do the weekly shop. Fresh fruit and vegetables are the mainstay, with the pick of the season's best on display, and Cornish bacon and sausages are always in great demand.

Other local and regional specialities include cider, scrumpy, wines and award-winning ales, cheeses and other dairy products, Original Cornish fairings (spiced crunchy biscuits), Cornish sea salt, Cornish gingerbread, Cornish clotted cream shortbread, and Cornish spring water. The shop also sells everyday food and household essentials, along with shrubs, herbs and plants and often a display of local arts and crafts. Since opening its doors, Tredinnick Farm Shop has attracted a loyal and growing local clientele, and it also supplies a number of restaurants, pubs, hotels and guest houses in the area.

The excellent produce is the basis of the food served daily in the tea rooms, from all-day breakfasts to cream teas and Sunday roasts.

Tina Lapthorne and her family and staff also provide a unique service that allows visitors, holidaymakers (and locals returning from holiday) to order from home or while on holiday. It offers 'chef-selected quality Cornish produce plus all the essentials delivered to your holiday accommodation. With 48 hours notice they will deliver all over Cornwall and the South Devon border area. Options include vegetarian packs, barbecue packs, holiday welcome packs even a supply of pet food; and another service **www.cornish-food-hamper.co.uk** will deliver gift hampers anywhere in the UK.

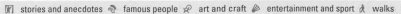

stories and anecdotes 　famous people 　art and craft 　entertainment and sport 　walks

town. Something of a jack-of-all-trades, over the years Looe has had a pilchard fishing fleet, has served the mineral extractors of Bodmin Moor and has also been a smugglers' depository. However, it is only the fishing industry that remains from the town's colourful past. Looe is still Cornwall's second most important port with fish auctions taking place at East Looe's busy quayside market. Nearby is the famous Banjo Pier, which is actually part of the harbour wall with a circular area at its sea end and it does vaguely resembles a banjo.

Looe Island

Of the two distinct parts, East Looe, with its narrow streets and twisting alleyways, is the older. Here, housed in a striking 15th-century building, is the **Old Guildhall Museum**, where can be seen the old magistrates' bench and original cells as well as displays detailing much of Looe's history. After the opening of the Looe Valley Line to passengers in 1879, the development of the twin towns as a holiday resort began. Fortunately, the character of East Looe has been retained while West Looe is, essentially, a residential area.

More recently, Looe has established itself as Britain's major shark fishing centre and regularly plays host to an International Sea Angling Festival. River and estuary trips are also available from the harbour.

Once a refuge for one of Cornwall's most notorious smugglers, Black Joan, **Looe Island**, just off the coast, is now a bird sanctuary. The island was made famous by the Atkins sisters who lived there and featured it in their books, *We Bought an Island* and *Tales from our Cornish Island*.

Around Looe

ST KEYNE
5 miles N of Looe on the B3254

🏛 St Keyne's Well   🏛 Stone Circle

🌿 Paul Corin's Magnificent Music Machines

Named after one of the daughters of a Welsh king who settled here during the 5th century, St Keyne is home to the famous holy well – **St Keyne's Well** – that lies beneath a great tree about a mile outside the village. Newly married couples came here to drink – the first to taste the waters was said to be the one to wear the trousers in the marriage. Romanticised by the Victorians, the custom is still carried out by newly-weds today.

Though a small village, St Keyne sees many visitors during the year as it is home to **Paul Corin's Magnificent Music Machines**, a wonderful collection that opened in 1967. Housed in the old mill buildings, where Paul was the last miller, this collection of mechanical instruments covers a wide range of sounds and music from classical pieces to musicals, and includes a Wurlitzer from the Regent Cinema, Brighton. Paul's collection has featured on numerous radio and TV programmes. Incidentally, Paul's grandfather was Bransby Williams, the only great star from the music hall days to have his own BBC TV show, in the early 1950s.

Just to the south of St Keyne, in the village of Daloe, is a **Stone Circle** of eight standing quartz stones, said to be older than Stonehenge.

ST GERMANS

7 miles NE of Looe on the B3249

🏛 St German's Church 🏛 Port Eliot

Before the Anglo-Saxon diocese of Cornwall was incorporated with Exeter in 1043, this rural village was a cathedral city. The present **St German's Church** stands on the site of the Saxon cathedral. Dating from Norman times, the present building was built as the great church for the Augustinian priory founded here in 1162. As well as curiously dissimilar towers dating from the 13th and 15th centuries, the church contains several striking monuments to the Eliot family, including one by Rysbrack commemorating Edward Eliot who died in 1722. Other treasures in the church include a glorious east window with stained glass by Burne-Jones, a superb Norman doorway as its west front and an old chair that bears a series of carvings depicting Dando, a 14th century priest from the priory. According to local stories, one Sunday Dando left his prayers to go out hunting with a group of wild friends. At the end of the chase, the priest called for a drink and was handed a richly decorated drinking horn by a stranger on a black horse. While

Port Eliot House

quenching his thirst Dando saw the stranger stealing his game. Despite his calls, the horseman refused to return the game. In a drunken frenzy, Dando swore that he would follow the stranger to Hell in order to retrieve his prizes, whereupon the stranger pulled Dando up onto his horse and rode into the River Lynher. Neither the stranger on the horse nor the priest was ever seen again.

Adjoining the village is the **Port Eliot** estate, the home of the Earl and Countess St Germans. At the centre of the estate is the magnificent stately house that has a history dating back to AD937 when it was built as an Augustinian Priory. At the Dissolution of the Monasteries it became the property of the earl's ancestors. The present building has 100 rooms, 82 chimneys, 13 staircases and a kitchen almost 100 yards from the nearest dining room. The rooms are hung with family portraits, including some by Reynolds, Hoppner and Ramsey Robert. It is very much a lived-in house, but a long period of neglect before the present earl inherited means that some of the furnishings and decoration are rather worn. As the present Countess has written: "Some may recoil at what might be described as the 'thread-bareness' of it all…some poetic friends consider the house to be a classic example of opulent and gilded decay".

The house is all but joined to St Germans Church that was once the cathedral of Devon and Cornwall. Church and house stand on the banks of the Lynher estuary, surrounded by a semi-circle of densely planted woodland and a stunning landscaped park laid out by Humphrey Repton in the 1790s. The house and park are only open for 100 days from spring to early summer, an arrangement with the Treasury that cedes inheritance taxes in lieu of art treasures being made available to public viewing for certain periods each year.

SALTASH
11½ miles NE of Looe on the A38

> 🏛 Royal Albert Bridge   🏛 Tamar Bridge
> 🏛 Guildhouse   🏛 Mary Newman's Cottage
> 🏚 Saltash Museum

A medieval port on the River Tamar, Saltash was once the base for the largest river steamer fleet in the southwest. Today, it remains the Gateway to Cornwall for many holidaymakers who cross the river into Cornwall via one of the town's mighty bridges. Designed by Isambard Kingdom Brunel in 1859, the iron-built **Royal Albert Bridge** carries the railway, while alongside is the much more slender **Tamar Bridge**, a suspension road bridge that was opened in 1961, replacing a ferry service that had operated since the 13th century.

Though older than Plymouth, on the other side of the Sound, Saltash is now becoming a suburb of its larger neighbour, following the construction of the road bridge. However, Saltash has retained much of its charm and Cornish individuality. There's an impressive

17th-century **Guildhouse**, which stands on granite pillars and is now home to the town council and tourist information centre. Close by is **Mary Newman's Cottage**, a quaint 15th-century building overlooking the Tamar that was the home of Sir Francis Drake's first wife. The interior has a kitchen and bedroom and the garden has been planted in the Elizabethan style.

Saltash Museum and Local History Centre opened in 2000 and contains a small permanent display about the history and well-known characters of Saltash.

TORPOINT
11½ miles E of Looe on the A374

> 🏛 Antony House   🌿 Antony Woodland Gardens

This small town grew up around a ferry service that ran across the Hamoaze (as the Tamar estuary is called at this point) to Devonport in the 18th century. From here there are excellent views over the water to the Royal Navy Dockyards and *HMS Raleigh*, the naval training centre for ratings and artificer apprentices. Commissioned in 1940, *HMS Raleigh* is also the home of the Royal Marine Band (Plymouth).

To the north of the town, overlooking the River Lynher as it meets the Tamar, is **Antony House** (National Trust), a superb example of a Queen Anne house. Built of pale silver-grey stone between 1711 and 1721, it has been the ancestral home of the influential Carew family for almost 600 years. It contains a wonderful collection of paintings (many by Sir Joshua Reynolds), tapestries and furniture. Surrounding the house are the gardens and grounds landscaped by Humphry Repton in the late 18th century, including the delightful **Antony Woodland Gardens**, which are at their best in the spring and autumn. The

Mount Edgcumbe Orangery

formal gardens contain the National Collection of Day Lilies.

CREMYLL
12½ miles E of Looe on the B3247

🏛 Mount Edgcumbe House 🏔 Rame Head

🏛 Eddystone Lighthouse

Linked to Plymouth by a passenger ferry, Cremyll is an excellent place from which to explore **Mount Edgcumbe House**, the 16th-century home of the Earls of Mount Edgcumbe. They moved here from Cotehele House after Piers Edgcumbe married Jean Durnford, an heiress with considerable estates including the Cremyll ferry. The gardens here, overlooking Plymouth Sound, have been designated as one of the Great Gardens of Cornwall. The 10 acres of grounds feature classical garden houses, statues, follies, an exotic Shell Seat, and the National Camellia Collection.

To the southwest of Cremyll are the two small and attractive villages of Cawsand and Kingsand. By some administrative quirk, for centuries they were placed in different counties: Cornwall and Devon respectively.

Though it is hard to believe today, it was from here that one of the largest smuggling fleets in Cornwall operated. At the peak of their activities in the late 18th and early 19th century, thousands of barrels of brandy, silk and other contraband were landed here in secret and transported through sleeping villages to avoid the attentions of the revenue men. It was also at Cawsand Bay that the Royal Navy fleet used to shelter before the completion of the Plymouth Breakwater in 1841, leaving the welcome legacy of a large number of inns.

Further southwest again, and at the southernmost point of Mount Edgcumbe Country Park, rises the spectacular **Rame Head**, which guards the entrance into Plymouth Sound. From the 400 foot-high cliffs there are superb views, but this beautiful headland has its own special feature – the ruined 14th-century St Michael's Chapel, from which a blazing beacon warned of the coming of the Armada. In the little hamlet of Rame itself is the older Church of St Germanus, which is still lit by candles; for centuries its west tower and spire acted as a landmark for sailors. The **Eddystone Lighthouse**, which can be seen on a clear day, lies 10 miles offshore from Rame Head.

WHITSAND BAY
8 miles E of Looe off the B3247

🐒 Monkey Sanctuary

Running between Rame Head and the hamlet of Portwrinkle, this bay has an impressive stretch of beach that is more a series of coves than one continuous expanse of sand. The

WESLEY HOUSE GALLERY

Big Green, Polperro, Cornwall PL13 2QT
Tel: 01503 272759
e-mail: enquiries@wesleyhousegallery.co.uk
website: www.wesleyhousegallery.co.uk

Located in the heart of the picturesque fishing village of Polperro is the **Wesley House Gallery**, owned and run by Wendy Carr and Maggie Livesey who took over the business in 2006. The house, incidentally, is named for John Wesley who stayed here in 1760. As well as displaying the work of a wide range of artists, whose work often focuses on Polperro and the surrounding area, the beautifully appointed gallery caters for collectors of Carn Pottery, Winstanley cats and fine art. The gallery is also renowned for its quality gifts, jewellery and cards

The gallery's pottery includes pieces from Carn Pottery, based at Nancledra in West Penwith, all hand-made and beautifully decorated by J M Beusmans. Dunoon Pottery is famous for its range of mugs in fine bone china and fine stoneware. Also available are items from Jane Adams' quirky collection of sheep, cats, dogs, chickens and cows. Not to be missed are Mark Smith's delightfully humorous boats and beach huts. He also creates unique ceramic "paintings" representing the Cornish landscape.

Artists represented in the gallery include Mike Praed, a very well-known artist from West Cornwall, whose Cornish scenes are instantly recognisable. Glyn Macey is a growing name in the art world, with his vibrant depictions of Cornish seascapes. Nicholas Smith is building a reputation for his detailed portraits of specific locations.

If you are planning to stay in this lovely spot, Wendy and Maggie can offer you comfortable bed and breakfast accommodation above the gallery. You will find yourself very much part of the family, which consists of your two hosts and their enthusiastic pets, Freddie (the dog) and Magic (the cat). The room features a king-size bed, en-suite shower, tea- and coffee-making facilities, colour TV, DVD and VCR. After a good night's sleep, you have a choice of full English or Continental breakfast. The menu features local, free-range and organic wherever possible. Free parking is available for those travelling by car, while for those arriving on public transport in Plymouth, Looe or Liskeard, a collection service is offered for a small fee.

seaside village of Portwrinkle developed around its medieval harbour. Further west along the coast, at the coastal village of Murrayton, is the famous **Monkey Sanctuary**, the world's first protected colony of Amazonian woolly monkeys. The sanctuary was set up in 1964 to provide a safe environment for monkeys rescued from zoos or abandoned as pets, and its inhabitants roam freely in the gardens of the outdoor enclosures. Plants for the monkeys to eat are grown in a forest garden, while the Tree Top Café takes care of hungry humans.

POLPERRO

3 miles SW of Looe off the A387

🏛 Polperro Heritage Museum of Smuggling

Polperro is many people's idea of a typical Cornish fishing village as its steep, narrow streets and alleyways are piled high with

fisherman's cottages built around a narrow tidal inlet. All routes in this lovely village seem to lead down to its beautiful harbour. It is still a busy fishing port, where there is normally an assortment of colourful boats to be seen. Boat trips from the harbour to Fowey, Looe and Polruan are available during the summer months.

For centuries dependent on pilchard fishing for its survival, Polperro also has a long association with smuggling. During the 18th century, the practice was so rife that nearly all of the inhabitants were involved in the shipping, storing or transporting of contraband. To combat this widespread problem, HM Customs and Excise established the first 'preventive station' in Cornwall here in the 1800s. At the **Polperro Heritage Museum of Smuggling**, housed in a former pilchard factory, a whole range of artefacts

---

ANGEL

8 Lansallos Street, Polperro, Cornwall PL13 2QU
Tel: 01503 272077
e-mail: info@angelinspire.co.uk
website: www.angelinspire.co.uk

Inspiration is certainly an important part of **Angel**, an exciting new gift shop and gallery close to the harbour in Polperro. Owner Kerry Bromfield can be found painting in her open studio at the back of the shop, where she will be displaying and selling her own work as well as that of many other local artists and craftspeople. Some of these will also be visiting to demonstrate their talents in the shop, whose walls and shelves are filled with a whole host of beautifully-made, unique gift items.

Angel is located inside what is quite an inspirational building itself, a picturesque old place from the early 1600s, with low ceilings and the intimate feel of walking into someone's sitting room rather than into a store. It isn't surprising that it looks so appealing and inspiring, as Kerry has worked in the interior design business since the 1980s, and as well as the arts and crafts she sells she also offers an interior design service. Her talents speak for themselves as soon as you walk through the door.

---

and memorabilia are used to illustrate the myths and legends surrounding the characters who dodged the government taxes on luxury goods. A model of *Lady Beatrice*, a traditional gaff-rigged fishing boat, can also be seen.

From Polperro, the coastal walk westwards to Polruan provides five miles of scenic splendour and gives access to some enchanting secluded sandy beaches.

FOWEY

8 miles W of Looe on the A3082/B3269

🏠 Fowey Museum	🐦 Sir Arthur Quiller-Couch
🐦 Daphne du Maurier	🦋 Fowey Royal Regatta
🏰 St Catherine's Castle	🕱 Coastal Footpath
🔱 Polruan	🏰 Polruan Blockhouse

Guarding the entrance to the river from which it takes is name, Fowey (pronounced Foy – to rhyme with joy) is a lovely old seafaring town with steep, narrow streets and alleyways leading down to one of the most beautiful natural harbours along the south coast. An important port during the Middle Ages, the town exhibits architectural styles ranging from Elizabethan to Edwardian. St Fimbarras Church was rebuilt in 1460 by the Earl of Warwick after being destroyed by French marauders; nearby the architecturally flamboyant Place House dates back to the 13th century and has been home to the Treffry family since that time.

As a busy trading port, Fowey naturally attracted pirates and was the home of the 'Fowey Gallants', who preyed on ships in the Channel and engaged in raids on the French coast. Brought together during the Hundred Years' War to fight the French, these local mariners did not disband at the end of the hostilities but continued to terrorise shipping along this stretch of coast and beyond. A devastating raid by the French in 1457, that saw much of Fowey burnt to the ground, was in direct retaliation for attacks made by the Gallants.

Later, in the 19th century, much of the china clay from St Austell was exported through Fowey. It is still a busy place as huge ships continue to call at this deep water harbour alongside fishing boats and pleasure craft. The town's **Fowey Museum**, housed in part of the medieval town hall, is an excellent place to discover Fowey's colourful past, from the days of piracy through to the china clay exports of the 19th century.

Naturally, there are many inns here including the King of Prussia, named after Frederick the Great whose victories in the Seven Years' War made him a popular figure in England; and the Ship Inn, originally a town house built by the influential Rashleigh family in 1570.

Fowey has two important literary connections. **Sir Arthur Quiller-Couch** (or Q), who lived for over 50 years at The Haven, on the Esplanade just above the Polruan ferry. Sir Arthur was a Cambridge professor, sometime Mayor of Fowey, editor of the *Oxford Book of English Verse* and author of several books connected with Fowey – he

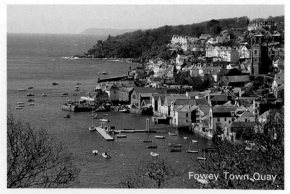
Fowey Town Quay

CRY OF THE GULLS

2 Webb Street, Fowey, Cornwall PL23 1AP
Tel: 01726 833838 e-mail: info@cryofthegulls.co.uk
website: www.cryofthegulls.co.uk

Open all year: Monday - Saturday: 10.00 am – 5.30 pm
                   Sunday: 11.00 am – 4.00 pm

The sound of the gulls is never far from Cry of the Gulls, a beautiful gallery situated in the heart of the stunning Cornish estuary town of Fowey. The gallery provides a visual feast for the eyes and a warm welcome making it a pleasure to visit at any time of the year.

Cry of the Gulls has a strong reputation for promoting work of the utmost excellence produced by a wide range of highly skilled British artists drawn from throughout the UK. The gallery showcases an eclectic range of work by many well-established and emerging artists, jewellers, potters and sculptors. The successful website includes an online shop, news page, map and opening time information.

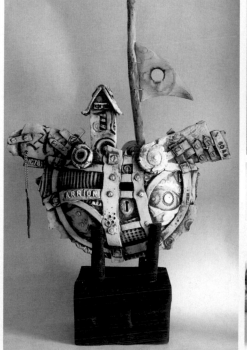

called it Troy Town. He died in 1944 after being hit by a car and was buried in St Fimbarrus churchyard. Sir Arthur Quiller-Couch is remembered by a monolithic memorial that stands on the coast facing Fowey. It was close to the site of this monument that, in 1644, Charles I narrowly escaped death from a sniper's bullet while making a survey of Cromwell's forces at Fowey. From the Bodinnick ferry there is a delightful walk across mainly National Trust land that leads up to the 'Q' memorial and then back via the Polruan ferry to Fowey.

The second literary figure was the novelist **Daphne du Maurier** who lived at Menabilly house (private), which featured as 'Manderley' in her most famous novel *Rebecca* (1938). Each year in mid May, a general arts and literature festival is held in her memory. A 'tented village' is set up overlooking the picturesque Fowey Estuary and the events include talks by a sparkling mix of star names, guided walks, drama, community events and free entertainment. There's also a permanent exhibition featuring her life and work at the Literary Centre at the tourist office.

Another major event is the **Fowey Royal Regatta and Carnival**, which takes place in mid August (usually the third full week). In addition to the sailing events there are firework displays on the Quay, Red Arrow displays, raft races, children's events, live music on the Quay, grand draws and carnival processions.

To the south of Fowey is Readymoney Cove whose expanse of sand acts as the town's beach. Further along are the sparse remains of **St Catherine's Castle**, built by Henry VIII as part of a

chain of fortifications to protect the harbours along the south coast. From Readymoney Cove, the **Coastal Footpath** is clearly marked all the way around to Polkerris. The walk takes in many fine viewpoints, including the castle and the wonderful daymark on Gribbin Head. This beacon was built in 1832 to help seafarers find the approaches into Fowey harbour.

Facing St Catherine's Castle across the mouth of the River Fowey and reached by ferry from Fowey, **Polruan** is an impossibly picturesque village. Tiny cottages cling to the steep hillside, threaded with winding steps, alleys and passageways. Life here revolves around the quay where the ferry lands. Beside the harbour, busy with pleasure craft and some industrial vessels, stands the late 15th-century **Polruan Blockhouse**, one of a pair of artillery buildings constructed to guard the narrow entrance into Fowey.

Just to the north of Polruan, and facing Fowey, is the pretty hamlet of Bodinnick where the actor Gerald du Maurier bought a holiday home beside the landing slip. He named it Ferryside and it was here that his daughter Daphne lived before her marriage and where she wrote her first novel *The Loving Spirit*. The house is still owned by

Polruan Village

the Du Maurier family but not open to the public. If you arrive in Bodinnick by the ferry, you pass the gates to the house as you walk off the landing slip.

GOLANT
8 miles W of Looe off the B3269

🏛 Castle Dore Earthworks

Close to this delightful waterside hamlet, which is home to yet another of Cornwall's many holy wells, are the **Castle Dore Earthworks**. This densely overgrown Iron Age lookout point is thought to be the site of King Mark's palace and is therefore linked with the legend of Tristan and Iseult.

Upriver and found in a sleepy creek is the quiet village of Lerryn, which was once a busy riverside port. Those familiar with Kenneth Grahame's novel, *The Wind in the Willows*, may find the thickly wooded slopes of Lerryn Creek familiar as they are believed to have been the inspiration for the setting of this ever-popular children's story.

LOSTWITHIEL
10 miles NW of Looe on the A390

🏛 Lostwithiel Museum

🏛 St Bartholomew's Church 🏛 Restormel Castle

Nestling in the valley of the River Fowey and surrounded by wooded hills, Lostwithiel's name – which means lost in the hills – perfectly describes its location. This small market town was the 13th-century capital of Cornwall. As one of the stannary towns, tin and other raw materials were brought here for assaying and onward transportation until the mining activity caused the quay to silt up and the port moved further down river.

Lostwithiel was also a major crossing point

Restormel Castle

on the River Fowey and the granite bridge seen today was completed in the 15th century. Set beside the river is the tranquil Coulson Park, named after the American millionaire Nathaniel Coulson who grew up in Lostwithiel. On the opposite bank of the river from the town lies Bonconnoc Estate, the home of the Pitt family who gave Britain two Prime Ministers: William Pitt the Elder and his son, William Pitt the Younger.

Throughout the town there are reminders of Lostwithiel's once important status. These include the remains of the 13th-century Great Hall, which served as the stannary offices, and the early 18th-century Guild Hall which is now occupied by the **Lostwithiel Museum**. It tells the story of this interesting town as well as displaying photographs of everyday life from the late 1800s to the present day. Nearby is **St Bartholomew's Church** with its striking octagonal spire. It was built in the 13th century and dedicated to the patron saint of tanners - tanning at that time was an important trade in the town.

Lostwithiel's strategic position as a riverside port and crossing place led to the construction of **Restormel Castle** upstream from the town, high on a mound overlooking

THE DELI

6-8 Church Street, Launceston, Cornwall PL15 8AP
Tel: 01566 779494
e-mail: shelley@thedeli.me.uk

Located in the historic Cornish town of Launceston,
The Deli is a family run business serving delicious
homemade food. The Deli opened in November 2009
and has gone from strength to strength. It is owned
by Shelley Alexander and Kate Akielan and there is
seating for around 17 diners. A tasty selection of
gourmet sandwiches are available as well as food
from around the world and a large selection of quality
cheese on sale.

The owners have developed a strong catering
section of the business and Shelley and Kate cater for
a wide range of events including weddings and
birthdays. Homemade 'ready meals' are also available
from The Deli as well as hampers, which can be sent
in the post. Ring for details.

Shelley and Kate's passion for good quality food is
fairly clear to see and The Deli is well worth a visit.
The attractive establishment can be found off the A30 trunk road at the Gateway to Cornwall, in
the ancient Cornish capital of Launceston.

DAVID PARISH MENSWEAR

5-7 Broad Street, Launceston, Cornwall PL15 8AA
Tel: 01566 772987
e-mail: richard.parish@hotmail.co.uk
website: www.davidparishmenswear.co.uk

David Parish Menswear is a popular gentleman's outfitters
located in the historic town square of Launceston, which is
the gateway to and ancient capital of Cornwall. The
independent menswear shop stocks an extensive range of
quality clothing to suit a wide range of ages and sizes at
affordable prices.

Owner Richard Parish prides himself on providing the kind
of traditional, one-to-one, personal service that is not so
widely seen these days.

As well as a fine selection of items on the shelves and
rails, which offer everything a gentleman needs to look well
presented, the shop also offers a few extra services. A full
hire wear collection for weddings and dinners is available as
well as bespoke tailoring. Choose from a wide selection of
cloths, including fine Italian wools to heavy Scottish Tweed,
and have your suit made in the style you require.

David Parish Menswear is a delightful place to shop and sells top brands such as Ben Sherman,
Gabicci, Double Two and Brook Taverner and Jockey. Off-road parking is not a problem.

the wooded Fowey valley. The Black Prince stayed here in 1354 and 1365, but following the loss of Gascony soon afterwards, most of the contents of any value were removed and the castle was deserted. The ruins of the huge circular keep with its deep moat remain impressive. In summer, the site is one of the best picnic spots in Cornwall, boasting stunning views of the peaceful surrounding countryside.

Launceston

🏛 Launceston Castle	🏛 Southgate Arch
🏛 St Mary Magdalene Church	🏛 Lawrence House
🚃 Launceston Steam Railway	
🚶 Tamar Valley Discovery Trail	

Situated on the eastern edge of Bodmin Moor close to the county border with Devon, Launceston (pronounced locally Lawnson) is one of Cornwall's most pleasant inland towns and was a particular favourite of Sir John Betjeman. The capital of Cornwall until 1838, it guarded the main overland route into the county. Shortly after the Norman Conquest, William I's half-brother, Robert of Mortain, built the massive **Launceston Castle** overlooking the River Kensey. Visited by the Black Prince and seized by Cornish rebels in 1549, the castle changed hands twice during the Civil War before becoming an assize court and prison. George Fox, the founder of the Society of Friends, was detained here in 1656. The court was famous for imprisoning and executing 'on the nod'. Although now in ruins, the 12-foot thick walls of the keep and

tower are still mightily impressive.

Also imposing is the 12th century **Southgate Arch**, the only remaining gateway of the three that once provided access to Cornwall's only walled town.

The most striking building in the town however is **St Mary Magdalene Church**. Its walls of sturdy Cornish granite are covered with delicate carvings that include angels, roses, pomegranates and heraldic emblems. The church was built by a local landowner, Sir Henry Trecarrel, in the early 1500s. He had started building a manor house nearby when both his beloved wife and infant son died within days of each other. Overwhelmed with grief, Sir Henry abandoned the manor house and devoted the rest of his life to building this magnificent church in their memory.

Elsewhere in the town, the streets around the castle are filled with handsome buildings, including the impressive **Lawrence House** that was built in 1753 for a wealthy local lawyer. Given to the National Trust to help preserve the character of the street, the house is now a museum that dedicates its numerous displays to the history of the area.

To the west of the town, and running through the beautiful Kensey Valley, the

Launceston Steam Railway

Launceston Steam Railway takes visitors on a nostalgic and scenic journey. Travelling in either open or closed carriages, passengers can enjoy a round trip along five miles of narrow-gauge track to Newmills and back. The locomotives used to haul the trains were built in the 1880s and 1890s by the famous Hunslet Engine Company of Leeds and once worked on the slate carrying lines high in the mountains of North Wales.

Launceston is also the start, or the finish, of the **Tamar Valley Discovery Trail**, a 30-mile footpath from here to Plymouth that takes in many of the villages scattered along the Cornwall-Devon border. Passing through old mining country, past market gardens and through ancient river ports, walkers of the trail will also see the wealth of bird, plant and wildlife that the varying habitats along the way support.

Around Launceston

GUNNISLAKE
10 miles SE of Launceston on the A390

Often referred to as the first village in Cornwall, it was here in the 1520s that Sir Piers Edgcumbe built the New Bridge over the River Tamar. It continues to serve as one of the major gateways into the county. In fact, this 180-foot-long granite structure remained the lowest crossing of the river by road right up until the 1960s when the massive suspension bridge linking Saltash with Plymouth was opened. The 16th-century bridge meant that this charming village also had an important strategic value. During the Civil War, it was the centre of bitter fighting. In the 18th and 19th centuries the village came alive with mining. Though the mines

---

MIDDLE TREMOLLET FARM

Coads Green, Launceston, Cornwall PL15 7NA
Tel: 01566 782416
e-mail: btrewin@talk21.com
website: www.cornish-farm-accommodation.co.uk

Brian and Vivien Trewin have run this traditional 19th-century Victorian farmhouse as a B&B for over 30 years, so there's nothing about the local area they don't know. **Middle Tremollet Farm** is set in half an acre of its own mature gardens, and there are breathtaking views across fields to Caradon Hill and to the outstanding natural beauty of nearby Bodmin Moor.

The owners really go that extra mile to make their guests' visit something special, which starts with a Cornish cream tea on arrival and providing a book of circular walks in the area. Guests also have a conservatory to enjoy, with barbecue facilities available in the summer and a roaring log fire in the winter.

The accommodation is rated 4-star by the English Tourist Board, with an extra Silver Award which only goes to the very best establishments. The farm has two ensuite double rooms and one twin room with a super-sized bed and its own private bathroom. All rooms have the latest flat-screen TVs, tea- and coffee-making facilities, and hairdryers. There's a generous breakfast too, cooked on the Aga, and in the evening a choice of nearby pubs and restaurants.

🏠 historic building   🏛 museum and heritage   🏚 historic site   🦆 scenic attraction   🌡 flora and fauna

have closed, some of the mine buildings have been immortalised by Turner in his great painting, *Crossing the Brook*, which also captures Gunnislake's famous bridge. The River Tamar is tidal as far as the weir upstream near Newbridge, and salmon fishermen continue to come to Gunnislake, as they have done since medieval times, to catch the fish as they travel up river to their spawning grounds.

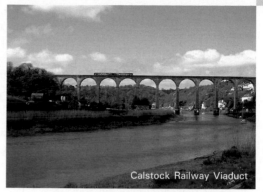

Calstock Railway Viaduct

CALSTOCK

12 miles SE of Launceston off the A390

- 🚉 Railway Viaduct
- 🚉 Cotehele
- 🏛 Cotehele Quay
- 🚣 Tamar Valley Line

Well known for its splendid views of the Tamar Valley, the village of Calstock was an important river port in the 19th century when vast quantities of tin, granite and copper ore were brought here for loading on to barges to be transported down the Tamar to the coast. In the countryside surrounding Calstock the remains of old mine workings, along with the

spoil heaps, can still be seen, along with the remains of the village's boat-building industry. The decline of Calstock as a port came with the construction of the huge **Railway Viaduct**, which carries the Tamar Valley Line southwards to Plymouth. Completed in 1908, this giant 12-arched viaduct, the first in the country to be constructed of concrete blocks, stands 120 feet above the river. Probably one of Britain's most picturesque branch lines, the **Tamar Valley Line** can still be taken down to the coast. Though the river has lost most of

Cotehele

St Dominick, nr Saltash, Cornwall PL12 6TA
Tel: 01579 351346
e-mail: cotehele@nationaltrust.org.uk
website: www.nationaltrust.org.uk

At the heart of this riverside estate sits the granite and slatestone house of **Cotehele**, built mainly between 1485 and 1627 and a home of the Edgcumbe family for centuries. Intimate chambers feature large Tudor fireplaces and rich hangings. Outside, the formal gardens overlook the richly planted valley garden below, with medieval dovecote, stewpond and Victorian summer house. At the quay interesting old buildings house the Edgcumbe Arms tea-room and an outstation of the National Maritime Museum. The restored sailing barge Shamrock is moored alongside.

its commercial traffic, it is a starting point for Tamar River canoe expeditions.

Just to the southwest of the village, **Cotehele** (see panel on page 113) represents one of the best-preserved medieval estates held by the National Trust. Mainly built between 1485 and 1539, this low granite fortified manor house was the principal home of the Edgcumbe family until the mid 16th century when they moved their main residence to Mount Edgcumbe. Along with its Great Tudor Hall, fabulous Flemish and Mortlake tapestries and period furniture, the house incorporates some charming features such as the secret spy hole in the Great Hall and a tower clock with a bell but no face or hands. Surrounding the house are, firstly, the grounds, containing exotic and tender plants that thrive in the mild valley climate and, beyond that, the estate with its ancient network of pathways that allow exploration of the valley.

The River Tamar runs through the estate and close to an old cider house and mill is **Cotehele Quay**, a busy river port in Victorian times. The quay buildings now house an outstation of the National Maritime Museum, an art and craft gallery and a licensed tearoom. The restored Tamar sailing barge *Shamrock* is moored alongside the museum.

CALLINGTON
9½ miles S of Launceston on the A388

🎨 Mural Project	🏛 Dupath Holy Well
🏛 Cadsonbury Hillfort	🌿 Kit Hill

Situated on the fertile land between the rivers Tamar and Lynher, Callington is now rich fruit-growing country. During the 19th century, the surrounding landscape was very different as it was an active mining area. The area's heritage, landscape and character are depicted on many of the walls of Callington's buildings, thanks to the town's interesting and unusual **Mural Project**.

About a mile outside the town, **Dupath Holy Well** is enclosed in a fine granite building of 1510. The water in the basin was believed to cure whooping cough.

Overlooking the River Lynher, southwest of this old market town, is **Cadsonbury Hillfort** – a massive Iron Age bank and ditch that are thought to be the remains of a local chief's residence. To the northeast rises **Kit Hill**, now a country park, where a 19th-century chimney stack built to serve one of the area's mines adds a further 80 feet to the hill's summit.

Cotehele Quay

HAMPTON MANOR

Alston, Stoke Climsland, Callington PL17 8LX
Tel: 01579 370494
e-mail: hamptonmanor@sapanet.com
website: www.hamptonmanor.co.uk

Hampton Manor is a country house hotel set in beautiful, secluded gardens in the peaceful countryside within the Tamar Valley, on the border of Devon and Cornwall. This impressive establishment is located in a designated Area of Outstanding Natural Beauty and offers six high quality en-suite guest rooms. Hampton Manor is extremely popular with walkers visiting the area to make the most of the spectacular surroundings. Within a half hour drive are numerous attractions; the market towns of Tavistock and Launceston; the seaside city of Plymouth, the grandeur of Dartmoor and many tranquil National Trust gardens and houses.

This four star country house hotel is an ideal retreat for people wanting to get away from the hustle and bustle of every-day life. Evenings can be spent relaxing in the wonderful conservatory, which overlooks more than two acres of land.

Guests can dine in the hotel's licensed restaurant at reasonable prices. Discounts are offered for groups, for short breaks and for longer stays. Small conference facilities are available and are regularly used by Christian church groups. In the summer months it doubles as a games room for families with children.

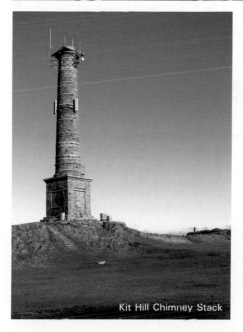

Kit Hill Chimney Stack

NORTH PETHERWIN
5 miles NW of Launceston off the B3254

🐾 Tamar Otter Sanctuary

Found above the River Ottery, this village is home to the **Tamar Otter Sanctuary**, a branch of the well-known Otter Trust, dedicated to breeding young otters for release into the wild to prevent the species from becoming extinct in lowland England. Visitors can watch the otters playing in large natural enclosures, see them in their breeding dens, or holts, and watch the orphans in the rehabilitation centre. Also here are a dormouse conservation project, refreshment and gift shop, lakes with waterfowl and an area of woodland where fallow and Muntjac deer roam freely.

📖 stories and anecdotes 🐿 famous people 🎨 art and craft 🎭 entertainment and sport 🥾 walks

LOCATOR MAP

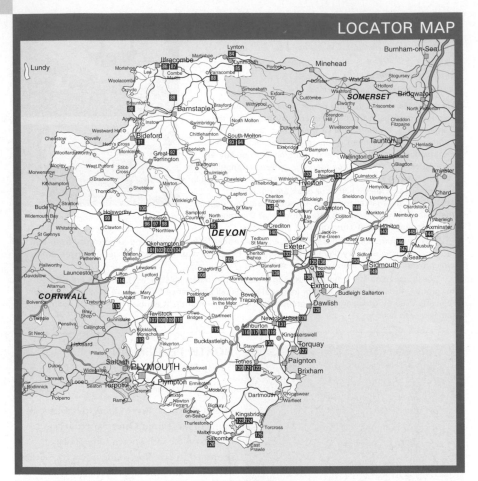

ADVERTISERS AND PLACES OF INTEREST

Continued on Page 118

🏠 historic building   🏛 museum and heritage   🏛 historic site   🍃 scenic attraction   🌿 flora and fauna

2| Devon

Asked to describe the 'ideal' English countryside, many people would conjure up a landscape of green rolling hills, of bright, fresh streams tumbling through wooded valleys, of white thatched cottages clustering around a venerable church, with a picturesque inn nestling beside it. Devon, of course, but only part of it. The whole of the Dartmoor National Park lies within its boundaries, a huge area of dome-shaped granite where the most frequently seen living creatures are the famous Dartmoor ponies that have roamed here since at least the 10th century.

The moor is notorious for its abundant rainfall – an annual average of 60 inches, twice as much as falls on Torbay, a few miles to the east. In some of the more exposed westerly fringes, an annual rainfall of 100 inches is common. In prehistoric times the climate was much drier and warmer. The moor then was dotted with settlements and this Bronze Age population left behind them a rich legacy of stone circles, menhirs, burial chambers and single, double or even triple rows of stones.

Then there's the busy port of Plymouth with its proud maritime history and associations with Sir Francis Drake and the Pilgrim Fathers. The rugged coastline to the north contrasts with the almost Mediterranean character of Torbay – the English Riviera. There are hundreds of picture postcard villages, of which Clovelly and Inner Hope are perhaps the most famous, and scores of delightful small towns such as Salcombe, Totnes and Dartmouth.

The county also boasts some outstanding buildings. The Gothic masterpiece of Exeter Cathedral has been described as "one of the supreme architectural pleasures of England", and it was a 14th-century Bishop of Exeter who built the glorious parish church of Ottery St Mary. The sumptuous mansion of Saltram House near Plymouth contains fine work by Robert Adam, Sir Joshua Reynolds and Thomas Chippendale, while Buckland Abbey is famed as the home of the Drake family and their most famous son, Sir Francis. Arlington Court is notable for the eclectic collections amassed by its last owner, Rosalie Chichester, during the course of a long life, and the now redundant church at Parracombe is a time warp building, still just as it was in the 18th century.

Part of Devon's enormous charm derives from the fact that it is so lightly populated. Just over one million people, roughly equivalent to the population of Birmingham, occupy the third largest county in England, some 670,000 acres in all. And most of those million people live in towns and resorts along its coastline, leaving huge tracts of countryside where the villages, the lanes and byways are still magically peaceful.

Lynch Tor, Dartmoor

🏛 historic building   🏛 museum and heritage   🏛 historic site   ⌘ scenic attraction   ❧ flora and fauna

Lynton

🏛 Lyn and Exmoor Museum   🪶 Scarecrow Festival
🐾 Valley of the Rocks

Lynton and Lynmouth, though often mentioned in the same breath, are very different in character. Lynton is the younger of the two settlements and sits atop a great cliff 600 feet high; Lynmouth, far below, clusters around the junction of the East and West Lyn rivers just before they reach the sea.

Lynton is a bright and breezy village, its houses and terraces mostly Victorian. The **Lyn and Exmoor Museum**, housed in a restored 16th-century house, has an interesting collection of tools and products of bygone local craftsmen and other exhibits relating to the area, including a reconstructed typical Exmoor kitchen of around 1800.

If you are visiting Lynton in August, you won't be able to avoid the strange characters lurking in gardens and doorways, sitting on roofs or shinning up drainpipes. Don't worry – they are just participating in the **Lynton & Lynmouth Scarecrow Festival**, a popular event that has become the largest and longest running such festival in the West Country.

To the west of Lynton, about a mile or so along a minor road, is one of the most remarkable natural features in Devon, the **Valley of the Rocks**. When the poet Robert Southey visited the area in 1800, he was most impressed by this natural gorge "covered with huge stones...the very bones and skeletons of the earth; rock reeling upon rock, stone piled upon stone, a huge terrific mass". In *Lorna Doone*, the author RD Blackmore transforms the site into the "Devil's Cheesering" where Jan Ridd visits Mother Meldrun who is sheltering under "eaves of lichened rock". And it was after walking along the clifftop

🎭 stories and anecdotes 🍄 famous people 🎨 art and craft 🎪 entertainment and sport 🥾 walks

Valley of the Rocks

path, more than 1300 feet above the sea, in company with William Wordsworth and his sister Dorothy, that ST Coleridge was inspired to write his immortal *Rime of the Ancient Mariner*.

An unusual attraction in the valley is its herd of feral goats, introduced here in the 1970s. A good time to see them is in January when the nannies give birth to their kids.

Around Lynton

LYNMOUTH

1 mile E of Lynton on the A39

🐾 Watersmeet   🐾 Cliff Railway

🐾 Glen Lyn Gorge   🕎 The *Louisa* lifeboat

Lynton is connected to its sister-village Lynmouth by an ingenious **Cliff Railway**,

which, when it opened on Easter Monday 1890, was the first of its kind in Britain. A gift from Sir George Newnes, the publisher and newspaper tycoon, the railway is powered by water, or rather by two 700-gallon water tanks, one at each end of the 450 feet track. When the tank at the top is filled, and the one at the bottom emptied, the brakes are released and the two passenger carriages change place.

For centuries, the people of Lynmouth subsisted on agriculture and fishing, especially herring fishing and curing. By good fortune, just as the herring shoals were moving away to new waters, the North Devon coast benefited from the two new enthusiasms for 'romantic' scenery and sea bathing. Coleridge and Wordsworth arrived here on a walking tour in the 1790s, Shelley wrote fondly of his visit in 1812, and it was Robert Southey, later Poet Laureate, who first used the designation "the English Switzerland" to describe the dramatic scenery of the area. The painter Gainsborough had already described it as "the most delightful place for a landscape painter this country can boast". One of the most picturesque villages in Devon, Lynmouth also has a tiny harbour surrounded by lofty wooded hills, a curious Rhenish Tower on the

---

LYNMOUTH LEISURE

7 Lynmouth Street, Lynmouth, Devon EX35 6EH
Tel: 01598 753634

There's no such thing as bad weather, outdoors people say, only the wrong gear. Well, whatever the West Country weather you'll find the right gear here at **Lynmouth Leisure**, from waterproofs and umbrellas, warm fleeces and scarves through to stylish sports shirts. There are top brands like Mountain Pass and Portwest, and ranges for all ages, for men and for women, in a rainbow of colours.

🏛 historic building   🖼 museum and heritage   🏚 historic site   🐾 scenic attraction   🌱 flora and fauna

Lynmouth Cliff Railway

pier, and do seek out Mars Hill, an eye-ravishing row of thatched cottages.

Lynmouth's setting beside its twin rivers is undeniably beautiful, but it has also proved to be tragically vulnerable. On the night of 16 August 1952, a cloudburst over Exmoor deposited nine inches of rain onto an already saturated moor. In the darkness, the normally placid East and West Lyn rivers became raging cataracts and burst their banks. Sweeping tree trunks and boulders along with it, the torrent smashed its way through the village, destroying dozens of houses and leaving 34 people dead. That night saw many freak storms across southern England, but none matched the ferocity of the deluge that engulfed this pretty little village. The Flood Memorial Hall has an exhibition that details the events of that terrible night.

Another testament to the ferocity of the storm can be seen in **Glen Lyn Gorge** where boulders and other debris still litter the ground. But the glen also provides some lovely woodland walks by the waterfalls and paths along the valley. An exhibition here demonstrates how water from West Lyn River now produces hydro-electricity. Children can have fun with giant waterwheels and water cannons. There's also a collection of steam

engines and models operated by water.

An earlier exceptional storm, in 1899, involved the Lynmouth lifeboat in a tale of epic endurance. A full-rigged ship, the *Forest Hall,* was in difficulties off Porlock, but the storm was so violent it was impossible to launch the lifeboat at Lynmouth. Instead, the crewmen dragged their three-and-a-half ton boat, the **Louisa**, the 13 miles across the moor. Along the way they had to negotiate Countisbury Hill, with a gradient of 1000 feet over two miles, before dropping down to Porlock Weir where the *Louisa* was successfully launched and every crew member of the stricken ship was saved.

Just to the east of the town is the popular beauty spot of **Watersmeet** where the East Lyn river and Hoar Oak Water come together. An 1832 fishing lodge, Watersmeet House, stands close by. A National Trust property, it is open during the season as a café, shop and information centre where you can pick up leaflets detailing some beautiful circular walks, starting here, along the East Lyn valley and to Hoar Oak Water.

MARTINHOE
4 miles W of Lynton on minor road off the A39

⚑ Hollow Brook Falls

Set amidst rolling fields above spectacular cliffs some 700 feet high, the small village of Martinhoe was occupied in Roman times as a signal station keeping an eye out for any aggressive activity by the Silurian tribes of Wales on the other shore of the Bristol Channel.

Martinhoe boasts what some argue is the highest waterfall in the West Country - it all depends on how you define a waterfall. **Hollow Brook Falls** descend 600 feet to the sea in a series of cascades, including two drops of 150 feet each. Coastal waterfalls are quite common on the North Devon and Exmoor coast but unusual elsewhere in Europe, apart from the Norwegian fjords.

Ilfracombe

🦢 The Landmark Theatre	🏛 Ilfracombe Museum
🏚 Chapel of St Nicholas	🏚 Tunnel Baths
🌿 Ilfracombe Aquarium	🏚 Old Corn Mill
🏚 Chambercombe Manor	

Like Barnstaple, Ilfracombe takes its floral decorations very seriously – during the 1990s the town was a consistent winner of the Britain in Bloom Competition. Between June and October the town goes "blooming mad" with streets, parks and hotels awash with flowers. Ilfracombe also promotes itself as a Festival Town offering a wide variety of events. They include a Victorian Celebration in mid-June when local people don period costumes. A grand costume ball and a fireworks display all add to the fun. There's a Fishing Festival in early August, a Carnival Procession later that month, a Birdman Competition, a Rescue Day and many more.

The Landmark Theatre is a striking building with what look like two gleaming white truncated cooling towers as its main feature. This multi-purpose arts centre has a 480-seat theatre, cinema screening facilities, a spacious display area and a café-bar with a sunny, sea-facing terrace. Next door to the Landmark Theatre, in Runnymede Gardens, is the **Ilfracombe Museum**, which opened in 1932 and has a variety of displays ranging from bats to Buddhas.

With a population of around 11,000, Ilfracombe is the largest seaside resort on the North Devon coast. Up until 1800, however, it was just a small fishing and market town relying entirely on the sea both for its living and as its principal means of communication. The boundaries of the old town are marked by a sheltered natural harbour to the north and, half-a-mile away to the south, a part-Norman parish church boasting one of the finest medieval waggon roofs in the West Country.

The entrance to Ilfracombe harbour is guarded by Lantern Hill, a steep-sided conical rock, which is crowned by the restored medieval **Chapel of St Nicholas**. For centuries, this highly conspicuous former fishermen's chapel has doubled as a lighthouse, the light being placed in a lantern at the western end of the building. St Nicholas must surely be the only ecclesiastical building in the country to be managed by the local Rotary Club – it was they who raised the funds for its restoration.

🏚 historic building 🏛 museum and heritage 🎞 historic site 🍃 scenic attraction 🌿 flora and fauna

SMUGGLERS NEEDLECRAFT

3 Capstone Place, Ilfracombe, Devon EX34 9TQ
Tel: 01271 863457
e-mail:chris.shaw93@yahoo.co.uk

Once upon a time Chris Shaw had a hobby: needlecraft. Back in 1981 she decided to try to turn her hobby into a business, and the result is **Smugglers Needlecraft**. The business has been so successful that Chris, her husband Geoff and daughter Penny can now boast customers from all over the world. Such is the range of products they offer that people from as far away as the USA, South Africa and Australia all come to Chris for their supplies.

Based near the Quay just along from Ilfracombe's harbour, Smugglers Needlecraft stocks an impressive range of fabrics and threads, alongside kits from Heritage, Derwentwater and others. They also sell accessories such as frames and needles, and offer visitors chance to create an unusual souvenir by making their own needlecraft scene of the Devon coast and countryside.

Don't be deceived by the outside of the shop, as the business has been described as both a Tardis and an Aladdin's Cave. It was originally a fisherman's cottage built in the 1600s but step inside this unique shop today and you're greeted by rainbow displays of metallic threads, space-dyed silks and just about everything the keen needlecrafter could possibly want.

From the chapel's hilltop setting there are superb views of Ilfracombe, its busy harbour and the craggy North Devon coastline.

Like so many west country resorts, Ilfracombe developed in response to the early 19th-century craze for sea bathing and sea water therapies. The **Tunnel Baths**, with their extravagant Doric facade, were opened in Bath Place in 1836, by which time a number of elegant residential terraces had been built on the hillside to the south of the old town.

Around the same time, two tunnels were bored through the cliff to reach rocky Tunnels Beach, which is still privately owned and for which a modest charge is made for access.

The arrival of a branch railway line from Barnstaple in 1874 brought an even larger influx of visitors to Ilfracombe. Much of the town's architecture, which could best be described as "decorated Victorian vernacular", dates from this period, the new streets spreading inland in steeply undulating rows. Around the same time the harbour was enlarged to cope with the paddle steamers bringing in tourists from Bristol and South Wales. Today, visitors can take advantage of regular sailings from that harbour to Lundy Island, as well as cruises along the spectacular Exmoor coast.

Standing beside the harbour is the **Ilfracombe Aquarium**, housed in the former lifeboat house. It contains an impressive collection of both freshwater and marine species in carefully re-created natural habitats. Worth a visit is the fun fish retail area here.

Chocaholics will surely seek out Walker's Chocolate Emporium in the High Street, which offers an irresistible choice of confectionery handmade on the premises. There's also a café selling hot chocolates and sweet snacks while upstairs is a chocolate museum.

For walkers, the **South West Coast Path** from Ilfracombe provides some spectacular scenery, whether going west to Capstone Point, or east to Hillsborough Hill.

Just to the east of Ilfracombe, at Hele Bay, **The Old Corn Mill and Pottery** is unique in North Devon. Dating back to the 16th century, the mill has been lovingly restored from near dereliction and is now producing 100% wholemeal stone-ground flour for sale. In Robin Gray's pottery, you can watch him in action at the potter's wheel and try your own skill in fashioning slippery clay into a more-or-less recognisable object. If you really want to keep the result, the pottery will fire and glaze it, and post it on to you.

Half a mile or so south of the mill, set in a secluded valley, **Chambercombe Manor** is an 11th-century mansion that was first recorded in the Domesday Book. Visitors have access to eight rooms displaying period furniture from Elizabethan to Victorian times, can peek into the claustrophobic Priest's Hole, and test their sensitivity to the spectral presences reputed to inhabit the Haunted Room. The Coat of Arms bedroom was once occupied by Lady Jane Grey and it is her family's arms that are displayed above the fireplace. Outside, the four acres of beautiful grounds contain wildfowl ponds, a bird sanctuary and an arboretum.

BERRYNARBOR

3 miles E of Ilfracombe off the A399

🏛 St Peter's Church   🏛 Watermouth Castle

Nestling in a steep-sided combe, Berrynarbor is a wonderfully unspoilt village set around **St Peter's Church**, which, with its 96 feet high tower, is one of the grandest churches in North Devon. Inside, there's an interesting collection of monuments, many of them memorials of the Berry family, once the owners of the nearby 15th-century manor house which later became the village school.

On the coast here is the pretty cove of Watermouth and the Victorian folly, **Watermouth Castle**, which has been transformed into a family theme park. In the castle's great hall, there's a collection of suits of armour and visitors can enjoy mechanical music demonstrations. Elsewhere, there are displays on Victorian life, antique pier machines, a room devoted to model railways and, down in the depths of the dungeon labyrinths, fairy tales come to life.

COMBE MARTIN

4 miles E of Ilfracombe on the A399

🏛 Combe Martin Museum

🌱 Wildlife and Dinosaur Park   🏛 Pack o' Cards Inn

✐ Exmoor Brass Rubbing Centre

Just a short distance from Berrynarbor, on the other side of the River Umber, is another popular resort, Combe Martin. There's a good sandy beach here and a short walk will take you to one of the secluded bays. An added attraction, especially for children, is the large number of rock pools amongst the bays. In the village itself, the main street is more than two miles long, reputed to be the longest in the country and featuring a wide selection of inns, cafés and shops. As well as the **Combe Martin Museum**, there is also the **Wildlife and Dinosaur Park** where life-sized animated dinosaurs lurk in the woods. The 25-acre site also shelters 250 species of real animals, including a large and lively collection of apes and monkeys. Within the park are animal handling areas, an Earthquake Ride, a dinosaur museum and oriental gardens. There's an otter pool and daily sea lion shows and falconry displays, and if you book ahead you can experience the unique thrill of swimming with the sea lions.

Also within the park is the **Exmoor Brass Rubbing Centre**. The first collection of brass rubbings was made by a man named Craven Ord between 1790 and 1830. His collection is now housed in the British Museum but because of his method – pouring printer's ink into the engraved lines and then pressing a sheet of damp tissue paper on the brass – the results are often very poor. It was the Victorians who developed a process using heelball (shoemaker's black wax) and white paper that is still in use today. The Centre provides all the necessary materials and friendly instruction.

A remarkable architectural curiosity in the village itself is **The Pack o' Cards Inn**, built by Squire George Ley in the early 18th century with the proceeds of a highly successful evening at the card table. This Grade II listed building represents a pack of cards with four decks, or floors, 13 rooms, and a total of 52 windows. Inside there are many features representing the cards in each suit.

PARRACOMBE
13 miles SE of Ilfracombe off the A39

- 🏛 Church of St Petroc
- 🚂 Lynton & Barnstaple Railway

The redundant **Church of St Petroc** is notable for its marvellously unspoilt interior, complete with 15th-century benches, 17th-century box pews, a Georgian pulpit and a perfectly preserved musician's gallery. Perhaps most striking of all is the unique gated screen between the chancel and the nave, which bears a huge tympanum painted with the royal arms, the Lord's Prayer, the Creed and the Ten Commandments. We owe the church's survival

---

THE FOX AND GOOSE

Parracombe, nr Barnstaple, North Devon EX31 4PE
Tel: 01598 763239

Located in the delightful village of Parracombe on the edge of Exmoor, **The Fox and Goose** is a well-known hostelry renowned for its good food, fine wines and real ales. The excellent steaks and specialities such as venison sausages and home-made pizzas are particularly popular. So too are the superb ploughman's lunches with a choice of 7 different cheeses, the game dishes in season, and fish dishes like the whole lemon sole and cod. Mine hosts, Paul Houle and Nikki Baxter, are both accomplished cooks and their home-made puddings are distinctly memorable. In the summer afternoons, they also serve cream teas with home-made scones and jam.

The Fox and Goose also offers quality accommodation in 4 newly refurbished en suite rooms. All rooms are equipped with TV/DVD and WiFi. Visitors at the inn will find plenty to see and do nearby. Parracombe village has its own pottery, and the Lynton and Barnstaple Railway is just a mile away. And just a few miles north along the A39, near the village of Lynton, is one of Devon's most famous scenic attractions, the Valley of the Rocks.

📖 stories and anecdotes 🐦 famous people 🎨 art and craft ✐ entertainment and sport 🚶 walks

to John Ruskin who led the protests against its intended demolition in 1879 after another church was built lower down the hill.

Barricane Beach

To the north of Parracombe is Woody Bay Station, the operating base for the **Lynton & Barnstaple Railway**, which offers a mile-long journey across Exmoor in trains drawn by vintage steam locomotives. The trip opens up grand views of the moor, the Bristol Channel and South Wales. There are ambitious plans to extend the line southwards via Parracombe to Wistlandpound and northwards for four miles to Lynton.

MORTEHOE
4 miles W of Ilfracombe off the B3343

🏛 St Mary's Church 🏛 Mortehoe Heritage Centre

🍃 Barricane Beach

Mortehoe is the most north-westerly village in Devon and its name, meaning raggy stump, reflects the rugged character of the Morte Peninsula. In this pretty stone-built village set on the cliff-top, Mortehoe's part-Norman **St Mary's Church** is certainly worth a visit. It's a small cruciform building with a 15th-century open-timbered waggon roof, an interesting early 14th-century table tomb, a bell in the tower, which may be the oldest in Devon, and a wonderful series of grotesquely carved Tudor bench ends. The church is also notable for the large mosaic of 1905, which fills the chancel arch. Designed by Selwyn Image, the Slade Professor of Art at Oxford, the mosaic was created by the same craftsmen who did the mosaics in St Paul's Cathedral.

In the village centre, the **Mortehoe Heritage Centre** occupies the Cart Linhay

building and also serves as a local Tourist Information Centre. It contains a museum that has sections dealing with the local farming communities, the railway and the history of shipwrecks in the area,

A short walk from Mortehoe village leads you to the dramatic coastline, mortally dangerous to ships, but with exhilarating views across to Lundy Island. Much of this clifftop area is in the guardianship of the National Trust, which also protects nearby **Barricane Beach** (remarkable for being formed almost entirely of sea shells washed here from the Caribbean), and the three-mile stretch of Woolacombe Sands.

WOOLACOMBE
7 miles SW of Ilfracombe on the B3343

The wonderful three-mile-long stretch of golden sands at Woolacombe is justifiably regarded as the finest beach in North Devon. This favoured resort lies between two dramatic headlands, both of which are now in the care of the National Trust. The sands and rock pools lying between these two outcrops are a delight for children (along with the swing boats and donkey rides), and surfers revel in the monster waves rolling in from the Atlantic.

🏛 historic building 🏛 museum and heritage 🏛 historic site 🍃 scenic attraction 🍃 flora and fauna

Back in the early 1800s, Woolacombe was little more than a hamlet whose few residents sustained a precarious livelihood by fishing. Then, suddenly, the leisured classes were seized by the craze for sea bathing initiated by George III at Weymouth and enthusiastically endorsed by his successor George IV at Brighton. Inspired by the economic success of those south coast towns, the two families who owned most of the land around Woolacombe, the Fortescues and the Chichesters, began constructing villas and hotels in the Regency style, elegant buildings that still endow the town with a very special charm and character. Many friends of the Fortescue and Chichester families regarded their initiative as a suicidally rash enterprise. Woolacombe was so remote and the roads of North Devon at that time still so primitive, little more than cart tracks. "Who," they asked, "would undertake such an arduous journey?" During the first few years only a trickle of well-to-do visitors in search of a novel (and comparatively inexpensive resort) found their way to Woolacombe. But their word of mouth recommendations soon ensured a steady flow of tourists, a flow that has swelled to a flood over subsequent years. The town recently won the England for Excellence Gold Award for best family resort, and was dubbed Best British Beach by the *Mail on Sunday*.

Barnstaple

🏛 Pannier Market	🏛 Butchers Row	🏛 Guildhall
🏛 Church of St Peter & St Paul	🏛 St Anne's Chapel	
🏛 Queen Anne's Walk		
🏛 Barnstaple Heritage Centre		
🏛 Museum of North Devon	⚲ Tarka Trail	

Barnstaple enjoys a superb location at the head of the Taw estuary, at the furthest point downstream where it was possible to ford the river. The first bridge across the Taw was built in the late 1200s, but the present impressive structure, 700 feet long with 16 arches, dates from about 1450 although it has been altered and widened many times.

Visitors will immediately realise that Barnstaple takes its floral decorations very seriously. The town began its association with the Britain in Bloom movement in 1991 and just five years later crowned its efforts by winning the Gold award for the Prettiest Floral Town in Europe in the Entente Florale Competition. Wherever you turn you may well find a magnificent display - a hay cart full of flowers outside the police station and civic centre, for example, a giant postage stamp modelled in blossoming plants outside the Post Office, or a stunning model of a train (again, all created in flowers) at the entrance to the railway station.

The town's love of floral exuberance may be one of its most endearing features, but Barnstaple is also the administrative and commercial capital of the region, a pre-eminence it

Barnstaple Long Bridge

already enjoyed when the Domesday Book recorded the town as one of only four boroughs in the county. Back then, in 1086, Barnstaple had its own mint and, already, a regular market. More than nine centuries later, the town still hosts produce markets every Tuesday and Friday, but the **Pannier Market** is open every weekday. This huge, glass-roofed building covering some 45,000 square feet was built in 1855 and its grandiose architecture resembles that of a major Victorian railway station, (London's St Pancras springs to mind). The Market takes it name from the pannier baskets, (two wicker baskets connected by a leather strap draped across the back of a donkey, pony or horse), in which country people in those days would carry their fruit and vegetables to town.

Pannier Market

Just across the road from the Pannier Market is **Butchers Row**, a quaint line of booth-like Victorian shops constructed mostly of wood with brightly painted wooden canopies. When they were built, facing north for coolness, back in 1855 and were occupied exclusively by butchers. Today, you'll find a much wider variety of goods on sale – seaweed amongst them. Every week during the summer season at least 300lb of this succulent algae are sold, most of it ending up as a breakfast dish, served with bacon and an egg on top.

In the pedestrianised High Street stands the rather austere **Guildhall**, built in the Grecian style in 1826 and now housing some interesting civic memorabilia – portraits, municipal regalia and silverware – which are occasionally on display. Nearby, the **Church of St Peter and St Paul** dates back to the early 1300s. After having its spire twisted by a lightning strike in 1810, it

suffered even more badly later that century under the heavy hand of the Victorian restorer, Sir Gilbert Scott. Much more appealing are the charming 17th-century Horwood's Almshouses nearby, and the 15th-century **St Anne's Chapel**, which served for many years as the town's Grammar School. During the late 17th century John Gay, author of *The Beggar's Opera,* was numbered amongst its pupils. The town has other literary associations. William Shakespeare visited in 1605 and it was the sight of its narrow streets bustling with traders that inspired him to write *The Merchant of Venice.* The diarist Samuel Pepys married a 15-year-old Barnstaple girl in 1655.

As at Tiverton, the 17th-century well-to-do residents of Barnstaple were much given to charitable endowments. As well as Thomas Horwood's almshouses, Messrs. Paige and Penrose both bequeathed substantial funds for almshouses, and in 1659 Thomas' wife, Alice, paid for the building in Church Lane of a school for "20 poor maids". It is now a coffee house.

A slightly later building of distinction is **Queen Anne's Walk**, a colonnaded arcade with some lavish ornamentation, surmounted by a large statue of the Queen herself. Opened in 1708, it was used by the Barnstaple wool merchants who accepted that any verbal bargain they agreed over the Tome Stone was legally binding. The building stands on the old town quay from which, in 1588, five ships set sail to join Drake's fleet against the Armada. The building is now home to the **Barnstaple Heritage Centre** where more can be found out about this ancient town and one of its most enduring industries, pottery, which has been made here continuously since the 13th century. As in those days, local Fremington red clay is used.

There's more pottery on display in the **Museum of North Devon** where a whole room is devoted to Barum Ware created by local potter CH Brannam (1855-1937). With its strident dark blues, greens and earthy tones on red clay, the range was vastly popular in late Victorian times.

Barnstaple has two railway stations but only one is still functioning. This is the northern terminus of the Tarka Line, a lovely 39-mile route that follows the gentle river valleys of the Yeo and the Taw where Tarka the Otter had his home. The railway is actually the main line route to Exeter but has been renamed in honour of one of the area's major visitor attractions.

Walkers along the **Tarka Trail** will know Barnstaple well as the crossover point in this figure-of-eight long-distance footpath. Inspired by Henry Williamson's celebrated story of *Tarka the Otter*, the 180-mile trail wanders through a delightful variety of Devon scenery – tranquil countryside, wooded river valleys, rugged moorland, and a stretch of the North Devon coast, with part of the route taking in the Tarka Line railway in order to get the best views of the locations described in the novel.

Around Barnstaple

MUDDIFORD
4 miles N of Barnstaple on the B3230

🐦 Marwood Hill Gardens

From Barnstaple to Ilfracombe, the B3230 winds through a pretty valley, passing along the way through attractive small villages. Despite the rather unappealing name, Muddiford is one of them. The village really did get its name from the muddy ford by which medieval travellers used to cross the river here.

About two miles southwest of Muddiford, **Marwood Hill Gardens** offer visitors some

---

BROOMHILL FARM

Muddiford, nr Barnstaple, North Devon EX31 4EX
Tel: 01271 850676 e-mail: rwmmills@hotmail.co.uk
website: www.broomhillfarmhouse.co.uk

Nestled in a rural woodland location yet only five minutes from the market town of Barnstaple, Broomhill Farm is a family run smallholding and livery stables offering comfortable,quality B&B accommodation.There are three tastefully furnished double rooms all with en-suite facilities,colour TV,hair dryers, tea and coffee. Home cooked breakfasts,using locally sourced produce and eggs from the free range chickens is served at a mutually arranged time. A very homely feel and an excellent base for visiting Exmoor, superb golf courses at Saunton and wonderful surfing beaches at Woolacombe and Croyde.

📖 stories and anecdotes 🐦 famous people ✍ art and craft 🎭 entertainment and sport 🚶 walks

18 acres of trees and shrubs, many of them rare and unusual. The collection was started more than half a century ago and now includes an enormous number and variety of plants. The three lakes, linked by the largest bog garden in the West Country, are busy with ducks and multi-coloured carp. From spring, when camellias and magnolias are in bloom, through to the brilliant hues of autumn, the gardens provide a continuous spectacle of colour. The gardens are home to the national collections of astilbe, iris and tulbaghia.

ARLINGTON
6 miles NE of Barnstaple on the A39

🏛 Arlington Court   🌿 Exmoor Zoological Park

Arlington Court is an imposing National Trust property, which was home to the Chichester family from 1534 until the last owner, Rosalie Chichester, died childless in 1949. (Sir Francis Chichester, famous as an aviation pioneer and as the first solo round-the-world sailor, was born two miles away at Shirwell.) The present house was built in 1822 to an unambitious design by the Barnstaple architect, Thomas Lee, and extended some 40 years later by Sir Bruce Chichester who also added the handsome stable block. When he died in 1881, he left the house and its 2775-acre park to his daughter Rosalie, along with a staggering mountain of debts. Only 15 years old when she inherited the estate, Rosalie managed to keep it intact and stayed on at Arlington Court until her death at the age of 83.

The interior today is really a museum reflecting Rosalie's varied interests. There are displays of her collections of porcelain, pewter, shells, snuff boxes, and more than one hundred model ships, some made by French soldiers captured during the Napoleonic wars.

Intriguingly, Rosalie never saw the most valuable work of art amongst her possessions. After her death, a watercolour by William Blake was discovered on top of a wardrobe where it had lain forgotten for over 100 years. It is now on display in the white drawing room.

During her lifetime, Rosalie Chichester transformed the grounds of Arlington Court into something of a nature reserve. She ordered the building of an eight-mile long perimeter fence to protect the native wildfowl and heron populations. The Shetland ponies and Jacob sheep grazing the fields today are descendants of those introduced by Rosalie. Another of her eclectic interests is evident in the 18th century stable block that houses a unique collection of horse-drawn carriages she saved from destruction.

About three miles southeast of Arlington Court, **Exmoor Zoological Park** is home to more than 170 species of unusual and exotic animals and birds. The residents of the 12 acres of gardens here range from pygmy marmosets to tarantulas, from penguins to catybara. Children can enjoy close encounters with many of the more cuddly animals, there are informative talks by the keepers but, as at any zoo,

Arlington Court

🏛 historic building   🏛 museum and heritage   🏛 historic site   🏞 scenic attraction   🌿 flora and fauna

the most magnetic visitor attraction is the feeding time for the various animals.

LANDKEY

2 miles SE of Barnstaple off the A361

North Devon Farm Park

Landkey boasts a fine church with some impressive memorials (well worth visiting) and also the distinction of being the only village bearing this name in Britain. Historians believe that it is derived from Lan, the Celtic word for a church, and the saint to which it was dedicated, Kea. An enduring legend claims that St Kea rowed over from Wales with his personal cow on board determined to convert the pagans of North Devon to Christianity. Sadly, these benighted people were not persuaded by his eloquence and chopped off his head. Not many public speakers could cope with that kind of negative response, but St Kea calmly retrieved his severed head and continued, head in hand, to preach the Gospel for many years.

Just outside the village, **North Devon Farm Park** has been trading as a farm park and rare breed centre since 1992 with the aim of providing an educational glimpse into times and lifestyles past. It is set in beautiful, unspoilt North Devon countryside, and centres around a Grade II listed, 15th-century Devon farm house. There are more than 50 acres of lovely countryside and nature walks to explore, including lime kilns, badger sets, rivers and lakes. There are many animals to see and feed as well as activities for the young ones, whatever the weather.

SWIMBRIDGE

5 miles SE of Barnstaple on the A361

Rev "Jack" Russell   Church of St James

For almost half a century from 1833 this attractive village was the home of the **Rev John "Jack" Russell**, the celebrated hunting parson and breeder of the first Jack Russell terriers. A larger than life character, he was an enthusiastic master of foxhounds and when his bishop censured him for pursuing such an unseemly sport for a man of the cloth, he transferred the pack into his wife's name and continued his frequent sorties. He was still riding to hounds in his late 70s and when he died in 1880 at the age of 87 hundreds of people attended his funeral. Russell was buried in the churchyard of St James', the church where he had been a diligent pastor. He was gratefully remembered for his brief sermons, delivered as his groom waited by the porch with his horse saddled and ready.

Mostly 15th century, the **Church of St James** is one of Devon's outstanding churches, distinctive from the outside because of its unusual lead-covered spire. Inside, there is a wealth of ecclesiastical treasures: a richly carved rood screen spanning both the nave and the aisles, an extraordinary 18th-century font cover in the shape of an elongated octagonal 'cupboard', a fine 15th-century stone pulpit supported by a tall pedestal and carved with the figures of saints and angels, and a wonderful nave roof with protective angels gazing down. Collectors of unusual epitaphs will savour the punning lines inscribed on a monument here to John Rosier, a lawyer who died in 1658:

> *Lo, with a Warrant sealed by God's decree*
> *Death his grim Seargant hath arrested me*
> *No bayle was to be given, no law could save*
> *My body from the prison of the grave.*

The village itself has some elegant Georgian houses and a pub, which in 1962 was renamed after Swimbridge's most famous resident. Jack Russell societies from around the world frequently hold their meetings here.

stories and anecdotes   famous people   art and craft   entertainment and sport   walks

Cobbaton Combat Collection

COBBATON

6 miles SE of Barnstaple off the A377

🏛 Cobbaton Combat Collection

The hamlet of Cobbaton is home to the largest private collection of military vehicles and wartime memorabilia in the southwest. Owner Preston Isaac started the **Cobbaton Combat Collection** as a hobby but admits that "it got out of hand!" His schoolboy's box of treasures has grown to comprise more than 60 World War Two military vehicles, including tanks and artillery, along with weapons and equipment from all over the world as well as thousands of smaller items. For visitors' convenience, a NAAFI truck is on duty to provide snacks and drinks and the Quartermaster's Stores offers a range of surplus uniforms, de-activated guns, militaria, books and souvenirs.

BISHOPS TAWTON

2 miles S of Barnstaple on the A377

Bishop's Tawton takes its name from the River Taw and the medieval Bishop's Palace that stood here until the reign of Henry VIII and of which a few fragments still stand. The village today is not over-endowed with listed buildings but it can boast a very unusual one, a sociable three-seater outside lavatory that has been accorded Grade II listed status. This amenity has not been used for 40 years or more (and the brambles that have invaded it would make it rather uncomfortable to do so) but it still looks perfectly serviceable.

ATHERINGTON

7 miles S of Barnstaple on the B3217

🏛 St Mary's Church

A landmark for miles around, **St Mary's Church** stands in the picturesque square of this hilltop village and is notable for a feature that is unique in Devon – a lavishly carved and alarmingly top-heavy rood loft. Created by two carvers from Chittlehampton in the 1530s, it is an exceptionally fine example of their craft. The church also contains striking effigies of Sir John Wilmington, who died in 1349, and his wife; a window of medieval glass; and well-preserved brasses of Sir John Basset, (died 1529), his two wives and 12 children.

HIGH BICKINGTON

8 miles S of Barnstaple on the B3217

Two miles south of Atherington is another hilltop village. Standing at almost 600 feet above sea level, the village commands excellent views in all directions. It boasts a fine 16th-century inn, The George, which is set amongst a delightful group of thatched cottages, and a parish church dating back to the 1100s, which is renowned for its exceptional collection of carved bench and pew ends. There are around 70 of them in all: some are Gothic (characterised by fine tracery); others are Renaissance (characterised by rounded figures). More recent carving on the choir stalls depicts an appealing collection of animals and birds.

BRAUNTON

6 miles NW of Barnstaple on the A361

🏛 Church of St Brannoc   🏛 Braunton Great Field

Braunton claims the rather odd distinction of being the largest village in Devon. It is certainly a sizeable community, spreading along both sides of the River Caen with some handsome Georgian houses and a substantial church reflecting Braunton's relative importance in medieval times. The church is dedicated to **St Brannoc**, a Celtic saint who arrived here from Wales in the 6th century. It's said that his bones lie beneath the altar of the present 13th-century church, a story that may well be true since the building stands on the site of a Saxon predecessor. What is certainly true is that the church contains some of the finest 16th-century carved pews to be found anywhere in England. Many of the carvings depict pigs, a clear allusion to the ancient tradition that St Brannoc was instructed in a dream to build a church where he came across a sow and her litter of seven pigs. Arriving in North Devon the saint happily discovered this very scene at the spot where Braunton's church now stands.

There is further evidence of Saxon occupation of this area to be found in **Braunton Great Field**, just to the southwest of the village. This is one of very few remaining examples of the Saxon open-field strip system still being actively farmed in Britain. Around 350 acres in total, the field was originally divided into around 700 half-acre strips, each of them a furlong (220 yards) long, and 11 yards wide. Each strip was

---

KITTIWAKES
HOME-GARDEN-BEACH

*15 Caen Street, Braunton, nr Barnstaple,
North Devon EX33 1AA
Tel: 01271 815314
e-mail: sarah@kittiwakes-shop.co.uk
website: www.kittiwakes-shop.co.uk*

Sarah Kirby describes her shop **Kittiwakes**, as "the home of shabby chic in North Devon". In fact, she sells beautiful soft furnishings and general home wares. With the focus on flair and presentation Sarah strives to make sure that her shop is a fantastic place to find gifts that have that extra little something, that touch of beauty, that makes a gift special. You'll find cushions and quilts by A.U. Maison, Nigella Lawson's kitchen range, candles, soaps, mirrors, wall decorations and oil cloth. Kittiwakes is also an approved Cath Kidston stockist.

The shop also stocks some great garden decorations, garden furniture and other products. Tins for seeds, string and matches, baskets, buckets and containers, plant labels, picnic blankets, outdoor thermometers, hand soaps, creams and salves - you'll definitely find that perfect gift for a garden lover somewhere here. And for the beach – think of Kittiwakes if you need: a beach BBQ, a picnic blanket, thermos, lantern or bucket and spade. "All with a tasteful twist or retro charm... of course!" says Sarah. Kittiwakes is open from 10am to 5pm, Monday to Saturday. Out of season hours may vary slightly, please telephone or check the website.

📰 stories and anecdotes   🐦 famous people   🎨 art and craft   🎭 entertainment and sport   🚶 walks

separated by an unploughed 'landshare' about one foot wide. Throughout the centuries, many of the strips have changed hands and been combined, so that now only about 200 individual ones remain.

CROYDE
9 miles NW of Barnstaple on the B3231

🐦 Braunton Burrows   🐦 Baggy Point

One of the prettiest villages in Devon, Croyde is renowned for its excellent beach with, just around the headland, another three-mile stretch of sands at Saunton Sands, one of the most glorious, family-friendly sandy beaches in the West Country. The sands are backed by 1000 acres of dunes known as **Braunton Burrows**, a UNESCO-designated Biosphere Reserve, which is the largest sand dune system in England. The southern part of this wide expanse is noted for its fluctuating population of migrant birds as well as rare flowers and insects.

Also noted for its abundant wildlife is **Baggy Point**, just northwest of Croyde. This headland of Devonian rock (so named because the rock was first identified in this county) is a popular nesting place for seabirds, including herring gull, fulmar, shag

and cormorant. Grey seals can often be seen from here.

Running north-westwards from the cliffs is a shoal known as Baggy Leap. In 1799, *HMS Weazle* was driven onto the shoal during a gale and all 106 people on board perished.

GEORGEHAM
9 miles NW of Barnstaple off the B3231

🐦 Henry Williamson

It was in Georgeham that **Henry Williamson** settled in 1921 and where he wrote his most famous novel, *Tarka the Otter,* published in 1927. Tarka lived in the land between the Taw and Torridge rivers and many of the small villages and settlements feature in the story. After World War Two, Williamson farmed for a while in Norfolk but returned to Georgeham where he died in 1947. He is buried in the graveyard of St George's Church. Skirr Cottage, which he rented while writing *Tarka*, is now a self-catering holiday home.

Bideford

🏛 Pannier Market   🏛 Royal Hotel
🏛 Burton Museum   🐦 Lundy Island

Dubbed the Little White Town by Charles Kingsley, this attractive town set beside the River Torridge was once the third busiest port in Britain. The first bridge across the shallow neck of the Torridge estuary was built around 1300 to link Bideford with its aptly-named satellite village, East-the-Water. That bridge must have been very impressive for its time. It was 670 feet long, and built of massive oak lintels of varying length, which created a series of irregular arches between 12

Baggy Point

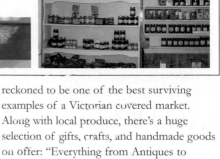

PANNIER PANTRY

9-11 Butchers Row, Market Place, Bideford,
Devon EX39 2DR
Tel: 01237 473957

Located in Bideford's historic Victorian covered market of 1883, the **Pannier Pantry** places great emphasis on achieving the minimum amount possible of "food miles" for all its produce. Owner Carol Wawrychuk, who established her shop in 2007, sources all her stock if possible from within a 10 miles radius of Bideford. Meat, game, cheeses, jam, eggs are all local, and even the herbs are plucked from local gardens.

The pantry has a very inviting atmosphere, with café-style gingham curtains and fresh flower displays. Carol is also a qualified cake maker and will make birthday, wedding and other cakes to order. She is also planning to introduce hampers which are ideal for picnics and self-catering.

and 25 feet apart. These erratic dimensions were preserved when the bridge was rebuilt in stone around 1460 (the old bridge was used as scaffolding), and despite widening during the 1920s, they persist to this day. Unusually, Bideford Bridge is managed by an ancient corporation of trustees, known as feoffees, whose income, derived from property in the town, not only pays for the upkeep of the bridge, but also supports local charities and good causes. A high-level bridge a mile or so downstream, opened in 1987, has relieved some of the traffic congestion and also provides panoramic views of the town and the Torridge estuary.

Bideford received its Market Charter from Henry III in 1272 (on 25 May to be precise), and markets still take place every Tuesday and Saturday. Since 1883 they have been held in the splendid **Pannier Market** building,

reckoned to be one of the best surviving examples of a Victorian covered market. Along with local produce, there's a huge selection of gifts, crafts, and handmade goods on offer: "Everything from Antiques to Aromatherapy!"

Devon ports seemed to specialise in particular commodities. At Bideford it was tobacco from the North American colonies that brought almost two centuries of prosperity until the American War of Independence shut off supplies. Evidence of this golden age can still be seen in the opulent merchants' residences in Bridgeland Street, and most strikingly in the **Royal Hotel** in East-the-Water, a former merchant's house of 1688 with a pair of little-seen plasterwork ceilings, which are perhaps the finest and most extravagant examples of their kind in Devon.

It was while he was staying at the Royal

Hotel that Charles Kingsley penned most of *Westward Ho!* A quarter of a million words long, the novel was completed in just seven months. There's a statue of Kingsley, looking suitably literary, on Bideford Quay. Broad and tree-lined, the Quay stands at the foot of the narrow maze of lanes that formed the old seaport.

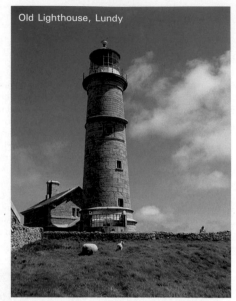

Old Lighthouse, Lundy

Just round the corner from the Quay, on the edge of Victoria Park, is the **Burton Museum and Art Gallery**, opened in 1994. The museum contains some interesting curios, such as Bideford harvest jugs of the late 1700s, and model ships in carved bone made by French prisoners during the Napoleonic wars. The gallery has frequently changing exhibitions with subjects ranging from automata to kites, quilts to dinosaurs, as well as paintings by well-known North Devon artists. The museum also has a craft gallery, shop, workshop, lecture area and coffee shop.

Starting at the Burton Gallery, guided walks around the town are available.

Around Bideford

LUNDY ISLAND
25 miles W of Bideford via MS Oldenburg

One excursion from Bideford that should not be missed is the day trip to Lundy Island on the supply boat, the *MS Oldenburg,* a journey that takes about two hours. Lundy is a huge lump of granite rock, three miles long and half a mile wide, with sheer cliffs rising 500 feet above the shore. Its name derives from the Norse lunde ey, meaning puffin island, and these attractive birds with their multi-coloured beaks are still in residence, along with many other species. More than 400 different species of birds have been spotted on Lundy, and you might also spot one of the indigenous black rats, which have survived only on this isolated spot. The island

has a 13th-century castle and a lighthouse, both offering accommodation through the Landmark Trust, a church, a pub and a shop selling souvenirs and the famous stamps.

WESTWARD HO!
2 miles NW of Bideford on the B3236

🐦 Northam Burrows Country Park

🏵 Pot Walloping Festival

Is there any other place in the world that has been named after a popular novel? Following the huge success in 1855 of Charles Kingsley's tale of Elizabethan derring-do, a company was formed to develop this spectacular site with its rocky cliffs and two miles of sandy beach. The early years were troubled. A powerful storm washed away the newly-built pier and most of the houses. When Rudyard Kipling came here in 1874 as a pupil at the United Services College he described the place as "twelve bleak houses by the shore". Today, Westward Ho! is a busy holiday resort well worth visiting

🏤 historic building 🏛 museum and heritage 🏚 historic site 🏞 scenic attraction 🐦 flora and fauna

for its two miles of golden sands, recently awarded a Blue Flag, and the nearby **Northam Burrows Country Park**, almost 1000 acres of grazed burrows rich in flora, fauna and migratory birds, and offering tremendous views across Bideford Bay.

Westward Ho! is also home to the Royal North Devon Golf Club, founded in 1864 and the oldest golf course in England.

An unusual event at Westward Ho! is the **Pot Walloping Festival**, which takes place in late spring. Local people and visitors join together to throw pebbles that have been dislodged by winter storms back on to the famous ridge, after which pots of a different kind also get a walloping.

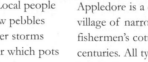

Cottages in Appledore

NORTHAM

2 miles N of Bideford on the A386

🏛 Bloody Corner

Northam is said to have been where Hubba the Dane attacked Devon and was repelled by either Alfred the Great or the Earl of Devon. Another tale recounts that in 1069, three years after King Harold had been slain at the Battle of Hastings, his three sons landed at Northam in an attempt to regain their father's throne. They came from Ireland with an invasion force of more than 60 ships but their rebellion was mercilessly suppressed at a site just to the south of the town. To this day, it is known as **Bloody Corner**.

APPLEDORE

3 miles N of Bideford on the A386

🏛 North Devon Maritime Museum

🎨 Appledore Visual Arts Festival

Overlooking the Taw-Torridge estuary,

Appledore is a delightful old-world fishing village of narrow winding lanes and sturdy fishermen's cottages from the 18th and 19th centuries. All types of fishing can be arranged here and you can even go crabbing from the quayside. The streets of the old quarter are too narrow for cars although not, it seems, for the occasional small fishing boat, which is pulled up from the harbour and parked between the buildings.

It seems appropriate that the **North Devon Maritime Museum** should be located in this truly nautical setting. Housed in a former ship-owner's residence, the museum contains a wealth of seafaring memorabilia, a photographic exhibit detailing the military exercises around the estuary in preparation for the D-Day landings during World War Two, a reconstructed Victorian kitchen, and much more.

A stroll along Bude Street is recommended. Art and craft galleries have gathered here amongst the Georgian style 'Captains houses', and it's particularly colourful during the **Appledore Visual Arts Festival** in late May-early June when one of the many events is a door decorating competition.

🏛 stories and anecdotes 🐦 famous people 🎨 art and craft 🎭 entertainment and sport 🚶 walks

INSTOW

3 miles N of Bideford on the B3233

The older part of this delightful village lies inland from the Torridge estuary while, looking out over the magnificent beach, there are some early 19th-century villas. Here, too, is the Instow Signal Box that was built in 1873 to control the crossing gates and the passing loop at Instow Station. It has been restored and is now the first Grade II listed signal box in the country. Visitors can see its machinery, gate wheel and instruments as well as 'pull off' a re-instated signal.

During the summer months, there's a ferry across the estuary to Appledore.

Just south of the village are Tapeley Park Gardens, some 35 acres of grounds on the eastern bank of the River Torridge. From here there are excellent views across the estuary and over to Lundy Island. Along with the lake reached by a woodland walk, there are masses of hydrangeas, rhododendrons and camellias. As well as the renovated Italian terraces and the restored walled kitchen garden, Tapeley has an organic perma culture garden where fruit, vegetables, nuts and herbs are mixed together using companion planting. There is also a children's play area and a variety of animals and pets to entertain the youngsters. The gardens are open daily, except Saturdays, from mid-March to the end of October; the Queen Anne house is open only to groups by appointment.

GREAT TORRINGTON

7 miles SE of Bideford on the A386

🏔 Castle Hill	🏛 Church of St Michael and All Angels
🏛 Torrington 1646	⚗ Dartington Crystal
🍃 May Fair	🌱 Rosemoor Garden

A good place to start exploring Great Torrington is at **Castle Hill**, which commands grand views along the valley of the River Torridge. (There's no view of the castle, which was demolished as long ago as 1228, its site is now a bowling green.) On the opposite bank of the river is the hamlet of Taddiport where the tiny 14th century church by the bridge was originally the chapel of a leper hospital; its inmates were not permitted to cross over into Torrington itself.

Not many churches in England have been blown up by gunpowder. That was the fate however of the original **Church of St Michael and All Angels**. It happened during the Civil War when General Fairfax captured the town on 16 February 1646. His Royalist prisoners were bundled into the church, which they had been using as an arsenal. In the darkness, the 80 barrels of gunpowder stored there were somehow set alight and in the huge explosion that followed the church was demolished, 200 men lost their lives, and Fairfax himself narrowly escaped death. The present spacious church was built five years later, one of very few in the country erected during the Commonwealth years.

Tapeley Park Gardens

The Civil War events are portrayed at **Torrington 1646**, a permanent exhibition near Castle Hill, where colourful characters dressed as 17th-century residents of Great Torrington speak in period language as they guide visitors through an indoor reconstruction of some of the lanes and streets of Great Torrington on the night of the fierce 1646 battle. Visitors then proceed to the linhay (an open sided barn) where they can try their hand at 17th-century games or perhaps try on some armour or have a go at wielding a pike.

But the town's leading tourist attraction is **Dartington Crystal** where visitors can see skilled craftsmen blowing and shaping the crystal, follow the history of glass-making from the Egyptians to the present day, watch a video presentation, and browse amongst some 10,000 square feet of displays. The enterprise was set up in the 1960s by the Dartington Hall Trust to provide employment in an area of rural depopulation. Today, the beautifully designed handmade crystal is exported to more than 50 countries around the world.

Torrington's **May Fair** is still an important event in the local calendar, as it has been since 1554. On the first Thursday in May, a Queen is crowned, there is maypole dancing in the High Street, and a banner proclaims the greeting "Us be plazed to zee 'ee".

About a mile south of Great Torrington, the Royal Horticultural Society's **Rosemoor Garden** occupies a breathtaking setting in the Torridge Valley. Notable as a centre for rose cultivation - there are some 200 varieties on show - the 40-acre site includes mature planting in Lady Anne Palmer's magnificent garden and arboretum; a winding rocky gorge

THE CRANFORD INN

nr St Giles in the Wood, Great Torrington, Devon EX38 7LA
Tel: 01805 623309
e-mail: cranfordinn@yahoo.com
website: www.cranfordinn.com

The **Cranford Inn** is a traditional Devon longhouse standing in lovely countryside on the B3227 just east of High Bullen (not in St Giles in the Wood). It has the look and feel of a true country pub and enjoys a super setting in 70 acres of grounds that include fishing lakes. The bar is a popular local meeting place, a convivial spot for a chat and a drink: the inn has its own microbrewery at nearby Yelland Manor Farm.

The Cranford is also a top-notch restaurant, with meat, game, fish and farm produce from the very best local sources; some of the fish is caught from the inn's own boat. They butcher their own meat, make their own sausages and smoke their own fish and game. The inn is a training establishment for a local catering college, and many students have gone on to cook in some of the top national restaurants.

The setting is rural but well-positioned, - 'in the middle of everywhere' - so it's an ideal base for exploring the glorious countryside. The guest accommodation, which can be booked on a B&B or self-catering basis, comprises three cottages, each with two bedrooms, a shower room, lounge and dining areas, a kitchenette, hot drinks tray and mini-bar. The inn specialises in catering for shooting parties and can also organise a day's fishing – on their own lakes, on local rivers or at sea.

with bamboos and ferns beside the stream, and a more formal area that contains one of the longest herbaceous borders in the country. There are trails for children, a picnic area and an award-winning Visitor Centre with a licensed restaurant, plant centre and shop.

MONKLEIGH
5 miles S of Bideford on the A388

🎭 Sir William Hankford

Monkleigh parish church contains a striking monument, an ornate canopied tomb containing the remains of **Sir William Hankford** who was Lord Chief Justice of England in the early 1400s. He lived at nearby Annery Park and the story goes that having been troubled by poachers Sir William instructed his gamekeeper to shoot anyone he found in the park at night. The gamekeeper did indeed see a figure passing through the park, fired and discovered to his horror that he had killed his master.

WEARE GIFFARD
5 miles S of Bideford off the A386

🏠 Weare Giffard Hall

This appealing village claims to be the longest riverside village in England, straggling for almost two miles along the banks of the Torridge. Weare Giffard (pronounced Jiffard) has a charm all its own, suspended in time it seems to belong to the more peaceful days of half a century ago. The villagers have even refused to have full street lighting installed, so avoiding the 'street furniture' that blemishes so many attractive places.

Another attraction in the village is a fine old 15th-century manor house, **Weare Giffard Hall**. Although its outer walls were partially demolished during the Civil War, the splendid gatehouse with its mighty doors and guardian

lions has survived. Inside, the main hall has a magnificent hammer-beam roof, and several of the other rooms are lined with Tudor and Jacobean oak panelling. For centuries, the house was the home of the Fortescue family and in the nearby church there is an interesting 'family tree' with portraits of past Fortescues carved in stone.

WOOLFARDISWORTHY
11 miles SW of Bideford off the A39

🐾 Milky Way Adventure Park

Naturally, you don't pronounce Woolfardisworthy the way it looks. The correct pronunciation is Woolsery. The extraordinary name goes back to Saxon times when the land was owned by Wulfheard who established a worthig, or homestead, here.

A mile or so north of the village, alongside the A39, is a family entertainment complex, the **Milky Way Adventure Park**. The park includes a huge indoor play area (for both children and adults) where you can test your archery and laser target shooting skills, a Pets Corner where children are encouraged to cuddle the animals, a Bird of Prey Centre, a Sheep Dog Training and Breeding Centre, Toddler Town - a safe play area for very young children - a Sports Hall, a miniature railway, and a Time Warp Adventure Zone.

CLOVELLY
12 miles SW of Bideford off the A39

🏛 Kingsley Museum   🏠 Fisherman's Cottage

🏺 Clovelly Pottery

Even if you've never been to Devon, you must have heard of this unbelievably quaint and picturesque village that tumbles down a steep hillside in terraced levels. Almost every whitewashed and flower-strewn cottage is worthy of its own picture postcard and from

Main Street, Clovelly

the story *A Message from the Sea* by Dickens and Wilkie Collins. Charles Kingsley (*The Water Babies; Westward Ho!*) was at school here in the 1820s and the **Kingsley Museum** explores his links with the village. Next door, the **Fisherman's Cottage** provides an insight into what life was like here about 80 years ago. And the award-winning Visitor Centre has an audio-visual show narrating the development of Clovelly from around 2000BC to the present day.

the sheltered little harbour there is an enchanting view of this unique place. One reason Clovelly is so unspoilt is that the village has belonged to the Rous family since 1738 and they have ensured that it has been spared such modern defacements as telegraph poles and 'street furniture'.

The only access to the beach and the beautifully restored 14th century quay is on foot or by donkey, although there is a Land Rover service from the Red Lion Hotel for those who can't face the climb back up the hill. The only other forms of transport are the sledges that are used to deliver weekly supplies. During the summer months there are regular boat trips around the bay, and the *Jessica Hettie* travels daily to Lundy Island with timings that allow passengers to spend some six hours there, watching the seals and abundant wildlife.

The owner of the *Jessica Hettie,* Clive Pearson, is also a potter. In 1992 he opened **The Clovelly Pottery**, which displays an extensive range of items made by Cornish and Devon potters. In the nearby workshop, for a small fee, you can try your hand at throwing a pot.

This captivating village has some strong literary connections. It features as Steepway in

HARTLAND
15 miles SW of Bideford on the B3248

🏛 Church of St Nectan		🏞 Hartland Point	
🏛 Hartland Museum		🏛 Hartland Abbey	

This pleasant village with its narrow streets and small square was once larger and more important than Bideford. Hartland was a royal possession from the time of King Alfred until William the Conqueror and continued to be a busy centre right up to the 19th century. It was at its most prosperous in the 1700s and some fine Georgian buildings survive from that period. But the most striking building is the parish **Church of St Nectan** (see panel on page 142) which stands about 1½ miles west of the village. This is another of Devon's 'must-see' churches. The exterior is impressive enough with its 128 feet high tower, but it is the glorious 15th-century screen inside that makes this church one of the most visited in the county. A masterpiece of the medieval woodcarvers' art, its elegant arches are topped by four exquisitely fretted bands of intricate designs. The arches are delicately painted, reminding one yet again how colourful English churches used to be before the vandalism of the Puritan years.

The Church of St Nectan

Lanepark Lane, Stoke, nr Hartland, Devon EX39 6HF
Tel: 01479 810000

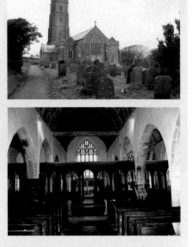

St. Nectan, the patron saint of this church and
parish, was one of many Celtic hermits and
missionaries associated with early Christian sites in
South-West Britain, South Wales and Ireland in the
fifth and sixth centuries.

The church as we have it is in the Perpendicular
style of the fourteenth century, subject to restoration,
particularly the windows, in 1848. Although situated
some 3 kilometres from the village of Hartland, the
centre of the manor, the church is one of the largest
in this part of Devon, Hartland parish being in the top
ten percent of Devon parishes by population till the
17th century.

The only major addition in the 1848 restoration
was an increase in the length of the chancel. The size
is best appreciated from beneath the tower arch, being enhanced by the areas of clear glass,
the exceptional height of the tower arch itself, and the width of the arches over the aisles.
The piers of the arcades (four in the nave and one in the chancel) are of limestone and appear
to be earlier than some other North Devon examples. The tower arch is over 8 metres high;
from an early date and up to 1848 it contained a musicians' gallery.

In the churchyard is the grave of Allen Lane
who, in 1935, revolutionised publishing by his
introduction of Penguin Books, paperback
books which were sold at sixpence (2½p) each.

From the village, follow the signs to
Hartland Abbey. Founded in 1157, the abbey
was closed down in 1539 by Henry VIII who
gave the building and its wide estates to
William Abbott, Sergeant of the Royal wine
cellars. His descendants still live here. The
house was partly rebuilt in the mid 18th
century in the style known as Strawberry Hill
Gothic, and in the 1850s the architect George
Gilbert Scott added a front hall and entrance.
The abbey's owner, Sir George Stucley, had
recently visited the Alhambra Palace in Spain,
which he much admired. He asked Scott to
design something in that style and the result is
the elegant Alhambra Corridor with a blue

vaulted ceiling with white stencilled patterns.
The abbey has a choice collection of pictures,
porcelain and furniture acquired over many
generations and, in the former Servants' Hall,
a unique exhibition of documents dating from
1160. There's also a fascinating Victorian and
Edwardian photographic exhibition, which
includes many early photographs.

A mile further west is Hartland Quay.
Exposed to all the wrath of Atlantic storms,
it seems an inhospitable place for ships, but it
was a busy landing-place from its building in
1566 until the sea finally overwhelmed it in
1893. Several of the old buildings have been
converted into a comfortable hotel; another
is now the **Hartland Museum**, which
records the many wrecks that have littered
this jagged coastline.

About three miles to the north of the Quay,

reached by winding country lanes, is **Hartland Point**. On Ptolemy's map of Britain in Roman times, he names it the Promontory of Hercules, a fitting name for this fearsome stretch of upended rocks rising at right angles to the sea. There are breathtaking sea and coast views and a lighthouse built in 1874.

South Molton

🏛 Town Museum   🏛 Medical Hall

🏛 Market Hall and Assembly Rooms   🏛 Guildhall

🐾 Quince Honey Farm

This pleasant old market town, thankfully now bypassed by the A361 North Devon link road, has been a focus of the local agriculture-based economy since Saxon times, and in common with many such towns throughout Devon was a centre of the wool trade in the late Middle Ages. The town still flourishes as a market town

with a main market day on Thursday and an extra pannier market on Saturday.

Unusually, the town has two Royal Charters, one from Elizabeth I in 1590 and another from Charles II in 1684. They are commemorated each year with an Old English Fayre held in June. The original charters can both be seen in the **Town Museum** along with one of the oldest fire engines in the country. It was bought by the town in 1746 for £46.

In the heart of the old town runs Broad Street, so broad as to be almost a square and distinguished by some handsome Georgian and Victorian civic architecture. Among the noteworthy buildings to be found here are the **Market Hall and Assembly Rooms**, the eccentric **Medical Hall** with its iron balcony and four Ionic columns, and the Palladian-style **Guildhall** of 1743, which overhangs the pavement in a series of arches. A useful Heritage Trail Guide, obtainable from the

📷 stories and anecdotes   🐦 famous people   🎨 art and craft   🎭 entertainment and sport   🚶 walks

THE CORN DOLLY TEASHOP

115a East Street, South Molton, Devon EX36 3DB
Tel: 01769 574249
e-mail: mail@corndollyteashop.co.uk
website: www.corndollyteashop.co.uk

Established in 1997, **The Corn Dolly Teashop** has garnered an impressive list of awards over the years. In 2005 it was the overall winner of the North Devon Food & Drinks Awards, and has received the Tea Guild's Award of Excellence every year from 2004 to 2010.

The Tea Shop is owned and run by Kevin and Jo Venison whose menu offers an extensive choice of home cooked treats ranging from the Corn Dolly Breakfast through various salads, jacket potatoes, 'things on toast' and specialities such as the Farmhouse Tea and the Kings Ransom - the latter being stilton melted onto a freshly toasted Corn Dolly Teacake. There is also a Pate of the Day, home made quiches and through the winter, hearty warming soups. Make sure you leave room for a delicious home made dessert or cake. There are many to chose from, from a scrumptious warm chocolate fudge cake, warm sticky treacle tart and planty of marvellous scones. As one appreciative customer put it "If you like scones with real Devon cream and jam, then this place serves the beat and the largest I have ever had!" The Corn Dolly is open from 9.30am to 5pm, Monday to Saturday; and from 11am to 5pm on Sunday.

Tourist Information Centre, provides an excellent introduction to these notable buildings.

Just to the north of South Molton is **Quince Honey Farm** where the mysterious process of honey-making is explained in a series of displays and demonstrations. This is the world's largest exhibition of living honey bees, their hives all safely behind glass. A viewing gallery gives an overhead view of the process of honey-making and the shop offers a full range of honey and honey products, including delicious Devonshire honey ice cream.

Around South Molton

NORTH MOLTON

3 miles NE of South Molton off the A399

🏛 Church of All Saints

Tucked away in the foothills of Exmoor,

North Molton was once a busy wool and mining town. At intervals from Elizabethan times until the late 1800s, copper and iron were extracted from the hills above the town and transported down the valley of the River Mole and on to the sea at Barnstaple. Evidence of abandoned mine workings are still visible around the town as well as remains of the old Mole Valley tramway.

North Molton's 15th-century parish **Church of All Saints** reflects the small town's former industrial importance. It's a striking building with a high clerestory and a 100 foot pinnacled tower, which seems rather grand for this somewhat remote community. Several notable features have survived. There's a part-medieval wine-glass pulpit complete with sounding board and trumpeting angel, a rood screen, some fine Jacobean panelling, and an extraordinary 17th-century alabaster monument to Sir Amyas Bampfylde depicting the reclining knight with his wife Elizabeth reading a book, and their 12 sons and five daughters kneeling nearby. The figures are delightfully executed, especially the small girl with plump cheeks holding an apple and gazing wide-eyed at her eldest sister.

Also interesting is the church clock, which was purchased in 1564 for the then exorbitant price of £16.14s 4d. However, it proved to be a sound investment since it remained in working order for 370 years before its bells chimed for the last time in 1934.

St Mary's Church, Molland

Just to the west of the church is a fine 16th-century house, Court Barton (private). The iconoclastic biographer and critic Lytton Strachey (1880-1932) stayed here with a reading party in 1908. It seems that the eminent writer greatly enjoyed his stay, reporting enthusiastically on the area's "mild tranquillities", and a way of life that encompassed "a surplusage of beef and Devonshire cream,.....a village shop with bulls'-eyes,.....more cream and then more beef and then somnolence".

MOLLAND
6 miles E of South Molton off the A361

St Mary's Church

Hidden away in a maze of lanes skittering across the foothills of Exmoor, Molland is one of Devon's 'must-visit' villages for anyone interested in wonderfully unspoilt churches. Following the sale of the village in the early 1600s, **St Mary's Church** stood within the estates of the Courtenay family. During and following the Commonwealth years, the Courtenays remained staunch Catholics and showed no interest in restoring or modernising the Protestant parish church. So today you will still find a Georgian screen and tiers of box-pews, whitewashed walls, an elaborate three-decker pulpit crowned by a trumpeting angel and a colourful Royal Arms blazoned with the name of its painter, Rowlands. Despite their Catholic principles, three late 17th and early 18th-century members of the Courtenay family are commemorated by some typically flamboyant monuments of the time. Also within Molland parish lies Great Champson, the farm where in the 18th century the Quartly family introduced and developed their celebrated breed of red North Devon cattle.

WEST ANSTEY
9 miles E of South Molton off the B3227

Two Moors Way

The tiny hamlet of West Anstey lies just a mile or so from the Somerset border. The **Two Moors Way** passes by just a little to the east and the slopes on which the hamlet stands continue to rise up to the wilds of Exmoor. Despite being so small, West Anstey nevertheless has its own church, which boasts a fine Norman font and an arcade from the 1200s, but is mostly 14th century. The area around West Anstey is one of the emptiest parts of Devon – grand open country dotted with just the occasional farm or a tiny cluster of cottages.

BISHOP'S NYMPTON
3 miles SE of South Molton off the A361

🎨 Lady Pollard

Bishop's Nympton, King's Nympton, George Nympton, as well as several Nymets, all take the Nympton or Nymet element of their names from the River Yeo, which in Saxon and earlier times was known as the Nymet, meaning river at a holy place. Bishop's Nympton has a long sloping main street, lined with thatched cottages, and a 15th-century church whose lofty, well-proportioned tower is considered one of the most beautiful in Devon. For many years the church had a stained glass window erected in Tudor times at the expense of **Lady Pollard**, wife of Sir Lewis, an eminent judge and leading resident of the village. Sir Lewis told the author of *The Worthies of Devon*, John Prince, that he was away on business in London at the time and the details of the window's design were entrusted to his wife. At the time Sir Lewis left for town, he and his wife already had 21 children, 11 sons and 10 daughters. "But his lady caused one more child than she then had to be set there: presuming that, usually conceiving at her husband's coming home, she should have another. Which, inserted in expectation, came to pass in reality". The oddest thing about the story is that Lady Pollard not only correctly predicted the forthcoming child, but also its sex.

CHULMLEIGH
8 miles S of South Molton off the A377

🌿 Eggesford Forest

With its narrow cobbled lanes,

courtyards and quiet squares, Chulmleigh is a delight to explore. Sprawled across the hills above the leafy valley of the Little Dart river, it is one of several attractive small towns in mid Devon which prospered from the wool trade in the Middle Ages and then declined into sleepy, unspoilt communities. Chulmleigh's prosperity lasted longer than most since it was on the old wagon route to Barnstaple that in 1830 one of the newfangled turnpike roads was constructed along the Taw valley, siphoning off most of its trade. A quarter of a century later the Exeter to Barnstaple railway was built along the same route, the final straw for Chulmleigh as a trade centre. But this charming small town has been left with many original thatched cob cottages that cluster around a fine 15th-century church noted for its lofty pinnacled tower and, inside, a wondrously carved rood screen that extends 50 feet across the nave and aisles.

To the south of Chulmleigh is **Eggesford Forest** where, in 1919, the newly-formed Forestry Commission planted its first tree. This event is commemorated by a stone unveiled by the Queen in 1956. The stone also marks the planting of more than one million acres of trees by the Commission. There are two walks

Eggesford Forest, nr Chulmleigh

through the forest, each about one mile long, which provide visitors with the opportunity of seeing the red deer that live here.

LAPFORD
12 miles S of South Molton on the A377

Remarkably, this small community still has its own railway station. Passenger numbers have been much augmented since British Rail's rather prosaic Exeter to Barnstaple route was re-christened as the Tarka Line. The original name may have been lacklustre but the 39-mile journey itself has always been delightful as it winds slowly along the gentle river valleys of the Yeo and the Taw.

Lapford stands high above the River Yeo, its hilltop church a famous local landmark for generations: "when yew sees Lapford church yew knaws where yew'm be". It's well worth a visit since the 15th-century rood screen inside is regarded as one of the most exquisitely fashioned in the country. There are five bands of the most delicate carving at the top and above them rise modern figures of the Holy Family (Jesus, Mary and Joseph), surmounted by the original ornamental ceiling with its carved angels gazing down from the nave roof.

WINKLEIGH
12 miles SW of South Molton on the A3124

This attractive village with its open views across to Dartmoor is believed to have been a beacon station in prehistoric times. When the Normans arrived they built two small castles, one at each end of the village. They were probably intended as bases for hunting in the nearby park – the only Devon park to be mentioned in the Domesday Book. For centuries Winkleigh was an important local trading centre with its own market, fair and borough court. Today, it's a peaceful little place with thatched cottages nestling up to the mainly 15th century church which has a richly carved and painted waggon roof where 70 golden-winged angels stand guard over the nave.

DOLTON
12 miles SW of South Molton on the B3217

Dolton clusters around its parish church of St Edmund's which boasts a real treasure - a Saxon font more than 1000 years old. Its intricate carvings depict a fantastic menagerie of winged dragons and writhing serpents, with yet more dragons emerging from the upturned face of a man. Their relevance to the Christian message may be a little obscure but there's no denying their powerful impact.

MEETH
14 miles SW of South Molton on the A386

🚶 Tarka Walkway

A mile or so north of Hatherleigh, the A386 crosses the River Torridge and a couple of miles further is the pleasant little village of Meeth whose Old English name means the meeting of the streams. Indeed, a small brook runs down the hillside into the Torridge. From the early 1700s, Meeth and the surrounding area was noted for its 'pipe' and 'ball clay' products, generically known as pottery clay. There are still extensive clay works to the northwest of the village.

But for cyclists and walkers Meeth is much better known as the southern terminus of the **Tarka Walkway**, which runs northwards through Bideford and Barnstaple.

NORTH TAWTON
16 miles SW of South Molton off the A3072

🏛 Bathe Pool

Wellknown nowadays to travellers along the

THE CHEESE COMPANY AT TAW VALLEY CREAMERY

North Tawton, Devon EX20 2DA
Tel: 01837 883400 Fax: 01837 82311
e-mail: jackie.eaton@cheese.co.uk
website: www.tawvalleycheese.co.uk

Since 1974 the **Taw Valley Creamery** has been producing award-winning cheeses in the heart of the Devon countryside, surrounded by lush green grass and rolling hills. The Creamery is part of the Milk Link group of companies owned by some 1600 British dairy farmers, most of them operating in the West Country. The milk for the Creamery is collected from more than 700 farms, many of them within a 30-mile radius, and the cheesemakers put a wealth of experience and expertise to use in producing the wonderful range of Cheddars, the Red Leicester and the Double Gloucester that are the mainstay of the business. They make other branded cheeses, and the shop sells a selection of prime cheeses from other producers.

The Creamery serves the public and also sells its produce to a large number of shops, delis, hotels, restaurants and pubs throughout Devon. Visitors come from all over the world to discover the scenic delights of this glorious part of the country, but no one should pass through without stopping off at the Taw Valley Creamery to sample and buy some cheese. The shop, which also sells crackers, chutneys and other complementary goods, as well as hampers and gift packs, is located just off the A3072 outside the village of North Tawton, between Crediton and Okehampton. Shop hours are 9 to 5 Monday to Friday, 9 to 12 Saturday.

Tarka Trail, the small market town of North Tawton was once an important borough governed by a portreeve, an official who was elected each year until the end of the 19th century. This scattered rural community prospered in medieval times but the decline of the local textile industry in the late 1700s dealt a blow from which it never really recovered - the population today is still less than it was in 1750. The little town also suffered badly from the ravages of a series of fires that destroyed most of the older and more interesting buildings. However, a few survivors can still be found, most notably Broad Hall (private), which dates back to the 15th century.

In a field close to the town is **Bathe Pool**, a grassy hollow that is said to fill with water at times of national crises or when a prominent person is about to die. The pool reportedly filled at the time of the death of Nelson, the Duke of Wellington and Edward VII, and also just before the outbreak of World War One.

HATHERLEIGH
17 miles SW of South Molton on the A386

- 🏺 Hatherleigh Pottery
- 🏛 Church of St John the Baptist
- 🌿 Abbeyford Woods 🏺 Hatherleigh Arts Festival

This medieval market town, which has held a market every Tuesday since 1693, has been popular for many years as a holiday base for fishermen trying their luck on the nearby River Torridge and its tributary, which runs alongside the small town.

A good starting point for an exploration of this attractive town with its cob and thatch cottages is the Tarka Country Information Point at **Hatherleigh Pottery** (see panel on

HATHERLEIGH POTTERY

20 Market Street, Hatherleigh, Devon EX20 3JP
Tel: 01837 810624
e-mail: hatherleighpots@aol.com
website: www.hatherleighpottery.co.uk

Located in a delightful and secluded cobbled courtyard off Market Street, **Hatherleigh Pottery** is owned and run by Jane Payne who has been a keen potter for more than 40 years. After retiring from teaching, she took a four-year course in ceramics and subsequently bought the pottery. Jane specialises in hand-thrown, practical domestic stoneware – jugs, mugs, bowls, dishes and the like. Much of her work is sgraffito decorated and her use of a wide range of glazes brings colour and variety to her wares. All Jane's pottery is trade-marked with a small fish imprinted near the base.

The light and airy showrooms at the Pottery also feature work by other craftspeople such as Michael Taylor, a local potter who shows mugs, vases and casseroles in a style that makes an interesting contrast with Jane's work. Also on display are Jane Ritchie's ranges of shoulder bags and handbags, all delightfully designed and beautifully made in rich, colourful textiles; and Gill Salway's original prints using a variety of techniques. The Pottery is open from Easter to New Year, Monday to Saturday, from 10am-5pm.

SALAR GALLERY

20 Bridge Street, Hatherleigh, nr Okehampton,
Devon EX20 3HY Tel: 01837 810940
e-mail: salar@hatherleigh.net website: www.salargallery.co.uk

The Salar Gallery opened in the centre of this market town in 1991 to provide an exhibition space for local artists and craftspeople. It displays and sells original work, mainly by Devon artists, much of it a celebration of the West Country – landscape, animals and rural subjects through the eyes of up to 50 artists and craftsmen. The works include local scenes by Eileen Gold; landscapes by Pam Cox, Richard Meyer and Sarah Woolfenden; seascapes by Mike Moss, animal paintings by Vivien Walters and Shan Miller and sculptures by Jo Seccombe, Joanna Martins and Paul Jenkins. Also on display are photographs by Sarah Gallifent and Jen Bryant, pottery by Maryjane Carruthers, glass by Inka Gabriel and Margaret Johnson and silk scarves by Isabella Whitworth. The gallery also has prints, including Dartmoor by Widgery and flowers by Anne Cotterill, plus a wide selection of cards, books, jewellery, church candles and so on. There are regularly changing exhibitions throughout the year.

The gallery, with its elegant Victorian interior, is on level ground, not far from the town car park. It is open from 10am to 1pm and 2pm to 5pm Tuesdays, Thursdays, Fridays and Saturdays and bank holidays, 10am - 1pm.

📖 stories and anecdotes 🐿 famous people 🎨 art and craft 🎭 entertainment and sport 🚶 walks

page 149) where there are exhibits detailing the life and countryside in and around this 1000-year-old town. You can also pick up leaflets to guide you around Hatherleigh's narrow streets. The Pottery itself has showrooms displaying colourful hand-thrown ceramics, textile items, original prints and greetings cards.

Hatherleigh was owned by Tavistock Abbey from the late AD900s until the Dissolution of the Monasteries in the 1540s, and the picturesquely thatched George Hotel is believed to have been built around 1450 as the abbot's court house. The London Inn also dates from around that time and the Old Church House is thought to be even older.

The town would have possessed an even finer stock of early buildings were it not for a devastating fire in 1840 that destroyed much of the old centre. Fortunately, the 15th-century **Church of St John the Baptist** escaped the flames. Set high above the Lew valley, the church's red sandstone walls and sturdy tower still provide a striking focus for this pleasant rural community. Although the church survived the great fire of 1840, a century-and-a-half later hurricane force winds, generated during the storms of January 1990, swashed against its spindly tower and tossed it through the roof of the nave. Thankfully, nobody was in the church at the time.

In mid-July, the **Hatherleigh Arts Festival** takes place, consisting of four days of contemporary arts, including theatre, concerts, art exhibitions, street theatre and workshops. All year round art is visible in the various sculptures scattered around the town, notably the larger than life Sheep sculpture in the town's car park.

For a superb view of the surrounding countryside, make your way to the Monument erected in memory of Colonel William Morris, a hero of the Charge of the Light Brigade.

Until 1966, the Okehampton to Bude

BRICKYARD FARM SHOP

Brickyard Farm, Holsworthy Road, Hatherleigh, Okehampton, Devon EX20 3LE
Tel: 01837 810204

This award-winning farm shop has been in business for over 40 years and is well worth the mile drive out of Hatherleigh along the Holsworthy Road. Look for the white building with the red awnings, and there's ample free parking when you get there. Just watch out for the peacocks and geese that roam around!

The shop has won a Daily Express Readers Award, numerous Gold Standard Product Awards, and has been both the National Lamb Barbecue Product Champion and the South-West Sausage Champion. At any one time there are usually at least a dozen different award-winning sausage varieties on offer, and half a dozen varieties of burger. All the shop's beef and lamb is sourced from local farms and markets, and slaughtered locally. The beef is then hung for up to three weeks to really bring out the flavour and give a supreme eating quality.

The **Brickyard Farm Shop** has one of the best selections of beef and lamb in the area, and also sells excellent metal-craft sculptures of birds.

🏚 historic building 🏛 museum and heritage 🏛 historic site 🐾 scenic attraction 🌿 flora and fauna

railway ran through Hatherleigh. In that year it was closed as part of the notorious Beeching Cuts. The last train on the Hatherleigh to Bude line, a prized local amenity, steamed its way into Cornwall on 16 May 1966, then to a siding, and then to rust. Long stretches of the old track bed of the railway now provide some attractive walking.

There's more good walking at **Abbeyford Woods**, about a mile to the east of the village, with a particularly lovely stretch running alongside the River Okement.

Holsworthy

⚑ St Peter's Fair   🚶 West Country Way

Wednesday is a good day to visit Holsworthy. That's when this little town, just four miles from the Cornish border, holds its weekly market. This is very much the traditional kind of street market, serving a large area of the surrounding countryside and with locally-produced fresh cream, butter, cheese and vegetables all on sale. The town gets even livelier in early July when it gives itself over to the amusements of the three-day-long **St Peter's Fair**. The Fair opens with the curious old custom of the Pretty Maid Ceremony. Back in 1841, a Holsworthy merchant bequeathed a legacy to provide a small payment each year to a local spinster, under the age of 30 and noted for her good looks, demure manner and regular attendance at church. Rather surprisingly, in view of the last two requirements, the bequest still finds a suitable recipient each year.

Holsworthy's most striking architectural features are the two Victorian viaducts that once carried the railway line to Bude. The viaducts stride high above the southern edge of the town and, since they now form part of a footpath along the old track, it's possible to walk across them for some stunning views of the area.

An interesting feature in the parish church is an organ built in 1668 by Renatus Hunt for All Saints Church, Chelsea. In 1723, it was declared worn out but was nevertheless purchased by a Bideford church. There it gave good service for some 140 years before it was written off once again. Removed to Holsworthy, it has been here ever since.

The area around Holsworthy is particularly popular with cyclists. There are three clearly-

Holsworthy Museum

Manor Offices, Holsworthy, Devon EX22 6DJ
Tel: 01409 259337
e-mail: holsworthy@devonmuseums.net
website: www.devonmuseums.net/holsworthy

Housed in an 18th century parsonage, this small museum gives you an insight into Holsworthy's heritage and traditions. Various themed displays cover the town, local railway, agriculture, trades, medical and the World Wars. Researchers into family and local history may view, by prior arrangement, a selection of local parish registers on microfiche, IGI fiche and Census data as well as information held in the Local History unit. The museum is run entirely by volunteers and is dependent on donations, a small entrance fee and support from local Councils. Open February to December.

designated routes starting and finishing in the town, and it also lies on the **West Country Way**, a 250-mile cycle route from Padstow to Bristol and Bath which, opened in the spring of 1997.

Around Holsworthy

SHEBBEAR
7 miles NE of Holsworthy off the A388

🏛 Devil's Stone

This attractive village is set around a spacious square laid out in the Saxon manner with a church at one end and a hostelry at the other. Lying in a hollow just outside St Michael's churchyard is a huge lump of rock, weighing about a ton, which is known as the **Devil's Stone**. According to local legend, the boulder was placed here by Old Nick who challenged the villagers to move it, threatening that disaster would strike if they could not. Every year since then, on 5 November (a date established long before the Gunpowder Plot of 1605), a curious ceremony has taken place. After sounding a peal of bells, the bell ringers come out of the church and set about the stone with sticks and crowbars. Once they have successfully turned the stone over, they return in triumph to the bell tower to sound a second peal. The story is recounted in greater detail in the village hostelry, The Devil's Stone Inn.

SHEEPWASH
9 miles E of Holsworthy off the A3072 or A386

🏛 Sheepwash Bridge

Sheepwash is yet another Devon community to have been devastated by fire. The conflagration here occurred in 1742 and the destruction was so great that for more than

---

THE BEAD CELLAR

Broad Street, Black Torrington, Devon EX21 5PT
Tel: 01409 231442
e-mail: kate@thebeadcellar.co.uk
website: www.thebeadcellar.co.uk

Nestled in the rolling Devonshire countryside, between Dartmoor and the North Devon coast, **The Bead Cellar** is a real gem! Selling a beautiful variety of imported beads, findings and jewellery making supplies, including Toho Japanese seed beads, bugles and cubes, new and vintage Swarovski, Czech glass beads and pearls, semi-precious gemstones, and ethnic & fair-trade wooden, paper, seed and shell beads. With such a shimmering array of items everyone will feel inspired to create their own gorgeous jewellery, gifts, interior design accessories, and embellishments.

To take real advantage of everything The Bead Cellar has to offer, it is essential you experience one of their fabulous classes and workshops. Based in the light and spacious purpose built workshop, which seats around 12 people, these illuminating classes cover everything from the very basics of beadwork for beginners, to unique and complex techniques which will help advanced beaders hone their craft. The classes are held throughout the year, by a team of accomplished beaders, and special masterclasses with visiting guest crafters an occasional treat. Private parties, of crafters at all ages and abilities, catered for. A visit to the wonderful website will keep you up to date on the latest events, and great new items for sale, or you could give them a phone during shop hours. The shop is open Tuesday to Saturday 10am-5pm.

🏛 historic building 🏛 museum and heritage 🏛 historic site ♧ scenic attraction 🌿 flora and fauna

Sheepwash Bridge

10 years the village was completely deserted. Slowly, the villagers returned, built new houses in stone, and today if you want the essence of Devon distilled into one location, then the village square at Sheepwash is just about perfect. Along one side stands the famous Half Moon Inn, renowned amongst fishermen; on another, the old church tower rises above pink-washed thatched cottages; while in the centre, cherry trees shelter the ancient village pump.

Just south of the village, a minor road crosses the River Torridge and there's a rather heartening story about the bridge here, **Sheepwash Bridge**. Until well into the 1600s, the only way of crossing the river was by means of stepping stones. One day, when the river was in full spate, a young man attempting to return to the village was swept away and drowned. His father, John Tusbury, was grief-stricken but responded to the tragedy by providing money to build a bridge. He also donated sufficient funds for it to be maintained by establishing the Bridgeland Trust and stipulating that any surplus income should be used to help in the upkeep of the church and chapel. The Trust is still in operation and nowadays also funds outings for village children and pensioners.

NORTHLEW

10 miles SE of Holsworthy off the A3072 or A3079

As at Sheepwash, the thatched cottages and houses stand around a large central square, which is dominated by a charming 15th century church standing on the hilltop above the River Lew. The church is noted for its Norman remains and the exceptional (mainly Tudor) woodwork in the roof, bench ends and screen. Also of interest is one of the stained glass windows, which features four saints. St Thomas, to whom the church is dedicated, is shown holding a model of the church; St Augustine, the first Archbishop of Canterbury, holds the priory gateway; while St Joseph carries the Holy Grail and the staff that grew into the famous Glastonbury thorn tree. The fourth figure is simply clad in a brown habit and carries a bishop's crozier and a spade. This is St Brannock who is credited with being the first man to cultivate the wild lands of this area by clearing woodland and ploughing and could therefore be regarded as the patron saint of farmers.

CLAWTON

3 miles S of Holsworthy, on the A388

A good indication of the mildness of the Devon climate is the number of vineyards that have been established over the past 30 years or so. **Clawford Vineyard** in the valley of the River Claw is a good example. Set in more than 78 acres of vines and orchards, the vineyard's owners welcome visitors to sample their home-grown wines and ciders, and in the autumn to watch that year's vintage being produced.

⟦ stories and anecdotes ⟡ famous people ⚲ art and craft ✐ entertainment and sport ⟰ walks

In and Around Dartmoor

Okehampton

🏠 Okehampton Castle   🏛 Museum of Dartmoor Life

🚂 Dartmoor Railway

The old travel-writer's cliché of a 'county of contrasts' can't be avoided when describing the landscape around Okehampton. To the north and west, the puckered green hills of North Devon roll away to the coast; to the south, lie the wildest stretches of Dartmoor with the great peaks of High Willhays and Yes Tor rising to more than 2000 feet. At this height they are, officially, mountains, but quite puny compared with their original altitude: geologists believe that at one time the surface of Dartmoor stood at 15,000 feet above sea level. Countless centuries of erosion have reduced it to a plateau of whale-backed granite ridges with an average height of around 1200 feet. After so many millions of years of erosion, the moor has become strewn with fragments of surface granite, or moorstone. It was because of this ready-to-use stone that Dartmoor became one of the most populous areas of early Britain, its inhabitants using the easily quarried granite to create their stone rows, circles, and burial chambers. Stone was also used to build their distinctive hut-circles of which there are more than 1500 scattered across the moor.

From Celtic times Okehampton has occupied an important position on the main route to Cornwall. Romantically sited atop a wooded hill and dominating the surrounding valley of the River Okement are the remains of **Okehampton Castle** (English Heritage). This is the largest medieval castle in Devon

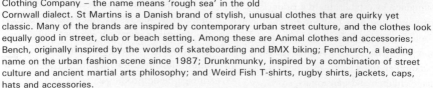

KUDOS CLOTHING

18 Red Lion Yard, Okehampton, Devon EX20 1AW
Tel: 01837 55102
e-mail: trisha.kudos@xln.co.uk

Okehampton is an interesting old market town, with two rivers, a heritage railway, plenty of eating places and the largest medieval castle in Devon. It's also a good place to shop, and many of the most interesting outlets are in red Lion Yard in the heart of town. **Kudos Clothing**, established by Trisha Shaw in 2004, is *the* place to go for distinctive, contemporary casual wear for men, women and children, and is the sole stockist in the region for many brands.

Amari, founded in 2007 by Amelia and Hari, produces creative, colourful stylish designer clothes featuring simple, flattering shapes and unique fresh prints – made in Katmandu, Nepal. Hager-Var specialises in edgy, abstract designs by some of Cornwall's most creative artists, sculptors and designers, made by the Cornish Surf Clothing Company – the name means 'rough sea' in the old Cornish dialect. St Martins is a Danish brand of stylish, unusual clothes that are quirky yet classic. Many of the brands are inspired by contemporary urban street culture, and the clothes look equally good in street, club or beach setting. Among these are Animal clothes and accessories; Bench, originally inspired by the worlds of skateboarding and BMX biking; Fenchurch, a leading name on the urban fashion scene since 1987; Drunknmunky, inspired by a combination of street culture and ancient martial arts philosophy; and Weird Fish T-shirts, rugby shirts, jackets, caps, hats and accessories.

🏠 historic building 🏛 museum and heritage 🏛 historic site 🍃 scenic attraction 🌿 flora and fauna

IN HOUSE

15 St James Street, Okehampton, Devon EX20 1DJ
Tel: 01837 53421
e-mail: tracie@inhouse-bytracie.co.uk

Okehampton has from ancient times occupied an important position on the main road to Cornwall, and visitors come here to look at the interesting old buildings, explore the ruins of the castle, indulge in a spot of nostalgia at the 1950s-style railway station, or discover the town's past in the museum. Others join the locals for a spot of shopping, and one of the best of the many excellent shops is **In House**, a gift boutique and interiors shop in a pleasant shopping street in the heart of town. Aromatic scents from the soaps and oils and gentle background music set a relaxed tone in Tracie Martin's shop, which started life as a butcher's shop owned by her husband's grandfather.

Behind the large display window and jazzy blind the shop is filled with a wide range of lovely things to enhance the home, something to wear, a spoiling treat or a special present for any occasion. Among the well-known brands usually in stock are Cath Kidston – homeware, clothing and accessories; East of India gifts and cards; Garden Trading Ltd accessories for home and garden; high-quality fair-trade Nomad Clothing; necklaces, bracelets, rings, earrings and brooches by One Button Jewellery; Gabriella Miller Pottery; home fragrances, pot pourri, candles and bath products from Green Leaf Fragrance; and a wide range of cards (personalised available) and gift wrap.

and the ruins are still mightily impressive even though the castle was dismantled on the orders of Henry VIII after its owner, the Earl of Devon, was convicted of treason.

A good place to start a tour of the town is the **Museum of Dartmoor Life**, housed in a former mill with a restored water wheel outside. Here, in the three galleries, the story of life on Dartmoor, down the ages, is told and, in particular, the museum displays illustrate how the moorland has shaped the lives of its inhabitants and vice versa. In the surrounding courtyard, you will also find a tearoom and the tourist information centre with books and gifts.

Amongst the town's many interesting buildings are the 15th-century Chapel of Ease, and the Town Hall, a striking three-storey building erected in 1685 as a private house and

Okehampton Railway Station

converted to its current use in the 1820s. And don't miss the wonderful Victorian arcade within the shopping centre, which is reminiscent of London's Burlington Arcade.

Okehampton is also the hub of the **Dartmoor Railway**, part of the former Southern Railway main line from London to Plymouth and Cornwall. This was once the

ANGEL

29 Fore Street, Okehampton,
Devon EX20 1HB
Tel: 01837 659300
e-mail: angelokehampton@aol.com
website: www.angelokehampton.com

The **ANGEL** ladies fashion boutique on Okehampton's main street is now celebrating its 10th year in business, during which time it has kept abreast of the changes in fashion and continued to seek out the top name brands to stock. The aim is to provide clothes that combine quality, style and individuality, in a range of sizes from 8-18, for a range of budgets too, and covering everything from the casual to clothes for a formal occasional.

At ANGEL there are names you don't see in every boutique, such as Ispirato, Noli, Nancy Mac, Jocavi, Masai, Sandwich, Pomodoro and Peppercorn. There is naturally a good range of accessories to match, too, including shoes from Menbur and Kazuri and Martina Wester Jewellery, Nica and Stone bags, and a good collection of hats and fascinators as well.

MASON JUDGE

33 Fore Street, Oakhampton, Devon EX20 1HB
Tel: 01837 658530
e-mail: enquiries@mason-judge.co.uk
website: www.mason-judge.co.uk

Always on the lookout for something a little bit special, the owner of **Mason Judge**, Meryl has a passion for quality unusual items - which is visible in the amazing array of pieces on show in her shop. This fabulous independent business is stocked full of gifts, homeware, toys, jewellery, the finest handbags and accessories, toiletries, and gadgets, searched out by Meryl and the Mason Judge team from local suppliers, genuine British traders, and ethically traded items from designers around the world, to bring their customers the best money can buy. Names synonymous with quality, such as Old Bag Co., Shruti Designs, Maxwell & Williams, The Puppet Co., and Heyland & Whittle, line the walls; mixed in with some fabulous pieces with names you won't know, but which will blow you away. A recent Limited Edition collection of handpainted mugs and plates from local artist Guy Cracknell, is just an example of the type of treasures you will find within Mason Judges' walls.

The shop offers a bespoke gift wrapping service, using their infinite collection of cool and classic wrapping papers and decorations, which is sure to add that finishing touch to the perfect gift.

route of the famous Atlantic Coast Express and the Devon Belle Pullman. Today, the company runs trains from Crediton and climbs into the National Park, terminating at Meldon Viaduct. Okehampton Station has been restored to its 1950s appearance, complete with buffet and licensed bar. Sampford Courtenay Station, 3½ miles to the east was re-opened in 2004 and provides access to pleasant walking routes, including the Devon Heartlands Way footpath. To the west, Meldon Quarry Station is the highest station in southern England. It has two visitor centres, a buffet with a licensed bar, a picnic area and a spectacular verandah giving wonderful views of Dartmoor's highest tors and the Meldon Reservoir dam.

Around Okehampton

SAMPFORD COURTENAY
5 miles NE of Okehampton

Prayer Book Revolt

A charming and unspoilt village with a fine medieval church, Sampford Courtenay is notable for its picturesque assortment of cottages, many of them thatched and built of cob. This local building material is created by mixing well-sieved mud with straw. This is then built up in sections. It was the local tradition to limewash the outside of the cottages at Whitsuntide, a process that helps to preserve the cob. This simple material is surprisingly durable and will

last indefinitely provided it has a 'good hat', that is, if the thatched roof is well looked after. Another unusual feature of the village is that every road out of it is marked by a medieval stone cross.

This peaceful and pretty village was the unlikely setting for the start of the **Prayer Book Revolt** of 1549. It was originally initiated as a protest against Edward VI's introduction of an English prayer book, but when the undisciplined countrymen marched on Exeter, it degenerated into a frenzy of looting and violence. Confronted by an army led by Lord Russell, the rioters were soon overwhelmed and several unfortunate ringleaders executed.

STICKLEPATH
2 miles E of Okehampton off the A30

Finch Foundry

The little village of Sticklepath boasts one of the most interesting exhibits of industrial archaeology in Devon. From 1814 to 1960, **Finch Foundry** (National Trust) was renowned for producing the finest sharp-edged

Finch Foundry

stories and anecdotes   famous people   art and craft   entertainment and sport   walks

tools in the West Country. The three massive waterwheels are regularly set working again driving the ancient machinery. The pounding rhythms of the steam hammer and rushing water vividly evoke that age of noisy toil.

SOUTH ZEAL
4 miles E of Okehampton off the A30

South Zeal is yet another of the many Devon villages that have good reason to be grateful for the major road-building undertakings of the 1970s. The village sits astride what used to be the main road from Exeter to Launceston and the Cornwall coast, a road, which as late as 1975, was still laughably designated on maps of the time as a 'Trunk (major) Road'. The 'Trunk Road' was actually little more than a country lane, but it was also the only route available for many thousands of holiday-makers making their way to the Cornish resorts. Today, the village is bypassed by the A30 dual carriageway.

Isolated in the middle of the broad main street stand a simple medieval market cross and St Mary's chapel, rebuilt in 1713. To the south of the village rises the great granite hump of Dartmoor. On its flanks, for the few years between 1901-1909, the villagers of South Zeal found sorely needed employment in a short-lived copper mine.

WHIDDON DOWN
7 miles E of Okehampton off the A30

🏛 Spinsters' Rock

About a mile south of the village stands the **Spinsters' Rock** , the best surviving chambered tomb in the whole of Devon. According to legend, three spinsters erected the dolmen one morning before breakfast, an impressive feat since the capstone, supported by just three uprights seven feet high, weighs 16 tons.

BELSTONE
2 miles SE of Okehampton off the A30

🏛 Nine Stones

Surrounded by the magnificent scenery of the Dartmoor National Park, Belstone is a picturesque village with a triangular village green, complete with stocks and a stone commemorating the coronation of George V, and a church dating back to the 13th century.

A path from Belstone village leads up to the ancient standing stone circle known as the **Nine Stones**, although there are actually well over a dozen of them. Local folklore asserts that these stones under Belstone Tor were formed when a group of maidens was discovered dancing on the Sabbath and turned to stone. The problem with this story is that the stone circle was in place long before the arrival of Christianity in England. It is also claimed that the mysterious stones change position when the clock strikes noon. What is certain is that the view across mid Devon from this site is quite breathtaking.

Another path from Belstone leads south to a spot on the northern edge of Dartmoor where the ashes of the Poet Laureate Ted Hughes were scattered and where a granite stone was placed to his memory.

For lovers of solitude, this is memorable country, unforgettably evoked by Sir Arthur Conan Doyle in *The Hound of the Baskervilles*. Recalling the villain's fate in that book, walkers should beware of the notorious "feather beds" – deep bogs signalled by a quaking cover of brilliant green moss.

DREWSTEIGNTON
10 miles SE of Okehampton off the A30

🏛 Castle Drogo

This appealing village stands on a ridge overlooking the valley of the River Teign and

🏛 historic building 🏛 museum and heritage 🏛 historic site 🌳 scenic attraction 🌿 flora and fauna

Castle Drogo

Drewsteignton, near Exeter EX6 6PB
Tel: 01647 433306
e-mail: castledrogo@nationaltrust.org.uk
website: www.nationaltrust.org.uk/castledrogo

Castle Drogo (National Trust) is spectacularly sited on a rocky outcrop with commanding views out over Dartmoor and the Teign gorge. It was built for Sir Julius Drewe, a self made millionaire, on land once owned by his Norman ancestor, Drogo de Teigne. Surrounding this 20th century dream country home, lies an equally impressive garden – the highest in the Trust.

The square shape of the castle and the large rotund croquet lawn exemplifies the simple ethos of the architect, Lutyens, of "circles and squares". From spring bulbs in the formal garden, the rhododendron garden, the stunning herbaceous borders, the rose garden and the winter garden there is colour and interest here all year round.

the celebrated beauty spot near the 400-year-old Fingle Bridge. Thatched cottages and a medieval church stand grouped around a square, very picturesque and much photographed. To the south of the village, Prestonbury Castle and Cranbrook Castle are not castles at all but Iron Age hilltop fortresses. **Castle Drogo** (National Trust - see panel above) on the other hand, looks every inch the medieval castle but in fact was constructed between 1911 and 1930 – the last castle to be built in England. Occupying a spectacular site on a rocky outcrop 900 feet above sea level, with commanding views over Dartmoor, it was built to a design by Lutyens for the self-made millionaire Sir Julius Drewe on land once owned by his Norman ancestor, Drogo de Teigne. Lutyens preliminary sketches envisaged a house of heroic size, but practicalities and the intervention of World War One caused the dimensions to be reduced

by about two-thirds. Nevertheless, the granite castle with walls 6 feet thick is one of Lutyens' most remarkable works. It combines the grandeur of a medieval castle with the comforts of the 20th century. Surrounding Sir Julius's dream home is an impressive garden that displays colour and interest all year round. There's also a croquet lawn for which you can rent mallets and balls.

CHAGFORD
10 miles SE of Okehampton off the A382

🎭 Mary Whiddon   🏠 Market House

An ancient settlement and Stannary town, Chagford lies in a beautiful setting between the pleasant wooded valley of the North Teign river and the stark grandeur of the high moor. In the centre of the town stands the former **Market House**, a charming 'pepperpot' building erected in 1862. Around the square are some old-style family shops providing interesting shopping, and scattered around the town are distinctive old thatched granite buildings, many dating from the 1500s.

St Michael's Church, mostly 15th century, has an elaborate monument to Sir John Wyddon who died in 1575. But the church is better known because of the tragic death of one of his descendants here in October 1641. **Mary Whiddon** was shot by a jilted lover as she was leaving the church after being married, an incident that is said to have inspired RD Blackmore's *Lorna Doone*. Her tombstone bears the inscription, "Behold a Matron yet a Maid". Her ghost is thought to haunt Whiddon Park Guest House - a young woman dressed in black appeared there on the morning of a wedding reception due to take place later that day.

The famous Dartmoor guide, James Perrot, lived in Chagford between 1854 and 1895, and is buried in St Michael's churchyard. It was he who noted that some of the farms around Chagford had no wheeled vehicles as late as 1830. On the other hand, Perrot lived to see the town install electric street lighting in 1891 making Chagford one of the first communities west of London to possess this amenity.

It was Perrot also who began the curious practice of letterbox stamp collecting. He installed the first letterbox at Carnmere Pool near the heart of the moor so his Victorian clients could send postcards home, stamped to prove they had been there. Today, there are hundreds of such letterboxes scattered all over Dartmoor.

To the west of Chagford, an exceptionally pleasant lane leads upstream from Chagford Bridge through the wooded valley of the North Teign river. (For one-and-a-half miles of its length, this lane is joined by the Two Moors

SHAMANKA

1 Mill Street, Chagford, Devon TQ13 8AW
Tel: 01647 433777
e-mail: cate@shamankatherapy.co.uk
website: www.shamankatherapy.co.uk

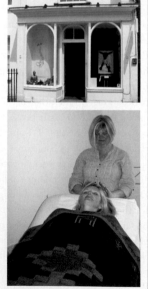

Occupying a Grade II listed building just off the main square in the beautiful Stannary town of Chagford, **Shamanka** is a unique centre where people come to relax, shop and receive a variety of therapies designed to promote improved levels of wellness. Shamanka (the name means "medicine woman") was established in the spring of 2010 by Cate Haynes following a twenty-five year career in the National Health Service as a Registered Nurse.

As you enter Shamanka you will instantly become aware of the relaxed atmosphere. Your senses automatically open, facilitated by the fragrant aroma of natural incense, oils and the gentle sounds of soothing music in the background. The treatments available include Bowen therapy, Reiki, herbal medicine and hypnotherapy, Thai yoga massage, reflexology, aromatherapy massage seated acupressure. All the therapists are fully qualified and insured.

The centre also has a gallery of artworks by local artists and people who simply enjoy the process of creating - which is therapy itself. In the gift shop you'll find an wide range of books, CDs, crystals and craftworks.

Way, the long-distance footpath that runs all the way from Ivybridge on the southern edge of Dartmoor to the Bristol Channel coast.) A rock beside the river known as the Holed Stone has a large round cavity. If you climb through this, local people assure you, a host of afflictions from rheumatism to infertility will be cured.

The land to the south of Chagford rises abruptly towards Kestor Rock and Shovel Down, the sites of impressive Bronze Age settlements and, a little further on, the imposing Long Stone stands at the point where the parishes of Gidleigh and Chagford end and Duchy of Cornwall land begins.

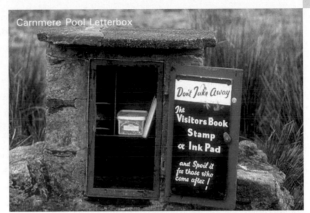

Carnmere Pool Letterbox

LYDFORD

8 miles SW of Okehampton off the A386

Lydford Castle   Lydford Gorge

In Saxon times, there were just four royal boroughs in Devon: Exeter, Barnstaple, Totnes and, astonishingly, Lydford, which is now a pleasant small town still occupying the same strategic position on the River Lyd that made it so important in those days. In the 11th century, the Normans built a fortification here, which was superseded 100 years later by the present **Lydford Castle**, an austere stone fortress which for generations served the independent tin miners of Dartmoor as both a court and a prison. The justice meted out here was notoriously arbitrary. William Browne of Tavistock (1590-1643) observed:

> *I oft have heard of Lydford law,*
> *How in the morn they hang and draw*
> *And sit in judgement after.*

Lydford parish is the largest in England, encompassing the whole of the Forest of Dartmoor. For many centuries the dead were brought down from the moor along the ancient Lych Way for burial in St Petroc's churchyard. A tombstone near the porch bears a lengthy and laboriously humorous epitaph to the local watchmaker, George Routleigh, who died in 1802. The inscription includes the statement that George's life had been "Wound up in hope of being taken in hand by his Maker and of being thoroughly cleansed and repaired and set going in the world to come".

To the southwest of the village, the valley of the River Lyd suddenly narrows to form the 1½ mile long **Lydford Gorge** (National Trust), one of Devon's most spectacular natural features. Visitors can follow the riverside path to the Devil's Cauldron, or wander along the two-mile walk to the White Lady, a narrow 100 foot high waterfall. Back in the 17th century, the then remote Lydford Gorge provided a secure refuge for a band of brigands who called themselves the Gubbinses. Their leader was a certain Roger Rowle (dubbed the Robin Hood of the West), whose exploits are recounted in Charles Kingsley's novel *Westward Ho!*

Tavistock

🏛 Guildhall   🪶 Goose Fair

This handsome old town is one of Devon's four stannary towns, so named from the Latin word for tin – *stannum*. These towns – the others are Ashburton, Chagford and Plympton – were the only places licensed to weigh and stamp the metal extracted from the moor.

For most of its recorded history, Tavistock has had only two owners. Tavistock Abbey and the Russell family. The Benedictine abbey was founded here, beside the River Tavy, in around AD974, close to a Saxon stockade or stoc, now incorporated into the town's name. The town grew up around the abbey and, following the discovery of tin on the nearby moors in the 12th century, both flourished.

Then, in 1539, Henry VIII closed the Abbey and gave the building, along with its vast estates to John Russell whose family, as Earls and Dukes of Bedford, owned most of the town until 1911. The present town centre is essentially the creation of the Russell family, who after virtually obliterating the once-glorious abbey, created a completely new town plan. Later, in the 1840s, Francis the 7th Duke diverted some of the profits from his copper mines to build the imposing **Guildhall** and several other civic buildings. He also remodelled the Bedford Hotel, and constructed a model estate of artisans' cottages on the western side of the town. A statue of the duke stands in Bedford Square while, at the western entrance to the town, there is a statue of Sir Francis Drake who is believed to have been born at nearby Crowndale.

One of the legacies of the abbey is the annual three-day fair, granted in 1105, which

🏛 historic building 🏛 museum and heritage 🏛 historic site 🍀 scenic attraction 🌿 flora and fauna

JELLY

1 Eastside Stores, The Market, Tavistock PL19 0AL
Tel: 01822 616897

Situated besides Tavistock's famous Pannier Market is Jelly, an independent fashion boutique offering an eclectic mix of fabulous ladieswear, jewellery and accessories.

Housed in a spacious converted barn, with white washed walls and wooden flooring, Jelly was established in 2003 by sisters-in-law Caren and Amanda Spicer. The pair do their utmost to make sure your shopping experience is a pleasant one and have provided a comfortable leather sofa for those who wish to relax whilst waiting, as well as a play area with train set for the children.

The shop specializes in a unique range of clothing suitable for stylish ladies of all ages, many items with a limited stock, therefore making the garment truly individual. Fresh labels are introduced regularly, which means there is always something new to tempt repeat customers. Favourite brands include Jackpot, Sandwich, Great Plains, Desigual, Avoca and Almost Famous. Also, why not complete your outfit with a piece of stunning jewellery by Martine Wester.

LIQUORICE LIVING

3c Barley Market Street,
Tavistock, Devon PL19 0JF
Tel: 01822 618158
email: info@liquoriceliving.co.uk
website: www.liquoriceliving.co.uk

Take a stroll to the top of Pepper Street in the ancient stannary town of Tavistock and you will find a fabulous boutique called **Liquorice**.

This little shop is full of great clothing and accessories cleverly mixed with a range of home interiors and gifts that will ensure you won't leave empty handed! Liquorice stocks labels such as **White Stuff, Seasalt, Noa Noa, Bohemia, Johnny Q Jeans** and their friendly staff will be on hand to help you with your wardrobe for the coming season. A range of contemporary jewellery and beautiful scarves will enable you to complete your look.

Gorgeous French furniture with a vintage twist nestles between the clothes giving you interior ideas for your home and inspiration for that 'special' gift. The shop is the perfect showcase for our limited and 'one of a kind' finds that will make your visit worthwhile.

So come and take a peep and experience Liquorice Living !

stories and anecdotes   famous people   art and craft   entertainment and sport   walks

N.H. CREBER DELICATESSEN

48 Brook Street, Tavistock,
Devon PL19 0BH
Tel: 01822 612266
e-mail: info@crebers.co.uk
website: www.crebers.co.uk

When you've been in business for 125 years you must know you're doing something right, and **N.H. Creber** has now passed that milestone with its delicatessen and fine wine store near the River Tay in the market town of Tavistock. The standards of service built up over those years are as high as ever, while the range of food and drink for sale still meets its own exacting standards. None of the many products they make themselves has any additives, colourings or other artificial ingredients added.

Those products include a wide range of wonderful foods, too. Even the salads are made in their own kitchens, while they also make their own paté and cure their own bacon. Other bacons and patés are sourced locally, along with cooked meats and cheeses, pickles, chutneys and jams. Other fare comes from further afield, with a good choice of Scottish smoked salmon, foie gras, caviar and truffles.

The fine wine section has over 150 different whiskies, vintage ports dating back to 1945, champagnes, clarets, and their own label house wines. It's a rare visitor who can enter Creber's and leave empty-handed.

has now evolved into **Goose Fair**, a wonderful traditional street fair held on the second Wednesday in October. Tavistock was also permitted to hold a weekly market, which, more than 900 years later, still takes place every Friday in the Pannier Market, a building that was another gift to the town from the 7th Duke. There's also an antiques and crafts market on Tuesdays, and a Victorian market on Wednesdays when many of the stallholders appear in period costume.

Around Tavistock

Tavistock Pannier Market

BRENT TOR
4½ miles N of Tavistock off the A386

🏛 Church of St Michael of the Rocks

Brent Tor, an 1100 foot-high volcanic plug that rears up from the surrounding countryside is one of the most striking sights in the whole of Dartmoor. Perched on its summit is the **Church of St Michael of the Rocks**, the fourth smallest complete church in England. St Michael's is only 15 feet wide and 37 feet long and has

🏛 historic building   📷 museum and heritage   🏛 historic site   🌤 scenic attraction   🌿 flora and fauna

walls only 10 feet high, but three feet thick. Constructed of stone that was quarried from the rock beneath, the church is surrounded by a steep churchyard that contains a surprising number of graves considering its precarious and seemingly soil-less position. Sometimes lost in cloud, the scramble to the summit of Brent Tor is rewarded on a clear day with magnificent views of Dartmoor, Bodmin Moor and the sea at Plymouth Sound.

LEWDOWN
8 miles N of Tavistock off the A30

🐦 Rev Sabine Baring-Gould

The completion of a bypass in the early 1990s took the main road between Exeter and Launceston away from the centre of this village, making Lewdown a much quieter and more enjoyable place to visit. The village lies within the parish of Lewtrenchard whose rector for 43 years, between 1881 and 1924, was the **Rev Sabine Baring-Gould**. Best known as the composer of the hymn, *Onward, Christian Soldiers*, Baring-Gould was also a prolific prose writer. He regularly produced two or three books a year – novels, historical works such as *Curious Myths of the Middle Ages*, and books on Devon legends and folklore. Baring-Gould nevertheless found time to restore St Peter's Church. His most remarkable success was the creation of a replica of a medieval screen that his grandfather, also a rector here, had destroyed. The grandson found enough pieces

remaining for the replica to be made. It is very impressive with an elaborate canopied loft decorated with paintings of 23 saints.

The Rev Sabine scandalised Victorian society by marrying a Lancashire mill girl, but the union proved to be a happy one and they had a huge family. One local story tells how, one day, emerging from his study, the rector saw a little girl coming down the stairs. "You look nice, my dear, in your pretty frock," he said, vaguely remembering that a children's party was under way. "Whose little girl are you?" "Yours, Papa," she answered and burst into tears.

MARY TAVY
3 miles NE of Tavistock on the A386

🏚 Wheal Betsy

The twin villages of Mary Tavy and Peter Tavy lie on opposite banks of the River Tavy and each takes its name from the saint of its parish church. Roughly twice the size of its east bank twin, Mary Tavy stands in the heart of Dartmoor's former mining area. Just to the north of the village stands a survivor from those days. **Wheal Betsy**, a restored pumping

Wheal Betsy

🎭 stories and anecdotes 🐦 famous people 🎨 art and craft 🏃 entertainment and sport 🚶 walks

engine house, was once part of the Prince Arthur Consols mine that produced lead, silver and zinc.

In the village, the grave of William Crossing, the historian of the moor whose magisterial guide first published in the early 1900s is still in print, can be found in the churchyard. Crossing moved to Peter Tavy in 1909 and described it as "a quiet little place, with a church embosomed by trees, a chapel, a school and a small inn". Inside the impressive medieval church there is a poignant memorial to the five daughters of a 17th-century rector. The oldest of them was less than a year when she died:

They breathed awhile and looked the world about
And, like newly-lighted candles, soon went out.

POSTBRIDGE
14 miles NE of Tavistock on the B3212

🏚 Clapper Bridge   🍴 Warren House Inn

In prehistoric times, the area around Postbridge was the 'metropolis' of Dartmoor as the wealth of Bronze Age remains bears witness. Today, the village is best known for its **Clapper Bridge**, which probably dates back to the 13th century and is the best preserved of all the Devon clapper bridges. Spanning the East Dart River, the bridge is a model of medieval minimalist construction with just three huge slabs of granite laid across solid stone piers. Not wide enough for wheeled traffic, the bridge would originally have been used by packhorses following the post road from Exeter into Cornwall.

Two miles along the road to Moretonhampstead, **Warren House Inn** claims to be the third highest tavern in England. It used to stand on the other side of the road, but in 1845 a fire destroyed that building. According to tradition, when the

present inn was built its landlord carried some still-smouldering turves across the road to the hearth of his new hostelry and that fire has been burning ever since. It's a pleasant enough sight in summer and must have been even more welcome in the winter of 1963. In that year, the Warren House Inn was cut off by heavy snow drifts some 20 feet deep for almost three months and supplies had to be flown in by helicopter. Such a remote inn naturally generates some good tales. Like the one about the traveller who stayed here one winter's night and opening by chance a large chest in his room discovered the body of a dead man. "Why!" said the landlord when confronted with the deceased, "tis only feyther! 'Twas too cold to take 'un to the buryin', so mother salted 'un down!"

MERRIVALE
4½ miles E of Tavistock on the B3357

🏚 Merrivale Rows

Set 1000 feet above sea level the tiny hamlet of Merrivale provides wonderful views that on a clear day extend as far as the Eddystone lighthouse in Plymouth Sound, some 30 miles away. The main attraction here is the impressive prehistoric site of **Merrivale Rows**, a double row of standing stones about one metre apart, which may have been erected as long ago as 2500BC. They extend for some 850 feet.

PRINCETOWN
9 miles E of Tavistock on the B3212

🏛 Dartmoor Prison Heritage Centre

Princetown, best known for its forbidding prison, stands 1400 feet above sea level in an area of the moor that is notorious for its atrocious climate. It gets doused with 80 to 100 inches of rain a year, more than three times the average for Exeter, which is less

---

🏛 historic building   🏛 museum and heritage   🏚 historic site   🌿 scenic attraction   🌱 flora and fauna

Dartmoor Prison

9000 French and, later, American inmates, but by 1816, with the cessation of hostilities, the prison became redundant and was closed. Princetown virtually collapsed as a result and it wasn't until 1823 that its granite quarries were given a new lease of life with the building of the horse-drawn Dartmoor Railway, another of Sir Thomas Tyrwhitt's initiatives. The prison was eventually re-opened for long-serving convicts in 1850 and since then it has been considerably enlarged and upgraded. It is currently in use as a medium security prison with around 640 inmates. The **Dartmoor Prison Heritage Centre** has exhibits detailing the history of the institution.

than 20 miles away.

That a settlement should be located here at all was the brainchild of one man, Sir Thomas Tyrwhitt, the owner of a local granite quarry. He proposed that a special prison should be built here to house the thousands of troops captured during the Napoleonic wars who were becoming too numerous and unruly for the prison ships moored in Plymouth Sound. The work was completed in 1809 by the prisoners themselves using granite from Sir Thomas' quarry. Paid at the rate of sixpence (2½p) a day, they also built the main east-west road across the moor, which is now the B3212. Yet another of their constructions was the nearby Church of St Mary, a charmless building in whose churchyard stands a tall granite cross in memory of all those prisoners whose bodies lie in unmarked graves. (The mortality rate of the inmates in the early 1800s was 50%.) Since around 1900, prisoners' graves have been marked just with their initials and date of death. The lines of small stones are a gloomy sight.

At one time the prison held as many as

Also in the town is the National Park's Moorland Visitors' Centre, which contains some excellent and informative displays about the moor, and also stocks a wide range of books, maps and leaflets. The centre is housed in the former Duchy Hotel where Sir Arthur Conan Doyle stayed while writing some chapters of *The Hound of the Baskervilles,* much of which is set in Dartmoor.

DARTMEET
13 miles E of Tavistock off the B3357

Dartmeet is a picturesque spot where the boulder-strewn East and West Dart rivers join together. At their junction, a single-span packhorse bridge was built in the 1400s; its remains can still be seen just upstream from the more modern road bridge.

Rising in the boggy plateau of north Dartmoor, the Dart and its tributaries drain a huge area of the moor. The river then flows for 46 miles before entering the sea at Dartmouth.

In the days when the tin mines were working, this area was extremely isolated, lacking even a burial ground of its own. Local people had to carry their dead across the moor to Lydford – "Eight miles in fair weather, and 15 in foul". In good weather, this is grand walking country with a choice of exploring the higher moor, dotted with a wealth of prehistoric remains, or following the lovely riverside and woodland path that leads to the famous Clapper Bridge near Postbridge, about five miles upstream.

To the east of Dartmeet, and hidden among bracken and gorse, is the Coffin Stone, a large boulder on which it was customary for bearers to rest the body while making the moorland crossing. A cross and the deceased's initials were carved into the stone while the bearers had some liquid refreshment and got back their breath before continuing on their journey.

YELVERTON
5 miles SE of Tavistock on the A386

🚉 Great Western Railway

In prehistoric times, the area around Yelverton must have been quite heavily populated to judge by the extraordinary concentration of stone circles and rows, hut and cairn circles, and burial chambers. The B3212 to Princeton passes through this once-populous stretch of moorland, part of which is now submerged beneath Burrator Reservoir.

EAST DART HOTEL

Postbridge, Dartmoor, Devon PL20 6TJ
Tel/Fax: 01822 880213
e-mail: info@eastdarthotel.co.uk
website: www.theeastdarthotel.co.uk

The **East Dart Hotel** is a 19th century former coaching inn located in the heart of Dartmoor National Park, in a sheltered valley on the main road. Paul and Rosie Joynson and their family provide a visit to remember, whether it's for a leisurely drink, a meal or an overnight or longer stay. Care and attention come top of the list, and the hosts know exactly what the customer wants, Paul through long experience in the licensed trade, Rosie through skills developed in her family's restaurant on Jersey. The bar, with its horse brasses, atmospheric photographs of the Moor and a historic hunting frieze, is a delightful place to meet for a chat and a drink, and there's plenty of space to enjoy good food in comfort; the options run from bar snacks to a full restaurant menu, daily specials and a popular Sunday carvery.

The guest accommodation comprises nine quiet, cosy en-suite rooms – five doubles, a twin, two singles and a family room. It's a great base for walking, fishing, riding and discovering the natural beauty of the region. The owners are dog-friendly, and they can provide stabling for guests' horses (or horses can be hired locally). Postbridge has a Dartmoor National Park information point that is central for all walks, and the staff and the hotel's owners can assist in organising guided walks, treks on horseback, fishing trips and falconry days.

🏠 historic building 🏛 museum and heritage 🏛 historic site ♨ scenic attraction 🌿 flora and fauna

Situated just inside the Dartmoor National Park, Yelverton itself is a large village with broad-verged streets, which has caused it to be described as "rather like a thriving racecourse". The village is one of very few in the country to have had its name bestowed by the Board of Directors of a railway company. **Great Western Railway** opened a station here in 1859 when the village was officially known as Elfordtown. The story goes that the London-based surveyors interpreted the Devon pronunciation of Elfordtown as Yelverton. So that was the name blazoned on the station signboard, and the name by which the village has been known ever since.

BUCKLAND MONACHORUM
5 miles S of Tavistock off the A386

🏛 Buckland Abbey 🌱 The Garden House

Tucked away in a secluded valley above the River Tavy, **Buckland Abbey** (National Trust) was founded in 1278 by Amicia, Countess of Devon, but became better known as the home of Sir Francis Drake. Drake purchased the former abbey in 1581 from his fellow-warrior (and part-time pirate) Sir Richard Grenville, whose exploits in his little ship *Revenge* were almost as colourful as those of Drake himself. The house remained in the Drake family until 1947 when it was acquired by the National Trust. Of the many exhibits at the abbey, Drake's Drum takes pride of place – according to legend, the drum will sound whenever England is in peril. The drum was brought back to England by Drake's brother, Thomas, who was with the great seafarer when he died on the Spanish Main in 1596 (rather ignominiously, of dysentery). Elsewhere at the abbey, visitors can see a magnificent 14th-century tithe barn, 154 feet long, housing an interesting collection of carts and carriages and a craft workshop, and a herb garden.

In the village itself, on the site of a medieval vicarage, **The Garden House** (see panel below) is surrounded by a delightful garden created after World War Two by Lionel Fortescue, a retired schoolmaster.

The parish church of St Andrew contains a

The Garden House

Buckland Monachorum, Yelverton, Devon PL20 7LQ
Tel: 01822 854769
e-mail: office@thegardenhouse.org.uk
website: www.thegardenhouse.org.uk

The Garden House is centred on an enchanting Walled Garden created by the plantsman Lionel Fortescue and his wife Katharine around the romantic ruins of a medieval vicarage. Lionel's successor Keith Wiley extended the garden into new areas such as the South African Garden, the Acer Glade, the Bulb Meadow and the Cretan Cottage Garden, creating vistas of stunning colour from Spring until Autumn in a pioneering naturalistic style inspired by great natural landscapes of the world. Now Head Gardener Matt Bishop is caring for this legacy, refurbishing some of the historic planting and developing exciting new designs.

📖 stories and anecdotes 🐾 famous people 🎨 art and craft 🎭 entertainment and sport 🚶 walks

tribute to the generations of Drakes who lived at Buckland Abbey, and there is a carving of the Golden Hind on the family pew.

GULWORTHY
2 miles SW of Tavistock on the A390

This little village lies at the heart of an area that, in the mid 1880s, had a worldwide reputation. A quarter of the world's supply of copper was extracted from this part of Devon and, more alarmingly, so was half of the world's requirements for arsenic. Mining for copper in this area has long been abandoned, due to the discovery of cheaper sources around the world, particularly in South America. Gulworthy's arsenic has also gone out of fashion as an agent of murder.

Today the village is best known for its luxury hotel and restaurant, The Horn of Plenty.

MILTON ABBOT
5½ miles NW of Tavistock on the B3362

🏛 Endsleigh House

Situated high above the Tamar Valley, Milton Abbot is home to the Regency masterpiece, **Endsleigh House**, that was designed for the Duke and Duchess of Bedford by the architect Sir Jeffry Wyattville and the landscape designer Humphry Repton. Built in the *cottage orne* in about 1810, the house comprises the main building and a children's wing that are linked by a curved terrace. The formal gardens were designed to form a setting for the house as well as frame views out across the surrounding countryside. Along with the three terraces, which were restored in

---

HAMPTON MANOR

Alston, Stoke Climsland, Callington PL17 8LX
Tel: 01579 370494
e-mail: hamptonmanor@sapanet.com
website: www.hamptonmanor.co.uk

Hampton Manor is a country house hotel set in beautiful, secluded gardens in the peaceful countryside within the Tamar Valley, on the border of Devon and Cornwall. This impressive establishment is located in a designated Area of Outstanding Natural Beauty and offers six high quality en-suite guest rooms.

Hampton Manor is extremely popular with walkers visiting the area to make the most of the spectacular surroundings. Within a half hour drive are numerous attractions; the market towns of Tavistock and Launceston; the seaside city of Plymouth, the grandeur of Dartmoor and many tranquil National Trust gardens and houses.

This four star country house hotel is an ideal retreat for people wanting to get away from the hustle and bustle of every-day life. Evenings can be spent relaxing in the wonderful conservatory, which overlooks more than two acres of land.

Guests can dine in the hotel's licensed restaurant at reasonable prices. Discounts are offered for groups, for short breaks and for longer stays. Small conference facilities are available and are regularly used by Christian church groups. In the summer months it doubles as a games room for families with children.

🏛 historic building 🏛 museum and heritage 🏛 historic site ᏪᎼ scenic attraction 🍃 flora and fauna

1998, there are less formal garden areas that include a Rock Garden with a mysterious underground grotto that leads to the Diary Dell. Little altered since they were first created, the grounds also include an internationally famous arboretum containing more than 1000 specimen trees. The house has recently been redeveloped as an upmarket hotel.

BERE ALSTON
5 miles SW of Tavistock on the B3257

Morwellham Quay

🏛 Morwellham Quay

For centuries, Bere Alston was a thriving little port on the River Tamar from whence the products of Dartmoor's tin mines were transported around the world. All that commercial activity has long since gone, but the river here is still busy with the to-ings and fro-ings of sleek pleasure craft. Just a few miles upstream from Bere Alston is one of the county's most popular visitor attractions, **Morwellham Quay**. The port fell into disuse following the arrival of the railway and by the 1980s it was a ghost harbour with the Tamar valley breezes whistling through its abandoned buildings. Now restored, this historic site faithfully re-creates the busy atmosphere of the 1860s when half the world's copper came through this tiny harbour. Visitors can journey through the mines on a riverside tramway, watch demonstrations in the blacksmith's and cooper's workshops, and explore the restored Tamar ketch *Garlandstone*. Although Morwellham lies some 20 miles upstream from Plymouth, the Tamar river at this point was deep enough for 300-ton ships to load up

with the precious minerals. Once known as the Devon Klondyke, Morwellham suffered a catastrophic decline when cheaper sources of copper were discovered in South America.

The quayside inn has also been restored. It was here that the dockside labourers used to meet for ale, food and the latest news of the ships that sailed from Morwellham. In those days, the news was chalked up on a blackboard, which is still here. Though out of date, the stories nonetheless remain intriguing.

LIFTON
9 miles NW of Tavistock on the A30

🏛 Dingles Fairground Heritage Centre

Situated on the banks of the River Lyd, Lifton was, in medieval times, an important centre of the wool trade. Dartmoor sheep tend to have rather coarse fleeces, due to the cold pastureland, so the weavers of Lifton petitioned Henry VII, "by reason of the grossness and stubbornness of their district" to allow them to mix as much lambs' wool and flock with their wool "as may be required to work it".

Just to the east of Lifton is **Dingles Fairground Heritage Centre** where visitors

LIFTON HALL HOTEL & VILLAGE INN

New Road, Lifton, Devon PL16 0DR
Tel: 01566 784863
e-mail: relax@liftonhall.co.uk
website: www.liftonhall.co.uk

Lifton Hall is the perfect place to get away from the hustle and bustle of urban life, a fine hotel set in the delightful Devon countryside. Positioned away from busy holiday resorts yet close enough to many of the tourist attractions that you might want to visit, such as The Eden Project, Dartmoor National Park and the beaches of North Cornwall. The Grade II listed building dates back in part to 1611, with Gothic-style extensions in the 19th century, and the traditional character has been carefully preserved alongside modern comfort and amenity. Many period features have been retained, and the décor throughout is in keeping with the Hall's age. The tone is set by the grand entrance hall with its Cornish slate floor, high ceiling, handsome chandelier and a staircase winding up to a galleried landing.

The guest accommodation comprises ten comfortable bedrooms with en suite bath or shower, crisp white cotton sheets and pillows, TV with radio-alarm, direct-dial phone, and drinks tray with scrumptious biscuits. Two of the rooms are suitable for families, and one room is located on the ground floor. The day starts with a full English breakfast featuring local produce, home-made preserves and a choice of teas and fair trade coffee.

The oldest part of the Hall was originally three cottages, and in what is now the Cottage Bar locals and guests can enjoy West Country real ales from the Ottery, Skinners and St Austell breweries. Food is an important part of the Hall's success, and fresh local produce is very much to the fore in the bar and restaurant menus. The chefs seek out prime raw materials from excellent local butchers and fishmongers and top fruit and vegetable suppliers (as well as some home-grown produce) for menus that cater for all tastes and appetites. The fine food is complemented by a well-chosen list of wines from Old and New Worlds. Tuesdays bring either Food Club nights, featuring the cuisines of different countries, or a popular quiz that's open to all.

Lifton Hall is a great choice for parties and weddings, and adaptable conference and meeting facilities make it an ideal base for business groups. The Hall has a large private car park and a split-level garden with mature trees – just the spot for a stroll or for a quiet read, a drink or a cream tea.

can see one of the best working steam collections in the country, including traction engines, steam rollers, fairground attractions and vintage machinery. There's also a collection of vintage road signs, play areas for children, a gift shop, café and riverside walks.

Ivybridge

🚶 Two Moors Way

The original bridge over the Erme at Ivybridge was just wide enough for a single packhorse, and the 13th-century crossing that replaced it is still very narrow. When the railway arrived here in 1848, Brunel constructed an impressive viaduct over the Erme valley. It was made of wood, however, so that too was replaced in 1895 by an equally imposing stone structure. The town grew rapidly in the 1860s when a quality paper-making mill was established to make good use of the waters of the Erme, and more recently Ivybridge has continued to grow as a commuter town for Plymouth.

Serious walkers will know Ivybridge as the southern starting point of the **Two Moors Way**, the spectacular but gruelling 103-mile path across both Dartmoor and Exmoor, finishing at Barnstaple. The trek begins with a stiff 1000 feet climb up Butterdon Hill, just outside Ivybridge – and that's the easy bit!

SOUTH BRENT
5 miles NE of Ivybridge off the A38

Standing on the southern flank of Dartmoor, just within the National Park, South Brent is a sizeable village of some 3000 souls. Set beside the River Avon, it has a 13th-century church with a massive Norman tower.

This was once the main church for a large part of the South Hams, as well as a considerable area of Dartmoor. Alongside the River Avon are some attractive old textile mills recalling the days when South Brent was an important centre for the production of woollens. In Victorian times, one of the mills was managed by William Crossing whose famous *Crossing's Guide to Dartmoor* provides a fascinating picture of life on the moor in the late 1800s.

In the days of stagecoach travel the town was a lively place with two posting houses servicing the competing coaches. It was said that four horses could be changed in 45 seconds and a full-course meal served in 20 minutes. The most famous of the coaches, the *Quicksilver*, left Plymouth at 8.30 in the evening and arrived in London at 4pm the following afternoon – a remarkable average speed of 11 mph, *including* stops.

BUCKFASTLEIGH
9 miles NE of Ivybridge off the A38

🏛 Valiant Soldier Museum 🚂 South Devon Railway

🦋 Buckfast Butterflies and Dartmoor Otter Sanctuary

🦦 Pennywell 🐦 Robert Herrick

A former wool town on the banks of the

South Devon Railway

🎭 stories and anecdotes 🐦 famous people 🎨 art and craft 🎟 entertainment and sport 🚶 walks

River Mardle, several old mill buildings still stand and the large houses of their former owners lie on the outskirts. A unique insight into the lives of local folk is provided by an old inn that has been restored and now houses the **Valiant Soldier Museum and Heritage Centre**. When the Valiant Soldier pub was closed in the 1960s, everything was left in place – even the money in the till. Rediscovered years later, this life-size time capsule features period public and lounge bars, as well as domestic rooms including the kitchen, scullery, parlour and bedrooms.

Buckfastleigh is the western terminus and headquarters of the **South Devon Railway**, (formerly known as the Primrose Line) whose steam trains ply the seven-mile route along the lovely Dart Valley to and from Totnes. The Dart is a fast-flowing salmon river and its banks abound with herons, swans, kingfishers,

badgers and foxes. The company also offers a combined River Rail ticket so that visitors can travel in one direction by train and return by boat. The railway runs regular services during the season with the journey taking about 25 minutes each way.

Another popular attraction close to the town is the **Buckfast Butterflies and Dartmoor Otter Sanctuary** where a specially designed tropical rain forest habitat has been created for the exotic butterflies. There's an underwater viewing area and both the butterflies and otters can be photographed, with the otters' thrice-daily feeding times providing some excellent photo-opportunities.

A couple of miles south of Buckfastleigh, **Pennywell** is a spacious all-weather family attraction that offers a wide variety of entertainments and activities. Pennywell also boasts the UK's longest gravity go-kart ride

---

CHURCH HOUSE INN

Holne, nr Ashburton, Devon TQ13 7SJ
Tel/Fax: 01364 631208
e-mail: info@churchhouseinndartmoor.co.uk
website: www.churchhouseinndartmoor.co.uk

Church House Inn in the hamlet of Holne, near Ashburton, has a history that goes back to 1329 when stonemasons built it to house them while they built the Church of St Mary the Virgin alongside. This quintessential Inn, now a Grade II listed building is full of character and charm, with two open fires bringing warmth in the cooler months. The appealing ambience is just part of the attraction. Mine hosts, Anthony and Helen Walker, have made good food a priority.

The inn offers a regular lunchtime menu and a different dinner menu, and the chef provides daily, a selection of interesting and appetising specials. Most of the meat is Dartmoor born and bred and fresh, locally sourced fish is always on the menu. To accompany your meal, there's a select grouping of hand drawn real ales from local breweries, and a good cross-section of draught ales and lagers. The wine list, too, has something to appeal to most palates. As you would expect from an inn of this character, the bedrooms are both delightful and comfortable. All 5 rooms are spacious, en-suite and are equipped with tea and coffee making facilities and colour TV. Wi-Fi is also available.

🏛 historic building 🏛 museum and heritage 🏛 historic site ⌘ scenic attraction ☙ flora and fauna

and promises that its hands-on activities provide something new every half hour.

Another mile or so south, the little church of Dean Prior stands beside the A38. The vicar here at the time of the Restoration was the poet and staunch royalist, **Robert Herrick** (1591-1674). Herrick's best-known lines are probably the opening of *To the Virgins, to make Much of Time:*

> *Gather ye rosebuds while ye may,*
> *Old Time is still a-flying*
> *And this same flower that smiles today*
> *Tomorrow will be dying.*

Herrick apparently found rural Devon rather dull and much preferred London where he had a mistress 27 years his junior. Perhaps to brighten up the monotony of his Devonshire existence, he had a pet pig that he took for walks and trained to drink beer from a tankard. Herrick died in 1674 and was buried in the churchyard where a simple stone marks his assumed last resting place.

BUCKFAST
10 miles NE of Ivybridge off the A38

🏛 Buckfast Abbey

Dominating this small market town is **Buckfast Abbey**, a Benedictine monastery built in the Norman and Gothic style between 1907 and 1938. If you've ever wondered how many people it takes to construct an abbey, the astonishing answer at Buckfast is just six. Only one of the monks, Brother Peter, had any knowledge of building so he had to check every stone that went into the fabric. A photographic exhibition at the abbey records the painstaking process that stretched over 30 years. Another monk, Brother Adam, became celebrated as the bee-keeper whose busy charges produced the renowned Buckfast

Abbey honey. The abbey gift shop also sells the famous Buckfast Tonic Wine, recordings of the abbey choristers and a wide range of religious items, pottery, cards and gifts. Nearby is an exhibition detailing the process of making the stained glass produced by the monks. The grounds contain Physic, Sensory and Lavender areas, which provide a peaceful and often colourful setting.

CORNWOOD
3 miles NW of Ivybridge off the A38

Cornwood is a pleasant village on the River Yealm, a good base from which to seek out the many Bronze Age and industrial remains scattered across the moor. One of the most remarkable sights in Dartmoor is the double line of stones set up on Stall Moor during the Bronze Age. One line is almost 550 yards long; the other begins with a stone circle and crosses the River Erme before ending at a burial chamber some two miles distant. There are no roads to these extraordinary constructions, they can only be reached on foot.

If you approach Dartmoor from the south, off the A38, Cornwood is the last village you will find before the moors begin in earnest. Strike due north from here and you will have to cross some 15 miles of spectacular moorland before you see another inhabited place. (Her Majesty's Prison at Princetown, as it happens.)

Bovey Tracey

🏛 Riverside Mill 🖌 House of Marbles

This ancient market town takes its name from the River Bovey and the de Tracy family who received the manor from William the Conqueror. The best-known member of the family is Sir William Tracy, one of the four

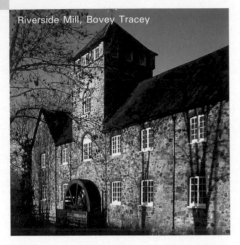

Riverside Mill, Bovey Tracey

knights who murdered Thomas à Becket in
Canterbury Cathedral. To expiate his crime, Sir
William is said to have endowed a church here,
dedicated to St Thomas. That building was
destroyed by fire and the present church is 15th
century with a 14th-century tower. Its most
glorious possession is a beautifully carved
screen of 1427, a gift to the church from Lady
Margaret Beaufort, the new owner of the
manor and the mother of King Henry VII.

Bovey Tracey, unlike so many Devon towns
and villages, has never suffered a major fire.
This is perhaps just as well since its fire-
fighting facilities until recent times were
decidedly limited. In 1920, for example, the
town did have an engine, and five volunteers
to man it, but no horses to draw it. The parish
council in that year issued a notice advising
"all or any persons requiring the Fire Brigade
with Engine that they must take the
responsibility of sending a Pair of Horses for
the purpose of conveying the Engine to and
from the Scene of the Fire".

For such a small town, Bovey Tracey is
remarkably well-supplied with shops as well as
the **Riverside Mill**, which is run by the

Devon Guild of Craftsmen. This is also the
southwest's leading gallery and craft
showroom with work selected from around
240 makers, many with national and
international reputations. The Guild presents
changing craft exhibitions and demonstrations
and the mill also houses a study centre, gallery
and a café with roof terrace.

A rather unusual shop is the **House of
Marbles**, a working glass and games factory
set in an historic pottery. They have been
manufacturing their range of traditional
games, puzzles, toys, marbles and glassware for
many years. Visitors can wander around the
old pottery buildings with their listed kilns,
explore the museums of glass, games and
marbles, watch glass-blowing demonstrations,
and be entertained by the wonderful collection
of marble runs and the giant floating marble
amongst other amusements.

Walkers will enjoy the footpath that passes
through the town and follows the track bed of
the former railway from Moretonhampstead
to Newton Abbot, which runs alongside the
River Bovey for part of its length

Just to the north of Bovey Tracey is Parke,
formerly the estate of the Tracy family but now
owned by the National Trust and leased to the
Dartmoor National Park as its headquarters.

Around Bovey Tracey

ILSINGTON
3 miles SW of Bovey Tracey off the B3387

Like so many Dartmoor communities,
Ilsington was once an important centre of the
wool industry. At the heart of the village is a
characteristic trio of late medieval buildings –
church, church house and inn. The interior of
St Michael's Church is well worth seeing, with

its impressive array of arched beams and roof timbers, which seem to hang in mid-air above the nave. The medieval pew ends are thought to be the only ones in Devon carved with the distinctive poppy head design; there's also a mid 14th-century effigy of a woman and an elaborately carved 16th-century rood screen.

Entry to the churchyard is by way of an unusual lych gate with an upper storey, which once served as the village schoolroom. The present structure is actually a replica of the original medieval gate that apparently collapsed when someone slammed the gate too energetically. The nearby church house, dating back to the 1500s, is now sub-divided into residential dwellings known as St Michael's Cottages.

This small village was the birthplace of the Jacobean dramatist John Ford (1586-1639) whose most successful play, *Tis Pity She's A Whore* (1633), is still occasionally revived.

Ilsington is a sizeable parish and includes the three wellknown tors of Rippon, Saddle and Haytor Rocks. The latter is perhaps the most dramatic, especially when approached from the west along the B3387, and with a height of almost 1500 feet provides a popular challenge for rock climbers.

In the early 1800s, the shallow valley to the north of Haytor Rocks was riddled with quarries that supplied granite for such famous buildings as London Bridge, the National Gallery and the British Museum.

BUCKLAND-IN-THE-MOOR
7 miles SW of Bovey Tracey off the A38

🏠 St Peter's Church

Another pretty village, surrounded by the wooded slopes of the Webburn Valley. St

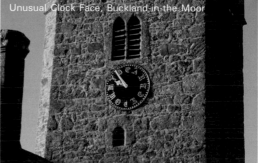
Unusual Clock Face, Buckland-in-the-Moor

Peter's Church, originally 14th century, boasts a fine Norman font and a medieval rood screen, which, unusually, is painted on both sides. Outside, the tower has a clock on which the numerals have been replaced by the words MY DEAR MOTHER. The timepiece was a gift to the parish in 1939 by the local squire William Whitley who, a decade earlier, had been instrumental in having two blocks of granite inscribed with the Ten Commandments. The slabs were intended to commemorate the rejection of the new Prayer Book of 1928. They were placed on top of Buckland Beacon, a mile to the east of the village and are still in place today. From this spot there are superb views across Dartmoor.

ASHBURTON
9 miles SW of Bovey Tracey off the A38

🏛 Ashburton Museum 🎵 Ashburton Blues Festival

This appealing little town lies just inside the boundary of the Dartmoor National Park, surrounded by lovely hills and with the River Ashburn splashing through the town centre. Municipal history goes back a long way here, to AD821 in fact, when the town elected its first portreeve, the Saxon equivalent of a mayor. The traditional office continues to the present day, although its functions are now purely ceremonial. But each year, on the

BIRDI'S EXQUISITE LINGERIE

8 West St, Ashburton, Devon TQ13 7DU
Tel: 01364 653713
e-mail: debbie@birdislingerie.co.uk
website: www.birdislingerie.co.uk

Bring a touch of glamour to your everyday lingerie, or pick up a little something special, at **Birdi's Exquisite Lingerie** boutique. Founded in December 2009, in the heart of the pretty moorland town of Ashburton, the boutique stocks a fabulous array of undergarments; from shapewear, nightwear and swimwear, to bridal, corsets and gorgeous vintage items. Relax in the lush pink and French-grey vintage boudoir-style boutique while you look over the many feminine luxuries to buy. The gorgeous accessories are all lovingly created and supplied by local jewellers and fashion designers.

Dedicated to finding the perfect fit and style for every customer, Birdi's personnel offer a brilliant fitting service and pay every attention to you underwear needs. From specialist corset fitting, and sourcing the most supportive and feminine mastectomy bras, to hosting ladies evenings for private parties, every need is catered for. In association with Ashburton's new Bizarre Bazaar Market, with its fabulous jazz and burlesque shows, Birdi's is a welcoming and glamorous treat already loved by the local female population. So shake your tail-feathers and give them a visit during your stay in Ashburton.

SILVER LION JEWELLERS

3 North St, Ashburton, Devon TQ13 7QJ
Tel: 01364 653718
e-mail: info@silverlionjewellers.co.uk
website: www.silverlionjewellers.co.uk

Hidden in the centre of the sublime countryside town of Ashburton is a real gem; Silver Lion Jewellers. The well-established shop has been part of the community here for over 25 years, and is a literal jewellery box for all that glitters (and is gold!). Customers are wondered by the Silver Lion's stunning collections of silver, gold, and delicate stone-set jewellery from all around the world; from beautiful traditional English and Celtic patterned gold-work, and funky contemporary pieces, to exotic and unusual pieces, infused with colour. However, it is in their bespoke jewellery creations that Silver Lion Jewellers really shine; their speciality being 9 or 18 ct gold bands, set inside and out with diamonds of every imaginable colour.

The Silver Lion, which has been under new ownership since 2008, remains popular with locals and visitors alike; their unusual and stunning pieces have attracted many brides and wedding guests looking for that extra special something to complete their outfits. The antique and vintage collection here too is very beautiful, and the hand or mechanical engraving service can add that special touch to any gift.If your favourite piece should be broken or damaged. they can repair, restring and resize with great care and skill. Watches, too, can have their batteries and straps replaced or altered.

🏛 historic building   🏛 museum and heritage   🏛 historic site   ♤ scenic attraction   🐾 flora and fauna

THE FISH DELI

7 East St, Ashburton, Devon TQ13 7AD
Tel: 01364 654833
e-mail: information@thefishdeli.co.uk
website: www.thefishdeli.co.uk

The fish deli is unique. A superb deli, but specialising in mainly fishy things. Fresh fish is sourced responsibly from local day boats. Customers are encouraged to buy the daily catch of what is available and in season. The deli was recently featured in the Marine Conservation magazine. Gentle advice is given about buying and trying more sustainable varieties.

Nick, Michele and their dedicated team also make wonderful fish dishes to take home such as Fish Cakes, Fish Pies, Bouillabaisse, Escabeche, Zarzuela, Curries, Fish pates etc. A fantastic friendly service, nothing too much trouble, the fish is offered whole, filleted, butterfly filleted, pin boned, whatever you want. The deli has been highly recommended by Seafish and the fish dishes have won Great Taste awards. There is a wide range of dry stores, delicious bread, classy cookware and cook books too.

It is an amazing shop bringing together all sorts of people from all walks of life to really enjoy/appreciate good food. The shop has been operating since 2004 and has a huge local following; it has also been featured in a number of national newspapers and Country Living magazine.

fourth Tuesday in November, officials gather in the St Lawrence chapel to appoint not just their portreeve, but also the Ale Tasters, Bread Weighers, Pig Drovers and even a Viewer of Watercourses.

In medieval times, Ashburton's prosperity was based on tin. As one of Devon's four stannary towns, it benefited from the trade generated by the Dartmoor tinners who were obliged to come here to have their metal weighed and stamped, and to pay the duty. Later, the cloth industry was the town's main money-spinner, with nine fulling mills along the banks of the Ashburn producing cloth that the East India Company exported to China.

The town is characterised by its many attractive houses and shops, with distinctive slate-hung front elevations. Housed in the former home and workshop of a brushmaker, **Ashburton Museum** offers a fascinating insight into the history of this stannary town as well as the domestic and rural life of Dartmoor down the centuries. The collections include old farming implements, Victorian toys, a model of the old

East Street, Ashburton

📖 stories and anecdotes 🦜 famous people 🎨 art and craft ✏ entertainment and sport 🚶 walks

PRESENCE

21-23 East St, Ashburton, Devon TQ13 7AQ
Tel: 01364 653369

Walk into **Presence** and enter a world of colour, imagination and ideas for unusual gifts.

Inside you will find a fine array of clothes, cushions, candles, natural bath and shower products, wooden toys, games and puzzles together with a large choice of life-enhancing essential oilsand incense.

Presence is also known for its wide variety of artistic, quirky and amusing cards. The shop is a great supporter of Fair Trade. All the clothes and much of the stock come from Fair Trade companies.

Zoe Williams established Presence 20 years ago - she is a working craftsperson in decoupage, patchwork and rag rug making and some of her work is for sale in the shop.

At Presence you will find a colourful and unique blend of clothes and gifts at reasonable prices so do pop in and see for yourself.

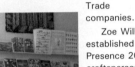

Market Hall and Native American artefacts donated by Paul Endicott, whose parents had left Ashburton for Oklahoma at the beginning of the 1900s.

Ashburton's Italianate Town Hall provides the main venue for the **Ashburton Blues Festival** over the last weekend in May.

WIDECOMBE IN THE MOOR
6 miles W of Bovey Tracey off the B3212

🏛 Cathedral of the Moors 🏛 Church House
🍃 Widecombe Fair 🗼 Grimspound

This pleasing village enjoys a lovely setting in the valley of the East Webburn river and its grand old church, with a massive 120 feet high granite tower rising against a backdrop of high moorland, has understandably been dubbed the **Cathedral of the Moors**. Dedicated to St Pancras, the church was built with funds raised by tin miners in the 14th

century, and enlarged during the next two centuries. A panel inside the church records the disastrous events of 21 October 1638. A sizeable congregation had gathered for a service when a bolt of lightning struck the tower, dislodging huge blocks of masonry on to the worshippers. Four were killed and a further 60 badly injured. (Local legend maintains that the Devil had been spotted earlier that day spitting fire and riding an ebony stallion across the moor.)

In addition to the church, two other buildings are worth mentioning. Glebe House is a handsome 16th-century residence, which has since been converted to a shop, and **Church House** is an exceptional colonnaded building which was originally built around 1500 to accommodate those travelling large distances across the moor to attend church services. It was later divided into almshouses then served in succession as a brewery and a school. It is now a National Trust shop and information centre.

The famous **Widecombe Fair** to which Uncle Tom Cobleigh, his boisterous crew and the old grey mare, were making their way is still held here on the second Tuesday in September, and although it is no longer an agricultural event, remains a jolly affair. A succession of real-life Tom Cobleighs have lived around Widecombe over the centuries, but the song probably refers to a gentleman who died in 1794. An amorous bachelor, this Uncle Tom Cobleigh had a mane of red hair and he refused to maintain any babies that did not display the same characteristic.

From Widecombe, a country lane leads to **Grimspound**, which is perhaps the most impressive of all Dartmoor's Bronze Age survivals. This settlement was occupied between 1800BC and 500BC and is remarkably well-preserved. There are 24 hut circles here, some of them reconstructed, and it's still possible to make out the positions of door lintels and stone sleeping shelves. Today, the area around Grimspound is bleak and moody, an atmosphere that recommended itself to Sir Arthur Conan Doyle who had Sherlock Holmes send Dr Watson into hiding here to help solve the case of *The Hound of the Baskervilles*.

NORTH BOVEY
6 miles NW of Bovey Tracey off the B3212

In any discussion about which is the loveliest village in Devon, North Bovey has to be one of the leading contenders. Set beside the River Bovey, it is quite unspoiled, with thatched cottages grouped around the green, a 15th-century church and a delightful old inn, the Ring of Bells, which like many Devon

hostelries was originally built, back in the 13th century, as a lodging house for the stonemasons building the church.

LUSTLEIGH
3 miles NW of Bovey Tracey off the A382

🍃 Becky Falls Woodland Park

🍃 Yarner Wood Nature Reserve

Lustleigh is one of Dartmoor's most popular and most photographed villages. Placed at all angles on the hillside are a ravishing assortment of 15th and 16th-century deeply-thatched, colour-washed cottages, picturesquely grouped around the church. Appropriately for such a genuinely olde-worlde village, Lustleigh keeps alive some of the time-honoured traditions of country life, enthusiastically celebrating May Day each year with a procession through the village, dancing round the maypole, and the coronation of a May Queen. From the village there are some delightful walks, especially one that passes through Lustleigh Cleave, a wooded section of the steep-sided Bovey valley. Also close by is the **Becky Falls Woodland Park**, with its waterfalls, rugged landscape and attractions for all the family. Here, too, is **Yarner Wood Nature Reserve**, home to pied flycatchers, wood warblers and redstarts.

MORETONHAMPSTEAD
7 miles NW of Bovey Tracey on the A382

🏛 St Andrew's Church   🏛 Almshouses

🍃 Miniature Pony Centre

Moreton, as this little town is known locally, has long claimed the title of Gateway to east Dartmoor, a role in which it was greatly helped by the branch railway from Newton Abbot, which operated between 1866 and 1964. This is the gentler part of Dartmoor, with many woods and plantations, and steep-sided river valleys. Within easy reach are picture-postcard villages such as Widecombe in the Moor, striking natural features like Haytor, and the remarkable Bronze Age stone hut circle at Grimspound.

The best approach to Moreton is by way of the B3212 from the southwest. From this direction you are greeted with splendid views of the little hilltop town surrounded by fields, and with the tower of **St Andrew's Church** piercing the skyline. Built using Dartmoor granite during the early 1400s, the church overlooks the Sentry, or Sanctuary Field, an attractive public park. In the south porch are the tombstones of two French officers who died here as prisoners of war in 1807. At one point during those years of the Napoleonic Wars, no fewer than 379 French officers were living in Moreton, on parole from the military prison at Princetown. One of them, General Rochambeau, must have sorely tested the patience of local people. Whenever news arrived of a French success, he would don his full-dress uniform and parade through the streets.

One of the most interesting buildings in Moreton is the row of thatched **Almshouses** in Cross Street, built in 1637 with a striking arcade supported by sturdy granite columns. The almshouses are now owned by the National Trust but are not open to the public. Just across the road from the almshouses is **Mearsdon Manor Galleries**, the oldest house in Moreton, dating back to the 14th century. The ground floor of the manor is now a very pleasant traditional English tearoom. In total contrast, the remaining rooms contain an astonishing array of colourful, exotic artefacts collected by the owner, Elizabeth Prince, on her trips to the Far East. There are Dartmoor-pony-sized wooden horses, Turkish rugs, Chinese lacquered furniture, finely-carved jade – a veritable treasury of Oriental craftsmanship.

Two miles west of Moretonhampstead, on the B3212, the **Miniature Pony Centre** is home to miniature ponies, donkeys and other horse breeds, as well as pygmy goats, pigs, lambs and many other animals. There are pony rides for children aged nine and under, a daily birds of prey display, indoor and outdoor play areas and a cafeteria.

Plymouth

🏛 Plymouth Hoe	🏛 The Citadel	🏛 Breakwater
🏛 Mayflower Steps	🏛 Eddystone Lighthouse	
🐦 National Marine Aquarium	🏛 Smeaton's Tower	

With around a quarter of a million inhabitants, Plymouth is now the largest centre of population in the southwest peninsula, but its development has been comparatively recent. It wasn't until the late 1100s that the harbour was recognised as having any potential as a military and commercial port. Another 300 years passed before it was established as the main base for the English fleet guarding the western channel

Plymouth Hoe

against a seaborne attack from Spain.

Perhaps the best way of getting to know this historic city is to approach **Plymouth Hoe** on foot from the main shopping area, along the pedestrianised Armada Way. It was on the Hoe on Friday, 19 July 1588, that one of the most iconic moments in English history took place. Commander of the Fleet, and erstwhile pirate, Sir Francis Drake was playing bowls here when he was informed of the approach of the Spanish Armada. With true British phlegm, Sir Francis completed his game before boarding *The Golden Hind* and sailing off to harass the Spanish fleet. A statue of Sir Francis, striking a splendidly belligerent pose and looking proudly to the horizon, stands on the Hoe, which is still an open space, combining the functions of promenade, public park and parade ground.

Just offshore, the striking shape of Drake's Island rises like Alcatraz from the deep swirling waters at the mouth of the River Tamar. In its time, this stark fortified islet has been used as a gunpowder repository (it is said to be riddled with underground tunnels where the powder was stored), a prison, and a youth adventure centre.

Two miles from the Hoe, Plymouth's remarkable **Breakwater** protects the Sound from the destructive effects of the prevailing southwesterly winds. Built by prisoners between 1812 and 1840, this massive mile-long construction required around four million tons of limestone. The surface was finished with enormous dovetailed blocks of stone, and the structure rounded off with a lighthouse at one end.

On a clear day, it's possible to see the

Plymouth Breakwater

famous **Eddystone Lighthouse**, 12 miles out in the Channel. The present lighthouse is the fourth to be built here. The first, made of timber, was swept away in a huge storm in 1703 taking with it the man who had built the lighthouse, the ship-owner Winstanley. In 1759, a much more substantial structure of dovetailed granite blocks was built by John Smeaton. It stood for 120 years and even then it was not the lighthouse but the rocks on which it stood that began to collapse. The lighthouse was dismantled and re-erected on the Hoe where, as **Smeaton's Tower**, it is one of the city's most popular tourist attractions. From the top, there are good views of Millbay Docks, Plymouth's bustling commercial port, which was once busy with transatlantic passenger liners. Today, the docks handle a variety of merchant shipping, including the continental ferry services to Brittany and northern Spain. To the east, the view is dominated by **The Citadel**, a massive fortification built by Charles II, ostensibly as a defence against seaborne attack. Perhaps bearing in mind that Plymouth had resisted a four-year siege by his father's troops during the Civil War, Charles' Citadel has a number of gun ports bearing directly on the city. The Citadel is still a military base, but there are guided tours on Tuesday and Thursday afternoons at 2.30pm.

Adjoining the Citadel is Plymouth's oldest quarter, the Barbican. Now a lively entertainment area filled with restaurants, pubs, and an innovative small theatre, it was once the main trading area for merchants exporting wool and importing wine.

Barbican Waterfront

Close by are the **Mayflower Steps** where the Pilgrim Fathers boarded ship for their historic voyage to Massachusetts. The names of the 102 pilgrims and their professions are listed on a board on nearby Island House. Many other emigrants were to follow in the Pilgrim Fathers' wake, with the result that there are now more than 40 communities named Plymouth scattered across the English-speaking world.

Opposite the Mayflower Steps is the Plymouth Mayflower Visitor and Exhibition Centre where the TIC has an interactive exhibition telling the story of the *Mayflower* and other famous voyages from Plymouth.

A number of interesting old buildings around the Barbican have survived the ravages of time and the terrible pasting the city received during World War Two. Prysten House, behind St Andrew's Church, is a 15th-century priest's house; the Elizabethan House in New Street has a rich display of Elizabethan furniture and furnishings; and the Merchant's House of 1608 in St Andrew's Street, generally regarded as Devon's finest Jacobean building, is crammed full of interesting objects relating to Plymouth's past. A particularly fascinating exhibit in the Merchant's House is the Park Pharmacy, a genuine Victorian pharmacy complete with its 1864 fittings and stocked with such

preparations as Ipecacuanha Wine ("one to two tablespoonfuls as an emetic") and Tincture of Myrrh and Borax, "for the teeth and gums". Another vintage shop is Jacka's Bakery which claims to be the oldest commercial bakery in the country and is reputed to have supplied the *Mayflower* with ship's biscuits.

Also in the Barbican area is the **National Marine Aquarium**, located on the Fish Quay. The Aquarium experience comprises a total of 50 live exhibits including three massive tanks, the largest of which – Britain's deepest tank – holds 2½ million litres of water. More than 4000 creatures from 400 species are displayed in realistic habitats from local shorelines to coral reefs. The tour includes encounters with brilliantly coloured fish, seahorses and even Caribbean sharks. The Explorocean zone focuses on ocean exploration and sustainability through innovative, interactive exhibits.

Locally, the Tamar estuary is known as the Hamoaze (pronounced ham-oys), and it's well worth taking one of the boat trips that leave from the Barbican landing stage. This is certainly the best way to see Devonport Dockyard, while the ferry to Cremyll on the Cornish bank of the Tamar drops off passengers at Mount Edgcumbe. During the season, there's also a ferry to the old

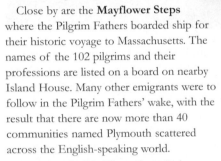

smuggling village of Cawsand. The trip also gives a grand view of the Royal Albert Railway Bridge of 1859, which spans the River Tamar and links Devon and Cornwall. It was the last major construction designed by Isambard Kingdom Brunel.

The blackest date in Plymouth's history is undoubtedly 21 March 1941. On that night, the entire centre of the city was razed to the ground by the combined effects of high-explosive and incendiary bombs. More than 1000 people were killed; another 5000 injured. After the war, the renowned town planner Sir Patrick Abercrombie was commissioned to design a completely new town centre. Much of the rebuilding was carried out in the 1950s, which was not British architecture's golden age, but half a century later the scheme has acquired something of a period charm. Abercrombie's plan included some excellent facilities, like the first-rate Museum and Art Gallery, the Theatre Royal with its two auditoria, the Arts Centre, and the Pavilions complex of concert hall, leisure pool and skating rink.

Plymouth's best-known export has to be Plymouth Gin which has been produced in the city since 1793. At the company's Black Friars Distillery visitors can take a guided tour and learn about the art of making this famous tipple. In the Refectory Bar here, it is said, the Pilgrim Fathers spent their last night before setting sail in the *Mayflower*. There's also a café and a shop.

Around Plymouth

PLYMPTON
4 miles E of Plymouth Plympton *on the B3416*

🏛 Saltram House   🌿 Plym Valley Railway

🏛 Hemerdon House

Plympton boasts one of Devon's grandest mansions, **Saltram House** (National Trust). Built during the reign of George II for the Parker family, this sumptuous house occupies a splendid site overlooking the Plym estuary. In the 1760s, Robert Adam was called in, at enormous expense, to decorate the dining room and 'double cube' saloon, which he accomplished with his usual panache. There are portraits of the Parkers by the locally born artist Sir Joshua Reynolds, and amongst the fine furniture, a magnificent four-poster bed by Thomas Chippendale. Other attractions include the great kitchen with its fascinating assortment of period kitchenware, an orangery in the gardens, and the former chapel, now a gallery displaying the work of West Country artists. The garden is mainly 19th century and contains several follies as well as some beautiful shrubberies and imposing specimen trees. The shop and gallery offer work for sale by contemporary local artists. Saltram House appeared as Norland House in the 1995 feature film of Jane Austen's *Sense and Sensibility* starring Emma Thompson and Hugh Grant.

From the village, the **Plym Valley Railway** (see panel on page 186) carries passengers on a short length of restored track, part of a Great Western Railway branch that ran from Plymouth to Launceston via Tavistock. Travelling in rolling stock redolent of the

Saltram House

Plym Valley Railway

Marsh Mills Station, Coypool Road, Plympton,
Devon PL7 4NW
Tel: 01752 330881
website: www.plymrail.co.uk

The object of the **Plym Valley Railway** is to relay and restore
a short section of the former Great Western Railway branch line from Plymouth to Launceston
via Tavistock and, in particular, the section that runs from Marsh Mills, Plympton to the local
beauty spot of Plym Bridge, a distance of around a mile and a quarter. A series of heritage
steam and diesel locomotives from the 1950s and 1960s operate the services that run on
Sundays and there is also a buffet and souvenir shop at Marsh Mills.

1950s and 1960s, passengers are conveyed to
local beauty spot, Plym Bridge.

To the north of Plympton is a fine
Georgian mansion that is often overlooked,
Hemerdon House, which is still occupied by
the original family. It contains family and other
portraits, silver, books and period furniture.
The house is open on a limited basis.

TURNCHAPEL
1 mile SE of Plymouth off the A379

Enjoying views across Cattewater to
Plymouth, the village of Turnchapel is strung
along the waterside. The village was declared
a Conservation Area in 1977 and, with its
two pubs, church, and waterfront, is a
pleasant place to wander around. From
Mountbatten Peninsula grand vistas open up
over to Plymouth Hoe and Drake's Island. It
was at RAF Mountbatten that Lawrence of
Arabia served as a humble aircraftman for
several years.

WEMBURY
6 miles SE of Plymouth off the A379

Wembury church provides a dramatic
landmark as it stands isolated on the edge of
the cliff, and the coastal path here provides
spectacular views of the Yealm estuary to the

east, and Plymouth Sound to the west. The
path is occasionally closed to walkers when the
firing range is in use, so look out for the red
warning flags. The Great Mew Stone stands a
mile offshore in Wembury Bay. This lonely
islet was inhabited until the 1830s when its last
residents, the part-time smuggler Sam
Wakeham and his family, gave up the unequal
struggle to make a living here. The Mew Stone
is now the home of seabirds.

NEWTON FERRERS
9 miles SE of Plymouth on the B3186

A picturesque fishing village of whitewashed
cottages sloping down to the river, Newton
Ferrers is beloved by artists and is also one of
the south coast's most popular yachting
centres. Part of the village sits beside the River
Yealm (pronounced Yam), the rest alongside a
large creek. When the creek dries out at low
tide, it is possible to walk across to Noss Mayo
on the southern bank. (When the tide is in, a
ferry operates, but only during the season.)

The South Hams

"The fruitfullest part of all Devonshire" said
an old writer of this favoured tract of land
lying south of Dartmoor, bounded by the

River Dart to the east and the River Erme to the west. The climate is exceptionally mild, the soil fertile and the pastures well watered. But the rivers that run off Dartmoor to the sea, slicing north-south through the area, created burdensome barriers to communications until fairly recent times. This comparative isolation kept the region unspoilt, but also kept it poor.

There are few towns of any size – only Totnes, Kingsbridge and Modbury really qualify, along with the picturesque ports of Dartmouth and Salcombe. For the rest, the South Hams is a charmed landscape of drowsy villages linked by narrow country lanes running between high banks on which wildflowers flourish and thanks to an enlightened County Council, the verges were never assaulted with massive quantities of herbicides as in other areas.

The area has been known as the South

Hams, the 'homesteads south of Dartmoor', since Saxon times, but one town at least claims a history stretching much further back in time. We begin our exploration of the South Hams at Totnes, which is the second oldest borough in England. The town sent its first Member of Parliament to London in 1295, and elected the first of its 630-odd Mayors in 1359.

Totnes

- Totnes Castle
- Ramparts Way
- Guildhall
- Orange Race
- St Mary's Church
- Elizabethan House Museum
- Rare Breeds Farm
- Devonshire Collection of Period Costume

This captivating little town claims to have been founded by an ancient Trojan named Brutus in

FINISHING TOUCHES OF TOTNES

Units 2-3 Brutus Centre, off Fore Street,
Totnes, Devon TQ9 5RW
Tel/Fax: 01803 862244
e-mail: shop@decocraft.co.uk
website: www.decocraft.co.uk

Established in 1990 as a home decorating store, over the years **Finishing Touches of Totnes** has diversified into craft materials as well. It is now one of the largest craft shops in the south-west. In 2010 the shop was runner-up in the "Craft Shop of the Year" for the south of England, including London. The range of products on sale in the shop is huge. The shop is a supplier of Personal Impressions items, Tseikiniko, Ranger, Tim Holtz and many other top brands. The shop also stocks Leyland and Nutshell Natural paints, as well as products from Jali MDF, Sandersons, Morris & Co., Galerie Willowprints and, indeed, just about everything for the home decorator. Owner David Dommett is a trained decorator himself so he can help with any technical problems.

David also holds many craft workshops throughout the year for all ages over nine. There are courses in card making, jewellery, scrapbook-making and Fimo. Finishing Touches is conveniently sited close to the Co-op car park just off the Fore Street. Totnes itself is well worth exploring with its many historic buildings, individually owned shops and its Friday and Saturday markets.

1200BC. The grandfather of Aeneas, the hero of Virgil's epic poem *The Aeneid,* Brutus sailed up the River Dart, gazed at the fair prospect around him and decided to found the first town in this new country that would take its name, Britain, from his own. The Brutus Stone, set in the pavement of the main shopping street, Fore Street, commemorates this stirring incident when both the town and a nation were born.

The first recorded evidence of this town, set on a hill above the highest navigable point on the River Dart, doesn't appear until the mid 10th century when King Edgar established a mint at Totnes. The Saxons already had a castle of sorts here, but the impressive remains of **Totnes Castle** are Norman, built between the 1100s and early 1300s. Towering over the town, it is generally reckoned to be the best preserved motte and bailey castle in

Devon. It affords grand views over the town and the Dart valley.

A substantial section of Totnes' medieval town wall has also survived and can be followed along the **Ramparts Way**. The superb East Gate, which straddles the steep main street is part of that wall.

Just a little way down the hill from East Gate is the charming 13th-century **Guildhall**, a remarkable little building with a granite colonnade that was originally part of a Benedictine priory. It houses both the Council Chamber (which is still in use) and the underground Town Gaol (which is not). The cells can be visited, as can the elegant Council Chamber with its plaster frieze and the table where Oliver Cromwell sat in 1646.

Another magnificent Elizabethan building, 16 High Street, was built in 1585 for Nicholas Ball who had made his fortune from the local

---

ALISON WARE

63 Fore Street, Totnes, Devon TQ9 5NJ
Tel: 01803 849222
e-mail: alisonware@btconnect.com
website: www.alisonware.co.uk

Opened in May 2005, **Alison Ware** occupies a charming 17th Century listed building with low ceilings, old beams, uneven floors, and lots of nooks and crannies. In this delightful setting, owner Alison has put together a fascinating collection of items that will enhance any interior. They include fabrics from leading designers such as Biggie Best, Vanessa Arbuthnott, Elanbach, Clarke & Clarke and James Hare Silk plus a measuring, making-up and fitting service for curtains, blinds and soft furnishings. Whilst not interior designers, they are always happy to help you put designs and schemes together. There is painted furniture from Sylvawood and china from Burleigh, both UK made. Upstairs, in a bedroom setting, there is a colourful array of quilts, throws, cushions, bed linen, lamps and French-influenced furniture and mirrors. Alison Ware stocks a stunning range of fake flowers which Alison, as a former florist, is always happy to arrange, including in customers' own vases.

Totnes is one of Devon's most appealing small towns with a main shopping street lined with historic buildings and fascinating privately-owned shops, all leading to the well-preserved Norman castle.

🏨 historic building 🏛 museum and heritage 🏚 historic site ⚘ scenic attraction 🌱 flora and fauna

CHINA BLUE

Station Road, Totnes, Devon TQ9 5JR
Tel: 01803 860905 (shop),
*   01803 860906 (café),*
*   01803 860908 (ceramic studio)*
e-mail: shop@china-blue.co.uk
website: www.china-blue.co.uk

China Blue is hard to describe and equally hard to resist. Based in the town of Totnes that is also noted for its quirky individuality, China Blue is a combination of many different things under one roof. If you're in the mood for shopping then the Homeware Store prides itself on offering as wide a range of home goods as any department store. They stock many exclusive brands and have been a 'shopping heaven' since 1997, as well as offering interior design advice for the home from their experienced team. The store is full of creative ideas for bedroom and bathroom, kitchen and living room, and outside in the garden too.

If you're hungry or just want a lovely place to sit down with a cup of coffee, the China Blue Café has a delightful conservatory dining room, and outdoor seating too. You can enjoy the complimentary newspapers over a cappuccino, a freshly-squeezed orange juice or a glass of wine, or perhaps have something more substantial. The all-day menu includes home-made cakes, wicked pastries, healthy salads, baked potatoes, baguettes and paninis, or a bowl of soup with a choice from the gourmet breads all baked on the premises.

Another indulgence available at China Blue is to treat yourself at the Blue Hair Studio. This cutting-edge hairdressing and design salon offers styling for weddings and other special occasions, or will suggest a hairstyle make-over, for men and for women. They also use and sell the top US brand, Redken.

As if all this wasn't enough, China Blue also has its fabulous Ceramic Studio, the biggest of its kind in south-west England. You can go in and put your creativity to the test by learning how to make original ceramic items, perhaps as gifts to take home as an unusual holiday souvenir. Advice is on hand to help you make plates, pots, mugs and more, with a range of colours, brushes and designs to choose from. If you're feeling really brave you can try one of the studio's state-of-the-art potter's wheels, while children can have their own fun and make robots, castles, or perhaps a little Devon duck.

You can also join in one of the classes teaching you how to create textiles and make your own jewellery, or visit the glass-blowing workshop and gallery too. In fact a visit to China Blue is almost a day out by itself.

stories and anecdotes   famous people   art and craft   entertainment and sport   walks

pilchard fishery. When he died, his wife Anne married Sir Thomas Bodley and it was the profit from pilchards that funded the world-famous Bodleian Library at Oxford University.

The town's Elizabethan heritage is celebrated on Elizabethan Tuesday in the summer. This is when the people of Totnes array themselves in crisp, white ruffs and velvet gowns for a charity market in the Civic Square. In August, the Elizabethan Society organises the **Orange Race**, which commemorates a visit to the town by Sir Francis Drake during which he presented "a fair red orange" to a small boy in the street. Today, contestants chase their oranges down the hill.

The parish church of Totnes is **St Mary's**. It was entirely rebuilt in the 15th century when the town's cloth industry was booming – at that time Totnes was second in importance only to Exeter. The church's most glorious possession is a rood screen delicately carved in stone from the quarry at Beer.

Close by at 70 Fore Street is the **Elizabethan House Museum**, housed in an attractive half-timbered Elizabethan building whose upper floors overhang the street. One of the fascinating exhibits here honours a distinguished son of Totnes, Charles Babbage (1791-1871) whose Analytical Machine is universally acknowledged as the forerunner of the electronic computer. The museum display records his doomed struggle to perfect such a calculator using only mechanical parts.

A little further up the hill, in High Street, the Butterwalk and Poultrywalk are two ancient covered shopping arcades whose upper storeys rest on pillars of granite, timber or cast iron.

River Dart, Totnes

In recent years, Totnes has earned the title of Natural Health Capital of the West Country. The first Natural Health Centre was established here in 1989. Visitors will find specialist shops offering natural medicines, organic food, aromatherapy, relaxation tapes and books on spiritual healing. A variety of craft and antique shops all add to the town's allure for shopaholics.

For centuries, Totnes was a busy river port and down by Totnes Bridge, an elegant stone structure of 1828, the quay was lined with warehouses, some of which have survived and been converted into highly desirable flats. Nearby, on the Plains, stands a granite obelisk to the famous explorer William Wills, a native of the town who perished from starvation when attempting to re-cross the Australian desert with Robert Burke in 1861.

One excursion from Totnes not to be missed is the breathtakingly beautiful river trip to Dartmouth, 12 miles downstream. This stretch of the river has been called the English Rhine and the comparison is no exaggeration. The river here is well away from roads, making it an ideal location for seeing wading-birds, herons, cormorants and even seals. During the summer, there are frequent departures from

---

🏠 historic building   🏛 museum and heritage   🏛 historic site   🐾 scenic attraction   🌿 flora and fauna

the quay near the bridge.

Another memorable journey is by steam train along the seven-mile stretch of the South Devon Railway, also known as the Primrose Line, which runs through the glorious scenery of the Dart Valley to Buckfastleigh. Most of the locomotives and carriages are genuine Great Western Railway stock and are painted in the GWR's famous chocolate and cream livery.

Next door to the railway, the **Rare Breeds Farm** includes a hedgehog rescue centre, some spectacular owls, red squirrels, goats, sheep, birds and much more. It also has a Garden Café with views of working steam trains and Totnes Castle.

Even that list of attractions isn't exhaustive. The **Devonshire Collection of Period Costume** is housed in one of the town's most interesting 16th-century houses and has a different display each year.

Around Totnes

BERRY POMEROY
2 miles E of Totnes off the A385 or A381

🏚 Berry Pomeroy Castle

For the past 1000 years this small village has been owned by just two families. The de la

Berry Pomeroy Castle

Pomerais dynasty arrived with William the Conqueror and held the land for almost 500 years. In the early 1300s they built **Berry Pomeroy Castle** in a superb position on a wooded promontory above Gatcombe Brook. Substantial remains of the castle still stand, including sections of the curtain wall and the 14th-century gatehouse. In 1548 the Pomeroys, as they were now known, sold the estate to Sir Edward Seymour whose sister, Jane, had been the third wife of Henry VIII. Sir Edward built a three-storey Tudor mansion within the medieval fortifications but this too is now a shell. Although the castle is still owned by Sir Edward's descendant, the Duke of Somerset, it is administered by English Heritage and open to the public daily during the season. In the village itself, St Mary's Church contains some interesting monuments to the Pomeroys and Seymours, as well as an outstanding rood screen.

ASHPRINGTON
2 miles SE of Totnes off the A381

Set in a stunning location above the River Dart, Sharpham Vineyard and Cheese Dairy offers two gastronomic experiences. Visitors can sample the international award-winning red and white wines, and watch the dairy cheese being made. The entrance fee includes complimentary tastings. An attractive way of visiting the vineyard is by taking one of the ferry boats along the River Dart, which will stop at Sharpham on request.

STOKE GABRIEL
5 miles SE of Totnes off the A385

A charming village of narrow lanes and alleys, Stoke Gabriel stands on a hillside above a tidal spur of the River Dart. A weir was built across the neck of the creek in Edwardian times and this traps the

🎭 stories and anecdotes 🐦 famous people 🎨 art and craft 🎟 entertainment and sport 🚶 walks

water at low tide, giving the village a pleasant lakeside atmosphere. The part 13th-century church of St Gabriel has a restored late-medieval pulpit and a truncated screen with some good wainscot paintings. In the churchyard are the rather forlorn remains of an oak tree reputed to be more than 1500 years old. To the west of the village, a lane leads to the riverside hamlet of Duncannon where, by general consent, the River Dart is at its most lovely.

Greenway, Dittisham

DITTISHAM
11 miles SE of Totnes off the A3122

🏛 Church of St George   🏛 Greenway

🌿 Barn Gallery

The best way to reach the pretty yachting village of Dittisham is by passenger ferry from Dartmouth. This village of atmospheric cottages, whose narrow streets drop down to the River Dart, is in an area renowned for its fruit farming; Dittisham plums were especially famous and are still grown on a small scale.

Dittisham's **Church of St George** has many interesting features, including the Royal Coat of Arms of Charles II hanging over a door (granted at the time of the Restoration in gratitude to the townspeople for their loyalty to the Royalist cause), a beautiful 15th-century carved stone wine glass pulpit, and windows in the north aisle inserted in about 1846 under the direction of Augustus Pugin.

The major attraction here is **Greenway** (National Trust), the home of Dame Agatha Christie for the last 30 years of her life. The house has a 1950s ambience and contains many of the family's collections, including archaeology, Tunbridgeware, silver, botanical china and books. Outside there's a large and romantic woodland garden with a restored

vinery, wild edges and rare plantings, which drift down the steep hillside towards the Dart estuary. Also within the grounds is the **Barn Gallery**, which mounts exhibitions of contemporary art by local artists. Parking at Greenway is limited and must be pre-booked, but there are ferries from Dartmouth, Torquay and Brixham.

DARTMOUTH
14 miles SE of Totnes on the A3122

🏛 Dartmouth Castle   🏛 Church of St Saviour's

🏛 Custom House   🏛 Dartmouth Museum

🏛 Britannia Royal Naval College

🌿 Dartmouth Regatta   🏛 Railway Station

For centuries, this entrancing little town clinging to the sides of a precipitous hill was one of England's principal ports. Millions of casks of French and Spanish wine have been offloaded onto its narrow quays. During the 1100s Crusaders on both the Second and Third Crusades mustered here, and from here they set sail. In its sheltered harbour, Elizabeth's men o'war lay in wait to pick off the stragglers from the Spanish Armada. In 1620, the *Mayflower* put in here for a few days for repairs before hoisting sail on 20 August for Plymouth and then on to the New World where the pilgrims arrived three months later. The quay from which they embarked later became the major location for the BBC TV series, *The Onedin Line,* and was also seen in the feature film *Sense and Sensibility* starring Emma Thompson and Hugh Grant.

Geoffrey Chaucer visited the town in 1373 in his capacity as Inspector of Customs and is believed to have modelled the Schipman of Dertemouthe in his *Canterbury Tales* on the character of the then Mayor of Dartmouth, John Hawley. Hawley was an enterprising merchant and seafarer who was also responsible for building the first **Dartmouth Castle** (English Heritage). Dramatically sited, it guards the entrance to the Dart estuary and was one of the first castles specifically designed to make effective use of artillery. In case the castle should prove to be an inadequate deterrent, in times of danger a heavy chain was strung across the harbour to Kingswear Castle on the opposite bank. (Kingswear Castle is now owned by the Landmark Trust and available for holiday rentals.)

There's a striking monumental brass to John Hawley and his two wives in the **Church of St Saviour's** a part 14th-century building against whose wall ships used to tie up before the New Quay was constructed in the late 1500s. Nearby is the **Custom House**, a handsome building of 1739, which has some fine internal plasterwork ceilings.

Also worth seeking out is The Butterwalk, a delightful timber-framed arcade dating from 1640 in which the **Dartmouth Museum** occupies the ground floor. The museum has a fine collection of model ships, ships in bottles and a nostalgic selection of vintage photographs of the town. In one of the galleries King Charles II held court while stormbound in Dartmouth in 1671. Some of the unique features of this magnificent room are the original wood panelling and the superb plaster ceiling.

Two other buildings in Dartmouth should be mentioned. One is the **Railway Station**, possibly the only one in the world that has never seen a train. It was built by the Great Western Railway as the terminus of their line from Torbay and passengers were ferried across to Kingswear where the railway actually ended. The station is now a restaurant. The other building of note is the **Britannia Royal Naval College** (guided tours during the season). This sprawling red and white building, built between 1899 and 1905, dominates the northern part of the town as you leave by the A379 towards Kingsbridge.

Those interested in industrial heritage will want to visit the Engine House, next door to the tourist office off Duke Street. Here you can see one of local man Thomas Newcomen's original engines at work.

Near the eastern boundary of the South Hams flows the enchanting River Dart, surely one of the loveliest of English rivers. Rising in

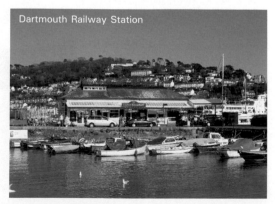
Dartmouth Railway Station

the great blanket bog of the moor, the Dart flows for 46 miles and together with its tributaries drains the greater part of Dartmoor. Queen Victoria called the Dart the English Rhine, perhaps thinking of the twin castles of Dartmouth and Kingswear that guard its estuary. It was her predecessor, Alfred the Great, who developed Dartmouth as a strategic base and the town's long connection with the senior service is reflected in the presence here of the Royal Naval College. The spectacular harbour is still busy with naval vessels, pleasure boats and ferries, and particularly colourful during the June Carnival and the **Dartmouth Regatta** in late August.

The most picturesque approach to the town is to drive to Kingswear and then take one of the two car ferries for the 10-minute trip across the river. Parking space in Dartmouth is severely restricted and it is strongly recommended that you make use of the Park & Ride facility located just outside the town on the A3122.

STOKE FLEMING
16 miles SE of Totnes on the A379

Blackpool Sands

Stoke Fleming is one of the most delightful villages in the South Hams, perched high on the cliffs 300 feet above Start Bay and with a prominent church that has served generations of mariners as a reassuring landmark. Inside is a brass of 1351, which is reckoned to be one of the oldest in Devon and another that commemorates the great-grandfather of the celebrated engineer, Thomas Newcomen. Less than a mile from the village are the misleadingly-named **Blackpool Sands**, a broad crescent of sandy beach overhung by

Monterey pines, which boasts a Blue Flag Award for its safe and healthy bathing.

HARBERTON
2 miles SW of Totnes off the A2381

St Andrew's Church

This delightful village is regarded as absolutely typical of the South Hams, a place where those two traditional centres of English village life, church and inn, sit comfortably almost side by side. **St Andrew's Church**, which is famous for its amazing, fantastically-carved, 15th-century altar screen, has been closely linked to the village hostelry for almost 900 years. Church House Inn, as the name suggests, was originally built to house the masons working on the church around AD1100. Harberton was then a major centre for church administration and a much more important place than Totnes. The inn became the Chantry House for the monks, the civil servants of their time, and what is now the bar comprised their Great Hall, chapel and workshop where they would congregate for a glass of wine.

In 1327, the Abbot handed the property over to the poor of the parish, but it was not until 1950 that it passed out of the Church's hands

Blackpool Sands

altogether. During restoration work ancient plaster was removed to reveal massive beams of fluted mellow oak and a fine medieval screen. Other treasures discovered then, and still in place, were a Tudor window frame and a latticed window containing priceless panes of 13th-century handmade glass. The inn's ecclesiastical connections are enhanced even more by the old pews from redundant churches that provide some of the seating.

DARTINGTON
2 miles NW of Totnes on the A384

🏠 Dartington Hall   🏠 High Cross House

When Leonard and Dorothy Elmhirst bought **Dartington Hall** and its estate in 1925, the superb 14th century Great Hall had stood roofless for more than a century. The buildings surrounding the two large quadrangles laid out in the 1390s by John Holand, Earl of Exeter, were being used as stables, cow houses and hay lofts. The Elmhirsts were idealists and since Dorothy (née Whitney) was one of the richest American women of her time, they possessed the resources to put their ideals into practice. They restored the Hall, re-opened it as a progressive school, and set about reviving the local rural economy in line with the ideology of the Indian philosopher, Rabindranath Tagore. The Elmhirsts were closely involved in the creation of the famed Dartington Glass. Sadly, long after their deaths, their school closed in 1995 as a consequence of financial problems and a pornography scandal. But the headmaster's residence, **High Cross House**, a classic Modernist building of the early 1930s has now been converted into an art gallery. Visitors are welcome here and also to wander around the 26-acre gardens, dotted with sculptures,

surrounding the Hall. There is no charge for entry to the quadrangle and Great Hall, but donations for its upkeep are welcomed. Guided tours are available by appointment.

Dartington Hall hosts more than 100 music performances each year during its International Summer School, a season that attracts musicians and artistes of the highest calibre from all over the world. All year round, even more visitors are attracted to the Dartington Cider Press Centre, a huge gallery on the edge of the estate, which displays a vast range of craft products – anything from a delicate handmade Christmas or birthday card to a beautifully modelled item of pottery.

Kingsbridge

🏛 Cookworthy Museum of Rural Life

The broad body of water to the south of Kingsbridge is officially known as Kingsbridge Estuary, although strictly speaking it is not an estuary at all – no river runs into it – but a ria, or drowned valley. Whatever the correct name, it provides an attractive setting for this busy little town, an agreeable spot in which to spend an hour or two strolling along the quayside or through the narrow alleys off Fore Street bearing such graphic names as Squeezebelly Lane.

In Fore Street is St Edmund's parish church, mostly 13th century, and well known for the rather cynical verse inscribed on the gravestone of Roger Phillips who died in 1798:

Here lie I at the chancel door
Here lie I because I'm poor
The further in the more you pay
Here lie I as warm as they.

Nearby is The Shambles, an Elizabethan market arcade whose late 18th-century upper

HEALTHWISE HEALTH AND WHOLEFOODS

81 Fore Street, Kingsbridge, Devon TQ7 1AB
Tel: 01548 857707
website: www.healthwisekingsbridge.com

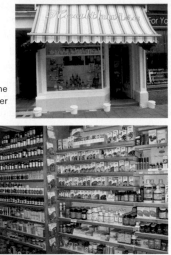

Healthwise is a health shop which occupies a Grade II listed building in the main shopping street of Kingsbridge. Behind the yellow-framed windows and jolly green and white blind, owner Irene Jeeninga, has stocked the shelves with a wide range of health-oriented products, including supplements, vitamins, minerals, homeopathic and herbal remedies, natural make-up, skin and body care items, magnetic bracelets, toiletries and eco-friendly household cleaning materials. The shop also sells a range of wholefoods – many of them organic – from local honey, apple juice to vegetarian pies and burgers.

Irene has a very broad product knowledge and long experience in her field, and makes a point of keeping up to date with new product launches. Service from Irene and her charming staff is invariably friendly and helpful, and they are always happy to track down a particular product that's not in stock. Brands normally to be found in the shop include A Vogel herbal remedies, vitamins from Viridian, Solgar, Bio. Health and FSC, INIKA mineral cosmetics from Australia and Ecover and Ecoleaf cleaning materials. Healthwise is open Monday to Saturday 9 to 5 (to 5.30 in summer).

🏚 historic building 🏛 museum and heritage 🏛 historic site 🌳 scenic attraction 🐑 flora and fauna

floor is supported on six sturdy granite pillars. Next door, the town hall hosts various markets during the season - a flea market on Monday, local produce on Wednesdays, and crafts on Fridays.

Above the church, the former Kingsbridge Grammar School, founded in 1670, now houses the **Cookworthy Museum of Rural Life**, named after William Cookworthy who was born at Kingsbridge in 1705. Working as an apothecary at Plymouth, William encountered traders from the Far East who had brought back porcelain from China. English pottery makers despaired of ever producing such delicate cups and plates, but Cookworthy identified the basic ingredient of porcelain as kaolin, huge deposits of which lay in the hills just north of Plymouth. Ever since then, the more common name for kaolin has been China clay.

During the season, a popular excursion from Kingsbridge is the river cruise to Salcombe. Coastal cruises and private charter boats are also available.

Around Kingsbridge

TORCROSS
7 miles E of Kingsbridge on the A379

Normally, the four-mile stretch of sand and shingle beach near Torcross is too extensive to ever become crowded, but back in 1943 things were very different. The beach had been selected by the Allied Commanders for a 'dress rehearsal' of the impending D-Day invasion of Normandy. The area was swarming with troops, and because live ammunition was being used in the training exercise, all the

local people were evacuated, more than 3000 of them from seven coastal villages.

Those D-Day preparations are recalled at Torcross where a Sherman tank recovered from the sea in 1984 is on display in the car park. While the exercises were in progress, an enemy E-boat attacked the landing forces and more than 600 Allied servicemen lost their lives. Beside the tank are memorial tablets to the men who died during this little-publicised military tragedy, and to the many who later perished on the Normandy beaches.

SLAPTON
8 miles E of Kingsbridge off the A379

🐦 Slapton Ley Field Study Centre

To the south of Slapton, the A379 runs for 2½ miles along the top of a remarkable sand and shingle bank, which divides the salt water of Start Bay from the fresh water of Slapton Ley, the largest natural lake in Devon. Continually replenished by three small rivers, this shallow body of water is a designated Nature Reserve and home to large numbers of freshwater fish, insects, water-loving plants and native and migrating birds. The **Slapton Ley Field Study Centre**, located in Slapton village, has leaflets detailing the delightful

Slapton Ley

🎭 stories and anecdotes 🐦 famous people 🎨 art and craft 🎫 entertainment and sport 🚶 walks

🏠 historic building 🏛 museum and heritage 🏛 historic site 🍃 scenic attraction 🌿 flora and fauna

circular nature trails through this fascinating Site of Special Scientific Interest.

An obelisk on the beach near Slapton, presented in 1954 by the US Army authorities to the people of the South Hams, commemorates the period in 1943 when the beach was used by Allied troops as a 'dress rehearsal' for the D-Day landings. The story is well told in Leslie Thomas's novel, *The Magic Army*.

CHIVELSTONE
7 miles SE of Kingsbridge off the A379

Even in Devon it would be hard to find anywhere farther away from the madding crowd than Chivelstone, an unassuming village hidden away in a maze of country lanes in the extreme southwest of the county and well worth seeking out. It's the tranquil rural surroundings that make Chivelstone so appealing, but the village also has a fine parish church, the only one in England dedicated to the 4th-century pope, St Sylvester. Historically, Sylvester is a misty figure, but an old tradition claims that his saintly ministrations cured the Roman emperor, Constantine, of leprosy. Chivelstone church was built at a time (the 15th century) when this disfiguring disease was still common in England; it seems likely the parishioners hoped that by dedicating their church to him, St Sylvester would protect them from the ravages of a deeply feared illness, which, once contracted, imposed total social exclusion on its innocent victims.

BEESANDS
8 miles SE of Kingsbridge off the A379

Beesands lies little more than a mile due south of Torcross and can easily be reached on foot along the coast path. By car, a four mile detour is required. If you don't want to walk, it's well worth negotiating the narrow Devon lanes to reach this tiny hamlet, just a single row of old cottages lining the foreshore of Start Bay. Less than 100 years ago, Beesands was a busy little fishing village. There are photographs from the 1920s showing fishermen who have drawn their boats laden with lobster, crab and mullet up the beach virtually to their cottage doors. Sadly, the fishing fleet is no longer operating, although some independent fishermen still land their catch at the Strand, but the mile-long shingle beach is as appealing as ever.

HALLSANDS
11 miles SE of Kingsbridge off the A379

South of Beesands, the only way to follow the coastline is by a well-trodden footpath. It's part of the South West Coast Path and the route takes you through the ruined village of Hallsands, which was almost completely demolished by a violent storm in January 1917. Another mile or so further brings you to the lighthouse at Start Point, built in 1836, and open for guided tours from Monday to

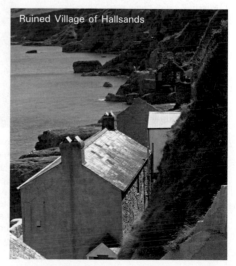
Ruined Village of Hallsands

VICTORIA INN

Fore Street, Salcombe, Devon TQ8 8BU
Tel: 01548 842604
e-mail: info@victoriainn-salcombe.co.uk
website: www.victoriainn-salcombe.co.uk

Traditional in all the best ways, the **Victoria Inn** is a gem set in the centre of picturesque Salcombe. Mine hosts, Liz and Tim Hore, are hugely proud of their reputation for great food. They aim to source the best local ingredients and keep the preparation and cooking of them relatively simple, to produce bags of flavour and taste on the plate. There's nothing too frilly or fancy – just good honest wholesome cooking! Executive chef James Chapman works hard with his team to make sure that the menu reflects the fact the inn is close to the sea and the countryside – so you'll find great fish dishes and fabulous cuts of meat. Vegetarians are not forgotten and there's a great, regularly changing 'Specials Board' with exciting meat, game, poultry, fish and shellfish creations. Cheeses are generally West Country in origin and all of our desserts are homemade. The Victoria's Sunday lunches are the best in the South Hams area and regularly offer a choice of three meats, plenty of fabulous crisp 'roasties', with home made Yorkshire puds, roast parsnips, plenty of fresh vegetables, and a gravy you'll want the recipe for. To accompany your meal, there are some fantastic Cask Marque ales, wines from around the world and Champagne by the glass.

The inn boasts something that no other pub in Salcombe has - a massive garden. It has two sun terraces, a huge grassy area for al fresco dining, a well-equipped children's play area and chickens. Children and dogs are most welcome at the Victoria, with a lollipop awaiting the best behaved children, whilst dogs have their own treat tin behind the bar - (and maybe a little titbit from the kitchen if especially good)!

Set in the beautiful pub garden is the newly opened 'Hobbit House' (so called because of its unique low front door). The Hobbit House offers two rooms; one double and one twin – both en suite with shower rooms. Comfortable beds, tea and coffee making facilities, television with CD and DVD player, heated towel rails, fluffy towels and hairdryers will ensure everything you need is to hand. Breakfasts are included in the price, and served at Captain Morgan's, a famous Salcombe institution for breakfasts literally just across the road from the Victoria Inn – and incidentally – owned by Tim & Liz as well.

Saturday during daylight hours. And if you want to be able to boast that you once stood at the most southerly point in Devon, continue along the Coast Path for about five miles to Prawle Point, an ancient lookout site where today there is a Coastguard Station.

MALBOROUGH
5 miles S of Kingsbridge on the A381

For anyone travelling this corner of the South Hams, the lofty spire of Malborough's 15th-century church is a recurrent landmark. It's a broach spire, rising straight out of the low tower. Inside, the church is wonderfully light, so much so that the splendid arcades built in Beer stone seem to glow.

SALCOMBE
7 miles S of Kingsbridge, on the A381

🌿 Overbecks Museum and Garden

🏛 Salcombe Maritime and Local History Museum

Standing at the mouth of the Kingsbridge 'estuary', the captivating town of Salcombe enjoys one of the most beautiful natural settings in the country. Sheltered from the prevailing westerly winds by steep hills, it also basks in one of the mildest micro-climates in England. In the terraced gardens rising from the water's edge, it's not unusual to see mimosa, palms, and even orange and lemon trees bearing fruit. The peaceful gardens at **Overbecks Museum and Garden** (National Trust), overlooking Salcombe Bar, have an almost Mediterranean character. Otto Overbeck, who lived in the charming Edwardian house here between 1918 and

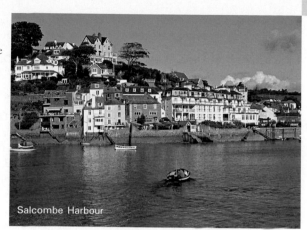
Salcombe Harbour

1937, amassed a wide-ranging collection that includes late 19th-century photographs of the area, local shipbuilding tools, model boats, toys and much more.

Like other small South Devon ports, Salcombe developed its own special area of trading. While Dartmouth specialised in French and Spanish wine, at Salcombe high-sailed clippers arrived carrying the first fruits of the pineapple harvest from the West Indies, and oranges from the Azores. That traffic has ceased, but pleasure craft throng the harbour and a small fishing fleet still operates from Batson Creek, a picturesque location where the fish quay is piled high with lobster creels. The town's seafaring history is interestingly evoked in the **Salcombe Maritime and Local History Museum** on Market Street. A unique gallery here is devoted to the work of Victorian 'pier head painters'.

The coastline to the south and west of Salcombe, some of the most magnificent in Britain, is now largely owned by the National Trust. Great slanting slabs of gneiss and schist tower above the sea, making the clifftop walk here both literally and metaphorically breathtaking.

HOPE COVE
6 miles SW of Kingsbridge off the A381

There are two Hopes here: Outer Hope, which is more modern and so gets less attention, and Inner Hope, which must be one of the most photographed villages in the country. A picturesque huddle of thatched cottages around a tiny cobbled square, Inner Hope once thrived on pilchard fishing, but nowadays only a few fishermen still operate from here, bringing in small catches of lobster and crab.

BANTHAM
6 miles SW of Kingsbridge off the A379

One mile to the north of Thurlestone (as the crow flies) is another popular sandy beach, at Bantham. This small village has a long history, since it was a centre of early tin trading between the ancient Britons and the Gauls. By the 8th century, Anglo-Saxons were well-established here, farming the fertile soil. The sea also provided a major source of income in the form of pilchard fishing. Bantham continued to be a busy little port until the early 1900s, with sailing barges bringing coal and building stone for the surrounding area.

THURLESTONE
5 miles W of Kingsbridge off the A381

One of the most attractive coastal villages, with many thatched and white-washed cottages, Thurlestone can boast not just one, but two beaches, separated by a headland. Both beaches are recommended, especially the one to the south with its view of the pierced, or 'thyrled', stone, the offshore rock from which the settlement gets its name and which was specifically mentioned in a charter of AD846. The village itself stands on a long, flat-topped ridge above the beaches and is an attractive mixture of flower-decked cottages, old farm buildings and long-established shops and inns.

BIGBURY ON SEA
10 miles W of Kingsbridge on the B3392

  🝔 Burgh Island

This popular family resort has a stretch of National Trust coastline and extensive sands. The most interesting attraction here though is **Burgh Island**, which is actually only a part-time island. When the tide is out, it is possible to walk across the sandbar linking it to the mainland. At other times, visitors reach the island by a unique sea tractor, specifically designed for this crossing. It can operate in seven feet of water, in all but the roughest conditions, and it's well worth timing your visit to enjoy this novel experience.

The whole of the 28-acre island, complete with its 14th-century Pilchard Inn, was bought in 1929 by the eccentric millionaire Archibald Nettlefold. He built an extravagant art deco hotel, which attracted such visitors as Noel Coward, the Duke of Windsor and Mrs Wallis Simpson, and Agatha Christie. The Queen of

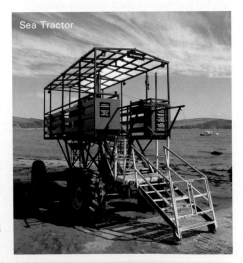
Sea Tractor

Crime used the island as the setting for two of her novels, *Ten Little Niggers,* (later renamed *And Then There Were None*), and *Evil Under the Sun*. A feature film of the latter was filmed on the island in 2001. The hotel, which has been described as "a white art deco cruise liner beached on dry land" is still in operation, its wonderful 1930s decor meticulously renovated in the 1990s.

AVETON GIFFORD
5 miles NW of Kingsbridge on the A379

🐦 Robert Macey

Pronounced Awton Jiffard, this pleasant small village, little more than one main street, had one of the oldest churches in Devon until it was almost completely destroyed by a German bomb in 1943. The modern replacement is surprisingly satisfying. The village's most famous son was born here in 1790, the son of a mason. After learning his father's trade, **Robert Macey** also studied as an architect. He then walked all the way to London where he successfully established himself and was responsible for designing many hospitals, factories, churches and theatres, of which the most notable were the Adelphi and the Haymarket.

At the southern end of the village, just before the three quarter-mile long medieval causeway, a lane on the right is signposted to Bigbury. This very narrow road runs right alongside the River Avon and is very beautiful, but be warned – the river is tidal here and when the tide is in the two fords along the way are impassable.

LODDISWELL
3 miles NW of Kingsbridge off the A379

🐦 Judhel of Totnes   🌱 Loddiswell Vineyard

After the Norman Conquest, Loddiswell became part of the 40,000 acre estate of **Judhel of Totnes**, a man with an apparently insatiable appetite for salmon. Instead of rent, he stipulated that his tenants should provide him with a certain number of the noble fish: Loddiswell's contribution was set at 30 salmon a year.

The benign climate of South Devon has encouraged several viticulturists to plant vineyards in the area. The first vines at **Loddiswell Vineyard** were planted in 1977 and since then its wines have been laden with awards from fellow wine-makers and consumer bodies. Visitors are welcome, Monday to Saturday.

MODBURY
9 miles NW of Kingsbridge on the A379

🏛 St George's Church   🐦 Rebecca Hoskins

Modbury's main street climbs steeply up the hillside, its pavement raised above street level and stepped. The many Georgian buildings give this little town an air of quiet elegance and the numerous antique, craft and specialist shops add to its interest. **St George's Church** contains some impressive, if damaged, effigies of the Prideaux and Champernowne families; the White Hart and Assembly Rooms are 18th-century, the Exeter Inn even older. Once a coaching inn, this inviting old pub dates back to the 1500s. Modbury's Fair Week in early May is a jolly affair, though perhaps not as riotous as it was in the 19th century when it lasted for nine days and the town's 10 inns stayed open from morning to night.

In May 2006, this quiet little town sparked off a green campaign that attracted national attention. It was master-minded by **Rebecca Hoskins**, a young Modbury-born-and-raised wildlife camerawoman who was appalled by the plastic bag pollution she found in remote parts of the Pacific Ocean. On her return to Devon she found the sea equally infested. She called a meeting of all 43 Modbury shopowners, showed them her film, and convinced them to stop handing out plastic bags to customers. The town is still a plastic-bag-free area and many other shops across the country have followed Modbury's lead.

Palm Trees, Torbay

Torbay

The most extensive conurbation in Devon, Torbay includes the three major towns of Torquay, Paignton and Brixham, strung around the deep indentation of Tor Bay. The excellent beaches and leisure facilities here have made it the county's busiest resort area with a host of indoor and outdoor attractions on offer. Torquay is the more sophisticated of the three, with elegant gardens, excellent shops and a varied nightlife. Paignton prides itself as being "unbeatable for family fun", and Brixham is a completely enchanting fishing town where life revolves around its busy harbour.

If you think Torbay's claim to be The English Riviera is a mite presumptuous, just take a look at all those palm trees. You see them everywhere here: not just in public parks and expensively maintained hotel gardens, but also giving a Mediterranean character to town house gardens, and even growing wild. They have become a symbol of the area's identity, blazoned on tourism leaflets, brochures, T-shirts, shop fronts, key-rings and hats.

The first specimen palm trees arrived in Britain in the 1820s and it was soon discovered that this sub-tropical species took kindly to the genial climate of South Devon. Today, there are literally thousands of them raising their spiky tufted heads above the more familiar foliage of English gardens. To the uninitiated, one palm tree may look much like another, but experts will point out that although the most common variety growing here is Cordyline Australis (imported from New Zealand), there are also Mediterranean Fan Palms, Trachycarpus Fortunei from the Chusan Islands in the East China Sea, and Date Palms from the Canary Islands. The oldest palm tree on record in the area is now over 80 years old and more than 40 feet high.

The Mediterranean similarities don't end there. Torquay, like Rome, is set on seven hills and the red-tiled roofs of its Italianate villas, set amongst dark green trees, would look equally at home in some Adriatic resort. The resemblance is so close that in one film in the Roger Moore TV series, *The Saint,* a budget-conscious producer made Torquay double for Monte Carlo.

Torquay

🐦 Edward VII 🏛 Torre Abbey

🐦 Agatha Christie 🏛 Torquay Museum

🏛 Kents Cavern 🏛 Bygones 🐦 Living Coasts

🏛 Cockington Village

🌿 Babbacombe Model Village

In Victorian times, Torquay liked to be known as The English Naples, a genteel resort of shimmering white villas set amongst dark green trees and spread, like Rome, across seven hills. It was indisputably the West of England's premier resort with imposing hotels like the Imperial and the Grand catering for "people of condition" from across Europe. At one time, the town could boast more royal visitors to the square mile than any other resort in the world. **Edward VII** came here on the royal yacht *Britannia* and anchored in the bay. Each evening he would be discreetly ferried across to a bay beneath the Imperial Hotel and then conducted to the first floor suite where his mistress, Lily Langtry, was waiting.

The town's oldest building is **Torre Abbey**, founded in 1195 but largely remodelled as a Georgian mansion by the Cary family between 1700 and 1750. Within its grounds stand the abbey ruins and the **Spanish Barn**, a medieval tithe barn so named because 397 prisoners

from the Spanish Armada were detained here in 1588. Torre Abbey was sold to Torbay Council in 1930 and, together with its extensive gardens, opened to the public until 2004 when the building was closed for major refurbishment. It re-opened in the summer of 2008 and now offers an impressive art collection, one of the largest in Devon, visiting exhibitions and a new brass-rubbing centre.

One of **Torquay Museum's** most popular attractions is the **Agatha Christie Gallery** on the second floor, which contains fascinating memorabilia loaned by her daughter. It includes manuscripts, photographs and even one of her fur coats. Dame Agatha was born in Torquay in 1890 and the town has created an **Agatha Christie Mile**, which guides visitors to places of interest that she knew as a girl and young woman growing up in the town.

The museum also has a pictorial record of Torquay over the past 150 years, and displays chronicling the social and natural history of the area. Amongst the museum's other treasures are many items discovered at **Kents Cavern**, an astonishing complex of caves regarded as "one of the most important archaeological sites in Britain". Excavations here in the 1820s revealed a remarkable collection of animal bones – the remains of mammoths, sabre-toothed tigers, grizzly bears, bison and cave lions. These bones proved to be the dining-room debris of cave dwellers who lived here some 30,000 years ago, the oldest known residents of Europe. The caves are open daily, all year, offering guided tours, a sound and light show, a gift shop and refreshment room.

Another popular attraction is **Bygones** in Fore Street where visitors can wander back in time through a real olde worlde street

Torre Abbey

complete with ironmongers, sweet shop, apothecary's shop, forge and pub. There are many original Victorian artefacts and other attractions include a giant model railway and railwayana collections, a children's fantasy land; a World War One exhibit, tearoom and shop.

A fairly new attraction is **Living Coasts**, which opened in 2003 on Torquay Harbour. It is operated by the same wildlife trust that runs Paignton Zoo and is best described as a coastal zoo that provides a natural habitat for seals, penguins, puffins, auks and sea ducks with the emphasis on the coast and environmental issues. There's an underwater viewing area, a café and a restaurant with grand views across Tor Bay.

Just a mile or so from Torquay town centre is **Cockington Village**, a phenomenally picturesque rural oasis of thatched cottages, a working forge, and the Drum Inn designed by Sir Edward Lutyens and completed in 1930. From the village there's a pleasant walk through the park to Cockington Court, now a Craft Centre and Gallery. Partly Tudor, this stately old manor was for almost three centuries the home of the Mallock family. In the 1930s they formed a trust to preserve "entire and unchanged the ancient amenities and character of the place, and in developing its surroundings to do nothing which may not rather enhance than diminish its attractiveness". The Trust has been spectacularly successful in carrying out their wishes.

About a mile north of Torquay is another village but this village is one-twelfth life size. **Babbacombe Model Village** (see panel below) contains some 400 models, many with sound and animation. Created by Tom

Babbacombe Model Village

Hampton Avenue, Babbacombe, Torquay, Devon TQ1 3LA
Tel: 01803 315315 Fax: 01803 315173
e-mail: mail@model-village.co.uk
website: www.babbacombemodelvillage.co.uk

Why not experience the ever changing miniature world of Babbacombe Model Village. Take time out from the hustle and bustle of every day life and feel on top of the world as you see it recreated in miniature. Thousands of miniature buildings, people and vehicles set in 4 acres capture the essence of England's past, present and future. It's not just the humour, nor the animation – it has a life of its own.

Towering above a medieval village, Merrivale Castle is a miniature tourist attraction full of visitors enjoying a day out re-living medieval England. The whole scene comes to life with superb animated effects featuring all the bawdy, comic events of old England. Dramatically illuminated at night, part of this feature is the Dastardly Dungeon, where characters are stretched to their limit, and hysterical scenes at the Celebrity Banquet- see who's been invited to the feast. Open all year, and summer evenings until late - times vary so phone or check website for details.

🏠 historic building 🏛 museum and heritage 🏛 historic site 🝞 scenic attraction 🌿 flora and fauna

Dobbins, a large number of the beautifully crafted models have been given entertaining names: Shortback & Sydes, the gents' hairdresser, for example, Walter Wall Carpets and Jim Nastik's Health Farm. The site also contains some delightful gardens, including a collection of more than 500 types of dwarf conifer, a 1000 foot long model railway, an ornamental lake stocked with koi carp and much more.

Around Torquay

COMBETEIGNHEAD
3 miles N of Torquay off the A380 or A379

🐦 John Keats

Standing across the river from Bishopsteignton, Combeteignhead is a charming village, which **John Keats** came to know well when he was staying with his consumptive brother Tom at nearby Teignmouth in 1818 In a letter to his family he often enclosed scraps of "happy doggerel" like this:

> *Here all the summer I could stay,*
> *For there's Bishop's Teign*
> *And King's Teign*
> *And Coomb at the clear Teign head -*
> *Where close by the stream*
> *You may have your cream*
> *All spread upon Barley bread.*

SHALDON
7 miles N of Torquay on the A379

🌿 Shaldon Wildlife Trust

Set on the southern bank of the Teign estuary, Shaldon's Marine Parade provides a grand viewpoint for watching the busy traffic sailing in and out of the river. A goodly number of

Regency houses add architectural dignity to the town, a reminder of the era when affluent Londoners, unable to holiday in a Europe dominated by Napoleon, began to discover the gentle charms of southwestern England. A more recent attraction for visitors is the **Shaldon Wildlife Trust's** breeding centre for rare small mammals, reptiles and exotic birds, just to the north of the town.

TEIGNMOUTH
9 miles N of Torquay on the A381 & A379

🏛 Church of St James 🏛 Assembly Rooms

🏛 The Quay

Teignmouth has something of a split personality. On the coastal side is the popular holiday resort with its two miles of sandy beaches, a splendid promenade almost as long, colourful gardens and a pier that once separated male and female bathers. There's also a 25 foot-high lighthouse which serves no apparent purpose apart from looking rather fetching. The residential area contains much fine Regency and Georgian building. Particularly noteworthy are the **Church of St James**, with its striking octagonal tower of 1820, and the former **Assembly Rooms**, a dignified colonnaded building, which now houses a café.

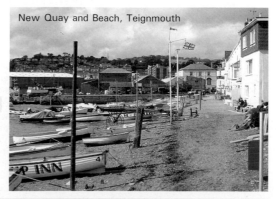
New Quay and Beach, Teignmouth

EARTH ANGEL GIFTS

16 Bank Street, Teignmouth, Devon TQ14 8AW
Tel/Fax: 01626 778957
e-mail: andytina78@supanet.com
website: www.earthangelgifts.co.uk

Located in the beautiful seaside town of Teignmouth Devon, **Earth Angel Gifts** offers some of the finest collectable gifts and teddy bears as well as many more unusual gift ideas for every occassion. Our product range is vast with prices from 10p upwards to £500, we stock some of the worlds best known brands, including the ever popular Charlie Bears, Steiff, Teddy Herman and many more bears and characters including Beatrix Potter, Paddington & The Great British Teddy Bear Co. Alongside our collection of bears and soft toys sits some of the best brand collectables from Royal Doulton, Nao, Willow Tree and many more, we are also a club store for many collectable brands including Hidden Treasures. We also stock a vast range of home fragrance products including Yankee Candle & Woodwick plus many more incense & Fragrance Oil products.

At Earth Angel you will also find a magical range of musical clocks from Seiko & Rhythm Clocks who are the worlds No.1 clocks. So if you are looking for something more unusual of the highest quality you will always receive a warm welcome and friendly honest service at Earth Angel Gifts. A mail order service is also available.

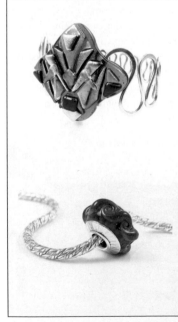

VIVIAN GALLERY

2 Queen Street, Dawlish, Devon EX7 9HB
Tel: 01626 867254
e-mail: mail@viviangallery.co.uk
website: www.viviangallery.co.uk

Look good and feel even better wearing jewellery as unique as you are, from the **Vivian Gallery**. This studio and workshop showcases the jewellery of Hazel Bunyan and her daughter Madeline. Each piece they make is individually crafted by hand with care, every item a work of *"wearable art"*.

The vibrant colours of kiln fired dichroic glass with the durable qualities of sterling silver are the mainstay of Hazel's work while Madeline creates colourful lampworked glass beads which feature in her sterling silver jewellery. Also she makes silver cored beads which will fit on your Troll, Pandora or similar bracelet systems.

They will be happy to tailor any of their designs to your requirements, gold instead of silver, or a particular colour, or something for a special occasion. Be sure to order early as their work is much in demand. The Gallery also displays work from other local artists and photographers. Open all year from 9.00am – 5.30pm Monday to Saturday. All major cards accepted.

🏚 historic building 🏛 museum and heritage 🏚 historic site ⚘ scenic attraction 🌱 flora and fauna

On the river side of the town is the working port, approached by the narrowest of channels. The currents here are so fast and powerful that no ship enters the harbour without a Trinity House pilot on board. **The Quay** was built in 1821 with granite from the quarries on Haytor Down. This durable stone was in great demand at the time. Amongst the many buildings constructed in Haytor granite were London Bridge (the one now relocated to Lake Tahoe in California), and the British Museum. Teignmouth's main export nowadays is potter's clay, extracted from pits beside the River Teign. From the Quay there's a passenger ferry across the estuary to Shaldon.

DAWLISH
12 miles N of Torquay on the A379

🌱 The Lawn 🌱 Dawlish Warren

This pretty seaside resort, which boasts one of the safest beaches in England, has the unusual feature of a main railway line separating the town from its sea front. The result is, in fact, much more appealing than it sounds. For one thing, the railway keeps motor traffic away from the beachside, and for another, the low granite viaduct that carries the track has weathered attractively in the century and a half since it was built. The arches under which beach-goers pass create a kind of formal entrance to the beach, and the Victorian station has become a visitor attraction in its own right.

By the time Brunel's railway arrived here in 1846, Dawlish was already wellknown as a fashionable resort. John Keats, with his convalescent brother, Tom, had visited the town in 1818. The great poet was inspired to pen the less-than-immortal lines:

Over the hill and over the Dale
And over the bourne to Dawlish
Where Gingerbread wives have a scanty sale
And gingerbread nuts are smallish.

Other distinguished visitors included Jane Austen (one of whose characters cannot understand how one could live anywhere else in Devon but here), and Charles Dickens who, in his novel of the same name, has Nicholas Nickleby born at a farm nearby. All of these great literary figures arrived not long after the first houses were built along the Strand. That had happened in 1803. Up until then, Dawlish was just a small settlement beside the River Daw, located about a mile inland in order to be safe from raiders. This is where the 700-year-old church stands, surrounded by a small group of thatched cottages.

At the time of John Keats' visit, the town was being transformed with scores of new villas springing up along the Strand. Earlier improvers had already "beautified" the River Daw, which flows right through the town, by landscaping the stream into a series of shallow waterfalls and surrounding it with attractive gardens like **The Lawn**. Until Regency times, The Lawn had been a swamp populated by herons, kingfishers and otters. Then in 1808, the developer John Manning filled in the marshy land with earth removed during the construction of Queen Street. Today, both The Lawn and Queen Street still retain the elegance of those early 19th-century days and the brook that runs through the area is the home of the famous Black Swans.

In August, Dawlish really comes to life with its colourful Carnival Week. It includes amongst other events a lively town procession and a display by the Red Arrows.

A couple of miles northeast of the town is **Dawlish Warren**, a mile-long sand spit, which almost blocks the mouth of the River Exe. There's a golf course here and also a 55-acre Nature Reserve, home to more than 450 species of flowering plants. For one of them, the Jersey lily, this is its only habitat in mainland England. Guided tours of the Reserve, led by the warden, are available during the season.

Sadly, the last surviving relic of Isambard Kingdom Brunel's Atmospheric Railway at Starcross has recently closed. The great engineer had intended that the stretch of railway between Exeter and Totnes should be powered by a revolutionary new system. The train would be attached to a third rail, which in fact was a long vacuum chamber, drawing the carriages along by the effects of air pressure. His visionary plan involved the building of 10 great Italianate engine houses at three-mile intervals along the line. Sadly, the project was a failure, partly for financial reasons, but also because the leather seals on the vacuum pipe were quickly eaten away by the combined forces of rain, salt and hungry rats. The exhibition at Starcross used to display a working model, using vacuum cleaners to represent the pumping houses, and volunteers are even propelled up and down the track to demonstrate the viability of the original idea.

Brunel had to fall back on conventional steam engines, but the route he engineered from Exeter to Newton Abbot is one of the most scenic in the country, following first the

western side of the Exe estuary, then hugging the seaboard from Dawlish Warren to Teignmouth before turning inland along the north bank of the River Teign.

PAIGNTON
3 miles SW of Torquay on the A379

🏛 Oldway Mansion	🐾 Paignton Zoo
🦋 Paignton and Dartmouth Railway	
🦋 Splashdown@Quaywest	

Today, Torquay merges imperceptibly into Paignton, but in early Victorian times Paignton was just a small farming village, about half a mile inland, noted for its cider and its "very large and sweet flatpole cabbages". The town's two sandy beaches, ideal for families with young children, were to change all that. A pier and promenade add to the town's appeal, and throughout the summer season there's a packed programme of special events, including a Children's Festival in August, fun fairs and various firework displays.

The most interesting building in Paignton is undoubtedly **Oldway Mansion**, built in 1874 for Isaac Singer, the millionaire sewing-machine manufacturer. Isaac died the following year and it was his son, Paris, who gave the great mansion its present exuberant form. Paris added a south side mimicking a music pavilion in the grounds of Versailles, a hallway modelled on the Versailles hall of mirrors, and a sumptuous ballroom where his mistress Isadora Duncan would display the new, fluid kind of dance she had created based on classical mythology. Paris Singer sold the mansion to Paignton Borough Council in 1946, and it is now used as a Civic Centre, but many of the splendid rooms (and the extensive

Dawlish Warren Beach

🏛 historic building   🏛 museum and heritage   🏚 historic site   🍃 scenic attraction   🐾 flora and fauna

Orang-utan at Paignton Zoo

with boa constrictors and pythons. The route of the Jungle Express miniature railway provides good views of these and many other animals.

Opened in the spring of 2006, the Occombe Farm Project is a 150-acre organic demonstration farm and educational venture. It incorporates a nature trail, a working farm, a butcher's, baker's, a shop selling local produce and an educational centre.

Located on Goodrington Sands, **Splashdown@Quaywest** claims to be Britain's "biggest, best, wildest and wettest waterpark", with the highest water slides in the country. Other amusements include go-karts, bumper boats, and crazy golf, and the site also offers a choice of bars, restaurants and cafés.

gardens) are open to the public free of charge and guided tours are available.

An experience not to be missed in Paignton is a trip on the **Paignton and Dartmouth Steam Railway**, a seven-mile journey along the lovely Torbay coast and through the wooded slopes bordering the Dart estuary to Kingswear where travellers board a ferry for the ten-minute crossing to Dartmouth. The locomotives and rolling stock all bear the proud chocolate and gold livery of the Great Western Railway, and the railway staff are in period costume. On certain services you can wine and dine in Pullman style luxury on the Riviera Belle Dining Train. During the peak season, trains leave every 45 minutes or so.

Another major attraction in the town is **Paignton Zoo**, set in 75 acres of attractive botanical gardens and home to some 300 species of animals. A registered charity dedicated to protecting the global wildlife heritage, the zoo is particularly concerned with endangered species such as the Asiatic lions and Sumatran tigers, which are now provided with their own forest habitat area. Orang-utans and gorillas roam freely on large outdoor islands, free from cages. Crocodiles from the River Nile and Cuba share a swamp

BRIXHAM
8 miles S of Torquay on the A3022

| 🌿 Battery Gardens | 🐿 Rev Lyte |
| 🌿 Berry Head Country Park | |

In the 18th century, Brixham was the most profitable fishing port in Britain, and fishing is still the most important activity in this engaging little town, although the trawlers now have to pick their way between flotillas of yachts and tour boats. On the quay there are stalls selling freshly caught seafood and around the harbour a maze of narrow streets where you'll find a host of small shops, tearooms and galleries. From the busy harbour, there are regular passenger ferries to Torquay and coastal cruises in the 80-year-old Brixham-built yacht *Vigilance* and other craft.

It was at Brixham that the Prince of Orange landed in 1688 to claim the British throne as William III; an imposing statue of him looks inland from the harbour. And in 1815, all eyes were focussed on the *Bellerophon*, anchored in

---

🎭 stories and anecdotes 🐿 famous people 🎨 art and craft ✏ entertainment and sport 🚶 walks

the bay. On board was Napoleon Buonaparte, getting his only close look at England before transferring to the *Northumberland* and sailing off to his final exile on St Helena.

Moored beside the quay is a full-scale reconstruction of the *Golden Hind*, the ship in which Sir Francis Drake circumnavigated the world in 1577-1580. Visitors can go below decks to view the tiny rooms in which the ship's surgeon and captain were housed.

A short walk from the quay brings you to **Battery Gardens**, so named because an Emergency Coastal Defence Battery was established on this site during World War Two. It is now a Scheduled Monument with many of the buildings and structures from that time - and from earlier wars - still standing. A museum on site tells their story.

Also close to the harbour is All Saints' Church where the **Rev Henry Francis Lyte** was the first Vicar from 1823 until his death in 1847. During his last illness, the Rev Lyte composed what is perhaps the best known and best loved English hymn – *Abide with me*. The church bells play the tune each day at noon and 8pm.

On the harbourside itself, the Strand Art Gallery is one of the oldest and largest art galleries in Devon and showcases the work of local artists. There are more than 400 original paintings on display and visitors can often see the artists at work, either in the gallery or on the slipway outside.

To the west of the town is **Berry Head Country Park**, which is noted for its incredible views (on a good day as far as Portland Bill, 46 miles away), its rare plants (like the white rock-rose), and its colonies of sea birds such as fulmars and kittiwakes nesting in the cliffs. The park also boasts the largest breeding colony of guillemots along the entire Channel coast. A

video camera has been installed on the cliffs to relay live close-up pictures of the guillemots and other seabirds. Within the park is a lighthouse that has been called "the highest and lowest lighthouse in Britain". The structure is only 15 feet high, but it stands on a 200-foot-high cliff rising at the most easterly point of Berry Head.

KINGSWEAR
10 miles S of Torquay off the A379

🐦 Coleton Fishacre

Kingswear sits on the steeply rising east bank of the River Dart, looking across to the picturesque panorama of Dartmouth stretched across the hillside on the opposite bank. The town is the terminus for the Paignton and Kingswear steam railway and passengers then join the ferry for the 10-minute crossing to Dartmouth. There's also a vehicle ferry. Above the town stand the impressive remains of Kingswear Castle, which is now owned by the Landmark Trust and has been converted to holiday flats. Together with its twin across the river, Dartmouth Castle, the fortresses guarded the wide estuary of the Dart. If an invasion seemed imminent, a huge chain was strung across the river from Dartmouth as an additional deterrent.

About three miles to the east of Kingswear, **Coleton Fishacre** (National Trust) has a delightful coastal garden basking in a mild climate that is ideal for growing exotic trees and shrubs. The garden was created between 1925 and 1940 by Lady Dorothy D'Oyly Carte whose grandfather had produced the Gilbert and Sullivan comic operas. Lady Dorothy introduced a wonderfully imaginative variety of plants. The 20-acre site, protected by a deep combe, contains formal gardens, wooded areas with wild flowers, tranquil pools and secret paths weaving in and out of glades. The house itself was built in the elegant Arts and Crafts style of the 1920s. Music plays, echoing the family's Gilbert and Sullivan connections and those able to do so can play the Blüthner piano in the saloon.

COMPTON
4 miles W of Torquay off the A381

🏠 Compton Castle

Dominating this small village, **Compton Castle** (NT) dates back to the 1300s and in Elizabethan times was the home of Sir Humphrey Gilbert, Walter Raleigh's half-brother and the coloniser of Newfoundland in 1583. Complete with battlements, towers and portcullis, the castle also boasts an impressive Great Hall, a solar and an ancient kitchen with a huge fireplace. The castle is still occupied by the Gilbert family although owned by the National Trust.

NEWTON ABBOT
7 miles NW of Torquay on the A380

🐦 William III   🖌 Racecourse

🏠 Bradley Manor   🏠 Tuckers Maltings

An ancient market town, Newton Abbot took on a quite different character in the 1850s when the Great Western Railway established its locomotive and carriage repair works here.

Neat terraces of artisans' houses were built on the steep hillsides to the south; the more well-to-do lived a little further to the north in Italianate villas around Devon Square and Courtenay Park.

The town's greatest moment of glory was on 5 November 1688 when William, Prince of Orange, "the glorious defender of the Protestant religion and the liberties of England", was first proclaimed king as **William III**. This climactic moment of the Glorious Revolution took place in front of St Leonard's Church of which only the medieval tower now remains. The new king had landed at Brixham and was on his way to London. Stopping off in Newton Abbot, he stayed at the handsome Jacobean manor, Forde House, which is now used as offices by the District Council.

To the south of the town is a delightful attraction in the shape of the Hedgehog Hospital at Prickly Hill Farm – where else?

On the northern outskirts of the town is **Newton Abbot Racecourse** where National Hunt racing takes place from the spring through to the autumn. For the rest of the year, the site is used for country fairs and other events.

On the western edge of the town stands **Bradley Manor** (National Trust), a notable

📽 stories and anecdotes   🐦 famous people   🖌 art and craft   🖌 entertainment and sport   🚶 walks

MAGPIES GIFTS
& THE NEST CAFÉ

11 Wolborough Street, Newton Abbot,
Devon TQ12 1JR
Tel: 01626 353456
e-mail: sales@magpies-gifts.co.uk
website: www.magpies-gifts.co.uk
     or www.charliebearsuk.com

'For Something Special'

Located close to Newton Abbot's famous clock tower you will find **Magpies Gifts**. Owners Carol and Richard Handley-Collins started the business in 1999 and since then, the shop has evolved into a specialist teddy bear business, with many collectables including new and retired bears and a tasteful range of teddy bear memorabilia.

Magpies Gifts is the largest stockist of the full range of Charlie Bears and Isabelle Collection based in Launceston, including many of the most unusual and hardest-to-find bears, each of them sold in a special collector's bag. Other teddy bear brands include Bearington Bears (from the USA), Kaycee Bears, Merrythought and Dean Bears (all made in the UK), Steiff, Hermann and Clemens (all made in Germany) and other collectables come from World of Minature Bears, Brigitte Rive Gollies, Deb Canham, Snoopy, Hansa Animals, Beatrix Potter and several makers of rag dolls as well as various artists from

around the world. Upstairs you will find **Mrs B's Bonnets & Gents Corner**. Mrs B's Bonnets offers a wonderful collection of some 100 varieties of hats for hire along with a variety of accessories for sale– just the place to select a hat for a day's racing at the nearby Newton Abbot National Hunt racecourse. Gents corner provides a wide range of male hats and accessories for sale.

Under the same roof and in the same ownership is **The Nest Café**, where browsers can take a break and treat themselves to some marvellous home cooking. The Café serves all-day breakfasts, lunches and afternoon cream teas, plus home-made cakes and speciality ice creams. At lunchtime there are daily specials such as local Brixham crab salad or chicken casserole served in a giant Yorkshire pudding. When the sun shines customers can enjoy their refreshment infront of the clock tower or on the secluded rear patio.

example of medieval domestic architecture. Most of it dates from around 1420 and includes a chapel, Solar, Great Hall and porch. By the mid 1750s this quaint style of architecture was decidedly out of fashion and the building became a farmhouse with poultry occupying the chapel. The house was given to the National Trust in 1938 by the then owner, Mrs AH Woolner. Her family continue to live here and manage the property.

Newton Abbot also boasts the only traditional working malthouse open to the public. **Tuckers Maltings** has been malting in Newton Abbot for more than 100 years and claims to offer the finest selection of bottled beers to be found in Devon. The speciality beer shop is open throughout the year and guided tours of the maltings are available during the summer months.

CHUDLEIGH
14 miles NW of Torquay off the A38

🏠 Ugbrooke House and Park

Activists who oppose the building of new roads will find little sympathy in this former coaching town on what used to be the main thoroughfare between Exeter and Plymouth. By the 1960s, the volume of traffic had reached unbearable levels, especially during the holiday season. Mercifully, the dual carriageway A38 now bypasses the little town and it is once again possible to enjoy Chudleigh's 14th-century church, containing some fine memorials to the Courtenay family, and its former Grammar School nearby, which was founded in 1668. (It is now a private house.) It was at the coaching inn here that William of Orange stayed after he landed at Torbay. From one of its windows, the new king addressed the good people of Chudleigh. The Dutchman's English was so bad, however,

they were unable to understand what he was saying. They cheered him anyway.

Clifford Street is named after Sir Thomas Clifford, Lord Treasurer to Charles II and a member of the king's notorious Cabal, his secretive inner cabinet. As was the custom then, Sir Thomas used his official position to amass a considerable fortune. This was later put to good use by his grandson who employed Robert Adam and Capability Brown to design **Ugbrooke House and Park**, a couple of miles southwest of Chudleigh and well worth visiting. Dating from the mid 1700s, and replacing an early Tudor manor house, Ugbrooke is named after the Ug Brook that flows through the estate and was dammed to create three lakes in the beautifully landscaped grounds. In the 1930s, the 11th Lord Clifford abandoned the estate as he could not afford to live there. During World War Two, Ugbrooke was used as a school for evacuated children and as a hostel for Polish soldiers. In the 1950s, some of the ground floor rooms were used to store grain, but today the house has been beautifully restored by the present Lord and Lady Clifford. It is noted for its collections of paintings, dolls, military uniforms and furniture.

Exeter

🏠 Rougemont Castle   🏠 St Peter's Cathedral

🏠 St Nicholas' Priory   🏠 Guildhall

🏠 Tucker's Hall   🏛 Piazza Terracina

🏛 Underground Passages   🏛 Sculpture Walk

🏛 Bill Douglas Centre   🏛 Exeter Ship Canal

A lively and thriving city with a majestic Norman cathedral, many fine old buildings, and a wealth of excellent museums, Exeter's history stretches back for more than two millennia. Its present High Street was already in place some 200 years or more before the Romans arrived, part of an ancient ridgeway striking across the West Country. The inhabitants then were the Celtish tribe of the Dumnonii and it was they who named the river Eisca, a river abounding in fish.

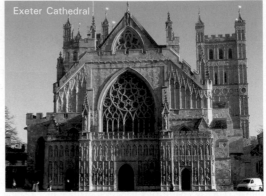

Exeter Cathedral

The Romans made Isca their southwestern stronghold, surrounding it with a massive defensive wall. Most of that has disappeared, but a spectacular caldarium, or Roman Bath House, was uncovered in the Cathedral Close in 1971. It was later grassed over but a model of it can be seen in the cathedral.

In the Dark Ages following the Roman withdrawal, the city was a major ecclesiastical centre, and in AD670 King Cenwealh founded an abbey on the site of the present cathedral. That, along with the rest of Exeter, was ransacked by the Vikings in the 9th century. They occupied the city twice before King Alfred finally saw them off.

The Normans were next on the scene, although it wasn't until 20 years after the Battle of Hastings that William the Conqueror finally took possession of the city after a siege that lasted 18 days. He ordered the construction of **Rougemont Castle**, the gatehouse and tower of which still stand at the top of Castle Street.

During the following century, the Normans began building **St Peter's Cathedral**, a work not completed until 1206. Half a century later, however, everything except the two sturdy towers was demolished and the present cathedral took shape. These years saw the development of the Decorated style, and Exeter is a sublime example of this appealing form of church architecture. In the 300-foot-long nave, stone piers rise 60 feet and then fan out into sweeping arches. Equally impressive is the west front, a staggering display of more than 60 sculptures, carved between 1327 and 1369. They depict a curious mix of Biblical characters, soldiers, priests and a royal flush of Saxon and Norman kings.

Other treasures include an intricately-carved choir screen from about 1320, an astronomical clock built in 1376, which is one of the oldest timepieces in the world, a minstrels' gallery with a wonderful sculpted band of heavenly musicians, a monumental organ, and a colossal throne with a canopy 59 feet high, carved in wood for Bishop Stapledon in 1316.

Another strange carving can be found beneath the misericord seats in the choir stalls where, amongst other carvings, there is one of an elephant. However, as the carver had no model to work from he has given the animal tusks that look like clubs and rather eccentric feet. It has been suggested that the carving was based on the first elephant to come to Britain as a gift for Henry III in 1253. The carver had probably heard stories of the creature and made up the rest.

In 1941 much of the old part of the city was destroyed by a German air raid and, although the cathedral survived, it was badly damaged. When restoration work began in

1943, a collection of wax models was discovered hidden in a cavity. Including representations of human and animal limbs, the complete figure of a woman and a horse's head, they are thought to have been brought here by pilgrims who would place their wax models on the tomb of Bishop Edmund Lacy. By placing a model of an injured or withered limb on the tomb the pilgrims believed that they would be cured of their affliction.

Such is the grandeur of the cathedral that other ecclesiastical buildings in Exeter tend to get overlooked. But it's well worth seeking out **St Nicholas' Priory**, an exceptional example of a small Norman priory. The Priory re-opened to the public in April 2008 after a two-year programme of conservation work. Adorned with quality replica furniture, and painted in the bright colours of the period, the Priory is now presented as the 1602 home of the wealthy Hurst family. Visitors can experience Tudor life including Elizabethan music, costume, food, games and stories, and view the original Priory cellar with its chunky Norman pillars, the 15th-century kitchens, and the parlour with its original Tudor plaster ceiling. The church of St Mary Steps also repays a visit just to see its beautifully-preserved Norman font, and its ancient 'Matthew the Miller' tower clock, named after a medieval miller noted for his undeviating punctuality. The church is currently only open for services. It stands in Stepcote Hill, a narrow cobbled and stepped thoroughfare, which until as late as 1778 was the main road into Exeter from the west.

The remarkable **Guildhall** in the High Street has been in use as a Town Hall ever since it was built in 1330, making it one of the oldest municipal buildings in the country. Its great hall was remodelled around 1450, and the Elizabethans added a striking, if rather fussy, portico, but the interior is still redolent of the Middle Ages.

Another interesting medieval building is **The Tucker's Hall** in Fore Street, built in 1471 for the Company of Weavers, Fullers and Shearmen. Inside there is some exceptional carved panelling, a collection of rare silver, and a huge pair of fulling shears weighing over 25lb and almost four feet long. Nearby Parliament Street claims to be the world's narrowest street, just 25 inches wide at one point.

Exeter's one-time importance as a port is reflected in the dignified Custom House, built in 1681, and now the centrepiece of Exeter Historic Quayside, a fascinating complex of old warehouses, craft shops and cafés. There are riverside walks, river trips, Canadian canoes and cycles for hire, and a passenger ferry across the river to the **Piazza Terracina**, which explores five centuries of Exeter's trading connections around the world. The museum contains an extraordinary collection of boats, amongst them an Arab dhow, a reed boat from Lake Titicaca in South America, and a vintage steam launch. A special attraction of the museum is that visitors are positively encouraged to step aboard and explore in detail the many craft on show.

Outstanding amongst the city's excellent museums is the Royal Albert Memorial Museum and Art Gallery, but it is currently undergoing a multi-million pound development and will not re-open until 2011. Other museums in the city include the Devonshire Regiment Museum (regimental history); the Rougemont House Museum near the castle, which has a copious collection of costumes and lace; and the **Bill Douglas Centre** for the History of Cinema and Popular Culture on the university campus, which follows the development of visual media from the late 1600s to the present day.

One of the city's most unusual attractions lies beneath its streets: the maze of **Underground Passages** (see panel below) constructed in the 14th and 15th centuries as service tunnels for the pipes bringing water from springs beyond the city walls. A guided tour of the stone-vaulted caverns is an experience to remember.

Although Exeter is linked to the sea by the River Exe, a 13th-century Countess of Devon, with a grudge against the city, built a weir across the river so that boats could sail no further upstream than Topsham. Some 300 years passed before action was taken by the city and the world's first ship canal was constructed to bypass the weir. Originally only three feet deep, this was changed to 14 feet over the years, and the **Exeter Ship Canal** continued to be used until the 1970s. However, the M5 motorway, which crosses the canal on a fixed height bridge too low to allow big ships to pass, finally achieved what the Countess of Devon began so many centuries ago.

Exeter University campus is set on a hill overlooking the city, and the grounds, laid out by Robert Veitch in the 1860s, offer superb views of the tors of Dartmoor. The landscape boasts many rare trees and shrubs, and the University has followed Veitch's example by creating many new plantings, including areas devoted entirely to Australasian plants. **Exeter University Sculpture Walk** comprises 24 sculptures, including works by Barbara Hepworth and Henry Moore, set out both in the splendid grounds and within the university buildings.

To the southwest of the city lies the Devon and Exeter Racecourse, one of the most scenic in the country and one that is considered to be Britain's favourite course.

Around Exeter

CADBURY
10 miles N of Exeter off the A3072

🏛 Cadbury Castle   🏛 Fursdon House

To the north of this delightful hamlet is **Cadbury Castle**, actually an Iron Age fort. It was built high on the hilltop, about 700 feet

Exeter's Underground Passages

Romangate Passage, Off High Street, Exeter, Devon EX4 3PZ
Tel: 01392 665887
website: www.exeter.gov.uk

Dating from 14th century, the medieval passages under Exeter High Street are a unique ancient monument: no similar system of passages can be

explored by the public elsewhere in Britain. They were built to house the pipes that brought fresh water to the city. Their purpose was simple: to bring clean drinking water from natural springs in fields lying outside the walled city, through lead pipes into the heart of the city. The pipes sometimes sprang leaks and repairs could only be carried out by digging them up as we do today. To avoid this disruption the passages were vaulted and it is down some of these vaulted passageways that visitors are guided.

🏛 historic building   🏛 museum and heritage   🏛 historic site   🏵 scenic attraction   🦅 flora and fauna

above sea level, and it's claimed that the views here are the most extensive in Devon. On a good day Dartmoor and Exmoor are in full view, and the Quantocks and Bodmin Moor can also be seen. A little more than a mile away stands **Fursdon House**, which has been lived in by the Fursdon family since around 1260. The varied architecture reflects the many additions made over the centuries. Some fascinating family memorabilia, including old scrapbooks, are on display, there's an excellent collection of 18th-century costumes and textiles. Amongst the family treasures is a letter from Charles I written during the Civil War. Opening times are restricted.

BICKLEIGH
12 miles N of Exeter on the A396

🏰 Bickleigh Castle   🏛 Devon Railway Centre

Running due north from Exeter, the Exe Valley passes through the heart of what is known as Red Devon. The soil here has a distinctive colour derived from the red Permian rocks that underlie it. Unlike most land in Devon, this is prime agricultural land, fertile, easily-worked and, for some reason, particularly favourable to growing swedes to which it gives a much sought-after flavour.

One of the most charming villages in the Exe Valley is Bickleigh. With its riverside setting, 17th-century bridge and picturesque thatched cottages with lovingly-tended gardens, Bickleigh is one of Devon's most photographed villages. **Bickleigh Castle** is actually a moated and fortified manor house with an impressive gatehouse dating back to the late 1300s. Even older is the detached chapel, built in the 11th century. Exhibits include Tudor furniture (including a massive four-poster), some fine oil paintings, and a Civil War Armoury. The nearby 17th-century farmhouse is very atmospheric

with its inglenook fireplaces, oak beams and ancient bread ovens. The castle is open daily from the late spring Bank Holiday until the first Sunday in October, and at any time for pre-booked groups.

Railway buffs will enjoy the **Devon Railway Centre** housed in the Victorian station buildings. It has 15 different working model railway layouts and various museum collections, and provides unlimited train rides on two railways. There's also a riverside picnic area, crazy golf and refreshments.

TIVERTON
16 miles N of Exeter on the A396

🏰 Tiverton Castle   🏰 St Peter's Church

🏰 St George's Church   🏰 Knightshayes Court

🏛 Tiverton Museum

The only town of any size in the Exe valley is Tiverton, originally Twyfyrde, or two fords, for here the Exeter University Sculpture Walk is joined by the River Lowman. The town developed around what is now its oldest building, **Tiverton Castle**, built at the command of Henry I in 1106. Unfortunately, the castle found itself on the wrong side during the Civil War. General Fairfax himself was in charge of the successful onslaught in 1645. A few years later, Parliament decreed that the castle should be 'slighted', destroyed beyond any use as a fortification. Cromwell's troops observed the letter of their instructions, sparing those parts of the castle that had no military significance, and leaving behind them a mutilated, but still substantial, structure. Today, it houses a variety of 17th-century armoury and guided tours are available on Sundays.

During the Middle Ages, the citizens of Tiverton seem to have had a very highly-developed sense of civic and social

THE HARTNOLL HOTEL

Bolham, Tiverton, Devon EX16 7RA
Tel: 01884 252777
e-mail: frontdesk@hartnollhotel.co.uk
website: www.hartnollhotel.co.uk

The former dower house of Knightshayes Court, this privately owned country house is now a luxury boutique-style hotel offering both elegance and comfort with stunning decor, sumptuous fabrics and a wonderful open log fire.

The Hartnoll Hotel has become one of Devon's premier gourmet restaurants. Head chef Steve Cox ensures the menu is suitable for all tastes, and uses honest, locally sourced ingredients. The lunchtime offering includes a comprehensive snack option for those wanting a lighter and speedier meal, whilst at dinnertime you can indulge in some quite spectacular dishes whilst you absorb the relaxed ambience of this lovely venue.

There are 18 superior double rooms, all with Egyptian cotton sheets and goose down pillows. With fine furnishings and understated elegance, the fully licensed hotel has a very friendly and welcoming atmosphere with many areas to enjoy, from the sitting room with its roaring fire in winter, to the airy atrium and function rooms.

The menu includes dishes such as; Goats Cheese Panna Cotta with Crispy Parma Ham, Pea Coulis & Beetroot Salad (starter), Pan Seared Seabass with Pesto Mash, Sauteed Spinach, Crispy Parma Ham, Sundried Tomato Veloute (main course) and Lemon Crème Brulee Served with a Strawberry Sorbet all encased in a Tuile Cage with Balsamic & Pepper Syrup (dessert).

Opening times are as follows:
Mon-Fri 7am onwards (Breakfast), noon-2pm (Lunch), 6.30pm-9.30pm (Dinner)
Sat 8am onwards (Breakfast), noon-2pm (Lunch), 6.30pm-9.30pm (Dinner)
Sun 8.30am onwards (Breakfast) noon-2.30pm (Lunch), 6.30pm-9.30pm (Dinner)
Coffee and Cream teas available all day

🏚 historic building 🏛 museum and heritage 🏛 historic site 🐾 scenic attraction � flora and fauna

River Exe, Tiverton

1604, by the Lowman Bridge, that the author RD Blackmore received his education. He later used the school as a setting for the first chapter of his novel, *Lorna Doone*. Now a highly-regarded public school, Blundell's moved to its present location on the edge of town in 1880.

The **Tiverton Museum** is one of the largest social history museums in the southwest, containing some 15 galleries in all. It's particularly strong on agriculture – it has a nationally important collection of farm wagons - and the Great Western Railway. One entire gallery is devoted to John Heathcoat's original lace-making machine.

The more one reads of Devon in the early to mid 18th century, the more one becomes convinced that there must have been a serial arsonist abroad. So many Devonshire towns during this period suffered devastating fires. Tiverton's conflagration occurred in 1731, but one happy outcome of the disaster was the building of **St George's Church**, by common consent the finest Georgian church in the county, furnished with elegant period ceilings and galleries.

responsibility. Throughout the town's golden age as a wool town, from the late 1400s until it reached its zenith in the 18th century, prosperous wool merchants put their wealth to good use. Around 1613, George Slee built himself a superb Jacobean mansion in St Peter Street, the Great House, and in his will bequeathed the huge sum of £500 to establish the Slee Almshouses, which were duly built right next door. Later almshouses, founded by John Waldron (in Welbrook Street), and John Greenway (in Gold Street) are still in use. As well as funding the almshouse, John Greenway also devoted another sizeable portion of his fortune to the restoration of **St Peter's Church** in 1517. He added a sumptuous porch and chapel, their outside walls richly decorated with carvings depicting sailing ships of the time.

Peter Blundell chose a different method of demonstrating his beneficence by endowing Tiverton with a school. It was in the Old Blundell's School (National Trust) building of

A quay on the southeastern edge of Tiverton marks the western end of the Grand Western Canal, which was built in the early 1800s with the idea of linking the River Exe to Bridgewater and the Bristol Channel. It was never fully completed and finally closed in 1920. In recent years, an attractive stretch from Tiverton quay to the Somerset border has been restored and provides a pleasant easy walk. Horse-drawn barge trips along the canal are also available.

A few miles north of Tiverton, up the Exe Valley, is **Knightshayes Court**, a striking Victorian Gothic house designed by William Burges in 1869. It is a rare survivor of his

LITTLE TURBERFIELD FARM SHOP

Tiverton Parkway, Sampford Peverell,
Devon EX16 7EH
Tel: 01884 820908

Little Turberfield Farm Shop can be found in the lovely mid-Devon village of Sampford Peverell, on the road leading to the Tiverton Parkway Station. Open Tuesday-Saturday from 8am, it stocks a wide range of some of the best locally-produced foods. This includes free-range meat, home-made sausages and burgers, a choice of items for the summer barbecue, and plenty of home-baked pies and pasties. Real Devon ice cream is another tasty treat that can be found here, and there's a good choice of fruit and vegetables, and local and international cheeses. Local jams and home-made bread can also be found in the shop, which is full of old-world charm with its attractive beamed ceilings.

All their meat comes from within a 20-mile radius of the shop. And for anyone who lives or is staying within a 15-mile radius, Little Turberfield Farm Shop is offering a free home delivery service every Thursday. It's the kind of extra service you get from a local business that has been here for over 20 years and run by the present owner, Sue Clifford-Parry, for the last five of those.

---

work. The grand and opulent interiors, blending medieval romanticism with lavish Victorian decoration, became too much for the owner, Sir John Heathcoat-Amory, the lace manufacturer. So he sacked Burges and employed the less imaginative but competent John Diblee Crace. Discreetly covered during the time of the backlash against the High Victorian style, the rooms have been returned to their original grandeur by the National Trust, who were given the building by the builder's son in 1973. The house is surrounded by extensive grounds that include a water-lily pond, topiary and some rare shrubs.

BAMPTON

21 miles N of Exeter on the B3190/B3227

🌿 Exmoor Pony Sale

In medieval times Bampton was quite an important centre of the wool trade but it's now best known for its dazzling floral displays and its annual **Exmoor Pony Sale**, held on the last Thursday in October. A local farm hosts a collective sale of horses, ponies and tack, while the village itself is filled to overflowing with around 100 stalls, entertainments including craft and music workshops, demonstrations and concerts, and a funfair.

Throughout the rest of the year, though, it's a wonderfully peaceful place with some handsome Georgian cottages and houses, set beside the River Batherm, a tributary of the Exe. To the north of the village, a tree-crowned motte marks the site of Bampton Castle. Bampton's parish church of St Michael and All Angels is popular with collectors of unusual memorials. A stone on the west side of the tower replicates a memorial of 1776, which records the strange death of the parish clerk's son who was apparently killed by a

---

🏠 historic building 🏛 museum and heritage 🏛 historic site 🌳 scenic attraction 🌿 flora and fauna

falling icicle. The inscription is remarkably insensitive and reads:

> Bless my 1 1 1 1 1 1 (eyes),
> Here he lies,
> In a sad pickle,
> Killed by an icicle.

BROADCLYST
5½ miles NE of Exeter on the B3181

🏠 Killerton

Just to the north of the village and set within the fertile lands between the Rivers Clyst and Culm, lies the large estate of **Killerton** (National Trust) centred around the grand 18th-century mansion house that was the home of the Acland family. Furnished as a comfortable family home, the house contains a renowned costume collection and a Victorian laundry. While the house provides some interest, it is the marvellous grounds laid out by John Veitch in the 1770s that make a visit here special. Veitch introduced many rare trees to the arboretum along with rhododendrons, magnolias and herbaceous borders, and in the parkland are several interesting structures, including a 19th-century chapel and the Dolbury Iron Age hill fort. Here, too, can be found **Marker's Cottage**, dating from the

15th century and containing 16th-century paintings, and **Forest Cottage**, originally a gamekeeper's cottage. Circular walks around the grounds and estate provide ample opportunity to discover the wealth of plant, animal and birdlife that thrives in this, the largest estate owned by the National Trust.

CLYST ST MARY
4 miles E of Exeter on the A376/A3052

🌿 Crealy Park

A couple of miles east of Clyst St Mary is **Crealy Park**, a large all-weather entertainment centre offering a wide range of attractions for children, including the largest indoor PlayZone in the country, bumper boats and go-karts, a farm nursery and pony rides.

WOODBURY
7 miles SE of Exeter on the B3179

🏠 St Swithin's Church   🚶 Woodbury Common

St Swithin's Church at Woodbury has achieved a rather sad kind of fame because of the Rev J Loveband Fulford who, in 1846, cut great chunks out of its medieval rood screen so that his parishioners could see him more clearly. Fortunately he left untouched the fine 15th century font made from Beer stone, the Jacobean pulpit, and the interesting memorials.

A mile or so to the east of the village is the famous **Woodbury Common** viewpoint. More than 560 feet high, it provides spectacular vistas across the Exe estuary to Dartmoor, and along the south Devon coast. It's easy to understand why an Iron Age tribe chose this spot to build their massive fort whose huge ramparts lie close to the viewpoint.

Marker's Cottage, Broadclyst

DARTS FARM

Topsham, Nr Exeter, Devon, EX3 0QH   Tel: 01392 878200
e-mail: shop@dartsfarm.co.uk   website: www.dartsfarm.co.uk

Darts Farm near the historic estuary town of Topsham is fortunate to be situated in a region that is rich in high quality artisan food producers. With all this wonderful local produce on the doorstep and still with their own working farm it's easy to understand why The Guardian described Darts Farm as..

'like finding Selfridges Food Hall dumped in the middle of a field'

Visit the deli, the cider maker, the florist or sample a bit of everything in the restaurant which uses the food hall as its larder with the chefs preparing fresh dishes everyday letting the good basic ingredients speak for themselves. This philosophy runs throughout Darts Farm whether it be the master butchers – Gerald David and family with their locally reared, naturally fed meat or The Fish Shed which only sells locally caught fish straight off the day boats. The choice is yours, either beautiful wet fish to take home and cook or try their famous fish and chips also open in the evenings for takeaway.

Combine all this with the Aga shop, Fired Earth, Orange Tree and the unusual design led gifts for the home and garden, florist, children's clothes, toys, The Treatment Loft beauty salon, Cotswold Outdoor and the RSPB shop and you will understand why your first visit won't be your last.

As Nick Wyke of The Times said.. *'I've seen the future of shopping and it's not in London, Manchester or Edinburgh but on a road that runs alongside the Exe Estuary in Devon, a few miles south of Exeter.'*

LYMPSTONE

8 miles SE of Exeter off the A376

Set beside the estuary of the River Exe, Lympstone looks across the water to the impressive outline of Powderham Castle. There's a tiny harbour with a slipway and, on the beach, an Italianate clock tower erected in 1885 by a Mr WH Peters in commemoration of his wife, Mary Jane, who was noted for her good works amongst the poor of the village. It's a delight to wander around the old part of Lympstone with its narrow streets, small courts and ancient cottages.

TOPSHAM

4 miles SE of Exeter off the A376

🏛 Topsham Museum

It's not surprising to find that the whole of the old town of Topsham has been declared a conservation area. Its narrow streets are lined with fine examples of 17th and 18th-century merchants' houses, many built in the Dutch style with curved gable ends. One of these contains **Topsham Museum**, which has a model of the town as it was in 1900, local craftwork and records of prominent local families. There's also an exhibit with memorabilia connected with the film star Vivien Leigh whose brother-in-law founded the museum.

Sunset at Topsham

The town has a wealth of specialist and antique shops, and some stunning views over the Exe estuary with its extensive reed beds, salt marshes and mud banks. These provide an important winter feeding ground and summer breeding area for birds from all over the world. The estuary is also home to the largest winter flocks of avocets in the county. There are walks along the banks of the estuary

🎬 stories and anecdotes 🦜 famous people 🎨 art and craft 🎭 entertainment and sport 🚶 walks

THE QUAY CENTRE

Topsham, nr Exeter, Devon, EX3 0JB
Tel: 01392 874006
Open: 10am – 5pm 7 days a week
website: www.quayantiques.com

This vast riverside warehouse on Topsham Quay is 'home' to 65 dealers in almost every facet of the antiques and collectables world. By virtue of its location geographically one will naturally expect to find Exeter Silver, Torquay Pottery, Honiton Lace, Cornish Studio pottery and contemporary art by local artists, but you will also find examples of the best of British design in glass, pottery, cutlery , woodworking tools, furniture, textiles, jewellery and home furnishings, ranging from 1800 – 2000!

Taking advantage of the huge diversity of stock in The Quay Centre, TV programmes like Bargain Hunt, Flog It, Cash in the Attic and The Antiques Road Trip have been regular visitors, and as a result brought customers from all parts of the world!

Specialist interests include Quimper and Gouda Pottery, Whitefriars Glass, Vintage Clothing and Textiles, 50s/60s Retro furnishings, Antique Lighting, Telephones, Books and Prints, Coins, Medals, Stamps, Tools, Clocks, Postcards, Costume Jewellery, Silver – something for everyone.

The Quay Centre is in a spectacular position right on the River Exe; climb to the top floor and you will get a commanding view, up and downstream, of the river and its wealth of bird life, along with an amazing assortment of eclectic merchandise!

Topsham is an interesting and historically important town with a huge variety of shops, restaurants, pubs and cafes, all close to the river and within walking distance of the Bird Reserve on the Marsh. It is well worth a visit and you can be assured of a "Grand Day Out". Get to Topsham by Bike, Train, Bus, on Foot or by Boat. If you come by Car we have a large carpark adjacent to the Quay Centre!

photographs by cdw design artist

that lead right from Exeter to the coast at Exmouth, and also river and bird-watching cruises from Topsham quay.

POWDERHAM
7 miles S of Exeter off the A379

🏛 Powderham Castle

Powderham Castle has been the home of the Courtenay family, Earls of Devon, since 1390. The castle stands in a beautiful setting alongside the River Exe and is at the centre of a large traditional estate of about 4000 acres. The present building is mostly 18th-century and contains some fine interiors, a breathtaking Grand Staircase, and historic family portraits – some of them by Sir Joshua Reynolds, a Devon man himself. The guided tours take in an 18th-century music room designed by James Wyatt, and a restored Victorian kitchen.

KENTON
7 miles S of Exeter on the A379

🏛 All Saints Church

Founded in Saxon times, this picturesque village is famed for its glorious 14th-century **All Saints Church**. The tower stands over 100 feet high and is decorated with a wonderful assortment of ornate carvings. Inside, there is more rich carving in the south porch and in the Beer stone arcades of the nave. The pulpit is a 15th-century original, which was rescued and restored after it was found in pieces in 1866, and the massive rood screen, one of the finest in Devon, is a magnificent testimony to the 15th-century woodcarver's art.

DUNCHIDEOCK
7 miles SW of Exeter off the A30

A beautifully located village, Dunchideock hugs the sides of a deeply-sloping combe. At

THE TURF

Exeter Canal, Exminster, Devon EX6 8EE
Tel: 01392 833128 Fax: 01392 832545
e-mail: info@turfpub.net
website: www.turfpub.net

When they extended the Exeter Ship Canal in 1827 they built **The Turf** to provide accommodation and sustenance for the lock-keeper and the crews of vessels using the canal. Since 1990 this isolated inn has been owned and run by Clive and Ginny Redfern, who have worked hard to maintain this historic timber-framed, slate-hung building and enhancing its reputation as a place to seek out for good food and drink.

The interior has abundant period charm, and outside is a large beer garden with the Exe Estuary on one side and the Turf Locks on the other. As much as possible of the produce that goes into the kitchen is locally sourced, and the West Country also features strongly among the drinks, with two local real ales and a lager, cider, apple juice and two wines. The bar is open all day from 11, and food is served every lunchtime and evening except Sunday evening. The inn has two barbecues that can be hired for a party. They supply the food, cutlery and plates and you do the cooking.

Half the fun is getting to The Turf, as there is no road access. Drivers can leave their cars in car parks off the mini-roundabout on the A379 at the south end of the Exminster by-pass and walk or cycle along the towpath. Alternatively, visitor can take a ferry from the Quay at Topsham direct to the Inn, or to Old Topsham Lock then a walk – or moor by the pub in their own boat!

stories and anecdotes 🦜 famous people 🎨 art and craft 🚴 entertainment and sport 🚶 walks

NOBODY INN

Doddiscombsleigh, Exeter, Devon EX6 7PS
Tel: 01647 252394
e-mail: info@nobodyinn.co.uk
website: www.nobodyinn.co.uk

Dating back to the sixteenth century, the **Nobody Inn** is set in rolling Devon countryside between the Haldon Hills and the Teign Valley. It is one of the country's leading inns and is renowned for its imaginative wine and whisky list, comprehensive selection of local cheeses and creative cooking based on fresh local produce. The inn has plenty of character and the low ceilings, blackened beams, inglenook fireplace, antique furniture and timeless atmosphere retain its unspoilt olde worlde charm.

The delightful Nobody Inn offers five comfortable guest bedrooms, four of which have en-suite facilities. It is an ideal place for keen walkers, cyclists and horse riders to stay because this traditional English country inn is located about six miles to the south west of the cathedral town of Exeter and on the outskirts of Dartmoor National Park.

The AA four star inn has recently undergone major refurbishment. The bar retains its own traditional charm, but the restaurant and guest rooms have had a makeover, giving them a more modern twist.

the northern end, the modest red sandstone church of St Michael has an unusual number of noteworthy internal features. There's a medieval font, a set of carved pew ends and a richly-carved rood screen, which at one point makes a surprising diversion around three sides of an octagonal roof column. Amongst the monuments is one to Major-General Stringer Lawrence, the Father of the Indian Army, who in 1775 left a legacy of £50,000 to his lifelong friend, Sir Robert Palk. Palk proceeded to build himself a mansion, Haldon House, half a mile to the south, along with a folly in memory of his benefactor. Known locally as Haldon Belvedere, or Lawrence Castle, this tall triangular structure stands on the summit of Haldon Ridge and can be seen for miles around.

CREDITON

8 miles NW of Exeter on the A377

🦅 St Boniface   🏛 Church of the Holy Cross

Very few Britons have managed to become fully-fledged Saints, so Crediton is rather proud that one of this small and distinguished group, **St Boniface**, was born here around AD680. The infant was baptised as Wynfrith but on becoming a monk he adopted the name Boniface. He rose swiftly through the ranks of the Benedictine Order and in AD731 was sent by the then pope to evangelise the Germans. Boniface was remarkably successful, establishing Christianity in several German states. At the age of 71, he was created Archbishop of Mainz, but three years later he and 53 members of his retinue were

SUSAN'S

131 High Street, Crediton, Devon EX17 3LQ
Tel: 01363 775818
e-mail: susanscrediton@live.co.uk

Having been in business now for 20 years, **Susan's** knows its flowers. Susan Tucker established her shop in November 1990 and has, appropriately enough, seen it bloom and blossom into the successful florist's it is today. Customers are greeted not just by the heady aroma and bright colours of the fresh flowers and bouquets, but also by the friendly staff who are happy to go the extra mile to prove that nothing is too much trouble. All the staff are well trained and can offer plenty of experienced advice on choosing the right flowers for weddings and other special occasions.

Susan's likes to source as many of its fresh flowers as possible locally, but will order anything from anywhere if a customer wants it. The shop has a wide range of silk and dried flowers too, alongside its bouquets and individual flowers. There's also a good choice of quality vases to display flowers in, as well as baskets and wicker items. The floral displays spill over onto the pavement, drawing the eye (and the nose!) to this lovely period listed building on Crediton's pleasant High Street where thankfully many independent shops like Susan's still flourish.

THORNES FARM SHOP

Hawthorn Gardens, Stockleigh Pomeroy,
Crediton, Devon EX17 4BH
Tel: 01363 866933   Fax: 01363 866541
e-mail: athorne@thornesfarmshop.co.uk
website: www.thornesfarmshop.co.uk

Anthony Thorne admits he was definitely born with the 'farming bug' and his enthusiasm and passion for farming is clearly evident to customers at the farm shop he owns. The idea for **Thornes Farm Shop** in Crediton, Mid Devon, developed after nearby residents started calling in asking if they could buy produce from the farm. A small shop was soon built on the land, which was replaced 17 years later with the current farm shop in the middle of the 'Pick Your Own' field. The owners started growing strawberries on the site in 1986 and now a varied selection of soft fruit and vegetables are grown over an area of 125 acres.

It is an extremely successful and professional business and the Thorne's now supply not only their own farm shop, but many other local shops and wholesalers. The produce is top quality and there is a fine range of preserves on sale in the shop as well as cream, eggs, milk etc. There are toilet facilities for customers and it is hoped there will soon be a coffee shop and a 'walk' created down to a small lake at the bottom of the valley. Ring for details.

THE DEVON WINE SCHOOL

Redyeates Farm, Cheriton Fitzpaine, Crediton,
Devon EX17 4HG
Tel: 01363 866742
e-mail: alastair@devonwineschool.co.uk
website: www.devonwineschool.co.uk

Described by the *Daily Telegraph* as "One of the top 10 places in the UK to learn about wine", **The Devon Wine School** occupies a lovely 17th century farmhouse in a delightfully rural spot conveniently located just 10 miles north of Exeter. The school was established by Alastair and Carol Peebles and is the only truly residential wine school in the UK. Alastair is a member of the exclusive group of Masters of Wine and was previously the wine director at Royal Warrant Holders Berry Bros. & Rudd in St James's, London. The school offers a range of courses, each limited to 12 people, from beginners to budding Masters of Wine. Participants sample wines sourced from some of the best producers in the world.

The school boasts a coveted VisitBritain 5-star Gold Award for its outstanding accommodation. The 5 en suite bedrooms, which enjoy lovely views over the garden and beautiful Devon countryside, are all provided with super king size beds draped with Egyptian cotton sheets. Carol is a professionally trained cook and all the delicious food is cooked on the farmhouse Aga. As one appreciative course member put it: "Perfect in every way, location, accommodation, food, wine and knowledge".

---

ambushed and murdered. They were on their way to the great monastery at Fulda in Hesse, which Boniface had founded and where he was laid to rest.

Boniface was greatly revered throughout Germany and a few years later the pope formally pronounced his sanctification, but it was to be almost 1200 years before the town of his birth accorded him any recognition. Finally, in 1897, the people of Crediton installed an east window in the town's grand, cathedral-like **Church of the Holy Cross** depicting events from his life. A few years later, a statue of the saint was erected in the gardens to the west of the church.

The interior of the early 15th-century church is especially notable for its monuments, which include one to Sir John Sully who fought alongside the Black Prince and lived to the age of 105, and another to Sir William

Peryam, a commissioner at the trial of Mary, Queen of Scots. Most impressive of all, though, is the richly ornamented arch in memory of Sir Henry Redvers Buller, commander-in-chief during the Boer War and the hero of the Relief of Ladysmith. Also of interest is the Lady Chapel of 1300, which housed Crediton's famous grammar school from the time of Edward VI until 1859 when it moved to its present site at the western end of the High Street.

East Devon

No less a traveller than Daniel Defoe considered the landscape of East Devon the finest in the world. Acres of rich farmland are watered by the rivers Axe, Otter and Madford, and narrow, winding lanes lead to villages that are as picturesque and interesting

---

🏠 historic building 🏛 museum and heritage 🏚 historic site ⚘ scenic attraction 🌳 flora and fauna

as any in England. Steep-sided hills rise towards the coastline where a string of elegant Regency resorts remind the visitor that this part of the coast was one of the earliest to be developed to satisfy the early 19th-century craze for sea bathing.

Bounded by the rolling Blackdown Hills to the north, and Lyme Bay to the south, much of the countryside here is designated as of Outstanding Natural Beauty. The best, and for much of the route, the *only* landward way to explore the glorious East Devon coastline is to follow the South West Coast Path, part of the 600-mile South West Peninsula Coast Path, which starts at Minehead in Somerset and ends at Shell Bay in Dorset.

East Devon's most famous son is undoubtedly Sir Walter Raleigh who was born at Hayes Barton near Yettington in 1552 and apparently never lost his soft Devon burr – a regional accent regarded then by 16th-century London sophisticates as uncouth and much mocked by Sir Walter's enemies at the court of Elizabeth I. The Raleighs' family pew can still be seen in Yettington parish church. The famous picture by Sir John Everett Millais of *The Boyhood of Raleigh* was painted on the beach at Budleigh Salterton with the artist using his two sons and a local ferryman as the models.

Honiton

🏛 Allhallows Museum	🏛 Thelma Hulbert Gallery
🏛 Bishop's Tower	🏛 St Margaret's Hospital
🏛 Copper Castle	⛰ Dumpdon Hill

Honiton is the 'capital' of east Devon, a delightful little town in the valley of the River Otter and the 'gateway to the far southwest'. It was once a major stopping place on the Fosse Way, the great Roman road that struck diagonally across England from Lincoln to Exeter. Honiton's position on the main traffic artery to Devon and Cornwall brought it considerable prosperity, and its broad, ribbon-like High Street, almost two miles long, testifies to the town's busy past. By the 1960s, this 'busyness' had deteriorated into appalling traffic congestion during the holiday season. Fortunately, the construction of a by-pass in the 1970s allowed Honiton to resume its true character as an attractive market town with a street market held on the High Street every Tuesday and Saturday.

Surrounded by sheep pastures, Honiton was the first town in Devon to manufacture serge cloth, but the town became much better known for a more delicate material, Honiton lace. Lace-making was introduced to east Devon by Flemish immigrants who arrived here during the early years of the reign of Elizabeth I. It wasn't long before those who could afford this costly new material were displaying it lavishly as a signal of their wealth and status. By the end of the 17th century, people were engaged in the lace making industry, most of them working from their own homes making fine 'bone' lace by hand. Children as young as five were sent to 'lace schools' where they received a rudimentary education in the three Rs of Reading, (W)Riting, and (A)Rithmetic, and a far more intensive instruction in the skills of lace-making. Almost wiped out by the arrival of machine-made lace in the late 1700s, the industry was given a new lease of life when Queen Victoria insisted upon Honiton lace for her wedding dress and created a new fashion for lace that persisted throughout the 19th century.

The traditional material is still made on a small scale in the town and can be found on

Allhallows Museum

High Street, Honiton, Devon EX14 1PG
Tel: 01404 44966
email: info@honitonmuseum.co.uk
website: www.honitonmuseum.co.uk

The building housing the museum is the oldest in Honiton, dating from 1327. It started life as part of a chapel when people from the 'new town' grew tired of climbing the hill to St. Michael's. They got permission for a chapel in the town centre and called it All Saints or Allhallows. The first gallery is the chancel of the chapel, which was shortened last century to make room for St. Paul's, just outside. Fifty years ago the chapel was bought by the townspeople and opened as a museum. It has three galleries, Murch, Nicoll and Norman, in which are housed selections of an extensive lace collection as well as local antiquities.

sale in local shops, and on display in **Allhallows Museum** (see panel above). This part 15th-century building served as a school for some 300 years, but is now an interesting local museum housing a unique collection of traditional lace and also, during the season, giving daily demonstrations of lace making. Other exhibits include the bones and tusks of the Honiton Hippos, which have been dated back some 100,000 years.

Allhallows Schoolroom was one of the few old buildings to survive a series of devastating fires in the mid 1700s. However, that wholesale destruction had the fortunate result that the new buildings were gracious Georgian residences and Honiton still retains the pleasant, unhurried atmosphere of a prosperous 18th-century coaching town.

Another building that escaped the flames unscathed was Marwood House (private) in the High Street. It was built in 1619 by the second son of Thomas Marwood, one of Queen Elizabeth's many physicians. Thomas achieved great celebrity when he managed to cure the Earl of Essex after all others had failed. (He received his Devonshire estate as a reward.) Thomas was equally successful in

preserving his own health, living to the extraordinary age of 105.

Honiton boasts the only public art gallery in East Devon. The **Thelma Hulbert Gallery** occupies Elmfield House, an attractive Grade II listed late Georgian/early-Victorian town house that was the home and studio of the artist Thelma Hulbert (1913-1995). Now owned by East Devon District Council, the gallery has strong links with the Hayward Gallery in London, which enables it to exhibit works by artists such as David Hockney, Andy Warhol and Roy Lichenstein.

Some buildings on the outskirts of the town are worth a mention. **St Margaret's Hospital**, to the west, was founded in the middle ages as a refuge for lepers who were denied entry to the town itself. Later, in the 16th century, this attractive thatched building was reconstructed as an almshouse. To the east, on Axminster Road, an early 19th-century toll house known as **Copper Castle** can be seen. The castellated, pink-washed building still retains its original iron toll gates. And just a little further east, on Honiton Hill, stands the massive folly of the **Bishop's Tower**, erected in 1843 next to his house by Bishop

Edward Copplestone, apparently to enable him to see his diocese of Llandaff across the Bristol Channel.

On the northern edge of Honiton rises the National Trust-owned **Dumpdon Hill**, an 850 feet high steep-sided outcrop which is crowned by a sizeable late-Iron-Age fort. Both the walk to the summit and the views over the Otter Valley are breathtaking.

Around Honiton

DUNKESWELL
5 miles N of Honiton off the A30

🏛 Dunkeswell Abbey

🏛 Dunkeswell Memorial Museum

A pleasant country lane leads past **Dunkeswell Abbey** of which only the 15th-century gatehouse survives, the rest of the site now occupied by a Victorian church of no great charm. A couple of miles further and the road climbs up the hillside to Dunkeswell itself. This little village lies in the heart of the Blackdown Plateau and its main claim to fame is a 900-year-old Norman font in St Nicholas' Church on which is carved a rather crude depiction of an elephant, the earliest known representation of this animal in England. Almost certainly the stonemason had never seen such a beast, but he made almost as good a fist of it as he did with his satirical carvings of a bishop and a doctor. The font was originally located in Dunkeswell Abbey.

To the west of the village, **Dunkeswell Memorial Museum** stands on the site of the only American Navy air base commissioned on British soil during World War Two. It is dedicated to the veterans of the US Fleet Air Wing 7 and RAF personnel who served at the base.

DALWOOD
6 miles E of Honiton off the A35

🏛 Loughwood Meeting House   🏛 Shute Barton

🏛 St Michael's Church   🌿 Burrow Farm Gardens

By some administrative freak, until 1842 the little village of Dalwood, despite being completely surrounded by Devon, was actually part of Dorset. Its other main claim to fame is as the home of the **Loughwood Meeting House**, one of the earliest surviving Baptist chapels in the country. When the chapel was built in the 1650s, the site was hidden by dense woodland, for the Baptists were a persecuted sect who could only congregate in out-of-the-way locations. Under its quaint thatched roof, this charming little building contains a simple whitewashed interior with early 18th-century pulpits and pews. The chapel was in use until 1833, then languished for many years until it was acquired by the National Trust in 1969. It is now open all year round with admission by voluntary donation.

About three miles south of Dalwood is another National Trust property, **Shute**

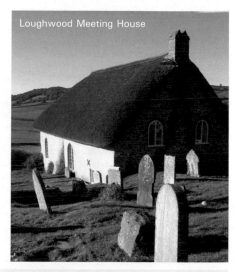
Loughwood Meeting House

Barton, an exceptional example of a medieval manor house, which dates from the 1380s. Only two wings of the original building have survived, but they include some remarkably impressive features, such as the Great Hall with its massive beamed ceiling, and the ancient kitchen with a huge range capable of roasting an ox whole. Entry is by way of a Tudor gatehouse. Shute Barton was owned by the Pole family, a local dynasty, commemorated by some grand monuments in **St Michael's Church**. Amongst them is an overbearing memorial to Sir William Pole, which depicts the Master of the Household to Queen Anne standing on a pedestal dressed in full regalia. More appealing is the 19th-century sculptured panel, seven feet high and framed in alabaster, which shows Margaret Pole greeting her three little daughters at the gates of heaven.

Close by are **Burrow Farm Gardens**, beautifully landscaped gardens that provide a peaceful place for a relaxing afternoon's outing, as well as plenty of interest for keen gardeners.

AXMINSTER
10 miles E of Honiton on the A35/A358

Thomas Whitty   Axminster Museum

This little town grew up around the junction of two important Roman roads, the Fosse and the Icknield, and was important in medieval times because of its Minster beside the River Axe. Its name has entered the language as the synonym for a very superior kind of floor-covering, which first appeared in the early 1750s. Wandering around London's Cheapside market, an Axminster weaver named **Thomas Whitty** was astonished to see a huge Turkish carpet, 12 yards long and 8 yards wide. Returning to the sleepy little market town where he was born, Thomas spent months

---

BUSY BEE FLORIST

The Ground Floor Shop, South Street, Axminster, Devon EX13 5AD
Tel: 01297 33192 / 33136
e-mail: busybee@xln.co.uk

Winner of "Business of the Year, 2006", the **Busy Bee Florist** was established in 1987. Alison Ayshford-Harris and her staff between them have more than 50 years experience in the floristry business. Alison is passionate about flowers and also makes personal customer service a priority. She likes to offers something a little bit unusual as well as traditional varieties. As well as providing flowers for all occasions, the Busy Bee produces traditional and contemporary design bouquets, basket and vase arrangements, and hand-made confetti. The shop also stocks indoor and outdoor plants, balloons, Filberts Bee products and, during the summer months, a selection of vegetable plants from a local gardener. Alison will also create sympathy tributes from customers' own garden flowers. The Busy Bee has a very green ethos - all waste from the shop, such as cuttings, cardboard and plastic, is recycled or composted. Annual flower arranging classes are available.

The Busy Bee is open from 9am to 5pm, Monday to Friday, Saturday 9am - 1pm.

🏛 historic building   🏛 museum and heritage   🏛 historic site   ♘ scenic attraction   🌱 flora and fauna

MILLERS FARM SHOP

Kilmington Cross, Kilmington, Axminster EX13 7RD
Tel: 01297 35290
website: www.millersfarmshop.com

Run by Malcolm Miller and his family, Millers Farm Shop in Devon has been growing and selling locally sourced produce for over 30 years. The shop is an 'Aladdin's Cave' of most sumptuous food imaginable. Most of the vegetables are grown on the farm, the rest is provided by local suppliers passionate about good quality food. Apart from the fresh fruit, veg, herbs and grow bags, you will also find award-winning products like Colyton butcher pies, preserves and chutneys. You can pick up fresh fish, beef, pork and lamb from local farms, daily deliveries of local milk, cider from Lyme Bay Winery and Perrys Cider Mill and sample a variety of local cheeses. Also very popular with customers are the mouth watering array of breads and pastries, along with an impressive selection of teas, coffees and juices.

In addition to the local produce, Malcolm and Angela travel to France once a week to scour markets in different regions for quality produce for the shop. The friendly atmosphere of a family-run working farm with people who really know their stuff, and are passionate about great food, completes this heavenly shopping experience.

puzzling over the mechanics of producing such a seamless piece of work. By 1755 he had solved the problem, and on midsummer's day that year the first of these luxurious carpets was revealed to the world. The time and labour involved was so prodigious that the completion of each carpet was celebrated by a procession to St Mary's Church and a ringing peal of bells. Ironically, one distinguished purchaser of an Axminster carpet was the Sultan of Turkey who, in 1800, paid the colossal sum of £1000 for a particularly fine specimen. But the inordinately high labour costs involved in producing such exquisite hand-tufted carpets crippled Whitty's company. In 1835, their looms were sold to a factory at Wilton. That was the end of Axminster's pre-eminence in the market for top-quality carpets, but echoes of those glorious years still reverberate. St Mary's Church must be the only house of worship in Christendom whose floor is covered with a richly-woven carpet.

Opposite the church is the former court-house, which is now home to the **Axminster Museum** where the old police cells can be visited, and there are collections of vintage agricultural tools and Axminster carpets.

COLYTON

7 miles SE of Honiton off the A3052

🏠 Church of St Andrew

The tramway that starts at Seaton runs by way of Colyford to this ancient and very appealing small town of narrow winding streets and interesting stone houses. Throughout its long history, Colyton has been an important agricultural and commercial centre with its own corn mill, tannery, sawmill and iron foundry.

Many of the older buildings are grouped around the part-Norman **Church of St**

MILL HOUSE FINE ART PUBLISHING LTD

Bellflower Gallery, Market Place,
Colyton, Devon EX24 6JS
Tel: 01297 553100
Fax: 01297 553608
e-mail: info@millhousefineart.com
website: www.millhousefineart.com

Mill House Fine Art Publishing is located in the Bellflower Gallery, a delightful find in the charming market town of Colyton, Devon.

Lilacs and other Blossom - Greetings Card

Pink Roses - Giclee Print

The Bellflower Gallery specialises in beautiful art work by Anne Cotterill, who is one of the foremost contemporary floral artists in the UK. Inside, visitors are presented with a display of Anne's eminently collectable fine art Greetings Cards, Lithographic and Giclee prints faithfully reproduced from her original oil paintings.

Anne Cotterill's paintings are distinguished by her skill in portraying the natural character and vitality of freshly picked flowers from hedgerows, lanes, meadows and gardens.

The gallery is also home to the wholesale side of the business distrbuting to galleries and shops throughout the UK and Europe.

Customers of the Bellflower Gallery can be sure of an efficient and friendly service. The gallery is open Monday - Friday between 10.30am and 3.30pm.

WHITE HART INN

Swan Hill Road,
Colyford, Colyton,
Devon EX24 6QF
Tel: 01297 553201

The thriving little riverside village of Colyford is known for the Seaton Tramway that passes through it and for possessing a fine old traditional hostelry, the **White Hart Inn**. It has a warm and friendly ambience, and features such as the stone floor in the bar area, lots of nooks and crannies, and a feature brick-built fireplace in the lounge all add to the charm.

Mine host is Bob Sellins who bought the pub in 2001 and now has an established reputation for selling quality food and well-maintained ales. The bar stocks a good range of local brews, including Otter and Branoc, as well as ciders and lagers, and a tempting selection of fine wines, malt whiskeys and other spirits. Unusually, Bob also stocks lovage, shrub, grenadine and Stone's ginger wine as mixers. There's a restaurant seating 43 and customers can also eat in the bar area or in the beer garden at the rear. Families and dogs are welcome; and there's ample parking.

🏛 historic building   🏛 museum and heritage   🏛 historic site   ⚘ scenic attraction   🌱 flora and fauna

Andrew, a striking building with an unusual 15th-century octagonal lantern tower, and a Saxon cross brilliantly reconstructed after its broken fragments were retrieved from the tower where they had been used as building material. Nearby is the Vicarage of 1529, and the Old Church House, a part-medieval building enlarged in 1612 and used as a Grammar School until 1928.

OTTERY ST MARY
5m SW of Honiton on the B3177

🏛 Church of St Mary 🐦 Samuel Taylor Coleridge

🏛 Cadhay 🌿 Escot Park and Gardens

The glory of Ottery St Mary is its magnificent 14th-century **Church of St Mary**. From the outside, St Mary's looks part mini-cathedral, part Oxford college. Both impressions are justified since, when Bishop Grandisson commissioned the building in 1337, he stipulated that it should be modelled on his own cathedral at Exeter. He also wanted it to be "a sanctuary for piety and learning", so accommodation for 40 scholars was provided.

The interior is just as striking. The church's medieval treasures include a brilliantly-coloured altar screen, canopied tombs, and a 14th-century astronomical clock showing the moon and the planets, which still functions with its original machinery.

Ottery's Vicar during the mid 18th century was the Rev John Coleridge whose 13th child became the celebrated poet, **Samuel Taylor Coleridge**. The family home near the church has since been demolished but in one of his poems Samuel recalls

> *"my sweet birth-place, and the old church-tower*
> *Whose bells, the poor man's only music, rang*
> *From morn to evening, all the hot Fair-day"*

A bronze plaque in the churchyard wall

honours Ottery's most famous son. It shows his profile, menaced by the albatross that features in his best-known poem, *The Ancient Mariner*.

It's a delight to wander around the narrow, twisting lanes that lead up from the River Otter, admiring the fine Georgian buildings amongst which is an old wool manufactory by the riverside, a dignified example of early industrial architecture.

An especially interesting time to visit Ottery is on the Saturday closest to 5 November. The town's Guy Fawkes celebrations include a time-honoured, if rather alarming, tradition of rolling barrels of flaming tar through the narrow streets.

About a mile northwest of Ottery, **Cadhay** is a beautiful Tudor mansion built around 1550 but incorporating the Great Hall of an earlier mansion built between 1420 and 1470. The house was built for a Lincoln's Inn lawyer, John Haydon, whose great-nephew Robert Haydon later added the exquisite Long Gallery, thus forming a unique and attractive courtyard. Opening times are restricted.

Close by is **Escot Park and Gardens** where visitors can see an arboretum and rose garden, along with a collection of wildlife that includes wild boar, pot-bellied pigs, otters and birds of prey. The original gardens in this 1200-acre estate were set out by Capability Brown and have been restored by the land artist and television gardener, Ivan Hicks.

BLACKBOROUGH
10 miles NW of Honiton off the A373

Most of the villages in this corner of East Devon nestle in the valley bottoms, but Blackborough is an exception, standing high on a ridge of the Blackdown Hills. It's a comparatively new settlement that sprang up when whetstone mining flourished here for a

THE OLD VICARAGE BED AND BREAKFAST

Broadhembury, Honiton, Devon   EX14 3ND
Tel: 01404 841648
e-mail: enquiries@broadhemburybandb.co.uk
website: www.broadhemburybandb.co.uk

If you are looking for a luxury and stylish B&B in the picturesque South West county of Devon then look no further than **The Old Vicarage Bed and Breakfast**. The Grade II listed B&B overlooks the 14th century church in the timeless village of Broadhembury.

Owned by mother and daughter - Sarah Carter and Christine Roberts, there are four spectacular guest rooms available. All of them offer striking fabrics, luxurious carpets, crisp linen, waffle towels and Chinese antiques, which blend in beautifully with the gracious elegance of the 18th century Georgian building.

Guests can look forward to a delicious and hearty breakfast. Each is prepared to order and the ingredients and produce are all sourced locally, really adding to the quality of the dish. Breakfast can be served in the modern dining room, the privacy of your own bedroom or, on warmer days, out in the garden.

There are two acres of garden for guests to explore. It has an outdoor heated swimming pool, chickens, an exotic vegetable garden and stunning views of the Blackdown Hills. It is the scenic surroundings that attract many visitors to this part of Devon and The Old Vicarage B&B offers the perfect place to enjoy the area.

Sarah and Christine are both very friendly and guests are left to make themselves at home and indulge in the added luxuries here. The B&B offers a unique combination of Georgian elegance and modern design and is located in one of the most picturesque cob-and-thatch villages in Devon.

Many wedding receptions have been held here and it isn't hard to see why many couples choose to come here. The five-star establishment is impressive and the outdoor area is extremely beautiful, providing the perfect place to have photographs taken.

Whether your visit is for rest and relaxation, outdoor pursuits, historical curiosity or simply to sample the delicious menu at the Drewe Arms, book your accommodation at the Old Vicarage and make your stay a memorable one. Children and pets are welcome here. Ring for further details.

🏛 historic building 🏚 museum and heritage 🏛 historic site 🜨 scenic attraction 🌸 flora and fauna

period in the early 1800s. RD Blackmore's novel *Perlycross* presents a vivid picture of life in these makeshift mining camps where the amenities of a comfortable life were few and far between.

UFFCULME

13 miles NW of Honiton off the A38

🏚 Coldharbour Mill

In medieval times, the charming little village of Uffculme, set beside the River Culm, was an important centre for the wool trade. Profits from this booming business helped build the impressive parish church of St Mary around 1450 and to install its splendid rood screen, believed to be the longest in Devon.

Coldharbour Mill, to the west of the village, is one of the few surviving reminders of the county's industrial wool trade. It closed down in 1981 but has since been converted into a Working Wool Museum where visitors can watch the whole process of woollen and worsted manufacture, wander around the carpenter's workshop, a weaver's cottage and the dye room. On most Bank Holidays, the massive 300 horsepower engine in the boiler house is 'steamed up'- a spectacular sight. Conducted tours are available by advance arrangement and the complex also includes a Mill Shop and a waterside restaurant.

CULMSTOCK

14 miles NW of Honiton on the B3391

🐦 RD Blackmore   🏛 Church of All Saints

🏛 Hemyock Castle

Lovers of **RD Blackmore's** novel *Lorna Doone* will be particularly interested in Culmstock since it was here that the author lived as a boy during the years that his father was the Vicar. One of his playmates in the village was Frederick Temple, another bright boy, and the two friends both went on to Blundell's School at Tiverton where they shared lodgings. Blackmore was to become one of the most successful novelists of his time; Temple entered the church and after several years as Headmaster of Rugby School reached the pinnacle of his profession as Archbishop of Canterbury.

In the centre of the village stands Culmstock's parish **Church of All Saints** with its famous yew tree growing from the top of the tower. The tree has been growing there for more than 200 years and, despite the fact that its only nourishment is the lime content of the mortar in which it is set, the trunk has now achieved a girth of 18 inches. It's believed that the seed was probably carried up in the mortar used to repair the tower when its spire was demolished in 1776. The church's more traditional kind of treasures include a magnificently embroidered cope of the late 1400s, now preserved in a glass case; a remarkable 14th-century tomb rediscovered during restoration in the 19th century; and a richly-coloured memorial window designed by Burne-Jones.

About three miles east of Culmstock is **Hemyock Castle**, built around 1380. Four turrets, a curtain wall, a moat with mallard and moorhen in residence, and a dungeon are all that remain of the Hidon family's sturdy manor house, but it is a peaceful and evocative place. The castle stands behind the church in beautiful grounds and, since it lies close to the head of the lovely Culm valley, is very popular as a picnic spot. Opening times are limited.

The Jurassic Coast

🚶 East Devon Way

The coastal stretch to the east of Exmouth

has been named the Jurassic Coast because it was formed during the Jurassic period some 185 million years ago. England's first natural World Heritage Site, the 95 miles of coastline from Exmouth to Studland in Dorset is spectacularly beautiful.

Three river valleys, those of the Axe, the Sid and the Otter, cut through the hills of east Devon to meet the sea at Lyme Bay. They provide the only openings in the magnificent 20-mile-long stretch of rugged cliffs and rocky beaches. Virtually the only settlements to be found along the seaboard are those which developed around the mouths of those rivers: Seaton, Sidmouth and Budleigh Salterton. The intervening cliffs discouraged human habitation, and even today the only way to explore most of this part of the coast is on foot along the magnificent **East Devon Way**, part of the South West Coast Path. Signposted by a foxglove, the footpath travels through the county to Lyme Regis just over the county border in Dorset. Four other circular paths link in with the East Devon Way providing other options for walkers to enjoy and explore the quieter and more remote areas away from the coast.

For centuries the little towns along the coast subsisted on fishing and farming until the early 1800s when the Prince Regent's fad for sea bathing brought an influx of comparatively affluent visitors in search of healthy relaxation. Their numbers were augmented by others whose accustomed European travels had been rendered impossible by Napoleon's domination of the Continent. Between them, they transformed these modest little towns into fashionable resorts, imbuing them with an indefinable 'gentility' which still lives on in the elegant villas, peaceful gardens and wide promenades.

Exmouth

| 🏛 World of Country Life | 🏛 Exmouth Museum |
| 🏚 A La Ronde | 🏚 Point-in-View |

With its glorious coastal scenery and splendid two-mile-long beach, Exmouth was one of the earliest seaside resorts to be developed in Devon, "the Bath of the West, the resort of the tip-top of the gentry of the Kingdom". Lady Byron and Lady Nelson came to stay and found lodgings in The Beacon, an elegant Georgian terrace overlooking the Madeira Walk and Esplanade. This early success suffered a setback when Brunel routed his Great Western line along the other side of the estuary (incidentally creating one of the most scenic railway journeys still possible in England), and it wasn't until a branch line reached Exmouth in 1861 that business picked up again. The town isn't just a popular resort. Exmouth Docks are still busy with coasters, and in summer a passenger ferry crosses the Exe to Starcross. There are also services to Dawlish Warren.

Exmouth's major all-weather attraction is **The World of Country Life**, which offers an Adventure Exhibition Hall, a collection of vintage cars and rare steam engines, a Victorian street, safari train, pirate ship, pets centre and restaurant.

Occupying converted 18th-century stables and an adjoining cottage, **Exmouth Museum** provides fascinating insights into the town's rich history and its strong maritime links. Exhibits include the reconstruction of a Victorian kitchen and a 1930s dining room.

While in Exmouth, you should make a point of visiting what has been described as "the most unusual house in Britain". **A La Ronde** (National Trust) is a fairy-tale thatched house

East of Exmouth

BUDLEIGH SALTERTON
4 miles E of Exmouth on the B3180

Sir John Everett Millais

Fairlynch Museum

With its trim Victorian villas, broad promenade and a spotlessly clean beach flanked by 500 feet-high red sandstone cliffs, Budleigh Salterton retains its 19th-century atmosphere of a genteel resort. Victorian tourists "of the better sort" noted with approval that the two-mile-long beach was of pink shingle rather than sand. (Sand, apparently, attracted the rowdier kind of holiday-maker.) The steeply-shelving beach was another deterrent, and the sea here is still a place for paddling rather than swimming.

One famous Victorian visitor was the celebrated artist **Sir John Everett Millais** who stayed during the summer of 1870 in the curiously-shaped house called The Octagon. It was beside the beach here that he painted his most famous picture, *The Boyhood of Raleigh*, using his two sons and a local ferryman as the models. Raleigh's birthplace, Hayes Barton, lies a mile or so inland and remains virtually unchanged.

The town centre has a good number of independently owned shops and the main street to the beach is bordered by a stream. Close to the seafront is the **Fairlynch Museum**, one of very few thatched museums in the country. Built in 1811 as a cottage orne, it houses numerous collections covering all aspects of life through the ages in the lower Otter Valley. There are weekly demonstrations of lace-making, a collection of locally-made Edwardian dolls, and an interesting collection

A La Ronde, Exmouth

built in 1765 by the sisters Jane and Mary Parminter who modelled it on the church of San Vitale in Ravenna. Despite its name, the house is not in fact circular but has 16 sides with 20 rooms set around a 45-foot-high octagon. The sisters lived here in magnificent feminist seclusion, forbidding the presence of any male in their house or its 15 acres of grounds. What, therefore, no gentleman saw during the lifetime of the sisters, was the wonderfully decorated interior that the cousins created. These fabulous rooms, common in Regency times, are rare today. Due to their delicacy, the feather frieze and shell-encrusted gallery can be seen only via closed circuit TV. Throughout the house the vast collection of pieces that the ladies brought back from their extensive travels is on display.

The Parminter sisters also paid for the building in 1812 of nearby **Point-in-View**, a tiny Congregational chapel with adjacent almshouses for "four spinsters over fifty years of age and approved character". The odd design includes a pyramidal roof with triangular windows, topped by a fanciful weathervane. Services are still held in the church.

of Victorian and Edwardian costumes.

The name Budleigh Salterton derives from the salt pans at the mouth of the River Otter, which brought great prosperity to the town during the Middle Ages. The little port was then busy with ships loading salt and wool, but by 1450 the estuary had become blocked by a pebble ridge and the salt pans flooded.

YETTINGTON
7 miles NE of Exmouth off the B3178

🦅 Sir Walter Raleigh 🌿 Bicton Park

Just to the south of the village of Yettington is Hayes Barton (private), a fine E-shaped Tudor house in which **Sir Walter Raleigh** was born in 1552. The Raleighs' family pew can still be seen in All Saints' Church, dated 1537 and carved with their (now sadly defaced) coat of arms. The church also contains a series of more than 50 16th-century bench-ends, which were carved by local artisans into weird and imaginative depictions of their various trades.

A mile or so in the other direction is **Bicton Park**, best known for its landscaped gardens, which were laid out in the 1730s by Henry Rolle to a plan by André Le Nôtre, the designer of Versailles. There is also a formal Italian garden, a remarkable palm house known as The Dome, a world-renowned collection of pine trees, and a lake complete with an extraordinary

summer house, The Hermitage. Its outside walls are covered with thousands of tiny wooden shingles, each one individually pinned on so they look like the scales of an enormous fish. Inside, the floors are made from deer's knucklebones. The Hermitage was built by Lady Louise Rolle in 1839 as an exotic summer-house; any occupation during the winter would have been highly inadvisable since the chimney was made of oak.

OTTERTON
7 miles NE of Exmouth off the B3178

🏚 Otterton Mill

This delightful village has a charming mix of traditional cob and thatch cottages, along with other buildings constructed in the distinctive local red sandstone, amongst them the tower of St Michael's parish church. Nearby stands a manor house, which was built in the 11th century as a small priory belonging to Mont St Michel in Normandy. It is now divided into private apartments.

The Domesday Book recorded a mill on the River Otter here, almost certainly on the site of the present **Otterton Mill**. This handsome, part-medieval building was restored to working order in the 1970s by Desna Greenhow, a teacher of Medieval Archaeology, and visitors can now buy packs of flour ground by the same methods that were in use long before the compilers of the Domesday Book passed through the village. The site also includes a craft centre, art gallery, shop and restaurant.

An interesting feature of this village of whitewashed thatched cottages is the little stream that runs down Fore Street. At the bottom of the hill, this beck joins the River Otter, which at this point has only a couple of miles to

Orangery, Biction Gardens

go before it enters the sea near Budleigh Salterton. There's a lovely riverside walk in that direction, and if you go northwards, the path stretches even further, to Ottery St Mary some nine or ten miles distant. En route, this path passes the village of East Budleigh where Sir Walter Raleigh's father was warden of the church. Inside, you can still see the family's pews prominently placed at the front on the left hand side.

HARPFORD

11 miles NE of Exmouth off the A3052

🔖 Rev Augustus Toplady 🍴 Aylesbeare Common

Attractively located on the east bank of the River Otter with wooded hills behind, Harpford has a 13th-century church with an impressive tower and, in its churchyard, a memorial cross to the **Rev Augustus Toplady** who was vicar of Harpford for a couple of years in the mid 1700s. In 1775 Augustus wrote the hymn *Rock of Ages, cleft for me*, which has proved to be one of the most durable contributions to English hymnody.

If you cross the footbridge over the river here and follow the path for about a couple of miles you will come to **Aylesbeare Common**, an RSPB sanctuary, which is also one of the best stretches of heathland in the area. Bird-watchers may be lucky enough to spot a Dartford warbler, stonechats, or tree pipits, and even hear the strange song of the nightjar.

SIDMOUTH

11 miles NE of Exmouth on the A375

🔖 Duke of Kent 🏛 Sidmouth Museum

🏚 Old Chancel ✏ Sidmouth Folk Week

Sidmouth's success, like that of many other

SIDMOUTH TRAWLERS

Fisherman's Yard, The Ham, Port Royal, Sidmouth, Devon EX10 8BG
Tel: 01395 512714

Tucked away in Fisherman's Yard at the far eastern end of the Esplanade is **Sidmouth Trawlers**, a fishmonger well known in the area for the excellent quality of its locally caught fish and shellfish. Established in the 1960s by Stan Bagwell, from a long line of fishermen, this family-run business maintains the highest standards in endeavouring to provide for all lovers of seafood a large variety of fish and shellfish sourced from local fishermen.

The family take great pride in the various national craftsmanship awards they have won over the years, and filleting and preparation is all part of the service. No one coming to Sidmouth should miss the opportunity to visit this superb fishmonger's. Insulated packaging is available to take home a selection of the freshest seafood - from brill, Dover sole, mackerel and scallops to freshly cooked lobster and crab - to be found anywhere in the country. A ready-to-eat service is also available for whelks, cockles, mussels, prawns and crabmeat, and generously filled sandwiches are made to order.

THE BARN & PINN COTTAGE

Bowd Cross, Sidmouth, Devon EX10 0ND
Tel: 01395 513613
e-mail: barnpinncottage@btinternet.com
website: www.thebarnandpinncottage.co.uk

Just a 5-minute drive from Sidmouth, **The Barn & Pinn Cottage** is a stunning 15th Century thatched cottage surrounded by glorious award winning gardens which received a Gold award from the Sidmouth in Bloom competition in 2009. This lovely old dwelling is the home of Peter and Kim Clinch who extend a genuinely warm welcome to all their guests. Finding the right bed and breakfast can be difficult, especially in Devon, but if you take a look around their website you may just find the decision making process has been made a whole lot easier for you!

Guests have the use of a comfortable and welcoming lounge with a 42" television, games and books. During the cooler months, a log-burning stove adds to the appeal. The 4-star accommodation comprises 10 individually decorated en suite rooms with full central heating, TV and hospitality tray. There's one single with a 4ft bed; 3 doubles, 2 twins, 1 holiday let, 1 king size and 2 luxury rooms with King size 4-poster beds and private patio and garden. Peter and Kim are happy to welcome guests with well-behaved dogs. There are three bedrooms suitable for use by guests with dogs.

Breakfast is served in a cosy room overlooking the garden and many guests enjoy watching the birds and squirrels who are active there. Dinner is available from Thursday to Sunday and is served in 'The Barn', a large vaulted room which in days gone by was a hay barn. This room also enjoys the comfort of a wood-burner and also enjoys lovely views over the gardens. The menu offers good home cooking with a varied menu to choose from. There's also a well-stocked bar.

Guests at the Barn & Pinn Cottage will find plenty to see and do in the area. Sidmouth itself was described by the late Poet Laureate, John Betjeman, as having "beautiful gardens and leisurely walks, Regency history, clean beaches and friendly shops. It's all here in this lovely seaside town that nestles beneath majestic red cliffs and the green hills of the glorious Sid Valley". Other attractions within easy reach include the historic houses of Cadhay, Ugbrooke Park and Powderham Castle; Escot Gardens and the manifold attractions of the historic city of Exeter.

English resorts, had much to do with Napoleon Bonaparte. Barred from the Continent and their favoured resorts by the Emperor's conquest of Europe, the leisured classes were forced to find diversion and entertainment within their own island fortress. At the same time, sea bathing had suddenly become fashionable so these years were a boom time for the south coast, even as far west as Sidmouth, which until then had been a poverty-stricken village dependent on fishing.

Sidmouth's spectacular position at the mouth of the River Sid, flanked by dramatic red cliffs soaring to over 500 feet and with a broad pebbly beach, assured the village's popularity with the newcomers. A grand Esplanade was constructed, lined with handsome Georgian houses, and between 1800 and 1820 Sidmouth's population doubled as the aristocratic and well-to-do built substantial 'cottages' in and around the town. Many of these have since been converted into impressive hotels, such as the Beach House, painted strawberry pink and white, and the Royal Glen, which in the early 19th century was the residence of the royal **Duke of Kent**. The duke came here in 1819 in an attempt to escape his numerous creditors, and it was here that his infant daughter, Princess Victoria, later Queen Victoria, saw the sea for the first time.

To evade his many creditors, the Duke had his mail directed to Salisbury. Each week he would ride there to collect his letters, but in Sidmouth itself he couldn't conceal his delight in his young daughter. He would push Victoria in a little carriage along the mile-long Regency Esplanade, stopping passers-by to tell them to look carefully at the little girl – "for one day she would be their Queen". Half a century later, his daughter presented a stained-glass window to Sidmouth parish church in dutiful memory of her father.

One of the town's early visitors was Jane Austen, who came here on holiday in 1801 and, according to Austen family tradition, fell in love with a clergyman whom she would have married if he had not mysteriously died or disappeared. Later, in the 1830s, William Makepeace Thackeray visited and the town featured as Baymouth in his semi-autobiographical work *Pendennis* (published in 1848). During the Edwardian age, Beatrix Potter was a visitor on several occasions.

A stroll around the town reveals a wealth of attractive Georgian and early-Victorian buildings. Amazingly for such a small town, Sidmouth boasts nearly 500 listed buildings. Curiously, it was the Victorians who let the town down. Despite being the wealthiest nation in the world at that time, with vast resources at its command, its architects seemed incapable of creating architecturally interesting churches, and the two 19th-century Houses of the Lord they built in Sidmouth display a lamentable lack of inspiration. So ignore them, but it's worth seeking out the curious structure known as the **Old Chancel** in Coburg Terrace, a glorious hotch-potch of styles using bits and pieces salvaged from the old parish church and from just about anywhere else, amongst them a priceless window of medieval stained glass.

Also well worth a visit is **Sidmouth Museum**, near the sea-front, which provides a vivid presentation of the Victorian resort, along with such curiosities as an albatross's swollen foot once used as a tobacco pouch. There's also an interesting collection of local prints, a costume gallery and a display of fine lace. One of the most striking exhibits in the museum is the 'Long Picture' by Hubert Cornish, which is some eight feet (2.4 metres) long and depicts the whole of Sidmouth seafront as it was around 1814.

📖 stories and anecdotes   🐦 famous people   🎨 art and craft   ✏ entertainment and sport   🚶 walks

Fishing Boats, Sidmouth

The town also boasts one of the few public access observatories in Britain: the **Norman Lockyer Observatory**. It has a planetarium and large telescopes, and a radio station commemorating the contribution of Sir Ambrose Fleming, a local hero, to the invention of the radio valve. Opening times are limited.

Demure though it remains, Sidmouth undergoes a transformation in the first week of August each year when it plays host to the **Sidmouth Folk Week**, a cosmopolitan event that attracts a remarkable variety of morris dancers, folk singers and even clog dancers from around the world.

SIDBURY
12 miles NE of Exmouth on the A375

St Peter & St Giles   Sidbury Castle

St Peter & St Giles' church at Sidbury boasts the unique amenity of a Powder Room. In fact, the room over the porch contained not cosmetics, but gunpowder, which was stored there by the military during the fearful days when Napoleon was expected to land in England at any moment. The church is also notable for its Saxon crypt, rediscovered during restoration in 1898. It's a rough-walled room just nine feet by ten feet, located under the chancel floor. Other treasures include a remarkable 500-year-old font with a square iron

lock intended to protect the holy water in the basin from witches, and a number of curious carvings on the Norman tower.

Above the village to the southwest stands **Sidbury Castle**, not a castle at all but the site of a hilltop Iron Age fort from which there are some spellbinding views of the coastline extending from Portland Bill to Berry Head.

BRANSCOMBE
14 miles NE of Exmouth off the A3052

Old Bakery, Manor Mill & Forge

MSC Napoli

The coastal scenery near Branscombe is some of the finest in the southwest with great towers of chalk rising from overgrown landslips. The village itself is a picturesque scattering of farmhouses and thatched cottages with an interesting National Trust property within its boundaries – **Old Bakery, Manor Mill and Forge**. Regular demonstrations are held at the Manor Mill, which is still in working order. The water-powered mill provided flour for the adjacent bakery, which, until 1987, was the last traditional bakery operating in Devon. Its vintage baking equipment has been preserved and the rest of the building is now a tearoom. The Forge is still working and the blacksmith's ironwork is on sale to visitors.

The land around Branscombe's beach, with its long expanse of pebbles and painted coastal huts, is also owned by the National Trust. The beach entered the national consciousness in January 2007 when a container ship, the *MSC Napoli* got into difficulties during a gale and was grounded about 100 yards from the beach. Some of the ship's containers broke open and their contents were washed on to the beach. The flotsam included barrels of wine, shoes, hair care products, beauty cream, steering wheels, exhaust pipes, gearboxes, nappies, foreign language bibles and even BMW motorbikes. As the word spread, the beach was invaded by scavengers, many of whom made away with rich pickings until the police closed the beach 24 hours after the *Napoli* had grounded. It was not until seven months later that the stricken ship was taken by tug to a dry dock at the Harland and Wolff shipyard in Belfast.

BEER
16 miles NE of Exmouth on the B3174

> ✎ Pecorama ⚒ Beer Quarry Caves
>
> ⚒ Beer Head

Set between the high white chalk cliffs of Beer Head and Seaton Hole, this stunningly picturesque fishing village is best known for the superb white freestone that has been quarried here since Roman times. Much prized for carving, the results can be seen in countless Devon churches, and most notably in the cathedrals at Exeter, Winchester and St Paul's, as well as at the Tower of London and in Westminster Abbey. Conducted tours around the vast, man-made complex of the **Beer Quarry Caves** leave visitors astonished at the sheer grandeur of the lofty halls, vaulted roofs and massive supporting pillars of natural stone. Not surprisingly, this complex underground network recommended itself to smugglers, amongst them the notorious Jack Rattenbury who was a native of Beer and published his *Memoirs of a Smuggler* in 1837.

A family attraction here is **Pecorama**, which sits on the cliff top high above the village and has an award-winning miniature railway, spectacular Millennium Gardens, the Peco Model Railway Exhibition, play areas and superb sea views.

South of Beer, the coastal path climbs to the summit of **Beer Head**, an imposing 425 feet high, which marks the beginning of the south coast's white chalk cliffs.

SEATON
17 miles NE of Exmouth on the B3172

> ✎ Seaton Tramway
>
> ⚓ South West Coast Path

Set around the mouth of the River Axe, with red cliffs on one side and white cliffs on the other, Seaton was once a quite significant port. By the 16th century, however, the estuary had filled up with stones and pebbles, and it wasn't until moneyed Victorians came and built their villas (and one of the first concrete bridges in the world, in 1877) that Seaton was accorded a new lease of life. The self-confident architecture of those times gives the little town an attractive appearance, which is enhanced by its pedestrianised town centre and well-maintained public parks and gardens.

From Seaton, an attractive way of travelling along the Axe Valley is on the **Seaton Tramway** whose colourful open-topped tramcars, the oldest of which was built in 1904, trundle through an area famous for its bird life to the villages of Colyford and Colyton. The three-mile route follows the course of the River Axe, which is noted for its abundant wild bird life. Really dedicated tram fans, after a short lesson, are even permitted to take over the driver's seat.

From Seaton, eastwards, the **South West Coast Path** follows the coastline uninterruptedly all the way to Lyme Regis in Dorset. Considered by naturalists as the last and largest wilderness on the southern coast of England, this area of unstable cliffs, wood and scrub is also a haven for wildlife.

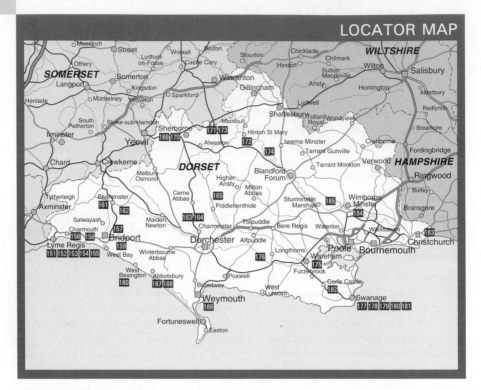

LOCATOR MAP

ADVERTISERS AND PLACES OF INTEREST

🏠 historic building   🏛 museum and heritage   🏚 historic site   🗝 scenic attraction   🌿 flora and fauna

3| Dorset

"Dorset has no high mountains and no coal. Everything else of beauty and almost everything of utility can be found within its borders."

This was Ralph Wightman's description of one of England's most enchanting counties. Twenty-five miles of the county's spectacular coastline has been awarded World Heritage Site status by UNESCO for its outstanding geology, an accolade that ranks it alongside the Grand Canyon and the Great Barrier Reef. The glorious coastal scenery includes beautiful Lulworth Cove, the strange natural formations of Durdle Door and the 10-mile long stretch of pebbles known as Chesil

Beach. South of Weymouth, the Isle of Purbeck – famous for the marble that has been quarried here since Roman times – falls like a tear-drop into the English Channel. To the west is the charming resort town of Lyme

Cheap Street, Sherborne

🎭 stories and anecdotes 🕊 famous people ✏ art and craft 🎟 entertainment and sport 🚶 walks

Regis, famous for its curved harbour wall, The Cobb, its associations with Jane Austen and for the remarkable fossils discovered in what is now known as the Jurassic Coast.

Dorchester Water Meadows

Inland, gently rolling hills, woodlands and gentle river valleys epitomise the charms of unspoilt rural England. Delightful old market towns like Shaftesbury, Bridport, Blandford Forum and Sherborne have a settled graciousness, while villages such as Milton Abbas, Cranborne and Breamore are almost impossibly picturesque.

The county has more than its fair share of historic castles. Corfe Castle, set high on a hill, is one of the most impressive man-made sights in the southwest; Sherborne Castle was the home of Sir Walter Raleigh and Portland Castle is the best-preserved of Henry VIII's coastal fortresses. Stately homes range from the Tudor gem of Athelhampton House, to the splendour of Kingston Lacy House with its outstanding collection of Old Masters. Then there are the magnificent abbeys of Wimborne Minster, Forde and Sherborne, and the fine church at Bere Regis, famed for its superbly carved and painted roof, and the priory at Christchurch with its imposing Norman exterior and wealth of tombs and chantries.

Dorchester, one of England's most appealing county towns, stands at the heart of 'Hardy Country' – most of the scenes in Thomas Hardy's novels are set within a dozen or so miles of the town. Hardy was born in the nearby village of Higher Bockhampton; the humble house where he grew up is open to the public. He spent the last four decades of his life in Dorchester at Max Gate, a modest villa he designed himself, which is now a National Trust property. Many of Dorset's most striking features – the Cerne Abbas hill carving of a naked giant, for example – feature in Hardy's novels, either as themselves or lightly disguised.

Lyme Regis

🦆 The Cobb 🦆 Golden Cap

🏃 South West Coast Path 🌿 Jane Austen Garden

🏛 Lyme Regis Museum 🏛 Dinosaurland

🏮 Town Mill 🌿 Regatta and Carnival

Known as The Pearl of Dorset, Lyme Regis is a captivating little town enjoying a setting unrivalled in the county, an Area of Outstanding Natural Beauty where the rolling countryside of Dorset plunges to the sea. The town itself is a maze of narrow streets with many charming Georgian and Regency houses, and the picturesque harbour will be familiar to anyone who has seen the film *The French Lieutenant's Woman*, based on the novel by Lyme resident, the late John Fowles. The scene of a lone woman standing on the wave-lashed Cobb has become one of cinema's most enduring images.

The Cobb, which protects the harbour and the sandy beach with its clear bathing water from south-westerly storms, was first recorded in 1294, but the town itself goes back at least another 500 years to Saxon times when there was a salt works here. A charter granted by Edward I allowed Lyme to add Regis to its name, but during the Civil War the town was staunchly anti-royalist, routing the forces of Prince Maurice and killing more than 2000 of them. Some 40 years later, James, Duke of Monmouth, chose Lyme as his landing place to start the ill-fated rebellion that would end with ferocious reprisals being meted out to the insurgents by the notorious Judge Jeffreys. Happier days arrived in the 18th century when Lyme became a fashionable resort, famed for

THE OLD BOATHOUSE

1 Marine Parade, Lyme Regis, Dorset DT7 3JE
Tel: 07767 390321

When the sun shines there's no better place to spend an hour or two than the seafront at Lyme Regis, with the English Channel stretching out ahead and glorious sweeping views in both directions. Marine Parade is a great place to walk, to sit, to enjoy the sun and the views – and to pause for a snack and a tea or coffee.

Rain or shine, there are always plenty of customers at the **Old Boathouse**, the first café you see when stepping out onto the beach, down from the car park with its big clock. Once a store for boats, and later a tourist information centre, this popular beach café has recently seen a complete facelift and a change of focus by long-term owner Gail Morris. The tables and chairs are now located outside (along with parasols) and the Old Boathouse is now primarily a takeaway, reflecting the fact that people like to sit outside just a few steps from the sea.

The straightforward menu remains much the same, with locally sourced produce to the fore. There are sandwiches and baguettes, pastries and delectable West Country ice creams, with teas, coffees and soft drinks to accompany a snack. One of the favourite orders is the crab sandwiches, making use of the bountiful year-round supply of crabs caught in the Bay.

🎬 stories and anecdotes 🦜 famous people 🎨 art and craft 🌿 entertainment and sport 🏃 walks

its fresh, clean air. Jane Austen and her family visited in 1803 and part of her novel *Persuasion* is set in the town. The **Jane Austen Garden** commemorates her visit.

Occupying a row of former fishermen's cottages on the Cobb, the **Marine Aquarium** has a good display of local marine life, including poisonous weaver fish, sea horses and sea scorpions.

A few years after Jane Austen's visit to the town, a 12-year-old girl called Mary Anning was wandering along the shore when she noticed bones protruding from the cliffs that stretch in both directions away from Lyme. She had discovered the first ichthyosaur to be found in England. Later, as one of the first professional fossil collectors, she also unearthed locally a plesiosaur and a pterodactyl. The six-mile stretch of coastline on either side of Lyme is world-famous for its fossils and some fine specimens of local discoveries can be seen at the award-winning **Lyme Regis Philpot Museum** in Bridge Street and at **Dinosaurland & Fossil Museum** in Coombe Street, which also runs guided fossil walks along the beach. The museum is housed in a magnificent Grade I listed building, which was once a church and where Mary Anning was baptised and where she used to worship.

Just around the corner from Dinosaurland, in Mill Lane, you'll find one of the town's most interesting buildings. It was in January 1991 that a group of Lyme Regis residents got together in an effort to save the old **Town Mill** from destruction. There has been a mill on the River Lim in the centre of the town for many centuries, but most of the present buildings date back to the mid 17th century when the mill was rebuilt after being burned down during the Civil War siege of Lyme in 1644. Today, back in full working order, Town Mill is one of Lyme's major attractions, incorporating two Art Galleries that stage a wide range of exhibitions, concerts, poetry readings and other live performances. There is also a stable building that houses craft workshops and a café/bistro.

If you enjoy walking, the **South West Coast Path** passes through Lyme: if you follow it eastwards for about five miles it will bring you to **Golden Cap** (617ft), the highest point on the south coast with spectacular views from every vantage point. Or you can just take a pleasant stroll along Marine Parade, a traffic-free promenade stretching for about a mile from the Cobb.

For its size, Lyme Regis has an extraordinary range of activities on offer, too many to list here, although the famous week-

🏠 historic building   🖼 museum and heritage   🏛 historic site   🦢 scenic attraction   🌿 flora and fauna

LYME FOSSIL SHOP

4 Bridge Street, Lyme Regis, Dorset DT7 3QA
Tel: 01297 442088
e-mail: lymefossilshop@aol.com
website: www.lymeregisfossilshop.co.uk

Established more than 30 years ago, The Lyme Regis Fossil Shop stocks a huge variety of local fossils probably the largest selection in Britain. Their professional palaeontologist visitors frequently tell them that is the best fossil shop in the UK. The Titchener family are constantly travelling the world to find the best specimen fossils or minerals.

So you'll find a wide choice of amber and copal from the Baltic, Dominican Republic, Columbia and Madagascar, many of them with inclusions of insects. There's also a huge variety of fish plates with specimens originating in America, France, Germany, China, Lebanon and Brazil.

The shop is also well known for its vast range of local fossils with prices ranging from 99p to £1,500. Another interesting fossil available here is the Portland Titanites Gigantus, the largest ammonite in the world, and the very similar Moroccan Agadir ammonites - these range in price from £45 to £400. The shop doesn't confine itself to fossils and minerals. It also sells dinosaur toys, sea shells, carved stone products in soapstone, coal, and onyx, as well as jewellery which is mostly handmade with either sterling silver or 9ct and 18ct gold.

GINGER BEER

12 Broad Street, Lyme Regis, Dorset DT7 3QD
Tel: 01297 444443
e-mail: gingerbeersw@aol.com website: www.ginger-beer.biz

Ginger Beer is *the* shop to visit for the very best in outdoor living.

Dawn Lathey, Nigel & Susie Cole have brought together a fascinating collection of new & vintage products distinguished by their classic design, simple elegance, all of the highest quality.

Sandstorm Bags handcrafted in Kenya, traditional Panama hats from Ecuador, Millican rucksacks & field bags. The fabulous Kelly Kettle, a must for the great outdoors! You'll also find Bill Brown roll up beds, a wide range of Lilyflame candles, Burt Bees ointments & balms. Their vintage stock is constantly changing but you will find Turkish urns still smelling of olive oil, beautiful old garden furniture & an extensive range of gardening tools.

Always on the look out for new & exciting products they aim to promote items that are ethically traded, recyclable, & from a sustainable source. For everyone at Ginger Beer, the ambition is simple... to ensure their customer's enjoy outside living as much as they do!

Their sister interiors shop, 'Susie Cole' is just up the street.

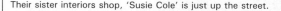

SUSIE COLE

15 Broad Street, Lyme Regis, Dorset DT7 3QE
Tel: 01297 444933
e-mail: susie@susiecole.co.uk
website: www.susiecole.co.uk

Located in the main shopping street of this charming seaside town, **Susie Cole** is a highly acclaimed interiors and gift shop, overflowing with romance and intrigue. Susie opened the shop in 2003 and has put together an enticing array of products for the home – and for yourself. There are some wonderful leather handbags, brief cases and suitcases from Rome, for example, stylish jewellery by both local craftspeople and foreign producers and unusual British vintage fashion accessories. Or you could indulge yourself with some of the bath gels, hand creams and perfumes from her Now and Forever range.

Among items for the home, antique and vintage china features prominently, and there are old and new quilts from Denmark, kitchenware, dressing table items, retro and industrial homeware and vintage toys. Susie also stocks a range of painted furniture, old books and the Anzu and Willemien ranges of greetings cards. Just along the street, with Susie one of the owners, Ginger Beer stocks a brilliant selection of outdoor living and garden products.

long **Regatta and Carnival** held in August deserves a mention. Bands play on the Marine Parade, there are displays by Morris Men and folk dancers, and an annual Town Criers Open Championship. Lyme has maintained a town crier for more than 1000 years without a break and the current incumbent in his colourful 18th-century costume can be seen and heard throughout the town during the summer months.

Around Lyme Regis

River Char, Charmouth

CHARMOUTH
2 miles NE of Lyme Regis off the A35

🏛 Charmouth Heritage Coast Centre

What better recommendation could you give the seaside village of Charmouth than the fact that it was Jane Austen's favourite resort? "Sweet and retired" she called it. To quote Arthur Mee, "She loved the splendid sweep of country all

Charmouth Heritage Coast Centre

Lower Sea Lane, Charmouth, Dorset DT6 6LL
Tel: 01297 560772
website: www.charmouth.org

Charmouth Heritage Coast Centre is one of the country's leading coastal geological visitor centres. The Centre's displays introduce the visitor to the amazing geology and fossils of the West Dorset coast. There are fossils for you to look at and touch, interactive fossil identification displays and a "fossil beach" to practice fossil hunting.

Two large aquariums house a variety of local marine life, while a computerised display lets you dive into Lyme Bay and discover the secrets of the underwater world. For a small charge you can visit the Jurassic Theatre and discover "Finding Fossils at Charmouth" or "Secrets of the Sea". A wide selection of books, postcards and gifts are on sale.

The Centre is run by three wardens who organise a series of guided walks throughout the season. As well as the popular fossil hunting walks, there are rockpooling sessions and walks in the local countryside. Details are available from the Centre or from the website.

round it, the downs, the valleys, the hills like Golden Cap, and the pageantry of the walk to Lyme Regis." Charmouth remains an attractive little place with a wide main street lined with Regency buildings, and a quiet stretch of sandy beach that gradually merges into shingle. This part of the coast has yielded an amazing variety of fossils, many of which can be seen at the **Charmouth Heritage Coast Centre** (see panel above). Two large aquariums house a variety of local marine life, while a computerised display enables you to 'dive' into Lyme Bay and explore the secrets of the underwater world. The centre is run by three wardens who, throughout the season, organise a series of guided fossil-hunting walks along this scenic stretch of the Jurassic Coast.

WHITCHURCH CANONICORUM
4 miles NE of Lyme Regis off the A35

🏛 Church of St Candida 🏛 St Wite

🕊 Georgi Markov

Clinging to the steep hillside above the valley of the River Char, Whitchurch Canonicorum is notable for its enchanting setting and for its **Church of St Candida and the Holy Cross**. This noble building with its Norman arches and an imposing tower built around 1400 is remarkable for being one of only two churches in England still possessing a shrine to a saint. (The other is that of Edward the Confessor in Westminster Abbey.) St Candida was a Saxon woman named Wite – the Anglo-Saxon word for white, which in Latin is Candida. She lived as a hermit but was murdered by a Viking raiding party in AD831. During the Middle Ages a major cult grew up around her memory. A large shrine was built of golden Purbeck stone, its lower level pierced by three large ovals into which the sick and maimed thrust their limbs, their head or even their whole body, in the hope of being cured.

The cult of **St Wite** thrived until the Reformation when all such "monuments of feigned miracles" were swept away. That might have been the end of the story but during the winter of 1899-1900 the foundations of the church settled and cracked open a 13th century tomb chest. Inside was a lead casket with a Latin inscription stating that "Here rest the relics of St Wite" and inside the casket the bones of a small woman about 40 years old. The shrine still attracts pilgrims today, the donations they leave in the openings beneath the tomb now being devoted to causes that aid health and healing.

A martyr of a different kind lies in the churchyard with English words on one side of his tombstone and Bulgarian on the other. In 1978, **Georgi Markov**, "Bulgaria's most revered dissident", was assassinated on Waterloo Bridge by a communist agent using a gas-gun disguised as an umbrella to inject him with a pin-sized pellet of the lethal toxin ricin.

BROADWINDSOR
9 miles NE of Lyme Regis on the B3163

Just to the south of this pretty terraced village is a trio of hill forts, Pilsdon Pen, Lambert's Castle and Coney's Castle (all National Trust). They are connected by a network of paths and all provide magnificent views out across Marshwood Vale to the sea. William Wordsworth took a house on Pilsdon Pen for

a while and declared that there was no finer view in England.

FORDE ABBEY
11 miles N of Lyme Regis off the B3162

🏛 Forde Abbey

About as far west as you can get in Dorset, **Forde Abbey** enjoys a lovely setting beside the River Axe. Founded as a Cistercian monastery more than 800 years ago, it is now the home of the Roper family. The abbey church has gone but the monks of those days would still recognise the chapter house, dormitories, kitchen and refectories. The Upper Refectory is particularly striking with its fine timbered roof and carved panelling. After the Dissolution of the Monasteries, the abbot's residence became a private house and was greatly extended in 1649 by Cromwell's Attorney-General, Sir Edmond Prideaux. The mansion's greatest treasures are the superb Mortlake tapestries of around 1630, which are based on cartoons by Raphael and have borders probably designed by Rubens. Gardens extending to 30 acres, and with origins in the early 1700s, are landscaped around this enchanting house.

Bridport

🏛 Town Hall 🐾 Purbeck Brewery 🐿 Charles II

🏛 Bridport Museum 🏚 Mangerton Mill

With its broad streets, (from the days when they were used for making ropes), Bridport is an appealing little town surrounded by green hills and with a goodly number of 17th and 18th-century buildings. Most notable amongst these are the stately Georgian **Town Hall** of 1786, and the pleasing collection of 17th-century houses in the street running south from the Town Hall. An even older survivor is the medieval Prior's House, known as The Chantry. If you visit the town on a Wednesday or Saturday you'll find its three main streets chock-a-block with dozens of stalls participating in the regular Street Market. The Town Council actively encourages local people who produce goods at home and not as part of their regular livelihood to join in. So there's an extraordinary range of artefacts on offer, anything from silk flowers to socks, fossils to fishing tackle. Another popular attraction is **Palmers Brewery** in West Bay Road. Established in 1794, part of the brewery is still thatched. During the season, visitors are welcomed Monday to Friday for a tour of the historic brewery, the charge for which includes a commemorative certificate and also a glass or two of beer.

The focal point of the town is the oddly-named Bucky Doo Square, which has at its centre a magnificent carved centrepiece of Portland and Purbeck stone by a local stone mason, Karl Dixon. The octagonal piece has eight bas-relief panels depicting aspects of the town's past, present and future.

Based in a Tudor town house dating back to the early 16th century, **Bridport Museum** tells the story of the town from its origins to the present day. There are notable displays on artefacts from a nearby Roman hillfort and the world-famous rope and net making industries which has produced everything from hangman's nooses, the 1966 World Cup net and the nets that catch space shuttles as they return to earth. As well as the permanent displays, there is a programme of temporary exhibitions that change throughout the April to November season. A street away is Bridport Museum's Local & Family History Centre where you can further research the town and its industries, or

SPRAY COPSE FARM

Lee Lane, Bradpole, Bridport, Dorset DT6 4AP
Tel: 01308 458510

Spray Copse Farm occupies a lovely riverside position just outside Bridport and close to the Jurassic Coast. This 4-star bed & breakfast establishment is owned and run by Helen McReavie and her family who pride themselves on delivering excellence as standard across all areas, from hospitality and the quality of the rooms to the generous and delicious 'Dorset Fry' breakfasts, locally sourced

and perfect for setting you up for the day ahead. Guests have the use of a spacious, bright and airy lounge area with TV, as well as a large conservatory area, perfect for those long and balmy summer's evenings.

Families are welcome, and there's a large paddock complete with goalposts and a trampoline, where children will be fully entertained during their stay. Anglers will appreciate of fishing in the River Asker within the grounds.

📖 stories and anecdotes 🐿 famous people 🎨 art and craft 🎭 entertainment and sport 🚶 walks

do family history research for the local area and the whole of the UK.

Two distinguished visitors to the town should be mentioned. One was Joan of Navarre who landed at Bridport in 1403 on her way to become queen to Henry IV; the other, the future **Charles II** who arrived in the town after his defeat at the Battle of Worcester in 1651. He was fleeing to France, pretending to be the groom in a runaway marriage. As he attended to his horses in the yard of an inn, an ostler approached him saying, "Surely I know you, friend?" The quick-thinking future monarch asked where the ostler had been working before. When he replied "In Exeter," Charles responded "Aye, that is where we must have met." Charles then excused himself and made a speedy departure from the town. If the ostler's memory for faces had been better, he could have claimed the £1000 bounty for Charles' capture and subsequent English history would have followed a very different course.

Just to the north of Bridport, **Mangerton Mill** is a working 17th-century watermill in a peaceful rural setting. On the same site is a Museum of Rural Bygones, a tearoom and craft shop.

In recent years, the area around Bridport has featured extensively in TV chef Hugh Fearnley-Whittingstall's popular "live off the land" cookery series, *Return to River Cottage*.

ARTWAVE WEST

Morcombelake, Dorset DT6 6DY
Tel: 01297 489746
e-mail: info@artwavewest.com
website: www.artwavewest.com

A stunning new contemporary art gallery displaying work by professional local and international artists set in a beautifully restored former country pub. **Artwave West** concentrates its exhibiting around artists who have shaped a distinctive personal vision around the discourse between abstraction and figuration.

The gallery ensures that a close working relationship with its artists is maintained and customers can be assured of well chosen portfolios and thorough knowledge of work. Exhibitions change every six weeks guaranteeing visitors to always see something new and exciting. The programme also includes mixed exhibitions that attract a range of visiting and emerging artists to the gallery to enhance and supplement the presentation. The combined artist complement brings an impressive national and international exhibiting profile to Artwave West.

The gallery has been designed to make viewing the art work an enjoyable experience and the inclusion of a coffee bar allows visitors to relax whilst taking in the atmosphere. Artwave West can be found on the main road in the village of Morcombelake between Bridport and the seaside resort of Lyme Regis. The gallery has a large car park and there is also a bus stop directly outside.

NORBURTON HALL

Shipton Lane, Burton Bradstock, Bridport,
Dorset DT6 4NQ
Tel: 01308 897007
e-mail: info@norburtonhall.com
website: www.norburtonhall.com

Located in the picturesque village of Burton Bradstock at the western edge of Dorset's famous Chesil Beach. **Norburton Hall** offers award winning bed and breakfast and luxury self catering accommodation in the elegant surroundings of a country retreat built in the Arts and Crafts style amongst 6 acres of peaceful grounds. Within weeks of opening Norburton Hall received top accolades and has been consistently graded as 5 stars gold award by VisitBritain.

All of their self-catering cottages and apartments are situated within the historic environs of Norburton Hall, close to the main house. A sensitive refurbishment programme in 2005 has transformed the traditional estate buildings, some of which date from the 16th century. Much of the original fabric, the features and character have been retained. These are now blended with the very latest in contemporary living to provide outstanding self-catering convenience and stylish top quality comfort. Quality feather and down duvets and pillows with cotton bedding and towels are provided with an emphasis on comfort and relaxation. Fresh local organic produce can be ordered, to be available on your arrival including a Norburton Breakfast box.

Conveniently positioned off-road parking is provided adjacent to each property, for easy access. And guests are welcome to relax in the beautifully maintained gardens and woodland.

WEST BAY

1 mile S of Bridport off the A35

When Bridport's own harbour silted up in the early 1700s, the townspeople built a new one at the mouth of the River Brit and called it West Bay. During the 19th century, hundreds of ships docked here every year, and West Bay had its own shipbuilding industry until 1879. The little town never became a fashionable resort but the beach, backed by 100ft high sandstone cliffs, is much enjoyed by holiday-makers, and there's still a stall at the little harbour where you can treat yourself to a tub of cockles. From the harbour you can take a mackerel boat round the bay or go for the deeper waters in search of cod, conger, skate or pollock – and keep a lookout for one of the friendly dolphins.

West Bay

TAMARISK ORGANIC FARM

Tamarisk Farm, West Bexington, Dorset DT2 9DF
Tel: 01308 897781
e-mail: farm@tamariskfarm.co.uk
website: www.tamariskfarm.co.uk

Tamarisk Farm is a 600-acre mixed organic farm and organic market garden behind Chesil Beach on the stunning Dorset Heritage Coast with holiday cottages (including two specifically for disabled) and a farm shop. It is run by Arthur and Josephine Pearse, their daughter Ellen and son-in-law Adam, the main farm being owned by the family with additional land rented from the National Trust. The family were early members of the Soil Association and have been producing wholesome organic food since 1960. From the beginning they maintained a close link between growing food and wildlife conservation. Their land incorporates a wide variety of valuable habitats supporting a fascinating wealth of wildlife including many rare plants and animals.

The shop sells the very finest organic produce, all grown or raised on the farm. The beef – well hung - comes from their 'Ruby Red' Devon cattle, the lamb, hogget and mutton from Dorset Down sheep and specialist breeds. Burgers and sausages are made from their meat by a local butcher. Also sold here are fruit and vegetables, wool and sheepskins, wholemeal wheat and rye flours stone-milled here by Adam. The shop has limited opening hours so do phone or check the website.

Close to the harbour is the Bridport Arms Hotel, an historic old thatched building that in parts dates back as far as the 1500s. The inn's picturesque qualities earned it two roles in the BBC-TV series *Harbour Lights* starring Nick Berry and Tina Hobky. The inn appeared as both The Piers Hotel and the Bridehaven public house.

BEAMINSTER
5 miles N of Bridport on the A3066

📷 Beaminster Museum 🐾 UK Llamas

In Hardy's novel, when Tess Durberville arrives in Beaminster, (Emminster in the novel), she finds a delightful little market town. Visitors today will find that remarkably little has changed. The whole of the town

centre is a conservation area and contains an impressive 200 listed buildings. Amongst them are the 17th-century almshouse, the majestic church tower in gold-tinted Ham stone, the 16th-century former Pickwick's Inn (now called the Wild Garlic and owned by the 2009 Master Chef winner, Mat Follas), and the charming Market Square with its stone roofed market cross. What have disappeared are the many small industries that thrived in those days – rope and sailcloth, embroidered buttons, shoes, wrought ironwork and clock-making were just some of the artefacts produced here. Housed in the former Congregational Chapel of 1749, **Beaminster Museum** displays objects relating to the life of the town from

NICK TETT - FAMILY BUTCHER

19 The Square, Beaminster, Dorset DT8 3AU
Tel: 01308 862253
e-mail: nicholas.tett@tiscali.co.uk

Over recent years, Beaminster has become something of a Foodie Town. The owner of the Wild Garlic restaurant won TV's Masterchef in 2008 and the town has an excellent butcher's shop, **Nick Tett - Family Butcher**. Nick started as a butcher at the age of 14 and opened his own shop in the summer of 2009. It's now a thriving business selling locally sourced meats and game in season. The shop also sells a wide selection of pastries, pies, soft and hard cheeses, pâtés and dairy products. As Nick says "It's all about selling what the customers want".

medieval times to the present day.

Visitors to Beaminster's imposing 15th-century church tend to be overwhelmed by the grandiose, over-lifesize sculptures of the Strode family who lived at Parnham House, a gem of Tudor architecture about a mile south of the town. Unfortunately this house is now closed to the public as a result of its recent sale into private ownership.

For a rather different mode of exploring rural Dorset, drop in at **UK Llamas**, located two miles north of the town at Mosterton. Guided llama trekking tours are available and the owners will also modify the tours to suit your individual requirements and pace. There's a variety of routes throughout the area and a full day's trek starts at approximately 10.30am with a stop for lunch.

MAPPERTON
5 miles NE of Bridport off the A3066

Mapperton

It's not surprising to find that the house and gardens at **Mapperton** (see panel below) have featured in three major films – *Tom Jones, Emma* and *Restoration*. Home of the Earl and Countess of Sandwich, this magnificent Jacobean mansion set beside a lake, and with its very own church, is stunningly photogenic. The house has been restored to

Mapperton Gardens

Beaminster, Dorset DT8 3NR
Tel: 01308 862645 Fax: 01308 863348
e-mail: office@mapperton.com
website: www.mapperton.com

Two miles from Beaminster, five miles from Bridport, **Mapperton Gardens** surround a fine Jacobean manor house with stable blocks, a dovecote and its own Church of All Saints. The grounds, which run down a gradually steepening

valley, include an orangery and an Italianate formal garden, a 17th century summer house and a wild garden planted in the 1960s. The gardens, which are open to the public from March to October, are a natural choice for film location work, with *Emma* and *Tom Jones* among their credits.

📖 stories and anecdotes 🐿 famous people 🎨 art and craft 🖉 entertainment and sport 🚶 walks

its original style and contains paintings by Joshua Reynolds and Hogarth. The Italianate upper gardens contain some impressive topiary, an orangery, dovecote and formal borders descending to fish ponds and shrub gardens. The house stands in an Area of Outstanding Natural Beauty with some glorious views of the Dorset hills. The gardens are open during the season; opening times for the house are limited.

Dorchester

🏛 Maumbury Rings		🏛 Roman Town House	
🏛 Dorset County Museum		🏛 Church of Our Lady	
🏛 Tutankhamun Exhibition		🕊 Thomas Hardy	
🏛 Terracotta Warriors		🏛 Dinosaur Museum	
🏛 Dorset Teddy Bear Museum			
🏛 Old Crown Courts		🏛 The Keep Military Museum	
🏛 Max Gate		🕊 Judge Jeffreys	

One of England's most appealing county towns, Dorchester's known history goes back to AD74 when the Romans established a settlement called Durnovaria at a respectful distance from the River Frome. At that time the river was much broader than it is now and prone to flooding. The town's Roman origins are clearly displayed in its street plan, in the beautiful tree-lined avenues known as The Walks, which follow the course of the old Roman walls, at **Maumbury Rings**, an ancient stone circle thatthe Romans converted into an amphitheatre, and in the well-preserved **Roman Town House** behind County Hall in Colliton Park. As the town's most famous citizen put it, Dorchester "announced old Rome in every street, alley and precinct. It looked Roman, bespoke the art of Rome, concealed dead men of Rome". **Thomas Hardy** was in fact describing Casterbridge in

his novel *The Mayor of Casterbridge*, but his fictional town is immediately recognisable as Dorchester. One place he describes in great detail is Mayor Trenchard's House, easily identified as what is now Barclays Bank in South Street and bearing a plaque to that effect. Hardy made his home in Dorchester in 1883 and two years later moved into **Max Gate** (National Trust) on the outskirts of the town, a strikingly unlovely two-up-and-two-down Victorian villa designed by Hardy himself and built by his brother at a total cost of £450. Here Hardy entertained a roll-call of literary luminaries – Robert Louis Stevenson, GB Shaw, Rudyard Kipling and HG Wells amongst many others.

The most accessible introduction to the town and the county can found at the excellent **Dorset County Museum** in High Street West. This grand Victorian building houses a comprehensive range of exhibits spanning the centuries, from a Roman sword to a 19th-century cheese press, from dinosaur footprints to a stuffed Great Bustard, which used to roam the chalk uplands of north Dorset but became extinct in this country in 1810. However, in 2009, a programme of re-introducing them to Salisbury Plain proved successful with the birth of a brood of chicks.

Founded in 1846, the museum moved to its present site in 1883, into purpose-built galleries with lofty arches of fine cast ironwork inspired by the Great Exhibition of 1851 at the Crystal Palace. The building was designed by GR Crickmay, the architect for whom Thomas Hardy worked in 1870. The great poet and novelist is celebrated here in a major exhibit that includes a fascinating reconstruction of his study at Max Gate, his Dorchester home. The room includes the original furnishings, books, pictures and fireplace. In the right hand corner are his musical instruments, and the very pens with which he wrote *Tess of the d'Urbervilles, Jude the Obscure,* and his epic poem, the *Dynasts.* More of his possessions are displayed in the Gallery outside – furniture, his watch, music books, and some of his notebooks. Also honoured in the Writers Gallery is William Barnes, the Dorset dialect poet, scholar and priest, who was also the first secretary of the Dorset Natural History and Archaeological Society which owns and runs the museum.

Just outside the museum stands the Statue of William Barnes and, at the junction of High Street West and The Grove, is the Statue of Thomas Hardy. There are more statues outside St George's Church, a group of lifesize models by Elizabeth Frink representing Catholic martyrs who were hanged, drawn and quartered in the 16th century.

Opposite the County Museum, the Antelope Hotel and the 17th-century half-

Thomas Hardy Statue, Dorchester

timbered building beside it (now a tearoom) was where **Judge Jeffreys** (1648-1689) tried 340 Dorset men for their part in Monmouth's Rebellion of 1685. As a result of this 'Bloody Assize', 74 men suffered death by being hanged, drawn and quartered. A further 175 were transported for life. Jeffreys' ferociousness has been attributed to the agony he suffered from gallstones for which doctors of the time could provide no relief. Ironically, when his patron James II was deposed, Jeffreys himself ended up in the Tower of London where he died. A century and a half after the Bloody Assize, another infamous trial took place in the Old Crown Court nearby. Six farm labourers, who later became known as the Tolpuddle Martyrs, were condemned to transportation for their part in organising a Friendly Society – the first agricultural trade union. The **Old Crown Courts** are now open to the public where they are invited to "stand in the dock and sit in the dimly-lit cells...and experience four centuries of gruesome crime and punishment".

There can be few churches in the country with such a bizarre history as that of **Our Lady, Queen of Martyrs, & St Michael**. It was first erected in Wareham, in 1888, by a Roman Catholic sect who called themselves the Passionists, a name derived from their obsession with Christ's passion and death. When they found that few people in Wareham shared their fixation, they had the church moved in 1907, stone by stone, to Dorchester where it was re-assembled and then served the Catholic community for almost 70 years. By the mid 1970s the transplanted church had become too small for its burgeoning congregation. The Passionists moved out, ironically taking over an Anglican church whose communicants had become too few to sustain it. A decade later, their abandoned church was acquired by an organisation called World Heritage, which has transformed its interior into the **Tutankhamun Exhibition**. The life, death and legacy of Tutankhamun exerts an abiding fascination and the exhibition pulls all the various strands of the extraordinary tale together. The Exhibition has won international renown and has been featured in many major TV documentaries.

Keep Military Museum, Dorchester

Also owned by World Heritage is the **Dinosaur Museum**. Dorchester is just seven miles from Dorset's world-famous coastline and in the heart of dinosaur country. The award-winning museum is the only one on mainland Britain dedicated to dinosaurs.

Under the same ownership are two more museums. For those who want to get in touch with their softer side a visit to the **Dorset Teddy Bear Museum** is a must. Marvel at the evocative and atmospheric displays of the history of the teddy bear, featuring examples from the very earliest about a century ago up to the present day. Famous bears such as Rupert Bear, Winnie the Pooh and Paddington are on display, along with bears representing the signs of the zodiac. Many collectors, limited editions, and artists, bears are also present. In Teddy Bear House meet Edward Bear and his extended family of human-sized teddy bears as they busy themselves or relax around their Edwardian style home.

A gem of a museum is **Terracotta Warriors Museum**. It is the only museum outside China devoted to the terracotta

warriors who are now regarded as the eighth wonder of the Ancient World. Featured are unique replicas of the warriors, plus reconstructions of costumes and armour, and multimedia presentations.

Also well worth a visit is **The Keep Military Museum** housed in an interesting, renovated Grade II listed building. Audio technology and interactive computerised displays tell the remarkable story of those who have served in the regiments of Dorset and Devon. An additional bonus is the spectacular view from the battlements across the town and surrounding countryside.

An oddity in the town is an 18th-century sign set high up in a wall. It carries the information that Bridport is 15 miles distant and Hyde Park Corner 120. Apparently, the sign was placed in this position for the convenience of stagecoach drivers, although one would have thought that they, of all people, would have already known the mileage involved.

On the western outskirts of Dorchester, less than a mile from the town centre, is **Poundbury**, the Prince of Wales' controversial experiment in creating a new

---

🏠 historic building   📷 museum and heritage   ⌂ historic site   ⌘ scenic attraction   🌱 flora and fauna

community based on old principles. The prince wanted to show how traditional quality architecture and modern town planning could combine to create urban life in a rural setting. One objective was to make it possible for no one to be more than 10 minutes away from his or her workplace. The enterprise began in 1993 and when completed will consist of four different quarters, each with its own public buildings, shops, pubs, offices and workshops. The enterprise has attracted much scorn from cutting-edge architects who deride the whole concept as "living in the past", but the traditionally-built properties are much sought-after.

Around Dorchester

MAIDEN CASTLE
2 miles SW of Dorchester off the A35

Maiden Castle

Maiden Castle is one of the most impressive prehistoric sites in the country. This vast Iron Age fortification covering more than 45 acres dates back some 4000 years. Its steep earth ramparts, between 60 and 90 feet high, are nearly two miles round and, together with the inner walls, make a total of five miles of defences. The settlement flourished for 2000 years until AD44 when its people were defeated by a Roman army under Vespasian. Excavations here in 1937 unearthed a war cemetery containing some 40 bodies, one of which still had a Roman arrowhead embedded in its spine. The Romans occupied the site for some 30 years before moving closer to the River Frome and founding Durnovaria, modern Dorchester. Maiden Castle was never settled again and it is a rather

forbidding, treeless place, but the extensive views along the Winterborne valley by contrast are delightful.

WINTERBOURNE ABBAS
4 miles W of Dorchester

Nine Stones

The village of Winterbourne Abbas stands at the head of the Winterborne valley, close to the river, which is notable for running only during the winter and becoming a dry ditch in summer. The second part of the name, Abbas, comes from having been owned by the abbots of Cerne. The village is surrounded by ancient barrows, amongst which are the **Nine Stones**, Dorset's best example of a standing stone circle. Not the best location, however. The circle lies beside the busy A35, isolated from the village to the west and surrounded by trees. Despite the constant din of passing traffic, the circle somehow retains an air of tranquillity.

CHARMINSTER
1 mile N of Dorchester on the A52

Wolfeton House

An attractive town on the River Cerne, Charminster has a 12th-century church with an impressive pinnacled tower added in the 1400s. Inside are some striking memorials to the Trenchard family whose noble mansion, **Wolfeton House**, stands on the northern edge of the town. A lovely medieval and Elizabethan manor house, it is surrounded by water meadows near the meeting of the rivers Cerne and Frome. The house contains a great stone staircase, remarkable plaster ceilings, fireplaces and carved oak panelling – all Elizabethan – some good pictures and furniture. Opening times are restricted. There is also a cider house here from which cider can be purchased.

GREEN VALLEY FARM SHOP

Longmeadow, Godmanstone, Dorchester, Dorset DT2 7AE
Tel: 01300 342164
website: www.greenvalleyfarmshop.co.uk.

Green Valley Farm Shop is located in the charming village of
Godmanstone in the heart of rural Dorset. They stock Longmeadow
Organic Vegetables and locally sourced organic meat, a selection of
local cheese and a range of organic wine. Green Valley sources much of its produce locally and
estimates that 90% of its stock is organic. The extensive range of products also includes organic
wholefoods, bread from Leakers bakery in Bridport, Manna Organic's award winning and healthy
ready meals and popular local cheese such as Woolsery goat's cheese and Dorset Blue Vinny.
Described as a 'one-stop shop for organic foodies', Green Valley Farm Shop is indeed about as
green as it's possible to be.

LONGMEADOW ORGANIC VEGETABLES

Godmanstone Dorset DT2 7AE
Tel: 01300 341779

Owned and run by Hugh and Patsy Chapman, Longmeadow Organic Vegetables is set beside the
River Cerne and nestles beneath Cowden Hill. Their impressive range of vegetables includes
potatoes, beetroot, carrots, beans, broccoli, leeks, onions, tomatoes and salads. They also grow
a variety of apples which, along with the vegetables, are on sale in Green Valley Farm Shop.
When visiting the shop you are welcome to walk around the fields of vegetables and peek into
the polytunnels.

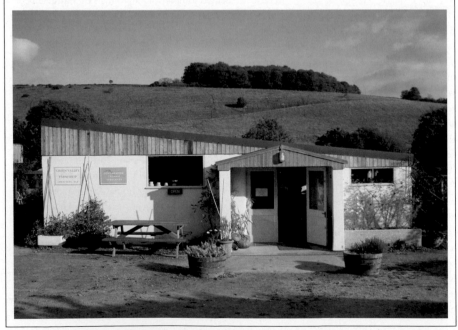

GODMANSTONE
4 miles N of Dorchester on the A352

🍺 Smith's Arms

Dorset can boast many cosy, intimate pubs, but the **Smith's Arms** at Godmanstone is in a class of its own, claiming to be the smallest inn in the country with a frontage just 11 feet wide. This appealing 14th-century thatched building was originally the village smithy. According to tradition, Charles II happened to stop here to have his horse shod. Feeling thirsty, the king asked for a glass of ale and was not best pleased to be told that as the blacksmith had no licence, no alcoholic drink was available. Invoking the royal prerogative, Charles granted a licence immediately and this tiny hostelry has been licensed ever since. Given the cramped interior, elbow-bending at the Smith's Arms can be a problem at busy times, but fortunately there is a spacious terrace outside.

PIDDLETRENTHIDE
6 miles N of Dorchester on the B3143

Mentioned in the Domesday Book, this village is named after the river beside which it stands and the "30 hides" of land for which it was assessed. A beautiful place in a beautiful location, Piddletrenthide is believed to have been the home of Alfred the Great's brother, Ethelred.

CERNE ABBAS
7 miles N of Dorchester on the A352

🍺 Cerne Abbey   🏛 Cerne Abbas Giant

This pretty village beside the River Cerne takes its name from **Cerne Abbey**, formerly a major Benedictine monastery of which an imposing 15th-century gatehouse, a tithe barn of the same period, and a holy well still

The Cerne Abbas Giant

survive, all well worth seeing. So too are the lofty, airy church with grotesque gargoyles and medieval statues adorning its west tower, and the old Market House on Long Street. In fact, there is much to see in this ancient village where cottages dating back to the 14th century still stand.

But the major visitor attraction is to be found just to the north of the village – the famous **Cerne Abbas Giant** (National Trust), a colossal 180ft-high figure cut into the chalk hillside. He stands brandishing a club, naked and full-frontal, and there can be absolutely no doubt about his maleness. An ancient tradition asserts that any woman wishing to become pregnant should sit, or preferably sleep the night, on the giant's huge erect penis, some 22 feet long. The age of this extraordinary carving is hotly disputed but a consensus is emerging that it was originally created by ancient Britons as a fertility symbol and that the giant's club was added by the Romans. (There are clear similarities between the giant and the representation of Hercules on a Roman pavement of AD191, preserved at Sherborne Castle.) As with all hill-carvings, the best view is from a distance, in this case from a layby on the A352. A curious puzzle remains. The giant's outlines in the chalk need a regular scouring to remove grass and weeds. Should this be neglected, he would soon fade into the hillside. In medieval centuries, such a non-essential task of conservation could only have been authorised by the locally all-powerful Abbots of Cerne. What possible reason did those Christian advocates of chastity have for carefully preserving such a powerful pagan image of virility?

MINTERNE MAGNA
9 miles N of Dorchester, on the A352

🌿 Minterne Gardens

A couple of miles north of the Cerne Giant, Minterne Magna is notable for its parish church, crowded with memorials to Napiers, Churchills and Digbys, the families who once owned the great house here and most of the Minterne valley. The mansion itself, rebuilt in the Arts and Crafts style around 1900 is not open to the public but its splendid **Minterne Gardens** are. The gardens are laid out in a horseshoe shape below the house and landscaped in the 18th-century style of Capability Brown. They contain an important collection of Himalayan rhododendrons and azaleas, along with cherries, maples and many other fine and rare trees. The gardens are open daily from March to early November.

On Batcombe Hill, to the west of the village, stands a stone pillar known as the Cross and Hand that is said to date from the 7th century. Its purpose is unknown, but in *Tess of the d'Urbervilles*, Hardy relates the local legend that the pillar marks the grave of a criminal who was tortured and hanged there,

PLUSHART
Plush, Dorchester, Dorset DT2 7RJ
Tel: 01300 348280
e-mail: gallery@plushart.co.uk
website: www.plushart.co.uk

In the folds of the Dorset landscape at the head of the Plush valley, Millers Barn is a series of interlinked spaces, daylight is ever present and the modern interior a background for contemporary art. The house dissects landscaped gardens, green swathes bounded by woodland to the north, the south surrounded by stone walls, long brick terrace, curving spaces and traditional planting with swimming pool, deck and mediterranean planting at a lower level.

PlushArt through commission, corporate rental, private view and art@plush exhibitions, showcase ceramics, paintings, photography, sculpture and wood through the house and garden with artists invited for the quality and integrity of their work.

Breast Cancer LIFE launches 25 & 26 September 2010 at Millers Barn - 40 life studies in pencil, pastel and oils by Harriet Barber, raise awareness, recognise the strength of women overcoming illness, radical surgery and aggressive therapies, demonstrating to those at the beginning of their journey through Breast Cancer, that there is a very positive life ahead. The exhibition moves to Poundbury Garden Centre 16/10–14/11; Malthouse Gallery, Lyme Regis 1-20/02/2011; The Lighthouse, Poole 05/2011 – then ten further venues around the UK.

Guests can stay in 'The Art House' and enjoy calming, thought provoking and innovative work.

🏛 historic building   🏛 museum and heritage   🏛 historic site   � scenic attraction   🌿 flora and fauna

and whose mournful ghost appears beside the column from time to time.

STINSFORD
1 mile NE of Dorchester, off the A35

🐿 Thomas Hardy 🌱 Kingston Maurward Gardens

It was in St Michael's Church at Stinsford that **Thomas Hardy** was christened at the Norman font, which is still in place, and where he attended services for much of his life. He sang hymns to the accompaniment of the village band, (amongst whom were several of his relatives), which played from a gallery at the back of the church. The gallery was demolished in Hardy's lifetime, but many years later he drew a sketch from memory that showed the position of each player and the name of his instrument. A copy of this drawing is on display in the church, alongside a tablet commemorating the Hardys who took part in services here. There's also a fine memorial window designed by Douglas Strachen in 1930.

Although Thomas Hardy was cremated and his ashes buried in the Poets' Corner of Westminster Abbey, his heart was brought to Stinsford to be interred in a graveyard tomb here. According to a scurrilous local tradition, it is shared with the village cat, which had managed to eat the heart before it was buried. Several of Hardy's relatives, including his parents and two wives, are buried in the churchyard. So too is the former Poet Laureate Cecil Day Lewis (1904-1972).

Just to the east of the village, **Kingston Maurward Gardens** are of such historical importance that they are listed on the English Heritage Register of Gardens. The 35 acres of classical 18th-century parkland and lawns sweep majestically down to the lake from the stately Georgian house. The formal Edwardian Gardens include a croquet lawn, rose garden, herbaceous borders and a large display of tender perennials, including the National Collection of Penstemons and Salvias. There's also an Animal Park with an interesting collection of unusual breeds, a lovely ornamental lake, nature trails, plant sales and the Old Coach House Restaurant serving morning coffee, lunches and teas.

HIGHER BOCKHAMPTON
2 miles NE of Dorchester off the A35

🏠 Hardy's Cottage

In the woods above Higher Bockhampton, reached by a series of narrow lanes and a 10-minute walk, is a major shrine for devotees of Thomas Hardy. **Hardy's Cottage** is surrounded by the trees of Puddletown Forest, a setting he evoked so magically in *Under the Greenwood Tree*. The delightful thatched cottage and gardens are now owned by the National Trust and the rooms are furnished much as they would have been when the great novelist was born here in 1840. Visitors can see the very room in which his mother gave birth only to hear her child proclaimed still-born. Fortunately, an observant nurse noticed that the infant was in fact breathing and so ensured that such classics of English literature as *Tess of the*

Hardy's Cottage, Higher Bockhampton

d'Urbervilles and *The Return of the Native* saw the light of day. This charming cottage was Hardy's home for the first 22 years of his life until he set off for London to try his luck as an architect. In that profession his record was undistinguished, but in 1871 his first novel, *Desperate Remedies,* was published. An almost farcical melodrama, it gave few signs of the great works that would follow, but was sufficiently successful for Hardy to devote himself thereafter to writing full time.

PUDDLETOWN
5 miles NE of Dorchester off the A35

🏛 Athelhampton House

Originally called Piddletown (piddle is the Saxon word for clear water) the village's name was changed by the sensitive Victorians. It was at Piddletown that Hardy's grandfather and great-grandfather were born. Renamed Weatherbury, it features in *Far From the Madding Crowd* as the place where Fanny's coffin was left out in the rain, and Sergeant Troy spends the night in the porch of the church after covering her grave with flowers.

Just to the east of Puddletown, **Athelhampton House** is a delightful, mostly Tudor house surrounded by a series of separate 'secret' gardens. It's the home of Sir

Edward and Lady du Cann and has the lived-in feeling that adds so much interest to historic houses. One of the finest houses in the county, Athelhampton's most spectacular feature is its magnificent Great Chamber with its hammer beam ceiling and original fireplace, all built during the reign of Elizabeth I. In the grounds are topiary pyramids, fountains, the Octagonal Garden designed by Sir Robert Cooke in 1971, and an unusual 15th-century circular dovecote. It is almost perfectly preserved, with its potence, or revolving ladder used to collect eggs from the topmost nests, still in place and still useable.

TOLPUDDLE
8 miles E of Dorchester off the A35

🏛 Martyrs' Museum

The small village of Tolpuddle is a peaceful little place today, but in the early 19th century, Tolpuddle was far sleepier than it is now. Not the kind of place you would expect to foment a social revolution, but it was here that six ill-paid agricultural labourers helped lay the foundations of the British Trade Union Movement. In 1833, they formed a "confederation" in an attempt to have their subsistence wages improved. The full rigour of the landowner-friendly law of the time was immediately invoked. All six were found guilty of taking illegal oaths and sentenced to transportation to Australia for seven years. Even the judge in their case was forced to say that it was not for anything they had done, or intended to do, that he passed such a sentence, but "as an example to others". Rather surprisingly, public opinion sided with the illegal "confederation". Vigorous and sustained protests eventually forced the

Athelhampton House, Puddletown

government to pardon the men after they had served three years of their sentence. They all returned safely to England, honoured ever afterwards in trade union hagiography as the Tolpuddle Martyrs. In the centenary year of their conviction, 1934, six memorial cottages were built in Tolpuddle, one of which has been set up as the **Martyrs' Museum**. It tells an inspiring story, but it's depressing to realise that the seven-shilling (35p) weekly payment those farm-workers were protesting against actually had more buying power in the 1830s than the current legally-enforced minimum wage.

WINTERBORNE CAME
2 miles SE of Dorchester off the A352

⚘ William Barnes

This tiny hamlet is a place of pilgrimage for admirers of Dorset's second most famous man of letters who is buried in the graveyard here. **William Barnes** was Rector of Winterborne Came from 1862 until his death in 1886 and in the old Rectory (not open to the public) he entertained such luminaries of English literature as Alfred Lord Tennyson and Hardy himself. Although Barnes was highly respected by fellow poets, his pastoral poems written in the distinctive dialect of the county never attracted a wide audience. At their best, though, they are marvellously evocative of the west Dorset countryside:

> *The zwellen downs, wi' chalky tracks*
> *A-climmen up their zunny backs,*
> *Do hide green meads an zedgy brooks...*
> *An' white roads up athirt the hills.*

Winterborne Came's unusual name, incidentally, derives from its position beside the River Winterborne and the fact that in medieval times the village was owned by the Abbey of Caen in France.

OWERMOIGNE
6 miles SE of Dorchester off the A352

🏛 Mill House Cider Museum

🏛 Dorset Collection of Clocks

Just north of the village is a dual attraction in the shape of the **Mill House Cider Museum** and **A Dorset Collection of Clocks**. Housed in a mill that featured in Hardy's *The Distracted Preacher*, the Cider Museum has a collection of 18th and 19th-century cider-making mills and presses, reflecting the importance of cider as a main country drink in the past. The Collection of Clocks showcases numerous timepieces ranging from longcase clocks to elaborate turret clocks. Visitors get the opportunity to see the intricate movements that are usually hidden away in the large clocks found on churches and public buildings.

Weymouth

🏛 Timewalk Journey 🎨 Brewers Quay

🏛 Museum of Coastal Defence 🌿 Nothe Gardens

🏰 Nothe Fort 🌿 Lodmoor Country Park

🏛 Deep Sea Adventure

No wonder the good citizens of Weymouth erected a statue to George III to mark the 50th year of his reign in 1810. The troubled

Old Harbour, Weymouth

Clock Tower, Weymouth

king had brought great kudos and prosperity to their little seaside resort by coming here to bathe in the sea water from the long sandy beach. George had been advised that sea-

bathing would help cure his 'nervous disorder' so, between 1789 and 1805, he and his royal retinue spent a total of 14 holidays in Weymouth. Fashionable society naturally followed in his wake and left as its legacy the wonderful seafront of Georgian terraces. Not far away, at the head of King Street, George's granddaughter Victoria is commemorated by a colourful **Jubilee Clock** erected in 1887, the 50th year of her reign.

Nearby, the picturesque harbour is always busy – fishing boats, paddle steamers, pleasure boats, catamarans servicing the Channel Islands and St Malo in France and, if you're lucky, you may even see a Tall Ship or two.

One of the town's premier tourist venues is **Brewers Quay** (see panel below), an imaginatively redeveloped Victorian brewery offering an enormous diversity of visitor attractions within a labyrinth of paved courtyards and cobbled streets. There are no fewer than 22 different establishments within the complex, ranging from craft shops and

Brewers Quay

Old Harbour, Weymouth, Dorset DT4 8TR
Tel: 01305 777622 Fax: 01305 761680
website: www.brewers-quay.co.uk

Brewers Quay is an imaginatively converted Victorian brewery in the heart of the picturesque Old Harbour. Amid the paved courtyards and cobbled alleys is a unique under-cover shopping village with over 20 specialist shops and attractions.

The Timewalk tells the fascinating story of the town as seen through the eyes of the brewery cat and her family, and in the Brewery Days attraction Hope Square's unique brewing heritage is brought to life with an interactive family gallery, audio-visual show and Victorian-style Tastings Bar.

Weymouth Museum contains an important record of local and social history; its latest exhibition is called Marine Archaeology and Associated Finds from the Sea. The Discovery Hands-on Science Centre has over 60 interactive exhibits, and this entertaining complex also has a bowling alley, gift shops, a traditional pub and a self-service restaurant.

🏛 historic building   🖼 museum and heritage   🏛 historic site   ♣ scenic attraction   🌱 flora and fauna

restaurants through a fully automated tenpin bowling alley to the **Timewalk Journey**, which promises visitors that they will "See, hear and smell over 600 years of Weymouth's spectacular history", and the Discovery exhibition, which reveals some fascinating scientific facts with interactive displays.

From Brewers Quay, a path leads through **Nothe Gardens** to **Nothe Fort**, built between 1860 and 1872 as part of the defences of the new naval base being established on Portland. Ten huge guns face out to sea; two smaller ones are directed inland. The fort's 70 rooms on three levels now house the **Museum of Coastal Defence**, which has many interesting displays illustrating past service life in the fort, history as seen from the Nothe headland, and the part played by the people of Weymouth in World War Two. Nothe Fort is owned and operated by the Weymouth Civic Society, which also takes care of **Tudor House** just north of Brewers Quay. One of the town's few remaining Tudor buildings, the house originally stood on the edge of an inlet from the harbour and is thought to have been a merchant's house. It's now furnished in the style of an early17th-century middle class home and the guided tour gives some fascinating insights into life in those days.

Just a 15 minute walk from the town along the Esplanade and through Greenhill Gardens, **Lodmoor Country Park** is another popular attraction. Access to most of the park is free and visitors can take advantage of the many sport and recreation areas, wander around the footpaths and nature reserve, or enjoy a picnic or barbecue.

A major family attraction is **Deep Sea Adventure** on Custom House Quay, which offers two separate attractions under one roof. Deep Sea Adventure tells the story of underwater exploration and marine exploits from the 17th century through to the modern day. This entertaining and educational exhibition fills three floors of an imposing Victorian grain warehouse with a wealth of animated and interactive displays recounting compelling tales of shipwreck survival and search and rescue operations, a Black Hole in which you can experience what it is like to be a deep sea diver, and a unique display that tells the epic story of the *Titanic* in the words of the officers, crew and survivors, along with the original *Titanic* signals and one of the largest models in the world of the doomed ship. A fairly recent addition to Deep Sea Adventure is Sharky's, a huge, all-weather adventure play area for children of all ages (with a height limit of 5ft), and a separate area for toddlers.

OSMINGTON
4 miles NE of Weymouth on the A353

🕊 White Horse 🏠 Smugglers Inn

There are several White Horses carved into hillsides around the country, but the **White Horse** near Osmington, apart from being one of the largest (354ft high and 279ft wide), is

Osmington White Horse

the only one that also has a rider. The horse was created in 1807, the rider was added about three years later. Wearing a tall cocked hat and carrying a whip, the horseman represents George III. The king was a frequent visitor to nearby Weymouth and his royal patronage naturally attracted many free-spending courtiers to the town. The town fathers of Weymouth decided to express their appreciation by paying the local militia to add the royal rider. The result was an unrecognisable, if undoubtedly loyal, tribute to His Majesty. Like all the other white horses in England, it looks much better when seen from a few miles away; close up, it is meaningless.

A mile south of Osmington, at Osmington Mills, the area's notorious history in trading contraband liquor lingers in the name of the **Smugglers Inn**. Unlike many similarly-named hostelries, this one really was a regular haunt for smugglers. Dating back to the 13th century, this former fisherman's cottage enjoyed a secluded position and the nearby beach provided safe landing. The inn's landlord in the early 1800s was Emmanuel Carless who, together with his French partner, Pierre Latour, or French Peter, ran a thriving business importing thousands of gallons of brandy each year. Unfortunately, the liquor was so inferior locals refused to

drink it and the spirit had to be carried inland on stagecoaches, disguised as luggage, to be distilled again.

ISLE OF PORTLAND
4 miles S of Weymouth, on the A354

🔎 Tout Quarry Sculpture Park	🏛 Portland Castle
🏛 St Andrew's Avalanche Church	🐦 The Fleet
🔱 Chesil Beach	🏛 Portland Museum

Portland is not really an island at all, but a four-and-a-half mile long peninsula, well known to devotees of shipping forecasts and even more famous for the stone from its quarries. Numerous buildings in London are constructed of Portland stone, amongst them St Paul's Cathedral, Inigo Jones' Banqueting Hall in Whitehall, and Buckingham Palace. The stone was also favoured by sculptors such as Henry Moore. The quarries still provide the renowned stone and are also used as study centres. In the huge **Tout Quarry Sculpture Park** are some 50 pieces carved out of the rock face – look out for Anthony Gormley's figure of a man falling down the rock face.

The island's most famous building is **Portland Castle** (English Heritage), one of the finest of Henry VIII's coastal fortresses. Its active role lasted for 500 years, right up to World War Two when it provided a D-Day embarkation point for British and American forces. Oliver Cromwell used the castle as a prison and in Victorian times it was the residence of Portland's governors. Visitors can try on the armour, meet Henry VIII in the Great Hall, and enjoy the special events that are held regularly throughout the year. The battlements command superb views of Portland Harbour whose breakwaters were constructed by convict labour to create the second largest man-made harbour in the

Portland Castle

world. On the highest point of the island is Verne Citadel, which was a base for troops defending Portland and Weymouth. It became a prison in 1950.

At Southwell is **St Andrew's Avalanche Church**, built in 1879 chiefly as a memorial to those who perished when the clipper *Avalanche* sank off the Portland coast at the beginning of a passage to New Zealand. Also in Southwell is **Portland Museum**, which was founded by the birth control pioneer Marie Stopes who lived in the old lighthouse on the island. Housed in a charming pair of thatched cottages, the museum tells the story of life on the island from smuggling and shipwrecks to traditions and customs. One of the cottages inspired Thomas Hardy to centre his novel *The Well-Beloved* around it, making it the home of Avice, the heroine of the story.

At the southernmost tip of the island, the Bill of Portland, the first lighthouse to be built here, is now a base for bird-watchers. The current Portland Bill Lighthouse offers guided tours during the season and also has a visitor centre. Nearby are some particularly fascinating natural features: the tall, upright Pulpit Rock, which can be climbed, and some caves to explore.

The Isle provides some good cliff-top walks with grand views of the harbour and of **Chesil Beach**, a vast bank of pebbles worn smooth by the sea. It stretches for some 10 miles to Abbotsbury and it's been estimated that the 200 yard wide and 50 feet high bank contains 100 million tonnes of pebbles. Inexplicably, the pebbles are graded in size from west to east. Fishermen reckon they can judge whereabouts on the beach they are landing by the size of the pebbles. In the west they are as small as peas and usually creamy in colour; at Portland they have grown to the size

of cooking apples and are more often grey. The long, narrow body of water trapped behind the beach is known as **The Fleet**. It is now a nature reserve and home to a wide variety of waterfowl and plants, as well as fish that can be viewed by taking a trip in a glass-bottomed boat.

CHICKERELL
3 miles NW of Weymouth off the 3157

🦆 Water Gardens

A pretty village of thatched cottages, Chickerell is best known for its **Water Garden**, which were created in 1959 by Norman Bennett. He began by growing water lilies in the disused clay pits of a brickworks, using lilies from the same nursery in France that supplied plants to Monet's garden in Giverny. The gardens are now home to the National Collection of Water Lilies. Within the gardens is a museum telling the story of the village, which featured in the Domesday Book.

PORTESHAM
6 miles NW of Weymouth on the B3157

🏛 Hardy's Monument

On the Black Downs northeast of Portesham stands **Hardy's Monument** (National Trust), which commemorates not Thomas Hardy the great novelist of Wessex, but Sir Thomas Hardy, the flag-captain of *HMS Victory* at Trafalgar to whom the dying Lord Nelson spoke the immortal words, "Kiss me, Hardy", (or possibly, "Kismet, Hardy"). Sir Thomas was born in Portesham and, like his novelist namesake, was descended from the Hardys of Jersey. After Trafalgar, he escorted Nelson's body back to London and soon afterwards was created a baronet and, eventually, First Sea Lord. Sir Thomas's stunningly graceless memorial has been

Abbotsbury

Abbotsbury Tourism Ltd, West Yard Barn,
West Street, Abbotsbury, Dorset DT3 4JT
Tel: 01305 871130 Fax: 01305 871092
e-mail: info@abbotsbury-tourism.co.uk
website: www.abbotsbury-tourism.co.uk

Surrounded by hills, with the sea close at hand, **Abbotsbury** is one of the county's most popular tourist spots and by any standards one of the loveliest villages in England. Very little remains of the Benedictine Abbey that gives the village its name, but what has survived is the magnificent Great Abbey Barn, a tithe barn almost 250ft long that was built in the 14th century to house the Abbey's tithes of wool, grain and other produce.

The village's three main attractions, which bring the crowds flocking in their thousands to this lovely part of the world, are the **Swannery**, the **Sub-Tropical Gardens** and the **Tithe Barn Children's Farm**. The most famous of all is Abbotsbury Swannery, which was established many centuries ago, originally to provide food for the monks in the Abbey. For at least 600 years the swannery has been a sanctuary for a huge colony of mute swans. The season for visitors begins in earnest in March, when the swans vie for the best nesting sites. From May to the end of June cygnets hatch by the hundred and from then until October the fluffy chicks grow and gradually gain their wings. Cygnets who have become orphaned are protected in special pens until strong enough to fend for themselves. By the end of October many of the swans move off the site for the winter, while other wildfowl move in. An audio-visual show is run hourly in the old swanherd's cottage, and a few lucky visitors are selected to help out at the spectacular twice-daily feeding sessions. The swans' feed includes eelgrass from the River Fleet. In May of this year the Swanherd, who has looked after the colony for 40 years, Dick Dalley, retired. When he first started the birds were still being raised for the table, but today, the 159 breeding pairs - including 2 black swans - are protected by law. Also on site are a shire horse and cart service, a gift shop and a café housed in a delightful building that was converted from Georgian kennels.

At the western end of the village, Abbotsbury Sub-Tropical Gardens, established by the first Countess of Ilchester as a kitchen garden for her nearby castle, occupy a 20-acre site close to Chesil Beach that's largely protected from the elements by a ring of oak trees. In this micro-climate a huge variety of rare and exotic plants and trees flourish, and the camellia groves and the collections of rhododendrons and hydrangeas are known the world over.

There's a woodland trail, a children's play area, visitor centre, plant nursery, gift shop and restaurant with a veranda overlooking the sunken garden. Most of the younger children will make a beeline for the Tithe Barn Children's Farm, where they can cuddle the rabbits, bottle feed the lambs, race toy tractors, feed the doves and meet the donkeys and horses. The Farm's latest attraction is the Smugglers Barn, where the little ones can learn and play at the same time.

🏛 historic building 🏛 museum and heritage 🏛 historic site 🐦 scenic attraction 🌿 flora and fauna

variously described as a "huge candlestick", a "peppermill", and most accurately as a "factory chimney wearing a crinoline". But if you stand with your back to it, there are grand views over Weymouth Bay. Currently, the monument is closed due to erosion and no date has been given for its re-opening.

ABBOTSBURY
8 miles NW of Weymouth on the B3157

🏛 St Catherine's Chapel 🦢 Abbotsbury Swannery

🏛 Great Abbey Barn

🦢 Abbotsbury Sub-tropical Gardens

Surrounded by hills, picturesque Abbotsbury is one of the county's most popular tourist spots and by any standards one of the loveliest villages in England. Its most striking feature as you approach is the 14th-century **St Catherine's Chapel**, perched on the hill-top.

Only 45 feet by 15 feet, it is solidly built to withstand the Channel gales with walls more than four feet thick. St Catherine was believed to be particularly helpful in finding husbands for the unmarried, and in medieval times spinsters would climb the steep hill to her chapel chanting a dialect jingle which concludes with the words *"Arn-a-one's better than narn-a-one"* – anyone is better than never a one.

Abbotsbury takes its name from the important Benedictine Abbey that once stood here but was comprehensively cannibalised after the Reformation, its stones used to build the attractive cottages that line the village streets. What has survived however is the magnificent **Great Abbey Barn**, 247 feet long and 31 feet wide, which was built in the 1300s to store the abbey's tithes of wool, grain and other produce. With its thatched roof, stone walls and a mightily impressive entrance, it is

---

WHEELWRIGHTS TEA ROOM, GIFT SHOP AND B&B

14 Rodden Row, Abbotsbury, Dorset DT3 4JL
Tel: 01305 871800
e-mail: suenigel@wheelwrights.co.uk
website: www.wheelwrights.co.uk

Close to the car park in the historic village of Abbotsbury, **Wheelwrights** is not just a traditional tea room ~ it is also a gift shop, and it offers a room for Bed & Breakfast.

For centuries a wheelwright's workshop, and later a glass engraver's studio, Sue and Nigel Melville turned it into a tea room in 1996. They quickly built a fine (and international) reputation for excellent home baking: locals and visitors tuck into their cream teas, rich cakes and light sponges in the tearoom itself or in the garden with its views of the hilltop St Catherine's Chapel.

The gift shop sells a selection of stylish, contemporary gifts, including tableware, ceramics, glassware, stationery and greetings cards. The third string to Wheelwrights' bow is the Garden Room, which offers 21st century comfort in a 17th century setting. The one-time apprentice wheelwrights' dormitory has been completely transformed into a stylish, versatile and self-contained guest bedroom in a garden setting under a thatched roof. The Garden Room has twin beds that can become a super-kingsize double, with an en-suite shower room and toilet, a hot drinks tray, TV with Freeview and DVD player, and internet access. Guests are treated to a cream tea or tea and cakes on arrival.

🎭 stories and anecdotes 🦜 famous people 🎨 art and craft 🎟 entertainment and sport 🥾 walks

one of the largest and best-preserved barns in the country. It now contains a children's farm where they can cuddle small animals, watch goats racing, ride tractors or just play in the soft play area.

About a mile south of the village is the famous **Abbotsbury Swannery** (see panel on page 276), established in Saxon times to provide food for the abbey during the winter months. Up to 600 free-flying swans have made their home here and visitor figures rocket from the end of May to the end of June – the baby swans' hatching season. Quills from the fully-grown swans are still sent to Lloyds of London where they have been used for centuries to write the names of ships lost at sea in their official insurance records. There's also a children's Ugly Duckling Trail, a maze laid out in the shape of a swan, and the oldest known still working duck decoy.

Just to the west of the village, **Abbotsbury Sub-Tropical Gardens** enjoy a particularly well-sheltered position and the 20 acres of grounds contain a huge variety of rare and exotic plants and trees. The gardens were originally laid out in 1765 for the Countess of Ilchester as a kitchen garden. Other attractions here include an 18th-century walled garden, beautiful lily ponds and a children's play area.

Sherborne

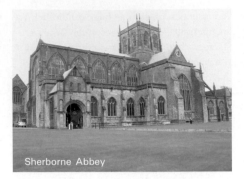
Sherborne Abbey

🏛	Sherborne Abbey	🏛	Sherborne Old Castle
🏛	Sherborne New Castle	🏛	Sherborne Museum
🏛	Almshouses	🏛	Sandford Orcas Manor House
🏛	Conduit House	🌱	Pageant Gardens

One of the most beautiful towns in England, Sherborne beguiles the visitor with its serene atmosphere of a cathedral city, although it is not a city and its lovely **Abbey** no longer enjoys the status of a cathedral. Back in AD705 though, when it was founded by St Aldhelm, the abbey was the Mother Cathedral for the whole of southwest England. Of that original Saxon church only minimal traces remain: most of the present building dates back to the mid 1400s, which, by happy chance, was the most glorious period in the history of English ecclesiastical architecture. The intricate tracery of the fan vaulting above the nave of the abbey looks like the supreme culmination of a long-practised art: in fact, it is one of the earliest examples in England. There is much else to admire in this majestic church: 15th-century misericords in the choir stalls, which range from the sublime (Christ sitting in majesty on a rainbow), to the scandalous (wives beating their husbands); a wealth of elaborate tombs amongst which is a lofty six-poster from Tudor times, a floridly baroque late 17th-century memorial to the 3rd Earl of Bristol, and another embellished with horses' heads in a punning tribute to Sir John Horsey who lies below alongside his son.

As well as founding the abbey, St Aldhelm is also credited with establishing Sherborne School which numbered amongst its earliest pupils the two elder brothers of King Alfred, (and possibly Alfred himself). Later alumni

include the Poet Laureate Cecil Day-Lewis and the writer David Cornwell, better known as John le Carré, author of *The Spy Who Came in from the Cold* and many other thrillers.

Perhaps the bestknown resident of Sherborne however is Sir Walter Raleigh. At a time when he enjoyed the indulgent favour of Elizabeth I he asked for, and was granted, the house and estate of **Sherborne Old Castle** (English Heritage). Sir Walter soon realised that the medieval pile with its starkly basic amenities was quite unsuitable for a courtier of his sophistication and ambition. He built a new castle alongside it, **Sherborne New Castle** (see panel on page 280), a strange three-storeyed, hexagonal structure that must rate, from the outside, as one of the most badly-designed, most unlikeable mansions to be erected in an age when other Elizabethan architects were creating some of the loveliest

Almhouses, Sherborne

Sherborne Castle

Sherborne, Dorset DT9 3PY
Tel: 01935 813182
e-mail: enquiries@sherbornecastle.com
website: www.sherbornecastle.com

As soon as Sir Walter Raleigh was given the Old Castle and its estates by Queen Elizabeth I, he realised that the stark, comfortless castle was not his ideal residence, and instead of restoring it he built a new castle alongside the old one. He called it Sherborne Lodge to distinguish it from the Old Castle, and this unusual rectangular, six-turreted building became his home. Upon Sir Walter Raleigh's death on the block his estates were forfeited to the Crown, but in 1617 King James I allowed Sir John Digby to purchase the new castle and this gentleman added four wings in a similar style to the old building. During the Civil War, the Old Castle was reduced to a ruin by Cromwell's Parliamentary forces - the siege in 1645 lasted 16 days and prompted Cromwell to talk of this 'malicious and mischievous castle'. The name Sherborne Castle came to be applied to the new building, where today splendid collections of Old Masters, porcelain and furniture are on display.

Other attractions at the castle, which is still in the care of the Digby family, include the library, a Tudor kitchen and an exhibition of finds from the Old Castle. Lancelot 'Capability' Brown was called in to create the lake in 1753 and gave Sherborne the very latest in landscape gardening. The Castle, which was a Red Cross Hospital for wounded soldiers in the First World War and the HQ for D-Day Commandos in the Second, was opened to the public in 1969 and hosts a variety of events in the summer season. The gardens, tea room and shop are open every day except Mondays and Fridays (open Bank Holiday Mondays), from April to October.

buildings in England. Inside Sir Walter's new castle, it is quite a different story: gracious rooms with elaborately-patterned ceilings, portraits of the man who single-handedly began the creation of the British Empire, and huge windows, which at the time Sir Walter ordered them proclaimed a clear message that its owner had the wealth to pay the enormous cost of glazing such vast expanses. After Sir Walter's execution, the castle was purchased in 1617 by Sir James Digby and it has remained with his descendants ever since. They added exquisite gardens designed by Capability Brown and, in the late 1800s, redecorated the interior

in Jacobean style. Amongst the castle's greatest treasures is the famous painting by Robert Peake the Elder depicting Elizabeth I in procession, being carried on a litter and surrounded by a sumptuously dressed retinue. The old cellar of the castle is now a museum housing an eclectic display of items, most gruesome of which is the skull of a Royalist soldier killed in the seige of 1645. A bullet is still lodged in his eye socket. Sherborne New Castle, incidentally, is one of several locations claiming to be the genuine setting for the old story of Sir Walter enjoying a pipe of tobacco and being doused with a bucket of water by a servant who believed his master was on fire. Sherborne Castle is open from April to October, and also offers visitors an attractive lakeside tearoom, a well-stocked gift shop, and various special events throughout the year.

This appealing small town, with a population of around 8500, has much else to interest the visitor. The **Almshouse of Saints John the Baptist and John the Evangelist**, near the abbey, was founded in 1437 and the original buildings, completed in 1448, are still in use as an almshouse, accepting both men and women. The almshouse chapel boasts one of the town's greatest treasures, a late 15th-century Flemish altar tryptich, which can be viewed on afternoons during the summer. Close by, the **Conduit House** is an attractive small hexagonal building from the early 1500s, originally used as a lavatorium, or washroom, for the abbey monks' ablutions. It was moved here after the Reformation and has served variously as a public fountain and a police phone box. The Conduit House is specifically mentioned in Hardy's *The Woodlanders* as the place where Giles Winterborne, seeking work, stood here in the market place "as he always did at this season of the year, with his specimen apple tree".

Another striking building is the former Abbey Gatehouse, which frames the entrance to Church Lane where the **Sherborne Museum** has a collection of more than 15,000 items relating to local history. Particularly notable are two major photographic collections recording events and people in the town since 1880.

To the south of the town, near the railway station, **Pageant Gardens** were established in 1905 using funds raised by a great pageant of that year celebrating the 1200th anniversary of the founding of the town by St Aldhelm.

About two miles north of Sherborne, **Sandford Orcas Manor House** is a charming Tudor building with terraced gardens, topiary and a herb garden. Since it was built in honey-coloured Ham Hill stone in the 1550s, only three different families have lived here. The present owner, Sir Mervyn Medlycott, whose family has lived here for more than 250 years, personally conducts guided tours that take in the manor's Great Hall, stone newel staircases, huge fireplaces, fine panelling, Jacobean and Queen Anne furniture and family portraits.

Around Sherborne

MELBURY OSMOND
6 miles SW of Sherborne off the A37

It was in the Church of St Osmund in this pretty village that Thomas Hardy's parents, Jemima Hand and Thomas Hardy, were married in 1839. At the northern end of the footpath through the churchyard is a thatched house where Hardy's mother is thought to have lived as a child.

In Hardy's novels the village appears as Great Hintock, which provides the setting for *The Woodlanders*. Melbury Osmond is still unspoilt and picturesque with many oak trees – do find time to walk down from the church to the water splash, and beyond to some 17th-century thatched stone cottages.

Shaftesbury

🏛 Abbey Museum   🌱 Gold Hill

🏛 Gold Hill Museum   ✒ Shaftesbury Arts Centre

Set on the side of a hill 700ft high, Shaftesbury was officially founded in AD880 by King Alfred who fortified the town and

Gold Hill, Shaftesbury

also built an abbey of which his daughter was first Prioress. A hundred years later, the King Edward who had been murdered by his stepmother at Corfe Castle was buried here and the abbey became a major centre of pilgrimage. A few remains of Shaftesbury Abbey have survived – they can be seen in the walled garden of the **Abbey Museum**, which contains many interesting artefacts excavated from the site as well as some illuminated manuscripts. The museum is on Park Walk, an elegant promenade laid out in the 1760s, which provides some wonderful views across the surrounding countryside.

Shaftesbury is a pleasant town to explore on foot. In fact, you have to walk if you want to see its most famous sight, **Gold Hill**, a steep, cobbled street, stepped in places and lined with 18th-century thatched cottages. Already well-known for its picturesque setting and grand views across the Vale of Blackmoor, Gold Hill became even more famous when it was featured in the classic TV commercial for Hovis. Also located here is the **Gold Hill Museum**, which vividly evokes the story of this ancient market town.

The 17th-century Ox House, referred to in Thomas Hardy's *Jude the Obscure*, is just one of a number of interesting and historic buildings in

the town. Others include the Church of St Peter, the Tudor-style Town Hall dating from the 1820s, and the Grosvenor Hotel, a 400-year-old coaching inn.

Shaftesbury boasts one of the liveliest arts centres in the country, the **Shaftesbury Arts Centre**, which, remarkably, is completely owned by its membership and administered entirely by volunteers. The results of their efforts are anything but amateur, however. The centre's Drama Group is responsible for three major productions each year, performed in the well-equipped theatre that also serves as a cinema for the centre's Film Society, screening a dozen or more films during the season. One of the most popular features of the centre is its Gallery, which is open daily with a regularly changing variety of exhibitions ranging from paintings, etchings and sculpture, to batiks, stained glass, embroidery and quilting.

Around Shaftesbury

ASHMORE
5 miles SE of Shaftesbury off the B3081

🏛 Compton Abbas Airfield

To the northwest of Ashmore is **Compton Abbas Airfield**, generally considered to be the most picturesque airfield in the country. Situated at more than 800 feet above sea level, the airfield is surrounded by an Area of Outstanding Natural Beauty and 50% of the airfield is organically farmed. One of the most popular displays is the collection of famous aeroplanes, special effects and memorabilia from film and TV productions. For the more adventurous, flights are available with a qualified instructor for a trip over this scenic part of the county; training courses for a full pilot's licence are also conducted here. The airfield hosts regular events throughout the year, including aerobatic displays. There's a shop selling a range of stunt and power kites and a bar and restaurant.

To the west of Ashmore are Fontwell and Melbury Downs, two estates that cover an important stretch of chalk downland that is cut by steep-sided valleys. Both areas are owned by the National Trust and evoke the landscapes described by Thomas Hardy – they are also notable for their population of butterflies.

TOLLARD ROYAL
7 miles SE of Shaftesbury on the B3081

🌿 Larmer Tree Gardens

About a mile outside Tollard Royal, so named because there was once a royal hunting lodge there, are **Larmer Tree Gardens**, which were established in the 19th century by General Augustus Pitt-Rivers. It's an idyllic spot with colourful shrubs and trees flourishing in secret enclosures. There are sunken dells, water gardens, and some delightful walkways shared with peacocks and macaws. Not surprisingly, it's a popular venue for wedding receptions.

MARNHULL
7 miles SW of Shaftesbury on the B3092

🏠 Tess's Cottage

The scattered village of Marnhull claims to be the largest parish in England, spread over a substantial area with a circumference of 23 miles. The village itself is well worth exploring for its part-Norman St Gregory's church with a fine 15th-century tower, and who knows what you might find along Sodom Lane? This now-prosperous village appears in *Tess of the d'Urbervilles* as Marlott, the birthplace of the heroine. The thatched **Tess's Cottage** (private, but visible from the lane) is supposedly the house Hardy had in mind, while the Crown Inn (also thatched) is still recognisable as the Pure Drop Inn in the same novel.

STALBRIDGE
9 miles SW of Shaftesbury on the A357

🏠 Market Cross

The 15th-century church here has a lofty 19th-century tower which provides a landmark throughout the Vale of Blackmoor. Perhaps even more impressive is the town's **Market Cross** standing 30 feet high and richly carved with scenes of the Crucifixion and

---

GUGGLETON FARM ARTS PROJECT

Station Road, Stalbridge, Dorset DT10 2RQ
Tel: 01963 363456 or 01963 370219

The **Guggleton Farm Arts Project** was founded within converted stone farm buildings during 1995 for recently graduated young artists to have studio space and a gallery from which to show their work.

These small beginnings have developed into a full programme of arts related subjects for the community to participate in. As well as the Gallery and studios we have a large workshop and dutch barn from which our courses are run. Our programme includes stone carving, sculpture, painting, drawing, picture framing and children's courses. Contact Isabel de Pelet (9am-5pm) for the full programme, or details of hiring studio, workshop or Gallery space.

🎬 stories and anecdotes 🐦 famous people 🎨 art and craft ✒ entertainment and sport 🚶 walks

Resurrection. Just outside the town, Stalbridge Park (private) sheltered Charles I after his defeat at Marston Moor. The house (now demolished) was built by Richard Boyle, 1st Earl of Cork, and it was here that his seventh son, the celebrated physicist and chemist Robert Boyle carried out the experiments that eventually led to his formulation of Boyle's Law.

STURMINSTER NEWTON
11 miles SW of Shaftesbury on the A357

🏠 Riverside Villa 🏠 Sturminster Mill

This unspoilt market town – the 'capital' of the Blackmore Vale – is an essential stop for anyone following in Thomas Hardy's footsteps. It was at Sturminster Newton that he and his first wife Emma had their first real home together. From 1876 until 1878, they lived in "a pretty cottage overlooking the Dorset Stour, called **Riverside Villa**". Here, Hardy wrote *The Return of the Native* and he often referred later to their time at Sturminster Newton in his poems. It was, he said, "our happiest time". The house is not open to the public but is visible from a riverside footpath.

Until Elizabethan times, Sturminster and Newton were separate villages standing on opposite sides of the River Stour. Shortly after the graceful Town Bridge linked the two communities, a mill was built some 250 yards upstream. Once again restored to working order, **Sturminster Mill** offers guided tours explaining the milling process, and the delightful setting attracts many amateur and professional artists and photographers. Incidentally, the fine old six-arched bridge still bears a rusty metal plaque carrying the dire warning: "Any person wilfully injuring any part of this county bridge will be guilty of felony and upon conviction liable to be transported for life by the court. P. Fooks."

LYDLINCH
13 miles SW of Shaftesbury on the A357

The small hamlet of Lydlinch in the Vale of Blackmore features in a poem by the Dorset dialect poet, William Barnes. He recalls as a young boy hearing the sound of Lydlinch church bells wafting across meadows to his home in nearby Bagber:

> *Vor Lydlinch bells be good vor sound,*
> *And liked by all the neighbours round.*

The five bells he heard still hang in the tower of the 13th-century church.

THE NEW CURIOSITY SHOP

2 The Parade, Station Road, Sturminster Newton, Dorset DT10 1BA
Tel: 01258 473944
e-mail: mikeandmarianhollamby@btinternet.com

For anyone looking for something for the home or a present that's out of the ordinary, the place to head for is the **New Curiosity Shop**. Owners Mike and Marian are great champions of the region's artistic talent, and all of the paintings on display are by local artists. Other items in this browser's delight include jewellery, sculpture and fairly traded pieces from overseas. Every visit is certain to reveal new surprises and new curiosities – even maybe a guitar or two.

🏠 historic building   🏛 museum and heritage   🏚 historic site   ⚘ scenic attraction   🌱 flora and fauna

ELSE FAMILY BUTCHERS

High Street, Stalbridge,
Dorset DT10 2LH
Tel: 01963 362276
website: www.rogerelse.co.uk

At Else Butchers Ltd the shop is run by Roger who has been a butcher for 48 years and bought the business from his boss. He is helped by his wife Brenda, son Julian and several other members of staff who are all very proud of the excellent quality fresh meat and meat products displayed, all labelled and priced with full traceability information available.

We have a large stock of well hung beef, local pork and lamb, free range poultry, several different varieties of our home made pork sausages, game when in season, home made burgers, oven baked meat pies, a fantastic BBQ range, home cured bacon, home cooked meats and a cheese and deli counter.

We are able to send fresh meat of your choice in our special boxes to anywhere in the UK via our overnight courier service, for further information please visit www.postaroast.com.

We are also very proud to be part of our village superstore Dike & Son which is open 7 days a week where we supply and run the butchery department alongside the fresh fish counter run by Martyn and Nicki Else. All three of us were winners in the Best of Dorset Food Awards 2008 and have recently been awarded the Taste of Dorset Best Butchers award 2010.

Julian owns Else Family Butchers Hog Roast EFB and outside catering using all our meats for private functions, weddings, BBQs, parties, with a choice of menus available. Please phone for details(hostaroast.com).

The shop is open from 6:30am - 1pm Monday, 6:30am - 5:30pm Tues - Fri closing for lunch 1pm - 2pm and 6am til 1pm on Saturdays.

Come and visit our shop or Dike & Son to see for yourselves what an excellent choice of meats we have on display.

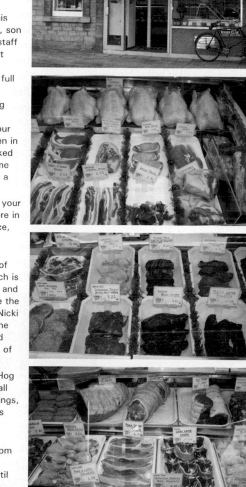

EAST STOUR
4 miles W of Shaftesbury on the A30

🐦 Henry Fielding

East Stour's literary connections are not with Dorset's omnipresent Thomas Hardy, but with the man who has been dubbed Father of the English Novel, **Henry Fielding**. When he was three years old, Fielding's family moved to the Manor House here, which stood close to the church. Fielding spent most of his childhood in the village before leaving to study at Eton and Leyden. He then spent a few years in London writing plays before returning to East Stour in 1734 with his new young wife, Charlotte Cradock. She was to provide the model for Sophia Western in his most successful novel, *Tom Jones*. By the time that book was published in 1749, Charlotte was dead, Fielding was seriously ill and he was to die just five years later while visiting Lisbon in an attempt to recover his health.

GILLINGHAM
4 miles NW of Shaftesbury on the B3081

🏛 Gillingham Museum

The most northerly town in Dorset, Gillingham was once an important centre for the milling of silk and the manufacture of the distinctive Victorian red-hot bricks. The parish church has a 14th-century chancel but the rest of the building, like much of the town, dates from after the arrival of the railway in 1859. **Gillingham Museum** charts the history of the town and the surrounding villages from prehistoric times; an interesting exhibit here is a manual fire engine dating from 1790.

Blandford Forum

🏛 Church of St Peter & St Paul

🏛 Blandford Museum   🏛 Fashion Museum

🏛 Royal Signals Museum

Blandford Forum, the administrative centre of North Dorset, is beautifully situated along the wooded valley of the River Stour. It's a handsome town, thanks mainly to suffering the trauma of a great fire in 1731. The gracious Georgian buildings erected after that conflagration, most of them designed by local architects John and William Bastard, provide the town with a quite unique and soothing sense of architectural harmony. Three important ancient buildings escaped the fire of 1731: the Ryves Almshouses of 1682, the Corn Exchange, and the splendid 15th-century Old House in The Close, which was built in the Bohemian style to house Protestant refugees from Bohemia. The old parish church did not survive the fire, but its 18th-century replacement, the **Church of St Peter & St Paul**, crowned by an unusual cupola, now

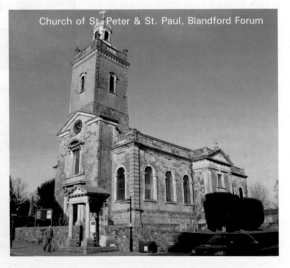
Church of St. Peter & St. Paul, Blandford Forum

SAXON INN

Gold Hill, Child Okeford, Blandford Forum, Dorset DT11 8HP
Tel: 01258 860310
e-mail: peterturner@saxoninn.co.uk
website: www.saxon inn.co.uk

Set amidst the captivating landscape of the Blackwater Vale, the **Saxon Inn** is a delightful old Dorset Freehouse nestling in the picturesque village of Child Okeford. It was originally built some time in the 1600s and became a pub in 1950. Today's customers receive a warm welcome from mine hosts Peter and Helen Turner who arrived here in the spring of 2003. Cosy log fires, a warm rustic atmosphere and traditional values all add to the appeal of this friendly hostelry.

The bar area has been sympathetically extended to allow more room for drinkers and diners. Those homely log fires in winter and access to an appealing covered patio and beer garden in summer make for an agreeable tipple whatever the weather. The bar stocks an excellent range of cash conditioned ales from local breweries throughout the year. The house beers are Butcombe Best and Ringwood Best, supported by guest beers from 'The Hidden Brewery', Palmers of Bridport, Otter Ales of Devon, and Goddards from the Isle of Wight, to name just a few. The bar also offers a select range of world class wines from the local vintner, guaranteeing a wine for every occasion. There's also a wide range of spirits and liqueurs and, for the non-drinker, a healthy choice of soft drinks.

Helen heads up the kitchen team and offers a diverse menu of traditional home-cooked food based on local produce from local suppliers wherever possible. The regular menu, featuring dishes such as home-cooked ham with local eggs, is supplemented by daily specials such as fresh fish dishes, steaks and seasonal delights.

The accommodation at The Saxon comprises four guest bedrooms which have been lovingly accessorised by Helen with reclaimed wood from parts of the old pub used to make the headboards and doors in all the rooms. This invests the rooms with a wonderful character, complemented by the luxurious en suite bathrooms. Contemporary flat screen televisions and access to WiFi internet give the rooms an extra dimension of modern day living.

dominates the marketplace. It's well worth stepping inside the church to see the box pews, an organ presented by George III, the massive columns of Portland stone, and the elegant pulpit, designed by Sir Christopher Wren, removed here from St Antholin's Church in the City of London.

In front of the church, the Fire Monument (known locally as Bastard's Pump) has a dual purpose – to provide water for fire fighting and as a public drinking fountain. Opposite the church, the **Blandford Museum** features a diorama of the Great Fire along with a wonderful collection of artefacts illustrating many aspects of life in and around Blandford over the years.

Housed in one of the fine town houses designed by the Bastard brothers, the **Blandford Fashion Museum** displays a fantastic collection of costumes from the 1730s through to the 1950s. Originally amassed by the late Mrs Betty Penny, the collection comprises more than 500 items. The museum also has a garden, shop and tearoom.

Just outside the town centre, at Blandford Camp, the **Royal Signals Museum** explores the arcane world of military communications with displays featuring spies, codes and code-breaking, the enigma machine, and Dorset's involvement in the preparations for D-Day.

Around Blandford Forum

IWERNE MINSTER
6 miles N of Blandford Forum on the A350

Unusually for Dorset, the church at Iwerne Minster has a spire. It also has one of the few examples of a Victorian church restoration that was actually an improvement. The Lady Chapel here was reconstructed by the architect JL Pearson in elaborate Gothic style, roofed with a stone vault and decorated with intricate floral bosses. The beautiful stained glass is a reproduction of 16th-century Flemish glass.

The old village was completely rebuilt in the early 1900s by a very wealthy Lord of the Manor and is notable for its varied cottages all built of red brick.

TARRANT HINTON
5 miles NE of Blandford Forum on the A354

  🌿 Great Dorset Steam Fair

This small village is the setting for the **Great Dorset Steam Fair**, held in late August/early September. Occupying a huge 600-acre site, this is one of the world's largest international steam events, attracting some 200 steam engines and more than 220,000 visitors. The annual extravaganza includes working engine displays, an old-time steam funfair, demonstrations of rural crafts, displays of working Shire horses and live music.

TARRANT GUNVILLE
7 miles NE of Blandford Forum off the A354

A tablet in the church here commemorates the death in 1805 of Thomas Wedgwood, son of the famous potter Josiah. Thomas's own claim to fame is as a pioneer of photography. He treated a sheet of white paper with a solution of nitrate of silver, placed a fern leaf on it and exposed the sheet to the sun. The resulting image, according to historians of photography, qualifies as possibly the first photograph ever made.

CHETTLE
7 miles NE of Blandford Forum off the A354

  🏚 Chettle House

A picturesque village with a charming manor

Chettle House

brewery expanded quickly thanks to a contract to supply ale to the Army during the Napoleonic Wars. Its Badger Ales trademark is one of the oldest known. The brewery is still thriving and visitors can take a tour of the premises by arrangement.

MILTON ABBAS
6 miles SW of Blandford Forum off the A354

🏛 Abbey Church

house, **Chettle House**. It was designed by Thomas Archer in the English baroque style and completed in 1720. Archer's work includes the north front of Chatsworth and the Church of St John in Smith Square and his buildings are typified by lavish curves, inverted scrolls and their large scale, a style that owed much to the Italian architects Bernini and Borromini. Chettle House was bought in 1846 by the Castleman family who added an ornate ceiling. The house contains portraits of the Chafin family, earlier owners, and the beautifully laid out gardens include herbaceous borders, a rose garden and croquet lawn. Opening times are limited.

BLANDFORD ST MARY
1 mile SW of Blandford Forum off the A354

🍺 Badger Brewery

The main attraction here is the **Badger Brewery**, founded at Ansty near Dorchester in 1777, but moved to its present site beside the River Stour in 1899. The original brewery was founded by Charles Hill, a farmer's son who learnt the brewing art along with farming. The

This picture-postcard village of thatched cottages and broad streets was created in the 1770s by Joseph Damer, 1st Earl of Dorchester. The earl lived in the converted former abbey from which the village takes its name, but he decided to demolish the medieval buildings and build a more stately mansion surrounded by grounds landscaped by Capability Brown. The earl's ambitious plans required that the small town that had grown up around the abbey would have to go, so more than 100 houses, four pubs, a brewery and a school were razed to the ground. The residents were moved more than a mile away to the present village for which Brown had made the preliminary plans. The earl's new mansion is now a private school and the only part of the abbey that has survived is the Milton Abbas **Abbey Church**, which contains some wonderful Pugin glass and an extraordinary tomb to the earl and his wife Caroline. Designed by Robert Adam and exquisitely carved by Agostino Carlini, the monument shows the earl propped up on one elbow gazing out across his beautiful wife.

📖 stories and anecdotes   🐦 famous people   🎨 art and craft   🎭 entertainment and sport   🚶 walks

MILBORNE ST ANDREW
9 miles SW of Blandford Forum on the A354

⚑ John Morton

An attractive village in the valley of a tributary of the River Piddle, Milborne St Andrew was owned in medieval times by the Morton family. One of them gave his name to the expression 'Morton's Fork'. As Lord Chancellor to Henry VII (and Archbishop of Canterbury), **John Morton** devised a system of parting the rich, and the not-so-rich, from their money. He proposed the thesis that if a man was living in grand style he clearly had money to spare; if he lived frugally, then he obviously kept his wealth hidden away. This ingenious argument became known as Morton's Fork and many a citizen was caught on its vicious prongs. However, the system enriched and delighted the king who made Morton a Cardinal in 1493. Morton spent his remaining years spending lavishly on the building and restoration of churches, most notably in the magnificently carved and painted roof of Bere Regis church.

Wareham

🏛 Church of St Mary   🏛 Wareham Museum
🌿 TE Lawrence Memorial   🎬 Rex Cinema

Situated between the rivers Frome and Piddle, Wareham is an enchanting little town lying within the earthworks of a 10th-century encircling wall. Standing close to an inlet of Poole Harbour, Wareham was an important port until the River Frome clogged its approaches with silt. Then, in 1726, a devastating fire consumed the town's timber buildings, a disaster which produced the happy result of a rebuilt town centre rich in handsome Georgian stone-built houses.

Wareham's history goes back much further than those days. Roman conquerors laid out its street plan: a stern grid of roads that faithfully follows the points of the compass. Saxons and Normans helped build the **Church of St Mary**, medieval artists covered its walls with devotional paintings of remarkable quality. It was in the grounds surrounding the church that King Edward was buried in AD978 after his stepmother, Queen Elfrida, contrived his murder at Corfe Castle. Elfrida added insult to injury by having the late king buried outside the churchyard in unhallowed ground.

Occupying the 12th-century Holy Trinity Church near the quay, the Purbeck Information and Heritage Centre offers copious information about the town; while in East Street, **Wareham Museum** has some interesting displays and artefacts illustrating the town's history.

In the Saxon St Martin's Church, notable for its early medieval wall paintings, there's a striking memorial to what appears at first glance to be a medieval crusader dressed in Arab robes, holding an Arab dagger and resting his head on a camel's saddle. This is a **Memorial to TE Lawrence**, Lawrence of Arabia, who is actually buried at Moreton.

Wareham boasts one building that is unique – the privately owned **Rex Cinema**, which was built pre-1914 and is the only gas-lit cinema in the country. The original antique carbon arc projectors are still used to show the latest blockbusters. The Rex is unusual, too, in having its own bar so that patrons can enjoy a drink while watching the film.

An ancient survival in Wareham is the custom of the Court Leet. In Norman times these courts were the main judicial institution in many parts of the country. On four evenings in November, strangely dressed men

PETER HEDLEY GALLERY

10 South Street, Wareham, Dorset BH20 4LT
Tel: 01929 551 777
e-mail: peter-hedley@btconnect.com
website: www.peterhedleygallery.co.uk

The **Peter Hedley Gallery** is located in the centre of Wareham, an attractive Saxon riverside town between Poole Harbour and the beautiful Purbeck hills and coast. The gallery has always specialised in original paintings and bronzes and considers itself one of the well-established and well-stocked galleries in the south of England. It opened in 1983 to specialise in promoting the work of contemporary painters and sculptors, chosen from all over the British Isles as well as some from Europe.

Peter initially worked in the West End with Frost and Reed, the Tryon Gallery and the Sladmore Gallery from 1971 to 1976, before moving to manage Windsor and Eton Fine Arts for six years. After such an excellent grounding he decided to open his own gallery which has had many fine exhibitions over the years and has established a 'stable' of many talented artists and sculptors, several of whom have shown with him since the opening of the gallery and have a considerable following of clients who collect their work. The gallery is open from 10am to 5pm, Monday to Saturday, or by appointment.

visit the town's inns to check the quality and quantity of the food and ale on offer. The officials include ale-tasters, bread-weighers and carnisters, who sample the meat. Although they have no powers nowadays, it is a quaint tradition.

Around Wareham

ORGANFORD
3 miles N of Wareham off the A35

🌱 Farmer Palmer's

The tiny village of Organford stands on the edge of the tree-covered expanses of Gore Heath. The settlement is so small it doesn't possess either a church or a pub, but it does have a Manor House, which enjoys a wonderfully quiet and secluded position surrounded by woods. It's also home to **Farmer Palmer's** where children can feed

lambs and goats, watch cows being milked, enjoy a wild trailer ride, drive pedal tractors, or work off some energy in the bouncy castles and soft play zone.

WORTH MATRAVERS
7 miles SE of Wareham off the B3069

🎭 Benjamin Jesty   🏛 Chapel of St Aldhelm

In the graveyard of St Nicholas' Church is the grave of a local farmer, **Benjamin Jesty**, whose tomb inscription is worth quoting in full:

An upright and honest man, particularly noted for having been the first person known that introduced the Cow Pox by inoculation, and who, from his great strength of mind, made the experiment from the cow on his wife and two sons in the year 1774.

His family's "great strength of mind" might also have been noted since the inoculation was made using a knitting needle. The man usually credited with discovering inoculation, Edward Jenner, didn't make his first successful experiment until 1796 – 22 years after Benjamin's.

High on the cliffs of St Aldhelm's Head, a couple of miles south of the village and accessible only by a bridleway, the **Chapel of St Aldhelm** stands alone. It is one of the oldest churches in Dorset, a low square building with a fine Norman doorway and one solitary window. Uniquely, the chapel has no east wall as the corners of the walls are aligned to the points of the compass. In its dank, dim interior the stonework is bare of decoration, just a central column from which eight ribs extend to the walls. According to legend, the church was built in 1140 by a local man in memory of his newly-married daughter and her husband. He was watching from this clifftop as the boat in which they were sailing to a new home was caught in a sudden squall and capsized. All on board perished.

FURZEBROOK
4 miles S of Wareham off the A351

🐾 Blue Pool

If you are interested in natural curiosities, follow the brown and white signs for the **Blue Pool**. In what was originally a clay pit, tiny particles of clay in the pool diffract light and create an astonishing illusion of colour, varying from sky blue to deepest azure. There's a tea house, shops and museum here and the tree-lined shore is a popular picnic place.

CHURCH KNOWLE
5 miles S of Wareham off the A351

🐾 Margaret Green Animal Sanctuary

This small village is home to the **Margaret Green Animal Sanctuary** where there are usually many animals awaiting a new home. In addition to small domestic animals, there are also some goats, sheep and horses.

TYNEHAM
8 miles SW of Wareham off the A351

During World War Two, the entire population of the village of Tyneham was evacuated - and never returned. It's possible to walk round the ruins and also visit the church and the schoolroom where the desks, blackboard, and textbooks are still in place.

WINFRITH NEWBURGH
9 miles SW of Wareham off the A352

🐾 Lulworth Cove   🐾 Durdle Door

🏛 Lulworth Castle

The charming little village of Winfrith Newburgh with its thatched stone cottages stands on a minor road that leads to one of the county's best known beauty spots, **Lulworth Cove**. An almost perfectly circular bay, the Cove is surrounded by towering 440 foot cliffs. Over the centuries, the sea has gnawed away at a weak point in the limestone here, inadvertently creating a breathtakingly beautiful scene. Best to visit out of season,

Lulworth Cove, Winfrith Newburgh

Durdle Door, Winfrith Newburgh

however, as parking places nearby are limited.

About a mile to the west of Lulworth Cove stands another remarkable natural feature that has been sculpted by the sea. **Durdle Door** is a magnificent archway carved from the coastal limestone. There's no road to the coast at this point, but you can reach it easily by following the South West Coast Path from Lulworth Cove. Along the way, you will also see another strange outcrop - a forest of tree-stumps that have become fossilised over the centuries.

A couple of miles inland, **Lulworth Castle** (English Heritage) looks enormously impressive from a distance: close-up, you can see how a disastrous fire in 1929 destroyed much of it. Amongst the remains, though, is a curious circular building dating from 1786: the first Roman Catholic church to be established in Britain after Henry VIII's defiance of the Pope in 1534. Sir Thomas Weld was given permission to build this unique church by George III. The king cautiously added the proviso that Sir Thomas' new place of worship should not offend Anglican sensibilities by looking like a church. It doesn't, and that's a great part of its appeal. The castle's other attractions include indoor and outdoor children's play areas, an animal farm, pitch and putt, woodland walks, and a café and shop.

BOVINGTON CAMP
6 miles W of Wareham off the A352

🏛 Tank Museum 🐒 Monkey World

🦅 TE Lawrence 🏠 Cloud's Hill

It was at Bovington Camp that TE Lawrence served as a private in the Royal Tank Corps. Today, the camp is home to the **Tank Museum** (see panel on page 294) which has more than 150 armoured vehicles on display dating from World War One to the present day. Audio tours are available, there's a children's play area, restaurant and gift shop, and during the summer tanks take part in live action displays. Also here is **Jumicar**, a children's fun and educational activity where road awareness skills are taught using real junior-sized cars on a mini road layout complete with traffic lights and zebra crossings. Open every weekend and school holidays except December and January.

Hardy may be Dorset's most famous author, but one mile north of Bovington Camp it is another distinguished writer (also a scholar, archaeologist and military hero), who is remembered. In 1935 **TE Lawrence**, Lawrence of Arabia, left the RAF where he was known simply as Aircraftsman TE Shaw and retired to a spartan cottage he had bought 10 years earlier. It stands alone on the heath outside Moreton village and here Lawrence lived as a virtual recluse, without cooking facilities and with a sleeping bag as his bed. He was to enjoy this peaceful, if comfortless, retreat for only a few weeks. Lawrence loved speeding along the Dorset lanes on his motor-cycle and one sunny spring day his adventurous driving led to a fatal collision

The Tank Museum

Bovington, Dorset BH20 6JG
Tel: 01929 405096 Fax: 01929 405360
e-mail: info@tankmuseum.co.uk
website: www.tankmuseum.co.uk

The Tank Museum, defined by the Government as a Designated Collection, houses the world's finest and most extensive indoor collection of armoured fighting vehicles. It tells the story of tanks and armoured warfare illustrated through scientific and technological developments, woven together with the stirring story of human endeavours on the battlefield.

In 1919 the tanks came back from France and hundreds of them, awaiting scrap, filled the fields around Bovington, where tank training had started in 1916. A few were rescued from the scrapman and fenced off from the rest. The plan was to provide young Tank Corps soldiers with an idea of their heritage and tank designers with historical references. When Rudyard Kipling visited Bovington in 1923 he suggested that a proper tank museum be established, and the museum, its stock much expanded after the Second World War, opened to the public in 1947. The Museum has a large model, book and gift shop, fully licensed restaurant, grass picnic area, outdoor play area and ample car and coach parking. Bovington still trains all branches of the Army in tracked vehicle driving and its tank repair workshops are one of the largest employers in the county.

with a young cyclist. The King of Iraq and Winston Churchill attended the hero's burial in the graveyard at nearby Moreton and the home Lawrence occupied for such a short time, **Cloud's Hill** (National Trust), is now open to the public.

A very different kind of attraction, to the east of the camp, is **Monkey World** whose 65 acres are home to some 240 rescued primates. Most of them have been acquired from circuses, zoos or laboratories. The site also includes the largest children's adventure play area on the south coast, an education centre, woodland walk, pets corner, café, picnic areas and full disabled facilities.

BERE REGIS

7 miles NW of Wareham on the A35

🏠 Church of St John

Most visitors to the **Church of St John** at Bere Regis are attracted by its associations with Hardy's *Tess of the D'Urbervilles*. They come to see the crumbling tombs of the once-powerful Turberville family whose name Hardy adapted for his novel. It was outside the church, beneath the Turberville window, that Hardy had the homeless Tess and her family set up their four-poster bed. A poignant fictional scene, but the church itself is definitely worth visiting for its unique and magnificent carved and painted wooden roof. Large figures of the 12 Apostles (all in Tudor dress) jut out horizontally from the wall and there are a number of humorous carvings depicting men suffering the discomforts of toothache and over-indulgence. There's also a carving of Cardinal Morton who had this splendid roof installed in 1497. The church's history goes back much farther than that. In Saxon times, Queen Elfrida came here to spend the remainder of her days in penitence for her part in the murder of young King

Edward at Corfe Castle in AD979. Further evidence of the church's great age is the fact that around 1190 King John paid for the pillars of the nave to be "restored".

Swanage

🐦 Durlston Country Park   🔗 Swanage Railway

🏛 Town Hall   🏛 King Alfred Column

🌍 Great Globe   🌿 Studland Bay

Picturesquely set beside a broad, gently curving bay with fine, clear sands and beautiful surrounding countryside, Swanage is understandably popular as a family holiday resort. A winner of Southern England in Bloom, the town takes great pride in the spectacular floral displays in its parks and gardens. The town's other awards include the prestigious European Blue Flag for its unpolluted waters, and the Tidy Britain Group's Seaside Award. Swanage offers its visitors all the facilities necessary for a traditional seaside holiday, including boat trips, (with sightings of bottle-nosed dolphins if you're lucky), water sports, sea angling and an attractive old-fashioned pier and bandstand. The Mowlem Theatre provides a seasonal programme of films, shows and plays, and on Sunday afternoons the Recreation Ground resounds to the strains of a brass band. On the clifftops, **Durlston Country Park** covers some 260 acres of delightful countryside; on the front, the Beach Gardens offer tennis, bowls and putting, or you can just rent a beach hut or bungalow and relax.

One attraction not to be missed is a ride on the **Swanage Railway** along which magnificent steam locomotives of the old Southern Railway transport passengers some six miles through lovely Dorset countryside to Norden, just north of Corfe Castle.

THE PURBECK DELI

26 Institute Road, Swanage,
Dorset BH19 1BX
Tel: 01929 422344
e-mail: thepurbeckdeli@yahoo.co.uk
website: www.thepurbeckdeli.co.uk

Located in the heart of Swanage, **The Purbeck Deli** has proved very popular with both locals and visitors. It was established by Diane Littleton who prides herself on selecting only the very best produce, whether it be locally sourced, from other regions of the UK, or from anywhere in Europe. One thing she will not do is compromise on quality.

Her shop offers a huge range of comestibles and food items. The cheese counter, in particular, presents a dazzling range of cheeses from across Britain and Europe. There's also an extensive choice of cooked meats, breads, olives, pickles, coleslaw, preserves and chutneys, and much, much more. Diane and her staff are very knowledgeable about their products and will happily put together a hamper for you, based on your personal preferences. The Deli also offers an outside catering service.

📖 stories and anecdotes   🍄 famous people   🎨 art and craft   🎭 entertainment and sport   🏃 walks

In the town itself, the **Town Hall** is worth seeing for its ornate façade, the work of Christopher Wren. Wren didn't build it for Swanage, however. It was originally part of Mercers Hall in Cheapside, London. When the Hall was being demolished, a Swanage man named George Burt scavenged the fine frontage and rebuilt it here. He also brought the graceful little Clock Tower that stands near the pier, but once used to adorn the Surrey end of London Bridge; a gateway from Hyde Park for his own house; and cast-iron columns and railings from Billingsgate Market. No wonder older residents of the town refer to Swanage as Little London.

There is, however, one monument that is purely Swanage – the **King Alfred Column** on the seafront. This commemorates the king's victory here over a Danish fleet in AD877. The column is topped by cannonballs that would have been of great assistance to Alfred had they been invented at the time.

Collectors of curiosities will want to make their way to Tilly Whim Hill, just south of Swanage, which is also well-known for its murky caves. High above the caves stands the **Great Globe**, a huge round stone of Portland limestone, some 10 feet in diameter and weighing 40 tons, its surface sculpted with all the countries of the world. At its base, stone slabs are inscribed with quotations from the Old Testament psalms, Shakespeare and other poets. They include moral injunctions such as, "Let prudence direct you, temperance chasten you, fortitude support you", and the information that, "if a

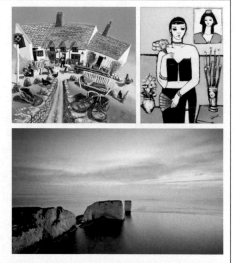
🏚 historic building   🏛 museum and heritage   🏛 historic site   🏞 scenic attraction   🌱 flora and fauna

THE MULBERRY TREE GALLERY

57 High Street, Swanage, Dorset BH19 2LT
Tel: 01929 423141
e-mail: info@mulberrytreegallery.co.uk
website: www.mulberrytreegallery.co.uk
Mon - Sat: 9.30am to 5.00pm

On the corner of Swanage High Street, **The Mulberry Tree Gallery** brings a touch of class to a town best known for its seaside charm. In two large window displays, artwork, glassware and ceramics are exhibited with a refreshing uniqueness that owners Sonia and Emma have learnt in the years they have run the business. Themed around an artist, hand-crafted pottery, stationery and glassware is displayed alongside the artist whose style it suits. It's an holistic way to window dressing, reflecting their approach to the business of selling art.

They set out to bring art to a cross section of people in a down-to-earth way. The simplest way to achieve this is to offer affordable art, which they have done in stocking originals, limited edition prints and canvases ranging in value from ten pounds, to thousands of pounds.

You can while away the time looking at the hugely entertaining spectrum of greetings cards or come in for a chat whilst choosing a frame for your artwork or memorabilia. The gallery is proud to have two Fine Art Trade Guild Commended Framers, of which there are just over 1000 worldwide. We know you will leave the gallery happy with your purchase whether it is simply a greetings card, a newly framed canvas or an original piece of artwork chosen to spoil yourself or a loved one!

It's a seasonal business, with the town enjoying an influx of summer visitors before settling into quiet, windswept winters. When the sun shines, Sonia's preference for bright, 'naive' art comes into its own. The walls are hung with beachy, fresh pieces from Rebecca Lardner, Sasha and Sophie Harding, Hannah Cole and other nationally acclaimed artists. In the colder months, the mood changes to reflect the season and Emma's taste for richer, spicier work comes to the fore. Over the festive season you can mooch about with a glass of mulled wine, taking in Ben Spurling's cool coastal scenes, Ges Wilson's warmly lit nudes or Tony Chance's famous crashing waves.

Their other big aim was to make the gallery part of the community. Swanage is a small, close-knit town with a huge proliferation of artists. They have taken time to build lasting relationships with the artists they represent, by promoting and supporting them through regular exhibitions.

As a result, the Mulberry Tree Gallery is not just on the corner but is a cornerstone of Swanage High Street, and well worth a look.

© Hester Viney

CANDLEWORLD

14 High Street, Swanage, Dorset BH19 2NT
Tel: 01929 421611
e-mail: candleworld@mac.com
website: www.candleworld.co.uk

A well-established business, Candleworld has been supplying its customers with quality candles for more than a quarter of a century. Owner Vicky Clarke was a costumier based in London before taking over here. Her flair has been thoroughly utilised with the introduction of new lines which have enhanced the range on offer. Candleworld now stocks top quality candles from companies such as Woodwicks, Colony, St Eval, Broste, Spaas and Gisela Graham. The shop also offers accessories produced by Think Pink, Faerie Flames and Glick papers.

Candleworld provides lighting for all occasions, whether it be household interiors with different ranges dependent on the season and including lanterns, mobiles and outdoor lights. You'll also find organic bath products, greeting cards, bunting and a range of paper products for all occasions. The shop stands on Swanage's main street and its window displays change throughout the year based on themes such as Halloween, Christmas or the beach. Candleworld's products are also available by mail order and from its website.

SWANAGE BAY FISH

48 High Street, Swanage,
Dorset BH19 2NY
Tel: 01929 422288
e-mail: swanagebayfish@live.com

Julia and Terry have lived and worked in the fishing community all of their lives, Terry and his family have fished from swanage for the past 5 generations before opening their own fishmongers shop, **Swanage Bay Fish**, in 2009. The idea was to sell all the fish that they caught.

Almost all of the fish in their shop is locally caught in the bay. They strive to sell what ever their catch, from Lobster and crab, sea bass and mackerel to the more unusual fish such as trigger fish, wrasse and gar fish. However they do have to source outside dorset, cod, haddock and farmed fish to keep the counter topped up and their customers happy, especially during bad weather when they cannot get out to sea.

As well as selling fish, Julia has some great ideas for recipes for fish dishes. So if you are struggling to come up with a meal idea, Julia can point you in the right direction.

🏠 historic building   🏛 museum and heritage   🏚 historic site   ⚘ scenic attraction   🌱 flora and fauna

globe representing the sun were constructed on the same scale, it would measure some 1090 feet across".

A couple of miles north of Swanage, **Studland Bay** offers a lovely four-mile stretch of sandy beach, with views of Old Harry Rocks and the Isle of Wight. Part of the beach is clearly designated as an exclusive resort for naturists only.

Around Swanage

LANGTON MATRAVERS
2 miles W of Swanage, on the B3069

🏠 Coach House Museum

🌱 Putlake Adventure Farm

Before tourism, the main industry around Swanage was quarrying the famous Purbeck stone that has been used in countless churches, cathedrals and fine houses around the country. **The Coach House Museum** at Langton Matravers tells the story of Purbeck Marble, a handsome and durable material that was already being cut and polished back in Roman times. This sizeable village with many houses built of Purbeck stone is also home to **Putlake Adventure Farm** where visitors are encouraged to make contact with a variety of friendly animals, bottle-feed the lambs, or have

a go at milking cows. There are pony and trailer rides, picnic and play areas, a farm trail, gift shop and tearoom.

CORFE CASTLE
5 miles NW of Swanage on the A351

🏰 Corfe Castle   🏘 Model Village

One of the grandest sights in the county is the impressive ruin of **Corfe Castle** (National Trust) standing high on a hill and dominating the attractive grey stone village below. Once the most impregnable fortress in the land, Corfe dates back to the days of William the Conqueror, with later additions by King John and Edward I. The dastardly John threw 22 French knights into the castle dungeons and left them to starve to death. Later, Edward II was imprisoned here before being sent to Berkeley Castle and his horrible murder.

Corfe Castle remained important right up until the days of the Civil War when it successfully withstood two sieges before it fell into Parliamentary hands through treachery. A month later, Parliament ordered the castle to be slighted – rendered militarily useless.

Although Corfe now stands in splendid ruin, you can see a smaller, intact version at the **Model Village** in West Street. This superbly accurate replica is built from the same Purbeck stone as the real thing and the

📖 stories and anecdotes 🦜 famous people 🎨 art and craft 🎭 entertainment and sport 🚶 walks

details of the miniature medieval folk going about their daily business are wonderful. Surrounded by lovely gardens, this intriguing display is well worth a visit. You might also want to explore the local museum, which is housed in the smallest Town Hall building in the country.

NORDEN
7 miles NW of Swanage, on the A351

🏛 Swanage Railway

About half a mile north of Corfe Castle, Norden Station is the northern terminus of the **Swanage Railway** and there's a regular bus service from the station to the castle. The hamlet of Norden itself is actually another mile further to the northeast, a delightful place surrounded by pine trees and heathland.

Bournemouth

🏛 Pier   🏛 Russell-Cotes Art Gallery and Museum

🏛 St Peter's Church   🏛 Bournemouth Eye

🏛 Oceanarium   🏛 Teddy Bear Museum

🏛 Bournemouth Aviation Museum

🏛 Adventure Wonderland

Bournemouth used to be known as a retirement town for the elderly, but in the 1990s its character changed, and today, it's been calculated that Bournemouth has "more nightclubs than Soho" as well as a huge range of hotels, shops, bars, restaurants and entertainment venues. The largest town in Dorset, Bournemouth also supports two symphony orchestras. In

July 2009, in the hope of attracting more of Britain's 250,000 surfers to the town, Bournemouth council completed the construction of a 1600 foot-long artificial reef capable of producing breakers up to 16 feet high. Beach users will also benefit as the reef will create a peaceful lagoon.

Already, some five and a half million visitors each year are attracted to this cosmopolitan town, which has been voted the greenest and cleanest resort in the UK. There are more than 2000 acres of Victorian parks and gardens, and the town centre streets are washed and scrubbed every morning.

Two hundred years ago, the tiny village of Bourne was a mere satellite of the bustling port of Poole, a few miles to the west. The empty coastline was ideal for smugglers and Revenue men were regularly posted here to patrol the area. One of them, Captain Louis Tregonwell, was enchanted by Bourne's glorious setting at the head of three deep valleys, or chines. He and his wife bought land here, built themselves a house and planted the valleys with the hundreds of pine trees that give the present-day town its distinctive appearance. Throughout Victorian times,

Bournemouth Pier

🏛 historic building   🏛 museum and heritage   🏛 historic site   🏛 scenic attraction   🏛 flora and fauna

Bournemouth, as it became known, grew steadily and the prosperous new residents beautified their adopted town with wide boulevards, grand parks, and public buildings, creating a Garden City by the Sea.

They also built a splendid **Pier** (1855) and, around the same time, **St Peter's Church**, which is much visited for its superb Gothic Revival interior, and the tomb in which Mary Shelley, the author of *Frankenstein*, is buried along with the heart of her poet-husband, Percy Bysshe Shelley. A few yards from the Promenade, the **Russell-Cotes Art Gallery and Museum** is based on the magnificent collection of the globe-trotting Sir Merton Russell-Cotes and housed in his cliff-top mansion. The **Teddy Bear Museum** is housed in the Expocentre and, north of the town, the **Bournemouth Aviation Museum** at Bournemouth International Airport, home to a collection of vintage jet aircraft – including the last flying Sea Fury fighter – that are flown on a regular basis.

Opposite the airport and set in seven acres of landscaped grounds, the **Adventure Wonderland** (formerly the Alice in Wonderland Family Park) is designed for children aged 2-12 and offers a wide variety of rides and attractions, a huge Alice Maze, indoor play centre, and a daily panto-style Storyline.

Back in town, the **Oceanarium**, located alongside the pier, explores the wonders of the natural world beneath the surface of seas, lakes and rivers. Displays include life under the Amazon, the Caribbean and the lagoons of Hawaii. A popular feature here is Turtle Beach, home to rescued green turtles.

And if you're looking for a novel experience, and a really spectacular aerial view of the town and coastline, the **Bournemouth Eye**, in the Lower Gardens near the pier, offers day or night ascents in a tethered balloon that rises up to 500 feet.

Around Bournemouth

CHRISTCHURCH
5 miles E of Bournemouth on the A35

Blue Plaques Millennium Trail   Double Dykes
Christchurch Priory   Christchurch Castle
St Michael's Loft Museum   Place Mill
Red House Museum   Museum of Electricity

An excellent way of exploring Christchurch is to follow the **Blue Plaques Millennium Trail**, which commemorates sites around the town from Neolithic times to the 20th century. A booklet detailing this trip through time is available from the tourist information centre in the High Street.

Pride of place on the trail goes to **Christchurch Priory**, a magnificent building begun in 1094 and reputedly the longest parish church in England, extending for 311 feet. It has an impressive Norman nave, some superb medieval carving, and a vast 14th-century stone reredos with a Tree of Jesse. Other treasures include the magnificent Salisbury Chantry, some fine misericords and, in the beautiful Lady Chapel, a pendant vault believed to be the earliest of its kind in the country. From the Lady Chapel, a stairway of 75 steps leads to St Michael's Loft, originally a school for novice monks and later a grammar school for boys. It now houses **St Michael's Loft Museum**, which tells something of the long history of the priory. Another stairway – a spiral one of 176 steps – winds its way up the tower of the church; from the top there are extensive views over the town and harbour.

Just north of the priory are the remains of

Christchurch Castle, built in the late 11th century and slighted (rendered militarily useless) after the Civil War. The site here contains the Constable's Hall, which boasts the oldest Norman chimney in Britain, constructed around 1150.

Other nearby attractions include the **Red House Museum and Gardens**, which is housed in a former Georgian workhouse and provides some interesting local history as well as a peaceful enclave in the heart of the town; and the **Museum of Electricity**, which occupies a stately Edwardian power station and has something for everyone – from dozens of early domestic appliances to a pair of boot warmers.

On Town Quay, at the meeting of the rivers Stour and Avon, is **Place Mill**, which dates back to Anglo-Saxon times and was mentioned in the Domesday Book. The mill has been restored and, although it is unable to grind corn, you can still see the wheel turning when tidal conditions are right. The body of the mill is now an art gallery with changing exhibitions by local artists, interesting displays of artefacts and a gift shop.

To the south of Christchurch are the ancient ditches known as **Double Dykes**, an area that offers great walking along with superb views. The dykes cut across the heathland of Hengistbury Head, which forms the southern side of the town's large natural harbour. The headland is now a nature reserve, one of the few uninhabited parts of this otherwise built-up stretch of coastline.

Not far from Double Dykes, in 1910, Britain's first air show took place. It was attended by some of the greatest names of early aviation, amongst them Wilbur Wright, Blériot, and the Hon Charles Rolls (of Rolls-Royce fame) who was killed when his plane crashed at this event.

Mudeford Quay, Christchurch

MUDEFORD
7 miles E of Bournemouth off the A337

Standing at the entrance to Christchurch Harbour, Mudeford has a picturesque quay with piles of lobster pots, a fresh fish stall, fishermens' cottages and an old inn. It is still the centre of the local fishing industry and the quay provides a great vantage point for watching yachts and windsurfers as they come up The Run into the harbour. The beach here is clean and sandy with a lifeguard service during the summer months when beach huts, deck chairs and canoes can all be hired, and ferry services cross the harbour to Mudeford Sandbank. Day cruises to the Needles and Yarmouth on the Isle of Wight are also available.

HIGHCLIFFE
9 miles E of Bournemouth on the A337

🏛 Highcliffe Castle

The most easterly community in Dorset, Highcliffe has a fine beach and views of the eastern tip of the Isle of Wight. The bustling village centre hosts a Friday market, but the major attraction here is **Highcliffe Castle** (English Heritage), an imposing mansion of gleaming white stone originally built between 1831 and 1835. It was damaged by fire in the

MONICA'S CRUSTY CRUST LTD

314 Lymington Road, Highcliffe, nr Christchurch,
Dorset BH23 5ET
Tel: 01425 273888 e-mail: crustycrust.uk@hotmail.com
website: www.crustycrust.com

Monica's Crusty Crust Ltd is based in Highcliffe, the most easterly community in Dorset, with a fine beach and views across to the tip of the Isle of Wight.

Gérard Lazéras bought this outstanding baker and patisserie in the spring of 2010, having owned and worked in catering outlets all over the world. He bought the business from the previous owners, who are still involved here, helping to maintain the highest standards of quality and reliability for the people of Highcliffe and the neighbouring towns and villages.

Everything is the best, from the daily baked bread and rolls to cakes and pastries, doughnuts, dinky little gingerbread men, pasties and quiches. Monica's sells not just to the public but to numerous local restaurants, pubs and hotels, and orders come from as far afield as London and Scotland. Customers can place orders in advance by phone, and this friendly, well-run place also bakes cakes for birthdays, weddings and other special occasions. Try any of Monica's baked delights and you'll never want to go to the supermarket again for your bread and cakes.

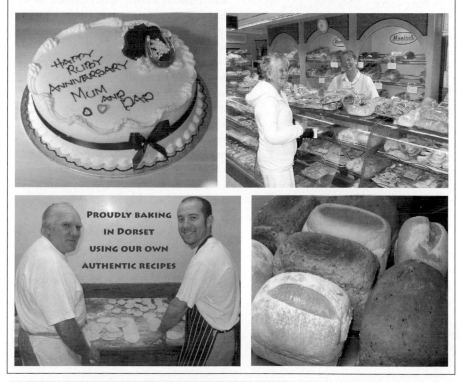

1960s but the exterior was restored in the 1990s although most of the interior remains unrepaired. Guided tours are available every Tuesday afternoon during the summer; the grounds, visitor centre, galleries and gift shop are open all year round.

POOLE
4 miles W of Bournemouth, on the A35/A350

🏛 Waterfront Museum   🏺 Poole Pottery

🌿 Compton Acres   🏛 Brownsea Island

Once the largest settlement in Dorset, Poole is now a pleasant, bustling port. Its huge natural harbour, the second largest in the world, is actually a drowned river valley. It has a shoreline of some 50 miles and is the most extensive anchorage in Europe with a history going back well beyond Roman times. A 33 feet long Logboat, hollowed from a giant oak tree and dating back to around 295BC, has been found off Brownsea Island, the largest of several islands dotting the harbour. Poole's extensive sandy beaches boast more Blue Flag awards than any other UK strand, and every Thursday evening in August there's a beach party with sports, calypso bands, barbecues and a spectacular firework finale.

The Quay is a great place to relax with a drink and watch people "just messing about in boats" or participating in one of the many water sports available. Near the Quay is the internationally famed **Poole Pottery**, which has been producing high-quality pottery for more than 125 years, although its main production is now in Stoke-on-Trent. Its visitor centre stands on the site of the old factory. Here, visitors can watch a 12-minute video summarising two millennia of ceramic production, see the age-old processes under way, and children can have a go themselves at this tricky craft. The Pottery Shop offers factory-direct prices and special savings on seconds. There are superb displays of the Pottery's distinctively designed creations, and a brasserie and bar overlooking the harbour.

In the town centre, the **Waterfront Museum** celebrates 2000 years of maritime heritage, and displays the Logboat mentioned above. Next door is Scaplens Court, a striking medieval house with a Tudor herb and physic garden, which is only open in August.

Poole is well-provided with public parks offering a wide range of activities, and the town also boasts one of the county's great gardens, **Compton Acres**, which was created in the 1920s by Thomas William Simpson who spent the equivalent of £10 million in today's money. Amongst its varied themed areas, which include a lovely Italian Garden, the Japanese Garden enjoys an especially fine reputation. Japanese architects and workmen were brought over to England to create what is reputed to be the only completely genuine Japanese Garden in Europe, an idyllic setting in which only the most troubled spirit could not find solace. Magnificent sculptures enhance the grounds, which also contain restaurants, a delicatessen, model railway exhibition and shops. From the Colonnade viewpoint there are grand views over Poole Harbour to the Purbeck hills beyond. To the south of Compton Acres, a narrow peninsula divides Poole Bay from Poole Harbour. Known as Sandbanks, it has become notorious as having the most expensive residential properties in Europe.

From Poole Quay there are regular cruises along the coast and ferries to **Brownsea Island** (National Trust), where there are quiet beaches with safe bathing. Visitors can wander through 500 acres of heath and woodland, which provide one of the few remaining refuges for Britain's native red squirrel. In 1907, General Robert Baden-Powell carried out an experiment on the island to test his idea of teaching boys from all social classes the scouting skills he had refined during the Boer Wars. Just 20 boys attended that first camp - in its heyday during the 1930s, the world-wide Scouting Movement numbered some 16 million members in more than 120 countries.

WIMBORNE MINSTER
7 miles NW of Bournemouth on the A349/A31

🏛 Wimborne Minster   🌿 Knoll Gardens and Nursery

🖋 Wimborne Model Town   🏛 Stapehill Abbey

🌿 Honeybrook Country Park   🏛 Kingston Lacy

🏛 Museum of East Dorset Life

🌿 Dean's Court Garden

Happily, the A31 now bypasses this beguiling old market town set amongst meadows beside the rivers Stour and Allen. The glory of the town is **Wimborne Minster**, which, in 2005,

celebrated 1300 years of ministry. It's a distinctive building of multi-coloured stone boasting some of the finest Norman architecture in the county and also notable for its 14th-century astronomical clock, and the Quarterjack, a life-sized figure of a grenadier from the Napoleonic wars, who strikes the quarter hours on his bells. Inside, the unique Chained Library, founded in 1686, contains more than 240 books, amongst them a 14th century manuscript on vellum.

In the High Street, the Priest's House is a lovely Elizabethan house set amidst beautiful gardens. It houses the **Museum of East Dorset Life**, which re-creates 400 years of history in a series of rooms where the decoration and furnishings follow the changing fashions between Jacobean and Victorian times. There's also an archaeology gallery with hands-on activities, a Gallery of Childhood, delightful walled garden and summer tearoom.

In King Street you can see Wimborne as it was in the early 1950s – but at one-tenth the size. **Wimborne Model Town** presents a meticulous miniature version of the town, complete with an Old English fair and a working small-scale model railway.

Also close to the town centre, **Dean's Court Garden** is a 13-acre expanse of partly wild gardens surrounding an old house that was once the Deanery to the Minster. There are many fine specimen trees, lawns and borders, as well as a fascinating old kitchen garden stocked with some of the oldest varieties of vegetables.

On the outskirts of Wimborne,

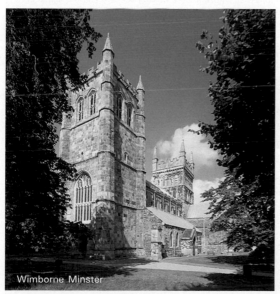
Wimborne Minster

VANESSA BLUNDEN FINE ART

10 Highland View Close, Wimborne, Dorset BH21 2QX
Tel: 01202 886470
e-mail: vanessa@vbfineart.co.uk
website: www.vbfineart.co.uk

Located in the beguiling old market town of Wimborne, **Vanessa Blunden Fine Art** displays a wide range of work by contemporary artists. The gallery was established by Vanessa Blunden some 16 years ago and she prides herself on finding the very best artists up and down the country. The paintings are on display in her home and include works by painter Terry Grundy who discovered his passion for art at an early age, although he remained an amateur whilst focusing on a career in engineering. However, in the 1980's his passion for art was reignited whilst living in Cornwall by the beauty of the landscape and spectacular coastline. Focusing his efforts on improving his completely self-taught technique Terence has achieved his ambition of ranking amongst the top Bristish landscape artists of the 21st Century. Terence's unique ability to capture the timeless beauty of the English countryside is testament to his meticulous attention to detail and natural ability.

Richard Price gained a degree in Fine Arts in 1983. He has shown work at the Royal Academy and several society exhibitions, such as the New English Art Club, and has won numerous prizes. Richard is interested in the application of paint in order to create different effects and images that are not just mere representations of the world about us but works of art and beauty. Ken Hammond is a self-taught artist whose love of coastal scenery and old ships has brought him to the south coast where he now lives. He has been greatly influenced by the Dutch Masters and the Norwich School of Painters.

Honeybrook Country Park has a family yard with lots of pure breed animals, dray and pony rides, an adventure playground, a period farmhouse, a natural maze, river and countryside walks, farm shop, tearoom and picnic areas. The park also hosts events such as country sports days, tug-of-war competitions, beer tasting and barn dances.

About a mile from the town centre, Wimborne Market is the largest covered market in the south of England. There are more than 400 stalls, selling everything from local produce, crafts and antiques, to plants and home-made cakes.

A mile or so northwest of Wimborne, **Kingston Lacy** (National Trust - see panel below) is an imposing 17th-century mansion that has been the home of the Bankes family for more than 300 years. The house exerts an

irresistible attraction for anyone who loves the paintings of such Old Masters as Brueghel, Titian, Rubens and Van Dyck. Apart from those owned by the Queen, the pictures on display here are generally acknowledged by experts as forming the finest private collection in the country. Kingston Lacy's fabulous gilded-leather Spanish Room and elegant Grand Saloon, both with lavishly decorated ceilings, and a fascinating exhibit of Egyptian artefacts dating back to 3000BC, all add to the interest of a visit. Outside, you can wander through 250 acres of wooded parkland which contains a genuine Egyptian obelisk c150BC and a herd of splendid Red Devon cattle. A fairly recent addition is the Edwardian Japanese Tea Garden, which follows traditional Japanese design with features such as a waiting pavilion, a dry

Kingston Lacy House

Wimborne, Dorset BH21 4EA
Tel: 01202 883402 Fax: 01202 882402
website: www.nationaltrust.org.uk

The Kingston Lacy estate was bequeathed in 1981 to the National Trust, along with 8,000 acres on the Isle of Purbeck, in the will of Ralph Bankes. Much of the land has been declared inalienable, meaning that it can never be sold, developed or mortgaged. Kingston Lacy House, home of the Bankes family for over 300 years, is a beautiful 17th century building with an outstanding collection of Old Masters, Egyptian artefacts and the amazing Spanish room with gilded leather hanging on the walls. All four floors are open to visitors, and the Edwardian laundry gives a fascinating insight into life below stairs 100 years ago.

The garden has two formal areas, the parterre and the sunken garden. The Victorian Fernery supports over 25 types of fern, the Blindwalk contains flowering shrubs and groundcover plants, and the 18th century Lime Avenue leads to Nursery Wood, where specimen trees, rhododendrons, azaleas and camellias grow. The landscaped park covers 250 acres and is home to the North Devon herd of cattle. There are lovely walks through the woodland areas, some suitable for wheelchairs, and Coneygar Copse has three different areas of woodland play equipment.

stories and anecdotes 🐦 famous people 🎨 art and craft ✍ entertainment and sport 🚶 walks

stream raked with gravel, and a thatched tea house. Also within the grounds of the Kingston Lacy estate are Badbury Rings, an Iron Age hill fort reputedly the site of a great campaign by King Arthur.

A couple of miles to the east of Wimborne, **Stapehill Abbey** was built in the early 1800s for a silent order of nuns to provide a peaceful place for retreat and contemplation. Visitors can now enjoy the serenity of the restored Nuns' Chapel, stroll around the cloisters and enjoy the glorious award-winning gardens. Inside, there are reconstructions of a Victorian parlour, kitchen and washroom, and an outstanding Countryside Museum recording rural life in the area. Stapehill is also home to a group of working craftspeople, special events are held throughout the year, and the site contains a licensed coffee shop and picnic areas.

Just to the east of Stapehill are **Knoll Gardens and Nursery**, whose gardens were planted more than 30 years ago and are famous for the mature trees and shrubs that provide a wealth of colour throughout the seasons. The gardens specialise in grasses and perennials, but in all there are more than 6000 plant species, including many fine trees. Tumbling waterfalls and ponds in an informal English setting add to the appeal.

WIMBORNE ST GILES
15 miles NW of Bournemouth off the B3081

🏛 Church of St Giles

A pretty village set beside the River Allen, Wimborne St Giles is notable for its **Church of St Giles**. It was rebuilt after a fire by the distinguished architect Sir Ninian Comper who also contributed the fine stained glass. Also worth seeing are the marvellous monuments, notably to Sir Anthony Ashley

and to the 7th Earl of Shaftesbury (who is even more memorably honoured by the statue of Eros in Piccadilly Circus, London).

Verwood

12 miles N of Bournemouth on the B3081

🐂 Dorset Heavy Horse Centre

🌿 Verwood Heathland Heritage Centre

Located in the heart of the town, **Verwood Heathland Heritage Centre** has permanent displays of the local Verwood pottery industry. The centre occupies a former pottery drying shed and visitors may get the opportunity to throw a pot or two themselves.

Just north of Verwood village, **The Dorset Heavy Horse Centre** offers a real hands-on experience with these mighty beasts. You can drive a horse and wagon or a vintage tractor, or have a go at logging or ploughing with the heavy horses. Suitable for all ages and weather conditions, the centre also has a display of gypsy caravans, animal feeding and handling, pedal tractors and go-carts, a straw slide barn and a resident menagerie of donkeys, llamas, kunekune pigs, miniature ponies and pygmy goats. There's also a café, picnic area and gift shop.

CRANBORNE
15 miles N of Bournemouth on the B3078

🏛 Church of St Mary   🏛 Cranborne Manor

🏛 Edmonsham House and Gardens

A picturesque village in a glorious setting, Cranborne sits on the banks of the River Crane with a fine church and manor house creating a charming picture of a traditional English village. The large and imposing **Church of St Mary** is notable for its Norman doorway, 13th-century nave, and exquisite

14th-century wall-paintings.

Cranborne Manor was built in Tudor and Jacobean times and acquired by Robert Cecil, Elizabeth I's Chief Minister. It is lived in today by his descendant, Viscount Cranborne. The house is not open to the public but visitors can explore the gardens on Wednesdays during the season, and the Cranborne Manor Garden Centre, which specialises in old-fashioned roses, is open all year. The present manor house stands on the site of a royal hunting lodge built by King John for his hunting forays in Cranborne Chase. Much of the huge forest has disappeared, but detached areas of woodland have survived and provide some splendid walks.

To the south of the village stands **Edmondsham House and Gardens**, a superb Tudor manor house with Georgian additions that has been owned by the same family since the 1500s. Guided tours of the house and its Victorian dairy are conducted by the owner on Wednesday afternoons. The grounds (open Wednesday and Sunday afternoons) contain a walled organic garden, a six-acre garden with unusual trees and spring bulbs, and a stable block that is a fine example of Victorian architecture.

Edmondsham House and Gardens

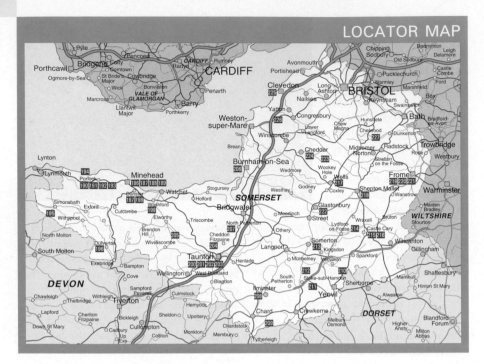

ADVERTISERS AND PLACES OF INTEREST

🏛 historic building   🏛 museum and heritage   🏛 historic site   ⚘ scenic attraction   🐦 flora and fauna

4| Somerset

Was Cadbury Castle really King Arthur's Camelot? Did Joseph of Arimathea really walk through England's green and pleasant land to plant a thorn from Christ's crown of thorns at Glastonbury, where it blossomed once a year on the day of Christ's resurrection? Was it really at Athelney that King Alfred, deep in thought, allowed the cakes to burn? Myth and legend seem to be as integral to Somerset as its cider orchards and Cheddar cheese, its free-roaming ponies on Exmoor and the olde-worlde pubs with their skittle alleys.

Many literary luminaries found inspiration here. Exmoor provided

the setting for RD Blackmore's great historical romance *Lorna Doone*; Wordsworth and Coleridge both lived in the county for several

River Barle, Exmoor

📖 stories and anecdotes 🐿 famous people 🎨 art and craft 🎭 entertainment and sport 🚶 walks

years and it was during their countless walks over the Somerset hills that they fashioned their *Lyrical Ballads*, a new kind of plain speaking verse that inspired the Romantic Revolution. Tennyson was a frequent visitor to the county and it was for his Clevedon friend, Arthur Hallam, that he spent 17 years perfecting his great lyrical poem *In Memoriam*.

Somerset Levels near Othery

Hallam was a member of the Elton family whose great house, Clevedon Court, is just one of many fine mansions within the county borders. Others include the late-medieval stone manor house of Lytes Cary, the Palladian Hatch Court and the exquisite Montacute House, built in the late 16th century for Elizabeth I's Master of the Rolls. The fine houses are sometimes overshadowed by their gardens. There are some splendid examples here, particularly those, such as Barrington Court, Hestercombe Gardens and Tintinhull House Gardens, that were planted, or influenced by, the early 20th-century landscape gardener, Gertrude Jekyll.

A wealth of prehistoric remains have been found within the county, but two of the area's most popular and famous attractions are both natural – Cheddar Gorge and the caves at Wookey Hole. With cliffs over 400 feet high on either side of the road that runs through the bottom of the gorge, Cheddar is indeed a spectacular sight, while the caves at Wookey Hole, from which the River Axe emerges, are famous for their echos and for their fantastic stalagmite and stalactite formations.

Somerset also contains the smallest city in England, Wells. It is also one of the country's most delightful cities, clustered around its superb cathedral. This magnificent building boasts a truly wonderful Astronomical Clock, which was installed in the 14th century and is still functioning perfectly.

To the north of the Mendip Hills lies the city of Bath, which in the 18th century became the most fashionable spa town in the country. Some 1600 years earlier, it was equally fashionable among the Romans. Close by is the West Country's largest city, Bristol, Sir John Betjeman's favourite English city, which, he asserted, had "the finest architectural heritage of any city outside London".

Minehead

🐦 North Hill Nature Reserve

🌿 West Somerset Railway

Minehead Beach

Award-winning floral displays and gardens, a tree-lined avenue leading to a recently constructed promenade and a sandy beach, a wide range of shops, pubs, restaurants and open-air cafés, and an extensive choice of family attractions and amusements – Minehead has everything you expect of a successful English seaside resort. There are still thatched cottages in the picturesque Higher Town, and the unspoilt acres of the Exmoor National Park stretch away to the west and south.

Despite sounding like a product of the industrial age, Minehead is an attractive and popular seaside town, lying at the foot of the wooded promontory known as North Hill. It is one of the oldest settlements in Somerset. A busy Bristol Channel port since the time of the Celts, the old harbour lies in the lee of North Hill, making it one of the safest landing places in the West Country. At one time, ships

---

FAVOURITE THINGS – JEWELLERY & GIFTS

47 The Avenue, Minehead, Somerset TA24 5BB
Tel: 01643 709403
e-mail: sally.chilton@virgin.net
website: www.favouritethingsonline.co.uk

On Minehead's tree-lined main shopping street, **Favourite Things** sells a wide range of contemporary jewellery, things to wear, things for the home and gifts for any occasion. Owner Sally Chilton ensures that shopping is fun with her fun and funky jewellery, some glass, some beaded, some made of porcelain and some in classic silver. Among the other best-sellers are beaded bags, pashminas, scarves, decorative glass, wooden toys and puzzles, scented candles, soaps, crystals and many local and fair trade products. Shop hours are 10.30 to 5.30 Monday to Saturday and 11 to 4 on Sunday. Everything in stock here can also be ordered online.

GERALD DAVID & FAMILY

3 Park Street, Minehead, Somerset TA24 5NQ
Tel 01643 702843
website: www.geralddavid.co.uk

Three Generations of Master Butchers

Our family have taken pride in selecting what we believe to be the best fresh, not frozen beef, lamb and pork for over 40 years.
Come and meet our friendly Master Butchers who will happily give you advice on cuts, cooking times and delicious recipes. If you are travelling we can pack your purchase in dry ice to ensure it reaches your onward destination in pristine condition.

🎞 stories and anecdotes 🐓 famous people ✏ art and craft ✿ entertainment and sport 🚶 walks

EXPLORE West Somerset - by STEAM TRAIN!

935

Family Fares • Round Trip & Day Rover Tickets • Party Rates • Wheelchair Friendly • Bar/Buffet Cars
West Somerset Railway, The Railway Station, Minehead, Somerset TA24 5BG
Tel: 01643 704996   www.West-Somerset-Railway.co.uk
Photograph © Don Bishop

arrived here with wool and livestock from Ireland, crops from the plantations of Virginia, coal from the South Wales valleys and day trippers from Cardiff and Bristol. The merchants and paddle steamers have gone and nowadays the harbour is the peaceful haunt of sailing dinghies and pleasure craft.

There is a good view of the old port from the **North Hill Nature Reserve**, and a three-mile-walk starting near the lifeboat station on the harbour side is an excellent way to explore this area of Minehead and its surroundings. The 14th-century parish Church of St Michael stands in a prominent position below North Hill. For centuries, a light was kept burning in its tower to help guide ships into the harbour. Inside, the church contains a number of unusual features, including a rare medieval prayer book, or missal, which once belonged to Richard Fitzjames, a local vicar who went on

to become Bishop of London in 1506.

The decline of Minehead as a port was offset by its gradual expansion as a seaside resort and the town went to great lengths to attract a suitably genteel clientele. So much so, in fact, that there was a local bylaw in force until 1890 that forbad anyone over 10 years of age from swimming in the sea "except from a bathing machine, tent or other effective screen". The arrival of the railway in 1874 failed to trigger the rapid expansion experienced by some other seaside resorts. Nevertheless, during World War One, Minehead was able to provide an escape from the ravages of war at timeless establishments like the Strand Hotel, where guests were entertained by such stars as Anna Pavolva and Gladys Cooper.

Changes to Minehead over the years have been gradual, but the most momentous change came in 1962 when Billy Butlin opened a

---

🏠 historic building 🏛 museum and heritage 🏚 historic site 🌿 scenic attraction 🌱 flora and fauna

STUART LOWEN FARM SHOP

4B Hawksworth Road, Minehead, Somerset TA24 5BZ
Tel: 01643 706034
e-mail: stuart.lowen@live.com
website: www.stuartlowen.co.uk

Located next door to Tesco on the A39 seafront road just outside Minehead, the **Stuart Lowen Farm Shop** specialises in top quality local meat and poultry. Stuart is a qualified butcher and rears his own lambs on 17 acres at nearby Hopcott. The shop also sells a superb range of sausages, local fresh vegetables, some excellent cheese, local home-made cakes, ready made meals and ice cream from Styles of Rodhuish. The shop offers free local delivery and the produce is also available by mail through the website.

holiday camp at the eastern end of the esplanade. Now updated, this popular attraction has done much to transform present-day Minehead into an all-round family resort.

The town is also the northern terminus of the **West Somerset Railway** (see panel opposite), the privately-owned steam railway that runs for 20 miles between the resort and Bishop's Lydeard, just northwest of Taunton. Vintage locomotives up to 80 years old trundle along the route that follows the coast as far as Blue Anchor, which has a station next to the beach and a small Great Western Railway museum, then on to Watchet, which has a Victorian station with a small gift shop. The route then turns inland and travels through peaceful countryside to Bishop's Lydeard.

were in fact built in the 19th century by the local lord of the manor to provide housing for his estate workers.

Just to the northwest of the village rises Selworthy Beacon, one of the highest points on the vast **Holnicote Estate**. Covering some 12,500 acres of Exmoor National Park, the estate includes a four-mile stretch of coastline between Minehead and Porlock Weir. There are few estates in the country that offer such a variety of landscape. There are north-facing cliffs along the coast, traditional villages and hamlets of cottages and farms and the **Horner and Dunkery National Nature Reserve** where Dunkery Beacon, the highest point on Exmoor, rises to 1700 feet. Virtually the full length of the Horner Water lies within the estate, from its source on the high

Around Minehead

SELWORTHY
3 miles W of Minehead off the A39

🐑 Holnicote Estate

🐑 Horner & Dunkery National Nature Reserve

🏛 Allerford Museum

This picturesque and much photographed village is situated on the side of a wooded hill. Its cob and thatch cottages look timeless, but

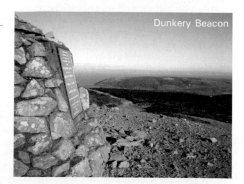

Dunkery Beacon

moorland to the sea at Bossington Beach, one of the best examples of a shingle storm beach in the country. The whole area is noted for its diversity of wildlife and the many rare plant species to be found.

This National Trust-owned estate has more than 100 miles of footpaths through fields, moors and villages for walkers to enjoy. The South West Coast Path curves inland at Hurlstone Point to avoid landslips in the soft Foreland sandstone. West of this model village is another estate village, Allerford, which has an elegant twin-arched packhorse bridge. In Allerford's old school is a **Museum** dedicated to the rural life of West Somerset. Among its many imaginatively presented displays are a Victorian kitchen, a laundry and dairy, and an old school room complete with desks, books and children's toys. The museum also houses the ever-growing West Somerset Photographic

Archive covering most villages and hamlets in the area from late Victorian times.

PORLOCK
7 miles W of Minehead off the A39

🏛 Dovery Manor   ⚐ Porlock Hill

🚶 Coleridge Way

An ancient settlement once frequented by Saxon kings, in recent decades Porlock has become a popular riding and holiday centre. The charming village is filled with lovely old buildings, most notably the 15th-century **Dovery Manor** (now a museum) with its striking traceried hall window, and the largely 13th-century parish church that lost the top section of its spire during a thunderstorm in the 17th century. Porlock has the feel of a community at the end of the world as it lies at the foot of **Porlock Hill**, a notorious incline

---

HARTSHANGER EXMOOR HOLIDAYS
VB★★★★

Toll Road, Porlock, Somerset TA24 8JH
Tel: 01643 862700
e-mail: hartshanger@lineone.net
website: www.hartshanger.com

Hartshanger Exmoor Holidays is based in a handsome Edwardian villa set above the village of Porlock in the heart of Exmoor National Park. Alanna Edward and her family offer self-catering accommodation in two beautifully appointed flats with beams, sloping ceilings and patchwork quilts. High Hanger, with a double and a twin bedroom, is on the top floor of the main house, while Little Hanger, with three bedrooms, is located in the coach house. Both flats have a fully equipped kitchen, comfortable sitting room, hairdryer, ironing facilities, TV with video/DVD and radio-alarm. Wi-Fi is available.

It's a lovely, quiet place to stay, with five acres of gardens and grounds (including an all-weather tennis court) and glorious views over Porlock Bay and the Bristol Channel across to Wales, and the loudest noises guests are likely to hear are the surf and the seabirds. The shops and pubs and restaurants of Porlock are a short walk away, and there are facilities nearby for sea and river fishing, horse riding and cycling – for guests who bring their own bikes Hartshanger has secure storage and a washing down area.

🏛 historic building   📷 museum and heritage   🏛 historic site   ⚐ scenic attraction   🐾 flora and fauna

DETAILS FOR THE HOME

1 Lowerbourne House, High Street, Porlock,
Somerset TA24 8PT
Tel: 01643 863511
e-mail: detailsforthehome@talktalkbusiness.net

Details for the Home was established in 2006.
The owners have a passionate interest in interior
decoration and have gathered together an
eclectic selection of unusual and intriguing
items. All of them are practical and useful and
are sold at very reasonable prices.

Amongst the furniture items are dressers and
cupboards in soft tones of white, cream or grey.
There's also a range of mirrors and clocks,
kitchenware, picture frames, candleholders,
vases, and much, much more. Fabrics include
tablecloths, napkins, cushions and throws.

The shop's reputation has spread far and
wide, with visitors from London and the Home
Counties, and it also has a loyal following among
local people.

CHURCHGATE GALLERY

High Street, Porlock, Somerset TA24 8PT
Tel: 01643 802238
website: www.churchgategallery.co.uk

Will and Rachel Rayner opened their first gallery
in Minehead in 1988 and in the summer of
2010 they opened the **Churchgate Gallery** on
Porlock's main street.

The Gallery, which is open daily from 11am,
displays a large and eclectic selection of original
paintings in oils, pastels and watercolours,
original prints and etchings, limited edition
prints, photography, jewellery, books and artist
greetings cards. Many of the pieces are inspired
by the local coast and countryside. The
excellent website includes details of some of
the artists currently shown.

The Gallery also offers high-quality framing
and giclée printing services, which are offered,
with similar high standards, at the sister
company Courtyard Farming & Gallery in Friday
Street, Minehead. Tel: 01643 705648.

GLEN LODGE COUNTRY HOUSE

Hawkcombe, Porlock, Somerset TA24 8LN
Tel: 01643 863371 Fax: 01643 863016
e-mail: glenlodge@gmail.com
website: www.glenlodge.net

Beautifully located overlooking Porlock bay, set within 21 lovely acres of woodland and lush landscaped gardens, **Glen Lodge Country House** is the perfect location for your escape to the countryside. Glen Lodge is perfectly situated for walking to and around Exmoor, bird watching, exploring the northern Somerset and Devon countryside, relaxing on one of the nearby beaches, or just staying around its gardens to unwind. A short walk from the house takes you to the centre of Porlock with unique local shops, pubs, museums, galleries and restaurants.

The accommodation is, as you would expect, elegant and kept to the highest standard; each room has been individually decorated and has its own unique character. Of the five rooms in the Hotel, three are en-suite and two have private bathrooms, and all have fabulous views of either the stunning coastline or the lovely sprawling acres of garden. The owners, who have lived here for five years, are wonderful hosts, and always endeavour to do their upmost to cater for all of their guests. This is reflected in the breakfast included with your stay, which has such a huge variety there will be something for any taste; you can have the traditional full English, waffles, pancakes, muffins, or soufflés, as well as a whole spread of fresh fruit, cereals and yogurts all organic, freshly cooked, and locally sourced where possible.

where the road rises 1350 feet in less than three miles, with a gradient of 1 in 4 in places.

Porlock lies at the western end of the **Coleridge Way**, a 36-mile-long walk that takes in some of the county's most beautiful landscapes and ends at Nether Stowey, one-time home of the poet Samuel Taylor Coleridge. Coleridge was a passionate walker and once walked from Nether Stowey to Porlock in a day. Most modern day walkers allow three to four days.

PORLOCK WEIR
9 miles W of Minehead off the A39

🏠 Doverhay Garage

🐦 Porlock Weir Marine Aquariums

🔍 Exmoor Glass ⚜ Submerged Forest

🏛 Culborne Church

Today, this hamlet has a small tide-affected

harbour full of fishing boats and yachts but Porlock Weir was once an important seaport. The Danes sacked it on a number of occasions in the 10th century. In 1052, Harold, the future king of England, landed here from Ireland to begin a short-lived career that ended at the Battle of Hastings in 1066. A pleasant and picturesque place, Porlock Weir offers a number of interesting

Porlock Weir

🏛 historic building 🏠 museum and heritage 🏚 historic site ⚜ scenic attraction 🐦 flora and fauna

NO. 7 HARBOUR STUDIOS

Porlock Weir, nr Minehead, Somerset TA24 8P
Tel: 01643 862468
e-mail: no7pashminas@hotmail.co.uk

Located opposite Porlock Weir's attractive harbour, No7 invites you into a den of delights. The air is gently scented from the range of Branche d'Olive soaps, candles, room diffusers and much more made in the South of France.

Your eye alights on the display of hand picked Pashminas, woven and embroidered by hand in Kashmir in an enticing palette of colours and designs.

There is an unusual selection of cushion covers and bedspreads

– from fine organza backed cutwork, sumptuous silks to richly textured Khambardia patched pieces. Arrays of wall panels decorate the walls along with cushion covers and hangings made from antique textiles interspersed with a few tribal artefacts.

Quality and beauty are the prime objective in this small space and you are always assured of find something different.

attractions, including a 100-year-old garage, **Doverhay Garage**, which is now a museum displaying vintage cars and motoring memorabilia. **Porlock Weir Marine Aquariums**, opened in 2009, celebrates the variety of marine life to be found in and along the shores of the Bristol Channel.

Visitors can watch flounder, bass, blennies and various kinds of wrasse in the numerous tanks, and spot turbot and rays and many other species in the large open pool. And at **Exmoor Glass** you can purchase items in its Cranberry Range glassware made in the traditional manner, as well as jewellery and other goods. A short distance offshore from Porlock weir is a **Submerged Forest**, a relic of the Ice Age that can be seen at low tide.

From Porlock Weir an attractive one-and-a-half-mile walk leads up through walnut and oak trees to **Culbone Church**, arguably the

smallest church in regular use in England, and certainly one of the most picturesque. A true hidden treasure, measuring only 33 feet by 14 feet, this superb part-Norman building is set in a wooded combe that once supported a small charcoal burning community, and was at other times home to French prisoners and lepers.

OARE
11 miles W of Minehead off the A39

🐚 RD Blackmore

Set deep in a secluded valley, Oare is one of the highlights for pilgrims following the Lorna Doone Trail. According to **RD Blackmore's** novel, it was in the narrow little 15th-century church here that his heroine was shot at the wedding altar by the villainous Carver Doone. Blackmore knew the church well since his grandfather was rector here in the mid 1800s.

EMMETT'S GRANGE COUNTRY HOUSE ACCOMMODATION

Simonsbath, Exmoor National Park, Somerset TA24 7LD
Tel: 01643 831138 Fax: 01643 831093
e-mail: mail@emmettgrange.co.uk
website: www.emmettsgrange.co.uk

Emmett's Grange offers quiet, comfortable accommodation in an oasis of friendly civilisation amid the glorious Exmoor National Park scenery on the Somerset-Devon border. The graceful Georgian-style house stands southwest of Simonsbath at the end of a half-mile private drive, set in its own 900-acre estate. The house has five beautifully decorated and furnished en suite guest bedrooms – doubles, twins and a family room. Each has its own particular charm and character: one has a super-king size bed with an additional single bed, another has a splendid antique four-poster. One room, the Linhay, a small barn conversion with a kitchen and eating area, can be booked on a B&B or self-catering basis.

Owners Tom and Lucy love cooking, and the breakfast here is definitely not to be missed. For those opting for an evening meal, breakfast is the time to discuss Tom's excellent four-course dinners, which often feature superb local produce including seafood, Red Devon beef and seasonal game. Guests have the use of three day rooms – a drawing room for drink and a chat, a library for a quiet read or gentle study and a morning room where guests can practise their skills on the Steinway – as well as the run of the lovely lawns, gardens and grounds. Emmett's Grange is an ideal base for touring, walking (the Two Moors Way and the Tarka Trail both pass nearby), cycling, riding, fishing – or just relaxing. Tom and Lucy can arrange hunting, shooting and fishing trips.

A placard inside the church indicates the most likely window used by Carver Doone to fire the shot that almost proved fatal to the novel's heroine, and a memorial to the author is set into the wall of the church beside the south door.

LISCOMBE
13 miles SW of Minehead off the B3223

🗿 Tarr Steps

Just west of the moorland village of Liscombe is an extraordinary survival from prehistoric times. **Tarr Steps** is the longest clapper bridge anywhere in the world, its huge stone slabs supported by low stone pillars extending 180 feet

across the River Barle. It's a mystery where the stones slabs came from since there are no similar rocks anywhere near. Geologists believe they were probably left here by retreating glaciers at the close of the Ice Age.

Tarr Steps

🏛 historic building 🏛 museum and heritage 🗿 historic site 🔱 scenic attraction 🐦 flora and fauna

WINSFORD

7 miles S of Minehead off the A396

One of the prettiest villages in Exmoor, with picturesque thatched cottages, a ford and no fewer than seven bridges, including an old packhorse bridge. On a rise to the west of the village stands the medieval church with a handsome tall tower that dominates both the village and the surrounding area. This idyllic spot was the birthplace of the firebrand Ernest Bevin, founder of the Transport & General Workers Union, World War Two statesman and Foreign Secretary in the post-war Labour government.

DULVERTON

12 miles S of Minehead on the B3222

🏛 Guildhall Heritage & Arts Centre

🐎 Exmoor Pony Centre

Dulverton is a lively little town set in the wooded valley of the River Barle on the southern edge of Exmoor. Small though it is, the town boasts a surprising variety of attractions and in recent years has come to challenge Dunster in popularity. The Exmoor National Park has an excellent Visitor Centre here, housed in what used to be the local workhouse. Close by is the **Guildhall Heritage & Arts Centre,** which has displays on Dulverton's history over the past century

and is also home to the Exmoor Photographic Archive, which stages special exhibitions throughout the year. An integral part of the centre is Granny Baker's Cottage with its authentic Victorian kitchen. There's also a gallery that provides a showcase for the work of local artists and craftspeople. The Centre is open from mid April to the beginning of November.

It's a pleasure to stroll around the town with its ancient bridge, traditional hostelries, cosy tearoom and family-run shops selling anything from antiquarian books to country clothing, gifts to old-fashioned fish and chips. Regular community markets offer a wide range of local crafts, while the highlights of the year in Dulverton are the Carnival, held on the first Saturday in October, and Dulverton by Starlight on the first Sunday in December.

Just outside Dulverton, at Ashwick, the **Exmoor Pony Centre** offers rides on these sturdy little beasts. Because of their size, the rider's weight is restricted to 76kg.

DUNSTER

2 miles SE of Minehead on the A396

🏠 Dunster Castle 🏠 Dunster Working Watermill

🏠 Dunster Priory 🏠 Luttrell Arms 🏠 Dovecote

🏠 Church of St George

Although Dunster is one of the most popular

📖 stories and anecdotes 🦅 famous people 🎨 art and craft 🎭 entertainment and sport 🚶 walks

of Exmoor's villages, this ancient
settlement is also one of the least
typical as it lies in the fertile valley of
the River Avill. No visitor will be
surprised to learn that this landscape
inspired Mrs Alexander to compose the
hymn *All Things Bright and Beautiful*. The
village is dominated by **Dunster Castle**
standing outside the village on the top
of the wooded Conygar Hill. Founded
by William de Mohun on this natural
promontory above the River Avill, just
a few years before the Domesday Book
was completed in 1089, the castle passed into
the hands of the Luttrell family in 1379. It
remained in that family until it was given to
the National Trust in 1976 by Lt Col GWF
Luttrell. The medieval castle was remodelled
in 1617 by William Arnold. During the
English Civil War, Dunster Castle was one of
the last Royalist strongholds in the West

Dunster Castle

Country to fall. The garrison only surrendered
after a siege lasting 160 days. While several
Jacobean interiors have survived, the castle
underwent major alterations during the latter
part of the 17th century. Some of the finest
features date from that period, in particular
the superb plasterwork in the dining room and
the magnificent balustraded main staircase

THE DUNSTER CASTLE HOTEL

Exmoor National Park, Dunster, Somerset TA24 6SF
Tel: 01643 823030
e-mail: thedunstercastlehotel@googlemail.com
website: www.dunstercastlehotel.co.uk

The Dunster Castle Hotel offers contemporary style with
traditional comfort at the foot of the historic National
Trust property Dunster Castle, in the Exmoor National
Park. The hotel building, with its medieval cobblestone
pavement, dates back to about 1750 and was once the
home of the outgoing dowager of Dunster Castle The hotel
has recently been fully refurbished to a very fine standard
and the owners are highly proud of their accommodation;
eight luxury en-suite bedrooms each individually designed by
'jennyd interiors' to reflect the understated elegance that
runs throughout the hotel.

A stay of at least 2 to 3 nights is essential to really enjoy
the area and relax in style. The beautiful Exmoor National
Parkland and West Somerset railway are only ten minutes
drive away, and the coast is only half a mile from the town. Horse riding, shooting and safaris can
be organised for you by the hotel and, of course, you can visit the Castle which is almost next
door. You can also enjoy a drink or dine in the fabulous Cellar Bar or Squires Brasserie, both of
which serve the finest food prepared from local fresh produce wherever possible.

🏚 historic building   🏛 museum and heritage   🏚 historic site   ✿ scenic attraction   🐾 flora and fauna

THE CROOKED WINDOW GALLERY

7 High Street, Dunster, Somerset TA24 6SF
Tel: 01643 821606
e-mail: bob.ricketts@tiscali.co.uk
website: www.thecrookedwindow.co.uk

Opening Times:
Mon-Sat 10.30am-5.30pm
Sunday variable - please enquire
Other times by appointment

The Crooked Window Gallery is situated in Dunster's picturesque High Street and is so named because the movement in its timber framed construction has caused one of the shops bay windows to become distorted and bowed. The building dates from the 15th century and is unusual for its decorative 18th century plasterwork, or 'pargeting', a feature quite untypical of this area.

The gallery is owned and run by Robert Ricketts. Robert buys, sells, collects and lectures on antiques. You might be surprised to find an impressive collection of ancient Chinese ceramics - not normally seen outside London.

Robert also stocks a good selection of qaulity gemstones from which he designs and makes his own jewellery in a choie of precious metals. Why not commission your own piece of unique jewellery for that special occasion. He can also alter or repiar your existing jewellery.

Within the atmospheric interior you will find an exciting range of jewellery in gold, silver, precious and semi-precious stones. There are quality crafts from other artists as well as interesting and unusual antique items - all eminently suitable as gifts.

stories and anecdotes famous people art and craft entertainment and sport walks

Dunster Watermill

with its delicately carved flora and fauna. However, the overall medieval character of the exterior of the present day castle is due to restoration work undertaken by Anthony Salvin in the 1860s when the castle was transformed into a comfortable and opulent country mansion. The steeply terraced gardens with their striking collection of rare shrubs and subtropical plants were also laid out around this time, and the castle and gardens are surrounded by a 28-acre deer park through which there are several footpaths, as well as the Arbutus Walk through the National Collection of strawberry trees.

The parkland of Dunster Castle is also home to another National Trust property, **Dunster Working Watermill**, built in the 18th century on the site of a pre-Norman mill. Now restored to working order, the mill, which is run as a private business, has a shop selling mill flour, muesli and mill souvenirs. There's also a tearoom by the riverside.

Remnants of the ancient feudal settlement that grew up in the shelter of the castle can still be seen in the village today, particularly in the wide main street. At the north end of this street stands a small octagonal building, the former Yarn Market. This was erected by the Luttrells in the early 17th century when the village was an important cloth trading centre. Such was

Dunster's influence in this trade that a type of woollen cloth, renowned for its quality and strength, bears the village's name. The nearby **Luttrell Arms** was converted from a private residence into an inn in the mid 1600s. Distinguished by its fine 15th-century porch, the inn is one of the few places in the country where the once common custom of burning the ashen faggot is still observed. On Christmas Eve, the faggot, a bundle of 12 ash branches bound with green ash bands, is burnt in the inn's great fireplace. As each band burns through, another round of hot punch is ordered from the bar. While the ash is burning, the company sings the ancient Dunster Carol and when the faggot is finally consumed, a charred remnant is taken from the embers ready to light the following year's fire.

The inn once belonged to Cleeve Abbey, while the village's principal religious house, **Dunster Priory**, was an outpost of Bath Abbey. Now largely demolished, the only parts of the priory to survive are the splendid priory church and an unusual 12th-century **dovecote** that can be seen in a nearby garden. It has a revolving wooden ladder inside, which gave access to the 500 nesting boxes and their eggs. The squabs, or fledgling doves, provided a staple element of the medieval monk's diet. The priory **Church of St George**, rebuilt by the monks in a rose pink sandstone as early as 1100, is one of the most impressive of Somerset's parish churches. The church tower was added in the 15th century but its most outstanding feature is undoubtedly the fan-vaulted rood screen that extends across the nave and aisles. At 54 feet it is the longest in England and was built in 1498 after a squabble between the priory and the townspeople. The magnificent screen served to separate the monk's choir from the parish church.

On the southern edge of the village, the ancient Gallox Bridge, a medieval packhorse bridge, spans the River Avill.

CARHAMPTON
3 miles SE of Minehead on the A39

🎭 Madam Carne

A small inland village that was the site of a Viking victory in the 9th century. Carhampton's original village church was named after St Carantoc, an early Celtic missionary from across the Bristol Channel. He is reputed to have chosen this site for his ministry by throwing his stone altar overboard and following it to shore. The present church building, though much restored, contains a remarkable 15th-century painted screen that extends across the entire church. The old inn, near the churchyard lych gate, has the date 1638 set into its cobbled floor in sheep's knuckle bones.

Each January, the residents of Carhampton re-enact the ancient custom of wassailing the apple trees. A toast is made to the most productive apple tree in the district and cider is poured on to its trunk in a charming ceremony that probably has pagan origins.

Local folklore tells of a mysterious woman from the village, **Madam Carne**, who died in 1612 having done away with three husbands. According to legend, her ghost returned home after her funeral to prepare breakfast for the mourners.

WASHFORD
6 miles SE of Minehead on the A39

🏛 Cleeve Abbey   🐦 Tropiquaria

📻 Radio Museum

This village is spread out across Vallis Florida, the flowery valley dedicated to Our Blessed Lady of the Cliff. Washford is dominated by **Cleeve Abbey** (see panel below), the only monastery in Somerset that belonged to the austere Cistercian order founded in 1198 by

Cleeve Abbey

Washford, Somerset TA23 0PS
Tel: 01984 640377
website: www.english-heritage.org.uk

On 25th June 1198 the new Abbey of Cleeve was founded, dedicated to the Blessed Virgin and originally named Vallis Florida or Vale of Flowers. Since then the Black Death, the dissolution of the monasteries, destruction of the Abbey Church and use as a farmhouse, have all played a part in the 800 year history of Cleeve Abbey. Today, it survives as a haven of peace and tranquillity, one of the undiscovered jewels of Somerset boasting magnificent architecture and hidden treasures.

Some of the finest cloister buildings in England can be seen including the magnificent 15th century timber roof in the refectory with its exquisite carved angels, the unique medieval wall paintings of the Painted Chamber and the heraldic tile pavements. One of the greatest pleasures however is to explore the numerous nooks and crannies, which reveal hidden carvings and paintings, from the hands of craftsmen long ago.

the Earl of Lincoln. This abbey is fortunate in that it was not allowed to fall into disrepair after the Dissolution of the Monasteries in 1539 like many great monastic houses. The cloister buildings at Cleeve were put to domestic use and they are now among the most complete in the country. Although the cruciform abbey church has been reduced to its foundations, the refectory, chapter house, monks' common room, dormitory and cloisters remain. Most impressive of all is the great hall, a magnificent building with tall windows, a wagon roof decorated with busts of crowned angels and medieval murals, and a unique set of floor tiles with heraldic symbols. The curved dormitory staircase has particularly fine archways and mullion windows, while the combined gatehouse and almonry, the last building to be constructed before the Dissolution, makes an imposing entrance to the abbey precinct.

A short distance northeast of the village is a more recent attraction, **Tropiquaria**, a wildlife park featuring a wide range of tropical animals. There is an aquarium here as well as an aviary and visitors are offered the chance to stroke snakes, tickle tarantulas and to get in touch with their wilder side. Children can swarm over the full-size pirate ships or work off some energy in the indoor play castle; grown-ups may be more interested in the **Radio Museum**, which is housed within an old radio transmitting station. There are hundreds of vintage radios to look at as well as a wealth of other radio memorabilia

Watchet Harbour

from Watchet that Coleridge's imaginary crew set sail in *The Rime of the Ancient Mariner*, the epic poem written while the poet was staying at nearby Nether Stowey. A statue of the Ancient Mariner himself stands on the promenade.

The scale of Watchet's parish church reflects the town's long-standing importance and prosperity. It is set well back from the town centre and contains several fine tombs belonging to the Wyndham family, the local lords of the manor who did much to develop the potential of the port. There is a local story that suggests that one 16th century member of the family, **Florence Wyndham**, had to be buried twice. The day after her first funeral the church sexton went down into church vaults secretly to remove a ring from her finger. When the coffin was opened, the old woman suddenly awoke. In recent years, the town has become something of a coastal resort and one of its attractions is the small museum dedicated to local maritime history.

WATCHET
7 miles SE of Minehead on the B3191

🎭 Florence Wyndham

Once a busy industrial port, Watchet is now a thriving marina for yachts and boats. It was

WILLITON
7 miles SE of Minehead on the A39/A358

🏛 Bakelite Museum

The large village of Williton was once a Saxon royal estate. During the 12th century the manor was the home of Sir Reginald FitzUrse, one of the knights who murdered Thomas à Becket. To atone for his terrible crime, Sir Reginald gave half the manor to the Knights Templar.

The village today is the home of the diesel locomotive workshops of the West Somerset Railway and the **Bakelite Museum**, a fascinating place providing a nostalgic look at the 'pioneer of plastics'. Housed within an historic watermill, the museum displays the largest collection of vintage plastics in Britain, with thousands of quirky and rare items, including spy cameras, monstrous perming machines and even a Bakelite coffin.

MONKSILVER
8 miles SE of Minehead on the B3188

🏠 Combe Sydenham Hall 📷 Drake's Cannonball

🏠 Nettlecombe Court 🌳 Brendon Hills

This pretty village of charming old houses and thatched cottages has, in its churchyard, the graves of Elizabeth Conibeer and her two middle-aged daughters, Anne and Sarah, who were murdered in June 1775 in the nearby hamlet of Woodford. Their tombstone bears a message to the unidentified murderer:

> *Inhuman wretch, whoe'er thou art*
> *That didst commit this horrid crime,*
> *Repent before thou dost depart*
> *To meet thy awful Judge Divine.*

Just to the south of the village is a particularly handsome manor house, **Combe Sydenham Hall**, built in the middle of the reign of Elizabeth I by George Sydenham on the site of a monastic settlement. Above the entrance, there is a Latin inscription that translates as; This door of George's is always open except to ungrateful souls. This was also

the home of Elizabeth Sydenham, George's daughter, who was to become the second wife of Sir Francis Drake. After becoming engaged, Sir Francis left his fiancée to go off looting for Spanish gold. Elizabeth grew so weary waiting for her betrothed to return that she resolved to marry another gentleman. According to local stories, she was on her way to the church, when a meteorite flew out of the sky and smashed into the ground in front of her. Taking this as a sign that she should wait for Sir Francis she called off the wedding and, eventually, the couple were reunited. The meteorite, now known as **Drake's Cannonball**, is on display in the great hall; it is said to bring good luck to those who touch it. The 500-acre grounds around the hall have been designated a country park and they contain a working corn mill complete with waterwheel, a herb garden, a peacock house and a herd of fallow deer. The estate also incorporates a modern trout farm that stands on the site of a fully restored Tudor trout hatchery dating from the end of the 16th century.

A mile or so to the west stands another ancient manor, **Nettlecombe Court**, once the home of the Raleigh family, relations of another great Elizabethan seafarer, Sir Walter

Combe Sydenham, Monksilver

Raleigh. Later, the manor passed by marriage to the Cornish Trevelyan family and it is now a field studies centre open only by appointment.

To the southwest of the village are the **Brendon Hills**, the upland area within the Exmoor National Park from where, in the mid 19th century, iron ore was mined in significant quantities. The ore was then carried down a steep mineral railway to the coast for shipment to the furnaces of South Wales. At one time the Ebbw Vale Company employed almost 1000 miners here. The company was a strictly Nonconformist concern and imposed a rigorous teetotal regime on its workers. Those wanting a drink had to walk across the moor all the way to Raleigh's Cross. The company also founded a miners' settlement with a temperance hotel and three chapels that became renowned for the achievements of its choir and fife and drum band. Those walking the slopes of the hills can still see sections of the old mineral railway. A two-mile stretch of the track bed leading down to the coast at Watchet is now a pleasant footpath.

EAST QUANTOXHEAD
11 miles SE of Minehead off the A39

🏛 Trendle Ring   🐾 Beacon Hill

From the village there is a pleasant walk to the southeast, to Kilve, where the ruins of a medieval chantry, or college of priests, can be found. From here a track can be taken from the churchyard down to a boulder-strewn beach reputed to be a favourite haunt of glats – conger eels up to 10 feet long that lie in wait among the rocks near the shore. Once known as St Keyna's serpents, local people used to search for them using trained fish dogs.

Further to the southeast lies the

village of Holford, in the Quantocks, and a track from here leads up to the large Iron Age hill fortification known as Dowsborough Fort. Close by are also the dramatic viewpoints **Beacon Hill** and Bicknoller Hill. On the latter is another Iron Age relic, a livestock enclosure known as **Trendle Ring**. This is one of many archaeological sites in this area, which lies within the Quantock Hills Site of Special Scientific Interest.

Taunton

🏛 Taunton Castle   🏛 Somerset County Museum

🏛 Somerset Military Museum   ⚜ Bath Place

🏛 Somerset County Cricket Museum

🍃 Vivary Park   🍃 Taunton Racecourse

🏛 St Mary Magdalene Church

🕴 Bridgwater & Taunton Canal

Despite a settlement being founded here by the Saxon King Ine in the 8th century, Taunton, the county town of Somerset, has only been its sole centre of administration since 1935. Before that date, both Ilchester and Somerton had served as the county town. By Norman times the Saxon settlement had grown to have its own Augustinian monastery,

Taunton Castle

🏛 historic building   🏛 museum and heritage   🏛 historic site   🐾 scenic attraction   🍂 flora and fauna

a minster and a **Castle** – an extensive structure whose purpose had always been more as an administrative centre than as a military post. However, this did not prevent the castle from being the focus of two important sieges during the English Civil War. A few years later, the infamous Judge Jeffreys sentenced more than 150 followers of the Duke of Monmouth to death here during the Bloody Autumn Assizes. Even today, the judge's ghost is said to haunt the castle grounds on September nights.

The castle houses the **Somerset County Museum**, which is currently closed for refurbishment and is scheduled to re-open in 2011 as the Museum of Somerset. It contains the **Somerset Military Museum**, which is also closed, but some charming medieval almshouses can still be found at the castle site. Another of the town's old buildings is still making itself useful today. Somerset's County Cricket Ground occupies part of the priory grounds that once extended down to the river. A section of the old monastic gatehouse, known as the Old Priory Barn, can still be seen beside the cricket ground. Now restored, this medieval stone building is home to the fascinating **Somerset County Cricket Museum**.

Soaring above the town is the exquisite 163 foot high tower of **St Mary Magdalene Church**. A church has occupied this site since at least the 12th century but the present tower was rebuilt to its original design in 1862. In order to raise the stone during this construction, a pulley system was used, operated by a donkey walking down Hammet Street. When the work was completed, the builders hauled the donkey to the top of the tower so that it could admire the view it had

---

OLIVE TREE DELICATESSEN AND COFFEE SHOP

10-10A The Bridge, Taunton, Somerset TA1 1UG
Tel: 01823 353707
email: enquiries@theolivetreetaunton.co.uk
website: www.theolivetreetaunton.co.uk

If you can make it past the temptations of the delicatessen, the Olive Tree also has a licensed Coffee Shop upstairs. It's an intimate place where diners know they will need to arrive early or reserve a table. The breakfast dishes are available all-day and include hot bacon baguettes, a breakfast panini, or simply a few slices of hot thick toast. Just as appealing are the luxury cream teas, including the Olive Tree's home-made scones with strawberry jam and lots of clotted cream. Hot dishes include soup-of-the-day, jacket potatoes, a choice of home-made quiche, pasta dishes and that traditional British dish, homity pie.

The Olive Tree also prides itself on its impressive collection of cheeses from around the world which include the local Somerset Brie and the infamous Stinking Bishop. In the Deli you can buy many of these items and much more, such as speciality tea and coffee, olives, local jam and honey. There is also a selection of Somerset cider, wine and liqueurs.

ALPHA
EXCLUSIVE FASHIONS
FOR MEN AND WOMEN

2 The Courtyard, St James Street,
Taunton, Somerset TA1 1JR
Tel: 01823 324488

Alpha is located in a small complex of shops called The Courtyard near to the County cricket ground. For more than 10 years this family run boutique has catered for the fashion conscious citizens of Taunton and the surrounding area with an impressive collection of clothes and accessories to suit all. Many of the brands are exclusive to Alpha in Taunton.

Brands for men include Gant, Hackett, Polo Ralph Lauren and Barbour. Brands for women include Barbour, Stills, 120% Lino, James Jeans, Avoca, and Karen Cole. Among the many accessories are belts and buckles by Hamilton Davies and Butterfly Blue, handbags by Drift, Blondie Mania, scarves by Glen Prince and jewellery by About Face and Tutti & Co.

FINE FABRICS

Magdalene Lane, Taunton, Somerset TA1 1SE
Tel: 01823 270986
website: www.finefabricstaunton.co.uk

Located in central Taunton, **Fine Fabrics** have been suppliers of high quality fabrics for 27 years. With an extensive range of dress patterns, including those from 'Vogue' and many beautiful fabrics to choose from, you can find all you need to accomplish that special and individual bridal gown or evening dress. As a haberdashery, you can find everything you need to make your outfit and a wide selection of accessories are also available to complete your look.

Fine fabrics are stockists of many hobby craft materials including cross-stitch, embroidery and tapestry materials together with wool and knitting accessories. They are also suppliers of daylight and needlework lamps to aid you in your chosen past-time. There are many furnishing fabrics in stock and a variety of curtain accessories to meet you home furnishing requirements.

Fine fabrics offer private appointments to give customers professional advice with each stage of the dress making process, from choosing the patterns and selecting the fabrics, to the finished product.

GERALD DAVID & FAMILY

The Orchard, Taunton, Somerset TA1 3TP
Tel 01823 334400
website: www.geralddavid.co.uk

Three Generations of Master Butchers

Our family have taken pride in selecting what we believe to be the best fresh, not frozen beef,lamb and pork for over 40 years.
Come and meet our friendly Master Butchers who will happily give you advice on cuts,cooking times and delicious recipes. If you are travelling we can pack your purchase in dry ice to ensure it reaches your onward destination in pristine condition.

helped to create. The main body of the church is medieval and its interior distinguished by a host of carved saints, apostles and gilded angels floating above the congregation. The road leading to the church, Hammet Street, retains an impressive number of original Georgian houses.

Ardent shoppers will want to seek out **Bath Place**, a delightful narrow street of cottages mixed with an assortment of individual shops offering a huge range of goods and services. In medieval times, when this street was owned by the Bishop of Winchester, it was called Swains Street and was well known for its brothels, one of the few services not on offer here today. But you can have your hair done, your body pierced, lunch or dine in a choice of restaurants, and shop for arts and crafts, jewellery, glassware, books, computer games and much more.

Like many other West Country towns and villages, Taunton was a thriving wool, and later silk, cloth-making centre during the Middle Ages. The profits earned by the medieval clothiers went into buildings. Here their wealth was used in the construction of two huge churches: St James' and St Mary's. The rest of the town centre is scattered with fine buildings including the timber-framed Tudor House in Fore Street. Taunton is still a thriving place with an important commercial centre, a weekly market and a busy light industrial sector that benefits from some excellent transport links with the rest of the country.

Today, the **Bridgwater and Taunton Canal** towpath has been reopened following an extensive restoration programme and it provides pleasant waterside walks along its 14 miles. A relative latecomer, the canal first opened in 1827 and was designed to be part of an ambitious scheme to create a freight route between Exeter and Bristol to avoid the treacherous sea journey around the Cornwall peninsula. For many years, the canal was the principal means of importing coal and iron from South Wales to the inland towns of Somerset, and of exporting their wool and agricultural produce to the rest of Britain.

Taunton's major open space is the extensive **Vivary Park**, located at the

Bridgwater and Taunton Canal

southern end of the High Street and approached through a magnificent pair of Victorian ornamental gates. Fully restored with lottery money in 2002, the 70-acre park is home to the Vivary Golf Course, the Taunton Bowling Club and Taunton Deane Cricket Club. Other features include tennis courts, a wildlife lake, a model boat pond, a bandstand, an ornate fountain commemorating Queen Victoria, a model train track and children's play areas.

Taunton's attractive **National Hunt Racecourse** lies on the opposite side of the motorway from the town and the combination of good facilities, excellent racing and glorious location make it one of the best country racecourses in Britain.

Around Taunton

CHEDDON FITZPAINE
3 miles N of Taunton off the A358

🐾 Hestercombe Gardens

Spreading across the south-facing lower slopes of the Quantock Hills, the gorgeous **Hestercombe Gardens** (see panel below) form part of an estate that has been in existence since Saxon times. In 1872, the estate was acquired by the 1st Viscount Portman and it was his grandson, the Hon Edward Portman, who commissioned Sir Edwin Lutyens to create a new formal garden that was planted by Gertrude Jekyll between 1904 and 1908. Within the 40-acre site are temples, streams and lakes, formal terraces, woodlands, cascades and some glorious views. Of all the gardens designed by the legendary partnership of Lutyens and Jekyll, Hestercombe is regarded as the best preserved.

STOKE ST GREGORY
7 miles NE of Taunton off the A378

🐾 Willows & Wetlands Visitor Centre

A straggling village in the heart of the Somerset Levels, Stoke St Gregory provides an appropriate location for the **Willows and Wetlands Visitor Centre**, established by the Coates family, which has more than 170 years

Hestercombe Gardens

Cheddon Fitzpaine, near Taunton,
Somerset TA2 8LG
Tel: 01823 413923 Fax: 01823 413747
e-mail: info@hestercombegardens.com
website: www.hestercombegardens.com

Lying on the southern slopes of the Quantocks, **Hestercombe Gardens** can be found on an estate that dates back to Saxon times but, from the 14th to the late 19th century it was continuously owned by one family, the Warres. It was Coplestone Warre Bampfylde who designed and laid out the magnificent landscaped garden in the mid 18th century. In 1873, the estate was acquired by the 1st Viscount Portman and it was his grandson, the Hon Edward Portman who, in 1904, commissioned sir Edwin Lutyens to create a new formal garden that was planted by Gertrude Jekyll.

🏠 historic building　🏛 museum and heritage　🏚 historic site　🦆 scenic attraction　🐾 flora and fauna

experience in the willow industry. Their 80 acres of willow provide the natural material for craftsmen to weave a wide variety of baskets, furniture and garden items for sale. Guided tours are available.

BURROW BRIDGE

9 miles NE of Taunton on the A361

⚲ Somerset Levels Basket & Craft Centre

⚶ Burrow Mump ⌂ Maunsel House

This village, on the River Parrett, is home to one of several pumping stations built in Victorian times to drain the Somerset Levels. The Pumping Station is open to the public occasionally throughout the year. Burrow Bridge is also the home of the **Somerset Levels Basket and Craft Centre**, a workshop and showroom stocked with handmade basket ware.

Rising dramatically from the surrounding wetlands is the conspicuous conical hill, **Burrow Mump** (National Trust). Situated at a fording point on the River Parrett, this knoll has at its summit the picturesque remains of an unfinished chapel to St Michael begun in 1793, but for which funds ran out before its completion. Burrow Mump is located in the heart of the low-lying area known as **King's Sedge Moor**, an attractive part of the

Burrow Mump

Somerset Levels drained by the Rivers Cary and Parrett. A rich area of wetland, the moor is known for its characteristic pollarded willows, whose straight shoots, or withies, have been cultivated on a substantial scale ever since the taste for wicker developed during the 19th century. The traditional craft of basket-weaving is one of Somerset's oldest commercial activities and it once employed thousands of people. Although the industry has been scaled down over the past 150 years, it is still alive and currently enjoying something of a revival.

The isolated Burrow Mump is reputed to be the site of an ancient fortification belonging to King Alfred, King of Wessex. He is said to have retreated here to escape from invading Vikings. It was during this time that he is rumoured to have sought shelter in a hut in the nearby village of Athelney. While sitting at the peasant's hearth, absorbed in his own thoughts, legend has it he allowed the cakes that the housewife had been baking to burn. Not recognising the king, the peasant boxed his ears for ruining all her hard work. In the 19th century, a stone was placed on the site recalling that in gratitude for his hospitality, King Alfred founded a monastery on the Isle of Athelney.

Just to the west of Burrow Bridge, the Bridgwater and Taunton Canal winds its way through some of the most attractive countryside in the Somerset Levels. The restored locks, swing bridges, engine houses and rare paddle gearing equipment add further interest to this picturesque walk. The canal also offers a variety of recreational facilities including boating, fishing and canoeing, while the canal banks are alive with both bird and animal life. At the canal's southern end, boats have access to the River Tone via Firepool

Lock in the heart of Taunton.

North Newton, one of the pretty villages along the canal, is home to the magnificent country manor of **Maunsel House**, which dates back to the 13th century. The house is set in 100 acres of stunning parkland at the heart of a sprawling 2000-acre estate, comprising farms, lakes, woodlands, walnut groves, orchards, Somerset wetlands, cottages and ancient barns. The house can boast such visitors as Geoffrey Chaucer, who wrote part of *The Canterbury Tales* whilst staying here. Occasionally open to the public, the house is always available for functions such as weddings and conferences.

HATCH BEAUCHAMP
5½ miles SE of Taunton on the A358

Hatch Beauchamp is a pleasant village that has managed to retain much of its rural atmosphere despite being on the major route between Ilminster and Taunton. Its name originates from *Hache*, a Saxon word meaning gateway, which refers to the ancient forest of Neroche whose boundary was just to the north and west. The Beauchamp element comes from the Norman family who owned the local manor and whose house stood on the land now occupied by one of the finest country houses in the area, Hatch Court, which, sadly, is now closed to the public.

PITMINSTER
3 miles S of Taunton off the B3170

⌂ Poundisford Park

Recorded as Pipeminster in the Domesday Book, although there is no evidence of a minster ever having been built here, the village does have an old church containing 16th-century monuments to the Colles family. Just to the north of Pitminster is

Poundisford Park, a small H-shaped Tudor mansion standing within a delightful, wooded deer park that once belonged to the bishops of Winchester. The house is renowned for its fine plasterwork ceilings and the grounds incorporate a formal garden laid out in the Tudor style.

BRADFORD-ON-TONE
4 miles SW of Taunton off the A38

🏛 Sheppy's Cider

Sheppy's Cider has been making its renowned ciders since the early 1800s and now boasts more than 200 awards, including two gold medals. Visitors can stroll through the orchards with their wide variety of apples, visit the museum for an insight into the farming of the past, watch a video following the cider-maker's year, and sample the finished product in the shop. Professional guided tours are available for parties of 20 or more. Other amenities on site include a licensed tearoom, picnic area and children's play area.

WELLINGTON
6 miles SW of Taunton on the A38

🏛 Town Hall 🏛 Wellington Monument

This pleasant old market town was once an important producer of woven cloth and serge and it owes much of its prosperity to Quaker entrepreneurs and, later, the Fox banking family. Fox, Fowler and Co was the last private bank in England to issue its own notes - they only ceased in 1921 when they were taken over by Lloyds. The broad streets around the town centre are peppered with fine Georgian buildings, including the neoclassical **Town Hall**. At the eastern end of the town, the much altered church contains the ostentatious tomb of Sir John Popham, the judge who presided at the trial of Guy Fawkes.

To the south of the town rises the **Wellington Monument**, a 175-foot obelisk erected not long after the Duke of Wellington's great victory at Waterloo. The foundation stone was laid in 1817 by Lord Somerville, but the monument was only completed in 1854. The duke himself visited the site and the town from which he took his title only once, in 1819.

WIVELISCOMBE
9 miles W of Taunton on the B3227

🏛 Gaulden Manor

This is an ancient market town where the Romans once had a fort. A cache of 3rd and 4th-century coins has been uncovered in the area. Later, in medieval times, the local manor house was used as a summer residence of the bishops of Bath and Wells. The remains, including a striking 14th-century archway, have now been incorporated into a group of cottages. During World War Two, the church's crypt was used to store priceless historic documents and ecclesiastical treasures brought here from other parts of Somerset that were more at risk from aerial attack.

Known to locals as Wivey, this thriving local centre has numerous small shops, some with their original Victorian frontages, and several pubs that stock ales from the town's two breweries.

To the northeast of Wiveliscombe, close to the village of Tolland, is the delightful **Gaulden Manor** (see panel below), an estate that dates from the 12th century, although the present house is largely 17th century. It is currently not open to the public because of family illness and no date has been set for its re-opening. The house contains some outstanding early plasterwork, fine furniture, and many examples of embroidery by the owner's wife. The interesting gardens include a herb garden, old-fashioned roses, a bog garden and a secret garden beyond the monks' fish pond. Gaulden Manor once belonged to the Turberville family whose name was adapted by Thomas Hardy for use in his novel, *Tess of the D'Urbervilles*.

To the north and west of Wiveliscombe, below the Brendon Hills, are two reservoirs, Wimbleball and Clatworthy, which offer

Gaulden Manor Gardens and House

Tolland, nr Taunton, Somerset TA4 3PN
Tel: 01984 667213

Set in a beautiful valley between the Brendon and the Quantock hills is the historic **Gaulden Manor**, a medieval house parts of which are believed to date back to the 12th century. The house is famous for its plasterwork, the date of which can be assessed by the coats of arms on the overmantels and depict two families joined by marriage in 1639. Parties can view the interior of the house by appointment.

The house is surrounded by a series of gardens that include the rose garden, a well-stocked herb garden, a bog garden and a butterfly garden. Tucked away lies the Secret Garden planted with white shrubs and roses whilst beyond is the Monk's Fish Pond and island and a grassy walk with old shrub roses and geraniums leading back to the house. Not an overly neat garden, this is a place to explore with something new and different around each corner. Plants propagated from the garden are for sale.

🎬 stories and anecdotes 🐦 famous people 🎨 art and craft 🎭 entertainment and sport 🚶 walks

excellent facilities for picnickers, anglers and water sports enthusiasts.

NORTON FITZWARREN
2 miles NW of Taunton on the B3227

Large finds of Roman pottery have been excavated in and around this village, helping to confirm that Norton Fitzwarren was the Roman settlement of Theodunum. The village's name comes from the Saxon north tun (meaning north farm) and the Norman family who were given the manor here after the Conquest. Norton Fitzwarren's antiquity and former importance gave rise to the old rhyme, "When Taunton was a furzy down, Norton was a market town". Today, although the village has all but been consumed by its much larger neighbour, it has still managed to retain some of its individuality.

The land around Norton Fitzwarren is damp and fertile and, for hundreds of years, cider apples have been grown here. Cider made here is now transported all over the world, but until the early 19th century, cider was a beverage very much confined to Somerset and the West Country. It was the Rev Thomas Cornish, a local clergyman, who first brought cider to the attention of the rest of the nation, when he produced a drink so appetising that it found great favour with Queen Victoria.

BISHOP'S LYDEARD
5 miles NW of Taunton off the A358

🌿 West Somerset Railway   🏛 St Mary's Church
🏛 Bishop's Lydeard Mill

This large village is the southern terminus of the **West Somerset Railway**, a nostalgic enterprise that recaptures the era of the branch line country railway in the days of steam. This privately operated steam railway runs to

West Somerset Railway

Minehead on the Bristol Channel coast and, extending for nearly 20 miles, is the longest line of its kind in the country. It was formed when British Rail's 100-year-old branch line between Taunton and Minehead closed in 1971. There are 10 stations along the line and services operate between Easter and the end of October. The railway's special attractions include a first-class Pullman dining car and the *Flockton Flyer* locomotive, named after the 1970s children's drama series of that name, which centred on the adventures of a family running a preserved railway.

St Mary's Church has a magnificent tower built of local red stone around 1450. Fortunately, it was spared any insensitive Victorian restoration of the interior. Look out for the 'hunky punks' on the outside of the tower. Hunky punk is the local term for the carved creatures, which, unlike gargoyles that carry off rainwater, serve no useful function. St Mary's has five hunky punks – the one on the southwest corner of a dragon with a stone in its mouth looks particularly menacing.

The Grade II listed **Bishop's Lydeard Mill** has been painstakingly restored over many years by the Back family and is now fully working. Among the many traditional trades and crafts displayed here are a wheelwright's shop, transported from Devon and preserved exactly as it was left on the day the owner shut up shop, and an equally authentic blacksmith's shop. Other attractions include fun interactive displays, a gift shop and Dusty Miller's tearoom.

Admiral Blake Statue

Bridgwater

🏛 Blake Museum

🏛 Somerset Brick & Tile Museum

🌿 Carnival 🌿 Somerset Space Walk

Situated at the lowest bridging point of the River Parrett, Bridgwater is an ancient inland port and industrial town. Despite having been fortified since before the Norman Conquest, the settlement that grew up around the castle remained little more than a village until an international trade in wool, wheat and other agricultural products began to develop in the late Middle Ages. Bridgwater grew and, at one time, was the most important town on the coast between Bristol and Barnstaple. For a short period, it was the fifth busiest port in the country. The largely 14th-century parish church, with its disproportionately large spire, is the only building to remain from that prosperous medieval era. The castle was dismantled after the English Civil War and the 13th-century Franciscan friary and St John's Hospital disappeared long ago. Although the street layout here is still medieval, the buildings in the

area between King Street and West Quay provide some of the best examples of domestic Georgian architecture in the county.

Bridgwater's most famous son is the celebrated military leader, Robert Blake, who was born here in 1598. When in his 40s, Blake became an important officer in Cromwell's army and twice defended Taunton against overwhelming Royalist odds. Just a decade later, he was appointed General at Sea and went on to win a number of important battles against the Dutch and the Spanish. In so doing, he restored the nation's naval supremacy in Europe. The house in which he was born is now home to the **Blake Museum**, which contains a three-dimensional model of the Battle of Santa Cruz, one of Blake's most famous victories, along with a collection of his personal effects. Blake was not the only military leader connected with Bridgwater. During the late 1600s, the Duke of Monmouth stayed here before his disastrous defeat at the nearby Battle of Sedgemoor. The museum suitably illustrates this decisive battle in the duke's quest for the English throne. Recently upgraded and re-opened in March 2010, this is also a museum of local history with a large collection of locally discovered artefacts on display that date from Neolithic times right up to World War Two.

The highlight of Bridgwater's events calendar is its **Carnival** commemorating Guy Fawkes' Day. Believed to be the largest such event in the world, the celebration involves hundreds of themed 'carts', each ablaze with as many as 25,000 light bulbs, which join a procession more than two miles long, accompanied by various town bands. Following the procession, 'squibs', or giant fireworks, are carried through the town and set alight in the High Street.

An attractive amenity of the town is the Bridgwater and Taunton Canal which was completed in 1827 and can still be explored on water by canoe, trail boat or narrow boat, or along the towpath on foot or by cycle. Before the construction of a canal dock, the ships arriving at Bridgwater used to tie up on both sides of the river below the town's medieval bridge. Here, too, can be seen the last remnant of the medieval castle, The Water Gate, on West Quay.

The arrival of the canal gave a great boost to local industries. The manufacture of Bridgwater glass, which had begun the previous century, expanded greatly. The river mud that caused the decline of the town's port also proved to have hidden benefits, because when baked in oblong blocks it was found to be an excellent scourer. As Bath Brick, it was used for nearly a century to clean grates and stone steps. The canal terminus, where the brickworks also stood, was finally closed in 1970, but has now been restored as a fascinating area of industrial archaeology.

More of the county's industrial heritage can be explored at the **Somerset Brick & Tile Museum** on East Quay. The last surviving kiln at the former Barham Brother's yard is a poignant reminder of the brick and tile industry that was once so important in the county. The kiln has been repaired by Somerset County Council and now provides the centrepiece of the museum.

An interesting feature on the canal is based at Lower Mounsel Locks, about five miles south of Bridgwater. **The Somerset Space Walk** uses the 13-mile length of the canal to represent the solar system with scale models of each of the planets. The sun is placed at the locks with the inner planets nearby; Pluto can be found on the outskirts of Taunton.

Around Bridgwater

HIGHBRIDGE
6 miles N of Bridgwater on the A38

🐾 Alstone Wildlife Park

The small coastal town of Highbridge was once a busy port on the Glastonbury Canal. Today its main visitor attraction is **Alstone Wildlife Park**, a small non-profit making, family-run park, which devotes all its proceeds to the welfare and upkeep of the animals. Open daily from Easter to November, the park is home to a variety of animals including Theadore the camel, a herd of red deer, wallabies, owls, pigs, emus and ponies.

BURNHAM-ON-SEA
7 miles N of Bridgwater on the B3140

🏛 St Andrew's Church   🏛 Low Lighthouse

🍃 Brent Knoll

A traditional seaside resort as well as a thriving market town, Burnham-on-Sea has acres of sandy beach, a fine Edwardian Esplanade, a Pier Pavilion and a 15th-century church that was built close by the shore. This turned out to be a not very good idea. Because of the sandy foundations, the 80 foot tower of **St Andrew's Church** now leans three feet from the vertical. But the structure is apparently quite stable and has not shifted for many decades. Inside are parts of a massive altarpiece designed by Inigo Jones and carved by Grinling Gibbons. Originally installed in James II's Whitehall Palace, it survived the great fire that destroyed the palace and was re-installed in Westminster Abbey. But when the abbey was being prepared for the coronation of George IV the huge structure was deemed out of place and surplus to requirements. Somehow, the vicar of Burnham learned of its impending fate and managed to acquire it for his country church. The parts are now dispersed over various parts of the chancel.

In the early 1800s, the local curate, the Rev Davies, discovered mineral springs in the gardens of Burnham Hall. An attempt was made to turn Burnham into a spa town to rival Cheltenham and Bath. A series of buildings was erected around the springs, the most notable of them being the Bath House, now Steart House, on the Esplanade. Unfortunately, the waters were too sulphurous and stinking for most convalescents to endure and the venture fizzled out. The town would have to depend on its wide sandy beach to attract visitors.

A distinctive feature on the beach is the unique nine-legged **Low Lighthouse**, a curious square structure raised above the beach on tall stilts. An earlier lighthouse, the High Lighthouse, erected in 1750, still stands inland behind the dunes, but because of the huge rise and fall of tides in the Severn estuary, its light was ineffective at low tides.

Hence the need for the Low Lighthouse.

To the northeast of Burnham rises **Brent Knoll**, a conspicuous landmark that can be seen from as far away as South Wales. Before the Somerset Levels were drained, this isolated hill would almost certainly have been an island. As with many other natural features that appear out of place in the landscape, there are several stories that suggest that the knoll owes its existence to the Devil. The 445-foot summit is crowned with the remains of an Iron Age hill fort. The summit, which can be reached by footpaths beginning near the churches at East Brent and Brent Knoll, offers walkers a spectacular view out over the Bristol Channel, the Mendips and the Somerset Levels.

BREAN
11 miles N of Bridgwater off the A370

🐦 Animal Farm Adventure Park   🌿 Steep Holm

This elongated, mainly modern resort village is sheltered, to the north, by the 320 feet-high Brean Down (National Trust), an imposing remnant of the Mendip hills that projects out into the Bristol Channel. Another fragment can be seen in the form of the offshore island, **Steep Holm**. A site of settlement, ritual and defence for thousands of years, the remains of an Iron Age coastal fort and a Roman temple have both been found on Brean Down along with some medieval 'pillow' mounds. The tip of the promontory is dominated by the Palmerston fort of 1867, built as part of the defences to protect the Bristol Channel. There are also some 20th-century gun emplacements. As well as its archaeological and geological interest, this peninsula has been designated a Site of Special Scientific Interest because of its varied habitats. Oystercatcher and dunlin can be seen along the foreshore and estuary;

the scrubland is an important habitat for migrating birds such as redstart, redpoll and reed bunting; rare plants take root in the shallow and exposed soil; and the south-facing slopes are home to a variety of butterflies. Subject to one of the widest tidal ranges in Europe, the currents around the headland can be dramatic and very dangerous.

About a mile inland from Brean Sands beach, at Berrow, **Animal Farm Adventure Park** promises fun for all the family with a mix of domestic and rarer animals, including llamas, alpacas and emus; adventure play areas, ride-on tractors and a miniature railway.

WESTONZOYLAND
3½ miles SE of Bridgwater on the A372

🏚 Battle of Sedgemoor   🏛 Pumping Station

Just to the northwest of the village, and on the southern bank of what is now the King's Sedgemoor Drain, is the site of the last battle to be fought on English soil. In July 1685, the well-equipped forces of James II heavily defeated the followers of the Duke of Monmouth in the bloody **Battle of Sedgemoor**. This brought an end to the ill-fated Pitchfork Rebellion that aimed to replace the Catholic King James with the Protestant Duke of Monmouth, an illegitimate son of Charles II. Around 700 of Monmouth's followers were killed on the battlefield, while several hundred survivors were rounded up and taken to Westonzoyland churchyard, where many of them were hanged. The duke himself was taken to London where, 10 days after the battle, he was executed on Tower Hill. However, it was during the infamous Judge Jeffrey's Bloody Assizes that the greatest terror was inflicted on the surviving followers of the duke when well over 300 men were condemned to death.

🏚 historic building 📷 museum and heritage 🏛 historic site 🌿 scenic attraction 🐦 flora and fauna

CLAVELSHAY BARN RESTAURANT

Lower Clavelshay Farm, North Petherton, nr Bridgewater, Somerset TA6 6PJ
Tel: 01278 662629
e-mail: query@clavelshaybarn.co.uk
website: www.clavelshaybarn.co.uk

Clavelshay Barn Restaurant nestles in an idyllic valley on the edge of the Quantock Hills within an area of outstanding natural beauty. It is set in the heart of a family-owned dairy farm and is in easy reach of Taunton, Bridgewater, and the M5.

Sympathetically converted from a beamed 17th Century Somerset Barn, the restaurant offers a monthly-changing menu, showcasing the very best in local seasonal produce. Where possible, free-range ingredients are sourced from the farm itself: fresh herbs and vegetables from our walled garden; eggs from our own Clavelshay hens; smoked meats and fish from our onsite smokery; pigeon and rabbit from the farm and fresh water from nearby springs.

Clavelshay Barn Restaurant is a flexible venue: generously proportioned, it stretches over two floors and offers al fresco dining on its picturesque patio. It is an ideal space for intimate dining; anniversaries; birthdays; Christmas parties; corporate events and weddings and has ample grounds for marquees both large and small.

Not only does Clavelshay Barn Restaurant offer the cream of local Somerset ingredients but also prides itself on the excellence of its friendly, professional service

So set your sat. nav. to TA6 6PJ and discover *" a hidden gem of a place – off the beaten track but well worth finding " ."* It's worth a trip to Somerset to dine at Clavelshay Barn on the edge of the Quantock Hills," Country Living - August 2010

Quantock Hills

Neolithic and Bronze Age remains, including around 100 burial mounds, many of which now resemble nothing more than a pile of stones. The richer soil in the south sustains arable farms and pockets of dense woodland, and this varied landscape offers some magnificent walking with splendid views over the Bristol Channel, the Vale of Taunton Deane, the Brendon Hills and Exmoor. It was this glorious classical English landscape that the poets Wordsworth and Coleridge so admired while they were living in the area.

A further 600 were transported to the colonies. Today, a stark memorial marks the site of the lonely battlefield.

The village lies in the Somerset Levels and a steam-powered **Pumping Station** was built here in the 19th century to drain the water from the levels into the River Parrett. The oldest pumping station of its kind in the area, the engine on show here was in operation from 1861 until 1952. Now fully restored, it can be seen in steam at various times throughout the year. The station itself is a Grade II listed building. Also on the site is a small forge, a tramway and a number of other exhibits from the steam age.

Southwest of Enmore in one of the loveliest areas of the southern Quantocks is **Fyne Court** (National Trust), which houses both the headquarters of the Somerset Wildlife Trust and a visitor centre for the Quantocks. The main house here was built in the 17th century by the Crosse family. It was largely destroyed by fire in the 1890s and the only surviving parts are the library and music room that have been converted into the visitor centre. The grounds, which incorporate a walled garden, two ponds, an arboretum and a lake, have been designated a nature reserve.

ENMORE
4 miles SW of Bridgwater off the A39

⚅ Quantock Hills   🏠 Fyne Court   🎦 Andrew Cross

To the west of Enmore the ground rises up into the **Quantock Hills**, an Area of Outstanding Natural Beauty that runs from near Taunton to the Bristol Channel at Quantoxhead. Rising to a high point of 1260 feet at Wills Neck, this delightful area of open heath and scattered woodland supports one of the country's last remaining herds of wild red deer. The exposed hilltops are littered with

Fyne Court

The most renowned occupant of the house was **Andrew Cross**, an early 19th-century scientist who was a pioneer in the field of electrical energy. Known locally as the 'thunder and lightning man', one of Crosse's lightning conductors can still be seen on an oak tree in the grounds. Local stories tell how, during one of his electrical experiments, Crosse created tiny live insects. It was this claim that helped to inspire Mary Shelley to write her Gothic horror story, *Frankenstein*, in 1818.

NETHER STOWEY
10 miles W of Bridgwater off the A39

🏛 Stowey Court   🏛 Coleridge Cottage

🚶 Quantock Forest Trail

🐦 Samuel Taylor Coleridge

This attractive village of 17th and 18th-century stone cottages and houses is best known for its literary connections, but Nether Stowey has a much longer history. At one time, it was a small market town. A castle was built here in Norman times and the earthwork remains can be seen to the west of the village centre, while its substantial manor house, **Stowey Court**, stands on the eastern side of the village. The construction of the manor house was begun by Lord Audley in 1497 shortly before he joined a protest against Henry VII's taxation policy. Sadly, he was not able to see the project through to completion as he was executed soon afterwards.

In 1797, a local tanner, Tom Poole, lent a dilapidated cottage at the end of his garden to his friend, **Samuel Taylor Coleridge**, who stayed here for three years with his wife and child. So began Nether Stowey's association with poets and writers. It was here that Coleridge wrote most of his famous works, including *The Rime of the Ancient Mariner* and

the opium-inspired *Kubla Khan*. When not writing, he would go on long walks with his friend and near neighbour William Wordsworth, who had moved close to Nether Stowey from a house in Dorset at around the same time. Other visitors to the cottage included Charles Lamb. But it was not long before Coleridge's opium addiction and his rocky marriage began to take their toll. These were not the only problems for the poet as local suspicion was growing that he and Wordsworth were French spies. The home in which the Coleridges lived for three years is now **Coleridge Cottage**, a National Trust property where mementoes of the poet are on display.

A lane leads southwest from the village to the nearby village of Over Stowey and the starting point of the Forestry Commission's **Quantock Forest Trail**, a three-mile walk lined with specially planted native and imported trees.

Ilminster

🏛 Dillington House

One of Somerset's most beguiling towns, Ilminster is perched on the side of a hill with its main street running round, rather than up and down the slope. For centuries, it stood on the main London to Exeter route; today the A303 bypasses the town allowing its special charm to be enjoyed in comparative peace.

During the Middle Ages, it expanded further into a thriving wool and lace-making town. This period of prosperity is reflected in the town's unusually large parish church, whose massive multi-pinnacled tower is modelled on that of Wells Cathedral. Any walk around the old part of Ilminster will reveal a number of delightful old buildings,

A TOUCH OF ELEGANCE

5 West Street, Ilminster, Somerset TA19 9AA
Tel: 01460 85992
e-mail: sue@atouchofelegancesomerset.co.uk
website: www.atouchofelegancesomerset.co.uk

Sue Woodbury developed her love of interiors after renovating a Somerset cottage and in 2000 she established **A Touch of Elegance**, a home interiors shop supplying furnishings of the highest quality. There is a vast range of contemporary and traditional wooden, glass and bespoke furniture from companies including 'Zoffany' and 'Duresta'.

The collections of high quality designer fabrics come from suppliers such as 'Colefax & Fowler', Sanderson, Designers Guild and Osborne Little among others lending themselves to the beautiful scatter cushions, bedspreads, curtains and the many curtain trimmings and accessories available. Old furniture can be revamped with quality upholstery and loose covers, and curtains and blinds can be made to measure with a choice of luxurious fabrics.

No part of the room is forgotten in A Touch of Elegance. With paints from 'The little green paint company' and 'Zoffany' and a wide range of wall coverings in a variety of designs and colours, there is something for every taste. To add interest, complete the room with one of the beautiful wall, ceiling or standing lights or choose from the collections of smaller ornamental pieces and giftware.

---

many constructed in golden Hamstone, including the chantry house, the old grammar school and a colonnaded market house. Another, the George Inn, proudly displays a sign proclaiming that it was the first hotel that Queen Victoria stayed at, as Princess Victoria, in 1819. The future queen was on her way with her parents to Sidmouth in Devon.

On the outskirts of Ilminster is another lovely old building, the handsome part Tudor mansion, **Dillington House**. It is now owned by Somerset County Council and used as a Residential Centre for Adult Education, but it was originally the home of the Speke family. In the time of James II, John Speke was an officer in the Duke of Monmouth's ill-fated rebel army that landed at Lyme Regis in 1685. Following the rebellion's disastrous defeat at the Battle of Sedgemoor, Speke was

forced to flee abroad, leaving his brother, George, who had done no more than shake the duke's hand, to face the wrath of Judge Jeffreys. The infamous 'hanging judge' sentenced George to death, justifying his decision with the words, "His family owes a life and he shall die for his brother."

Around Ilminster

BARRINGTON
3 miles NE of Ilminster off the B3168

🏛 Barrington Court

To the east of the village is the beautiful National Trust-owned **Barrington Court**, famous for its enchanting garden influenced by the great 20th-century garden architect Gertrude Jekyll. This estate originally

Barrington Court

belonged to the Daubeney family but it passed through several hands before becoming the property of William Clifton, a wealthy London merchant, who was responsible for building the house in the mid 16th century. In 1907, the by then dilapidated Barrington Court became the first country house to be purchased by the National Trust. It was restored in the 1920s by Col AA Lyle, to whom the Trust had let the property. The garden, too, was laid out during this time in a series of themed areas including an iris garden, a lily garden, a white garden and a fragrant rose garden. Gertrude Jekyll was brought in to advise on the initial planting and layout and the garden remains the finest example of her work in the Trust's care. There is also an exceptionally attractive kitchen garden with apple, pear and plum trees trained along the walls that, in season, produces fruit and vegetables for the licensed restaurant that can be found here.

DOWLISH WAKE
2 miles SE of Ilminster off the A303 or A358

🐦 John Hanning Speke ⌀ Perry's Cider Mills

In the parish church of this attractive village is the tomb of **John Hanning Speke**, the intrepid Victorian explorer who journeyed for more than 2000 miles through Africa to confirm that Lake Victoria was, indeed, the source of the River Nile. After his epic journey, Speke returned to England a hero but, tragically, on the very morning of the day that he was due to report his findings to the British Geographical Association, he accidentally shot himself while on a partridge shoot.

This picturesque village is also the home of **Perry's Cider Mills** where the cider presses are installed in a wonderful 16th-century thatched barn. If you visit in the autumn you can see the cider-making in progress, but the presses and an interesting collection of vintage farm tools and equipment are on view all year round. The full range of ciders, including cider brandy, is available in the shop and can be sampled from the barrel before you buy. The shop also stocks a huge range of country-style pottery, stone cider jars, baskets, terracotta kitchenware, country jams and pickles and much more.

HINTON ST GEORGE
11 miles SE of Ilminster off the A356

🐦 Sir Amyas Poulett 🌳 Lower Severalls

This wonderfully unspoilt former estate village has a broad main street, thatched houses, a medieval village cross and a striking 15th-century church. For centuries the village was owned by the Poulett family and it is thanks to them that Hinton St George has been left virtually untouched. The Pouletts arrived here in the 15th century and the house that they rebuilt then, Hinton House, now forms the main structure of the present day mansion, which has been converted into apartments.

Several ostentatious monuments to members of the Poulett family can be seen in the village's 15th-century Church of St George. Commemorated by a superb alabaster memorial is the most famous member of the family, **Sir Amyas Poulett**. A loyal and honourable courtier of Elizabeth I, Sir Amyas fell out of favour when he declined to act on the queen's suggestion that he murder Mary, Queen of Scots, who was in his custody. "A dainty and precise fellow," was the queen's scornful response to the knight's over-scrupulous behaviour.

On the last Thursday in October, called Punkie Night, it is traditional for Hinton children to beg for candles to put inside their intricately fashioned turnip and pumpkin lanterns. It is considered very unlucky to refuse to give a child a candle as each lantern is thought to represent the spirit of a dead person who, unless illuminated, will rise up at Halloween.

Hinton seems to have a special interest in light. It was the first village in England to install gas street lighting in 1863, and recently its modern street lighting scheme received an award from the International Dark Skies Association because its street lamps minimise light pollution.

Lower Severalls has an enchanting and original garden set in front of an 18th-century Hamstone farmhouse. The garden has an informal style with profuse herbaceous borders around the house and innovative features that include a living dogwood basket, a wadi and a scented garden.

CREWKERNE
13 miles SE of Ilminster on the A30/A356

🏛 Church of St Batholomew   ⛰ Windwhistle Hill
🏛 Crewkerne Heritage Centre
🌿 Clapton Court Gardens   🚶 River Parrett Trail

Another delightful small market town, noted for its antiques and book shops, and the famous auction house of Lawrence's, which is housed in a restored linen yard. A thriving agricultural centre during Saxon times, Crewkerne even had its own mint in the decades leading up to the Norman invasion. Evidence of this ancient former market town's importance and wealth can still be seen in the magnificence of its parish **Church of St Bartholomew**, built using money generated by the late medieval boom in the local wool industry. A building of minster-like proportions, this is one of the grandest of the many fine Perpendicular churches to be found in south Somerset. Unlike many other towns in Wessex, whose textile industries suffered an almost total decline in later years, Crewkerne was rejuvenated in the 18th century when the availability of locally grown flax led to an expansion in the manufacture of sailcloth and canvas webbing. Among the many thousands of sails made here were those for *HMS Victory*, Admiral Nelson's flagship at the Battle of

Church of St Bartholomew

🏛 historic building   🏛 museum and heritage   🏛 historic site   ⛰ scenic attraction   🌿 flora and fauna

Trafalgar. Nelson's captain in that engagement was Sir Thomas Hardy, educated at Crewkerne grammar school. Hardy's career is celebrated at the **Crewkerne Heritage Centre** recently relocated in a beautifully restored 18th century house.

The economic boost provided by the flax industry was further fuelled by the development of the London to Exeter stagecoach route. This led to the rebuilding of Crewkerne with elegant Georgian buildings, many of which can still be seen. The main areas, around Church and Abbey Streets, have now been designated an Area of Outstanding Architectural Interest.

To the west of Crewkerne rises the aptly named **Windwhistle Hill**, a high chalk-topped ridge from the top of which there are dramatic views, on a clear day, southwards to Lyme Bay and northwards across the Somerset Levels to the mountains of South Wales. The town also lies close to the source of the River Parrett. From here the 50-mile **River Parrett Trail** follows the river through some of the country's most ecologically sensitive and fragile areas, the Somerset Levels and Moors. Old mills, splendid churches, attractive villages and ancient monuments, as well as orchards, peaceful pastureland and traditional industries such as cider-making and basket-weaving can all be found along the route.

Just a couple of miles southwest of Crewkerne, close to the village of Clapton, are the varied and interesting **Clapton Court Gardens**. Among the many beautiful features of this 10-acre garden are the formal terraces, the rose garden, the rockery and a water garden. The grounds incorporate a large wooded area containing a massive ash tree that, at over 230 years old and 28 feet in girth, is believed to be the oldest and the largest in

mainland Britain. There is also a fine metasequoia that is already over 80 feet tall, although it was only planted in 1950 from a seed brought back from China.

HASELBURY PLUCKNETT
14 miles SE of Ilminster on the A3066

🏛 Haselbury Bridge

This delightfully named and particularly pretty village has a large part-Norman church whose churchyard contains a series of unusual 'squeeze stones', narrow entrances formed by two large slabs of stone. Just to the west of the village the lovely **Haselbury Bridge**, a medieval packhorse bridge, crosses the still young River Parrett.

CHARD
6 miles S of Ilminster on the A30

🏛 Chard Museum   🏛 Hornsbury Mill
🌿 Chard Reservoir Nature Reserve

The borough of Chard was first established in 1235 and, during the Middle Ages, became a prosperous wool centre with its own mayor, or portreeve, and burgesses. However, few buildings date from before 1577, when a devastating fire raged through the town and left most of it as ashes. One building that did survive the destruction was the fine Perpendicular parish church. The town was rebuilt and, today, many of these 16th and 17th-century buildings remain, including the courthouse and the old grammar school. Chard also has some striking Georgian and Victorian buildings. On the outskirts of the town the unusual round toll house, with its conical thatched roof, is a picturesque relic of the days of stagecoaches and turnpike roads.

Chard has expanded rapidly since World War Two; its population has more than doubled. Nevertheless, the centre of this light industrial town still retains a pleasant village-like atmosphere that is most apparent in its broad main shopping street. At the western end of the town's High Street, housed in the attractive thatched Godworth House, is the award-winning **Chard Museum** amongst whose exhibits are displays celebrating two very inventive former residents. James Stringfellow produced the first steam-powered aeroplanes in the 1840s, and James Gillingham pioneered artificial limbs a few decades later. Also featured is Margaret Bonfield, who was the first female British cabinet member as Minister of Labour in 1929.

To the northwest of the town is a 200-year-old corn mill, **Hornsbury Mill**, whose impressive water wheel is still in working order. It stands in five acres of beautiful informally landscaped water gardens. The old buildings have been given a new lease of life and now incorporate a restaurant and bed and breakfast guest rooms, and also provides a popular venue for weddings, special events and conferences.

To the northeast, **Chard Reservoir Nature Reserve** is a conservation area where kingfishers, great crested grebes and other rare species of birds have made their home in and around the lake. The nature reserve also has a two-mile circular footpath that takes in rustling reed beds, broad-leaved woodland and open hay meadows.

TATWORTH
8 miles S of Ilminster off the A358

🏛 Forde Abbey

To the northeast of Tatworth lies a meadow that is the last remaining vestige of common land that was enclosed in 1819. Changes in the ownership of the land during the 1820s allowed too many farmers grazing rights on the land, and the meadow suffered from being over-stocked. Therefore, in 1832, the holders of those rights met and, calling their meeting 'Stowell Court', they auctioned off the meadow for one year and shared the proceeds. So an annual tradition was born and the Stowell Court still meets on the first Tuesday after 6 April every year. Although many more customs have been added over the years, the auction proceedings are unique. They begin when a tallow candle of precisely one inch in length is lit and they end with the last bid before the candle goes out. Today, Stowell Mead is managed as a Site of Special Scientific Interest and, as the land is not treated with fertilisers, pesticides or herbicides, it is home to many rare plants. There is no right of way across the land but it can be seen from the road.

A short distance to the southeast of Tatworth, just over the county border in Dorset, is **Forde Abbey** (see panel opposite), founded in the 12th century by Cistercian monks after they had made an unsuccessful attempt to found an abbey in Devon. For more details, see the entry in the Dorset chapter of this book.

WAMBROOK
8 miles SW of Ilminster off the A30

🌿 Ferne Animal Sanctuary

Visitors interested in animal welfare will be keen to visit the **Ferne Animal Sanctuary** at Wambrook. Originally founded in 1939 by the Duchess of Hamilton and Brandon, the sanctuary moved to its present position in the valley of the River Yarty in 1975. This pleasant 51-acre site incorporates a nature trail, conservation area, dragonfly pools and picnic areas.

Forde Abbey

Tatworth, nr Chard, Somerset TA20 4LU
Tel: 01460 220231 Fax: 01460 220296

Originally founded by Cistercian monks in the 12th century, **Forde Abbey** lay empty for over 100 years after the Dissolution of the Monasteries before its was sold to Edmund Prideaux, Oliver Cromwell's Attorney General in 1649.

The remains of the abbey were incorporated into the grand private house of the Prideaux family – the old chapter house became the family chapel – and later additions include the magnificent 17th century plaster ceilings and the renowned Mortlake Tapestries that were brought over from Brussels by Charles I. Today, Forde Abbey is the home of the Roper family and it stands at the heart of this family run estate.

Along with the collection of tapestries, period furniture and paintings to see in the house, there is the refectory and dormitory that still survive from the time of the medieval monastery whilst the abbey is also home to the famous Eeles Pottery exhibition.

Meanwhile, the house is surrounding by wonderful gardens and they have been described by Alan Titchmarsh as "one of the greatest gardens in the West Country." There are sloping lawns, herbaceous borders, a bog garden, lakes and a working kitchen garden that supplies the abbey's restaurant with produce whilst rare and unusual plants are for sale at the Plant Centre. The estate is also known for its pedigree herd of cattle and the house, with its restaurant and tearoom, can be visited between April and October whilst the gardens and ground are open all year round.

Yeovil

🏛 Church of St John the Baptist

🏛 Museum of South Somerset

Yeovil takes its name from the River Yeo, sometimes called the River Ivel. There was a Roman settlement here, but the town really began to develop in the Middle Ages when a market was established that continues to be held every Friday. Yeovil's parish **Church of St John the Baptist** is the only significant medieval structure to survive as most of the town's other early buildings were destroyed by the series of fires that struck the town in the 17th century. A substantial structure with a solid-looking tower, the church dates from the late 14th century and has a surprisingly austere exterior given its exceptional number of windows. It has so many windows that it is sometimes referred to as the 'Lantern of the West'.

During the 18th century, Yeovil developed into a flourishing coaching centre due to its strategic position at the junction of several main routes. Industries such as glove-making, leather-working, sailcloth-making and cheese-producing were established here. This rapid expansion was further fuelled by the arrival of the railway in the mid 1800s. Then, in the 1890s, James Petter, a local ironmonger and pioneer of the internal combustion engine, founded a business that went on to become one of the largest manufacturers of diesel

RED BARN FARM SHOP

Hinton Farm, Mudford, Yeovil, Somerset BA22 8BA
Tel: 01935 850994
website: www.redbarnfarmshop.moonfruit.com

Our traditional, family-run farm shop sells a wide range of fantastic produce - our prize-winning Guernseys deliver unpasteurised milk and cream, our seasonal vegetables, fruit and flowers come straight into the shop from a field five minutes away or from neighbouring growers, and our free-range hens are often to be found just outside the shop, checking for any stray crumbs. In May and June our asparagus is on sale within hours of being cut; we also sell meat from named local producers, local cheeses, jams and chutneys, and bread and cakes.

engines in Britain. Although production was eventually transferred to the Midlands, a subsidiary set up to produce aircraft during World War One has since evolved into a helicopter plant.

Today, Yeovil retains its geographical importance and is south Somerset's largest concentration of population. It is a thriving commercial, shopping, and market town best known perhaps as the home of Westland Helicopters. Situated in Wyndham House, the **Museum of South Somerset** documents the social and industrial history of the town and surrounding area, from prehistoric times to the present. A reconstructed Roman dining room and kitchen and Georgian House provide settings for countless items from the museum's extensive collection. Amongst many other intriguing exhibits is one that explains how a patent stove was the basis for the town's world-leading helicopter industry.

Around Yeovil

ILCHESTER
7 miles N of Yeovil off the A37

🏠 Ilchester Museum

In Roman times, the settlement here stood at the point where the north-south route

between Dorchester and the Bristol Channel crossed the Fosse Way. However, it was during the 13th century that Ilchester reached its peak as a centre of administration, agriculture and learning. Like its near neighbour Somerton, Ilchester was, for a time, the county town of Somerset. Three substantial gaols were built here, one of which remained in use until the 1840s. Another indication of this town's former status is the 13th-century Ilchester Mace, England's oldest staff of office. Up until recently, the mace resided in the town hall, but today a replica can be seen here, while the original mace is on display in the County Museum at Taunton.

The tiny **Ilchester Museum** is in the centre of the town, by the Market Cross. Here the story of the town from pre-Roman times to the 20th century is told through a series of exhibits that include a Roman coffin and skeleton. Ilchester was the birthplace, in around 1214, of the celebrated scholar, monk and scientist, Roger Bacon, who went on to predict the invention of the aeroplane, telescope and steam engine, although he was eventually imprisoned for his subversive ideas.

YEOVILTON
7 miles N of Yeovil

🏠 Fleet Air Arm Museum

Yeovilton boasts one of the world's largest

🏠 historic building 🏠 museum and heritage 🏛 historic site ♧ scenic attraction ♚ flora and fauna

Fleet Air Arm Museum

aviation museums, the **Fleet Air Arm Museum**, which owns a unique collection of aircraft of which around half are on permanent display. Concorde is here along with a hangar full of fragile vintage aircraft. Visitors can 'fly' aboard the museum's own carrier; use interactive displays to explore the history and atmosphere of many of the aircraft stored here; and undertake the Merlin Experience that replicates a challenging flying mission. Other attractions include a children's adventure playground, a large book and souvenir shop, restaurant, airfield viewing galleries and a picnic area.

CHARLTON MACKRELL
9 miles N of Yeovil off the A37

🏛 Lytes Cary Manor

A couple of miles southeast of the town stands the charming manor house of **Lytes Cary Manor** (National Trust). This late medieval stone house was built by succeeding generations of the Lyte family, the best known member of which was Henry Lyte, the Elizabethan herbalist who dedicated his 1578 translation of Dodoen's *Cruydeboeck* to Queen Elizabeth "from my poore house at

Lytescarie". After the family left the house in the 18th century it fell into disrepair, but in 1907 it was purchased and restored by Sir Walter Jenner, son of the famous Victorian physician. Notable features include a 14th-century chapel and Tudor Great Hall. The present garden is an enchanting combination of formality and eccentricity. There is an open lawn lined with magnificent yew topiary, an orchard filled with quince, pear and apple trees, and a network of enclosed paths that every now and then reveal a view of the house, a lily pond or a classical statue.

SPARKFORD
8 miles NE of Yeovil on the A359

🏛 Haynes International Motor Museum

🏛 Cadbury Castle

The **Haynes International Motor Museum** is thought to hold the largest collection of veteran, vintage and classic cars and motorbikes in the United Kingdom. A living and working museum, it cares for more than 340 cars and bikes ranging from nostalgic classics to the super cars of today. The site contains 11 huge display halls; one of the UK's largest speedway collections; a kids' race track; adventure play area; gift shop and restaurant.

Just to the southeast of the village rises **Cadbury Castle**, a massive Iron Age hill fort first occupied more than 5000 years ago and believed by some to be the location of King Arthur's legendary Camelot. The Romans are reputed to have carried out a massacre here in around AD70 when they put down a revolt by the ancient Britons. A major excavation in the 1960s uncovered a wealth of Roman and pre-Roman remains on the site as well as

🎭 stories and anecdotes 🦜 famous people 🎨 art and craft 🎪 entertainment and sport 🚶 walks

Haynes International Motor Museum

BARWICK
2 miles S of Yeovil off the A37

🏠 Barwick Park

Pronounced barrik, this village is home to **Barwick Park**, an estate dotted with bizarre follies, arranged at the four points of the compass. The eastern folly, known as Jack the Treacle Eater, is composed of a rickety stone arch topped by a curious turreted room. According to local stories, the folly is named after a foot messenger who ran back and forth between the estate and London on a diet of nothing more than bread and treacle. The estate also possesses a curious grotto and a handsome church with a Norman font and an unusual 17th-century transeptal tower.

WEST COKER
3 miles SW of Yeovil off the A30

🏠 Brympton d'Evercy Manor

Close to the village of West Coker is the magnificent **Brympton d'Evercy Manor House** dating from Norman times, but with significant 16th and 17th-century additions. (The house is not normally open to the public but is available for civil weddings and other functions.) The superb golden Hamstone south wing was built in Jacobean times to a design by Inigo Jones. It boasts many fine internal features including the longest straight single span staircase in Britain and an unusual modern tapestry depicting an imaginary bird's-eye view of the property during the 18th century. When viewed from a distance, the mansion house, the little estate church and the nearby dower house make a delightful lakeside grouping.

In the church at nearby East Coker were

confirming that there was certainly a 6th-century fortification on the hilltop. This particular discovery ties the castle in with King Arthur who, at around that time, was spearheading the Celtic British resistance against the advancing Saxons. If Cadbury Castle had been Arthur's Camelot, it would have been a timber fortification rather than the turreted stone structure of the storybooks.

This easily defended hilltop was again fortified during the reign of Ethelred the Unready in the early 11th century. The poorly-advised king established a mint here in around 1000. Most of the coinage from Cadbury was used to buy off the invading Danes in an act of appeasement that led to the term Danegeld. As a consequence, most of the surviving coins from the Cadbury mint are now to be found in the museums of Scandinavia.

The mile-long walk around Cadbury Castle's massive earthwork ramparts demonstrates the site's effectiveness as a defensive position. This allowed those at the castle to see enemy's troop movements and it now provides spectacular panoramic views for today's visitors.

buried the ashes of the poet and playwright TS Eliot. His ancestors lived in the village before emigrating to America in the mid 1600s and it provides the title for the second of his *Four Quartets*. Its opening and closing lines are engraved on a plaque in the church:

> *In my beginning is my end.*
> *In my end is my beginning.*

MONTACUTE
4 miles W of Yeovil off the A3088

🏠 Montacute House   🏛 TV, Radio & Toy Museum

This charming village of golden hamstone houses and cottages has as its focal point the magnificent Elizabethan mansion, **Montacute House** (National Trust - see panel below), built in the 1590s for Edward Phelips, Queen Elizabeth's Master of the Rolls. There have been alterations made to the house over the centuries, most notably in the late 1700s when the west front was remodelled by the fifth Edward Phelips. In the 19th century the fortunes of the Phelips family began to decline and the house was leased out. In the

1920s, following a succession of tenants, the house was put up for sale. A gift from Ernest Cook (the grandson of the travel agent Thomas Cook) enabled the National Trust to purchase this outstanding Elizabethan residence. Constructed of Hamstone, the house is adorned with characteristic open parapets, fluted columns, twisted pinnacles, oriel windows and carved statues. The long gallery, one of the grandest of its kind in Britain, houses a fine collection of Tudor and Jacobean portraits on permanent loan from London's National Portrait Gallery. Other noteworthy features include magnificent tapestries and samplers on display from the Goodhart Collection; the stone and stained glass screen in the great hall, and Lord Curzon's bath, an Edwardian addition concealed in a bedroom cupboard. The house stands within a magnificent landscaped park that incorporates a walled formal garden, a fig walk, an orangery and a cedar lawn formally known as Pig's Wheaties's Orchard.

Some 500 years before Montacute House was built, a controversial castle was erected on

Montacute House

Montacute, Somerset TA15 6XP
Tel: 01935 823289
e-mail: montacute@nationaltrust.org.uk
website: nationaltrust.org.uk

Built in the late 16th century for Sir Edward Phelips, **Montacute** glitters with many windows and is adorned with elegant chimneys, carved parapets and other Renaissance features, including contemporary plasterwork, chimney pieces and heraldic glass. The splendid staterooms are full of fine 17th and 18th century furniture and textiles. Tudor and Elizabethan portraits, from the National Portrait Gallery are displayed in the Long Gallery, the longest of its kind in England. The House is surrounded by formal gardens with mixed borders, old roses and interesting topiary. The wider estate consists of landscaped parkland.

🎭 stories and anecdotes   🦜 famous people   🎨 art and craft   🎣 entertainment and sport   🚶 walks

the nearby hill by Robert, Count of Mortain. The count's choice of site angered the Saxons as they believed the hill to be sacred because King Alfred had buried a fragment of Christ's cross here. In 1068, they rose up and attacked the castle in one of many unsuccessful revolts against the Norman occupation. Ironically, a subsequent Count of Mortain was found guilty of treason and forced into donating all his lands in the area to a Cluniac priory on the site now occupied by Montacute village. The castle has long since disappeared, as has the monastery, with the exception of its fine 16th-century gatehouse, now a private home, and a stone dovecote.

The village is also home to the **Montacute TV, Radio and Toy Museum** where a vast collection of vintage radios, wireless receivers and TV sets, from the 1920s through to the present day, is on display. It developed from the keepsakes hoarded by Dennis Greenham who had been in the electrical business since 1930. The huge collection of radio and TV memorabilia includes toys, books and games. There are also tearooms, gardens and a museum shop.

TINTINHULL
4 miles NW of Yeovil

🌱 Tintinhull Garden

A couple of miles to the east of Martock is another enchanting National Trust property, **Tintinhull Garden**, set in the grounds of an early 17th-century manor house. The house itself, which is not open to the public, overlooks an attractive triangular green that forms the nucleus of the sprawling village of Tintinhull. The garden was laid out between 1933 and 1961 in a series of distinctive areas, divided by walls and hedges, each with its own planting theme. There is a pool garden with a

delightful pond filled with lilies and irises, a kitchen garden and a sunken garden that is cleverly designed to give the impression it has many different levels.

Other interesting buildings in the village include a remodelled, part-medieval rectory, Tintinhull Court; the 17th-century Dower House; and St Margaret's parish church, a rare rectangular single-cell church.

STOKE SUB HAMDON
5 miles NW of Yeovil off the A303

🏛 Stoke sub Hamdon Priory   🌄 Ham Hill

The eastern part of this attractive village is dominated by a fine Norman church; the western area of the village contains the remains of a late medieval priory. **Stoke sub Hamdon Priory** (National Trust) was built in the 14th and 15th centuries and later converted into a house with a very impressive Great Hall.

South of the village rises the 400 feet-high **Ham Hill** (or Hamdon Hill), the source of the beautiful honey-coloured stone used in so many of the surrounding villages. This solitary limestone outcrop rises abruptly from the Somerset plain and provides breathtaking views of the surrounding countryside. A substantial hill fort, built here during the Iron Age, was subsequently overrun by the invading Romans. The new occupants built their own fortification to guard their major route, the Fosse Way, and its important intersection with the road between Dorchester and the Bristol Channel at nearby Ilchester.

It was the Romans who discovered that the hill's soft, even-grained limestone made a flexible and highly attractive building material and they used it in the construction of their villas and temples. Later, the Saxons and then the Normans came to share this high opinion

ASH HOUSE HOTEL

41 Main Street, Ash, Martock,
Somerset TA12 6PB
Tel: 01935 822036
e-mail: reception@ashhousehotel.co.uk
website: www.ashhousehotel.co.uk

Ash House Hotel provides top quality accommodation set in 1.5 acres of beautiful gardens. The Ham stone building dates back to the early 18th century and inside the hotel has been restored to its former glory. The Georgian building, which has a flagstone floor dating back 300 years, contains nine en-suite rooms, which are all full of character and charm.

The rooms are comfortable and the beds have Italian cotton sheets and fluffy towels. All of the beds have mattress toppers and the bathrooms are equipped with power showers. Most of the rooms boast spectacular views over the hotel's gardens, which are floodlit at night and each have a hospitality tray of local treats. Produce is sourced locally and lunches and dinners are available in the hotel's Orangery, with daily changing menus, which are imaginative and finely executed.

The owner of Ash House Hotel, Gordon Doodson, has 25 years of experience in the hospitality trade, and he and his staff offer a warm and friendly welcome to all guests. For those on business trips the hotel has meeting rooms, business facilities and wireless internet connection. Well behaved dogs are also welcome. Ring for details.

There are plenty of things to do in the area with clay pigeon shooting, fishing, golf and bird watching among the most popular. For those seeking a cultural experience, there are plenty of museums and galleries in the vicinity as well as cider tasting. Walkers, cyclists and horse riders will be in their element with plenty of nature trails to explore. Passing through Martock, is the 50 mile long Parrett Trail. And for shopaholics there are plenty of shopping outlets nearby.

The hotel is located close to the village of Martock which is a mile from the A303 London to Exeter road. Yeovil is six miles away and the hotel is also within easy reach of the Blackdown Hills, the Mendips, the Quantocks, Exmoor and the Dorset coast. There are plenty of historical sites in the area including Montacute House, Barrington Court, Muchelney Abbey, East Lambrook Manor and Cadbury Castle.

stories and anecdotes 🐦 famous people 🎨 art and craft 🏊 entertainment and sport 🚶 walks

of Hamstone. By the time quarrying reached its height in the 17th century, a sizeable settlement had grown up within the confines of the Iron Age fort though, today, only a solitary inn remains. A war memorial to 44 local men who died during World War One stands on the summit of Ham Hill. Now designated a country park, the combination of the view, the old earthwork ramparts and the maze of overgrown quarry workings make this an attractive place for recreation and picnics.

MARTOCK
6 miles NW of Yeovil on the B3165

🏛 Treasurer's House　　🏛 Pinnacle Monument

This attractive, small town is surrounded by rich arable land and the area has long been renowned for its prosperous land-owning farmers. Martock's long-established affluence is reflected in its impressive part 13th-century parish church. A former abbey church that once belonged to the monks of Mont St Michel in Normandy, the church boasts one of the finest tie-beam roofs in Somerset with almost every part of it covered in beautiful carvings.

The old part of Martock is blessed with an unusually large number of fine buildings. Amongst these can be found the **Treasurer's**

House (National Trust), a small medieval house of two storeys built in the late 13th century for the Treasurer of Wells Cathedral, who was also rector of Martock. Visitors can see the Great Hall, an interesting wall painting and the kitchen added to the building in the 15th century. Close by is the Old Court House, a parish building that served as the local grammar school for 200 years. To the west is a 17th-century Manor House, once the home of Edward Parker, who exposed the Gunpowder Plot after Guy Fawkes had warned him against attending Parliament on that fateful night.

Outside the Market House stands the **Pinnacle Monument**, an unusual structure with four sundials arranged in a square on top of its column, the whole finished with an attractive weather vane.

EAST LAMBROOK
8 miles NW of Yeovil off the A303

🌿 East Lambrook Manor Garden

Just west of this charming hamlet is **East Lambrook Manor Garden**, which was planted with endangered species by the writer and horticulturist, Margery Fish, who lived at the medieval Hamstone manor house from 1937 until her death in 1969. Her exuberant planting and deliberate lack of formality created an atmosphere of romantic tranquillity that is maintained to this day. Now Grade I listed, the garden is also the home of the National Collection of the cranesbill species of geranium.

The low-lying land to the north of East Lambrook is criss-crossed by a network of drainage ditches or rhines (pronounced reens) that eventually flow into the rivers Parrett, Isle and Yeo.

Market House, Martock

🏛 historic building　📷 museum and heritage　🏚 historic site　🌄 scenic attraction　🌿 flora and fauna

East Lambrook Manor Gardens

Originally cut in the early 19th century, the ditches are often lined with double rows of pollarded willows, a sight that has come to characterise this part of Somerset. Despite having to be cleared every few years, the rhines provide a valuable natural habitat for a wide variety of bird, animal and plant life.

MUCHELNEY

12 miles NW of Yeovil off the A372

🏛 Muchelney Abbey 🏛 Midelney Manor

🎨 Muchelney Pottery 🎨 John Leach Gallery

This village's name means the Great Island and it dates from the time when this settlement rose up above the surrounding marshland, long since drained to provide excellent arable farmland. Muchelney is also the location of an impressive part-ruined Benedictine monastery thought to have been founded by King Ine of Wessex in the 8th century. This claim was, in part, confirmed when, in the 1950s, an archaeological dig unearthed an 8th-century crypt. During medieval times **Muchelney Abbey** (English Heritage) grew to emulate its great rival at Glastonbury. After the Dissolution in 1539, the buildings, dating mainly from the 15th and 16th centuries, gradually fell into disrepair.

Much of its stone was removed to provide building material for the surrounding village. In spite of this, a substantial part of the original structure, including the south cloister and abbot's lodge, still stands.

Opposite the parish church, which its noted for is remarkable early 17th-century illuminations, stands the **Priest's House** (National Trust), a late-medieval hall house built by the abbey for the parish priest. Little has changed since the 17th century when the building was divided. The interesting features to see include the Gothic doorway, the beautiful tracery windows and a massive 15th-century stone fireplace. Although it is still a dwelling, the house is opened on a limited basis.

At the **Muchelney Pottery**, John Leach continues the tradition of his famous grandfather, the potter Bernard Leach. Muchelney kitchen pots are used daily in kitchens all over the world, but the pottery is still very much a small family business. The pots are all lovingly hand-thrown, using local clays, and wood-fired in the three-chambered kiln to the high stoneware temperature of 1320°C, which creates their distinctive 'toasted' finish. Next door to the pottery is the kitchenware shop and the **John Leach Gallery**, which provides a showcase for the display and sale of signed work by John Leach and other potters, with a changing selection of paintings, ceramics, sculpture, textiles and woodwork by leading west country artists.

Just to the west of the village, near Drayton, stands the privately-owned **Midelney Manor**, originally an island manor belonging to Muchelney Abbey. A handsome manor house with architectural features from

🎞 stories and anecdotes 🦜 famous people 🎨 art and craft 🅿 entertainment and sport 🚶 walks

the 16th, 17th and 18th centuries, this has been in the hands of the Trevilian family since the early 1500s. The estate incorporates a heronry, a series of delightful gardens, a unique 17th-century falcon's mews and woodland walks. Although the house is not normally open to the public, there are self-catering cottages available on the estate.

LANGPORT

12 miles NW of Yeovil on the A378

🏛 Langport Gap   🏠 Stembridge Tower Mill

🏛 Langport & River Parrett Visitor Centre

The old part of this former market town stands on a rise above an ancient ford across the River Parrett. A short distance downstream from this point, the river is joined by the Rivers Isle and Yeo. Defended by an earthwork rampart during Saxon times, by AD930 Langport was an important commercial centre that minted its own coins. The only surviving part of the town's defences is the East Gate incorporating a curious 'hanging' chapel that sits above the arch on an upper level. It is now a Masonic Lodge and rarely open to the public. The impressive tower of the church at nearby Huish Episcopi can be seen through the barrel-vaulted gateway.

During the 18th and 19th centuries, Langport flourished as a banking centre and the local independent bank, Stuckey's, became known for its impressive branches, many of which can still be seen in the surrounding towns and villages, although the bank has long since been taken over by NatWest. At the time of this amalgamation in 1909,

Stuckey's had more notes in circulation than any other bank in the country save for the Bank of England. Stuckey's original head office is now Langport's branch of NatWest.

Throughout recorded history, the **Langport Gap** has been the site of a number of important military encounters. Two of the most significant occurred more than 1000 years apart. In the 6th century, Geraint, King of the Dumnonii, was involved in a battle here, and in July 1645 the Parliamentarian victory at the Battle of Langport gave Cromwell's forces almost total control of the West Country during the English Civil War.

More about life, past and present, on the Somerset Levels and Moors can be discovered at the **Langport and River Parrett Visitor Centre** through its series of hands-on exhibits and displays. Cycles are available for hire along with suggested cycle routes.

Just to the east, at Huish Episcopi, stands one of the finest examples in the country of a late medieval Somerset tower. At its most impressive in high summer when it can be viewed through the surrounding greenery, this ornate structure is adorned with striking tracery, pinnacles and carvings. The church

Floods on the Somerset Levels

🏠 historic building 🏛 museum and heritage 🏛 historic site 🍂 scenic attraction 🍃 flora and fauna

also has an elaborate Norman doorway, which still shows signs of the fire that destroyed much of the earlier building in the 13th century. A window in the south chapel was designed by Edward Burne-Jones, the 19th-century Pre-Raphaelite.

The church at Aller, just northwest of Langport, was the scene of another historic event. It was here, in AD878, that King Alfred converted Guthrum the Dane and his followers to Christianity following a battle on Salisbury Plain. The low wooded rise to the east of Aller is criss-crossed by a network of ancient country lanes that pass through some pleasant hamlets and villages including High Ham, the home of the last thatched windmill in England. Dating from 1822 and overlooking the Somerset levels, **Stembridge Tower Mill** (National Trust) continued to operate until 1910.

SOMERTON
13 miles NW of Yeovil on the B3151

🏠 Church of St Michael   🎨 Courthouse Gallery

This small town gave the county its name, and for 100 years between 1250 and 1350 was also its administrative centre. The prosperity this brought to the town is reflected in the fine **Church of St Michael**, which was later enhanced even further by the installation of a magnificent roof. Carved around 1500 by monks from Muchelney Abbey, the gloriously coffered structure is supported by tie beams on which rest pairs of Wessex wyverns, or dragons. These gradually increase in size as they near the altar, culminating in two ferocious monsters snarling across the aisle at each other.

Somerton today is a place of handsome old stone houses, shops and inns. The general

📖 stories and anecdotes   🐦 famous people   🎨 art and craft   🎭 entertainment and sport   🚶 walks

atmosphere of mature prosperity is heightened by the presence of a number of striking ancient buildings, most notably the 17th-century Hext Almshouses. Broad Street leads into the picturesque market place with its distinctive octagonal covered Market Cross and Town Hall. Between 1278 and 1371, Somerton was the location of the county gaol and the meeting place of the shire courts, as well as continuing to develop as a market town, reflected in the delightfully down-to-earth names of some of its streets such as Cow Square and Pig Street (now Broad Street).

The **Courthouse Gallery** in the Market Place provides a showcase for work by members of the Somerset Guild of Craftsmen. At any one time, as many as sixty members may be exhibiting here with artefacts ranging from pottery and ceramics, glass, metalwork and wood, through to furniture and textiles.

Castle Cary

🏛 Round House   📸 Castle Cary District Museum
🏛 War Memorial   ✒ John Boyd Textiles

This lovely little town, surrounded by meadows and woods, has an atmosphere of mature rural calm as well as some interesting old buildings, many of them built in the local hamstone that radiates a golden glow. There is a strikingly handsome 18th-century post office, a tiny 'pepper pot' lock-up gaol called the **Round House** dating from 1779, and a splendid Market House with a magnificent 17th-century colonnade. Largely constructed

---

THE COACH HOUSE

Alford, Castle Cary, Somerset BA7 7PN
Tel: 01963 240315
e-mail: liz@alfordcoachhouse.co.uk
website: www.alfordcoachhouse.co.uk

Liz Thring offers B&B and self catering accommodation at **The Coach House** in the village of Alford 2 miles west of **Castle Cary** on the B3153. The Coach House was converted recently into a comfortable and elegantly furnished family home with three guest bedrooms, two en suite and one with adjacent private bathroom. The self catering annex has one twin and one double bedroom, and can sleep up to six with z beds, and with access to a large garden. The Coach House is set in farmland and woodland with the river Brue running through the grounds. It is a lovely place to unwind and relax for a walking holiday and a perfect base for discovering the many scenic and historic attractions of the region.

HOLLY LANE

No.1 High Street, Castle Cary, Somerset BA7 7AN
Telephone: 01963 351259
Website: www.hollylane.co.uk

In Autumn 2008 **Holly Lane** opened their first shop here in Castle Cary – independent, stylish, full of delicious shoes, clothing and accessories. With a long list of well-known brands (including Out of Xile, Sandwich, Think & Manas), a great choice of shoes and clothes, and many happy customers, the shop is a real success. The guiding principle is simple – *offer original and exciting product, and give superb service...*

🏛 historic building   📸 museum and heritage   🏛 historic site   ⌘ scenic attraction   🌿 flora and fauna

in 1855, the Market House is now the home of the volunteer-run **Castle Cary District Museum**. Perhaps the most interesting site here is the town's **War Memorial**, which stands in the middle of a pond said to be part of the old castle moat. It was used for many years as a drive-through bath for muddy horses and carts, for washing horsehair, and as a convenient place for ducking scolds and witches.

Just to the west of the town at Higher Flax Mills is an interesting survival from earlier days. **John Boyd Textiles** have been weavers of horsehair fabric since 1837 and are still using looms that were first installed in 1870. Horsehair was especially popular in Victorian times because of its durability and for being easy to clean. Furniture designers such as Chippendale, Hepplewhite, Lutyens and Charles Rennie Mackintosh all used horsehair

fabrics, which were also used for Empire and Biedermeier furniture. Guided tours of the mill are available by arrangement.

Around Castle Cary

BRUTON
4 miles NE of Castle Cary on the A359

🏠 Sexey's Hospital 🏠 Patwell Pump

🏠 The Dovecote

This remarkably well-preserved former clothing and ecclesiastical centre, clinging to a hillside above the River Brue, is more like a small town than a village. In the middle of the High Street is the 17th-century **Sexey's Hospital**, with a beautiful quadrangle providing a stunning view across the Brue valley. It has a small, candle-lit chapel with dark Jacobean oak pews and pulpit. The

---

OATES AND MUSSON FINE FOODS

Fore Street, Castle Cary, Somerset BA7 7BG
Tel: 01963 359023
e-mail: katie@oatesandmusson.com
website: www.oatesandmusson.co.uk

Katie Lee-Pawsey opened her outstanding deli and grocery shop, **Oates and Musson Fine Foods**, in August 2009. The following April she won the award for 'Best Independent Food Shop in Somerset'. The shop had already won the "Best Independent Food Retailer" award from Taste of Somerset. "Our mission" says Katie, "is to provide locals and visitors alike with high quality, reasonably priced, sustainably sourced goods, and aim for 70% of all goods to be supplied within 50 miles of our doorstep". Her shop specialises in delicious local fayre, anything from scrumptious cakes to divine cheeses, ciders and ales, superb cold meats to yummy freshly prepared salads. Also on offer are organic, Fair Trade and sustainable produce, refillable cleaning products and Eco-friendly baby wares

Oates and Musson also offer a catering service, specialising in canapé parties, dinner parties and picnics for between 2 and 150 people. Everything you could possibly need for a romantic picnic for two, a family day out or to mark a special occasion. And if you are looking for an ideal present for someone who really appreciates fine foods and wine, why not check out the fine and bespoke hampers available?

🎬 stories and anecdotes 🐦 famous people 🎨 art and craft 🎭 entertainment and sport 🚶 walks

hospital was founded by Hugh Sexey, a courtier of Elizabeth I and James I. It still accommodates the elderly and also has a school that is one of the few state boarding schools in England.

A priory was first established at Bruton in the 11th century, and although much of this has disappeared, the former priory church is now the parish church. The Church of St Mary has a rare second tower built over the north porch in the late 1300s. The light and spacious interior contains a number of memorials to the Berkeley family, the local lords of the manor who also owned the land on which London's Berkeley Square now stands.

Across the river from the church is the **Patwell Pump**, a curious square structure that was the parish's communal water pump and remained in use until well into the 20th century. Further downstream a 15th-century packhorse bridge still serves pedestrians. However, **The Dovecote** is arguably Bruton's most distinctive building. Now roofless, it can be seen on the crest of a hill to the south of the bridge. Built in the 15th century, the dovecote is thought to have doubled as a watchtower.

WINCANTON
5 miles SE of Castle Cary off the A303

🏖 Wincanton Racecourse   ⚲ Discworld Emporium

Wincanton's broad main street is flanked by substantial houses and former coaching inns, a faint echo of the era when as many as 17 coaches a day would stop here, pausing about halfway between London and the long-established naval base at Plymouth. At that time, the inns could provide lodging for scores of travellers and stabling for more than 250 horses. A former cloth-making centre, the oldest part of this attractive town stands on a draughty hillside above the River Cale. An impressive number of fine Georgian buildings, some of which were constructed to replace earlier buildings destroyed in a fire in 1747, can be found here.

Modern day Wincanton is a peaceful light industrial town whose best known attraction, **Wincanton National Hunt Racecourse**, harks back to the days when horses were the only form of transport. Horse-racing began in the area in the 18th century and the racecourse moved to its present site to the north of the town centre in 1927. Wincanton is remembered as the course where the great *Desert Orchid* had his first race of each season during his dominance of steeple-chasing in the 1980s. For golf enthusiasts, the racecourse incorporates a challenging nine-hole pay and play course, which is open throughout the year.

Wincanton also has the distinction of being home to the only shop in the known universe devoted to artefacts inspired by the writings of Terry Pratchett, author of the *Discworld* novels, which have sold more than 40 million copies worldwide. At **The Cunning Artificer's Discworld Emporium** devotees will find all manner of wonderful objects ranging from the Mystic Prawn Medallion to the Dibbler Pie – "A culinary delight that will act as not just a superb paperweight, but also an appetite depressant".

TEMPLECOMBE
8 miles SE of Castle Cary on the A357

🏖 Gartell Light Railway

🏛 Templecombe Railway Museum

To the east of the village is the unusual **Gartell Light Railway**, a rare two-foot gauge line that runs for around a mile through the beautiful countryside of Blackmore Vale on

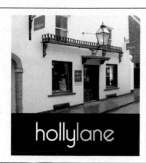

the track bed of the Somerset and Dorset
Railway, closed more than 30 years ago. The
trains run every 15 minutes from Common
Line Station, which also has a visitor centre,
refreshment room and shop. The nearby
Templecombe Railway Museum houses a
fascinating collection of artefacts,
photographs and models that tell the story of
the nearby station, once a busy junction where
some 130 railwaymen worked.

Wells

- 🏛 Cathedral of St Andrew
- 🔭 Astronomical Clock
- 🏛 Bishop's Palace
- 🏛 Penniless Porch
- 🏛 Wells & Mendip Museum

This ancient ecclesiastical centre derives its
name from a line of springs that rise up
from the base of the Mendips and deliver
water at the rate of some 40 gallons per
second. The first church here is believed to
have been founded by King Ine in around
AD700; the present **Cathedral of St
Andrew** was begun in the 12th century.
Taking more than three centuries to
complete, this magnificent building
demonstrates the three main styles of
Gothic architecture. Its 13th-century west
front, with more than 170 statues of saints,
angels and prophets gazing down on the

cathedral close, is generally acknowledged to
be its crowning glory. There used to be twice
as many statues, all painted in glowing colours.
Following the Civil War, Puritan fanatics
mutilated or destroyed as many as they could
and 700 years of exposure to the Somerset
weather has scoured away the colours. A few,
including the central figure of Christ in His
Glory, have been replaced with faithful copies.

Inside the cathedral there are many superb
features including the beautiful and unique
scissor arches and the great 14th-century
stained glass window over the high altar.
However, the cathedral's most impressive
artefact is its 14th-century **Astronomical
Clock**, one of the oldest working timepieces
in the world. It displays the minutes, hours
and phases of the moon on separate inner and

Bishop's Palace

stories and anecdotes   famous people   art and craft   entertainment and sport   walks

outer dials and marks the quarter hours with a lively battle between knights.

The west front of the cathedral has an internal passage with pierced apertures and there is a theory that choirboys might have sung through these openings to give the illusion to those gathered on the cathedral green that the then lifelike painted statues were singing.

To the south of the cathedral's cloisters is the **Bishop's Palace**, a remarkable fortified medieval building, which has been the home of the bishops of Bath and Wells since 1206. The palace is enclosed by a high wall and surrounded by a moat fed by the springs that give the city its name. A pair of mute swans on the moat can often be seen at the Gatehouse, ringing a bell for food. Swans were trained to do this in the 19th century and the present pair continue the tradition, passing it on to their young.

In order to gain access to the palace from the Market Place, visitors must pass under a 13th-century stone arch known as the Bishop's Eye and then cross a drawbridge that was last raised for defensive purposes in 1831. Although it is still an official residence of the Bishop of Bath and Wells, visitors can tour the palace's chapel, the 13th-century Great Hall and the beautiful gardens where many of the fine trees were planted in 1821. On the northern side of the cathedral green is the Vicar's Close, completed in 1363. This picturesque cobbled thoroughfare was built to house the cathedral choristers.

The cathedral green is surrounded by a high wall breached at only three castellated entrance points. One of these, the gateway into the Market Place, is known as **Penniless Porch**. It was here that the bishop allowed the city's poor to beg for money from those entering

the cathedral close. Set in the pavement here is a length of brass that extends over the prodigious distance leapt by local girl Mary Rand when she set a world record for the long jump at the Tokyo Olympic Games.

There is, of course, much more to Wells than its ecclesiastical buildings and heritage. The **Wells and Mendip Museum**, found near the west front of the cathedral, explains much of the history of the city and surrounding area through a collection of interesting locally found artefacts. Amongst these are some Roman coins and lead ingots, geological remains some 180 million years old when the Mendip Hills were a tropical paradise, and the remains of the 'Witch' of Wookey Hole.

The city also remains a lively market centre, with a street market held every Wednesday and Saturday. For a grand view of Wells from a distance, follow the attractive footpath that starts from the Moat Walk and leads up the summit of Tor Hill.

Around Wells

STRATTON-ON-THE-FOSSE
9 miles NE of Wells on the A367

🏛 Downside Abbey

This former coal mining village is home to the famous Roman Catholic boys' public school, **Downside Abbey**, which occupies the site of a monastery founded in 1814 by a group of English Benedictines. The steady expansion of the school during the 20th century encouraged the monks to move to a new site on higher ground near the existing abbey church, an impressive building that took over 70 years to complete and numbered among its architects Sir Giles Gilbert Scott.

🏛 historic building 🏛 museum and heritage 🏛 historic site 🐾 scenic attraction 🌱 flora and fauna

Midsomer Norton High Street

MIDSOMER NORTON
10 miles NE of Wells on the B3355

Radstock, Midsomer North & District Museum

The history of the area around this town is one of mining, with coal being hewn from nearby Norton Hill until as recently as the 1970s. In the churchyard of the town's parish church is a memorial to the 12 miners who were killed in an accident at Wellsway coal works in 1839. The surrounding countryside is beautiful and the sights and sounds of collieries have long since been replaced with that of open farmland. Midsomer Norton itself is a pleasant mix of old and new. There are excellent shopping facilities along with attractive Georgian buildings and a late medieval tithe barn.

At the interesting **Radstock, Midsomer North and District Museum**, housed in a converted 18th-century barn, more information can be sought about the Somerset coalfield as the museum is devoted to the people of the local coal mines, along with other exhibits relating to the railways, farms and schools of the area.

CAMELEY
10 miles NE of Wells off the A37

St James's Church

This attractive village is home to a church referred to by John Betjeman as "Rip Van Winkle's Church". When the village of Cameley was moved to nearby Temple Cloud in the 1700s, **St James's Church** was left alone on its low hill. Its old box pews are still in place and seem to have been custom-made for their owners. Those who couldn't afford their own box could worship from the gallery along the south wall, which bears the legend "for the free use of the inhabitants, 1819". A row of hat pegs was also conveniently provided. In the 1960s, a remarkable series of medieval wall paintings was discovered here, under layers of whitewash. The murals are believed to have been painted between the 11th and the 17th centuries and feature such diverse images as the foot of a giant St Christopher stepping through a fish and crab infested river, a charming 14th-century jester complete with harlequin costume, and a rare coat of arms of Charles I.

MELLS
13 miles NE of Wells off the A362

John Horner

Mells was at one time on the easternmost limit of the lands belonging to Glastonbury Abbey. In the 15th century, the Abbot of Glastonbury drew up plans to rebuild the village in the shape of a St Anthony's cross, with four arms of equal length. However, only one street, New Street, was ever completed. This architectural gem can still be seen to the south of St Andrew's parish church. While the exterior of the church is certainly imposing, the main interest lies inside where there is a remarkable collection of monuments designed by masters such as Lutyens, Gill, Munnings and Burne-Jones. One of the memorials is to Raymond, the eldest son of Herbert Asquith, the Liberal Prime Minister. Raymond was killed in the First World War. Raymond's sister was Violet Bonham Carter, whose grave is in the churchyard. Another memorial in the churchyard honours the pacifist and poet Siegfried Sassoon.

According to legend, the Abbot of Glastonbury, in an attempt to stave off Henry VIII's Dissolution of the Monasteries, dispatched his steward, **John Horner**, to London with a gift for the king consisting of a pie into which was baked the title deeds of 12 ecclesiastical manor houses. However, rather than attempting to persuade the king, Horner returned to Somerset the rightful owner of three of the manors himself. He paid a total of £2000 for Mells, Nunnery and Leigh-upon-Mendip. This blatant act of disloyalty is, supposedly, commemorated in the nursery rhyme *Little Jack Horner* that describes how Jack "put in his thumb and pulled out a plum". The manor house at Mells remained in the hands of the Horner family until the early 20th century, when it passed to the Asquith family by marriage.

LULLINGTON
19 miles NE of Wells off the B3090

🏭 Orchardleigh Park

A footpath leads southwards from this peaceful riverside village to **Orchardleigh Park**, an imposing Victorian mansion built in the mid 1800s and now a popular venue for civil weddings and conferences. In the 550 acres of parkland surrounding the house is a lake with an island on which is a small church whose graveyard contains the grave of Sir Henry Newbolt, the author of *Drake's Drum*.

SHEPTON MALLET
6 miles E of Wells on the A371

🏭 Church of St Peter & St Paul   🏭 Market Cross

🏭 The Shambles   🪶 Mid-Somerset Show

🪶 Royal Bath & Wells Show   🌾 Pilton Manor

🏭 Tithe Barn

Situated on the banks of the River Sheppey, just to the west of Fosse Way, this old market town has been an important centre of communications since before the time of the Romans. The settlement's name is Saxon and it means, quite simply, sheep town. This reveals its main commercial activity from before the Norman Conquest to the Middle Ages, when Shepton Mallet was, firstly, a centre of woollen production and then weaving. The industry reached its peak in the 15th century. It was around this time that the town's most striking building, its magnificent parish **Church of St Peter & St Paul** was constructed. It is notable for its superb wagon roof with 350 small painted panels and for its pulpit carved from a single block of stone.

🏭 historic building   🏛 museum and heritage   🏚 historic site   🌿 scenic attraction   🌾 flora and fauna

Other reminders of Shepton Mallet's past can be seen around its market place where there is a 50-foot **Market Cross**, dating from around 1500 and restored in Victorian times. There is also **The Shambles**, a 15th-century wooden shed where meat was traded. After the Duke of Monmouth's ill-fated Pitchfork Rebellion, several of his followers were executed at the Market Cross in 1685 on the orders of the infamous Judge Jeffreys. Although it is a relatively nondescript building, Shepton Mallet's old prison, built in 1610, was thought to be so well away from the threat of enemy bombing that it was here that the Domesday Book was hidden during World War Two. It was also used during that period by the US forces as a military prison.

Today, Shepton Mallet is a prosperous light industrial town that has a good selection of shopping and leisure activities. Each year the town plays host to two agricultural shows. The **Royal Bath and West Show**, which has a permanent showground to the southeast of the town takes place in late May/early June, followed in August by the **Mid-Somerset Show**.

To the southwest of the town stands a former residence of the abbots of Glastonbury, **Pilton Manor**, whose grounds have been planted with vines, mostly of the German Riesling variety. Visitors are encouraged to stroll around the estate and also take the opportunity of sampling the vineyard's end product. Another legacy of Glastonbury Abbey can be found at Pilton village where there is a great cruciform Tithe Barn that stands on a hill surrounded by beech and chestnut trees. Unfortunately, the barn lost its arch-braced roof when it was struck by lightning in 1963, but has since been restored.

At Croscombe, to the west of Shepton Mallet, is another fine 15th-century **Tithe Barn**, a reminder of the days when the local tenant farmers paid a proportion of their crops each year to their ecclesiastical landlords.

NUNNEY
12 miles E of Wells off the A361

🏠 Castle

This picturesque old market town is dominated by its dramatic moated **Castle**, begun in 1373 by Sir John de la Mare on his return from the French wars. Thought to have been modelled on the Bastille, the fortress consists of four solidly built towers that stand on an island formed by a stream on one side and a broad water-filled moat on the other. The castle came under attack from Parliamentarian forces during the English Civil War and, despite having a garrison of only one officer, eight men and a handful of civilian refugees, held out for two days. However, the bombardment damaged the building beyond repair and it had to be abandoned, leaving the romantic ruins that can still be seen today. One of the 30-pound cannonballs that were used by Cromwell's forces can be seen in the village's 13th-century church.

Nunney Castle

JENNY BARTON CERAMICS
AT THE ENIGMA POTTERY STUDIO

Enigma Pottery Studio, Vicarage Street,
Frome, Somerset BA11 1PX
Tel: 01373 452079
e-mail: jbarton@enigmapottery.co.uk
website: www.enigmapottery.co.uk

Jenny Barton's Ceramics can be found in the gallery shop of Enigma Pottery Studio. In the showroom on Vicarage Street visitors can browse and choose from the wide range of exquisite pieces created by Jenny in her studio in the walled garden behind the showroom. Random Ware is a full range of tableware for the discerning diner, in a choice of five textured designs. The plates and bowls, the mugs and jugs, the cups and saucers, the pots and cake stands are colour washed to suit the ambience of the customer's home and are high-fired to stoneware to make them dishwasher safe.

Romantic Mood Ware is a range of soap dishes, mugs, bowls, candle accessories and jewellery made from earthenware clay and finished in a smooth glaze with touches of colour to suit the mood. Bespoke Garden Ceramics are sculptures, plant pots and bird baths made to order, each piece hand-made and finished in stoneware ceramic for frost resistance. The range includes garden fairies (boys and girls) which can be dressed in the customer's chosen outfit. Jenny also organises adult and after-school pottery classes and pottery-making parties – please phone for details.

CREAM LUXURY KNITWEAR

33 Catherine Hill, Frome,
Somerset BA11 1BY
Tel: 01373 453311
e-mail: avril@luxuryknitwear.co.uk
website: www.luxuryknitwear.co.uk

Avril Mann, founder of **Cream Luxury Knitwear**, has long been passionate about knitwear and her designs are comfortable, easy to wear, suitable for all shapes and sizes, smart or casual, and equally suitable for town or country wear. She loves colour, and her collections move away from the drab monotone to vivid mix and match brights, giving her clothes a fresh, contemporary look and feel. Her luxury knitwear has graced the windows of top boutiques around the world, from New York and Beverley hills to Paris and London.

Originally based in London, Avril now lives, designs and makes everything here in Somerset with her team of expert knitters. Cream Luxury Knitwear offers a bespoke service, ensuring that every design in the shop can be ordered in the exact size and colour to suit each individual customer. This lovely boutique is open from 10 to 5 Tuesday to Saturday, and shoppers who can't get to Frome can order by phone.

🏠 historic building   🏛 museum and heritage   🏚 historic site   🐟 scenic attraction   🌱 flora and fauna

FROME

17 miles E of Wells off the A361

🏛 Blue House 🏛 Longleat House

The fourth largest settlement in Somerset, Frome is an attractive town built on steep hills with cobbled streets and boasting more listed buildings than anywhere else in Somerset.

The town developed beside the river from which it takes its name, its first recorded building being a mission station founded in AD685 by St Aldhelm, the Abbot of Malmesbury. Such was the expansion around St Aldhelm's stone Church of St John that, by the time of the Domesday Book, the settlement had a market, which suggests that it was already a place of some importance. General markets still take place every Wednesday and Saturday.

Frome continued to prosper during the Middle Ages on the back of its cloth industry until competition from the woollen towns of the north in the 19th century saw the industry begin to decline. The trade in Frome died out completely in the 1960s. Since then other industries, printing in particular, have flourished and the population has doubled to more than 20,000.

Fortunately, this new growth has not spoilt the charm of the town's old centre. Best explored on foot, the town's old quarter is an attractive conservation area where, amidst the interesting shops, cafés and restaurants, can be found the **Blue House**. Built in 1726 as an almshouse and a boy's school, it is one of the town's numerous listed buildings. Another is the fine bridge across the River Frome, a contemporary of Bath's Pulteney Bridge dating from 1667, and unusual in having buildings along its length.

A popular excursion from Frome is to **Longleat House**, about five miles to the south and just across the county border in Wiltshire. The magnificent home of the Marquess of Bath was built by his ancestor, Sir John Thynne, in a largely symmetrical style in the 1570s. The interior is a treasure house of Old Masters, Flemish tapestries, exquisite furniture, rare books and the present Lord Bath's racy murals. The superb grounds were landscaped by Capability Brown and now contain one of the country's best known venues for a marvellous day out. In the famous Safari Park the Lions of Longleat, first introduced in 1966, have been followed by a veritable Noah's Ark of exotic creatures, including rhinos, zebras and white tigers. The park also offers safari boat rides, a narrow-gauge railway, a children's amusement area, a garden centre, and the largest hedge maze in the world.

FROME WHOLEFOODS

Cheap Street, Frome, Somerset BA11 1BN
Tel: 01373 473334

Located in picturesque Cheap Street, noted for its speciality shops, **Frome Wholefoods**, established by Sheila Gore in 1997, offers an extensive choice of organic and natural whole foods. It also stocks a huge range of dried herbs and spices, organic beers and wines, Fairtrade products, and a selection of herbal medicines and cosmetics. Freshly delivered each day, you'll also find tasty bread made from local flour.

🎬 stories and anecdotes 🦜 famous people 🎨 art and craft ☕ entertainment and sport 🚶 walks

BALTONSBOROUGH
9 miles S of Wells off the A37

🐦 St Dunstan

Baltonsborough was one of the 12 manors owned by Glastonbury Abbey, which lies just to the northwest. In those days, the lives of the people of the village were completely governed by the monks. The permission of the abbey had to be sought before a daughter could be married, while on a man's death his chattels and beasts became the property of the abbey. **St Dunstan** is said to have been born here between AD909 and AD925 - the ancient flour mill in the village is thought to have been owned by Dunstan's father. Before entering Glastonbury Abbey, Dunstan found favour at the court of King Athelstan but, once he had given up his worldly possessions, Dunstan followed an austere regime. By setting himself apart from the abbey's other novices, Dunstan soon rose through the ranks of the religious house to become abbot, whereupon he enforced the strict Benedictine code. The wealth of Glastonbury grew under Dunstan and he also encouraged pilgrims to make their way here to see the holy relics. As well as being a great cleric and an entrepreneur, Dunstan was also an engineer. He was one of the first people to instigate the draining of the land in this area. From Glastonbury, Dunstan moved to Canterbury, where he was Archbishop until his death.

GLASTONBURY
6 miles SW of Wells on the A39

🏛 Glastonbury Abbey   🏚 Lake Village
🏛 George & Pilgrim Hotel   🏛 Rural Life Museum
🐊 Glastonbury Tor   🌿 Glastonbury Festival
🐦 King Arthur

Today, this ancient town of myths and legends, of tales of King Arthur and the early Christians, is an attractive market town still dominated by the ruins of its abbey. The dramatic remains of **Glastonbury Abbey** (see panel opposite) lie in the heart of the old town and, if the story of Joseph of Arimathea is to be believed, this is the site of the earliest Christian foundation in the British Isles. By the Middle Ages, Glastonbury was second only to Rome as a place of Christian pilgrimage.

Joseph of Arimathea, the wealthy Jerusalem merchant who had provided a tomb for the crucified Jesus, is said to have arrived at Glastonbury in around AD60. According to legend, while he was walking on the tor, Joseph drove his staff into the ground whereupon it took root and burst into leaf. Taking this as a sign that he should build a church, Joseph erected a simple church on the site now taken by the abbey. His staff is reputed to have grown into the celebrated Christmas-flowering Glastonbury hawthorn.

Today, the picturesque abbey ruins, with their associations with the legend of **King Arthur**, remain a great tourist attraction. It was Henry III who "caused search to be made for King Arthur's tomb" at Glastonbury. His workmen found it with suspiciously little difficulty. After digging down some seven feet, they unearthed a huge stone slab bearing a cross of lead. No body, however. So they continued digging another nine feet and then "found the bones of the great prince". This fortuitous find brought a further influx of sightseers to the town.

During the Middle Ages, Glastonbury Abbey was also an internationally renowned centre of learning, and scholars and pilgrims from all over Christendom made their way here. One of the guest houses built to

Glastonbury Abbey

Glastonbury, Somerset BA6 9EL
Tel: 01458 832267 Fax:: 01458 832267
e-mail: glastonbury.abbey@dial.pipex.com
website: www.glastonburyabbey.com

Set in the middle of the old market town, **Glastonbury Abbey** has been an influence on the lives of those who have lived in this part of the world for the past 1,950 years and there are many people who believe that the 'Somerset Tradition' makes the association even longer than that. It is said that it was here that the followers of Jesus landed shortly after His death and set up the first Christian settlement with its own church in Britain, whilst some traditions go further and suggest that Christ Himself came to Glastonbury as a boy on one of the boats of his great uncle, Joseph of Arimathea. The legends around Glastonbury would certainly indicate that it was Joseph of Arimathea, and not St Augustine centuries later, who started the Christian conversion of Great Britain in the 1st century.

What, however, can be said with more certainty is that Glastonbury Abbey was a major Christian sanctuary during the 5th and 6th centuries and, by the time of the Norman Conquest, it was considered to be the wealthiest and grandest abbey in the country. Such was its status within England during the Dark Ages that it would have been logical that the great Celtic monarch, King Arthur, should be buried here after his long struggle against the Saxons.

Following the Dissolution in the 16th century, the abbey fell into ruins and, along with it, King Arthur's tomb was destroyed. Nevertheless, a number of impressive remains have survived and these include **St Mary's Chapel**, the shell of the great church, and the 14th century **Abbot's Kitchen**. However, people coming here today come for three main reasons: to see where the first church might have existed; to see where King Arthur and Queen Guinevere might have been buried; and to enjoy the beautiful and peaceful parkland that surrounds the ruins.

The abbey is a private organisation run by trustees and, although a small concern, the abbey remains open throughout the year. Along with the ruins and the parkland, there is an award winning museum and a small abbey shop and visitors may also come across Brother Thomas Cleeve, the Guestmaster of 1538.

accommodate them is now the **George and Pilgrim Hotel**. Originally constructed in 1475, this striking building has old timber beams adorned with carved angels and an interior guarded by a series of curious monks' death masks. Close by is another 15th-century building, the handsome Tribunal that is home to the town's Tourist Information Centre.

Even the town's **Rural Life Museum**, which explores the life of farmers in this area during the 19th and early 20th centuries, cannot escape from the influence of the abbey. Although the museum itself is housed in a Victorian farmhouse, there is an impressive 14th-century barn here that once belonged to Glastonbury Abbey.

To the east of the town, **Glastonbury Tor** is a dramatic hill that rises high above the surrounding Somerset Levels. The 520-feet tor has been inhabited since prehistoric times and excavations on the site have revealed evidence of Celtic, Roman and pre-Saxon occupation. Because of its unusually regular conical shape the hill has long been associated with myth and legends. In its time, it has been identified as the Land of the Dead, the Celtic Otherworld, a Druid's temple, a magic mountain, an Arthurian hill fort, a ley line intersection and a rendezvous point for passing UFOs. Along with its mystical energy, the tor also offers magnificent panoramic views across Somerset to Wells, the Mendips, the Quantocks and the Bristol Channel. The striking tower at the summit is all that remains of the 15th-century Church of St Michael, an offshoot of Glastonbury Abbey. Between the tor and the town lies the wooded rise of Chalice Hill, where, it is said, Joseph buried the Holy Grail, the chalice used at the Last Supper.

In recent years, a new band of pilgrims has been making their way to Glastonbury every June. The first **Glastonbury Festival** took place in 1970 and 1500 people came; that figure has now multiplied by 100. Pop idols who have played here include Johnny Cash, David Bowie, Van Morrison, Led Zeppelin and many more. The event is now the largest open air festival in Europe.

To the northwest of the town is the site of a prehistoric **Lake Village** discovered in 1892 when it was noticed that the otherwise level fields were studded with irregular mounds. Thought to date from around 150BC, the dwellings were built on a series of tall platforms that raised them above the surrounding marshland.

STREET
7 miles SW of Wells on the A39

🏛 Friends' Meeting House   📷 Shoe Museum

The oldest part of this now sprawling town lies around the 14th-century parish Church of the Holy Trinity, although most of the town itself dates from the 19th century when Street began to expand from a small rural village into the light industrial town it is today. Much of this growth was due to one family, the Clarks. In the 1820s, the Quaker brothers, Cyrus and James Clark began to produce sheepskin slippers from the hides of local animals. Many of the town's older buildings owe their existence to the family. In particular, there is the **Friends' Meeting House** of 1850 and the building that housed the original Millfield School.

The oldest part of the Clark's factory has now been converted into a fascinating **Shoe Museum**. Although the company is one of the largest manufacturers of quality footwear in Europe, it continues to keep its headquarters in the town and also operates the Clarks Village Shopping Outlet where 90 leading brands offer discounts of up to 60% every day.

MEARE
6½ miles SW of Wells on the B3151

🏛 Abbot's Fish House

🌿 Shapwick Heath Nature Reserve

Just to the east of this attractive village is an unusual medieval building known as the **Abbot's Fish House**. Before 1700, this isolated building stood on the edge of Meare Pool, once a substantial lake that provided nearby Glastonbury Abbey with a regular supply of freshwater fish. Before the lake was drained, this early 14th-century building was used for storing fishing equipment and salting the catches.

To the southwest of Meare, in terrain scarred by years of peat extraction, is the **Shapwick Heath Nature Reserve**, which provides a safe haven for rare plants and wildlife. Parts of the neolithic 'Sweet Track', the oldest man-made routeway in Britain, still exist beneath the wet peat. This remarkable timber track was constructed around 3800BC to cross a mile or so of reed swamp. Many artefacts have been found beside the trackway including stone axes, pots containing hazelnuts, a child's toy tomahawk and a polished jadeite axe from the Alps.

WOOKEY
2 miles W of Wells off the A371

🏚 Burcott Mill

A rare and historic working watermill, **Burcott Mill** has its origins in pre-Domesday times. Visitors can see stone-ground flour being handmade and join a tour led by the miller himself. The site also has an adventure playground, country tearoom, pets and picnic area, a pottery. And B&B accommodation.

WEDMORE
7½ miles W of Wells on the B3139

🏚 Ashton Windmill

This remote village was the ancient capital of the Somerset marshes. King Alfred is said to have brought the newly baptised Danish King Guthrum to sign the Peace of Wedmore here in AD878. This treaty left Wessex in Alfred's hands but gave East Anglia, East Mercia and the Kingdom of York to the Danes. The village's main street, the Borough, is lined with fine stone buildings, including a lovely old coaching inn. The parish church's spectacular Norman south doorway is thought to have been carved by the craftsmen who built Wells Cathedral.

To the northwest of the village, near Chapel Allerton, is **Ashton Windmill**. It was built in the 1700s and has an unusual upturned boat-style roof. The site provides wonderful views over Cheddar Gorge and the Somerset levels.

WOOKEY HOLE
1½ miles NW of Wells off the A371

🪨 Great Cave 🪨 Ebbor Gorge

Throughout the centuries, the carboniferous limestone core of the Mendip Hills has been

---

PRIDDY GOOD FARM SHOP

Townsend Farm, Priddy, nr Wells, Somerset BA5 3BP
Tel: 01749 870171
website: www.priddygoodmeat.co.uk

Priddy Good Farm Shop is a family-run enterprise located on Townsend Farm, where the Simmons family have farmed for over 300 years. Will and Jo, who know many of their customers personally, supply high-quality produce that includes beef and lamb raised on their 400-acre farm, and locally sourced pork and poultry, all with full traceability and minimum food miles. Beside the cuts and joints they sell top-notch burgers, and their own prize-winning sausage rolls, pies and pastries. The shop also sells a wide variety of fresh fruit and vegetables, dairy produce, pickles and preserves and baked goods. Open from Monday - Saturday 8am to 5pm and Sunday 8am - 12.30pm. Plans for 2011 include opening a café-tea room.

🎦 stories and anecdotes 🐦 famous people 🎨 art and craft 🖋 entertainment and sport 🚶 walks

Ebbor Gorge

gradually dissolved away by the small amount of carbonic acid in rainwater. This erosion has created more than 25 caverns around Wookey Hole, of which only the largest half dozen or so are open to the public. The **Great Cave** contains a rock formation known as the Witch of Wookey that casts a ghostly shadow and is associated with gruesome legends of child-eating. During prehistoric times, lions, bears and woolly mammoths lived in the area. In a recess known as the Hyena's Den, a large cache of bones has been found, many of them showing signs of other animal's tooth marks. The river emerging from Wookey Hole, the River Axe, has been harnessed to provide power since the 15th century, and the present building here was originally constructed in the early 17th century as a paper mill.

Just to the northwest runs the dramatic **Ebbor Gorge**, now a National Nature Reserve managed by English Nature. There are two walks here, the shorter one suitable for wheelchairs accompanied by a strong pusher. The longer walk involves a certain amount of rock scrambling. However, the hard work is rewarded as there is a wealth of wildlife here, including badger and sparrow hawk in the woodland, lesser horseshoe bats in and around the caves and buzzards flying overhead.

CHEDDAR
8 miles NW of Wells on the A371

🍦 Cheddar Gorge   🍦 Pavey's Lookout Tower

🏛 Cheddar Man & Cannibal Museum

This sprawling village is best known for its dramatic limestone gorge, **Cheddar Gorge** (see panel opposite), which extends for some two miles and is one of the most famous and most often visited of Britain's natural attractions. It is characterised by its high vertical cliffs, from which there are outstanding views out over the Somerset Levels, the Quantock Hills and, on a clear day, across the Bristol Channel to South Wales. The National Trust owns most of the land around this magnificent ravine, which is a Site of Special Scientific Interest. Numerous rare plants grow here and it is also a haven for butterflies. A circular walk through the area takes in plantations, natural woodland and rough downland. This is a place that draws rock climbers, but the less ambitious may like to take the 274 steps of Jacob's Ladder that lead from the bottom of the gorge to the top of the cliffs. Here, **Pavey's Lookout Tower** offers yet more spectacular views of the surrounding area.

While the gorge is undoubtedly everyone's idea of Cheddar, the village is also renowned for its caves and, of course, its cheese. Although much embellished by modern tourist paraphernalia, its two main show caves, Gough's Cave – an underground 'cathedral' – and the brilliantly coloured Cox's

Cheddar Caves & Gorge

Cheddar, Somerset, BS27 3QF
Tel: 01934 742343
e-mail: caves@visitcheddar.co.uk
website: www.cheddarcaves.co.uk.

Cheddar Gorge, a place of wild and rugged beauty, is a karst limestone and calcareous grassland Nature Reserve and home to many rare plants and animals, including endangered Greater Horseshoe bats. Cheddar Caves, inhabited by our ancestors up to 40,000 years ago, were re-discovered by Messrs Gough & Cox, enterprising Victorian showmen, and are world famous for their spectacular stalactite and stalagmite decorations, whose beautiful colours are mirrored in pools of water. Easy-to-use audio-guides tell the story of the caves' formation and discovery. These caves also fired the imagination of JRR Tolkien, author of the trilogy "Lord of the Rings", on his honeymoon visit in 1916. "The Crystal Quest", the dark-walk fantasy adventure, creates a similar world of elven magic and bold adventure underground.

The Museum of Pre-history, "Cheddar Man & the Cannibals", explores 40,000 years of British Pre-history, with demonstrations of Stone Age survival skills and beautiful cave art. Here you can discover the truth about why our *Homo sapiens* ancestors, throughout the world for most of pre-history, were cannibals.

From April to September, an open-top double-decker bus takes you on a sight-seeing tour through Cheddar Gorge, beneath rocky pinnacles rising sheer above you, the home of Peregrine falcons. There are 274 steps to reach a Lookout Tower for stunning views of this limestone countryside, then a 3-mile cliff-top walk right around Britain's biggest Gorge, climbing 400ft above the road, through this internationally important Nature Reserve.

Cave, are both worth seeing for their sheer scale and spectacular calcite formations. In 1903 an almost complete skeleton, named Cheddar Man, was discovered in Gough's Cave and this can be seen in the **Cheddar Man & Cannibal Museum**, along with cannibalised human skulls and flint tools. There are demonstrations of Stone Age survival skills and some intriguing cave art.

The Cheddar Gorge Cheese Company is the only cheesemaker left in Cheddar itself. Visitors can watch the various stages as rich, local milk is turned into award-winning authentic Cheddar cheese. After seeing cheese being made you can treat yourself to a free taste at the taster bar and then visit the shop where the company's Cheddars are on sale together with local pickles, biscuits, hand-crafted cheese dishes, cheese knives and more.

Back in 1726, Daniel Defoe was already singing the praises of Cheddar's most famous product. "Without all dispute," he wrote, "Cheddar is the best cheese that England affords, if not that the whole world affords." Today, in south Somerset alone, some 50 tonnes of Cheddar cheese is produced each day by nine cheese-makers. The original unpasteurised handmade farmhouse Cheddar

---

📖 stories and anecdotes 🐦 famous people 💃 art and craft 🖋 entertainment and sport 🚶 walks

is still produced on just two farms: Montgomery's in North Cadbury, and Keen's near Wincanton. Their round half-hundredweight cheeses are wrapped in muslin, kept for more than a year and turned regularly as they mature. The result is Cheddar cheese at its most perfect.

Since the term Cheddar Cheese refers to a recipe and not a place, the cheese can be made anywhere in the world. Somerset itself is dotted with cheese manufacturers of various sizes and a number of these establishments supplement their income by offering guided tours, cheese demonstrations and catering facilities for the many visitors who come to gorge on the local speciality.

CHARTERHOUSE
9 miles NW of Wells off the B3134

🐾 Mendips   🐾 Black Down

Rising, in some places, to more than 1000 feet above sea level, the **Mendips** form a landscape that is like no other in the region. Although hard to imagine today, lead and silver were once mined from these picturesque uplands. The Mendip lead-mining activity was centred around the remote village of Charterhouse – the last mine in the district, at Priddy, closed in 1908.

Charterhouse takes its name from a Carthusian monastery, Witham Priory, which owned one of the four Mendip mining sectors, or liberties. This area has been known for its mineral deposits since the Iron Age and such was its importance that the Romans declared the mines here state property within just six years of their arrival in Britain. Under their influence, silver and lead ingots, or 'pigs', were exported to France and to Rome. The settlement grew into a sizable town with its own fort and amphitheatre, the remains of

which can still be seen today. Centuries later, improved technology allowed the original seams to be reworked and the area is now littered with abandoned mine buildings and smelting houses.

A footpath from Charterhouse church leads up onto **Black Down**, which is, at 1067 feet, the highest point in the Mendips. From here, to the northwest, the land descends down into Burrington Combe, a deep cleft said to have inspired the Rev Augustus Toplady to write the hymn *Rock of Ages*.

AXBRIDGE
10 miles NW of Wells off the A371

🏛 King John's Hunting Lodge   🎭 Frankie Howerd

A small town with a delightful centre, Axbridge is now a conservation area. In its ancient market square stands an exceptional example of a half-timbered merchant's house dating from around 1500. Three storeys high and known as **King John's Hunting Lodge** (National Trust), the building was extensively restored in the early 1970s and is now home to an excellent Local History Museum. Although the Lodge has nothing to do with King John or hunting, its name is a reminder that the Mendip hills were once a royal hunting ground. Elsewhere in the centre of Axbridge there are many handsome Georgian shops and town houses.

Back in 1960, the town was by-passed and to celebrate the liberation of the medieval square and narrow streets from traffic, the town organised a pageant re-enacting its fascinating history. This has since become a traditional event, celebrated every 10 years. The two-hour spectacular costume drama in which some 500 people take part will next take place over the August Bank Holiday, 2020.

About a mile west of Axbridge, near the village of Cross, is an unusual attraction. The late comedian **Frankie Howerd** lived in a cottage here for many years and, since he was a great hoarder, the cottage was full of hundreds of scripts, photographs and props, along with a pair of swords used in the film *Cleopatra* (a gift from Richard Burton and Elizabeth Taylor), two stone cats from Laurence Olivier, and a fossilised egg presented to Frankie by the Italian government after he starred in the film *Up Pompeii*.

In May 2008, the four-bedroom, pink cottage was put up for sale with an asking price of £800,000. The thousands of items of memorabilia, including Frankie's toupee, were available as optional extras for an additional £600,000. The property was acquired by the Frankie Howerd OBE Trust, but it is not clear whether it will re-open to the public.

Bristol

- 🏛 Castle Park   🏛 Bristol Cathedral
- 🏛 Floating Harbour   🏛 Clifton Suspension Bridge
- 🏛 Museum of Bristol   🖋 At Bristol
- 🐦 Blue Reef Aquarium
- 🖋 Isambard Kingdom Brunel   🖋 Theatre Royal
- 🏛 Maritime Heritage Centre   🏛 Redcliffe Caves
- 🏛 Church of St Mary Radcliffe   🏛 Goldney Grotto
- 🏛 John Wesley's Chapel
- 🏛 City Museum & Art Gallery   🏛 Cabot Tower
- 🐦 Avon Gorge Nature Reserve
- 🐦 Bristol Zoo Gardens

Bristol was Sir John Betjeman's favourite English city. It had, he said "the finest architectural heritage of any city outside London". Today it is also one of Britain's most vibrant and stimulating cities and offers a fascinating combination of grand buildings, reverberant history and contemporary creativity.

Situated at a strategically important bridging point at the head of the Avon gorge, Bristol was founded in Saxon times and soon became a major port and market centre. By the early 11th century, it had its own mint and was trading with other ports throughout western Europe, Wales and Ireland. The Normans quickly realised the importance of the port and, in 1067, began to build a massive stone keep. Although the castle was all but destroyed at the end of the English Civil War, the site of the fortification remains as **Castle Park**.

Situated just to the west of the castle site stands **Bristol Cathedral**, founded in around 1140 by Robert Fitzhardinge as the great church of an Augustinian abbey. While the abbey no longer exists, several original Norman features, such as the chapter house, gatehouse and the east side of the abbey cloisters, remain. Following the Dissolution in 1539, Henry VIII took the unusual step of elevating the abbey church to a cathedral and, soon after, the richly-carved choir stalls were added. However, the building was not fully completed until the 19th century, when a new nave was built. Among the cathedral's

Bristol Cathedral

🎞 stories and anecdotes   🐦 famous people   🖋 art and craft   🖋 entertainment and sport   🚶 walks

treasures is a pair of candlesticks donated in 1712 by the rescuers of Alexander Selkirk, the castaway on whom Daniel Defoe based his hero Robinson Crusoe.

During the Middle Ages, Bristol expanded as a trading centre and, at one time, it was second only to London as a seaport. Its trade was built on the export of raw wool and woollen cloth from the Mendip and Cotswold Hills, and the import of wines from Spain and southwest France. It was around this time that the city's first major wharf development took place when the River Frome was diverted from its original course into a wide artificial channel now known as St Augustine's Reach. A remarkable achievement for its day, the excavation created over 500 yards of new berthing and was crucial in the city's development. Later, in the early 19th century, the harbour was further increased when a semi-artificial waterway, the **Floating Harbour**, was created by diverting the course of the River Avon to the south. Another huge feat of engineering, the work took over five years to complete and was largely carried out by Napoleonic prisoners of war using only picks and shovels. Today, the main docks have moved downstream to Avonmouth and the Floating Harbour has become home port to a wide assortment of pleasure and small working craft.

Much of Bristol's waterfront has now been redeveloped for recreation. Down on the harbourside is **At Bristol**, one of Britain's largest and most exciting hands-on centres of science and discovery. There are more than 300 hands-on exhibits to explore, as well as live shows and a Planetarium. Close by, on Harbourside, the **Blue Reef Aquarium** transports visitors to the spectacular 'underwater gardens' of the Mediterranean and the stunning beauty of tropical waters -

home to everything from seahorses and puffer fish, to living corals and tropical sharks. Other displays reveal the diversity of the aquatic world with naturally themed mangrove, tropical rainforest and fast-moving river habitats alongside open-top tanks, caves, wooden walkways and bridges.

The aquarium hosts a programme of free daily events including entertaining talks and feeding displays as well as the awesome IMAX Cinema that will take you on an "immersive 3D journey".

Also in the old port area is the Bristol Industrial Museum, which is currently undergoing an extensive refurbishment and will re-open as the **Museum of Bristol** in 2011. It will present a fascinating record of the achievements of the city's industrial and commercial pioneers, including those with household names such as Harvey (wines and sherries), McAdam (road building), Wills (tobacco) and Fry (chocolate). Visitors will also find out about the port's history, view the aircraft and aero engines that have been made here since 1910 and inspect some of the many famous vehicles that have borne the Bristol name since Victorian times.

Another famous name, that of the engineer and inventor **Isambard Kingdom Brunel**, is closely associated with the city. His graceful **Clifton Suspension Bridge** soars 200 feet

Clifton Suspension Bridge

SS Great Britain

In medieval times, the city's prosperous merchants gave liberally for the building of one of the most impressive parish churches in the country. **The Church of St Mary Redcliffe** was described by Queen Elizabeth I as "the fairest, goodliest and most famous Parish Church in England". Along with its glorious exterior, the church contains monuments to Admiral Sir William Penn, whose son founded the state of Pennsylvania in the United States, and John Cabot, the maritime pioneer who in 1497 was the first non-Scandinavian European to set foot on Newfoundland. (A replica of the tiny boat, *The Matthew*, in which Cabot made his perilous journey can be seen alongside Brunel's *SS Great Britain*.) The sandstone beneath St Mary's church is riddled with underground passages known as the **Redcliffe Caves**. There are occasional guided tours of these unusual natural subterranean caverns.

above the Avon gorge to the west of the city centre. Opened in 1864, five years after the death of its designer, the bridge continues to be a major route into the city and provides magnificent views over Bristol and the surrounding countryside. Brunel's mighty *SS Great Britain*, the world's first iron-hulled passenger liner was launched in 1843 and is now berthed in a dry dock in the harbour. It forms part of the **Maritime Heritage Centre**, dedicated to the history of shipbuilding in Bristol. One exhibit tells Brunel's compelling and entertaining life story, including his strengths and achievements, failures and faults. And if you arrive in the city by train from London you will have travelled along the route Brunel engineered for the Great Western Railway. He also designed every one of the bridges and stations along the way, including Bristol's Temple Meads station.

Another ecclesiastical building of note is **John Wesley's Chapel**, the oldest Methodist building in the world. It was built in 1739 and remains completely unspoilt. Visitors can explore the preacher's rooms above the chapel, stand in Wesley's pulpit and see his preaching gown, riding whip and bed.

Elsewhere in the city are The Red Lodge, the only remaining Tudor domestic interior in Bristol, which also has a lovely walled garden with a re-created Elizabethan-style knot garden; and the elegant Georgian House in Great George Street, which was built in 1791. This is one of the most complete 18th-century townhouses to have survived in Britain, its four floors all fully furnished and providing a fascinating insight into life at that time both above and below stairs.

The city is also home to one of the oldest theatres in the country to still be in use. The **Theatre Royal** was built in the 1760s and is the home of the famous Bristol Old Vic theatre company. Backstage tours are available.

Next to the University, the **City Museum and Art Gallery** occupies a magnificent building, which contains no fewer than seven art galleries as well as temporary exhibitions. It also houses important collections of minerals and fossils, eastern art, world wildlife, Egyptology, archaeology and some exceptional Chinese glass.

Standing high on Brandon Hill above the harbour, the 150 metre-high **Cabot Tower** was built in 1897 to commemorate the 400th anniversary of John Cabot's voyage to Newfoundland. For the energetic, there's a spiral staircase inside leading to the top from where there are astounding views across the city and harbour.

The land just to the west of the Clifton Suspension Bridge is now the **Avon Gorge Nature Reserve** and there are some delightful walks here through Leigh Woods up to the summit of an Iron Age hill fort. On the eastern side of the gorge an old snuff mill has been converted into an observatory whose attractions include a camera obscura. Once a genteel suburb, Clifton is now an attractive residential area of elegant Georgian terraces. Here, too, is Goldney House, now a university hall, but also the home of the unique subterranean folly, **Goldney Grotto**, which dates from the 1730s. The walls of this fantastic labyrinth, filled with spectacular rock formations, foaming cascades and a marble statue of Neptune, are covered with thousands of seashells and Bristol diamonds, fragments of a rare quartz found in the Avon gorge.

Clifton is also home to **Bristol Zoo Gardens**, which cares for more than 400 exotic and endangered species. Its Monkey Jungle provodes an immersive forest experience where monkeys mingle with gorillas, and visitors can enjoy close-up walk-through encounters with lemurs. A new addition for the summer of 2008 is the Butterfly Forest featuring spectacular butterfly and moth species from across the world.

Around Bristol

CHEW MAGNA
6 miles S of Bristol on the B3130

🏛 Church House	🏚 Stanton Drew
🎞 The Wedding	🏚 Wansdyke
🐾 Blagdon Lake	🐾 Chew Valley Lake

Situated just to the north of Chew Valley Lake, this former wool village is a pleasant place with some handsome Georgian houses. The nucleus of the village is its three-sided green whose surrounding shops and pubs are linked by an unusual raised stone pavement. At the top of the green is the striking early 16th-century **Church House** that was originally intended to be the venue for the annual church sales and for brewing the ale and baking the bread to be sold on these occasions. The funds raised at this event were used to maintain the parish church for the coming year. These church houses, built in the 15th or early 16th century, were mainly confined to the counties of Somerset and Devon. Close by is the impressive parish Church of St Andrew, a testimony to the former prosperity of this village. Inside can be seen the interesting double effigy of Sir John Loe, a 15th-century local squire reputed to be seven feet tall. Behind a high wall adjacent to the churchyard stands Chew Court, a former summer palace of the bishops of Bath and Wells.

Just to the east of the village is **Stanton Drew**, an ancient settlement that stands

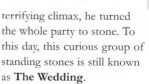

Stanton Drew Stone Circles

terrifying climax, he turned the whole party to stone. To this day, this curious group of standing stones is still known as **The Wedding**.

A couple of miles to the north of Stanton Drew, the line of the ancient **Wansdyke** runs in a roughly east-west direction around the southern fringes of Bristol. Built during the Dark Ages as a boundary line and defensive barrier against the Saxons, short sections of this great earthwork bank can still be seen, notably at Maes Knoll and along the ridge adjoining the Iron Age hill fort on Stantonbury Hill.

To the south of Chew Magna are two reservoirs constructed to supply Bristol with fresh water, but which also provide a first-class recreational amenity. The smaller **Blagdon Lake** was completed in 1899 and **Chew Valley Lake** in 1956. Together they have around 15 miles of shoreline and attract visitors from a wide area who come to fish, take part in water sports and observe the wide variety of waterfowl and other bird life that is drawn to this appealing habitat.

BARROW GURNEY
5 miles SW of Bristol on the B3130

Before the construction of the reservoirs of Blagdon and Chew Valley, Bristol's fresh water came from the three small reservoirs at Barrow Gurney. The first was opened in 1852, but within two years it developed a leak and had to be drained, causing a serious disruption to the city's water supply. Like many of the villages to the southwest of Bristol, Barrow Gurney has undergone considerable change since World

beside a prehistoric site of some importance – a series of stone circles over half a mile across that were constructed by the Bronze Age Beaker people between 2000 and 1600BC. This complex of standing stones consists of three circles, a lone stone known as Hauteville's Quoit and a large chambered burial tomb called The Cove. The stones are composed of three different types of rock: limestone, sandstone and conglomerate. They are thought to have been erected for religious, or perhaps astronomical, purposes. In common with many stone circles in western Britain, the origins of this stone circle are steeped in legend. The most widespread tale tells of a foolhardy wedding party who wanted to continue dancing into the Sabbath. At midnight, the piper refused to carry on, prompting the infuriated bride to declare that if she had to, she would get a piper from hell. At that point, another piper stepped forward to volunteer his services and the party resumed its dancing. As the music got louder and louder and the tempo faster and faster, the dancers realised, too late, that the good-natured piper was the Devil himself. When his playing reached its

War Two and is now becoming a dormitory settlement for the city's commuters.

CONGRESBURY
13 miles SW of Bristol on the A370

🏛 St Congar

This sizeable village, which today appears to be just another commuter town, has a long and eventful history that goes back to Roman times. Around 2000 years ago a settlement stood here at the end of a spur of the Somerset marshes. Fragments of Roman and pre-Saxon pottery have been found on the ancient hill that overlooks the present village.

The early Celtic missionary, **St Congar**, is believed to have founded an early wattle chapel at Congresbury in the 6th century. A tree bound by an iron hoop, on the eastern side of the church, is still referred to as St Congar's Walking Stick. This is reputed to

have grown from the saint's staff that miraculously sprouted leaves after he had thrust it into the ground outside the chapel.

CLEVEDON
15 miles SW of Bristol on the B3133

🏛 Clevedon Pier   🎋 Poet's Walk

🏛 Clevedon Court

Clevedon was developed in the late 18th and early 19th-century as a resort, but the lack of a railway prevented the town from expanding further. It was overtaken by Weston-super-Mare as the leading seaside town along this stretch of coast. As a result there are few of the attractions that are normally associated with a holiday resort. A notable exception is **Clevedon Pier**, a remarkably slim and elegant structure that was built in the 1860s from iron rails intended for Brunel's ill-considered South Wales Railway. When part of the pier

🏛 historic building   🏛 museum and heritage   🏛 historic site   🎋 scenic attraction   🌱 flora and fauna

collapsed in the 1970s, its long term future looked bleak but, following an extensive restoration programme, the pier is now the landing stage, during the summer, for large pleasure steamers such as the *Balmoral* and the *Waverley*, the only surviving sea-going paddle steamers in the world.

Beginning at Clevedon promenade and leading up to Church and Wain's Hills is the **Poet's Walk**, a flower-lined footpath that is said to have been popular with Victorian poets. On the top of Wain's Hill, are the remains of an Iron Age coastal fort, from which walkers can look out over the town, the Somerset Levels and the Severn Estuary.

The town's major attraction is **Clevedon Court** (National Trust), an outstanding 14th-century manor house. One of the earliest surviving country houses in Britain, Clevedon preserves many of its original 14th century features still intact, and incorporates a massive 12th-century tower and a 13th-century great hall. Once partly fortified, this imposing manor house has been the home of the Elton family since 1709. As long standing patrons of the arts, the family invited many of the country's finest poets and writers to Clevedon in the early 1800s. These included Coleridge, Tennyson and Thackeray. It was while staying here that Thackeray fell in love with one of his host's daughters, Mrs Brookfield. He was to spend some time here seeing her and writing *Vanity Fair*. Another member of the Elton family was Arthur Hallam, a student friend of Lord Tennyson who showed great promise as a poet but who died very young. Tennyson was devastated by his friend's untimely death and sought to assuage his grief by writing the great elegiac poem *In Memoriam, AHH*, which was published in 1850.

Although the Elton family is closely associated with literature, one member of the family in the Victorian era invented a special technique for making the type of brightly coloured pottery that was to become known as Eltonware. It was particularly popular in the United States. There are many fine examples on display in the house, along with a collection of rare glass from the works at Nailsea. Clevedon Court is is surrounded by beautiful 18th-century terraced gardens. A footpath leads through nearby woodland on to a ridge overlooking the low and once marshy Gordano valley.

BANWELL
16 miles SW of Bristol on the A368

Bone Caves Puxton Church

This pleasant village was once the site of a Saxon monastery and the parish church here is

---

---

 stories and anecdotes famous people art and craft entertainment and sport walks

certainly ancient. Banwell Castle, on the other hand, although it looks like an authentic medieval fortress, is in fact a Victorian mansion house now converted into a hotel. Just to the west of the village, on Banwell Hill, a remarkable discovery was made in 1821. A series of caverns were found containing the remains of prehistoric animals including bison, bear and reindeer. They are now known as the **Bone Caves**.

A couple of miles north of Banwell is the village of **Puxton**, noted for its eccentric church tower that leans at such an angle that it looks as if it might topple at any moment, causing its weathercock to nosedive into the churchyard.

WESTON-SUPER-MARE
22 miles SW of Bristol on the A370

🏚 Grand Pier 🐦 Seaquarium 🏞 Sand Point

🏛 North Somerset Museum 🏃 Mendip Way

🏛 Helicopter Museum 🏛 Worlebury Camp

This traditional seaside resort, whose greatest asset is undoubtedly its vast expanse of sandy beach, has in recent years also developed as a centre of light industry. As late as 1811, Weston was a fishing hamlet with just 170 residents. Within 100 years, it had grown to become the second largest town in Somerset and today has a resident population of around 70,000.

The commercial development of Weston began in the 1830s around the Knightstone, an islet joined to the shore at the northern end of the bay, and here were eventually built a large theatre and swimming baths. The arrival of the railway in 1841 stimulated the town's rapid expansion and, in 1867, a pier was

built on the headland below Worlebury Camp connecting Birnbeck Island with the mainland. Intended as a berth for steamer traffic, the pier was found to be slightly off the tourist track. Later, a more impressive pier was built nearer the town centre. Refurbished and extended, the **Grand Pier** was re-opened in July 2010 and now stands at the centre of an area crammed with souvenir shops, ice cream parlours, cafés and assorted attractions that are part and parcel of a British seaside resort. There are also the indoor attractions of the Winter Gardens, along the seafront, and the fascinating, family-friendly **North Somerset Museum**.

For anyone wishing to explore Weston on foot, the Museum Trail begins on the seafront and follows a trail of carved stones created by the artist Michael Fairfax. The **Seaquarium** has more than 30 intriguing marine displays, along with feeding times and demonstrations to amuse the whole family.

An excellent viewpoint to the north of the resort is **Sand Point**, a ridge overlooking a lonely salt marsh that is home to a wide variety of wading birds. At the southern end of Weston Bay, another spectacular view

Weston-Super-Mare Beach

🏚 historic building 🏛 museum and heritage 🏛 historic site 🏞 scenic attraction 🐦 flora and fauna

opens up from the clifftop site of the semi-ruined church at Uphill. This village lies at the start of the sometimes demanding **Mendip Way**, a 50-mile footpath that takes in the whole length of the Mendip Hills, including the broad vale of the Western Mendips, the high plateau of the central part and the wooded valleys in the eastern region.

Just to the southeast of the town is Weston Airport, home to the world's largest collection of helicopters and autogyros. The only museum in Britain dedicated to rotary wing aircraft, **The Helicopter Museum** has more than 70 helicopters with exhibits ranging from single-seater autogyros to multi-passenger helicopters. Visitors can see displays on the history and development of these flying machines and a conservation hangar where the aircraft are restored. Grown-ups can take a Helicopter Experience Flight; under-12s can stage a rescue in the Lynx helicopter play area.

The area around Weston has been inhabited since prehistoric times. The wooded promontory at the northern end of Weston Bay was the site of a sizeable Iron Age hill settlement known as **Worlebury Camp**. In the 1st century AD this is said to have been captured by the Romans after a bloody battle. Recent excavations, which revealed a number of skeletons showing the effects of sword damage, provided confirmation. A pleasant walk from the town centre now leads up through attractive woodland to this ancient hilltop site from where there are magnificent views out across the mouth of the River Severn to Wales.

WRAXALL
6 miles W of Bristol on the B3128

🏠 Tyntesfield   🐦 Noah's Ark Zoo Farm

One of the National Trust's most fascinating properties, **Tyntesfield** is an extraordinary Victorian Gothic Revival house that was home to four generations of the Gibbs family. The Gibbs' lived on a grand scale and spent lavishly on opulent furnishings for their magnificent mansion, including its stunning private chapel.

When the house was saved for the nation in June 2002, it needed a huge amount of conservation work, which still continues with parts of the house not open to the public. Visitors are no longer restricted to guided tours only and can see this work in progress as they wander at will through the permitted areas. Outside, there are formal gardens, an arboretum, walled garden and a working kitchen garden. Admission to the house is by timed ticket. Tickets are issued at visitor reception on arrival and cannot be booked.

Also at Wraxall is **Noah's Ark Zoo Farm**, a hands-on real working farm with a rare collection of more than 100 types of animals, including meerkats, camels, rhinos, wallabies, monkeys and giraffes. There are also 12 all-weather playgrounds and a huge indoor play barn. Daily events include animal shows, tractor rides, bird of prey displays and keeper talks.

HENBURY
4 miles NW of Bristol off the A38

🏠 Blaise Castle

In her novel *Northanger Abbey*, Jane Austen described **Blaise Castle** at Henbury as "one of the finest places in England". This impressive 18th-century house is set in parkland and boasts a large collection of everyday objects from the past, including model trains, dolls and toy soldiers. There's also a Victorian schoolroom, picture gallery and period costumes. Within the estate grounds is Blaise Hamlet, an impossibly picturesque group of nine detached and individual stone cottages designed in a romantic rustic style by John Nash in 1809. The cottages are owned by the National Trust but are not open to the public.

Bath

- 🏛 Roman Baths   🏛 Thermae Bath Spa
- 🏛 Bath Abbey   ⚘ 'Beau' Nash
- 🏛 Holburne Museum   🏛 Royal Crescent
- 🏛 Pump Room   ✐ Theatre Royal
- 🏛 Museum of East Asian Art   🏛 Pulteney Bridge
- 🏛 Assembly Rooms   🏛 Fashion Museum
- 🏛 Museum of Bath at Work
- 🏛 Bath Postal Museum   ⚘ Jane Austen Centre
- ⚘ Herschel Museum of Astronomy
- 🏃 Bath Skyline Walk
- ❦ Prior Park Landscape Garden

Designated a World Heritage City, Bath is Britain's finest Georgian city, replete with gracious buildings of which around 5000 are listed because of their architectural merit. Set in a sheltered valley, it is surrounded like Rome by seven hills, which may have been one reason why the Romans took to it with such enthusiasm. Another important reason was, of course, its natural hot springs.

Since time immemorial more than half a million gallons of water a day, at a constant temperature of 46°C, have bubbled to the surface at Bath. The ancient Celts believed the mysterious steaming spring was the domain of the goddess Sulis and they were aware of the water's healing powers long before the invasion of the Romans. However, it was the Romans who first enclosed the spring and went on to create a spectacular health resort that became known as Aquae Sulis. By the 3rd

century, Bath had become so renowned that high ranking soldiers and officials were coming here from all over the Roman Empire. Public buildings and temples were constructed and the whole city was enclosed by a stone wall. By AD410, the last remaining Roman legions had left and, within a few years, the drainage systems failed and the area returned to marshland. Ironically, the ancient baths remained hidden throughout the entire period of Bath's 18th-century renaissance and were only discovered in the late 19th century. The restored Roman remains can be seen today. They centre around the **Roman Baths**, a rectangular lead-lined pool standing at the centre of a complex system of buildings that took over 200 years to complete. It comprised a swimming pool, mineral baths and a series of chambers heated by underfloor air ducts.

One hundred yards from the Great Bath, the **Thermae Bath Spa** opened in the summer of 2006. Visitors can bathe in the natural thermal waters that the Romans enjoyed almost 2000 years ago. There's a spectacular rooftop pool, an innovative series of steam rooms, and an extensive range of spa treatments are available.

In a city crammed with beautiful buildings, **Bath Abbey** is still outstanding. The present great church was begun in 1499, after its Norman predecessor had been destroyed by fire. Building work was halted at the time of the Dissolution in the 1540s and the church remained without a roof for 75 years. It was not finally completed until 1901. It is now considered to be the ultimate example of English Perpendicular church architecture.

Inside, there is a memorial to **Richard 'Beau' Nash**, one of the people responsible for turning Bath into a fashionable Georgian spa town. Prior to Nash's arrival in the early

Royal Crescent

Bath's other 18th-century founding father was Ralph Allen, an entrepreneur who made his first fortune developing an efficient postal system for the provinces, and who went on to make a second as the owner of the local quarries that supplied most of the honey-coloured Bath stone to the city's Georgian building sites.

18th century, Bath was a squalid place with farm animals roaming the streets within the confines of the old Roman town. Notwithstanding, the town had continued to attract small numbers of rich and aristocratic people. Eventually, the town authorities took action to improve sanitation and their initiative was rewarded in 1702, when Queen Anne paid Bath's spa a visit. The elegant and stylish Beau Nash, who had only come to the town to earn a living as a gambler, became the Master of Ceremonies and, under his leadership, the town became a relaxing place for the elegant and fashionable of the day's high society. Among the entrepreneurs and architects who shared Nash's vision was the architect John Wood who, along with his son, designed many of the city's fine neoclassical squares and terraces. Among these is the **Royal Crescent**, John Wood the Younger's Palladian masterpiece and one of the first terraces in Britain to be built to an elliptical design. It has now been designated a World Heritage Building. Open to the public, No 1 Royal Crescent has been restored, redecorated and furnished so that it appears as it might have done when it was first built.

Famed for its wealth of Georgian architecture, Bath is a delightful city to wander around. Beside the original Roman Baths is the **Pump Room**, which looks much as it did when it was completed in 1796. The **Theatre Royal** is one of Britain's oldest and most beautiful theatres and offers a year-round programme of top quality drama, opera, dance and frequent Sunday concerts. Spanning the River Avon, in the centre of the city, is the magnificent **Pulteney Bridge**, designed by Robert Adam and inspired by Florence's Ponte Vecchio with its built-in shops.

The National Trust-owned **Assembly Rooms**, one of the places where polite 18th-century society met to dance, play cards or just be seen, were severely damaged during World War Two and not re-opened until 1963. They now incorporate the interesting **Fashion Museum** with a collection of more than 30,000 original items illuminating the vagaries of fashion over the past 400 years.

This is just one of the city's many excellent museums. Currently closed for refurbishment and not due to re-open until 2011, the **Holburne Museum** is housed in one of the city's finest examples of Georgian architecture and set in beautiful gardens. Originally a spa hotel, it was converted into a museum in the early 20th century and now contains the superb collection of decorative and fine art put together by Sir William Holburne in the 19th century. Landscapes by Turner and Guardi, and portraits by Stubbs, Ramsey, Raeburn, Zoffany and Gainsborough, are among its many treasures. The **Museum of Bath at Work** holds a fascinating collection that chronicles the city's unique architectural evolution; the **Museum of East Asian Art** displays artefacts from China, Japan, Korea and Southeast Asia; and the **Bath Postal Museum** illustrates 4000 years of communication from "clay-mail to e-mail" and has a reconstruction of a Victorian sorting office.

The city is closely associated with Jane Austen and her novels and, at the **Jane Austen Centre**, enthusiasts can learn more about the Bath of her time and the importance of the city to her life and works. Another famous resident is celebrated at the **Herschel Museum of Astronomy**, which occupies the mid-Georgian house where the famous astronomer and musician lived in the late 1700s and where he made his discovery of the planet Uranus.

An ideal way to gather a general impression of this magnificent city is to take the **Bath Skyline Walk**, an eight-mile footpath, through National Trust-owned land, taking in some superb landscaped gardens and woodland to the southeast of the city and from where there are extensive views out over Bath. The most striking feature of the skyline is Beckford's Tower, which was built for the eccentric William

Beckford in 1827. There are yet more magnificent views of the city from another National Trust property, **Prior Park Landscape Garden**, which is just a 10-minute walk or short bus ride from the city centre – there is no parking at the garden itself. Within the beautiful grounds of this intimate 18th-century garden are three lakes set in sweeping valleys, and a famous Palladian bridge, one of only four of its kind in the world.

Around Bath

DYRHAM
7 miles N of Bath off the A46

🏛 Dyrham Park

Set in an extensive deer park just minutes from the M4, **Dyrham Park** (National Trust) is a spectacular Baroque mansion containing a fabulous collection of 17th-century furnishings, textiles, paintings and Delftware reflecting the taste for Dutch fashions at the time it was built. Visitors can wander round the park with its woodlands and formal garden, and discover how Victorian servants worked 'below stairs'.

Deer at Dyrham Park

🏛 historic building 📷 museum and heritage 🏛 historic site 🌿 scenic attraction 🐦 flora and fauna

BATHFORD
3 miles NE of Bath off the A363

🏠 Eagle House 🏠 Brown's Folly

🏛 Bathampton Down

This residential community once belonged to Bath Abbey. Among the many fine 18th-century buildings to be seen here is **Eagle House**, a handsome residence that takes its name from the great stone eagle that stands with its wings outstretched on the gabled roof. On the hill above Bathford, there is a tall Italianate tower known as **Brown's Folly** built following the Napoleonic Wars to provide local craftsmen with work during the economic depression of the 1830s.

To the west lies Bathampton whose church is the last resting place of Admiral Arthur Phillip, the first governor of New South Wales, who took the initial shipload of convicts out to the colony and established the settlement of Sydney. He is regarded by some as the founder of modern Australia. A chapel in the south aisle, known as the Australian Chapel, contains memorials to the admiral's family.

Above the village lies **Bathampton Down**, which is crowned with an ancient hillfort that, according to some historians, was the site of the 6th-century Battle of Badon in which the forces of King Arthur defeated the Saxons.

CLAVERTON
2 miles E of Bath on the A36

🏠 Claverton Manor

🏛 American Museum in Britain

Just to the west of the village stands the 16th-century country mansion, **Claverton Manor**, bought in 1764 by Ralph Allen, the quarry-owning co-founder of 18th-century Bath. The mansion that Allen knew has been demolished, leaving only a series of overgrown terraces, but some of the stone from the old house was used in the construction of the new mansion on the hill above the village. It was here, in 1897, that Sir Winston Churchill is said to have given his first political speech. Claverton Manor is best known as the **American Museum in Britain**. Founded in 1961, it is the only establishment of its kind outside the United States. The rooms of the house have been furnished to show the gradual changes in American living styles from the arrival of the Pilgrim Fathers in the 17th century, to New York of the 19th century. The arboretum contains a collection of native American trees and shrubs.

HINTON PRIORY
3½ miles SE of Bath off the B3110

🏛 Stoney Littleton Long Barrow

All that remains of the early Carthusian monastery founded here by Ela, Countess of Salisbury, are atmospheric ruins. As in other religious houses belonging to this order, the monks occupied their own small dwellings set around the main cloister, often with a small garden attached. These communities were generally known for their reclusiveness. However, one outspoken monk from Hinton Priory, Nicholas Hopkins, achieved notoriety in Tudor times as the confessor and spiritual adviser to the 3rd Duke of Buckingham and his story is recounted by Shakespeare in *Henry VIII*. Several sections of the old priory remain, including the chapter house, parts of the guest quarters and the undercroft of the refectory.

Close by can be found one of the finest examples of a Neolithic monument in the west of England, **Stoney Littleton Long Barrow** (English Heritage), built more than

4000 years ago. This striking multi-chambered tomb has recently been restored following vandalism and the interior can be inspected by obtaining a key from nearby Stoney Littleton Farm.

FARLEIGH HUNGERFORD
5 miles SE of Bath on the A366

🏯 Farleigh Hungerford Castle 🌱 The Peto Garden

This old fortified settlement is still overlooked by the impressive remains of **Farleigh Hungerford Castle** that stands on a rise above the River Frome to the northeast of the village. It was built by Sir Thomas Hungerford, the first Speaker of the House of Commons, on the site of an old manor house that he acquired in the late 14th century. Legend has it that Sir Thomas failed to gain the proper permission from the Crown for his fortification and this oversight led to his downfall. The castle changed hands in the early 18th century and the incoming family saw it as a quarry for building stone rather than as a place to live. Much of the castle was left to go to ruin while the family built a new mansion on the other side of the village. Nevertheless, an impressive shell of towers and perimeter walls has survived intact, along with the castle's Chapel of St Leonard. This contains a striking 15th-century mural of St George, some fine stained glass and a number of interesting monuments, including the tomb of Sir Thomas Hungerford himself.

To the north, just inside Wiltshire, is Iford Manor, home to the **Peto Garden**, a Grade I listed Italian style garden famed for its tranquil beauty. A unique hillside garden, it was the creation of architect and landscape gardener

---

PITFOUR HOUSE

High Street, Timsbury, nr Bath, Somerset BA2 0HT
Tel: 01761 479554
e-mail: pitfourhouse@btinternet.com

Splendid food, convivial company and truly wonderful hospitality are to be found at **Pitfour House**, a contemporary English experience in a charming listed Georgian home. Situated in the countryside village of Timsbury, just 6 miles outside of Bath, Pitfour House dates from the 1790s and stands back from the High Street, with a wonderfully mellow stone façade. The surroundings are so picturesque and rural here it is easy to forget how close you are to so many great attractions and cities!

The delicious, expertly cooked modern menu at Pitfour House includes fresh home grown vegetables from the beautiful garden (when seasonal) and a wide selection of personally selected local ingredients. The 2 or 3 course dinners, as well as the hearty breakfasts, are served in the elegant dining room. Guests are also to relax during their stay in the cosy sitting room, and take in a little TV, or the even cosier snug, or enjoy the well maintained gardens, which can seem like a world away from the hustle and bustle of Bath! The two tastefully decorated bedrooms, one with ensuite shower, the other with a private bathroom have king size beds with top quality linen and towels providing all the amenities you need for your stay.

🏯 historic building 🏛 museum and heritage 🏛 historic site ♧ scenic attraction 🌱 flora and fauna

Harold Peto, who lived at the manor from 1899 until 1933.

NORTON ST PHILIP
5½ miles S of Bath on the A366

🍺 George Inn 🍃 Norwood Farm

In the 13th century, a group of Carthusian monks were given some land near here where they founded a Priory that was completed in 1232. The monks were also responsible for building the village's most famous landmark, the splendid **George Inn**, originally established as a house of hospitality for those visiting the priory. A wonderful fusion of medieval stonework, oriel windows and timber framing, it is still a hostelry today. The inn's timber framed upper floors were added in the 15th century when the inn doubled as a warehouse for storing the locally produced woollen cloth. In 1668, the diarist Samuel Pepys stayed here while on his way to Bath with his family and noted, "Dined well. 10 shillings." Just a short while later, the inn played host to the Duke of Monmouth, who made the George his headquarters shortly before his defeat at the Battle of Sedgemoor in 1685. According to a local story, 12 men implicated in the uprising were imprisoned here after the battle, in what is now the Dungeon Bar. They were later taken away to be hanged, drawn and quartered at the local market place.

To the north of the village, **Norwood Farm** offers an introduction to the objectives and practicalities of organic farming. A Farm Walk takes in a recycling area, explains the use of wind turbines and provides a view of more than 30 rare and beautiful animal breeds including Saddleback pigs, Shetland ponies and Wiltshire Horn sheep. A café and farm shop on site make good use of the organic food produced on the farm.

KEYNSHAM
6½ miles NW of Bath on the A4175

🍃 Avon Valley Country Park

A former industrial centre, Keynsham is now a dormitory town for Bristol. Despite its modern appearance, it has ancient roots. During the excavations for a chocolate factory, the remains of two Roman villas were discovered. These remains have since been incorporated into an interesting small museum near the factory entrance. In the late 12th century, an abbey was founded here, close to the River Chew, but it seems that the medieval monks were not as pious as they should have been. Eventually, they were banned from keeping sporting dogs, going out at night, employing private washerwomen and entertaining female guests in the monastery. Today, the abbey foundations lie under the bypass but the part 13th-century parish church has survived and, along with being a good example of the Somerset Gothic architectural style, it contains some impressive tombs to members of the Bridges family.

Much later, two large brass mills were established at Keynsham during the town's 18th-century industrial heyday, one on the River Avon and the other on the River Chew. Though production had ceased at both mills by the late 1920s, they are still impressive industrial remains.

Just to the east of Keynsham, **Avon Valley Country Park** provides a popular day out for families. There's a large adventure playground, indoor play area, friendly animals and pets corner, falconry displays, boating lake, 1½ mile nature trail walk, mini-steam train rides, land train rides, quad bikes, picnic and barbecue area, café and gift shop.

🎭 stories and anecdotes 🐦 famous people 🎨 art and craft 🎟 entertainment and sport 🚶 walks

TOURIST INFORMATION CENTRES

Cornwall

BODMIN

Shire Hall, Mount Folly Square, Bodmin,
Cornwall PL31 2DQ
e-mail: bodmintic@visit.org.uk
Tel: 01208 76616

BUDE

Bude Visitor Centre, The Crescent, Bude,
Cornwall EX23 8LE
e-mail: budetic@visitbude.info
Tel: 01288 354240

CAMELFORD

North Cornwall Museum, The Clease, Camelford,
Cornwall PL32 9PL
e-mail: manager@camelfordtic.eclipse.co.uk
Tel: 01840 212954

FALMOUTH

11 Market Strand, Prince of Wales Pier, Falmouth,
Cornwall TR11 3DF
e-mail: info@falmouthtic.co.uk
Tel: 01326 312300

FOWEY

5 South Street, Fowey, Cornwall PL23 1AR
e-mail: info@fowey.co.uk
Tel: 01726 833616

LAUNCESTON

Market House Arcade, Market Street, Launceston,
Cornwall PL15 8EP
e-mail: launcestontica@btconnect.com
Tel: 01566 772321

LOOE

The Guildhall, Fore Street, East Looe,
Cornwall PL13 1AA
e-mail: looetic@btconnect.com
Tel: 01503 262072

NEWQUAY

Marcus Hill, Newquay, Cornwall TR7 1BD
e-mail: newquay.tic@cornwall.gov.uk
Tel: 01637 854020

PADSTOW

Red Brick Building, North Quay, Padstow,
Cornwall PL28 8AF
e-mail: padstowtic@btconnect.com
Tel: 01841 533449

PENZANCE

Station Road, Penzance, Cornwall TR18 2NF
e-mail: penzancetic@cornwall.gov.uk
Tel: 01736 362207

ST AUSTELL

Southbourne Road, St Austell, Cornwall PL25 4RS
e-mail: tic@cornish-riviera.co.uk
Tel: 01726 879 500

ST IVES

The Guildhall, Street-an-Pol, St Ives,
Cornwall TR26 2DS
e-mail: stivestic@cornwall.gov.uk
Tel: 01736 796297

TRURO

Municipal Building, Boscawen Street, Truro,
Cornwall TR1 2NE
e-mail: tic@truro.gov.uk
Tel: 01872 274555

Devon

BARNSTAPLE

Museum of North Devon The Square, Barnstaple,
Devon EX32 8LN
e-mail: info@staynorthdevon.co.uk
Tel: 01271 375000

TOURIST INFORMATION CENTRES

BIDEFORD

Victoria Park, The Quay, Bideford, Devon EX39 2QQ
e-mail: bidefordtic@visit.org.uk
Tel: 01237 477676

BRAUNTON

The Bakehouse Centre, Caen Street, Braunton,
Devon EX33 1AA
e-mail: info@brauntontic.co.uk
Tel: 01271 816400

BRIXHAM

The Old Market House, The Quay, Brixham,
Devon TQ5 8TB
e-mail: holiday@torbay.gov.uk
Tel: 01803 211211

BUDLEIGH SALTERTON

Fore Street, Budleigh Salterton, Devon EX9 6NG
e-mail: info@visitbudleigh.com
Tel: 01395 445275

COMBE MARTIN

Seacot Cross Street, Combe Martin, Devon EX34 0DH
e-mail: mail@visitcombemartin.co.uk
Tel: 01271 883319

DARTMOUTH

The Engine House, Mayor's Avenue, Dartmouth,
Devon TQ6 9YY
e-mail: holidays@discoverdartmouth.com
Tel: 01803 834224

DAWLISH

The Lawn, Dawlish, Devon EX7 9PW
e-mail: dawtic@Teignbridge.gov.uk
Tel: 01626 215665

EXETER

Dix's Field, Exeter, Devon EX1 1GF
e-mail: tic@exeter.gov.uk
Tel: 01392 665700

EXMOUTH

Alexandra Terrace, Exmouth, Devon EX8 1NZ
e-mail: info@exmouthtourism.co.uk
Tel: 01395 222299

HONITON

Lace Walk Car Park, Honiton, Devon EX14 1LT
e-mail:honitontic@btconnect.com
Tel: 01404 43716

ILFRACOMBE

The Landmark, The Seafront, Ilfracombe,
Devon EX34 9BX
e-mail: info@ilfracombe-tourism.co.uk
Tel: 01271 863001

IVYBRIDGE

Global Travel, 19 Fore Street, Ivybridge,
Devon PL21 9AB
e-mail: bookends.ivybridge@virgin.net
Tel: 01752 897035

KINGSBRIDGE

The Quay, Kingsbridge, Devon TQ7 1HS
e-mail: advice@kingsbridgeinfo.co.uk
Tel: 01548 853195

LYNTON AND LYNMOUTH

Town Hall, Lee Road, Lynton, Devon EX35 6BT
e-mail: info@lyntourism.co.uk
Tel: 0845 660 3232

MODBURY

5 Modbury Court, Modbury, Devon PL21 0QR
e-mail: modburytic@lineone.net
Tel: 01548 830159

NEWTON ABBOT

6 Bridge House, Courtenay Street, Newton Abbot,
Devon TQ12 2QS
e-mail: natic@Teignbridge.gov.uk
Tel: 01626 215667

TOURIST INFORMATION CENTRES

OKEHAMPTON

Museum Courtyard, 3 West Street, Okehampton,
Devon EX20 1HQ
e-mail: okehamptontic@westdevon.gov.uk
Tel: 01837 53020

OTTERY ST MARY

10a Broad Street, Ottery St Mary, Devon EX11 1BZ
e-mail: tic.osm@cosmic.org.uk
Tel: 01404 813964

PAIGNTON

The Esplanade, Paignton, Devon TQ4 6ED
e-mail: holiday@torbay.gov.uk
Tel: 01803 211211

PLYMOUTH

Plymouth Mayflower Centre, 3-5 The Barbican,
Plymouth, Devon PL1 2LR
e-mail: barbicantic@plymouth.gov.uk
Tel: 01752 306330

SALCOMBE

Market Street, Salcombe, Devon TQ8 8DE
e-mail: info@salcombeinformation.co.uk
Tel: 01548 843927

SEATON

The Underfleet, Seaton, Devon EX12 2TB
e-mail: info@seatontic.freeserve.co.uk
Tel: 01297 21660

SIDMOUTH

Ham Lane, Sidmouth, Devon EX10 8XR
e-mail: sidmouthtic@eclipse.co.uk
Tel: 01395 516441

SOUTH MOLTON

1 East Street, South Molton, Devon EX36 3BU
e-mail: visitsouthmolton@btconnect.com
Tel: 01769 574122

TAVISTOCK

Town Hall, Bedford Square, Tavistock,
Devon PL19 0AE
e-mail: tavistocktic@westdevon.gov.uk
Tel: 01822 612938

TEIGNMOUTH

The Den Sea Front, Teignmouth, Devon TQ14 8BE
e-mail: teigntic@teignbridge.gov.uk
Tel: 01626 215666

TIVERTON

Phoenix Lane, Tiverton, Devon EX16 6LU
e-mail: tivertontic@btconnect.com
Tel: 01884 255827

TORQUAY

The Tourist Centre, Vaughan Parade, Torquay,
Devon TQ2 5JG
e-mail: holiday@torbay.gov.uk
Tel: 01803 211211

TORRINGTON

Castle Hill, South Street, Great Torrington,
Devon EX38 8AA
e-mail: info@great-torrington.com
Tel: 01805 626140

TOTNES

The Town Mill, Coronation Road, Totnes,
South Devon TQ9 5DF,
e-mail: enquire@totnesinformation.co.uk
Tel: 01803 863168

WOOLACOMBE

The Esplanade, Woolacombe, Devon EX34 7DL
e-mail: info@woolacombetourism.co.uk
Tel: 01271 870553

Dorset

BLANDFORD FORUM

1 Greyhound Yard, Blandford Forum, Dorset DT11 7EB
e-mail: blandfordtic@north-dorset.gov.uk
Tel: 01258 454770

BOURNEMOUTH

Westover Road, Bournemouth, Dorset BH1 2BU
e-mail: info@bournemouth.gov.uk
Tel: 01202 451700

CHRISTCHURCH

49 High Street, Christchurch, Dorset BH23 1AS
e-mail: enquiries@christchurchtourism.info
Tel: 01202 471780

DORCHESTER

11 Antelope Walk, Dorchester, Dorset DT1 1BE
e-mail: dorchester.tic@westdorset-dc.gov.uk
Tel: 01305 267992

LYME REGIS

Guildhall Cottage, Church Street, Lyme Regis,
Dorset DT7 3BS
e-mail: lymeregis.tic@westdorset-dc.gov.uk
Tel: 01297 442138

POOLE

Enefco House, Poole Quay, Poole, Dorset BH15 1HJ
e-mail: info@poole.gov.uk
Tel: 01202 253253

SHAFTESBURY

8 Bell Street, Shaftesbury, Dorset SP7 8AE
e-mail: tourism@shaftesburydorset.com
Tel: 01747 853514

SHERBORNE

3 Tilton Court, Digby Road, Sherborne,
Dorset DT9 3NL
e-mail: sherborne.tic@westdorset-dc.gov.uk
Tel: 01935 815341

SWANAGE

The White House, Shore Road, Swanage,
Dorset BH19 1LB
e-mail: mail@swanage.gov.uk
Tel: 01929 422885

WAREHAM

Holy Trinity Church, South Street, Wareham,
Dorset BH20 4LU
e-mail: tic@purbeck-dc.gov.uk
Tel: 01929 552740

WEYMOUTH

The Pavilion, The Esplanade, Weymouth,
Dorset DT4 8ED
e-mail: tic@weymouth.gov.uk
Tel: 01305 785747

WIMBORNE MINSTER

29 High Street, Wimborne Minster, Dorset BH21 1HR
e-mail: wimbornetic@eastdorset.gov.uk
Tel: 01202 886116

Somerset

BATH

Abbey Chambers, Abbey Church Yard, Bath,
Somerset BA1 1LY
e-mail: tourism@bathtourism.co.uk
Tel: 0906 711 2000

BRIDGWATER

Bridgwater House, King Square, Bridgwater,
Somerset TA6 3AR
e-mail: bridgwater.tic@sedgemoor.gov.uk
Tel: 01278 436 438

BRISTOL

E Shed, 1 Cannons Road, Bristol, Somerset BS1 4LH
e-mail: ticharbourside@destinationbristol.co.uk
Tel: 0333 321 0101

TOURIST INFORMATION CENTRES

BURNHAM-ON-SEA

South Esplanade, Burnham-on-Sea, Somerset TA8 1BU
e-mail: burnham.tic@sedgemoor.gov.uk
Tel: 01278 787852

CARTGATE

South Somerset TIC, A303/A3088 Cartgate Picnic Site,
Stoke-sub-Hamdon, Somerset TA14 6RA
e-mail: cartgate.tic@southsomerset.gov.uk
Tel: 01935 829333

CHARD

The Guildhall, Fore Street, Chard, Somerset TA20 1PP
e-mail: chardtic@chard.gov.uk
Tel: 01460 260051

FROME

The Round Tower, Justice Lane, Frome,
Somerset BA11 1BB
e-mail: enquiries@frometouristinfo.co.uk
Tel: 01373 467271

GLASTONBURY

The Tribunal, 9 High Street, Glastonbury,
Somerset BA6 9DP
e-mail: glastonbury.tic@ukonline.co.uk
Tel: 01458 832954

MINEHEAD

17 Friday Street, Minehead, Somerset TA24 5UB
e-mail: info@mineheadtic.co.uk
Tel: 01643 702624

SHEPTON MALLET

70 High Street, Shepton Mallet, Somerset BA4 5AS
e-mail: sheptonmallet.tic@ukonline.co.uk
Tel: 01749 345258

SOMERSET

Sedgemoor Services, Somerset Visitor Centre,
Road Chef Services, M5 Southbound, Axbridge,
Somerset BS26 2UF
e-mail: somersetvisitorcentre@somerset.gov.uk
Tel: 01934 750833

STREET

Clarks Village, Farm Road, Street, Somerset BA16 0BB
e-mail: info@streettic.co.uk
Tel: 01458 447384

TAUNTON

The Library, Paul Street, Taunton, Somerset TA1 3XZ
e-mail: tauntontic@tauntondeane.gov.uk
Tel: 01823 336344

WELLINGTON

30 Fore Street, Wellington, Somerset TA21 8AQ
e-mail: wellingtontic@tauntondeane.gov.uk
Tel: 01823 663379

WELLS

Town Hall, Market Place, Wells, Somerset BA5 2RB
e-mail: touristinfo@wells.gov.uk
Tel: 01749 672552

WESTON-SUPER-MARE

Beach Lawns, Weston-super-Mare, Somerset BS23 1AT
e-mail: westontouristinfo@n-somerset.gov.uk
Tel: 01934 888800

YEOVIL

Hendford, Yeovil, Somerset BA20 1UN
e-mail: yeoviltic@southsomerset.gov.uk
Tel: 01935 845946

ACCOMMODATION, FOOD AND DRINK

ACTIVITIES

INDEX OF ADVERTISERS

INDEX OF ADVERTISERS

INDEX OF ADVERTISERS

IMAGE COPYRIGHT HOLDERS

Some images in this book have been supplied by **http://www.geograph.org.uk** and licensed under the Creative Commons Attribution-Share Alike 2.0 Generic License. To view a copy of this license, visit **http://creativecommons.org/licenses/by-sa/2.0/** or send a letter to Creative Commons, 171 Second Street, Suite 300, San Francisco, California, 94105, USA.

COPYRIGHT HOLDERS ARE AS FOLLOWS:

Castle Remains, Tintagel ©*Richard Law*	*pg 3*
Egyptian House, Penzance ©*Tony Atkin*	*pg 7*
Harbour Lighthouse, Penzance ©*Amanda King*	*pg 11*
Wayside Folk Museum, Zennor ©*Pauline Eccles*	*pg 12*
Porthmeor Beach, St Ives ©*Andy F*	*pg 21*
St Michaels Mount, Marazion ©*Sheila Russell*	*pg 24*
Harbour Lighthouse, Mousehole ©*Martin Bodman*	*pg 27*
Minack Theatre, Porthcurno ©*Pennie Winkler*	*pg 28*
Gwennap Pit, Redruth ©*Rod Allday*	*pg 32*
Tin Mine, St Agnes ©*John Spivey*	*pg 33*
Blockhouse at Pendennis Castle, Falmouth ©*Chris Downer*	*pg 37*
National Maritime Museum, Falmouth ©*Martin Meggs*	*pg 41*
Mawes Castle, St Mawes ©*Tony Atkin*	*pg 49*
St Anthony Lighthouse, St Mawes ©*Tony Atkin*	*pg 49*
Grylls Monument, Helston ©*Tony Atkin*	*pg 55*
Lifeboat Station, Lizard ©*Pam Brophy*	*pg 59*
Cathedral, Truro ©*Richard Rogerson*	*pg 61*
Eden Project, St Blazey ©*RichTea*	*pg 63*
Surfing at Fistral Beach, Newquay ©*Geoff Tydeman*	*pg 69*
East Wheal Rose, St Newlyn East ©*Malcolm Kewn*	*pg 72*
Old Post Office, Tintagel ©*Mark Collins*	*pg 79*
Harbour, Port Isaac ©*Amanda King*	*pg 80*
Crooklets Beach, Bude ©*William Wells*	*pg 84*
St Swithins Church, Launcells ©*Pierre Terre*	*pg 87*
Dozmary Pool, Bolventor ©*Nick McNeill*	*pg 91*
St Nonna's Church, Altarnun ©*Michael Murray*	*pg 92*
The Cheesewring, Minions ©*Pete Chapman*	*pg 93*
Looe Island, Looe ©*Paula Goodfellow*	*pg 100*
Port Eliot House, St Germans ©*Rod Allday*	*pg 101*
Mount Edgcumbe Orangery, Cremyll ©*Tony Atkin*	*pg 103*
Town Quay, Fowey ©*Martin Bodman*	*pg 106*
Village, Polruan ©*Martin Bodman*	*pg 108*
Restormel Castle, Lostwithiel ©*Charles*	*pg 109*
Steam Railway, Launceston ©*Mick Heraty*	*pg 111*
Railway Viaduct, Calstock ©*Roger Geach*	*pg 113*
Cotehele Quay, Cotehele ©*Roger Cornfoot*	*pg 114*
Kit Hill, Callington ©*Sarah Charlesworth*	*pg 115*
Lynch Tor, Dartmoor ©*Nigel Mole*	*pg 117*
Valley of the Rocks, Lynton ©*Graham Horn*	*pg 120*
Cliff Railway, Lynmouth ©*Ruth Sharville*	*pg 121*
Barricane Beach, Morthoe ©*Darren Cummins*	*pg 126*
Long Bridge, Barnstaple ©*Humphrey Bolton*	*pg 127*
Pannier Market, Barnstaple ©*OLU*	*pg 128*
Arlington Court, Arlington ©*Linda Bailey*	*pg 130*
Baggy Point, Croyde ©*Roger A Smith*	*pg 134*
Old Lighthouse, Lundy ©*Pauline Eccles*	*pg 136*
Cottages, Appledore ©*Philip Halling*	*pg 137*
Tapeley Park Gardens, Instow ©*Richard Croft*	*pg 138*
Main Street, Clovelly ©*John Clive Nicholson*	*pg 141*
St Marys Church, Molland ©*John Salmon*	*pg 145*
Eggesford Forest, Chulmleigh ©*Barrie Cann*	*pg 146*
Bridge, Sheepwash ©*Roger A Smith*	*pg 153*
Railway Station, Okehampton ©*Clive Warneford*	*pg 155*
Fitch Foundry, Sticklepath ©*Ben Gamble*	*pg 157*
Carnmere Pool Letterbox, Chagford ©*Patrick Gueulle*	*pg 161*
Pannier Market, Tavistock ©*Glen Denny*	*pg 164*
Dartmoor Prison, Princetown ©*Lynda Poulter*	*pg 167*
Morwellham Quay, Bere Alston ©*Martin Bodman*	*pg 171*
South Devon Railway, Buckfastleigh ©*Jonathan Simkins*	*pg 173*
Riverside Mill, Bovey Tracey ©*Mike Crowe*	*pg 176*
Unusual Clock Face, Buckland in the Moor ©*Guy Wareham*	*pg 177*
East Street, Ashburton ©*Derek Harper*	*pg 179*
Plymouth Hoe, Plymouth ©*Ron Strutt*	*pg 182*
Plymouth Breakwater, Plymouth ©*Mick Lobb*	*pg 183*
Barbican Waterfront, Plymouth ©*Pierre Terre*	*pg 184*
Saltram House, Plympton ©*Shaun Ferguson*	*pg 185*
River Dart, Totnes ©*JThomas*	*pg 190*

IMAGE COPYRIGHT HOLDERS

ORDER FORM

To order any of our publications just fill in the payment details below and complete the order form. For orders of less than 4 copies please add £1 per book for postage and packing. Orders over 4 copies are P & P free.

Please Complete Either:

I enclose a cheque for £ [   ]   made payable to Travel Publishing Ltd

Or:

CARD NO: [   ]   EXPIRY DATE: [   ]

SIGNATURE: [   ]

NAME: [   ]

ADDRESS: [   ]

TEL NO: [   ]

Please either send, telephone, fax or e-mail your order to:

Travel Publishing Ltd, Airport Business Centre, 10 Thornbury Road, Estover, Plymouth PL6 7PP
Tel: 01752 697280   Fax: 01752 697299 e-mail: info@travelpublishing.co.uk

	PRICE	QUANTITY		PRICE	QUANTITY
HIDDEN PLACES REGIONAL TITLES			**COUNTRY LIVING RURAL GUIDES**		
Cornwall	£8.99	....	East Anglia	£10.99	....
Devon	£8.99	....	Heart of England	£10.99	....
Dorset, Hants & Isle of Wight	£8.99	....	Ireland	£11.99	....
East Anglia	£8.99	....	North East of England	£10.99	....
Lake District & Cumbria	£8.99	....	North West of England	£10.99	....
Lancashire & Cheshire	£8.99	....	Scotland	£11.99	....
Northumberland & Durham	£8.99	....	South of England	£10.99	....
Peak District and Derbyshire	£8.99	....	South East of England	£10.99	....
Yorkshire	£8.99	....	Wales	£11.99	....
HIDDEN PLACES NATIONAL TITLES			West Country	£10.99	....
England	£11.99	....			
Ireland	£11.99	....			
Scotland	£11.99	....			
Wales	£11.99	....			
OTHER TITLES					
Off The Motorway	£11.99	....	**TOTAL QUANTITY**	[ ]	
Garden Centres and Nurseries of Britain	£11.99	....	**TOTAL VALUE**	[ ]	

READER REACTION FORM

The **Travel Publishing** *research team would like to receive readers' comments on any visitor attractions or places reviewed in the book and also recommendations for suitable entries to be included in the next edition. This will help ensure that the* **Country Living series of Rural Guides** *continues to provide its readers with useful information on the more interesting, unusual or unique features of each attraction or place ensuring that their visit to the local area is an enjoyable and stimulating experience. To provide your comments or recommendations would you please complete the forms below and overleaf as indicated and send to:*

The Research Department, Travel Publishing Ltd, Airport Business Centre, 10 Thornbury Road, Estover, Plymouth PL6 7PP

YOUR NAME:

YOUR ADDRESS:

YOUR TEL NO:

Please tick as appropriate: COMMENTS   RECOMMENDATION

ESTABLISHMENT:

ADDRESS:

TEL NO:

CONTACT NAME:

PLEASE COMPLETE FORM OVERLEAF

READER REACTION FORM

COMMENT OR REASON FOR RECOMMENDATION:

....

....

....

....

....

....

....

....

....

....

....

....

READER REACTION FORM

The **Travel Publishing** *research team would like to receive readers' comments on any visitor attractions or places reviewed in the book and also recommendations for suitable entries to be included in the next edition. This will help ensure that the* **Country Living series of Rural Guides** *continues to provide its readers with useful information on the more interesting, unusual or unique features of each attraction or place ensuring that their visit to the local area is an enjoyable and stimulating experience. To provide your comments or recommendations would you please complete the forms below and overleaf as indicated and send to:*

The Research Department, Travel Publishing Ltd, Airport Business Centre, 10 Thornbury Road, Estover, Plymouth PL6 7PP

YOUR NAME:

YOUR ADDRESS:

YOUR TEL NO:

Please tick as appropriate: COMMENTS   RECOMMENDATION

ESTABLISHMENT:

ADDRESS:

TEL NO:

CONTACT NAME:

PLEASE COMPLETE FORM OVERLEAF

READER REACTION FORM

COMMENT OR REASON FOR RECOMMENDATION:

....

....

....

....

....

....

....

....

....

....

....

TOWNS, VILLAGES AND PLACES OF INTEREST

TOWNS, VILLAGES AND PLACES OF INTEREST

TOWNS, VILLAGES AND PLACES OF INTEREST

TOWNS, VILLAGES AND PLACES OF INTEREST

TOWNS, VILLAGES AND PLACES OF INTEREST

TOWNS, VILLAGES AND PLACES OF INTEREST

TOWNS, VILLAGES AND PLACES OF INTEREST

TOWNS, VILLAGES AND PLACES OF INTEREST

TOWNS, VILLAGES AND PLACES OF INTEREST

TOWNS, VILLAGES AND PLACES OF INTEREST

TOWNS, VILLAGES AND PLACES OF INTEREST

TOWNS, VILLAGES AND PLACES OF INTEREST

TOWNS, VILLAGES AND PLACES OF INTEREST

TOWNS, VILLAGES AND PLACES OF INTEREST

TOWNS, VILLAGES AND PLACES OF INTEREST

TOWNS, VILLAGES AND PLACES OF INTEREST

TOWNS, VILLAGES AND PLACES OF INTEREST

TOWNS, VILLAGES AND PLACES OF INTEREST